A Systems Perspec

To Richard, Katharina and Sophie

Nadine Pratt

A Systems Perspective on Sustainability
Contributing to Sustainability Science

Oldib
Verlag

Bibliografische Information der Deutschen Nationalbibliothek
Die Deutsche Nationalbibliothek verzeichnet diese
Publikation in der Deutschen Nationalbibliografie;
detaillierte bibliografische Daten sind im Internet
über http://dnb.ddb.de abrufbar.

© 2014, Oldib-Verlag, Essen
www.oldib-verlag.de
Oldib Verlag Oliver Bidlo
Waldeck 14
45133 Essen
www.oldib-verlag.de
Umschlaggestaltung: Oliver Bidlo
Herstellung: BoD, Norderstedt

ISBN 978-3-939556-43-5

Abstract

Human activity currently is altering the *environmental* and *social system* on a global scale and at an unprecedented pace. In efforts to meet this challenge and ensure that the measures taken affect humanity for the better, the business community (economy) is assigned an outstanding role by society – as both 'usurpator' and 'salvator'. *Corporate sustainability* therefore is crystallizing as one of the core topics of the current century. Many companies are beginning to accept the challenge and showing impressive success, but there remain numerous situations, where corporate sustainability measures remain modest or indeed prove counter-productive. In view of the increasing public awareness for sustainability issues, insufficient or failed sustainability-measures bear a serious risk of backfiring on the corporations, for example in form of increased Greenwashing accusations, social costs or environmental risks. This dissertation aims to discuss the potential of *a systems perspective* (systems thinking, systems science) to improve the success of corporate sustainability measures. The dissertation argues that measures of corporate sustainability often fall short, not primarily through individual failures of corporations, but rather due to *unsustainable systemic structures* arising from the *interaction* between a corporation and its shareholders and driven by *dynamics* unfolding in the process. The pitfall of these structures is that they remain undetected due to a lack of a systems perspective and run the risk of backfiring on the corporation itself. These structures constitute **Sustainability Traps:** Reoccurring *dynamic patterns* of failed sustainability measures that *backfire on corporations*. The dissertation aims to discuss why and how a systems perspective (systems thinking) as an organizational learning discipline, can be used to address Sustainability Traps and thus to improve success of corporate sustainability measures. To this end, the dissertation elaborates 'a systems perspective' (systems thinking principles) crucial for identifying and analyzing Sustainability Traps: *Thinking in Models, Re-thinking Boundary Judgments, System-as-Cause Thinking, Operational Thinking* and *Dynamic Thinking*. Subsequently the dissertation identifies *archetypical Sustainability Traps* from *business practice* and discusses *leverage points* to deal with the traps.

Acknowledgments

I would like to acknowledge my sincerest gratitude to various individuals and groups for their support during the time of my doctoral work. Though the following dissertation is an individual work, I could never have completed it without the support of the following people. First, I would like to thank my doctoral advisor, Prof. Birger P. Priddat, for being so supportive to work with. I would like to thank him especially for his openness to my ideas and for the freedom he granted me to develop my thoughts and scientific skills.

The first quarter of this dissertation stems from my academic experiences while attending the Sloan School of Management at the Massachusetts Institute of Technology, USA. It was here that I got inspired about the idea and importance of systems science. I most sincerely thank the department of Behavioral and Policy Sciences of the Sloan School as well as my fellow colleagues for this wonderfully enriching experience, which had a profound impact on my thinking and on my scientific development.

My special thanks go also to the staff members of the BPS department as well as those of the Society for Organizational Learning for their patient assistance in fulfilling the formalities regarding this phase of my research. My deepest gratitude and sincere thanks go to Dr. Peter Senge, for his assistance, generosity, and advice, which I received from him during my stay at MIT, for this dissertation and for the support of my endeavors. It is due to the many thought-provoking conversations I had with him and others, most important Dr. Macharia Waruingi from the Kenya Development Network, that the idea of Sustainability Traps developed. Therefore I want to thank Dr. Peter Senge especially for his comments and suggestions on my work and on the concept of Sustainbility Traps. His deep dedication to systems thinking and learning, his inexhaustible energy and interest for new ideas, and his inspiring personality have been a role model for me. Furthermore my sincere gratitude goes to Plug Power Inc., USA, for providing me the opportunity, interest and financial support to conduct my empirical analysis in the Transformation Laboratory on Sustainability. The findings of this micro-world simulation served to characterize and refine the mental models on sustainability used in this dissertation. I am especially grateful to the developers of the laboratory, Susan Svoboda and Gary Svoboda of Realia Group, for their generosity in placing the laboratory and their competence at my disposal. It was due to their commitment, experience and input that we developed a version of the laboratory, which met the requirements of this dissertation.

My thanks also go to the 'Studienstiftung des Deutschen Volkes' for a scholarship enabling me to write this dissertation and conduct my studies abroad as well as to my coordinative advisor for the scholarship program Prof. Dirk Baecker. Furthermore I would like to thank the Stefan Walter Besthorn Stiftung for the financial support of the laboratory.

My deepest thanks and respect go to the one person, who supported me above all others during the writing of this dissertation, my husband Richard Pratt. I would like to deeply thank him for his love, assistance and patience during this time. Also I would like to thank my father-in-law, William Pratt, for advising me on the subtleties of the English language. My thanks also go to Dr. Sarah Lubjuhn, who encouraged me to publish this book as well as to Dr. Oliver Bidlo for dealing with all the tricky aspects of formatting and layout.

Last but not least, I am very grateful to my family and friends for their understanding for missing out on some nice times together when writing this dissertation, and for their encouragement, affection and support. The dissertation was originally published online in 2007 since this was quicker as well as cheaper. However since then, there was a wish within me to publish it in a book version. Therefore I am very happy that years later, in 2014, this is finally happening (although in a shortened and slightly updated version). In my view – having worked for over seven years in the area of sustainability by now at the Collaborating Centre on Sustainable Consumption and Production (founded by the Wuppertal Institute and United Nations Environment Programme/UNEP) it has not lost its actuality.

On the private side, my husband and I, are blessed with two outstanding girls by now – Katharina and Sophie, to whom I would like to dedicate this book version, in the hope that they will be able to live in a world sustainable enough and that they find their way of contributing to a more sustainable living.

Table of Contents

List of Figures

Abbreviations

4CMR	Cambridge Centre for Climate Change Mitigation Research
AG	Aktiengesellschaft, Joint Stock Company
BMBF	Bundesministerium für Bildung und Forschung, German Federal Ministry for Education and Research
BMZ	Bundesministerium für wirtschaftliche Zusammenarbeit und Entwicklung; German Federal Ministry for Economic Cooperation and Development
BPS	Behavioral Policy Science
Btw.	Between
CA	California
CCC	Clean Clothes Campaign
CCSP	Climate Change Science Program
CEO	Chief Executive Officer
CERES	Coalition for Environmentally Responsible Economies
CLD	Causal Loop Diagram
CNN	Cable Network News
CR	Corporate Responsibility
CSCP	UNEP Wuppertal Institute Collaborating Center on Sustainable Consumption and Production
CSERGE	Centre for Social and Economic Research on the Global Environment
CSR	Corporate Social Responsibility
CT	Connecticut
DETR	UK Department for Environment, Transport and the Regions
e.g.	Exempli gratia, for example
ed.	Edition
Ed.	Editor
Eds.	Editors
EEA	European Environment Agency
EPA	Environmental Protection Agency
et al.	et alii, and others
etc.	Et cetera
f.	following
ff.	following
fig.	Figure
FLA	Fair Labor Association

FZKA	Forschungszentrum Karlsruhe, Research Center Karlsruhe
GDP	Gross Domestic Product
GTZ	Gesellschaft für Technische Zusammenarbeit, International cooperation enterprise for sustainable development
i.e.	Id est; that is
IEA	International Energy Agency
IFSR	International Series on Systems Science and Engineering
IGBP	International Geosphere-Biosphere Programme
IHDP	International Human Dimension Programme on Global Environmental Change
IIASA	International Institute for Applied Systems Analysis
ILO	International Labour Organization
Inc.	Incorporation
IPA	Institute of Public Affairs
IPCC	Intergovernmental Panel on Climate Change
ISO	International Organization for Standardization
IUCN	International Union for the Conservation of Nature and Natural Resources, The World Conservation Union
KDNC	Kenya Development Network Consortium
m	Million
MA	Massachusetts
MI	Michigan
MIT	Massachusetts Institute of Technology
MSN	Maquila Solidarity Network
NASA	National Aeronautics and Space Administration
NC	North Carolina
NGO	Non Governmental Organization
NJ	New Jersey
No.	Number
NY	New York
OMSC	Organic Milk Suppliers' Co-operative
OR	Operations Research
OTA	Organic Trade Association
p.	Page
PA	Pennsylvania
PLC	Public Limited Company

pp.	Pages
Prod.	Production
PSI	Policy Studies Institute
rev.	Revised
RFCE	Rose Foundation for Communities and Environment
RFF	Resources for the Future
SCORE!	Sustainable Consumption Research Exchange
SCP	Sustainable Consumption and Production
SEC	Securities and Exchange Commission
SETAC	Society of Environmental Toxicology and Chemistry
SETAC	Society of Environmental Toxicology and Chemistry
S.l.	Sine locatione; without place of publication
SoL	The Society for Organizational Learning
SWOP	South West Organizing Project
TNS	The Natural Step
TU	Technische Universtität
UK	United Kingdom
UMI	University of Michigan
UN	United Nations
UNCED	United Nations Conference on Environment and Development
UN-DESA	United Nations Department of Economic and Social Affairs
UNDP	United Nations Development Programme
UNEP	United Nations Environment Programme
URL	Uniform Resource Locator
US	United States
US$, USD	United States Dollar
USA	United States of America
VA	Virginia
Vol.	Volume
Vols.	Volumes
WB	World Bank
WBCSD	World Business Council for Sustainable Development
WBGU	Wissenschaftlicher Beirat der Bundesregierung Globale Umweltveränderungen, Scientific Advisory Council To The German Government On Global Environ-

mental Change

WCED	World Commission on Environment and Development
WRI	World Resources Institute
WTO	World Trade Organization
WVS	World Values Survey
WWF	World Wildlife Fund

1 Part I: Theoretical Background

1.1 Introduction

This chapter (1.1) defines the aim of the dissertation and discusses the actuality and problem context of the research question elaborated. Subsequently the design (structure of the dissertation), which the dissertation uses to address a systems perspective on sustainability, is outlined.

1.1.1 Research Question and Aim of the Dissertation

The research question this dissertation deals with is:

*Can – and if so **what** can - a systems perspective (systems thinking) contribute for improving corporate sustainability?*

The dissertation argues that a main contribution a systems perspective makes to corporate sustainability is that it reveals the importance of ***systemic, dynamic structures*** in the creation of *un*sustainability: It are often not primarily individual failures of corporations that lead to a shortcoming of sustainability measures, but rather *unsustainable systemic structures* (*dynamic patterns of unsustainability*). The dissertation refers to these structures as ***Sustainability Traps***: Reoccurring dynamic patterns of failed corporate sustainability measures that backfire not only on the environmental and social sphere, but also on the corporation itself. Sustainability Traps that backfire often remain unrecognized due to a lack of focus on systemic, dynamic structures in 'orthodox', linear thinking. The dissertation therefore aims to analyze why and how a systems perspective (systems thinking) enables corporations to better deal with characteristics of Sustainability Traps than does orthodox, linear thinking and to thus improve success of corporate sustainability measures.

1.1.2 Actuality and Problem Context

The following paragraph discusses the ***current problem context***, in which the dissertation' topic of a systems perspective on sustainability and Sustainability Traps in particular, is positioned in, with respect to *business practice* as well as with respect to *research on corporate sustainability*.

The National Research Council's Committee on Global Change Research points to the challenges ahead: Never before has human activity altered the Earth's environment on a global scale as well as in such high rate as at present (NRC 1999a: 2). Thereby global changes are occurring in people's natural environment (the ecosphere, environmental sustainability) as well as within society itself (anthroposphere, social sustainability) (WBGU 1994, 1995 and 1997). Significant changes presently occurring include land transformation, global warming and loss of biodiversity as well as globalization (including global markets), population increase in developing countries with explosion of numbers of young people seeking jobs, and decreasing and aging populations in industrialized countries (Europe), urbanization, persisting poverty and health issues (UNDP 2006, UNEP 2006, PRB 2006, Turner II et al. 1990). Hence we are living through a period of tremendous environmental and social transformation.

In efforts to meet this challenge the business community (economy) is assigned an outstanding role by society – as both 'usurpator'[1] and 'salvator'[2] (WBCSD 2006b). Corporate sustainability therefore is crystallizing as one of the core topics of the current century (Vries 2013: 1; Epstein 2008: 21f; Pohl; Tolhurst 2010: xv; Dunphy and Benveniste 2000). The concept of sustainability and the role it ascribes to business however is new to corporations and requires, in contrast to new *business* approaches, a broadening of system boundaries beyond the economic sphere towards the environmental and social sphere.

> *The dissertation argues that **systems thinking** thereby is essential for corporations and their stakeholders in order to successfully dealing with the challenges of sustainability. As the dissertation will show, corporations lacking a systems perspective risk getting caught up in **Sustainability Traps**, where – even well intended – corporate sustainability measures can lead to structures that leave environment and society as well as the corporation itself, worse off than before the sustainability measure. The reason is that interactions between the corporation, other social agents and environmental processes can create unsustainable systemic structures (Sustainability Traps), which remain unrecognized in orthodox thinking[3] and hold the agents prisoner.*

The dissertation argues that a systems perspective is better suited for dealing with Sustainability Traps than is orthodox thinking. The reason is that Sustainability Traps arise through dynamics unfolding between the corporate, social and environmental sphere. Orthodox thinking however is 'thinghood'[4] oriented, i.e. it analyzes the specifics of individual variables within their sectoral boundaries. Systems thinking in contrast focuses on 'systemhood', i.e. on *interrelations* between variables in a system and enables the analysis of interrelations between diverse spheres such as the corporate, social and environmental sphere. Furthermore orthodox thinking is

---

1 For example: Causer of environmental unsustainabilities (pollution) and social unsustainabilities (e.g. sweat-shops).
2 For example: Addressing environmental unsustainabilities through technology and tempering social unsustainabilities through rising living standards triggered by the economy.
3 Differences between orthodox, linear thinking and systems thinking will be thoroughly outlined in chapter 2.
4 This term has been introduced by Klir (2001), see below.

focused on linear processes, while systems thinking examines *non-linear, dynamic feedback processes*. Feedback processes are crucial for the unfolding of Sustainability Traps, because the traps are produced through corporate behavior, which impacts variables in the environmental and social sphere, which in turn backfire to the corporate sphere. Moreover orthodox thinking usually focuses on individual agents for explaining unsustainabilities (Senge 2006: 19, Sterman 2004: 10), which risks getting into the blame-game of 'bad guys' versus 'heroes' of sustainability.[5] Thereby very often the subliminal view of the 'unethical business' seems to be underlying, which has to be restricted ('to be set into limits'). As a consequence, many approaches to corporate sustainability have emerged, which are based on *ethical reasoning* and *moral appeals* to corporations to act less unsustainable, such as Corporate (Social) Responsibility (Carroll 1999, Harvard Business Review on Corporate Responsibility 2003, Hawkins 2006, Kotler and Lee 2005), Business Ethics (Ferrell, Fraedrich and Ferrell 2002, Priddat 2005a[6], Trevino and Nelson 2004, Velasquez 2006), Corporate Citizenship (Crane and Chapple 2003, Marsden 2000, Matten) and others. The dissertation will argue that social values, beliefs (mental models) and norms as they are put forward by these kinds of approaches are inevitably important for corporate sustainability.

They nonetheless constitute only one side of the problem and need to be complemented by approaches that address *systemic, dynamic structures*, to inhibit degenerating into blame-gaming in public argumentations. Systems thinking, in contrast to orthodox thinking, does not focus on individual agents to explain unsustainabilities, but rather on dynamic *structures* unfolding through feedback processes between the corporate, social and environmental sphere. The crucial point thereby is that even *well-intended* ('*moral*') sustainability measures can lead to unsustainability, if systemic, dynamic structures are not taken into account. A prominent example is that of eco-efficiency models, which often are celebrated as a crucial step forward in regard to corporate sustainability. But these measures can only play out their potential, if dynamic structures and their feedback processes are understood; otherwise they can backfire, creating even more unsustainability. In cases where this happens and corporations failed to fulfill their 'promises' (goals) of corporate sustainability, corporations are often accused of 'Greenwashing' without any further differentiation of circumstances. This in turn leads to even fiercer claims for *ethical reasoning, social responsibilities* and *moral appeals* to corporations. The leverage of such claims however remains questionable as long as the dynamic structures, which corporations are embedded – or even trapped – in, are not analyzed in a complementary

---

5 Failures and successes of sustainability are attributed to individual actors (e.g. corporations, NGOs, governments, customers, media etc.).
6 Priddat thereby does not only consider the ethics in business (in economy), but also – in turn – the economic aspects in morality; see also Priddat 1998.

manner. Systems thinking enables this corresponding analysis of the interplay between beliefs (mental models) of sustainability and systemic structures emerging on their basis. The dissertation therefore considers a systems perspective, and in particular the concept of Sustainability Traps, to be a valuable complement to the approaches of CR, CSR and Business Ethics, which currently are the focus of research in the field of corporate sustainability.

As will be discussed, there currently already are a variety of approaches to systems science, which use aspects of systems thinking (system science) to address issues of sustainability. The concept of Sustainability Traps and the systems thinking principles for addressing them, as they are elaborated in the dissertation, thereby constitute a contribution to this field, - particularly to the fields of Organizational Learning for Sustainability (Senge 2006 and Senge et al. 1994) and Sustainability Science.

1.1.3 Dissertation Design

The dissertation constitutes of four main parts:

Part I of the dissertation provides the theoretical background on sustainability (chapter 1.2) and systems thinking (chapter 1.3) relevant for the dissertation. The next chapter then deals with the combination of sustainability and systems thinking (chapter 1.4): It provides an overview of existing scientific fields applying systems thinking to sustainability, which to the best of the author's knowledge is the first extensive overview in this respect. The goal of this chapter is to outline the scientific context, which the dissertation' approach is positioned in.

Part II presents the dissertation' particular contribution to the scientific field: The concept and characteristics of Sustainability Traps (chapter 2.1). Subsequently, principles of systems thinking are elaborated, which are required for successfully managing (avoiding) Sustainability Traps. These are: Thinking in Models (chapter 2.2.1), Re-thinking Boundary Judgments (2.2.2), System-as-Cause Thinking (2.2.3), Operational Thinking (2.2.4) and Dynamic Thinking (2.2.5).

Part III identifies archetypical Sustainability Traps existing in business practice, which corporations holding a specific mental model of sustainability risk getting into. The dissertation uses case study analyses to outline and discuss the traps and will examine leverage points of how to manage the traps from a systems perspective. The mental models and potential traps discussed are: Trade-off Model (Job-Creation Trap and Fighting-the-enemy Trap), Compliance Model (Quick-Fix Trap with the special case: Fire-the-Supplier Trap), Efficiency Model (Efficiency Trap (rebound effects)), Reputation Leadership Model (Reputation Trap with special case: Financing Brand-Image through Low-Cost Production), Systemic Model and Mission-Driven Enterprises (Selling-(out) Trap).

Part IV of the dissertation draws conclusions on the findings of the dissertation and discusses their contributions to three fields: First, scientific contributions and directions for further research are discussed (chapter 4.1). Subsequently contributions to business practice (chapter 4.2) as well as contributions to the work of NGOs, international organizations and interested individuals (consumers) are presented (chapter 4.3).

The *dissertation' contribution to the scientific field* can be summarized the following: Part II and III constitute the main parts of the dissertation and outline the dissertation' contribution: Sustainability Traps, which become apparent when applying a systems perspective on sustainability. Part II elaborates the *theoretical concept* of Sustainability Traps, building on the existing scientific approaches discussed in Part I[7]. Part III analyzes the existence and application of the theoretical concept to *business practice*. Part II and III therefore are equally important and discuss complementary aspects: Theoretical concept and practical relevance of Sustainability Traps.

1.2   Sustainability

Chapter 1.2 provides a definition as well as a brief historical development of the concept of 'sustainability'. Subsequently the three dimensions of sustainability (environmental, social and economical) are discussed as they are used in the dissertation. Thereby it is important to mention, that, - as will be discussed further below, - the dissertation does not argue for a differentiation of the three dimensions, but rather for their integration (holistic perspective).

1.2.1   History and Definition of Sustainability

The term 'to sustain' has been in the language for a very long time. It has its etymological roots in the Latin verb 'sustenare' meaning 'to hold up' (Merriam Webster's Collegiate Dictionary 2004). The Chambers Concise Dictionary (1999) refers to the term 'sustainability' as "from the verb to sustain meaning: to hold up; to bear; to support; to provide for; to maintain; to sanction; to keep going; to keep up; to prolong; to support the life of." The verb 'to sustain' along with its derivatives (sustainability, sustainable, sustaining) for a long time were– and often still are – used in this general sense, which is applicable to any specific object or individual.

In 1713 however Hannß Carl von Carlowitz, a German national, for the first time introduced *sustainability as a principle* in the context of forest management. In his oeuvre Sylvicultura Oeconomica, he summarized the knowledge on forestry, much

---

7 As stated, an additional contribution of the dissertation with respect to Part I lies in the overview of scientific approaches using systems thinking principles to address sustainbility issues.

of which had been lost over the course of the thirty-year war, and enriched it with his own experiences. In the Sylvicultura Oeconomica he formulated sustainability as a principle, stating that lumbering should entail the removal of only as much wood as can re-grow again, so that the forest is never cleared entirely and can re-generate itself (von Carlowitz 1713: 105f). The idea then start to spread and the principle was applied to other environmental sectors (e.g. fisheries) as well as to social contexts. Starting in the 1960s and 70s the concept was increasingly applied on a macro-level referring to the need to sustain natural environment and human society as a whole (for example: UN 1972, Stivers 1976: 187; for an early use of the term see also Pirages 1977).

The development outlined led to a basic *dichotomy* of the term 'sustainability' as it is used today: Colloquially the term is often used in its historical context. In a more specific sense the term refers to the macro-level of the survival of the *natural system* and *human species*. Very often the concept encompasses not only the survival as such, but also a certain *quality* of survival (e.g. the ability to meet human needs).[8] The dissertation deals with the specific meaning of sustainability. It is often also referred to as 'Sustainable Development'.[9] However, within the context of this specific (macro-level) use, there are today a vast number of different definitions of the term 'sustainability' (Kates, Parris and Leiserowitz 2005: 20).[10]

In 1983 the General Assembly of the United Nations convened the World Commission on Environment and Development (WCED) in order to propose long-term environmental strategies for achieving sustainable development up to the year 2000 and beyond (UN 1983). The commission became known as the 'Brundtland Commission', named after the name of its Chairman Gro Harlem Brundtland, by then Prime Minister of Norway. The Commission focused its work on the unity of environment and development. Inter alia, the commission drew from the 1972 Stockholm Conference on the Human Environment, which was the first to acknowledge conflicts between environment and development (Declaration of the United Nations Conference on the Human Environment 1972) as well as from the 1980 World Conservation Strategy of the International Union for the Conservation of Nature and Natural Resources (IUCN/UNEP/WWF 1980), which sought

---

8 See sustainability definition of the Brundtland commission below.

9 The dissertation will use the terms 'sustainability' and 'sustainable development' synonymously. As various as the individual definitions of the two terms are, equally as various are their relationships outlined, e.g. synonyms, means versus end. As a differentiation of the two terms is not critical for the dissertation, the dissertation will use them synonymously, mainly referring to the term 'sustainability'. A specific definition of 'sustainable development/sustainability' will follow below.

10 Equally disputed remains consequently an understanding and approaches of corporate sustainbility, see Schulz, Geßner and Kölle (2006) and see below (three dimensions of sustainbility).

to explain how economic development and conservation of the environment can work together, thereby stressing conservation as a means to assist development and arguing for the sustainable development of species, ecosystems, and resources.[11] In 1987 the commission published its report 'Our common future', in which it defined 'sustainable development' as follows (WCED 1987: 43): "Sustainable development is development that meets the needs of the present without compromising the ability of future generations to meet their own needs. It contains within it two key concepts: the concept of needs, in particular the essential needs of the world's poor, to which overriding priority should be given; and the idea of limitations imposed by the state of technology and social organization on the environment's ability to meet present and future needs." The United Nations has adopted the term 'sustainable development' in its programs, e.g. Agenda 21 (UN 1992), which led to a broad diffusion of the concept itself and the definition in particular. The definition of the Brundtland report remains the most cited and wide-spread definition of sustainability today (Kates, Parris, Leiserowitz 2005: 10) and is also the one on which the dissertation builds on[12]. The 'creative ambiguity' of the definition, on the one side allowed "a range of disparate groups to assemble under the sustainable development tent", yet on the other side it "created a veritable industry of deciphering and advocating what sustainable development really means" (Kates, Parris, Leiserowitz 2005: 11, see also Parris and Kates 2003).

1.2.2 The Three (Traditional) Dimensions of Sustainability

Among the different definitions and interpretations of sustainable development, three dimensions (sectors) of sustainability have crystallized as crucial in sustainability literature: Environmental, social and economic sustainability. The three dimensional approach to sustainability however provides a *sectoral* perspective[13] and thus corresponds to orthodox thinking (focus on 'thinghood').

*The dissertation will argue that in order to deal with Sustainability Traps it is necessary to analyze **dynamic interrelations** between the three sustainability dimensions and thus to **overcome** sectoral boundaries by adopting a systems perspective (focus on 'systemhood').*

The dissertation uses the differentiation between the three dimensions (sectors) of sustainability as a *starting point* for its argumentation, because the differentiation is

---

11 See also: Kates, Parris, Leiserowitz 2005: 10 and Adams 1990.
12 The dissertation however expands the scope of the definition from the 'human species' to all 'living species'. For further definitions of the term "sustainable development" and the emphasis on its three dimensions, see also the dictionary of Schulz et al. 2001: 374ff. This three dimensional approach will be referred to in the following chapter.
13 That is three sectors: Environment, Society and economy.

commonly used. The differentiation allows the dissertation to show that it are however the *interactions* of variables commonly associated with different sectors, which are crucial for creating unsustainability rather than the specific sectors as such. As will be shown, a systems perspective therefore allows overcoming a sectoral perspective on sustainability.[14]

Because of this particular use of the three dimensions of sustainability in the dissertation, it is necessary to provide a brief overview of the use of the three dimensional approach in sustainability literature and contrast it to the use in the dissertation, before outlining the three dimensions of sustainability in detail in the following chapters.

Although the very differentiation between the three dimensions of sustainability as such has been criticized for many reasons, e.g. unfeasibility because of goal-conflicts, watering down the focus on environmental sustainability, the differentiation has become most common in sustainability literature as well as in public debates (see below). While there seems to be a broad consensus that these dimensions are key to establishing sustainable development, the *relationship* between the three sustainability dimensions remains hotly disputed as will be outlined. The three dimensional approach was originally popularized by the United Nations World Summit 1995, which stated that "economic development, social development and environmental protection are interdependent and mutually reinforcing components of sustainable development" (UN 1995: 5). Today the conception of the *three pillars of sustainability* is put forward by the United Nations, the European Union and national governments, e.g. the German government (Enquete-Kommission 'Schutz des Menschen und der Umwelt' 1998). In the business sector it has been particularly the *triple-bottom-line approach* (Elkington 1997) that contributed to the dispersion of the three dimensional concept by arguing not only to account for a financial bottom line but equally for social and environmental impacts (see also Lotter, Braun 2011: 15). As Gladwin, Kennelly and Krause (1995: 896ff) argue, economic sustainability alone is no sufficient condition for the overall sustainability of a corporation. The concept of sustainbility therefore requires departing from orthodox management conceptions. At present the three dimensions are the most common dimensions with regard to corporate sustainability (Blank and Clausen 2001: 374ff). However there exist strong disparities about the interpretations (contents) of the different dimensions and their weighting in corporations (see also part III of the dissertation). This is even more the case in the scientific sphere of sustainability: The US National Research Council (NRC 1999b: 21ff) has identified disparities in sustainability literature in reference to the three dimensions, with regard to which sustainability dimensions 'are to be sustained', i.e. which dimensions constitute the goals of sustainability (*normative*) and which dimensions 'are to be developed", i.e.

---

14 See in particular 'principle of the system boundary', chapter 2.2.2.1.

dimensions, which need to be changed (developed) as a means for *implementing* sustainability. The scientific debate about the relationship between the three dimensions culminates in the concept of weak versus strong sustainability, which deals with the substitutability between human-made and natural capital (Klassen and Opschoor 1990, Pearce and Atkinson, 1992, Pearce, Markandya and Barbier 1989, Pearce and Turner 1990, Turner 1992).

*The dissertation however focuses on a different aspect of the relationship between the three dimensions, which examines the **dynamics** between the three dimensions (rather than their substitutability).*

From a *normative* point of view, i.e. with respect to 'what is to be targeted' (sustained), the dissertation will argue that sustainability as a new holistic concept requires the reconciliation (re-evaluation) between holistic goals of sustainability (which relate to society and nature as a whole) and sectoral goals (e.g. profit maximization in the business sector). From an *implementation* point of view, i.e. 'how to reach what is desired', the dissertation will argue that it is crucial to focus on the **dynamics** between the three dimensions that drive unsustainable structures, i.e. *Sustainability Traps*.

How dynamics between the three dimensions of sustainability can form unsustainable structures, Sustainability Traps, is the core of the dissertation and will be discussed thoroughly later. At this point, the dissertation will first outline the three dimension of sustainability individually, in order to create an understanding of the dimensions as they are used in the dissertation. The aim of this outlining is *not* to discuss different definitions of each dimension, but rather to create a general understanding of the dimensions. The reason for this is the following: While some scholars have argued for precise definitions and differentiation between the three dimensions in order not to water environmental sustainability by elements of social and economic sustainability and to make the concepts operational (Goodland and Daly 1996), others have argued that precise definitions lead into a spiral of counter-definitions, which rather create confusion than enlightment (Dobson 1998: 33f). While both strands of argumentation have their eligibility, the reason for the dissertation to provide a general understanding of each sustainability dimension rather than to wage different definitions against each other, is of different nature and refers to the dissertation' intention stated above: As will be discussed more in-depth below, the three dimensions are based on a reductionist, 'thinghood'[15]-oriented concept of socially separated sectors, while a systems perspective focuses on dynamic interrelations between *variables attributed to* different sectors ('systemhood').[16] If a

---

15 For an explanation of this term see chapter 1.3.1.
16 See chapter 1.3.1 and 2.2.5.

variable is at all taken into account and if so, to which sustainability dimension (sector) the variable is attributed to, depends on how an organization sets its *system boundaries*. As will be discussed thoroughly in chapter 2.2.2, for dealing with Sustainability Traps it is crucial to be flexible on system boundaries and to *change* system boundaries (and thus to change the attribution of variables to specific sectors). Therefore providing static definitions of the different sustainability dimensions is not feasible for the dissertation. Rather the dissertation will show that it is necessary to *transcendent* and *overcome* sectoral boundaries of the three sustainability dimensions in order to deal with Sustainability Traps. Therefore the following overview provides a general understanding of the three sustainability dimensions rather then static definitions for the dissertation. How the dimensions are differentiated respectively how they are related to each other, then depends on the system boundaries of the individual agent (organization) and consequently on his ability for dealing with Sustainability Traps as the dissertation will show.[17]

1.2.2.1 Environmental Sustainability

This dimension relates to sustaining the *natural system*, the *ecosphere*, which encompasses the abiotic world (geosphere) and world of living species (biosphere) (Claussen 2001: 147). Correspondingly human health can also be attributed to the sphere of environmental sustainability. The emphasis of environmental sustainability in literature lies on *natural life support systems*, whereby the life considered to be supported in first place is *human* (NRC 1999b: 23). This view is inline with the Brundtland definition outlined above. An emphasis within this view lies on natural resources – renewables as well as non-renewables. While the focus on natural resources at first lied on products and production inputs, this concept in recent years has expanded to include the values of aesthetics, recreation as well as the absorption and cleansing of pollution and waste (Daily 1997, Daily et al. 1997). These utilitarian services of natural systems to humans are discussed under the term of *ecosystem services* (Costanza et. al. 1997, Mooney and Ehrlich 1997). Less frequently in literature are non-anthropocentric views, which claim to sustain the natural system itself for its own intrinsic value, because other living species have equal claims to existence and to meeting their needs (NRC 1999b: 23). The dissertation is inline with this latter argumentation. The dissertation refers the concept of environmental sustainability to living species in general (regardless to their 'utility' to humans), but nevertheless with a special emphasis on the human species, because of two reasons: First, because it is the species we belong to. Second, because it is the human species, which affects environmental sustainability the most.[18]

---

17 See chapter 2.2.2.

18 A most prominent concept regarding biological species is the one of biodiversity: "'Biological diversity' means the variability among living organisms from all sources including, in-

28

In the business context environmental sustainability previously was focused primarily on the manufacturing process, but today has been expanded over whole product life-cycles (Life Cycle Assessment) (Fava et al. 1991, Hawken 1993, SETAC 1993). In recent times a new focus has been laid on sustainable consumption, focusing on consumer demands for and utilization of products (Michaelis 2003, CSCP 2005a).[19] Today concepts, means as well as accounting and reporting instruments for corporate environmental sustainability are numerous (Baird and Freeman 2002, Dunphy, Griffiths and Benn 2003, Marshall and Brown 2003, Morhardt, Wheeler and Elkington 2001, Schaltegger, Burritt and Petersen 2003, Sharma and Aragon-Correa 2005). Thereby end-of-the-pipe solutions, which merely shift unsustainability (e.g. pollution) from one medium to another, increasingly are replaced by source reduction approaches (e.g. pollution prevention) (DeSimone and Popoff 2000: 1). A most prominent approach regarding environmental sustainability that the dissertation will deal with is eco-efficiency, which relates to optimal resource use, particularly resource productivity.[20]

Although business has made some significant improvements in reducing environmental unsustainability particularly on a local level, e.g. reducing air and water pollution, reducing chemical toxins in products, energy efficiency and alternative energies (Lash 2005 and 2006), the efforts seem like a drop in the ocean in the context of the anthroposophically triggered global changes currently developing, foremost climate change (Steffen 2004, WBGU 1994, 1995, 1999, 2000 and 2001; CCSP and The Subcommittee on Global Change Research 2006). A systems perspective helps better understanding these gaps and challenges.[21] Furthermore the research on human-caused environmental global change cited in chapter 1.1.2, clearly indicates that sustainability is not solely a corporate issue, but foremost a social issue. This stresses the crucial point the dissertation makes: That sustainability is to be analyzed from a systems perspective, which enables understanding *systemic structures of unsustainability* that are produced by actions of *various* agents and carried on by social and environmental dynamics.[22]

---

ter alia, terrestrial, marine and other aquatic ecosystems and the ecological complexes of which they are part; this includes diversity within species, between species and of ecosystems" (UNCED 1992: Article 2, see also Wilson and Peter 1988, Gaston and Spicer 2004).

19 While Life Cycle Assessment focuses on a cradle-to-grave perspective, McDonough and Braungart (2002a) have suggested a concept of eliminating downcycling and the concept of waste altogether by keeping two separate metabolisms, the biological and the technical, which each constitute closed cyclical material flows (cradle-to-cradle, see chapter 1.4.6 and 3.3.2.2).

20 See chapter 3.3.

21 See CO_2 example in chapter 2.2.4.1.

22 See especially chapters 2.2.5 and 3.

1.2.2.2 Social Sustainability

Goodland (2002: 2) proposes a very broad definition of social sustainability: "Social sustainability means maintaining social capital. Social capital is investments and services that create the basic framework for society. It lowers the cost of working together and facilitates cooperation: trust lowers transaction costs. Only systematic community participation and strong civil society, including government can achieve this. Cohesion of community for mutual benefit, connectedness between groups of people, reciprocity, tolerance, compassion, patience, forbearance, fellowship, love, commonly accepted standards of honesty, discipline and ethics. Commonly shared rules, laws, and information (libraries, film, and diskettes) promote social sustainability." The US National Research Council in its reconciliation of different sustainability conceptions focuses on sustaining cultural species (as opposed to biological species) comprising "distinctive *cultures,* particular *groups* of people, and specific *places*"(NRC 1999b: 25). Very often social sustainability is related to poverty reduction, i.e. elevating living standards in developing countries (in accordance with the emphasis of the Brundtland commission outlined above).[23]

Corporations increasingly are getting more involved in social sustainability. Basically three areas relating to corporate social sustainability can be distinguished: Cultural sponsoring, employee sustainability and community sustainability:

Cultural sponsoring (e.g. sponsoring of cultural or arts events, funding restoration or protecting of cultural places or heritage) has been executed by a number of businesses way before the sustainability movement (Hagan and Harvey 2000, Martorella 1996). Cultural sponsoring will not play a prominent role in the dissertation. The focus on employee health, well-being and motivation has been manifested in the concept of 'human capital' or 'human resource' (Becker 1964, Black and Lynch 1996) and today is accompanied by the approach of 'diversity management', that is eliminating discrimination of individuals due to specifics (e.g. gender, race, religion, disabilities, social class, sexual orientation, family situation) as well as valuing and harnessing diversity among employees (or other stakeholders) for gaining competitive advantage e.g. through new insights and perspective (Esty, Griffin and Schorr-Hirsch 1995, Flood and Romm 1996, Gilbert, Stead and Ivancevich 1999). With regard to employees in developing countries, aspects of working conditions are under the focus of social sustainability (e.g. working overtime, workplace safety, wages, sanitation etc). This particularly refers to workers in contract factories. Unsustainabilities in overseas contract factories have become known by the term of 'sweatshops' (Esbenshade 2004, Fung, O'Rourke and Sabel 2001, Kristof and WuDunn

---

23 A most prominent concept in this area are the United Nations Millennium Development Goals: At the Millennium Summit in September 2000 national governments as well as leading development institutions agreed on eight time-bound (until 2015) and quantified goals for human development (UN 2000, Sachs 2005).

2000). This aspect will play an important role in chapter 3.2.3 and 3.4.3 of the dissertation.

Very dominant in corporate social sustainability is the focus on communities, particularly local communities of business operations. Dyllick and Hockerts (2002: 16) even narrow their definition of corporate social sustainability to this aspect: "Socially sustainable companies add value to the communities within which they operate by increasing the human capital of individual partners as well as furthering the societal capital of these communities. They manage social capital in a way that stakeholders can understand its motivations and can broadly agree with the company's value system." As many multinational corporations produce in developing countries, the aspect of poverty reduction respectively elevation of living standards in local communities has equally become a topic for business (Contreras 2004, WBCSD 2004).[24] Interactions with local communities will play an important role in the development of unsustainable structures (Job Creation Trap) in the dissertation.

Last but not least Munro elaborates on an aspect characteristic to social sustainability, which is also hinted to in Goodland (2002) and Dyllick and Hockerts (2002) cited above. Social sustainability is closely linked to the development of social norms. An activity thereby is considered socially sustainable, if it conforms to or does not stretch to far from a society's tolerance for change (Munro 1995). Hence, social sustainability is subject to changing social norms and its limits and boundaries therefore harder to assess than environmental sustainability. The aspect of boundary judgments will play a crucial role in the dissertation in chapter 2.2.2.

1.2.2.3 Economical Sustainability

Economic sustainability can be defined as a "firm's ability to persist durably on the market under competition constraints" (Spangenberg and Bonniot 1998: 18). Spangenberg and Bonniot distinguish three groups of indicators for economic sustainability (Spangenberg and Bonniot 1998: 18): Liquidity/solvency, profitability and growth. For reason of simplicity, the dissertation will use profitability as the indicator for economic sustainability and *profit maximization* as the goal of economic sustainability.[25] The reason to choose this variable lies in the fact that profit maxi-

---

24 Furthermore an increasing number of multinational corporations start perceiving people in developing countries not only as cheap labor force (workers), but as an underserved market potential, that is as customers. This approach has become known under the name Base-of-the-Pyramid (BOP) (Prahalad and Hart 2002, Prahalad and Hammond 2002, Prahalad 2004). As Hart states, this approach bears high potential for sustainable approaches and alternative business models (Hart 2005 and 1997).

25 See also chapter 3.1.1. Profit here relates to the net income for a given period of time (Merriam Webster's Collegiate Dictionary 2004: 992, No.4). Profit maximization thereby

mization historically has been and today still is a dominant paradigm in corporate practice and within orthodox management theory (Anderson and Ross 2005: 31, Hirshleifer 1980: 265).

As stated, the above chapters discussed the three dimensions of sustainability individually in order to outline how each dimension is understood in the dissertation. Sustainability Traps, result through *dynamic interrelations* between variables of the three dimensions (environmental, social and economic). How dynamics between the three dimensions unfold and how they can lead to traps that backfire on corporations will be discussed in-depth in the dissertation: Chapter 2 of the dissertation will provide systems thinking skills for identifying and dealing with Sustainability Traps, while chapter 3 will discuss Sustainability Traps as they emerged and currently exist in business practice. The intention of the chapter above was to create a general understanding of the three dimensions of sustainability. As was equally stated above, the dissertation in later chapters will show that the individual differentiation respectively the relation between the three sustainability dimensions depends on system boundaries, which an individual agent (organization) sets. The ability of broadening boundary judgments and overcoming sectoral boundaries thereby will prove a crucial factor for an organization's capability to deal with Sustainability Traps.

1.3   Systems Thinking

The following chapter provides a definition of a 'system' and of 'systems thinking'. Subsequently the dissertation will outline the characteristics of systems thinking and their theoretical foundations, that constitute systems thinking as a new perspective as it is put forward in the dissertation, i.e. systems thinking as a new way of thinking compared to 'orthodox thinking'. As will be shown in later chapters, it are these characteristics of systems thinking that qualify systems thinking as a better way for dealing with Sustainability Traps than 'orthodox thinking'.

1.3.1   Definition of System and Systems Thinking

As Albert Einstein is heard to be said we cannot solve our problems with the same thinking we used when we created them. A lot of human-made sustainability problems (Sustainability Traps) we are facing today were caused through linear, sectoral thinking, which does not account for environmental or social feedbacks (backfiring) from economic activities. The dissertation argues that a new level of thinking, which enables to identify and better deal with Sustainability Traps is *sys-*

---

simply is the "behavioral assumption that a corporation maximizes its profit". Translation by the author. German original text: "Verhaltensannahme, nach der eine Unternehmung ihren Gewinn maximiert" (Gabler Wirtschaftslexikon 1994: 1364).

tems thinking, because it is based on a holistic perspective and enables to identify feedbacks between different systems, e.g. environmental, social and economic systems.

The dissertation departs from a broad ***definition of systems thinking*** equaling it to the definition of ***system science*** by Klir:

> Systems thinking (system science) thereby can be defined as
> "that field of scientific inquiry whose objects of study are systems" (Klir 2001: 3).

The dissertation chose to depart from this broad definition, because definitions and understandings of the term 'systems thinking' are vast (Ossimitz 2003: 2) and the dissertation draws from different approaches of systems thinking as will be discussed below and in chapter 1.4, particularly on Senge et al. The broad definition of Klir allows the integration of different systems thinking skills required for dealing with Sustainability Traps, which draw from different, yet related systems thinking approaches. In order to work with Klir's definition, two aspects need to further be elaborated in the following:

First, a definition of the term 'system' as it is used in the dissertation needs to be provided, which will be done in the following.

Second, the dissertation needs to further elaborate on the understanding of systems thinking used in the dissertation: This understanding is one of systems thinking as a new perspective, i.e. as a new way of thinking in contrast to 'orthodox' thinking, which is based on the concept of Senge et al. This understanding of systems thinking provides a (new) systems perspective on sustainability, which enables better dealing with Sustainability Traps. The understanding of systems thinking as a new perspective in contrast to 'orthodox' thinking will be discussed in the next chapter (1.3.2). As stated, the broad definition of systems thinking, based on Klir, requires to further defining the term 'system' for the dissertation. Senge et al., which the dissertation heavily builds, on define a system as "a perceived whole whose elements 'hang together' because they continually affect each other over time [...]"[26] (Kleiner in Senge et. al. 1994: 90). Ulrich and Probst provide a more detailed definition, which equally applies to the use of the term 'system' in the dissertation: "A system is a dynamic whole, which as such possesses distinctive qualities and behavior. It consists of parts, which are related thus that no part is independent from other parts and the behavior of the whole depends on the interaction of all parts"[27] (Ulrich and

---

26 Kleiner's definition ends by "[...] and operate towards a common purpose". The dissertation however does not perceive this as a necessary element for defining a system and considers the above sufficient.

27 Translation by the author. The German original text reads:" Ein System ist ein dynamisches Ganzes, das als solches bestimmte Eigenschaften und Verhaltensweisen besitzt. Es be-

Probst 1991: 30). Mathematically a system can be described through the following equation (Klir 2001: 5):"

$$S = (T, R)$$

where **S**, T, R denote, respectively, a *system*, a *set of things*, distinguished within **S**, and a relation (or, possibly, a set of relations) defined in T". Thereby the critical factor is the **relation** between objects of a system, which gives the system system-hood.[28] The importance of relations between elements as a characteristic of a system can be illustrated through the following example: A mere collection of books in a bookshelf does not constitute a system. Yet, if someone organizes the books in a special way (e.g. ordering by the author's name), it becomes a system (Klir 2001: 5). Klir stresses the point that system science studies "the systemhood properties of systems rather than their thinghood properties" (Klir 2001: 5). That is, system science (system thinking) focuses on the **interrelations** between elements of a system rather than on the specifics of individual elements.

How variables (factors) in a system are interrelated and interact, depends on the **structure of a system (systemic structure).** Senge, which as stated the dissertation builds on, defines systemic structure as "a set of unrelated factors that interact, even though they may be widely separated in time and place, and even though their relationship may be difficult to recognize" (Senge et al. 2000: 82).

As will be shown, Sustainability Traps are produced through specific **systemic structures***.*

The concept of 'structure' and its importance with respect to Sustainability Traps will be discussed more in depth later in the dissertation. What has been important at this point in the dissertation, is to introduce the concept of systems, which are characterized through their structure, i.e. how the variables of a system *interrelate*.

1.3.2 Systems Thinking as a New Perspective: Theoretical Foundations

This chapter will outline the **characteristics** of systems thinking and their theoretical foundations that constitute *systems* **thinking as a new perspective,** i.e. as a new way of thinking compared to '**orthodox thinking**'[29]. This will be done briefly. Chapters

---

steht aus Teilen, die so miteinander verknüpft sind, dass kein Teil unabhängig ist von anderen teilen und das Verhalten als Ganzes beeinflusst wird vom Zusammenwirken aller Teile."
28 The emphasis on relations also becomes evident in the etymological roots of the term. The term 'system' descended from the Greek term 'systema' meaning „formation, assembly" (Kluge 2002: 900). [Translation into English by the author. German term: Zusammenstellung.]
29 Orthodox thinking thereby is not a 'fix term'. Rather it relates to ways of thinking that often can be observed in social and organizational behavior. Similar to Senge (see below),

1.4 and 2 will then outline in detail, how these characteristics apply to the field of sustainability (Sustainability Traps) in particular. As will be argued in later chapters, the characteristics of systems thinking qualify systems thinking as most valuable for corporations for dealing successfully with sustainability, particularly with corporate Sustainability Traps.

The concept of systems thinking as a new way of thinking as it is put forward in the dissertation, heavily builds on Senge et al., who introduced systems thinking as an **organizational learning discipline** (Senge 2006 and Senge et al. 1994). Senge defines systems thinking as "a discipline for seeing wholes. It is a framework for seeing interrelationships rather than things, for seeing patterns of change rather than static 'snapshots.' It is a set of general principles - distilled over the course of the twentieth century, spanning fields as diverse as the physical and social sciences, engineering, and management" (Senge 2006: 68). As Senge's definition of systems thinking indicates, the concept of 'systems thinking as a new way of thinking' is based on a number of characteristics (principles) of systems thinking, which were developed over time by different historical approaches that took a new (systems) view compared to 'orthodox thinking'.[30] In the following the characteristics of systems thinking, which constitute systems thinking as a new perspective (compared to 'orthodox thinking') shall be discussed in the following. The characteristics relevant for the dissertation basically derive from three historical approaches of systems thinking:

a) General Systems Theory

The name and many of the principles of **general systems theory** have been defined by the biologist Ludwig von Bertalanffy (1968). In his book he traces the concept of systems back to the 17th century (Leibniz and other scholars). Bertalanffy proposed general systems theory as a counter-conception of traditional physics, which held a rather sectoral (reductionist) view. He argued that elements should not be analyzed isolatedly, but that it is the **interrelations** between elements that constituted significance (Bertalanffy 1968: 30ff and 54ff). As the term *general* systems theory suggests, the theory seeks to analyze generic characteristics and mechanisms innate to systems of different disciplines. Boulding has stressed this **generic nature** of general systems theory, referring to it as "*the skeleton of science*" (Boulding 1956). Each scientific discipline (e.g. physics, biology, chemistry, psychology, sociology,

---

the dissertation will therefore define what systems thinking *is* (its characteristics) and what it is not. The way of thinking that systems thinking 'is not' relates to orthodox thinking.

30 As becomes apparent in his definition, *orthodox thinking*, which Senge implicitly contrasts systems thinking with, is rather focused on things (see also Klir 'thinghood' above) and snapshots (individual events), while systems thinking focuses on interrelations between elements (things) and on non-linear dynamic patterns that change over time.

economics) separately developed specialized research methods, which yield content (understanding) relating to a specific segment of the empirical world.[31] These findings (contents) however remain unrelated to each other. *The quest of General Systems Theory therefore is to develop "a body of systematic theoretical constructs which will discuss the general relationships of the empirical world"* (Boulding 1956: 197).

Characteristics of Systems Thinking as a new perspective (compared to orthodox thinking) resulting from General Systems Theory relevant for the dissertation are:

*Systems thinking focuses on **interrelations** ('systemhood') rather than a perspective on the specifics of isolated variables ('thinghood').*

*Systems thinking has a **generic nature**, which allows integrating diverse systems (sectors), such as the economic, the social and the economic system.*

b) Cybernetics

A discipline closely related to general systems theory is **Cybernetics**. Cybernetics draws from fields such as electrical networks (engineering), modeling and neuroscience. Wiener defined Cybernetics as the science of "control and communication in the animal and the machine" (Wiener 1948). Wiener and his colleagues showed that technological and biological systems have many common characteristics, which laid significant groundwork for combining these systems, e.g. in sociotechnical systems, computer controlled machines such as automata and robots. What was important for a general system understanding was that cybernetics explained how systems control their actions through **regulatory feedback,** like e.g. a thermostat, which regulates temperature through adjustment processes based on the gap between desired and actual temperature. Cybernetics thus focuses on *how* a system functions. As Ashby states, "[c]ybernetics [...] treats, not things but *ways of behaving*. It does not ask 'what *is* this thing?" but '*what does it do?*' (Ashby 1956: 1).[32]

The characteristics of Systems Thinking as a new perspective (compared to orthodox thinking) resulting from Cybernetics relevant for the dissertation is:

---

31 For example: For systems thinking in physics and cybernetics see e.g. Wiener 1948 and Ashby 1956; for biology see e.g. Maturana and Varela (1980); for sociology see e.g. Luhmann (1986); for usage of systems thinking in behavioral science and psychology, see e.g. Schweitzer and Schlippe 2006, Schlippe and Schweitzer 2003, Schlippe, El Hachimi and Jürgens 2004 and for a special emphasis on teams ('reflective team') and systems thinking see Hargens and Schlippe (1998).

32 The concept of cybernetics was significantly enlarged through von Foerster, who introduced the concept of second-order cybernetics to refer to how observers construct models of systems, which they are part of and with which they interact (Foerster 1995 and 1979). This aspect will play a role in chapter 2.2.1 of the dissertation.

*Systems Thinking does not focus on the specifics of an individual variable, but rather on how variables are **interrelated** and drive behavior of a system: In dynamic systems, variables are not related one-way (linear), but through reciprocal **feedbacks (non-linear)**, which trigger regulation and control mechanisms in the system that drive **system behavior (organized complexity**, Bertalanffy 1968: 34ff and 93). As will be shown in the dissertation, the behavior of Sustainability Traps is that they produce unsustainability through dynamic feedback processes between variables from the economic, the social and the environmental sphere.*

c) (Qualitative) System Dynamics and Organizational Learning.

The field of System Dynamics was founded by Forrester in the early 1960s drawing from general systems theory (interrelations of variables) as well as from cybernetics (regulatory feedback mechanisms). Forrester defines systems dynamics as the following: "System dynamics deals with how things change through time which covers most of what most people find important. System dynamics involves interpreting real life systems into computer simulation models that allow one to see how the structure and decision-making policies in a system create its behavior" (Forrester 1999: 1). Thus, what is crucial to system dynamics is to examine how system behavior is created through the interrelation of a) decision-making policies based on specific mental models of agents and b) dynamic structures, which are created through the interplay of the actions, which the agents took based on the mental model they hold. While System Dynamics has its origins in quantitative (hard) systems thinking and computer modeling, a branch of qualitative system dynamics emerged in order to deal with ill-structured problem situations that include many qualitative variables. The field of qualitative system dynamics significantly developed through the approach of Organizational Learning of Senge et al. (Senge 2006, Senge et al. 1994), which focused on systems thinking as a discipline for organizational learning. The approach

The fields of System Dynamics and Organizational Learning are key approaches for the dissertation and will further be discussed in chapters 1.4.2 and 1.4.3. In this chapter what is relevant to outline are the characteristics of systems thinking relevant for the dissertation that constitute systems thinking as a new perspective resulting from System Dynamics and Organizational Learning. These are:

Systems Thinking focuses on how results, e.g. unsustainability, are created through the **interplay** of **mental models** of social agents and **dynamic, systemic structures**; rather than through 'unethical' behavior of individual social agents. Furthermore systems thinking allows **mapping** these dynamic, systemic structures, thus mapping the structure of Sustainability Traps, e.g. through *causal-loop-diagramming*[33]. Because structures entail dynamic complexity, systems thinking does not focus on fix, impeccable 'solutions' but rather on continuous *learning*.

The field of systems thinking is vast as will become apparent in the next chapter, its approaches manifold and in parts contradictory. The dissertation therefore in this chapter only discussed those *characteristics*, which constitute *systems thinking as a new perspective* (compared to orthodox thinking) as put forward in the dissertation and their theoretical foundations. As will be shown in following chapters, the dissertation argues that because of the characteristics of systems thinking elaborated on in this chapter, *systems thinking as a new perspective (a new way of thinking), is better suited to deal with issues of sustainability, particularly with Sustainability Traps, than 'orthodox' thinking, because Sustainability Traps arise through non-linear dynamic interrelations between the economic, social and environmental sphere.*

1.4 Applying Systems Thinking to Sustainability: Scientific Positioning

Chapter 1.2 has outlined the concept of sustainability and chapter 1.3 has introduced systems thinking as a new perspective, i.e. a new way of thinking. The following chapter now deals with the application of principles from systems thinking (systems science) to issues of sustainability. The number of scientific approaches currently existing that use principles of systems thinking (systems science) to analyze issues of sustainability, indicates the importance of a systems perspective for meeting the challenges of sustainability. However, the interconnectedness between many of the approaches yet still is slender and the field has not yet identified itself as a scientific field in its own right.[34] The following overview to the knowledge of the dissertation is the first overview of scientific approaches that use principles of systems thinking (systems science) to analyze issues of sustainability. The overview thus provides a *general* 'systems perspective on sustainability', which builds the *context* the dissertation is positioned in. It has to be stated clearly that the aim of this chapter is *not* to provide a complete list of all approaches applying system science to sustainability and to outline synergies and differences between them.[35] *Rather*

---

33 Causal-loop diagramming thus is a qualitative modeling language, which will be used in the dissertation and which will be outlined in-depth in chapter 2.2.5.

34 An effort for doing so can be considered Sustainability Science (see chapter 1.4.1).

35 This would be most interesting, considering the importance of the field. However this would constitute a dissertation in its own right. The aim of this dissertation is a particular 'system perspective on sustainability': Sustainability Traps. A complete overview of approaches applying system science to sustainability and an analysis of their synergies and differences thus constitute potential for future research (see chapter 1.4).

the aim of this chapter is to outline the existing scientific **context**, *which the dissertation' approach is positioned in.* As this context still is quite young and heterogeneous the following overview becomes necessary. That is:

The overview provides a ***general*** *'systems perspective on sustainability', which builds the* ***scientific context*** *the dissertation is positioned in. Part II will outline the dissertation' approach, which constitutes a* ***particular*** *'systems perspective on sustainability':* **Sustainability Traps** *and the specific principles of systems thinking required for managing them.*

The concept of Sustainability Traps elaborated thus is the *dissertation' contribution* to the scientific field of 'a systems perspective on sustainability'. Sustainability Traps are reoccurring **systemic** patterns of failed corporate sustainability measures that backfire, triggered through **dynamics** between the ***environmental, social*** and ***corporate*** sphere. The backfiring thereby impacts not only the environmental or social sphere, but equally the corporation itself. The introductory chapters 1.1.1 and 1.1.2 provided a first, basic understanding of Sustainability Traps. Their concept and characteristics will be elaborated in-depth in part II of the dissertation. First, the scientific approaches shall be discussed here that form the context, which Sustainability Traps are positioned in. Figure 1 provides the overview of existing scientific approaches with a systems perspective on sustainability. [36]

---

[36] It is important to state that the relationships (arrows) between the different fields in figure 1 are of theoretical nature, as boundaries between the fields are blur since most are very young, developing fast and heterogeneous between themselves as will become apparent in the discussion below. Therefore the illustration is to be understood as an orientation rather than a rigid, invariant categorization.

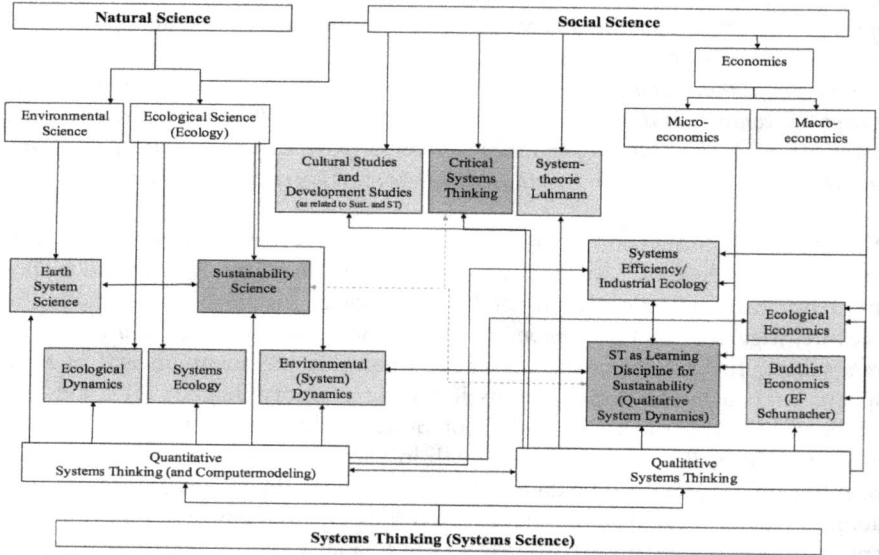

Fig. 1: Existing Scientific Approaches Applying Systems Thinking to Sustainability
Source: Produced by the author (ST = Systems Thinking; Sust. = Sustainability)

The *white boxes* in figure 1 constitute the broad context the dissertation is positioned in: On the one side, the three dimensions of sustainability (chapter 1.2.2),
represented through **natural science, social science**, which in turn includes
(micro)economics. On the other side: **Systems Thinking** (chapter 1.3), subdivided in
rather qualitative and quantitative branches. The *light shaded boxes* outline the different scientific approaches, using principles of systems thinking to analyze issues
of the sustainability dimensions, which build the scientific context for the dissertation' approach is positioned in. The *darker shaded boxes* thereby represent the approaches that are most fundamental to the dissertation' approach. As will be shown,
these are: 'Systems Thinking as a Learning Discipline for Sustainability' (Qualitative System Dynamics), Critical Systems Thinking and Sustainability Science.
While these three constitute the core basis, the dissertation will also resort to individual concepts or principles of other scientific approaches for elaborating specific
aspects important for successfully dealing with Sustainability Traps, as will be discussed. In the following the scientific approaches of figure 1 will be discussed,
which build the *context* of 'a systems perspective on sustainability' the dissertation is
positioned in. Thereby each subchapter has the following structure:
a) The **concept** of the scientific approach is discussed and
b) the **relation to the dissertation' approach** is elaborated.

1.4.1 Sustainability Science

a) Concept of Sustainability Science

Sustainability Science is a new scientific field, which is still in search of a homogenous definition and content. Sustainability Science can be defined as a transdisciplinary apparaoch to "construct a framework for understanding and acting in relation to (un)sustainable development" (Vries 2013: 5). Thereby Sustainability Science aims at integrating existing sustainability approaches under a roof that enables better meeting the sustainability challenges discussed in the introductory chapter (see also Clark 2003: 1f). Clark criticizes current scientific methods in the field of sustainability: "Present methods for addressing the environmental impacts of human activities impose a bias toward treating sustainability problems as though they were merely technocratic exercises in forecasting the impact of single stressors on simplified systems with linear responses and minimal uncertainty. In fact, many of the greatest challenges to sustainability could not be more different from this method-driven cartoon: They involve multiple, interacting stresses; complex, nonlinear responses; systemic uncertainty and multiple stakeholders" (Clark 2003: 4f). *To meet these challenges Clark et al. have introduced Sustainability Science as a new field of science, which relies on the work of the diverse disciplines dealing with sustainability, but will need to revise and build on them under a new paradigm that meets the holistic nature of the topic.* Sustainability science "differs to a considerable degree in structure, methods and content, from science as we know it" (Kates 2001, Kates et al. 2000: 2). Therefore Kates et al. argue for a "wide discussion within the scientific community [...] of the particular novelty of the approach, its key questions, appropriate methodologies and institutional needs. (Kates et al. 2000: 4). Thus, the concept of Sustainability Science still is in statu nascendi. As a start however, Kates et al. have identified four basic requirements of Sustainability Science (Clark 2003: 3-4; see also Kates et al. 2000, Kates et al. 2001, WBGU 1997)[37]:

- *An integrative, holistic approach to sustainability:* This approach points to the requirement not to focus on "single stressors (even climate change) or single solutions (even solar energy)" (Clark 2003: 3). "Sustainability Science focuses on the dynamic interactions between nature and society" (Kates et al. 2000: 1).
- *Coproduction of usable knowledge:* Clark does not only argue for a coproduction of different scientific disciplines, but also for a coproduction of science with stakeholders of sustainability: "[...A]n effective science of sustainability will almost certainly need to be a science in which academics, government,

---

37 The requirements for sustainability science put forward by Clark are the essence of dialogues executed by a vast number of scholars from different fields over several years, which are engaged to reach a shared vision of "what science for sustainability might seek to accomplish" (Clark 2003: 3).

business people and lay citizens see themselves vested in the production as well as the use of knowledge" (Clark 2003: 4).

- *A goal of findings solutions:* Scientists of sustainability science should not only restrict itself to analyzing, but should equally engage in the implementation of 'solutions'[38] (Clark 2003: 3), as the real challenge of sustainability starts with the implementations of workable solutions.
- *Scientists as facilitators for Social Learning:* Clark argues that scientists seeking to make a substantial contribution to sustainability will need to conduct themselves less as sources of social guidance, but more as facilitators of social learning (Clark 2003: 4). "Science has a great deal to contribute in helping society to design policy experiments from which it can learn, and in helping to design the monitoring and assessment systems necessary to carry through the learning" (Clark 2003: 4).

b) Relation to the dissertation' approach

As stated above, Sustainability Science aims to form a roof, under which sustainability approaches can be integrated that meet certain requirements identified by the field. The dissertation' approach heavily builds on 'systems thinking as a learning discipline for sustainability' (qualitative System Dynamics).

As 'systems thinking as a learning discipline for sustainability' however has not yet developed as a field on its own within the sustainability movement (see respective chapter below[39]), the dissertation positions itself within the field of Sustainability Science.

To reason this positioning, it shall be discussed in the following, how the concept of Sustainability Traps ties in with the four basic requirements of Sustainability Science outlined above.

The WBGU stresses the focus on 'an integrative, holistic approach Sustainability Science': "The interdependency of human and natural systems demands an approach which ensures that the complex problems of global change are analyzed in an integrated way from different perspectives and at a variety of levels" (WBGU 1997: 105). "The complex phenomena of global change cannot be analyzed in a purely sectoral manner or from the perspective of a single discipline, because they are the result of multilayered interactions between the ecosphere and the anthroposphere. It is virtually unthinkable that global change research could provide the basis for new response strategies without an analysis of the complex interactions between processes in the ecosphere and anthroposphere" (WBGU 1997: 105). The

---

38 The term solution here is used in opposition to mere analysis, not in the sense of ,the right solution' as will become apparent below.
39 See chapter 1.4.3.

dissertation' concept of Sustainability Traps meets this requirement as it focuses on the *interactions of factors from the environmental, social and economic sphere*. As will be discussed in chapter 2.1.3, this implies looking for *endogenous* rather than external 'causes' of unsustainability, which also is put forward by Clark with regard to Sustainability Science (Clark 2003: 3). Furthermore Sustainability Science requires a *problem driving* approach (Kates et al. 2000: 3). This aspect will be important for the dissertation, when talking about how to define problems (systems of Sustainability Traps)[40]. It relates to the postulation that a problem (system) definition should not be limited by sectoral boundaries, but should encompass any relevant variable that determines the behavior of the system. Moreover "Sustainability Science will need to [...] deal with functional complexity such as is evident in recent analyses of environmental degradation resulting from multiple stresses" (Kates et al. 2000: 1). Functional complexity as *complexity* based on systems structure will play a prominent role in the dissertation. As will be discussed in chapter 2.2.5, a main challenge of Sustainability Traps is that their systemic structure entails *dynamic complexity*, which defers causes and effects of unsustainability. Under the aspect of systems structure another of the requirements can be subsumed: "[A]ccount for both the temporal inertia and urgency of processes like ozone depletion" (Kates et al. 2000: 2). Inertia *(delays)* as a structural characteristic of Sustainability Traps plays an important role: Inertia is especially relevant for environmental feedback to social actions, which often only plays out after a considerable time span.[41] Furthermore Clark et al. claim that sustainability science should focus on *comparative* analysis rather than focusing on individual technologies or behaviors. Clark provides the following example: Sustainability science would spend little time on evaluating the absolute risks of genetic technologies, but it would focus on "whether a choice of Bt-cotton, or cotton-plus-orthodox pesticides, or polyester fibers was a more sustainable approach to providing the clothing fibers people want" (Clark 2003: 4). As will be discussed in-depth in chapter 3.1.2 the dissertation deliberately focused on not analyzing and modeling one particular sustainability trap in-depth, but rather chose to analyze a band-with of various Sustainability Traps in order to stress the concept of Sustainability Traps (realization through distinctions) and to reveal the different impacts of Sustainability Traps driven by particular underlying mental models of sustainability.

The 'coproduction of useable knowledge' is (Clark 2003: 3) is key to managing Sustainability Traps, as the traps are produced through dynamic interaction of a corporation and its stakeholders and thus can only be escaped from through co-operative approaches as will be discussed. With regard to 'scientists as facilitators for social learning' and the 'implementation of workable solutions' (Clark 2003: 3f), Clark ar-

---

40 See chapter 2.2.2.1.
41 See chapter 2.2.5.6.

gues that scientists seeking to make a substantial contribution to sustainability will need to conduct themselves less as sources of social guidance, but more as facilitators of social learning (Clark 2003: 4). "Science has a great deal to contribute in helping society to design policy experiments from which it can learn, and in helping to design the monitoring and assessment systems necessary to carry through the learning" (Clark 2003: 4). Social learning was implicit in the scientific enterprise since its beginning, yet the new quality of sustainability science (Kates et al. 2000: 2; see also Parson and Clark 1995) and the urgency of social change towards sustainability makes it explicit again. Social learning encompasses to admit that we do not know the 'right' solutions when it comes to sustainability, but that we as a society need to learn to become more sustainable. Scientists can facilitate the process. They need to reevaluate their own role however. For, as Clark states, the "'facilitator' role has not always come easily to scientists, especially those brought up in an earlier tradition of 'science advice to government'" (Clark 2003: 4)[42]. This aspect of sustainability science – science as facilitator for social learning – is core to the dissertation. As will be discussed thoroughly throughout the dissertation, the dissertation' approach is not to provide 'solutions' for managing Sustainability Traps, but rather concentrates on *learning skills* required for successfully dealing with them from a systems perspective (systems thinking as a learning discipline for sustainability).

1.4.2 (Environmental) System Dynamics

a) Concept of (Environmental) System Dynamics

Environmental System Dynamics is the study of complex interactions between natural systems and human activity at any scale - global and local -, whereby contributions on local scale (individual places) currently dominate (see e.g. Deaton and Winebrake 2000, Ford 1999, Ford and Cavana 2004, Jørgensen and Bendoricchio 2001). Environmental Dynamics is a subfield of *System Dynamics*. The System Dynamics Society holds a special interest group on Environmental Dynamics[43], which uses System Dynamics to analyze issues of environmental sustainability on global as well as on local level, whereby the emphasis lies on local perspectives. A definition of System Dynamics has already been given in chapter 1.3.2. The field was founded in the early 1960s by Forrester at the MIT Sloan School of Management, USA. System Dynamics has its origins in quantitative (hard) systems thinking. Hard systems thinking, focuses on optimizing means for best reaching a desired goal and usually relies on mathematical models and/or computer simulations. According to Jackson hard systems thinking still remains "the orthodoxy in applied systems work" (Jackson 1992: 73). Forrester developed System Dynamics by apply-

---

42 As for this statement Clark points to: The Social Learning Group 2001.
43 Homepage: http://www.systemdynamics.org/EnvSig, accessed 15. January 2005

ing concepts of electrical engineering (cybernetics) to social systems. His first work was concerned with industrial systems (Forrester 1961) and subsequently expended to various kinds of social and socio-ecological systems (Forrester 1989). Forrester considers System Dynamics crucial for dealing with the problems of the 21st century (Forrester 1994). However, his argumentation is rooted in hard systems thinking: Forrester argues that the most effective way for learning is modeling and computer simulation in interaction with revising mental models. His aim of learning thereby lies in the realization of *counter-intuitive behavior* of complex dynamic systems. In order to realize and understand counter-intuitive behavior Forrester considers computer models inevitable, because only they can calculate non-linear dynamics (Forrester 1995, 1991, 1994). Environmental Dynamics (Environmental System Dynamics) consequently is focused on quantitative approaches and often uses computer models to determine system behavior.

b) Relation to the dissertation' approach

The dissertation' relation to (Environmental) System Dynamics can be divided into three aspects:

First, the very **concept of a 'trap'**, which the dissertation uses, is derived from the concepts of 'counterintuitive behavior of systems', 'policy resistance' and 'backfiring' from system dynamics as will be discussed in-depth in chapter 2.1.1.

Second, many of the **principles for managing** Sustainability Traps (chapter 2.2) consequently are derived from System Dynamics. But as will be discussed, these are expanded by principles and concepts from other fields of system science, which allow meeting the specifics with respect to *sustainability.*

While the first two aspects have pointed out correspondences to the dissertation' approach, this *third* aspect discusses differences to the dissertation' approach: The most important difference of the dissertation' approach to (Environmental) System Dynamics lies in the use of a *qualitative* approach of the dissertation rather than a quantitative one: Forrester himself engaged into individual sustainability issues in his later work. Some of which can be considered a Sustainability Trap.[44] Most prominent are his works on Urban Dynamics (1969) and World Dynamics (1971). In Urban Dynamics Forrester showed that the interactions of policies for conserving old buildings, programs for low cost housing and for raising living standards caused socially unsustainable structures that actually *lowered* quality of living standards (1969). Urban Dynamics therefore can be considered a pertinent example of a Sustainability Trap, where (well-intended) intervention actually worsened the situation, because the dynamic interrelation of different variables respectively the system structure, were not analyzed. World Dynamics (Forrester 1971) constitutes the

---

44 Although focused on a macro-economic level, while the dissertation focuses on a micro-economic level.

first socio-economic System Dynamics model of the world (World 2 Model), mapping important interrelationships between world population, industrial production, pollution, resources, and food and problematic consequences of unchecked growth[45]. It constituted the basis for the World 3 Model developed by Forrester's students, which got famous through the report 'Limits-to-Growth' to the Club of Rome[46] (Meadows et al. 1972).[47]

Forrester's models - and even more so the models from Environmental Dynamics – however, are focused on quantitative modeling of socio-environmental dynamics of individual places or issues using computer simulations. The dissertation' approach in contrast is *qualitative* and holds a more general (generic), learning-centered approach. Its' emphasis does not lie in modeling as such, but rather on *learning skills* for dealing with Sustainability Traps. The dissertation' approach therefore is strongly related to Qualitative System Dynamics and Organizational Learning, which will be addressed in the chapter on 'Systems Thinking as a Learning Discipline for Sustainability' (chapter 1.4.3). Forrester's System Dynamics yet has built the basis for these approaches. The field of (Environmental) System Dynamics therefore is highly compatible with the dissertation' approach and can serve as a most valuable complement to the concept of Sustainability Traps: The dissertation is focused on sensitization for the issue of Sustainability Traps as a generic phenomenon for managers and presents *archetypes* of common Sustainability Traps, which can serve as an orientation point to identify if a corporation is caught up in a trap. Furthermore the dissertation elaborates principles for avoidance and management of Sustainability Traps from a focus of business practice. Once a corporation has realized it is caught up in a Sustainability Trap that backfires, it can be most helpful to build a System Dynamics computer simulation in order to analyze and quantify the *specifics* of the individual Sustainability Trap the corporation is caught up in.[48]

---

45 See figure 2 and 3 in chapter 1.4.3.
46 For the Club of Rome, see below.
47 Although limits-to-growth has its emphasis on computer-simulation, the work of Meadows et al., shall be discussed in the paragraph on 'Systems Thinking as a Learning Discipline', because later work, especially the one of Donella Meadows, departed from an emphasis on computer-modeling towards including soft-systems and learning skills.
48 As stated, the Sustainability Traps outlined in chapter 3 of the dissertation are archetypes.

1.4.3 Systems Thinking as a Learning Discipline for Sustainability (Qualitative System Dynamics)

a) Concept of Systems Thinking as a Learning Discipline for Sustainability

As stated above, this is the concept, which the dissertation most substantially is based on. Thereby 'Systems Thinking as a Learning Discipline for Sustainability' on contrast to the other approaches of figure 1, has not yet been proclaimed as on own scientific field (yet).

*Rather the dissertation subsumes hereunder approaches, which use **Qualitative System Dynamics** to deal with issues of sustainability. This does not exclude the use of quantitative modeling, yet the focus of these approaches lies on **learning about sustainability**, i.e. using **systems thinking as a new perspective**, which points to issues of sustainability that remain unrealized with 'orthodox thinking' and/or helps to better deal with specific sustainability issues than orthodox thinking.*

As this approach is crucial to the dissertation the chapter will be discussed in greater detail: In the following the dissertation will first outline the historical development of Qualitative System Dynamics out of System Dynamics. Subsequently the dissertation will outline individuals and organizations, which have developed approaches that can be subsumed under the field of 'Systems Thinking as a Learning Discipline for Sustainability'. These are: Senge (Organizational Learning), Vester, Meadows, Millennium Institute, Lazlo, Radermacher and The Natural Step. Thereby Senge is the one most crucial for the dissertation.

a1) Historical Development of Qualitative System Dynamics

This emphasis on quantification of variables and on computer modulation of Forrester's System Dynamics[49] was challenged by Senge (1990, 2006), Richmond (1994) and others. These approaches stressed systems thinking not primarily as a quantitative modeling technique, but as a new way of thinking and have become known under the term of *qualitative system dynamics* or *qualitative systems thinking*. The emergence of these approaches triggered discussions about two interrelated points within the System Dynamics community: First, discussions about the differentiation and relationships between system dynamics and systems thinking. Second, the validity of quantitative and qualitative system dynamics.

With regard to the first aspect, Forrester argued that systems thinking (in the sense of thinking about systems) is one part of systems dynamics, which only reveals a small fraction (5%) of understanding systems behavior (1994: 18). Forrester rea-

---

49 For an explanation of System Dynamics see (Environmental) System Dynamics, chapter 1.4.2.

soned this, because system dynamics deals with non-linear feedbacks, which can only be processed mathematically through computer simulations and not by a human brain. This view has been challenged by Richmond, which considered system dynamics part of systems thinking and later argued for an *equal* use of the terms (Richmond 1994: 2ff). Today the relationship between systems thinking and system dynamics is broadly perceived in Richmond's sense (Davidz, Nightingale and Rhodes 2004: 3). In regard to the second point of discussion, Richmond further argued for using systems thinking/system dynamics as a new way of thinking, without the need to quantify each variable and run computer-simulations[50] (Richmond 1994: 4ff, see also Wolstenholme 1990[51]). Sterman, head of the MIT System Dynamics Group and leading figure within the field, also discusses the limitations of computer simulation models in ill-structured problem contexts, which are characterized e.g. unawareness of decision rules, quantifying qualitative data, defining reasonable system boundaries, limited inside of modeler into specific situation, difficulty for organizational members to assess complex computer models (Sterman 1991). The discussion of the validity of quantitative versus qualitative systems dynamics is still ongoing in the field today. Thereby the dissertation, as has been pointed out in the above chapter (1.4.2), considers both complementary.

a2) Approaches of 'Systems Thinking as a Learning Discipline for Sustainability'
In the following the dissertation will outline individuals and organizations, which have developed approaches that use Qualitative System Dynamics to learn about issues of sustainability and thus can be subsumed under the field of 'Systems Thinking as a Learning Discipline for Sustainability'.

Peter Senge (Organizational Learning)
Senge (Senge 2006, see also Senge et al. 1994, 2000, 1999, 2004) within his concept of **Organizational Learning** brings together the potentials of system dynamics and elements of soft and critical systems thinking, although he does not outline the theoretical compatibility of the different perspectives explicitly (see also Jackson 2000: 272[52]). Senge et al. (Senge 2006 and Senge et al. 1994) distilled principles of system dynamics, such as interrelations of variables, holisms and feedback mechanisms and introduced them in form of systems thinking as an **organizational**

---

50 This does not exclude the *possibility* of quantification and computer-simulation, yet in contrast to Forrester this is not necessarily required and not perceived as the core potential (essence). Richmond considers the essence of this new thinking to be the operational thinking in stocks and flows. Operational Thinking will be discussed in-depth as a systems thinking skill for sustainability in chapter 2.2.4.
51 That is, Wolstenholme's argumentation for qualitative system dynamics approaches.
52 Jackson only refers to Senge combining system dynamics and soft systems thinking.

learning discipline. That is, systems thinking as a new, *qualitative way of thinking* rather than a quantitative tool. Senge far more than other scholars stresses the potential of systems thinking as a new paradigm. Additionally he points out that systems thinking is deeply intuitive. Senge states, "the underlying worldview [annotation of the author: of systems thinking] is extremely intuitive; experiments with young children show that they learn systems thinking very quickly" (Senge 2006: 7). But due to our socialization in linear and reductionist thinking we are not used to 'putting the different pieces together' (i.e. stock-and-flow thinking, circular causality and the other system thinking skills), that is to interrelate them and thus to see the 'larger picture' (see also Senge et al. 2000).

In Senge's approach of organizational learning, systems thinking as the fifth discipline, builds the framework for four other learning disciplines: Personal Mastery, Mental Models, Shared Vision and Team Learning (Senge 2006).[53] The term 'discipline' thereby indicates a "developmental path for acquiring certain skills and competencies" (Senge 2006: 10). Most important Senge et al., in addition to systems thinking as a learning discipline, introduce a qualitative modeling technique, *causal loop diagramming*, and use it to illustrate systems *archetypes* (Senge 2006: 92ff and 389ff; Senge et al. 1994: 150)[54]. Systems archetypes are reoccurring patterns of structure that drive organizational behavior, i.e. they are generic structures or 'nature's templates' as Senge refers to them (Senge 2006: 92f). One example is the prominent archetype of limits-to-growth, which gained popularity through the homonymous report to the Club of Rome (Meadows et al. 1972) (see appendix A.1). The organizational learning approach by Senge et al. refers primarily to business practice (business strategy) in general. Yet, in recent times the field of corporate sustainability is given rising intention (Senge 2006: 341-382 and 2004: 117-254). A new field of 'Organizational Learning for Sustainability' in the context of systems thinking is crystallizing (Senge, Laur, Schley and Smith 2006). According to Senge, systems theory is needed in the field of sustainability as it "continually reminds us that our perceptions of reality shape our actions and, consequently, that reality" (Senge, Laur, Schley and Smith 2006: 18). Systems Thinking thus allows better analyzing imbalances created by interdependencies, many of them eventually self-correcting (Senge, Laur, Schley and Smith 2006: 15).

---

53 As the other four disciplines, with the exception of mental models, will not play a particular role in the dissertation they should not be outlined here in-depth. For further information, see below.
54 For sources of this collection of archetypes see Senge et al. 1994: 121.

Frederic Vester (Bio-Cybernetic, Ecopolicy)[55]

The most prominent German representative in the field of 'Systems Thinking as a Learning Discipline for Sustainability' can be considered **Vester** (2005, 1999 and 2002[56]). Vester was a biocybernetic and member of the Club of Rome[57], which focused on dealing with dynamic complexity in the field of sustainability (Vester 1999, 1988, Bio-Cybernetics). Furthermore Vester was deeply engaged in the field of learning and developed a classification of different learning types (Vester 2001). Among other games and computer models, Vester developed Ecopolicy, a computer game for learning about interconnectedness and dynamics on global scale. Players are in power of a nation (industrial, developing and emerging country) and their decisions in combination with the decisions of their co-players result in structures effecting factors such as politics, production, environmental stress, quality of life, education and population.[58]

Donella and Dennis Meadows (Limits-to-Growth)

Within the field of System Dynamics Donella and Dennis **Meadows** are crucial contributors to the field of sustainability. They coauthored the book Limits to Growth, whose first version was published in 1972 commissioned by the Club of Rome (Meadows et al. 1972, 1992 and 2004, see also Meadows and Meadows 1973, Meadows, Richardson and Bruckmann 1982, Meadows et al. 1974). Limits-to-Growth analyzed the future consequences of unchecked growth due to finite resources on the planet using a computer model (World3 Model).[59] Further comments on sustainability issues from a systems perspective by Donella Meadows can be found in her bi-weekly column 'The Global Citizen', which was nominated for the Pulitzer Prize in 1991 (Meadows 1991). The first Limits-to-Growth report (Meadows et al. 1972) commissioned by the Club of Rome similarly represented a constitutive writing for the Club. The Club of Rome is an interdisciplinary global

---

55 Vester furthermore has become know for its sensivity model (Vester 2005: 185ff), which however will not be treated in the dissertation.

56 This book unfortunately has not yet been translated into English. Yet, for an extensive review in English see Ulrich 2005.

57 For further information on the Club of Rome see below.

58 For more information on the game visit homepage of the editor of the game Schulbuchverlag Bildungshaus Westermann (www.westermann.de; accessed 05. January 2005) or the Frederic Vester GmbH at the Malik Management Zentrum St. Gallen (http://www.frederic-vester.de/ecopolicy_engl.htm, accessed 05. January 2005). In Germany High school students organize Ecopolicy games (or battles) with politicians.

59 The concept of Limits-to-Growth, particularly the implication of steady-state-economy as experienced critiques (Wallich 1972, Solow 1973) as well as developments of alternative concepts so far (e.g. endogenous growth, see Aghion and Howitt 1998). For an overview of critiques and alternative models see Gerlagh and Keyzer 2001.

think tank dedicated to what it refers to as the 'world problematique': That is the complex set of the most crucial problems facing humanity – political, social, economic, technological, environmental, psychological and cultural.[60] Thereby the focus lies on dynamic complexity due to interdependencies between the issues. Figures 2 and 3 shows the so called World 3 Model used in the report 'Limits-to-Growth', which builds on World 2 Model of Forrester outlined above[61].

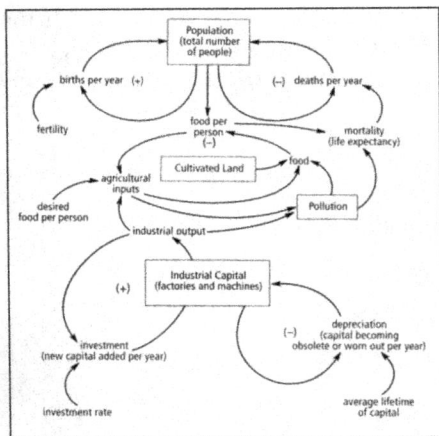

Fig. 2: Feedback Loops of Population, Capital, Services, and Resources

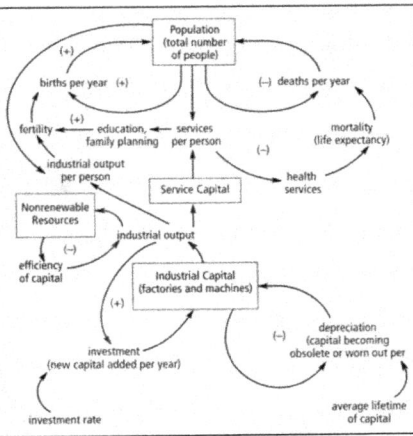

Fig. 3: Feedback Loops of Population, Capital, Agriculture, and Pollution

Source: Both figures constitute Feedback Loops extracted from World 3-03 Model, Meadows et al. 2004: 144f World

In contrast to Forrester, Donella Meadows can be considered to have held a broader approach to learning about systems thinking with a particular emphasis on sustainability. Her approach focused on internalizing and valuing how dynamic complex systems work, rather than controlling and predicting them. – Dancing with systems, i.e. knowing how to best move and behave in complex dynamic systems (Meadows 2002 and 1999). The work of Donella Meadows is continued by the Sustainability Institute, which was founded by her and analyzing issues of sustainability from a systems perspective (system dynamics).

---

60 For more information on the Club of Rome see the homepage: http://www.-clubofrome.org; accessed: 12. November 2004
61 World Dynamics, see chapter 1.4.2.

51

The Millennium Institute (Threshold 21)

Another extensive model based on system dynamics is Threshold 21 of the NGO "The Millennium Institute". Threshold 21 (T21) is a quantitative tool, customized to meet specific planning and analysis needs of countries or regions, for example poverty reduction. Currently there exist over 15 customized models with applications in less-industrialized countries such as Malawi and Bangladesh, emerging countries like China and India, and industrialized countries such as the United States and Italy. Thereby the Millennium Institute is working together with the Carter Center and the World Bank PRSP program. Underlying the model is a concept of the three dimensions of sustainability: Economy, Society and Environment. Figure 4 shows the basic T21 concept.

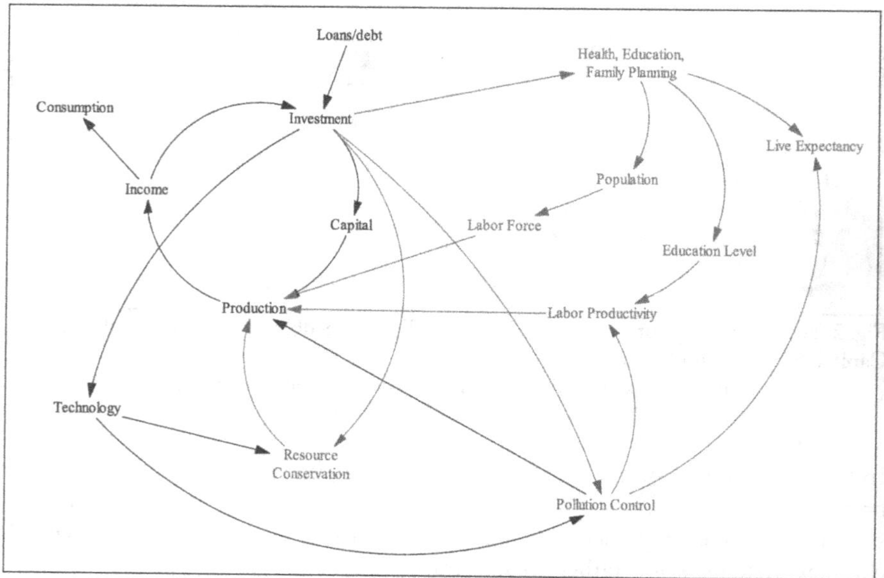

Fig. 4: T21 Basic Concept
Source: Retrieved from Threshold21 website[62]

Lazlo (Evolution Theory)

Another scholar related to this school of thought and equally a member of the Club of Rome is **Laszlo** (Laszlo 2006, 2003, 2001, 1996; Laszlo and Seidel 2006). Lazlo enlarges the systems perspective through an evolutionary point of view.

---

62 Model accessible online at http://www.threshold21.com/, accessed: 12. April 2005

Radermacher (Global Marshall Plan Initiative)

The last Club of Rome member which shall be mentioned within this context of the dissertation, is Radermacher. He focuses on building frameworks for reaching global sustainable development through an eco-social market economy including environmental, social and cultural guidelines (Radermacher 2004a and 2004b). Radermacher made a vital contribution to the practical field as main initiator of the Global Marshall Plan Initiative, - a global initiative aimed at the implementation of Radermacher's approach by striving for improved and binding frameworks for global economy, which integrate economy, environment, society and culture (Radermacher 2004a).

The Natural Step (TNS Framework)

A non-profit research and advisory organization, whose specific system-based approach (The Natural Step Framework) has found significant diffusion within the business community is The Natural Step (Cook 2004, Robèrt et al 2004). Related to this framework is the framework of a second organization to mention the 'Professional Practice for Sustainable Development', a partner organization to The Natural Step. Martin, Hall and other have developed a framework of 'earth as a system' and a corresponding workshop for professionals in education and business, which is related to critical systems thinking (Martin 2005 and 2002, Martin, Cohen, and Martin 2004, Martin and Hall 2002, see also Jucker 2002).

b) Relation to the dissertation' approach

The relation to the dissertation' approach shall equally be subdivided into two parts:
b1) The use and importance of Qualitative System Dynamics in the dissertation.
b2) The relation of the dissertation to the eight existing approaches of 'Systems Thinking as a Learning Discipline for Sustainability' discussed above, particularly to Senge et al.

b1) Relation to the dissertation' approach: Qualitative System Dynamics

As stated, the dissertation will not use quantitative system dynamics, but *qualitative* system dynamics. This can be reasoned by the following: Advantages and disadvantages of quantitative and qualitative systems thinking should be waged according to the intention of the dissertation: The intention of the dissertation is to create awareness and understanding about problematic structures of organizational sustainability measures (Sustainability Traps). The advantage of *quantitative* system dynamics lies in calculating non-linear feedbacks and in quantifying changes (results). This is valuable for well-structured problem contexts. But, organizational sustainability measures usually are ill-structured in the sense of Sterman (1991) outlined above (chapter 1.4.2): Decision rules are unclear; system boundaries are variable and a matter of social bargaining processes; the modeler (author) has limited inside into the organization; involvement of many qualitative variables (such as corporate responsibility, trust, image, blame etc.). These problem-characteristics make it hard and not feasible to quantify data and thus would not lead to reliable results. What the dissertation is interested in, is not to quantify particular sustainability issues, but rather to reveal and to create awareness for systemic *patterns* of unsustainability (Sustainability Traps). Identifying and illustrating these patterns, can be done without a necessity to quantify variables, e.g. by using causal loop diagramming as executed in the dissertation (chapter 3). The great advantage is that causal loop diagramming is far easier to grasp and to understand than mathematical computer models.[63] And it is specifically understanding and reflection of managers, which are key to trigger learning about Sustainability Traps through systems thinking as is intended by the dissertation. As outlined, it is the aim of the dissertation to stress the potential of systems thinking as a new perspective (a new way of thinking) on sustainability. As such, the approach of the dissertation needs to be feasible and easily accessible for business practice, i.e. for managers not yet familiar with systems thinking.[64] Thereby quantitative system dynamics still remains compatible with the approach of the dissertation and can be used to quantify and model an individual Sustainability Trap of a particular corporation as stated above.

b2) Relation to the dissertation' approach: Existing approaches to 'Systems Thinking as a Learning Discipline for Sustainability'

The core approach out of the eight approaches outlined above, which the dissertation builds on, is that of Senge et al. What is most relevant from Senge's conception for the dissertation is the *concept of systems thinking as a new way of thinking and organizational learning* as compared to 'orthodox' thinking based on characteristics of systems thinking. The other learning disciplines (Personal Mastery, Shared Vision and Team Learning) do not play a particular role in the dissertation, with the exception of the concept of mental models, which however is an innate part to the entire field of system dynamics (not only to Senge's concept) as outlined in chapter 1.3.2. The reason that the other three learning disciplines do not play a specific role in the dissertation is that Senge's original approach, as stated, is focused on organizational learning and change processes in general, while the dissertation holds a particular focus on sustainability respectively Sustainability Traps.[65]

---

63 See also chapter 2.2.5.2.

64 Computer models are likely to be outsourced to experts, risking missing out the opportunity for managers to gain systems thinking learning skills on their own.

65 However all of the four other learning disciplines of Senge are complementary with the systems thinking learning skills described in the dissertation. The dissertation however focused on learning skills, which particularly relate to Sustainability Traps. Senge's learning

For dealing with Sustainability Traps in particular other systems thinking skills are crucial as will be argued in the dissertation. These are: Thinking in Models, Re-thinking Boundary Judgments, System-as-Cause Thinking, Operational Thinking and Dynamic Thinking.[66] These five systems thinking skills are not only derived from Senge's 'fifth discipline', but also from other authors of qualitative system dynamics (Ossimitz 1997, Richmond 1994) and critical systems thinking (Ulrich 1998 and 2005). The very *concept* of using an integrated set of skills related to Systems Thinking in order to address learning about a topic as such (chapter 2 of the dissertation), in turn is based on the concept of Senge.[67] The systems thinking skills for dealing with Sustainability Traps and how they relate to Senge and the other authors, will further be discussed in-depth in chapter 2 and therefore shall not be further discussed at this point.

What is furthermore most relevant from Senge's concept for the dissertation is the technique of causal loop diagramming for illustrating the structure of Sustainability Traps (chapters 2.2.5 and 3). The dissertation thereby will focus on *archetypical* structures of Sustainability Traps, whereby some will build on systems archetypes of Senge et al. As will be discussed in in-depth however, there exists a difference between the use of the concept of Senge's archetypes and that of the dissertation.[68]

The relation of the other seven approaches of 'Systems Thinking as a Learning Discipline for Sustainability' to the dissertation' approach shall be summarized in the following:

Vester: A difference of the dissertation' approach to Vester lies in the focus on learning skills rather than on characteristics of systems themselves as well as a focus on the corporate sector, while Vester's analysis relates to the social sphere in general. Nevertheless, Vester's characteristics of systems thinking (qualitative system dynamics) ties in with the systems thinking skills of chapter 2 in the dissertation.

Meadows: The aspect of learning how to intuitively 'dance' with systems will play a role in the dissertation, insofar as systems cannot be 'controlled' and therefore there exist no 'right', 'fix' solution to Sustainability Traps (see chapter 1.4.2). Furthermore 'Limits-to-Growth' will play an important role in the dissertation as a systems

---

discipline of 'mental models' strongly relates to chapter 2.2.1 (thinking in models). Furthermore 'personal mastery' is required with regard to learning systems thinking for sustainbility, in the sense of reflecting upon someone's own actions (see also Pogo-attitude chapter 2.2.5.7). Moreover 'team learning' is important in respect to training and reflecting upon the systems thinking learning skills. Last but not least a shared vision about sustainability goals is inevitable in order to create sustainability.

66 See chapter 2.1.3 and 2.2.

67 That is, the 'content' of this set of five systems thinking skills is derived not only from Senge, but also from the other authors mentioned.

68 See chapter 3.1.2.

archetype (see also Senge 2006: 390) for a basis of specific Sustainability Traps (Job-Creation Trap and Reputation Trap).

The Natural Step: Aspects of the The Natural Step framework (The Four System Conditions) will become relevant in chapter 2.2.4.2 of the dissertation.[69]

Lazlo, Radermacher and *The Millennium Institute*: Will not play a particular role in the dissertation, but the approaches are compatible with the concept of Sustainability Traps developed in the dissertation and might provide potential for future research work on Sustainability Traps.

1.4.4 Critical Systems Thinking: Emancipatory System Approach

a) Concept of Critical Systems Thinking

The Critical Systems Thinking approach of Churchman and Ulrich (boundary critique) shall be discussed here, as these authors particularly focus on issues of sustainability.[70] The authors make a fully different use of systems thinking than other approaches presented here within the field of sustainability, which is: "[S]ystems thinking as a form of critique" (Ulrich 2003: 6; Ulrich 1983 and 2002). Constitutional for the approach of Critical Systems Thinking was the work of Churchman (1968 and 1982). Churchman shifted the focus from questions about 'what we know from a system' to the question of 'how to deal with the fact that we do not know enough', i.e. how to deal with uncertainty and imperfection. Considering all factors that will determine the quality of a decision is not possible. 'False consciousness' of knowing all factors and thus the one right, impeccable solution therefore risks distorting understanding. The core question, which Churchman therefore poses, is: "How can we design improvement without understanding the whole system?" (Churchman 1968: 3). Churchman argues that systems thinking can be beneficial to this aim as it allows critical reflection of the shortcomings and deceptions contained in proposed solutions. Ulrich builds on this work and develops the concept of boundary critique (Ulrich 1983, 2002 and 2005). Boundary setting decides on which variables (e.g. from the social and environmental field) as well as which participants (stakeholders) are *included* and which *excluded* in decision processes as well as how conflicting views are handled (Ulrich 2005: 7). A critical reflection on the boundaries set (boundary critique) can be of use in three respects to sustainabil-

---

69 Furthermore The Natural Step as an organization will play a role in the business case of the furniture company IKEA (chapter 3.2.2.3), which worked together with The Natural Step.

70 Critical Systems Thinking is also associated with the concept of Triple-Loop-Learning of Flood and Romm (1996). This approach however is not relevant for the dissertation and will only be used as a differentiation to another approach of Triple-Loop-Learning in chapter 2.2.1.2 of the dissertation.

ity in the view of Ulrich (1998: 7[71]): It enables critical self-reflecting of managers (respectively organizations) on the implications and consequences of the boundaries set, e.g. considering 'what' and 'who' is being left out of the relevant system (e.g. future generations). Equally boundary critique can be used for dialogical search for mutual understanding. Critical reflection and revision of the boundaries set, thus can lead to more sustainability. Third – and most important to Ulrich – boundary critique can be used as a means for *emancipation* of social groups (e.g. local communities) with less power or expertise than other social agents (e.g. corporations, scientists). The approach therefore is also referred to as *Emancipatory System Approach*. A critique of system boundaries, can serve as a means for emancipation, because system boundaries define the 'borders of concern' and therefore always imply *value judgments*, which are interdependent from 'facts' and therefore provide a basis for 'non-experts' to meet as equals with experts or other social agents of power (Ulrich 1998: 7). Thus, if social groups acquire knowledge of how to express boundary critique, this can help them in securing a symmetry (meeting as equals) even in situations of unequal distribution of power and expertise (Ulrich 1993). Ulrich provides a heuristic for how to execute boundary critique (Ulrich 1983 and 2005) and provides examples of its application, e.g. the use of boundary critique in the introduction of a new type of agricultural land use in the underprivileged region of North Rupununi District of south-west Guyana, in order to discuss and learn how ecological and socio-economic effects of the new land use would affect the lives of the people in the region in unintended and unequal ways (Ulrich 2005: 13f).

b) Relation to the dissertation' approach

The dissertation will **not** use Critical Systems Thinking as an emancipatory approach. Yet, Ulrich's concept of boundary judgments as such is most crucial for the dissertation. The dissertation uses Ulrich's concept of boundary judgments as a systems thinking skill for dealing with Sustainability Traps (chapter 2.2.2). As stated, Sustainability Traps relate to dynamic interrelations of variables from the economic, social and environmental sphere. Yet, which *system boundaries* an organization sets for its sustainability measures, i.e. which variables from the economic, social and environmental sphere it does considers and which it does not, is crucial with regard to Sustainability Traps as will be showed. Furthermore, because as Ulrich elaborated, setting system boundaries is a matter of value judgments, there is no one right, impeccable solution to manage Sustainability Traps. Rather, as will be discussed in-depth in chapter 2.2.2 of the dissertation, dealing with Sustainability

---

71 The explicit reference to the field of sustainability is made by the author of this dissertation. Ulrich outlines these three usages of boundary judgments in general.

Traps requires regularly re-thinking and adjusting system boundaries. Boundary judgments therefore are a continuous learning process.

1.4.5   Earth System Science

a) Concept of Earth System Science

Earth System Science (Earth System Analysis) is a scientific field closely related to Sustainability Science[72], as the latter fundamentally draws from approaches of Earth System Science (Clark, Crutzen and Schellnhuber 2003: 14ff). Earth System Science addresses the feedbacks and synergisms between the ecosphere and the anthroposphere, whereby each sphere (system) in turn encompasses various subsystems (Claussen 2001: 147, Schellnhuber Crutzen, Clark, Claussen and Held 2004)[73]. "The ecosphere or, the natural Earth system, encompasses the abiotic world, the geosphere, and the living world, the biosphere, whereas the anthroposphere includes all cultural and socio-economic activities of humankind which can be subdivided into subcomponents such as the psycho-social sphere etc" (Claussen 2001: 147). As the name indicates, Earth System Science has its roots in System Science, thereby focusing on *dynamic* interrelations between the ecosphere and the anthroposphere (Ehlers and Kraft 2001, Schellnhuber et al. 2003). These interrelations in Earth System Science often are illustrated in simplified models. A fundamental model thereby was the 'Bretherton Diagram' (figure 5), developed by the Earth System Science Committee NASA Advisory Council headed by Francis P. Bretherton in 1986.

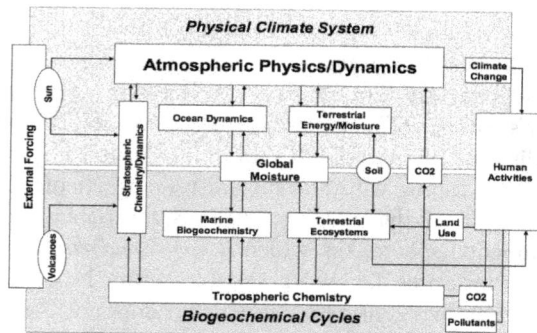

Fig. 5: Earth System Science: Bretherton Diagram
Source: NASA 1986

---

72 See chapter 1.4.1.

73 It has to be noted that although Earth System Science has arisen out of System Science it is focused on systems is based on 'thinghood'. A promising challenge would be to develop approaches of Earth System Science focused on 'systemhood' in order to focus on global and local dynamics that drive (un)sustainability.

Metaphorically, earth system science can be related to the *Gaia-Theory* (Schellnhuber 2001: 17ff). The Gaia-Theory has been developed by Lovelock and considers the earth as a living system in so far as different spheres (biosphere, atmosphere, oceans, soils) are dynamically interacting and influencing each other (Lovelock 2000 and 2006; also Margulis 1998). Scientifically, Earth System Science has its roots in *Global Change Science* (Ehlers and Krafft 2001: 7ff). Global Change Research started out as climate research and today is concerned with societal causes of global environmental changes in general (Ehlers and Krafft 2001; IHDP 2005; NRC 1999a and 2001; WBGU 1997; Kondratyev, Savinykh, Varotsos, Krapivin 2004). "For the first time in history, human activities are having impacts of planetary scale. The resultant changes in the global environment are reshaping the relationship between humankind and the natural basis on which its existence depends. This transformation process, called global change, is occurring at unprecedented speed and involves many risks" (WBGU 1997: 3). The current geological epoch, where humans emerged as a significant global force affecting the earth system and altering key processes in natural and biological systems also has become known as the 'anthropocene' (Mitchell and Lankao 2004: 388ff; see also Markl 1986).

Earth System Analysis tends to further combine traditional reductionist disciplines to provide a better understanding for the dynamics between the different spheres (Schellnhuber and Wenzel 1998, Schellnhuber 2001). Yet, it has to be stated that Earth System Science is still dominated by the natural science and contributions of social science are still low (Ehlers and Krafft 2001: 5f).

b) Relation to the dissertation' approach

The dissertation relates to Earth System Science and Global Change Science closely in so far as it basis its concept of Sustainability Traps on **dynamic interactions** between different systems (environmental, social and economic) and focuses on their **feedback** mechanisms. The dissertation differs from Earth System Science in so far as the latter focuses on *global environmental* changes triggered by society, whereby the dissertation focuses on the *corporate* (micro-economic) sphere. Furthermore the emphasis of the dissertation does not lie solely on *environmental impacts* of corporations, but similarly on *social impacts*. Yet, the dissertation considers Earth System Science and Global Change Science complementary and a most fruitful amendment for a systems perspective of corporate sustainability as it is elaborated here. For further research, feeding global environmental and social trends (see development studies below) into the concept of Sustainability Traps could be a promising enlargement.[74]

In regard to the Gaia Theory, the dissertation in-line with Earth System Science (Markl 2001: 87f) rejects conclusions resulting of Lovelock's hypothesis that due to

---

74 See chapter 4: Directions for further research.

a homeostatic, self-regulating feedback-system the earth will automatically sustain conditions for life on earth as it has done for millions of years. As Markl states, this is a dangerous misconception of feedbacks and autopoiesis[75] in dynamic systems.[76] The aspect that autopoetic systems are not free from the risk to collapse is a crucial implication to Sustainability Traps, as the traps due to backfiring (in extreme situations) indeed can lead to collapse of the system at issue.[77]

1.4.6   System Efficiency Approaches and Industrial Ecology
a) Concept of Systems Efficiency Approaches and Industrial Ecology
Industrial Ecology constitutes a scientific field in its own right. Out of reasons of simplicity, the field is subsumed into its larger context of Systems Efficiency Approaches in this overview. The concept of *Eco-Efficiency* focuses on reducing environmental impact, while increasing value of production (WBCSD 2006a). A fundamental approach to eco-efficiency has been 'Factor Four' (Weizsäcker, Lovins and Lovins 1997), another report to the Club of Rome[78]. The approach seeks to quadruple resource productivity so that wealth is doubled, and resource use is halved.[79] The concept of *Industrial Ecology* aims at reaching eco-efficiency by moving from open-loop, linear industrial systems to closed loop system, where wastes become input for new processes. The approach of Industrial Ecology thus is also closely related to the concept of *Biomimicry*[80] (Benyus 1997), i.e. learning from and imitating processes found in nature for the design of technological, industrial processes (here: closed-loop cycles). A core focus of Industrial Ecology thereby lies on material and energy flows between different industrial sectors, where waste of one industry can become the input for another (Ayres and Ayres 1996 and 2002; Socolow et al. 1994; Bourg and Erkman 2003; Van Den Bergh and Janssen 2005)[81]. A prominent example is the Industrial Park at Kalundborg, Denmark, where six companies exploit each other's residual or by-products on a commercial basis. For ex-

---

75 For the concept of autopoiesis see Maturana and Varela 1980 and 1987.

76 As will be outlined further below in the dissertation there are tipping points and bifurcation points, where structures and hence behavior of systems change. Markl argues for the evolution of the human mind and creativity to be such a factor. The global impact humans (due to cultural evolution) came to execute on natural and biological systems outlined above back this view (see chapter 1.1).

77 See chapters 2.1.2 and 2.2.5.6 for further information.

78 For more information on the Club of Rome see above.

79 Meanwhile it has also been argued for a more aggressive approach (Factor 10 Economics), which argues that per capita material flows caused by OECD countries should be reduced by a factor of ten.

80 Also referred to as Bionics.

81 For further information on the field of Industrial Ecology see the International Society of Industrial Ecology and the Journal of Industrial Ecology.

ample, excess steam from an electrical generating facility is used as a heat source for a refinery and a pharmaceutical plant; a wallboard producer purchases surplus gas from the refinery as a replacement for coal and removes the sulfur from the gas and sells it to a sulfuric acid plant (Ehrenfeld and Gertler 1997). Figure 6 represents the industrial ecology system at Kalundborg.

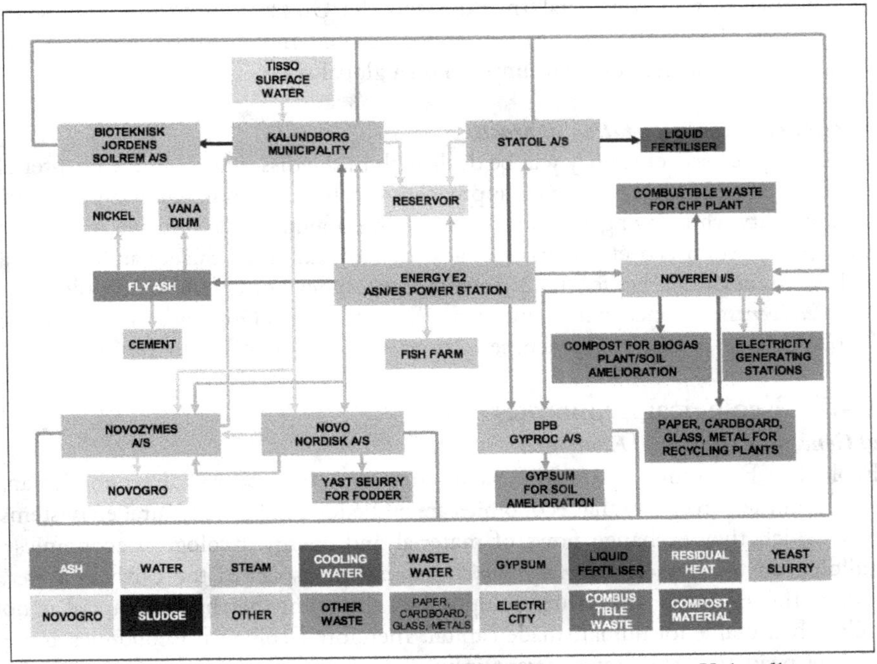

Fig. 6: Industrial Ecology: Example of Industrial Ecosystem Kalundborg
Source: Adapted from The Kalundborg Centre for Industrial Symbiosis[82]

Various organizations and approaches within the field of eco-efficiency have broad-ened their concepts and are working on eco-social *frameworks*, which are needed to move towards alternative business models that allow increase of resource efficiency and valuing natural and human capital (see e.g. Seiler-Hausmann, Liedtke and Weizsäcker 2004). Prominent examples are the Rocky Mountain Institute and the Wuppertal Institute for Climate, Environment and Energy. Both organizations where contributors to the approach of 'Factor Four' outlined above (Weizsäcker, Lovins and Lovins 1997). The Rocky Mountain Institute in cooperation with Paul Hawken (Hawken 1993, Natural Capital Institute) has developed the concept of

82 Available online at: http://www.symbiosis.dk, accessed: 07. January 2006.

Natural Capitalism as a framework for an alternative economy that regards the non-substitutable (economic) value of natural capital[83], which the authors consider the new limiting factor of production (Hawken, Lovins and Lovins 1999; Lovins, Lovins and Hawken 1999). The Wuppertal Institute, among other approaches, focuses on frameworks for sustainable production and consumption[84]. A Collaboration Center of the Wuppertal Institute and the United Nations Environmental Program (CSCP 2005a and 2006)[85] is focused on implementing approaches on sustainable production and consumption on a global scale.

b) Relation to the dissertation' approach
The concept of eco-efficiency will be dealt with in the dissertation in the chapter on the Efficiency Model. Efficiency approaches are highly promising for promoting sustainability while saving costs and therefore has found broad diffusion in business practice. However eco-efficiency can backfire and lead into a Sustainability Trap as will be discussed in chapter 3.3.2. Therefore eco-efficiency should be coupled with *eco-effectiveness*, a concept introduced by the authors McDonough and Braungart (2002a) (*cradle-to-cradle* approach, see also Stahlmann and Clausen 2000).

1.4.7 Ecological Economics
a) Concept of Ecological Economics
Ecological Economics is designed as an alternative to neoclassical economics and builds on the perception that economies are embedded in larger natural ecosystems, with which they exchange flows of material and energy. Ecological economics - building on the laws of *thermodynamics* – stress the aspect of the earth as a *closed system*. The approach furthermore emphasizes the point that natural capital is not fully substitutable for human-made capital. Therefore Ecological Economics argues for the need to move from current infinite, quantitative economic growth to an ecologically sustainable scale (Steady-State Economy) and qualitative growth (Daly and Farley 2003; Daly 1991; Daly 1996; Daly and Cobb 1986; Costanza 1991; Georgescu-Roegen 1971, 1976, 1977 and 1992, Gill 1998a and 1998b, Müller-Christ 2006).

b) Relation to the dissertation' approach
Although the dissertation does not refer to Ecological Economics explicitly in its approach, principles of Ecological Economics correspond to the 'systems perspec-

---

83 For example resources that currently still are not prized or ecosystem services.
84 See the research's group homepage for further information:
http://www.wupperinst.org/en/projects/rg4/index.html; accessed: 16. January 2007.
85 See the center's homepage for further information: http://www.scp-centre.org; accessed: 15. December 2005

tive on sustainability' in the thesis: The dissertation significantly stresses the point of the embeddedness of the economic system within the ecosystem. The dissertation thereby accentuates the *social* reference of the embeddedness, i.e. economy being a human (social) construct and humans stemming from and relying on the natural system.[86] However, the argumentation of ecological economics, that economy is an embedded subsystem of the natural system due to material and energy flows, equally applies. The law of thermodynamics respectively its consequence of limits of environmental variables (e.g. pollution limits, environmental sinks) play an important role in reference to Sustainability Traps as will be discussed in chapters 2.2.4 and 2.2.5. The concept of Sustainability Traps however does not only consider environmental dynamics but equally social dynamics, which are driven by social values.

1.4.8 Buddhist Economics
a) Concept of Buddhist Economics
An approach closely related to Ecological Economics is Buddhist Economics (school of Schumacher). Schumacher (Schumacher 1989 and 1977; Schumacher, Candre and Echeverri 1998) points to the earth's limitations for resource extraction and pollution emission and argues for perceiving nature as capital rather than as income[87]. Schumacher (1989) criticizes the emphasis of 'more' and 'bigger' (growth) in economic systems and argues for an 'appropriate' economy (technologies) tailored to human needs. Schumacher (1989: 56ff) thereby argues that Buddhist value systems and paradigms can significantly contribute in reaching these goals. Paradigms of Buddhist Economics put forward by Schumacher, among others, include: A focus on capacity building through someone's work, rather than working as a pure mechanical activity. Optimize consumption as a means to human well-being, rather than maximizing human consumption opportunities through optimizing production processes. Simplicity and non-violence as behavior norms, - not only with regard to other human beings, but equally to nature. The latter implies conscious use of natural resources as well as regeneration efforts, because environmental unsustainability risks triggering social violence and unsustainability due to the interdependent nature of the environmental and human sphere.
A scholar related to Schumacher's school of thought is Fritjof Capra (Capra 2002, 1982 and 2000; Capra, Matus and Steindl-Rast 1992; Callenbach et al. 1994). Capra is engaged in *learning from ecological systems* for a sustainable life (see Capra 2002, 2000, 2003). Capra in his works stresses the inter-connectedness of global factors and the need for a holistic perspective (Capra 1996, 2003, 1982). He argues for the need to learn form five principles, which he considers to be forming the

---

86 See chapter 2.2.2.4.2. The dissertation furthermore agrees on the limits of substitution of natural resources through human-made capital.
87 See also Hawken's concept of 'Natural Capital' in chapter 1.4.6.

structure of the ecological system: Interdependence; cycles in ecology; energy flows; co-operation and partnership; diversity and adaptation (Capra 1996).[88]

b) Relation to the dissertation' approach

While a relation of the dissertation' approach to the approaches of Schumacher and Capra is possible in some specific points, the dissertation does not use any of the two approaches explicitly. The concept of Buddhist Economics possesses strong *normative* implications for a more sustainable economy. The focus of the dissertation in turn rather lies on a new *perspective* (systems perspective) on sustainability, out of which in turn new values and norms might develop; but as a result of social bargaining processes. However, the 'systems perspective on sustainability' as it is put forward in the dissertation is compatible with many of the paradigms identified by Schumacher. This is because the Buddhist school of thought equals many aspects from systems thinking (e.g. thinking in loops, interconnectivity of variables, focus on continuous learning). The dissertation holds the same relation to Capra's approach, whereby here the compatibility is even higher, as Capra draws more explicitly from principles of systems thinking than Schumacher.

1.4.9   Cultural Studies and Development Studies

a) Concept of Cultural Studies and Development Studies

Within the fields that link systems thinking and sustainability presented here, it is striking that many approaches miss on drawing from the fields (findings) of Cultural Studies and Development Studies (particularly Development Economics). Vice-versa, systems thinking does not seem wide-spread in these fields either. The authors most related to these fields that deal with sustainability using systems thinking referred to in the dissertation are Diamond[89] (2005 and 1999) as well as Homer-Dixon (1999), who analyzed how humanly caused environmental unsustainability backfired on social agents up to the collapse of total societies. A scientific study devoted to an analysis of how different cultures (particularly national governments) are dealing with global environmental risk is The Social Learning Group (The Social Learning Group 2001). In the view of the dissertation it is crucially important in the future to further integrate these fields and their findings into the various fields linking systems thinking and sustainability, particularly Sustainability Science. For as the dissertation argues that a change towards sustainability is foremost a *cultural* change, which needs to value cultural specifics. Because of this perceived importance of Cultural and Development Studies they are included in

---

88 Capra's work also relates to emancipatory approaches of systems thinking (Critical Systems Thinking) due to his focus on human communities (see Jackson 2000: 302).
89 Diamond also particularly holds a historic perspective.

this overview (figure 1), although a prominent, specific subfield dealing with sustainability and system thinking is not existent yet.

b) Relation to the dissertation' approach
Sustainability Traps, particularly those relating to social sustainability in developing countries, are closely coupled with development issues such as poverty reduction, medical care and safety-issues as well as with issues relating to cultural understanding of sustainability. This will become apparent in Sustainability Traps relating to contract factories in emerging and developing countries (Fire-the-Supplier Trap, Financing Brand-Image through Low-Cost Production Trap; also Job Creation Trap).

1.4.10 Systemtheorie of Luhmann
a) Concept of Systemtheorie of Luhmann
Out of reasons of completeness Luhmann's Systemtheorie (System theory) shall be mentioned in this overview. Not because his emphasis lies in the field of sustainability, but because he is a significant contributor of systems thinking within the field of sociology (especially in German-speaking countries). Luhmann addresses the topic of *ecological communication* (1986) and focuses on the difficulties of communicating about unsustainabilities, because of the sectoral views of different social systems (e.g. economy, politics, science).

b) Relation to the dissertation' approach
The dissertation does not build on Luhmann's Systemtheorie. The dissertation however also stresses the difficulty of communicating about unsustainabilities due to sectoral perspectives. The dissertation thereby argues for the social agents to facilitate communication through joint analysis of how *systemic structures*, which the agents are involved in, produce unsustainability (Sustainability Traps). This implies communication about how the different agents affect the structures as well as how they are affected through the structure. Communication about boundary judgments (boundary critique) thereby can play an important role in overcoming – or at least in uncovering – specifics[90] of sectoral perspectives of social agents.

---

90 Particularly 'mental models' and 'values' on which boundary judgments are based on, see chapter 2.2.2.3.

1.4.11 Ecological Dynamics
a) Concept of Ecological Dynamics
Ecological Dynamics deals with the change of ecological systems over time using mathematical models, not particularly System Dynamics. One special emphasis is the branch of non-linear population theory (Gurney and Nisbet 1998; Cushing et al. 1996).

b) Relation to the dissertation' approach
The dissertation does not build Ecological Dynamics. Findings of the field on specific dynamics might however be an interesting amendment to specific Sustainability Traps. If and how such a contribution is feasible is up to future research work.

1.4.12 Systems Ecology
a) Concept of Systems Ecology
Systems Ecology is a branch of environmental science that focuses on a systems perspective insofar as it analyses how ecosystem's functions are determined on the basis of how their components cycle, retain or exchange energy and nutrients. Systems Ecology thereby builds on ideas of engineering and usually uses mathematical computer models, which allow predicting a system's responses to perturbations (Odum and Barrett 2005, Odum 1983)[91]. Departing from formalities of electronic circuits, the ecologist Howard Odum (1994) developed Energy Systems Language to model energy flows in ecological and socio-ecological systems (see also Brown 2004). This allows better understanding of behavior of any type of energy system, e.g. feedback patterns.[92]

b) Relation to the dissertation' approach
Systems Ecology, respectively Energy Systems Language, is related to System Dynamics insofar as both build on System Science and ideas of electronic circuits (see also Ossimitz 1997). Systems Ecology for the dissertation' approach however is not relevant.

The above chapter 1.4 discussed scientific fields applying facets of system science (system thinking) to sustainability issues and positioned the dissertation' approach in this field. It has been pointed out that the dissertation fundamentally draws from the field of 'Systems Thinking as a learning discipline for Sustainability', which uses (qualitative) System Dynamics to develop a new perspective on sustainability. As this field does not constitute a scientific sustainability field in its own right (yet),

---

91 Journals that relate to Systems Ecology are Ecological Modeling and Ecological Engineering.
92 An example of Energy Systems Language can be found in Swank, W.T. and D.R. Tilley, 2000: 101.

the dissertation argued for subsuming it as a contribution to the emerging field of *Sustainability Science*. Another approach, which the dissertation significantly draws from, is *Critical Systems Thinking* with its concept of boundary judgments. These three fields constitute the core, which the dissertation' approach of Sustainability Traps and the systems thinking skills systems for addressing them, i.e. the particular 'systems perspective on sustainability' of the dissertation, builds on.

As has further been described above, the dissertation additionally uses individual concepts or principles from other scientific fields to elaborate on individual aspects of Sustainability Traps, particularly Eco-Efficiency and Industrial Ecology, Ecological Economics and Cultural and Development Studies.

1.5 Chapter Summary (Part I)

Part I discussed the theoretical background important for the dissertation.

Chapter 1.1 provided an introduction to the dissertation and outlined its aim: The dissertation argues that a systems perspective reveals the importance for analyzing *Sustainability Traps*, because it very often are *systemic, dynamic structures* that cause unsustainability, rather than the failure of individual agents. The dissertation furthermore aims to analyze *how* a systems perspective enables managing Sustainability Traps successfully.

Chapter 1.2 discussed the concept of *sustainability*, including its 'traditional' three dimensions of *environmental, social* and *economic sustainability*. The three dimensions are important for the dissertation, because as will be shown in part II, it is dynamics triggered through an interplay of variables from these three dimensions, which produce Sustainability Traps.

Chapter 1.3 introduced the concept of *systems thinking* and its theoretical foundations. The focus thereby lay on the characteristics that constitute systems thinking as *a new perspective*, i.e. as a new way of thinking as compared to 'orthodox thinking'. This is important for the dissertation, because as will be shown later, it are these characteristics of systems thinking that constitute it as a most feasible perspective for dealing with Sustainability Traps.

Chapter 1.4 brought together the two pervious chapters and provided the first overview in this field of scientific approaches, which apply principles of systems thinking to issues of sustainability. Focus of this overview was to outline the context, which the dissertation' approach is positioned in. The following part II will now elaborate the dissertation' contribution to the scientific fields discussed in chapter 1.4, which consists in the concept of Sustainability Traps and how to deal with them from a systems perspective.

2 Part II: A Systems Perspective: Sustainability Traps

Part II of the dissertation elaborates the theoretical foundation for the concept of Sustainability Traps. First, a *definition* and *concept* of Sustainability Traps is elaborated (chapters 2.1.1 and 2.1.2). Then *characteristics* of Sustainability Traps are identified and the resulting requirements for recognizing and managing the traps (chapter 2.1.2). Subsequently five *principles of systems thinking* (*systems thinking skills*) are elaborated, which help corporations to manage (avoid) Sustainability Traps and thus to improve success of corporate sustainability measures (chapter 2.2).

2.1 Concept and Characteristics of Sustainability Traps
2.1.1 Definition and Derivation of the Concept of Sustainability Traps

The dissertation' contribution to the scientific field discussed in chapter 1.4 is the concept of Sustainability Traps. The dissertation **defines** Sustainability Traps as the following:

> *Sustainability Traps are reoccurring systemic patterns of failed corporate sustainability measures that backfire, triggered through dynamics between the corporate, social and environmental sphere. The backfiring thereby impacts not only the environmental or social sphere, but equally the corporation itself.*

The term 'pattern' thereby stands short for: The pattern of behavior of a system, which is produced through a specific, dynamic structure of that system (systemic structure). That is, in a Sustainability Trap, variables from the environmental, social or economic sphere interrelate and form a system, whose structure is thus that it produces a situation, where corporate sustainability measures fail and produce (more) unsustainability instead of reducing it, which backfires on the corporation itself.[93]

Derivation of the concept of Sustainability Traps
Before describing the concept of Sustainability Traps, the dissertation will outline the basis on which the dissertation *derived* the idea and concept of Sustainability Traps from. As part I of the dissertation indicated, the roots for the concept stem from the two fields of *systems thinking* and *sustainability*:

---

93 How this works in detail will be elaborated below.

*As will be shown, the concept of **traps** as such is derived from **system dynamics** and applied to the field of **corporate sustainability**.*

This shall be discussed more in-depth in the following, whereby
a) The first paragraph discusses the concept of traps derived from concepts of system dynamics
b) and the second paragraph outlines its application to sustainability.

a) Concept of Traps

The concept of Traps as such, is based on the concept of '*counterintuitive behavior of systems*' and resulting '*policy resistance*' and '*backfiring*' from **system dynamics**. As has been discussed in chapter 1.4.2, system dynamics is concerned with *counterintuitive behavior* of social systems (Forrester 1995 and 1991): Dynamics in a system's structure can lead to the effect that a system shows different behavior than intended or presumed.[94] This can lead to the effect that a system 'resists' policies, i.e. measures (policies) taken by social agents fail or even worsen a situation. Sterman (2004: 3) describes policy resistance the following: "All too often, well-intentioned efforts to solve pressing problems lead to *policy resistance*, where our policies are delayed, diluted, or defeated by the unforeseen reactions of other people or nature. Many times our best efforts to solve a problem actually make it worse."

The dissertation chose to use the term '*trap*' instead of policy resistance, because the dissertation focuses on particular cases of policy resistance, which refer to the latter point of Sterman's statement: Cases, where measures taken actually worsen the situation rather than ameliorating it. The crucial point, which makes these cases a *trap* is that the worsening of the situation **backfires**, i.e. the worsening in turn *negatively impacts the corporation itself.* The use of the term 'backfiring' is quite common in system dynamics (e.g. Stroh 2000, Senge 2006: 399[95]): If a variable in a system changes due to an action taken, it in turn can impact (backfire) on the agent, which caused the variable to change in the first place.[96] The dissertation considers focusing on cases of *backfiring* particularly important with respect to sustainability. If it can be mapped out how and why unsustainabilities are backfiring on corporations themselves, this has two advantages: First, corporations receive an *intrinsic* motivation for change towards sustainability. Second, once dynamics responsible for backfiring are identified, it gives corporations leverage points how to improve the suc-

---

94 For example: Producing unsustainability rather than increasing sustainability.
95 Backfiring stems from endogenous explanations see below. (Senge 2006: 399: Fixes that backfire (fail)).
96 In its simplest form thus: A impacts B, which leads B to impact A in turn (backfire on A). As will be outlined it is yet crucial to note, that this simplest form hardly applies. The crucial issue regarding traps is caused through dynamics triggered ,in the system itself'. This will further be outlined below.

cess of their sustainability measures (by reducing or even eliminating backfiring). The Backfiring on corporations, thereby need not necessarily to be easily quantifiable financial figures (e.g. direct costs), but equally comprise such factors as image, corporate responsibility, social risks.[97] The above are the reasons why the dissertation chose to use the concept of *systemic, dynamic traps,* which entail the concept of backfiring caused through dynamics in a system structure.

*The concept of systemic, dynamic **traps**, derived from system dynamics, constitutes the particular 'systems perspective' of this dissertation.*

That is: Chapter 1.4 presented the *general* 'systems perspective', i.e. the scientific field of approaches, which apply concepts of systems science to sustainability. The concept of *systemic, **dynamic traps derived from system dynamics** is the **particular systems perspective of this dissertation**,* which it applies to sustainability as a contribution to the scientific field.

b) Application to Sustainability
Applying the concept of systemic, dynamics traps as it has been derived from system dynamics by the dissertation to the field of sustainability, ties in with Proust's citation chosen as the introduction to the dissertation:

*When putting on the eyes (glasses) of the particular systems perspective just presented (systemic, dynamic traps) and looking through them at the field of sustainability, they enable to recognize that very often unsustainabilities, which we deal with in business practice is created through and driven by systemic, dynamic structures. That is, it enables to recognize the importance and frequentness of **Sustainability Traps** in business practice.*

Individual manifestations (cases) that can be considered Sustainability Traps have been addressed in the field of System Dynamics as well as in the field of Sustainability already. It is the contribution of the dissertation to elaborate Sustainability Traps as a *generic* phenomenon, i.e. Sustainability Traps as a *concept.* Therefore, prior to outlining Sustainability Traps as a concept, existing manifestations of Sustainability Traps shall be discussed and how they are addressed in *System Dynamics* and in *Sustainability* so far.

---

97 See chapter 2.1.3 b) for detailed argumentation of the advantages and importance of backfiring in the dissertation.

Manifestations in System Dynamics

As stated in the chapters 1.4.2 and 1.4.3, system dynamics has already dealt with cases that can be subsumed as Sustainability Traps. Prominent examples are Urban Dynamics (Forrester 1969) or Limits-to-Growth (Meadows et al. 1972, 1992 and 2004). The difference of the dissertation' approach to these models and particular to Environmental Dynamics has been discussed in the corresponding two chapters mentioned.[98]

Manifestations in Sustainability

With regard to the field of sustainability, basically two cases can be differentiated: Cases, where the particular systems perspective of dynamic, systemic traps *is used implicitly*[99] to deal with issues of sustainability. And cases, where a systems perspective is *not* used, but rather a perspective of 'orthodox thinking'.

In the field of sustainability, there are a variety of *individual* cases from scholars or journalists that *implicitly* analyze sustainability issues from a perspective congruent with the systems perspective presented above. In these cases the authors formulate Sustainability Traps, even though the term itself is not used and systems thinking is not addressed explicitly. Often these authors use facets of a systems perspective intuitively, i.e. without being familiar or trained in systems thinking (system dynamics). If so, the *full potential* of a systems perspective to analyze the issue *cannot be harnessed*. What was observed by the dissertation in the case-analyses used for chapter 3 e.g., was that some authors describe the *systemic* nature of an issue, i.e. they point out a structure of interaction, a pattern, which is responsible for a sustainability issue. What is yet not referred to and elaborated, are the *dynamics* that drive system behavior. Furthermore these cases again constitute analyses of *individual* traps, while as mentioned it is the aim of the dissertation to filter out the *generics* of such cases and thus to develop a *concept* of Sustainability Traps.[100]

The vast majority of literature dealing with corporate sustainability, however does *not* use a systems perspective, but rather argues out of a perspective from orthodox thinking. This was the case e.g. for the vast majority of the case studies analyzed for chapter 3 of the dissertation. In many of the cases however, it becomes possible –

---

98 It can be summarized the following: By far not all system dynamics models analyze such system behavior, which forms a trap and which relates to the field of sustainability. Those which do so focus on quantitative modeling and computer simulation in order to analyze the specifics of an individual case. The aim of the dissertation in contrast is to outline the *generic* nature of Sustainability Traps, i.e. Sustainability Traps as a *concept* (see below, see also archetypes in chapter 3). As stated, this requires a *qualitative* approach, focused on learning skills rather than on quantitative computer modulation.

99 The cases where it has been used *explicitly* have been outlined under the paragraph of System Dynamics.

100 That is: It often is systemic, dynamic structures that backfire.

through the analysis of various different sources relating to the business case – to identify a systemic pattern, which is underlying the sustainability issue in question. Once the pattern is identified for an individual case it is striking to note that it is applicable to many other cases, even though on a more generic level (archetypes of Sustainability Traps, see chapter 3). This is the aim and motivation of the dissertation: To show that, when looking at sustainability issues from a systems perspective, something new becomes visible: The fact that very often unsustainability is caused through systemic, dynamic structures. In existing sustainability literature the focus of analysis very often lies on identifying 'the causer' (the one responsible) or it lies on multicausality of different factors combined in a linear, additive way[101], e.g. unethical corporate behavior or lack of corporate responsibility; insufficient or inadequate governmental policies; lack of customer awareness. The dissertation does *not* deny the importance of these points. What the dissertation argues for, is for scholars and practitioners in the field of sustainability to stronger focus on how factors *interrelate* and form *systemic, dynamic structures*, because very often this is how corporate unsustainability is created (driven). Changes towards more sustainability thus need to take on a stronger *systemic* perspective on sustainability. The concept of Sustainability Traps is one contribution to this cause.

After Sustainability Traps have been defined and the basis for the derivation of their concept has been discussed, now the *concept* of Sustainability Traps shall be elaborated in the following, i.e. *what* constitutes a Sustainability Trap on a *generic* level.

2.1.2 Constitutives of the Concept of Sustainability Traps

This chapter is most important as it elaborates the *concept* of Sustainability Traps based on their definition above. As has just been outlined, individual cases of Sustainability Traps have been addressed in literature before, what shall be discussed here are the generics that constitute the nature of Sustainability Traps. Sustainability Traps as they are developed in the dissertation are constituted on two interrelated aspects:

a) First, the **interdependency** between **mental models** of social agents and **systemic structures**, which holds agents prisoner.

b) Second, the systemic structure in a Sustainability Trap is a **dynamic** one. That is, corporate sustainability measures unfold *dynamics* in a system's structure that produce the opposite than intended by corporate sustainability measures; i.e. they cause unsustainability to *increase* rather than to *decrease*, and risk to backfire on the corporation itself.

---

101 See 'laundry list thinking' in chapter 2.2.5.1.

a) Interdependency between Mental Models and Systemic Structures

The first important aspect with respect to a Sustainability Trap is that an agent is *caught up in a structure without being aware of it*, - at least when stepping into the structure (trap), but very often still when being in it for quite a time. Vickers has outlined the core fatality of a trap: "The nature of the trap is a function of the nature of the trapped. To describe either is to imply the other" (Vickers 1970: 15). Vickers provides the example of a trap to catch Lobsters, which successfully works for catching lobsters, because it is designed according to the nature ('thinking' and actions) of lobsters. A human being in contrast would not be caught within a lobster pot (even if big enough), because his thinking is thus that it enables him to see how to escape. Social agents (people, organizations) however get trapped by taking their own state of mind for granted. "A trap is a trap only for creatures which cannot solve the problems that it sets" (Vickers, 1970: 15). Thus, *our way of thinking influences how we deal with problems – and thus with traps*. The fatal nature of Sustainability Traps as they are examined in the dissertation therefore lies in the following:

> In a Sustainability Trap, there is an **interdependency** between the **mental models** of social agents and **systemic structures:**

> *The thinking - or more precisely the mental models[102] – of different agents guide their actions, which through their[103] interrelations create specific systemic structures. These structures in turn influence the behavior of the agents (Senge 2006: 42f, Sterman 2004: 28).*

> *The 'agents' with respect to sustainability are the corporation and its stakeholders; whereby these stakeholders can be corporate stakeholders (e.g. costumers, contract factories/suppliers, competitors), societal stakeholders (e.g. NGOs, international organizations, governments) and natural (environmental) processes.[104] Because of the existing interdependency between the mental models of social agents and systemic structures, in a Sustainability Trap, the same structure risks to be created over and over again by the agents. This is the case as long as the agents only per-*

---

102 These can be understood as believes of 'how the world works' (see chapter 2.2.1).
103 That is the interplay of the actions.
104 The interdependency of mental models and systemic structures, therefore of course only applies to social actors, i.e. actors from the corporate and societal sphere, which possess mental models. Environmental processes are triggered based on natural (e.g. biological, physical or chemical) principles, but equally contribute to the systemic structure by being impacted by human behavior and in turn impacting human behavior.

ceive and react upon the individual effects (symptoms) created by the structure that are backfiring (feedback) on the individual agents, and do not perceive the underlying structure itself. That way, agents hold themselves prisoner in a structure, which backfires on them without being aware of it. In these cases, agents, who seek to reduce unsustainability through their measures, can actually contribute to an increase of unsustainability that backfires on them, because the system's structure is thus that it increases unsustainability rather than reducing it.

A prominent example of a trap within the field of (social) sustainability is: Free food supply to developing countries in order to reduce undernourishment. The belief (mental model) underlying this trap is that those nations, which have food in abundance, should give to those who are in need (equity allocation). Yet, free food supply often leads to a destruction of local food markets, raising the need for more foreign food supply, which in turn destroys even more markets and increases undernourishment as well as dependency on foreign food supply. The suppliers – still acting upon their mental model – need to provide for even more food to developing countries free of charge. Thus, a vicious-circle is created, where the measure of free food supply actually increases the problem of undernourishment rather than reducing it as well as backfires on the supplier. Another Sustainability Trap is posed, when pharmaceutical corporations give away free drugs for medical treatment: At first sight, this seems to be a win-win situation as it promises reducing diseases in developing countries and promises to foster the corporation's image in reference to sustainability (i.e. corporate social responsibility). The drugs find broad diffusion, because they are free of charge or at very low cost. Yet, a trap is created, if resistance to the drug augments, because of its broad application and because expensive follow-up examinations on patients' resistance to the drug and corresponding adjustments in the treatment, are not provided simultaneously (either e.g. by the corporation itself, by NGOs or by local governmental bodies). Consequences are that the drug looses its effect with the disease further spreading and/or that more of the drug or 'harsher' drugs (with potentially more adverse reactions) need to be provided, thus worsening the medical situation. If this plays out, it risks at last to negatively impacting the image of the corresponding corporation or even its business in the long run, rather than increasing it.

b) Dynamics in the System's Structure

The examples outlined, point to the second aspect crucial to the concept of Sustainability Traps: **Dynamics** in the system structure. As the examples show, the variables in the system of a Sustainability Trap feed-back, i.e. react upon each other, recurrently. As the examples further indicate, there exists a **dynamic** when 'running' through the loop of the trap again and again: Not the same amount of food or drugs is needed, but more and more food is needed, because undernourishment increases respectively more of the drug or harsher drugs are needed, because the disease spreads. That is, while actions in a Sustainability Traps are reproduced (executed) by the agents again and again, the intensity of the actions and their effect (unsustainability)[105] does not stay the same in each 'round' (loop), but gets worse. This is the case because, the state of certain variables can alter, i.e. the state of a variable can add up or it can be reduced. For example, the variable 'number of local food suppliers in developing countries' can increase or decrease, equally the variables 'number of drug resistant strands' or 'amount of toxic chemicals in a lake' can augment or diminish. Depending on the level (state) of a variable, (new) effects are released or the intensity of its effect is increased, which in turn impacts the state of other variables in the system. Thus *dynamics* are created by the system 'itself'.[106] If these dynamics that drive the Sustainability Trap (the system's behavior) cause the system to pass a threshold (bifurcation point) this can – in extreme situations – even lead to a collapse of the entire system. A prominent example is the collapse of a lake due to the infiltration of toxic chemicals from manufacturing processes into the lake. Other examples are provided by Diamond, who examines the collapse of entire societies due to environmental backfiring on social activities (Diamond 2005). Thus, Sustainability Traps, in extreme situations, can ultimately lead to a collapse of the entire system. The dissertation yet will not deal with collapses particularly, because these are extreme situations, where thresholds (limits) are exceeded and the situation cannot be reversed anymore. The dissertation will rather deal with Sustainability Traps, which backfire and *worsen* a situation, though have not led to a collapse (yet). What is important to the dissertation to point out is that with regard to Sustainability Traps, it is important to be aware of (states) levels of variables and of limits in systems.[107] The tricky point is that limits - in general - are hard to assess and to quantify precisely. Therefore, what the dissertation lays emphasis on is to identify the *systemic structures* as such, which constitute a Sustainability Trap. That is, to identify (realize) that a corporation is caught up in a Sustainability Trap that backfires (i.e. worsens the situation) in the first place and how to get out of the trap. What is pivotal to realize with regard to systemic structures of Sustainability Traps therefore is the following:

---

105 That is the behavior (result) produced by the system.
106 This will further be outlined in chapters 2.2.5.6. and 2.2.5.7.
107 Thereby environmental limits (e.g. pollution limits) are usually far easier to estimate as limits from the social sphere (e.g. number of non-compliances with a company's code of conduct before it impacts a company's brand image and customers switch to other brands). For further information on level of variables and on limits see also chapters 2.2.4 and 2.2.5.6.

It is primarily __dynamics__ in the systemic structure that drive system be-
havior and not the number of agents or the number of different 'points
of view' involved. As the example of free food supply to developing coun-
tries illustrates, even if all agents have best intentions and act 'ethically'
and even if all agents strive for the goal of reducing unsustainability (re-
ducing undernourishment), measures taken can backfire, because of dy-
namics resulting in the structure and can actually lead to an increase of
unsustainability.[108] Therefore, what is crucial with respect to Sustainabil-
*ity Traps is, **how** the variables in a system are **interrelated**, i.e. the spe-*
cific dynamic structure of a system. Thereby dynamics can either reinforce
or balance (reduce) unsustainability in a system. In order to deal with
Sustainability Traps it is therefore important to analyze the structure of a
*trap by examining the **reinforcing** and **balancing dynamics** in a system*
in consideration of unsustainability. Systems Thinking Skills for analyz-
ing this will be provided in part II of the dissertation (chapter 2.2.4 and
2.2.5).

The above **defined** Sustainability Traps and elaborated their **concept** as it is put forward by the dissertation. In the following **characteristics** of Sustainability Traps will
be identified, because they determine the skills required for their management.

2.1.3 Characteristics and Requirements for Management of Sustainability Traps

The following chapter will outline the four main *characteristics* of Sustainability
Traps and the *requirements* for best dealing with them.

*As will be argued, the **properties of systems thinking identified in chapter 1.3.2** are bet-*
ter suited for meeting the requirements posed by the characteristics of Sustainability Traps
than properties of orthodox thinking[109].

The four characteristics discussed are:

---

108 For the illustration of these dynamics see chapter 2.2.5.1.
109 As stated in 1.3.2 already, orthodox thinking, thereby is no 'fix term'. Rather it relates to
ways of thinking that often can be observed in social and organizational behavior. The dissertation defined what systems thinking *is* (its characteristics) and what it is not. The way of
thinking that systems thinking 'is not' relates to orthodox thinking.

a) Sustainability Traps have *endogenous* causes.
b) Sustainability Traps *backfire* on the corporation.
c) Estimating Sustainability Traps depends on *system boundaries*.
d) There is *no 'right' solution* to a Sustainability Trap.

The characteristics will be discussed in the following.

a) Sustainability Traps have Endogenous Causes

The focus on endogenous explanations is prevalent in systems thinking and derives from a holistic system perspective, where the interrelation of the different parts is crucial and changes in one part of the system trigger effects in other parts of the system. Sterman states: "System dynamics seeks endogenous explanations for phenomena. The word 'endogenous' means 'arising from within'. An endogenous theory generates the dynamics of a system through the interactions of the variables and agents represented in the model. [...] Exogenous explanations are really no explanations at all, they simply beg the question, What caused the exogenous variables to change as they did?" (Sterman 2004: 95). This does not imply that exogenous variables cannot be included in a system at all, but their number should be very restricted and a thorough analysis is to be conducted to verify, if they are not rather endogenous (Sterman 2004: 95f).

> *As mentioned above, the decisive aspect is that a Sustainability Trap is caused through dynamics created in the system's structure due to the interplay of variables in the system. – And not through unethical behavior of an outside 'causer' or 'enemy'.*

Endogenous causes in form of dynamic structures are extremely hard to see and often remain unaware, because agents usually (i.e. in orthodox thinking) are focused to perceive and re-act upon events rather than on structures. As discussed above, structures therefore often remain unaware and can hold agents prisoner.
Conclusion: Managing this characteristic of a Sustainability Trap most importantly requires an analysis if and how a systemic structure produces unsustainability in a system and which mental models are underlying it.[110] Orthodox thinking is not focused on structure, but rather on events and linear processes. Systems thinking in this case is better suited for managing Sustainability Traps, as it is focused on the analysis of the interplay of mental models and systemic structures as the cause for (un)sustainability.[111]

---

110 As outlined above, it equally requires analyzing, which underlying mental models are contributing to the structure. This will not
111 As will be shown in chapter 2.2.3, systems thinking also explains how events as well as mental models tie into the systemic structure.

*This requires the systems thinking principle of '**System-as-Cause Thinking**' for managing Sustainability Traps, which will be elaborated in chapter 2.2.4.*

b) Sustainability Traps Backfire on the Corporation

The second characteristic of Sustainability Traps is that they *backfire*, in the sense that the systemic structure is thus that the aim of the corporate sustainability measure is not reached (e.g. fostering sustainability image, reducing energy-use through energy efficiency etc.), but rather the sustainability situation is worsened, which negatively impacts the corporation itself. For example, in the Fire-the-Supplier Trap (chapter 3.2.3) a corporation's image is damaged through scandals of unsustainabilities in their overseas contract factories (sweatshops). Many corporations in this situation sought to restore their image by 'showing an iron fist' against abuses of sustainability by rigidly quitting all business relationships with their suppliers (contract factories). This however risks leading into a trap, because it 1) leaves the workers unemployed and thus often worse off than before[112] and 2) the corporation is likely to get into the same situation of unsustainability scandals with their next suppliers, thus impacting the corporation's image even more. One way of avoiding this trap is to keep up working relationships with suppliers even though a scandal of unsustainability occurred and to engage in mutual communication and training relationships with the suppliers (e.g. safety measures, workers rights etc.), as more and more corporations currently pursue to do.

*With regard to Sustainability Traps, it was important to the dissertation to develop a concept that accounts for the risk of **backfiring on the corporation itself**. Many argumentations in reference to sustainability are based on 'external effects'. Yet, if an effect (or cause) is internal or external depends on system boundaries (see below). As discussed above, Sustainability Traps are based on **endogenous** explanations, where negative effects on environmental and social sustainability backfire on a corporation. This is **not** to deny, that there are situations, where a corporation does not experience any backfiring of its actions with regard to sustainability. The point the dissertation makes, is that if it can be shown **that** and **how** unsustainabilities can **backfire** on a corporation, corporations receive **higher incentives** for their successful change towards sustainability than through moral appeals alone. The advantage of systems thinking is that it allows mapping out the structure of how this backfiring can occur, i.e. to map out the structure of a trap.[113]*

---

112 That is, the situation with regard to social sustainability is worsened.
113 E.g. with causal-loop-diagramming, chapters 2.2.5 and 3.

The concept of backfiring implies **non-linearity**.[114] The crucial point of backfiring in Sustainability Traps yet is that the causal relationships leading to backfiring in a Sustainability Trap are not of the nature that a corporation 'does something wrong', which then backfires, i.e. negatively impacts, the corporation directly without any significant delay. Rather, backfiring in Sustainability Traps is driven through quite complex, non-linear dynamics (**dynamic complexity**). This is the case because, as has been elaborated above, the systemic structure, which creates backfiring, is 1) also driven by various other stakeholders and 2) variables can release feedback (backfiring) with a *delay*, i.e. after their state has piled up or is reduced to a certain amount, e.g. pollution limits. It is most crucial to note that because of dynamic complexity, causes and effects are deferred in *space* and *time* (Senge 2006: 71f).[115]

*Therefore a further challenging characteristic of Sustainability Traps is that because of **dynamic complexity** it often proves difficult 1) to forecast backfiring of a corporate measure as well as 2) to identify a negative impact on a corporation as a case of backfiring, i.e. as an endogenous cause.[116]*

Conclusion: Managing this characteristic of a Sustainability Trap requires a non-linear, dynamic perspective. Orthodox thinking is focused on linear causalities and is well suited, if the cause for an effect is 'nearby', i.e. time-wise and space-wise. Because of the dynamic complexity involved, systems thinking is better suited for managing Sustainability Traps, as it enables analyzing how dynamics operate in a system and create backfiring.

This requires the systems thinking principles of 'Operational Thinking' and of 'Dynamic Thinking', which will be elaborated in chapters 2.2.3 and 2.2.5.

c) Estimating Sustainability Traps depends on system boundaries

For a corporation, estimating if it is caught up in a Sustainability Trap that backfires, fundamentally depends on two factors: *Which* variables to include in the analysis and *how* the variables interrelate. As has been elaborated above, the latter point of *how* variables interrelate is determined by the dynamic system structure taken as the basis for analysis. The first point of *which* variables to include – and conse-

---

114 This is because very basically A impacts B (or more variables), which in turn impact A again.

115 Example with regard to *space*: corporate measures impact environment, which impacts social variables; or Example with regard to *time*: failed corporate sustainability measures backfire only on the corporation in five or ten years or potentially on future generations.

116 This again is the reason, why it often proves easier to blame an external agent to be the causer, than to track the corporation's own contribution to the backfiring.

quently which to leave out - is a matter of *system boundaries*. The very concept of sustainability requires broadening system boundaries beyond the economic sphere to include environmental and social factors. However, even in this larger perspective, system boundaries can be set rather narrow (e.g. contribution of a factory to pollution of a local lake) or rather broad (e.g. its contribution to global warming). Realizing if a corporation is caught up in a Sustainability Trap as well as estimating if it has escaped out of (exited) a Sustainability Trap, fundamentally depends on the system boundaries, which a corporation holds.[117]

The challenge thereby is that there are no 'right' and 'fix' system boundaries, but they are subject to social value judgments[118].

For example, corporate sustainability-behavior today is observed by stakeholders (e.g. NGOs, media, consumers) not only with regard to employees of a corporation, but has extended to local communities, schools etc. Equally a corporation's contribution to global warming (e.g. CO_2 emissions) today is becoming an accepted and relevant factor. Corporations, which do not broaden their system boundaries correspondingly, risk getting into Sustainability Traps, which not only produce unsustainability but risk to – at least – backfire on the image of the corporation, i.e. on its social license to operate.

Conclusion: Identifying and managing Sustainability Traps requires *re-considering* system boundaries. Orthodox thinking focuses on narrow system boundaries, i.e. on the division of problems and an analysis of their specifics. Sustainability Traps require broad system boundaries, which also consider factors from the social and the environmental sector, as well as a focus on interrelations between the variables, systems thinking is better suited. Furthermore Sustainability Traps require repeated re-consideration of system boundaries as they are subject to social value judgments.

This requires the systems thinking principle of 'Re-thinking Boundary Judgments' for managing Sustainability Traps, which will be elaborated in chapter 2.2.2.

---

117 For example, the dissertation in chapter 3 will deal with the case of the furniture company IKEA, which through a processes of running through various sustainability scandals, broadened its system boundaries from a formaldehyde problem in particleboards, to a formaldehyde problem in products, over to a problem of toxins in products, to environmental sustainability in general towards additionally considering social sustainability. Broadening its system boundaries has helped IKEA to come out of the Sustainability Trap of 'quick-fixing' its sustainability scandals. See chapter 3.2.2.3.

118 It might be argued that this also depends on scientific knowledge, which indeed is the case. How findings are achieved as well as interpreted however, is influenced by social values.

d) There is no 'right' solution to a Sustainability Trap

Because system boundaries that determine which variables constitute a system are subject to changing social values and because dynamic complexity that determines how variables interrelate, agents will always have to deal with uncertainty. Consequently, there is no one right solution to exit or even to avoid a Sustainability Trap. As the dissertation will thoroughly outline, an alleged solution to a trap can actually lead into a next trap. It therefore is key to realize that dealing with Sustainability Traps is a *continuous learning process*, which possesses no best solution, but only better solutions, - compared to what is intended to achieve. In this sense, systems thinking allows *better* dealing with Sustainability Traps than orthodox thinking for the reasons discussed above; yet, systems thinking cannot provide the one right, impeccable solution to the challenge of Sustainability Traps. Systems thinking does not allow controlling systemic structures. At best, if a social agent is skilled in systems thinking, it allows 'dancing' with systems as Meadows (Meadows 2002 and 1999) has phrased it. Thereby continuous reflection and adjustment between mental models (here: beliefs of how the world works) and learning about behavior of systemic structures is key, as will be discussed.

Conclusion: Positivistic thinking, in the sense of the existence of objectively 'right', impeccable solutions is not suited for dealing with Sustainability Traps. Sustainability Traps are produced through underlying systemic structures, whose variables change and continuously interact in non-linear dynamics. Dealing with Sustainability Traps therefore requires *continuous learning* and a *disposition for change*, not only for changing systemic structures but equally for changing the own mental models (beliefs).

This requires the systems thinking principle of 'Thinking in Models' for managing Sustainability Traps, which will be elaborated in chapter 2.2.1.

The above chapter discussed four main characteristics of Sustainability Traps
a) Sustainability Traps have *endogenous* causes.
b) Sustainability Traps *backfire* on the corporation.
c) Estimating Sustainability Traps depends on *system boundaries*.
d) There is *no 'right' solution* to a Sustainability Traps.

From the characteristics result specific requirements for how best to manage or even avoid Sustainability Traps. It has been shown that the properties of systems thinking as identified in chapter 1.3.2 are better suited for meeting these requirements than 'orthodox' thinking.

The following paragraph will outline the specific systems thinking principles needed to best manage Sustainability Traps.

2.2 Principles of A Systems Perspective for Managing Sustainability Traps

This chapter will outline five systems thinking principles for managing Sustainability Traps. Because there is no one right solution to Sustainability Traps and because whatever 'solution' to a Trap is taken eventually will influence the system in a way that is never one hundred percent predictable[119], *continuous learning* about system behavior is inevitable. The five systems thinking skills elaborated here build the basis for this learning.

*Therefore it is important to state that these principles constitute **learning skills**[120] in the sense of Senge (2006). Systems thinking skills can be considered filters of 'how' and 'what' we see (see also Richmond 1994: 7). The principles elaborated in the following are the skills, which enable managers to adopt the '**systems perspective on sustainability**', which is put forward in the dissertation and thus a perspective, which enables to recognize Sustainability Traps and to learn how best to manage them.*

Because of the broadness of the field of system science, the number of systems thinking skills that constitute a new way of thinking as compared to orthodox thinking, i.e. 'a systems perspective' in general is broad. There have been several attempts to crystallize and describe these skills that constitute a systems perspective (e.g. Senge 2006, Richmond 1994, Ossimitz 1995, Ulrich and Probst 1991, Vester 1999, Dörner 2005). Thereby the different skills closely interlink and their categorization is of rather theoretical nature.

The dissertation focuses on systems thinking skills, which are especially relevant for the field of *sustainability*.[121] The dissertation identified and developed five systems thinking skills crucial for managing Sustainability Traps, by drawing from principles of different fields of systems science discussed in chapter 1.4[122] and by tailoring these principles to the field of sustainability. A reference of all sources used for outlining/tailoring a specific skill, can be found in the individual chapter. However, the

---

119 Due to uncertainty caused by dynamic complexity; see also chapter 2.2.5.7.

120 Senge uses the term ‚discipline' (Senge 2006: 3ff): „Discipline is a development path for acquiring certain skills or competencies." The dissertation will use the term ‚skill' as it is more common and discipline colloquially often is associated with ‚enforced order'.

121 That is the dissertation does not seek to provide a full list of skills for the whole field of system science (which does not exists as a generally accepted list anyway), but will concentrate on those, which are especially relevant for sustainability.

122 The attribution of a principles (skill) to a specific system science however is blur, because fields of system science build on each other as outlined in chapter 1.4; e.g., organizational learning builds on qualitative system dynamics and thus the principles can be considered to stem from both fields.

following three systems science disciplines can be considered the *main* sources dissertation' principles stem from: *(Qualitative) System Dynamics* (Sterman 2004, Ossimitz 1997, Richmond 1994), *Organizational Learning* (Senge 2006, Senge et al. 1994) and *Critical Systems Thinking* (Ulrich 2005, 1998).

The five systems thinking principles for managing Sustainability Traps identified and processed by the dissertation are[123]:
- Thinking in Models (chapter 2.2.1)
- Re-thinking Boundary Judgments (chapter 2.2.2),
- System-as-Cause Thinking (chapter 2.2.3),
- Operational Thinking (chapter 2.2.4)
- Dynamic Thinking (chapter 2.2.5).

The five principles form an *integrated set* of skills, which need to develop coherently in the sense of Senge's learning disciplines (Senge 2006: 10f)[124]: The skills cannot be learned theoretically alone, but require being trained and developed in business practice over and over again. There is no full mastering of the skills that guarantees impeccable solutions to Sustainability Traps. To practice the skills is to be a lifelong learner. "You never arrive; you spend your life mastering disciplines" (Senge 2006: 10). Taking on a systems perspective thus is a developmental path.

In the following, the five systems thinking skills for dealing with Sustainability Traps will be elaborated in-depth. Thereby it is important to note, that chapter 2.2 focuses on the understanding of the *theoretical concept of each skill (principle)* and its *implications* for Sustainability Traps. How the principles can be applied to manage a particular Sustainability Trap in business practice will be discussed in *chapter 3*.

2.2.1 Thinking in Models
2.2.1.1 Mental Models and Epistemological Reasoning
In the following the term 'mental model' shall be defined as it is used in the dissertation. Subsequently the epistemological roots of systems thinking will be discussed, which constitute the importance of mental models for a systems perspective.

---

123 As this is a first attempt of providing learning skills for dealing with structures of unsustainability, the dissertation does not consider the list of skills to be complete. Rather with a commitment to critical systems thinking the dissertation would appreciate amplifications or deepening of the framework provided (see directions for future research in chapter 4).
124 Interdependencies between the different skills will become apparent later in the discussion of the skills.

a) Definition Mental Models

In systems thinking the concept of *mental models* is key. The understanding of mental models in systems thinking remained very heterogeneous for a long-time, until Doyle and Ford provided a definition, which today has found broad acceptance in the field of systems thinking, particularly system dynamics. Doyle and Ford (1998: 17) define a mental models as "a relatively enduring and accessible, but limited, internal conceptual representation of an external system whose structure maintains the perceived structure of that system."

Thus, the focus of mental models clearly lies on *structure*, or more precisely on structural identity (Doyle and Ford 1998: 14): "There is one important point on which virtually all of the definitions offered in cognitive science fields agree, namely, the idea that the structure of mental models 'mirrors' the perceived structure of the external system being modeled." (see also Johnson-Laird 1983). As has been mentioned above, structure relates to how variables interrelate and thus drive behavior of a system.[125]

Besides the focus on mirroring perceived *structures*, the term 'mental models' as it is used in the dissertation refers to such mental models that constitute *beliefs*.

*That is, mental models as referred to in the dissertation constitute **beliefs** of social agents (e.g. of corporations) about the **structure of a system** and how this structure produces behavior (results) the social agents observe (e.g. pollution increase, image damage). Most important, mental models (beliefs) drive the actions of social agents.*

This conception of mental models corresponds to Senge, who defines mental models as "deeply grained assumptions [...] that influence how we understand the world and how we take action" (Senge 2006: 8, see also Senge et al. 2000: 83). In-line with this understanding of *mental models as beliefs how 'the world' or a particular system works* is also Sterman. His definition stresses the aspect of beliefs about specific *structures*. Sterman defines mental models as "the implicit causal maps of a system we hold, our beliefs about the network of causes and effects that describe how a system operates, the boundary of the model [...] and the time horizon we consider relevant - our framing or articulation of a problem" (Sterman 1994: 294).

The conception of mental models as 'beliefs' needs to be set into context with the definition of Doyle and Ford outlined above, because the latter is the predominant definition of mental models in the field of system dynamics. Doyle and Ford outline that mental models *can* constitute beliefs, but it is not a necessary condition for mental models. As will be argued, in reference to Sustainability Traps, all mental models constitute beliefs.

---

125 See chapter 1.3.1.

Doyle and Ford state that although very often mental models are equaled with be-liefs, they argue for mental models to also encompass "knowledge or beliefs that are thought to be of doubtful validity" Doyle and Ford (1998: 17). Doyle and Ford (1998: 17) conclude: "From this perspective, the term 'belief', which implies a fairly high degree of confidence in one's knowledge, describes some but not all mental models." Thereby the classification if a mental model constitutes a belief (or merely an assumption), depends on the degree of confidence that is associated with it (Doyle and Ford 1998: 18).

In the dissertation all mental models constitute beliefs. This is the case, because getting caught up in a Sustainability Trap occurs in cases of high confidence, where an agent's own thinking is holding him prisoner as has been discussed. [126] In part III, the dissertation will differentiate five mental models of sustainability, based on different believes about how environmental and social sustainability *relate to* respec-tively *can contribute to* economic sustainability. [127] Very often agents are not aware of their mental models and the effects, which they have on their actions (Senge 2006: 8). It needs to be differentiated between *espoused mental models* (espoused theory) and *mental models in-use* (theory in-use). *Espoused* mental models are the ones ar-ticulated (communicated) by a corporation, e.g. towards its stakeholders (Argyris 1999: 232). Mental models *in-use* are the beliefs that actually drive corporate *be-havior* (Argyris 1999: 232, Senge 2006: 8). Mental models in-use and espoused mental models can be congruent, but very often they fall apart.

Mental models *in-use* driving behavior does not at all needs to be a deliberate process, but far more often this happens unrecognized (Argyris 1999: 232ff).

*With regard to Sustainability Traps it is mental models **in-use**, which are crucial, be-cause they are the ones that drive behavior of social agents, which can lead into a trap.*

Hence, if the dissertation speaks of mental models in the following, it refers to mental models *in-use*, if not stated otherwise.

b) Mental Models and Epistemological Roots of a Systems Perspective

The high relevance of mental models for systems thinking stems from the fact that - in contrast to orthodox thinking - systems thinking is epistemologically rooted in constructivism: Orthodox thinking, especially in science, is often still grounded in positivism. The observer is considered to stand outside the system he observes and thus can formulate an objective judgment (Foerster, von 1995: 3). Systems thinking in contrast holds a *radical constructionist* view (Glasersfeld 1995 and 2003). That is,

---

126 See chapters 2.1.1 and 2.1.2.
127 These five mental models of sustainability are: Trade-off Model, Compliance Model, Ef-ficiency Model, Reputation Leadership Model and Systemic Model.

in order to act, we need to build models of the world (reality). This is *not* to be confronted with solipsism, which states that no outside world exists. Constructivism argues that there *is* an outside (ontic) world. However this ontic world can never be perceived as such, because our perception is biased by our way of experiencing and by the mental model of the world which we are already holding (Glasersfeld 2003: 33). Ossimitz, who categorized 'thinking in models' as a crucial system thinking skill, phrases it the following way: "[W]e can only think according to our pictures and views of the world, which are necessarily models of the world itself" (Ossimitz 1997: 93). Therefore we seek to build our mental models of how the world works thus, that they best **match** the structure of the real world. So that through better 'understanding' how the world works, we can achieve the goals we want. Thus, mental models are build, changed and evaluated according to their ***viability*** (usefulness) ***to achieve what is desired*** (Glasersfeld 2003: 30). It is most important to understand the difference between *viable matching* of mental models and the reality on the one side and *objective consistence* between mental models and the reality, which we can never be sure of (Glasersfeld 2003: 30). So when do we really 'know for sure'? According to what has just been said the answer is: never. Is there the one right solution, the one right way? The answer is: This is unlikely. And if so, we do not know. Even if a desired goal is reached by using a certain solution, this does not entail that it must be the only viable solution (Glasersfeld 2003: 32). Therefore it is key to note that there can only be a *better* or *worse* matching of a mental model and the real world, measured by the extent to which the ***feedback*** of the real world corresponds to what we except respectively to what we desire. The real world reveals itself where we *fail* (Glasersfeld 2003: 30). This is why the concept of feedback is so important in the field of systems thinking. Regarding Sustainability Traps, 'social' and 'environmental' feedback from unsustainable structures to business behavior is crucial, as will be discussed below.

This constructionist view has been related to *cybernetics* by von Foerster in the concept of second-order cybernetics. Von Foerster treats the problematic how observers construct models of systems which they themselves are a part of and with which they interact (Foerster 1995).

Second order cybernetics represents a fundamental change in the way we conduct science and how we learn, because it threatens the basic principle of scientific discourse, which demands the separation of the observer from the observed. Foerster illustrates this point with the question, if an observer considers himself independent from the world, which he observes or as an interactive part of it. (von Foerster 1995: 310f). The irritating question than is: Where is the reference point from which to decide?

Von Foerster answers this question with what he calls "metaphysical postulate"; that is *only those questions that are in principle undecidable, we can decide*, simply because of the reason that the decidable questions are already decided by the choice of the framework in which they are asked (von Foerster 1995: 314f).

Thus, in consideration of a systems perspective it is crucial to realize that the basis on which we build our 'knowledge' on, our understanding of 'how the world works' is a *model* and not an obvious truth. Various authors from system dynamic have pointed to the challenge the constructionist roots of systems thinking poses for many agents: The "inevitable a priori" assumptions at the root of everything we think we know, i.e. acknowledging the limitations of our knowledge, is deeply threatening (Meadows 1980). "The concept that [...] there is no ultimate, absolute foundation for our beliefs, is so deeply counterintuitive, so threatening, that most people reject it as "obviously false" or become so dizzy with doubt that they run screaming as fast as they can to someone who claims to offer the Truth" (Sterman 2002: 526). Thus, as we never 'know for sure' the concept of **continuous learning** is key to a systems perspective on sustainability. Therefore the concept of *learning* shall be elaborated thoroughly in the following.

2.2.1.2 Single, Double and Triple Loop Learning for Sustainability

Learning for sustainability is not limited to intra-organizational learning, but most importantly is inter-organizational, including all relevant stakeholders as the individual cases in part III of the dissertation will outline in detail. The following concept of learning for sustainability as it is developed and used in the dissertation is based on the concept of Argyris and Schön (Argyris and Schön 1996, Argyris 1999) and Bateson (2000) and others on single, double and triple-loop learning (see figure 7).[128]

---

128 It has to be stated that this concept has significantly been developed over time and today there exist a variety of different interpretations and approaches. Therefore the following does not claim to incorporate all factors treated with respect to single, double and triple loop learning in literature, but rather the following sets the factors (variables) relevant for this dissertation into the context of single, double and triple loop learning.

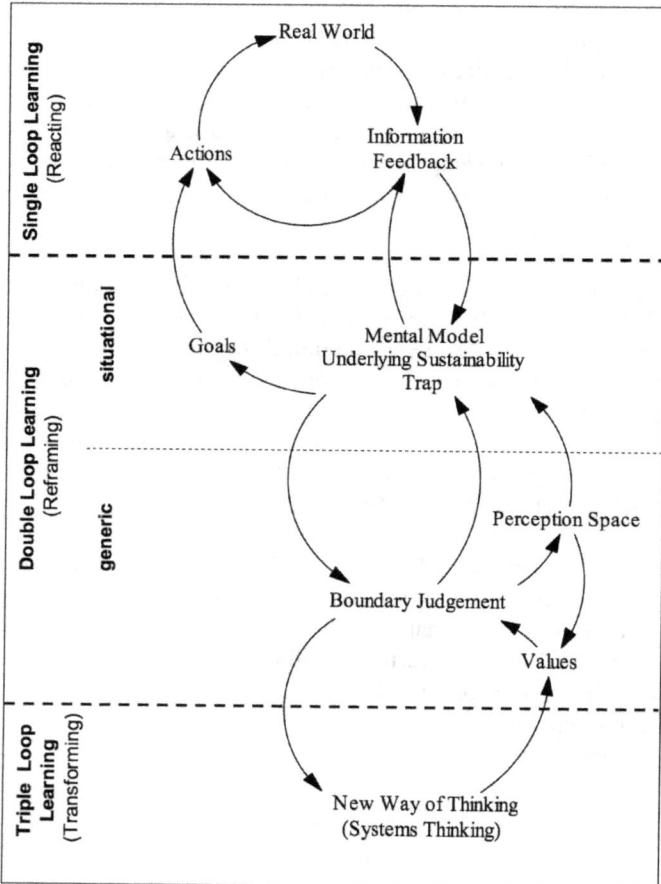

Fig. 7: Single, Double and Triple-Loop Learning as Referred to in the Dissertation
Source: Produced by the author; loosely based on Sterman 2004: 20

a) Single loop learning

Single loop learning is based on a simple balancing loop[129] from cybernetics: Actions are taken in order to meet a sustainability goal (economical, social and/or environmental sustainability). Information feedback from the real-world is compared to (matched with) the consequences desired and actions are adapted accordingly. "Single-loop learning occurs when matches are created, or when mismatches are corrected by changing actions" (Argyris 1999: 68). Single-loop learning therefore is

_____

129 See negative feedback and balancing loops in chapter 2.2.5.

focused on *reacting to events or trends*. In single-loop learning errors are "detected and corrected without questioning or altering the underlying values of the system (be it individual, group, intergroup, organizational or interorganizational)" (Argyris 1999: 68). Single loop learning relates to what Bateson has termed Learning I: "Learning I is *change in specificity of response* [emphasis by original text] by correction of errors of choice within a set of alternatives" (Bateson 2000: 293, see also 287ff). Other authors stress not only the point of 'correction', but consequently also the aspect of 'improvement' of single-loop learning. Flood and Romm argue that single-loop learning is means-end thinking, where managers focus on finding the best means to meet their goals. Therefore the basic question in single-loop thinking is 'Are we doing things right? How are we doing things?' (Flood and Romm 1996: 76ff, see also Flood and Romm 1997, Romme and Witteloostuijn 1999). Also Swieringa and Wierdsma stress the focus on improvement of single-loop learning that is being focused on more of the same, but better (Swieringa and Wierdsma 1992: 38). This level of learning therefore focuses on 'how'-questions rather than on why'-questions (Swieringa and Wierdsma 1992: 38). Hence, all authors point to the fact that single loop learning is concerned with correction and/or improvement, without tackling deeper, underlying causes. This however does not imply that single-loop learning is an easy endeavor. "[S]ingle loop learning cannot be confused with simple, easy, conflict-free or trouble-free learning" (Swieringa and Wierdsma 1992: 38).

b) Double loop learning

Double loop learning goes deeper than single-loop learning. "Double-loop learning occurs when mismatches are corrected by first examining and altering governing variables and then the actions. Governing variables are the preferred states that individuals strive to 'satisfice' when they are acting" (Argyris 1999: 68, see also Senge et al. 2000: 96). This requires asking *why*-questions in order to evaluate the theories, assumptions and arguments[130] that drive behavior of different individuals or groups (Swieringa and Wierdsma 1992: 39ff). This consequently can help answering the question 'are we doing the right things?' (Flood and Romm 1996: 127ff).[131] In or-

---

130 Swieringa and Wierdsma refer to these as 'insights' (1992: 38).

131 It has to clearly be stated however that the understanding of Flood and Romm (1996) of double and triple loop is a different one than in the dissertation. Flood and Romm relate 'why'-questions to *triple* loop learning, which they associate with power issues ('Is rightness buttressed by mightiness or vice versa'?, 1996: 169ff). *Double* loop learning for Flood and Romm results in the question 'are we doing the right things? What are we doing?' (Flood and Romm 1996: 127ff; see also Flood and Romm 1997, Romme and Witteloostuijn 1999), which yet can only be answered if underlying causes and motivations (why) are addressed. However, the question of 'are we doing the right things' does not lie at the heart of double loop learning as it is understood in the dissertation.

der to tackle underlying theories and assumptions, double loop learning requires dialogue and addressing *collective* knowledge and understanding. "The most significant cause for failure of double loop learning [...] is the avoidance of mutual debate or dialogue about the background to the problems" (Swieringa and Wierdsma 1992: 40).

*In systems thinking double loop learning usually refers to **reframing mental models**, i.e. reframing internal pictures of 'how a system works' and on which goals and actions are based on.*

As Sterman notes: "Feedback from the real world can also stimulate changes in mental models. Such learning involves new understanding of reframing of a situation and leads to new goals and new decision rules, not just new decisions." As already pointed out above, in the focus of the dissertation are ***mental models underlying a Sustainability Trap***, from which the dissertation in part III will outline five.[132]

*   **Reframing** (changing) these mental models **in-use** has two dimensions to it: First, changing **which** variables to consider in a system, i.e. for example to include 'new' variables from the environmental and the social sector. And second, reconsidering **how** these variables interrelate. While the latter depends on the **structure** of a system, the first (**which** variables to include) is determined by **system boundaries**.*

Deciding on (setting) system boundaries is of paramount importance: As discussed above, a mental model is a belief about how a particular system operates and thus produces a specific result, e.g. pollution increase, image damage. The mental model in-use of a corporation is key with respect to Sustainability Traps, as it constitutes the belief on which a corporation basis its actions on. Thereby it is key, *which* variables a corporation considers when determining its mental model of a system and how it operates, e.g. *if* – and *which* – variables from the environmental and social sector a corporation considers in its mental model. The space that a corporation considers to evaluate, which variables to include as relevant in its mental model of how a system operates and which to leave out, is referred to as ***perception space*** in the dissertation. The perception space therefore influences the boundaries of the mental models of a particular system (***system boundaries***). For example an organization that considers the natural environment as a non-substitutable basis for the functioning of social activities including economics (mental model of perception space), will use a different perception space (vantage point) to look at a sustainabil-

---

132 These five mental models are: Trade-off Model, Compliance Model, Efficiency Model, Reputation Leadership Model and Systemic Model.

ity issue in question, than an organization that perceives the natural system as means for resource input.

Furthermore it is important to note that boundary setting does not only occur on the basis of pure 'rational'[133], but is subject to *value judgments*. That is, 1) which *perception space* an agent holds and 2) consequently which *system boundaries* an agent sets regarding a particular mental model underlying a specific Sustainability Trap, is influenced by the **values**, which the agent holds. Referring to the example above e.g. if a social agent considers a well-functioning ecosystem inevitable and unsubstitutable for the well-functioning of the economic system, is influenced by the values, which the social agents holds. Because boundary setting is influenced by value judgments, boundaries of the perception space as well as boundaries of the particular system in question actually are *boundary judgments*.

Because boundary setting depends on values, *changing perception space* and consequently *changing system boundaries*, and thus ultimately *reframing mental models*[134], proves extremely difficult in business practice. Often the readiness to change (reframe) mental models only occurs, if a negative impact (backfiring) from the real-world is perceived by a corporation.

This is why double loop learning, in the sense of reframing mental models is key for successfully managing Sustainability Traps. Double-loop learning implies
*1) reflecting upon and changing **boundaries of perception space** and thus **system boundaries** and*
*2) reflecting upon and reframing **how** the variables in a system are perceived to **interrelate**, thus the perceived **structure** of a system.*

c) Triple loop learning

Triple loop learning in the dissertation refers to *transforming the way of thinking* – here in particular towards systems thinking.

Argyris and Schön use the concept of deuterolearning in order to refer to the underlying way of learning itself, i.e. *learning how to learn* (Argyris and Schön 1996: 28f). The authors differentiate two aspects of deuterolearning: The organizational structure of the learning system (e.g. channels of communication, information systems, procedures and routines that guide individual and interactive inquiry etc.) and the 'behavioral world' of the organization, i.e. "the qualities, meanings, and feelings that habitually condition patterns of interaction among individuals within the organization in such a way as to effect organizational inquiry" (Argyris and Schön 1996: 29). The dissertation uses triple loop learning in relation to Argyris and

---

133 That is, based on ‚fact' that are fed back by the real world.
134 That is beliefs about of a system works.

Schön in a very particular sense[135]: In the dissertation the aspect of 'learning how to learn' refers to *a new way of thinking* – *systems thinking* as compared to orthodox thinking, which thus changes the way we think and learn about sustainability as the dissertation aims to show. As is apparent in figure 7, systems thinking as a new way of thinking influences all variables in the figure. It is due to this fundamental quality, which 'changes in the way we think and learn' have on all other variables in figure 7, that the dissertation categorized 'a new way of thinking (systems thinking)' as a deeper level of learning, i.e. as triple loop learning.[136]

That is, while single loop learning refers to reacting upon events and double loop learning refers to reframing mental models and boundary judgments, triple loop learning as used in the dissertation refers to adopting a new way of thinking, a new perspective: systems thinking (in contrast to 'orthodox thinking). Transforming the way of thinking towards a systems perspective, constitutes the basis of the dissertation. It is important to point out 'a change in the way of thinking/ a change in perspective' as an separate level of learning in addition to single and double loop learning, because it is also possible to execute single loop learning (reacting upon events) and double loop learning (reframing mental models[137] and boundaries) within orthodox thinking. It is however the change in the way of thinking, towards a systems perspective, which is crucial for dealing with Sustainability Traps. Learning to look upon sustainability issues from a systems perspective is what constitutes triple loop learning in the dissertation. This correspondingly impacts mental models and boundary judgments perceived (double loop learning) as well as how an agent reacts upon events (single loop learning).

---

135 It has to be pointed out that this categorization differs from the one of Argyris and Schön and Bateson. Argyris and Schön subsume deuterolearning (learning how to learn) as a special aspect of *double* loop learning. They specifically refer to Bateson (see Argyris and Schön 1996: 29), who subsumes deuterolearning as Learning II, not Learning III (Bateson 2000: 292ff). It is however not unusual in literature to refer to deuterolearning (learning how to learn) as triple loop learning (see e.g. Eskildsen, Dahlgaard, and Norgaard 1999).

136 For the sake of completeness the following shall be mentioned: The concept of *Triple-loop learning* is treated very heterogeneous in literature. The concept of triple loop learning most prominent is the one of Flood and Romm (1996) relating to diversity management. Flood and Romm relate 'why'-questions to triple loop learning (not double-loop learning), but referring these to issues of power in organizations. That is, is power used as legitimation for an action, - 'is rightness buttressed by mightiness or vice versa'? (Flood and Romm 1996: 169ff). Swieringa and Wierdsma (1992: 44) relates triple loop learning to "changes in the commonly shared principles on which the organization is based; what kind of organization we wish to be, the contribution we want to make, the role we choose to play and what values we consider important." The dissertation however will use triple loop learning in a different sense as outlined.

137 That is, changing beliefs of 'how something works'.

Thereby it is important to point out that learning does not work one way (from triple to double and single loop learning), but is an iterative process as illustrated in figure 7. As pointed out in chapter 2.2.1.1 adopting a systems perspective is not a guarantee for 'right' answers and solutions. Rather the aspect of triple loop learning in regard to a systems perspective entails that the system perspective itself (i.e. its principles) can be subject to change itself.[138] That is, the principles of a systems perspective are not 'right' per se, but they constitute the basis (decision) for how the world is looked upon. This reverts to the 'uncomfortable', but crucial aspect of deciding upon in principle undecidable questions, outlined above.[139] As outlined above, learning remains a 'matching' process. If principles of systems thinking achieve greater success in reaching the corporate sustainability goals desired[140] than when applying orthodox thinking, principles of systems thinking are *better* suited for Sustainability Traps than those of orthodox thinking. This does however not imply that systems thinking principles are 'the best' nor that they are inerrant.

All three types of learning – single, double and triple-loop learning - are important and interdependent and all variables in figure 7 are subject to change. Although the learning process illustrated in figure 7 is quite complex, it only constitutes an idealized version. The learning process in reality is full of imponderabilities and biases. Some of these identified by Sterman (2004: 20) are:

- The real world has an unknown structure, is full of dynamic complexity and time delays and it is not possible to conduct fully controlled experiments.
- As for the information from the real world: It can be delayed, ambiguous or missing. Our perception is selective and often full of biases, distortion as well as errors.
- When building Mental Models, i.e. when constituting "how the system works" for us, we often have to deal with unscientific reasoning, judgmental biases, defensive routines.[141]

Thus the illustration of a learning process in figure 7 is a simplified one. In reality it has far more feedback loops and is full of non-linearities, which makes learning from information feedback very difficult (Senge 2006: 23f). Learning – from a systems perspective – therefore remains a continuous, lifelong process.

---

138 Changes in this triple loop, if ever, are far more seldom than changes on the level of single and double loop learning.
139 That is to be clear upon the basis, which a perspective is started from. And at the same time to be aware of the fact that this basis is not the unchangeable truth.
140 By avoiding or managing Sustainability Traps.
141 One very common and critical bias in this respect is linear thinking, while the real world is full of non-linearities.

2.2.1.3 Resulting Implications for Managing Sustainability Traps

In the following the implications for managing Sustainability Traps derived from the above chapter 2.2.1 will be summarized and the particular role of *double-loop learning* will be discussed.

As in a systems perspective there are no 'right' solutions, managing Sustainability Traps constitutes a continuous learning process, which (on a theoretical basis) can be differentiated into three levels. The basis of the learning process required to manage Sustainability Traps is constituted by a change towards *principles of a systems perspective* (triple loop learning), which for the reasons discussed are better suited to recognize and to deal with Sustainability Traps than orthodox thinking.

While a change towards a systems perspective (triple loop learning) constitutes the underlying, inevitable basis of the learning process, *double-loop learning* from a systems perspective constitutes the level most frequent and most relevant for managing individual, specific Sustainability Traps in question.

This is the case out of the following reason: If mental models, which a corporation holds, differ from the systemic, dynamic structures driving unsustainability in the real world[142], corporate measures risk falling short.

The higher the 'fit' (matching) between the mental models (beliefs) and systemic, dynamic structures existing in the real-world, i.e. the more a corporation is aware of how unsustainability is produced in a system, the better it can avoid Sustainability Traps and increase success of its sustainability measures.

A 'fit' can thereby basically be induced through two *interdependent* measures: First, changing/influencing the real-world systemic structure. Second, changing a corporation's mental models – and thus its actions - to better match the real world structure.

Therefore a systems perspective requires not only influencing systemic structures of the real world through corporate actions (single-loop learning)[143], but equally reflection and change in underlying mental models that drive actions (double loop learning). If single loop learning occurs without double loop learning[144], a corpora-

---

142 As outlined, the systemic structures existing in the real world can only be assumed, i.e. represented as models based on feedback from the real world. This process can be enhanced a) through stakeholder participation and dialogues, which enable to map a more ‚complete picture' of the real world structure and b) through computer simulation, which enables to calculate and quantify counter-intuitive effects of dynamics for the system behavior.

143 That is, merely re-acting upon the results of systemic structures.

144 That is, if a corporation just reacts upon real world feedback without reflecting (matching) it with the mental models and system boundaries the corporation holds. See also Iceberg Model in chapter 2.2.3.

tion risks re-creating unsustainable structures (Sustainability Traps) through its actions again and again as has been discussed in chapter 2.1. Without double-loop learning systemic structures in the real world risk to hold a corporation prisoner.

As has been discussed, double-loop learning, in the sense of reframing mental models, implies:

a) Reflecting upon and changing *boundaries* of *perception space* and thus *system boundaries*. This reframes, *which variables* are considered in the analysis of a system that constitutes a Sustainability Trap.

b) Reflecting upon and reframing *how* the variables in a system are perceived to *interrelate*, thus the perceived *structure* of a system. Because it is *how* the variables of a system interrelate, which determines how a system operates and thus forms a Sustainability Trap.

If core variables (system boundaries) and how they interrelate (systemic structure) remain insufficiently reflected upon, Sustainability Traps that backfire risk remaining unrecognized and/or cannot be dealt with successfully. Because there is no guarantee to possess the 'right' mental model and because systemic structures in the real world can change through the actions of social agents and through dynamics in a system, the learning process for managing Sustainability Traps constitutes a ***continuous learning process***, where systemic structures as well as mental models and their system boundaries need to be reevaluated continuously.

As mentioned, the dissertation in part III will exemplary discuss five mental models of sustainability frequent in business practice and will outline common Sustainability Traps, which corporations holding these mental models risk to get caught up in. The dissertation furthermore will discuss the learning required for best to deal with these traps.

These mental models discussed are[145]:

*   Trade-off Model,
*   Compliance Model,
*   Reputation Leadership Model,
*   Efficiency Model and
*   Systemic Model.

2.2.2 Re-thinking Boundary Judgments

The above chapter 'thinking in models' made it clear that systems thinking requires continuous learning. Thereby every factor – including values, mental models (beliefs) and what is perceived as 'facts' (information feedback) - needs to be open to change. If this is the case, the question arises where to depart from for this journey of change, i.e. what is a feasible reference respectively vantage point?

---

145 See chapter 3 for more information.

As the dissertation will show, the vantage point from which to look at a system depends on:

a) boundary setting of the *perception space* and

b) boundary setting of the *'relevant' system*, i.e. the system in question (situational). The term 'perception space' thereby is used by the dissertation to refer to the space where an agent looks for relevant variables for modeling a system, e.g. for identifying a Sustainability Trap. Within this perception space the agent identifies 'relevant variables', which do form part of the relevant system in question, while all other variables form part of the environment. This process of identifying 'relevant' variables is referred to as setting system boundaries (*boundary setting*). Building on Ulrich, system boundaries therefore can be defined as conceptual border lines, which distinguish the system in question from its environment and thus define what is considered 'relevant', i.e. the "borders of concern" (Ulrich 1998: 5).

Boundary setting is crucial for dealing with Sustainability Traps. As Sterman outlines, and as the dissertation aims to show, *crucial aspects of (Sustainability) Traps remain unperceived if boundaries are set **too narrow*** (Sterman 2002).

*Therefore **re-thinking** – in the sense of **re-considering** – on perception space and system boundaries is particularly crucial for the field of sustainability. As has been elaborated above[146], the very concept of sustainability requires looking at 'the larger system', i.e. **broaden system boundaries:** Larger in **space** in the sense not only to look at the economic system, but equally on the social and the environmental system. And larger in **time**, i.e. also to include the needs of future generations.*

Before outlining boundary setting for 'the relevant system' and for the 'perception space', it is necessary to elaborate on the theoretical foundations of this chapter. This chapter differs from the theoretical foundations of the other four chapters on systems thinking principles in so far as the other four chapters build on principles from (qualitative) system dynamics and closely related disciplines[147]. The current chapter on re-thinking boundary judgments differs hereof insofar, as it combines aspects of critical systems thinking (Ulrich 2005, 2002, 1998, 1994, 1983) and system dynamics (Sterman 2002 and 2004; Senge 2006), whose compatibility is still to show.

---

146 See chapter 1.2.

147 That is, the compatibility of aspects or principles from other systems thinking disciplines and system dynamics feeding into these four other skills have already been proven by the authors cited in the respective chapters and needs not to be done by the dissertation. The dissertation' contribution is to set these systems thinking principles into the context of sustainability.

Bringing together critical systems thinking (Ulrich)[148] *and qualitative system dynamics (Sterman and Senge*[149]*) with regard to boundary setting*

Boundary setting shares a similar fate as mental models: Although both concepts are acknowledged to play a crucial role in systems science their definitions vary significantly and often the disquisition remains superficial in regard to the importance of the issue. Regarding mental models this problem was raised and resolved by Doyle and Ford (1998) particularly relating to the fields of system dynamics.

Regarding boundary setting and boundary judgments the issue is treated in-depth by Ulrich (Ulrich 2005, 2002, 1994, 1983). Ulrich stresses the point that each boundary setting is subject to value judgments, so that it are indeed boundary *judgments*. Ulrich however restricts its approach to critique only[150]. So that for modeling, e.g. for modeling Sustainability Traps, there exist no satisfying approach yet, which accounts for the aspect of boundary judgments.

In turn, other scholars refer to boundary setting for modeling, but do not address the importance of *values* for boundary setting as Ulrich does. The latter however is especially crucial for the field of sustainability.

The dissertation therefore seeks to bring together the work of Ulrich on boundary judgments and the approach of qualitative system dynamics to model system structure as a means to better deal with issues of sustainability (here: Sustainability Traps). For this end, it is necessary to show that these two approaches are compatible. This shall be argued in the following.

Ulrich accuses the field of systems thinking to ignore the unavoidable *selectivity* of boundary setting for systems thinking (systems modeling) and the resulting lack of full comprehensiveness (Ulrich 1994, 1983). "Mainstream systems literature somehow always manages to ignore the fact that no conceivable methodology can secure comprehensively rational problem solutions" (Ulrich 1994: 27). Ulrich argues that systems thinking despite its effort of considering the 'whole relevant system' cannot alter the fact that all argumentations remain 'partial' in the double sense of "being selective with respect to relevant facts and norms and of benefiting some parties more than others" (Ulrich 2002: 41). Because considering the whole relevant system is always a matter of value judgments, no model can be 'true'/'right'. "The critical kernel of the systems idea consists in its reminding us of two fundamental limitations of knowledge. The first is that all our claims to knowledge, understanding, and rationality imply that we consider 'the whole' relevant system; the second, that in consequence we can rarely if ever be certain to know and understand enough" (Ulrich 1998: 5). Because of this "critical kernel of the systems idea", systems think-

---

148 See Ulrich 2005, 2002, 1998, 1994, 1983.
149 See Sterman 2002 and Sterman 2004; and Senge 2006.
150 That is using boundary judgments as a form of critique in argumentations and thus as a tool for emancipation as outlined in chapter 1.4.4.

ing in the view of Ulrich shall not be used primarily to model and analyze systems, but rather as a form of critique in the sense of pointing to value judgments underlying system boundaries (Ulrich 1998, 1994, 2002 and 2005). This limited use of systems thinking is rejected by the dissertation. Rather the dissertation considers the approach of boundary judgments of Ulrich not only *compatible* with analyzing systemic, dynamic structures as in the approach of system dynamics and organizational learning (Sterman 2002 and 2004, and Senge 2006), but the dissertation considers both approaches inseparable and their combination deeply enriching for managing Sustainability Traps. This shall be reasoned in the following.

The dissertation acknowledges that Ulrich's criticism on 'mainstream systems literature' cited above applies to *hard* systems thinking[151], where a model is used as a tool for advocacy, in the sense that it guarantees to show 'the proven truth'. This criticism is shared by qualitative systems thinking (qualitative system dynamics). Sterman points to the fact that although radical constructivism is the epistemological basis for systems thinking, among modelers the actual addressing of system boundaries is "surprisingly useful and shockingly rare. Often models are used not as tools of inquiry but as weapons in a war of advocacy. In such cases modelers seek to hide the assumptions of their models from potential critics" (Sterman 2004: 98, see also Sterman 2002: 518ff).

For *qualitative* systems thinking (qualitative system dynamics) Ulrich's criticism does not apply however as the dissertation argues. Rather qualitative systems thinking (qualitative system dynamics) fully *acknowledges* the fact that all models are influenced by value judgments on system boundaries and that therefore all models are wrong. Sterman, one of the leading figures in system dynamics states accordingly (Sterman 2002: 525): "All decisions are based on models, and all models are wrong. [...W]e [annotation of the author: systems thinkers] stress that human perception and knowledge are limited, that we operate from the basis of mental models, that we can never place our mental models on a solid foundation of Truth because a model is a simplification, an abstraction, a selection, because our models are inevitably incomplete, incorrect—wrong." This aspect has been stressed in-depth in the above chapter 2.2.1.

Thus, systems thinking (system dynamics) fully acknowledges Ulrich's criticism that all models are wrong and provide no foundation for knowing 'the truth'. The *difference* is that the dissertation, in-line with system dynamics, disputes the assumption that because all models are *wrong* (lack of comprehensiveness) this means that they are *useless*. Rather the dissertation argues that modeling and analyzing structures with the help of systems thinking, indeed is a means for learning that *mental* models, i.e. believes of 'how the world works', can be wrong and are subject to changing values. A systems perspective focuses on scientific inquiry skills in or-

---

151 See chapter 1.4.2.

der to uncover hidden assumptions and biases. It requires respect and empathy other's viewpoints. As Sterman further states, most important, and most difficult to learn, systems thinking requires acknowledging the limitations of our knowledge, because of the fact that all models are wrong (Sterman 2002: 501 and 526). Systems thinking "requires the humility we need to learn and the courage we need to lead, though all our maps are wrong" (Sterman 2002: 527). Thus system dynamics and organizational learning are aware of the problem that inevitably decisions have to be made upon models which are limited (wrong) and consequently comprehension and knowledge are limited and need constant critique and revision. This is the core foundation of the approach of organizational *learning* (Senge 2006, see also chapter 2.2.1). In-line with this view the dissertation hence argues that it is *indeed* the modeling and analysis of structures, which can help reveal the interdependency of 'modeling systemic structures', 'mental models' and 'system boundaries based on values'. That is, it is the modeling and analysis of systemic structures, which can reveal that mental models 'are wrong'. In this sense using systems thinking as a tool for analyzing structures constitutes also a form of critique, even more so a way of *learning*.

Therefore the concept of modeling systemic structures (system dynamics, organizational learning) and the aspect of boundary judgments (critical systems thinking) with respect to system boundaries are fully compatible. Both concepts argue for using systems thinking as a form of inquiry. Yet, Ulrich (critical systems thinking) restricts it to boundary critique, while boundary reflection forms only one part in system dynamics modeling.

As stated above, Ulrich's criticism applies insofar, as *although* the issue of boundary judgments is acknowledged by qualitative systems thinking (qualitative system dynamics) the issue is hardly addressed and examined by this discipline. There exist no detailed scientific approach in the discipline of qualitative system dynamics and organizational learning for addressing the issue of value judgments in boundary setting as it is put forward by Ulrich.

For the field of sustainability, boundary judgments however are crucial as stated above, because the very concept of sustainability requires broadening system boundaries beyond the economic sector to also encompass variables from the environmental and the social sector. Because of the crucial importance of boundary judgments for the field of sustainability and the compatibility of the approach to qualitative system dynamics, the dissertation will integrate Ulrich's approach of boundary judgments as a further systems thinking principle for dealing with Sustainability Traps. The dissertation through out its development of an instrument of systems thinking skills for Sustainability Traps will show that *analyzing systemic, dynamic structures* and *re-evaluating (re-thinking) boundary judgments* are interdependent and that both skills are necessary for successful managing Sustainability Traps.

In the following, the dissertation will outline **boundary setting** with regard to

a) the *'relevant' system*, i.e. the system which a specific Sustainability Traps refers to and whose structure is to be modeled and analyzed.

b) the *perception space*, i.e. the space where an agent looks for relevant variables for modeling a system, e.g. for identifying a Sustainability Trap. Within this perception space the agent identifies 'relevant variables', which do form part of the relevant system in question, while all other variables form part of the environment.

After boundary setting for these two points has been discussed, the dissertation will elaborate on the aspect of *value judgments* for the boundary setting of both – the relevant system and the perception space.

2.2.2.1 Setting System Boundaries

As has been discussed in chapter 1.3.1, a system is a perceived whole, whose parts (elements, variables) are interrelated and whose behavior is determined by the interaction of all parts. The question, which this chapter deals with is how to go about to define the *boundaries* of a system?

In order to answer this question it is important to distinguish between

    a)   Historical (sectoral) system boundaries and

    b)   Boundary setting in a systems perspective (principle of the system boundary), which is relevant for the dissertation.

a) Historical (sectoral) boundaries

At least since the enlightment in the 17th/18th century, we are used to think within boundaries of defined (sub)systems, which over the time have formed specialized disciplines and have earned us significant insights and achievements. In regard to sustainability the relevant sectors for the dissertation as discussed are *economic sector, social sector, environmental sector*.[152] It is important to state that these sectoral system boundaries are not what equals boundary setting in a systems perspective. For reasons of distinction the dissertation therefore refers to the latter as '*sectors*' or '*spheres*' or within the scientific context as '*disciplines*'. The term '*system*' in contrast will be used for entities (wholes), which are defined by using the principle of the system boundary.

For the difference it is most crucial to keep in mind that the classification into sectors (e.g. economical, social and environmental), is *purely social (theoretical)*. It is crucial to realize that the division into these sectors is one that has developed over time and we have been *trained* to think within these categories. Therefore they seem normal and coherent to us. But these system boundaries have been defined

---

152 See chapter 1.2.2.

historically over time ("socialized" system boundaries) and not by ourselves starting from today's problems and from there defining relevant system boundaries.

b) Boundary setting in a systems perspective (principle of the system boundary)

Systems thinking in contrast seeks to transcendent sectoral boundaries.[153] The risk and insufficiency of a sectoral perspective is that system boundaries are set to narrow and cannot provide a picture of the 'whole' (the system and how it operates). The problem of sectoral, narrow system boundaries can be illustrated by the Indian Sufi tale of the 'Blind Men and the Elephant' (Senge 2006: 66): As three blind men encounter an elephant for the first time, each one touches a different part of the animal. The man, who grasps the ear explains that an elephant is a large rough thing, wide and broad, like a rug. The second in contrast states, that it is a straight and hollow pipe, as he touches the trunk. The third one, touching the front leg of the elephant claims that it is mighty and firm, like a pillar.

The interpretations of the men are based on the particular part of the elephant (system) they happen to touch. Each is partly right, but no one has understood the system as a whole and it is most doubtful, if they will do so by reconciling their different interpretations.

*Therefore a systems perspective requires perceiving a relevant system **departing from a specific issue of unsustainability**, i.e. independent (beyond) sectoral boundaries. That is not to start by analyzing the specifics of individual parts of a system, but to depart from a particular system behavior (issue) in question (e.g. a system produces unsustainability).*

This has been summed up by Senge in the term of "principle of system boundary" (Senge 2006: 66). It requires that "the interactions that must be examined are those most important to the issue in question, *regardless* of parochial [...] boundaries" (Senge 2006: 66).

*That is the approach for defining a 'relevant system' in systems thinking is **bottom-up** and starts with a specific unsustainability issue in question, i.e. **which currently is observed**. Departing from there, all variables considered contributing to the problem and their interrelations are identified regardless from sectoral boundaries.[154]*

Figure 8, shows an example of a relevant system for analyzing the issue of 'undernourishment'.

---

153 See also chapter 1.3.
154 For an in-depth methodology for building models in system dynamics see Sterman 2000. What is relevant in this chapter is the issue of boundary setting.

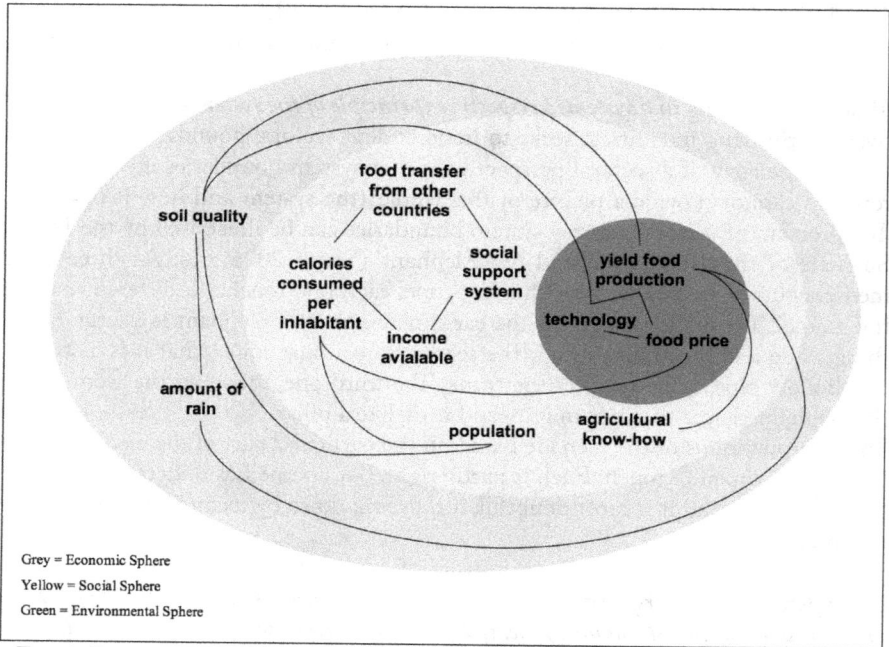

Fig. 8: Principle of System Boundary Using 'Undernourishment' as an Example
Source: Produced by the author

What is relevant to notice at this point is the difference between what *systems thinking* refers to as '*system*' (the *different variables and their interconnections*, e.g. food price, agricultural knowledge, rain) and *socially defined sectors* (*economical, social and environmental sector*).

As shown in figure 8, the variables that constitute the system stem from different sectors, i.e. from the economic, social and environmental sector.[155] Hence, a systems perspective ("principle of system boundary") leads to the effect that *sectoral boundaries* can be transcended (see colored areas (spheres) in figure 8). Therefore a systems perspective is ideally suited for interdisciplinary endeavors (Klir 2001), such as sustainability. The classification of the different variables to individual sectors (economic, social and environmental sector) as it is done in figure 8, constitutes a (social) attribution, which yet is not relevant for the system structure as such.

---

155 Variables influencing undernourishment might e.g. be "soil quality" (environmental sector), population size (social sector) and food price (economic sector). Another example of systems thinking transcending sectoral boundaries in existing literature can be found in Schellnhuber 2001: 36.

It is furthermore important to outline that argumentations that systems thinking means an effort to 'look at the whole' of an issue as it is often put forward (e.g. Ulrich 1993: 583) needs to be rejected (at least from a system dynamics point of view), as this represents a misconceived, shortened view of the systems idea: It is true, that systems thinking has been developed as an alternative to the reductionist view of the enlightment[156], which has led to the separation and specialization based on 'thinghood' within science (different scientific disciplines) as well as within society (specialized sectors), as has been discussed above. Already Bertalanffy however has outlined that systems thinking requires seeing 'the wholes' *and* 'the parts' (Bertalanffy 1968, see chapter 1.3). Thus the systems idea does *not* require holistic thinking in the sense of only seeing the whole, but in the sense of seeing **the whole and the parts**. Or more precisely: ***How the parts relate to each other and constitute the behavior of the whole***. Senge uses the metaphor of a forest to stress this point of view. Holistic thinking requires seeing the forest *and* the trees (Senge 2006). Put it more pointedly it can be referred to as seeing the trees *within* the forest, i.e. how the trees constitute the forest. Richmond refers to this aspect as seeing "both the generic and the specific - not just the latter!" (Richmond 1994: 7).

With regard to Sustainability Traps it is crucial to analyze *which* variables relate *how* to constitute a system, which produces unsustainability that backfires. Thereby **boundary setting** determines *which* variables to consider, i.e. which to include and – similarly – which to exclude. *How* variables interrelate is determined by the *structure* of a system. This will be dealt with in later chapters.[157] The current chapter deals with boundary setting, i.e. which variables to include when analyzing a system in order to determine if it forms a Sustainability Trap. As has just been shown, systems thinking requires to start with an *observed sustainability issue in question*, i.e. an event or trend, which is observed (e.g. undernourishment is a current problem), in order to start determining *which* variable constitute a relevant system to explain the issue of undernourishment.

2.2.2.2 Perception Space

The above chapter has laid emphasis to start setting system boundaries from an issue in question, regardless of sectoral boundaries. Yet, when looking for which variable to include (respectively which to leave out), we inevitably are looking within a specific space: The dissertation refers to this space as *perception space*.[158]

---

156 That is Descartes and other scholars of this time.
157 This will be dealt with in subsequent chapters 2.2.3 – 2.2.5.
158 As will be outlined below, a perception space can be rather congruent with a specific sector (e.g. considering variables from the economic sector) or can spread over various sectors.

The conception of *perception space* is neither raised in system dynamic literature (e.g. Sterman, Senge et al.) nor in Ulrich's concept of boundary judgments explicitly, but shall be introduced here, because of its particular relevance to the field of sustainability. Therefore the concept of perception space, first needs to be derived from respectively demarcated to the two fields (system dynamics and critical systems thinking), which this chapter builds on.

System Dynamics implicitly presumes that the perception space of agents is the largest system, i.e. the universe.[159] Ulrich (1998: 5f) in contrast makes more subtle distinctions. Similar to system dynamics, he distinguishes between the universe, i.e. the whole system, and the system of primary concern, which can be considered to equal the 'system' definition of system dynamics described above. Additionally he distinguishes the 'relevant environment' and the 'context of application'. "A part of the universe is 'relevant environment' if it does not belong to the system of concern but nevertheless influences the system; it is irrelevant environment (or simply a part of the universe) if it does not influence the system or if the way in which it influences the system is of no concern. [...] The context of application refers to that part of the universe which is influenced by the system" (Ulrich 1998: 5, see also Ulrich 1993: 11). Ulrich draws a distinction between those two environments, because he considers the context of application to be a counter-concept to the environment. Considerations about the 'relevant' environment are focused on a concern for success, while the context of application "implies a concern for the consequences that a proposal may impose upon third parties. The context of application is that conceptual part of the universe in which the normative content of a proposition or rationality claim becomes effective and visible" (Ulrich 1998: 5, see also Ulrich, 1987: 276 ff; Ulrich 1993: 592f).[160]

With regard to sustainability, the 'context of application' plays a crucial role, as it implies the consequences of corporate actions on the social or environmental sector, i.e. on 'third parties'. It is however the focus of the dissertation to specifically show that very often effects of corporate measures on 'third parties' are no side-effects, but can in turn trigger reactions from this field that contribute to structures, which backfire on the organization and thus become part of the 'relevant environment'. Consequently it does not make sense for the dissertation to differentiate between these two environments. Therefore the dissertation considers the perception space to be the set union of the 'relevant environment' and the 'context of application'

---

159 It might be interjected that system dynamics implicitly relates perception to existing mental models of agents. As the definition of Doyle and Ford presented above, suggests however, mental models refer to a representation of specific structures, which is far more concrete than the understanding of perception space outlined here.
160 Ulrich states that it is the context of application in which the normative content of a proposition becomes visible.

outlined by Ulrich[161]. Figure 9 illustrates the relationship between universe, perception space and relevant system as used in the dissertation:

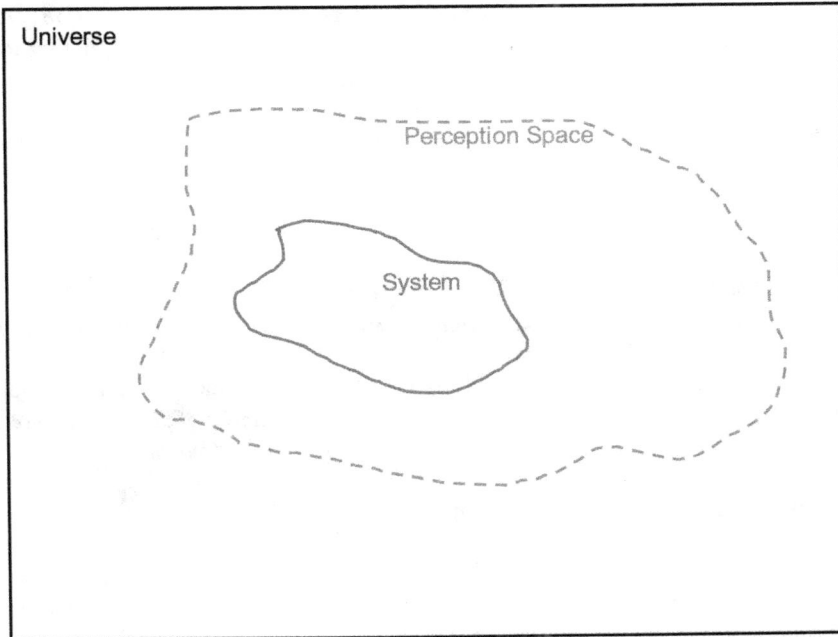

Fig. 9: Relationship Between Universe, Perception Space and Relevant System
Source: Produced by the author, adapted from Ulrich 1998: 6

Perception space as defined in the dissertation thus relates to parts of the universe considered to influence an issue (system) as well as parts of the universe that are

---

161 It has to be remarked critically that Ulrich designed this concept as a form of critique (Ulrich 2002) and therefore the context of application plays a critical role, because in his view it entails normative contents, which cannot be argued for on a pure basis of knowledge (see also Ulrich 1993: 594) and therefore provides a space that makes less-knowledgeable groups equal with professionals and therefore provides a space of emancipation (Ulrich 2003: 5f, see also chapter 1.4.4). The dissertation as outlined yet does not seek to use systems thinking means for emancipation in form of critique but rather as learning (self-reflection and group reflection). Thus, as outlined in the introduction to this paragraph Ulrich's concepts are used with a different intention in the dissertation. As equally been outline above this intention makes it feasible to view the relevant environment and context of application in combination as perception space. As will be outlined further below the normative, value-based implication which Ulrich attributes to the context of application, therefore equally does apply to the perception space – as it does to all kind of thinking anyway (see below).

considered to be influenced by an issue (system). It is within their perception space that social agents (e.g. corporations). The perception space is the space, which a social agent considers in order to *determine, which variables from his perception space to include as 'relevant'* (and which to exclude) with respect of a system relating to a particular unsustainability issue in question.

A perception space has two dimensions: *space* and *time*.

- *Space:* A perception space can be rather congruent with a specific sector (e.g. only considering variables from the economic sector) or can spread over various sectors.
- *Time*: A perception space can be rather short-term or long-term.

2.2.2.3 Boundary Setting as Value Judgment

It is most crucial to realize that all *boundary setting is subject to value judgments*. To outline and elaborate this point is the core merit of Ulrich (2005, 2003, 1993, 1998, 1983) on whose work the systems thinking skill of 're-thinking boundary judgments' crucially builds on. As will be shown, both, *boundaries of perception space* as well as boundaries of the specific system in question (*system boundaries*)[162], are subject to value judgments.

The importance of the notion that boundary setting never is based on rational assumptions only has already been perceived in system dynamics literature. Sterman for example states: "By model boundary I mean not only substantive assumptions such as whether the interest rate is endogenous or exogenous or whether the production function assumes constant returns to scale, but also the more subtle boundaries imposed by all modeling methodologies, such as the assumption that data are numbers, or that human beings make decisions to maximize expected utility. Most of the critical assumptions in any model, mental or formal, are the implicit ones, the ones buried so deep that the modelers themselves are unaware of them" (Sterman 2002: 513, Sterman also refers to: Meadows 1980; Meadows and Robinson 1985 and 2002). As stated in the introduction of this chapter, system dynamics however has not developed any approach to elaborate on *what* it is exactly what Sterman refers to as 'deeply buried, implicit assumptions' and which implications arise out of the fact that they influence boundary setting.[163]

---

162 That is, chapter 2.2.2.1 (particular system in question) and 2.2.2.2 (perception space).
163 System dynamics has developed different tools for describing the boundaries set: These are the 'model boundary chart', which consists of a table that indicates which key variables are endogenous, which are exogenous and which are excluded from a system model (Sterman 2000: 97f). Other tools are sophisticated protocols for group modeling (Sterman 2000: 512) and subsystem diagrams, which show how different subsystem couple to each other (see Sterman 2000: 99 for details). What is however missing in these concepts and where Ulrich can contribute too, is the importance of *values* in boundary settings and the implications

Ulrich states that it is *values*, which ultimately influence boundary setting of any system. Boundary setting therefore indeed is *judging* on boundaries (***boundary judgments***) based not only on rational assumptions, but eventually on underlying values."*[A]ny* partiality can and needs to be understood as amounting to boundary judgments; for any content we do or do not consider, and the way we consider it, implies corresponding boundary judgments. This consequence is the reverse side of the coin of 'clear and valid thinking', as it were; we cannot meaningfully talk about any aspect of a situation or an issue without implying boundary judgments" (Ulrich 2005: 3). The crucial contribution Ulrich therefore makes is that the analysis of every system requires boundary setting to define the borders of concern, and – this is the crucial aspect – that every boundary setting indeed is a ***boundary judgment***, which entails the ***duality of a rational (empirical) and a value-based justification (normative)*** (Ulrich 2005: 3, see also Ulrich 2003: 5).

This hence refers to setting boundaries for a *perception space* as well as for setting boundaries for a specific system in question (*system boundaries*), which relates to a specific Sustainability Trap. Both constitute boundary judgments, influenced not only by 'logical' argumentation and empirical findings, but equally through underlying values. Boundary judgments can be conscious and deliberate or unintended, but they always entail also a value-based justification (Ulrich 2005: 3).[164] These boundary judgments define the area of concern. Every decision on the 'adequate' perception space and on the 'relevant' system at some point reaches boundaries for its justification and so does the resulting analysis and its findings based on the perception space and system defined. This is why boundary judgments are so crucial in order to recognize and analyze Sustainability Traps. Boundary judgments are what lies *before* and *after* "justification break-offs", i.e. the analysis (justification) how an issue of unsustainability is produced. "It is of course also a normal fact that every attempt to justify a proposition or a design must start with some premises and end with some conclusions which it cannot question any further. That is, every chain of argumentation begins and ends with some *justification break-offs*" (Ulrich 1993: 594). That is, judging (deciding) on which boundaries to apply for perception space and for a particular system at case, comes down to what von Foerster has termed 'deciding upon in principle undecidable questions' (von Foerster 1995).[165] Here the undecidable question is:

---

arising from the relevance of values in boundary setting.

164 Thereby it is to expect that boundary judgments of the perception space remain less reflected than boundary judgments of a specific system, which an agent seeks to analyze (e.g. with regard to a Sustainability Trap).

165 See chapter 2.1.1.1.

*'Which **perception space (in time and space)** needs to be considered and which **system boundaries** (i.e. which variables) need to be considered by a corporation in order not to get caught up in a Sustainability Trap or, if it is caught up already, in order to deal with one?'*

That is in particularly: Which variables from the environmental and the social sector need to be considered by a corporation in order not to produce Sustainability Traps. How broad (or narrow) is broad (narrow) enough for perception space and for system boundaries?

It is the answer to this question that constitutes the core implication of Ulrich's concept of system boundaries. *The answer is that because boundary setting is boundary* ***judgment*** *there are no ex-ante 'right' and 'fix' boundaries; neither for a perception space nor for a particular system.* Boundary judgments come down to deciding upon in principle undecidable questions, because boundary judgments are made based on values an agent holds, the boundary judgments taken in turn, determine what an agent sees, i.e. what he perceives as 'relevant' and thus what he attaches value to. Hence there is no 'right' system boundary. As Ulrich states: "The 'right' boundary judgments depend on the subjective interests, values, and knowledge of those who judge, which is to say that boundary judgments (if recognized as such and laid open to everyone concerned) will tend to be disputed. A theoretically sufficient ('objective') justification will not be available" (Ulrich 1993: 593). Because boundary judgments determine, what is perceived and thus analyzed, *not* changing system boundaries is the most crucial factor that holds an agent prisoner in his thinking and thus caught up in a Sustainability Trap. *Re-thinking* and *changing* system boundaries therefore lies at the heart for successfully dealing with Sustainability Traps. Re-thinking (re-considering) system boundaries can be imagined as a process of zooming-out (broaden system boundaries) and zooming-in (narrowing system boundaries), which determines what an agent see (facts) and thus which he attaches value too.[166] "The 'facts' we observe, and how we evaluate them, depend on how we bound the system of concern [...]. Different value judgments can make us change boundary judgments, which in turn makes the facts look different. Knowledge of new facts can equally make us change boundary judgments, which in turn makes previous evaluations look different, etc." (Ulrich states 1998: 6). Thus, Ulrich stresses the interdependency between system boundaries, facts and values. Regarding Sustainability Traps, it is important to outline that boundary judgments influence even

---

166 The software Google Earth provides an illustrative analogy for zooming in and out and how it determines, what an agent sees; e.g. primarily a corporation in its economic sphere, its embeddedness in the social system (local community, city the corporation is based on) or the embeddedness of both, the corporation and the city, in the environmental system up to a global perspective.

more factors relevant for dealing with Sustainability Traps. *Re-thinking* and *changing* boundary judgments can be considered a pivotal part of the learning process elaborated in figure 7 in the previous chapter[167]: Changing boundary judgments with regard to *perception space*, influences *system boundaries*, i.e. which variables are considered as relevant for the analysis of a specific system in question. This in turn influences the perceived *system structure*, because if new variables (respectively more or less variables) are considered, this impacts *how* the variables *interrelate* and which *dynamics* they create in the system. The perception of system boundaries (which variables) and system structure, determines if a system is recognized as a *Sustainability Trap* that backfires or if it is not recognized as such. If (triggered by a change in boundary judgments) a system is recognized as a Sustainability Trap, this can change the *mental models* of a corporation of how (un)sustainability is produced. As discussed above, a change in mental models in turn alters the *goals* and *actions* of a corporation. Equally it alters the corporation's perception of *information feedback* ('facts', 'events') from the real-world; in particular effects of *backfiring* from a Sustainability Trap are perceived as caused *endogenously* and not by an outside enemy. The new mental model (belief) of how (un)sustainability and its backfiring is produced, can alter underlying *values*,[168] which in turn determine future boundary judgments. This constitutes the circular learning process elaborated in figure 7[169] and stresses the pivotal role, which boundary judgments play in this process:

As a decision (judgment) upon in principle undecidable questions, boundary judgments are what provides **stability** *for a corporation in the sense that they provide an* **anchor point (orientation point)** *from which social agents perceive and analyze systems. But,* **because** *of the very fact that they are an orientation point, boundary judgments at the same time provide the highest leverage for* **change** *in order to get out of a Sustainability Trap.*
Because there are **no one right system boundaries***, judging on system boundaries is a* **learning process***.*

---

167 See chapter 2.2.1.2.
168 For example, if a corporation (and equally a society) realizes that global warming (environmental sustainbility) is impacting its business (e.g. insurance company, agricultural company) it is likely to attach value to it and to consider it in future decisions.
169 As stated in chapter 2.2.1.2 this refers to double loop learning (as well as single loop learning in combination with double loop learning). Triple loop learning provides the system perspective, which enables to execute double and single loop learning in the form described above.

Thereby it is particularly interesting that, as discussed, in the learning process *boundary judgments* can also influence *values*, which a corporation – and a society – holds.[170] If system boundaries are broadened towards specific environmental or social factors, which reveal that a Sustainability Trap that backfires is at play, these environmental/social factors are approved (acknowledges) as valuable and considered in future boundary setting, because they contribute to a structure that risks to backfire on the agent. Anthropocentric contributions to the environmental factor 'global warming' are a prominent example, where the environmental factor is starting to be assigned value to by society as well as by corporations (e.g. corporations in the energy, insurance or agricultural industry). The learning process elaborated hence is a process, where changes in corporate values are motivated intrinsically through the realization of systemic patterns of unsustainability that risk backfiring. Approaches that deal with corporate *values* with regard to sustainability (or in a broader sense with corporate morals and norms), such as approaches of Corporate Responsibility, Corporate Social Responsibility and Business Ethics, are very important as they provide an orientation point for business behavior (e.g. Cannon 1992, Carroll 1999, Ferrell, Fraedrich and Ferrell 2002, Hawkins 2006, Moir 2001, Priddat 2005a, Trevino and Nelson 2004, Velasquez 2006). The learning process elaborated above has shown how *changes in corporate values* interrelate *with changes in boundary judgments* and thus *changes in how the corporation perceives a system* (respectively *a problem of unsustainability*). The learning process presented above therefore is complementary to such approaches as CSR, CR and Business Ethics, insofar as it provides a framework to explain how a motivation for *changing corporate values* can be created and compounded *intrinsically*.[171] The necessary complementary part for intrinsic corporate value changes thereby is an understanding of how underlying, unsustainable structures risks to backfire on corporations.

As mentioned already in chapter 2.2.1.2 the learning process elaborated above is an idealized one. Changing boundary judgments and resulting mental models in corporations is highly difficult, because they constitute deep rooted, implicit assumptions. Therefore it are often incisive events, like a *scandal* of unsustainability and/or *stakeholder dialogues* (e.g. with NGOs), which trigger the learning process in the course of which boundary judgments are reconsidered, i.e. new variables from the environmental and social sphere are considered as relevant, and mental models are reframed. Part III will outline business examples for this, which discuss the challenge and the learning required for changing boundary judgments.

---

170 That is, not only do values influence boundary judgments, but also vice versa as outlined (Ulrich 2005: 2).

171 Priddat also stresses the point that extending (broadening) system boundaries towards the social and environmental system and values attached to them, opens up behavior-alternatives for corporate (economic) decisions (i.e. economic moral, see Priddat 2005a).

2.2.2.4 Resulting Implications for Managing Sustainability Traps
2.2.2.4.1 Changing Boundaries of Perception Space and System Boundaries

It has been outlined above that perception spaces have two dimensions: *time* and *space*. In the following these two dimensions of perception spaces will be elaborated *with respect to sustainability*. As equally stated above, boundaries of the perception space influence the boundaries of a specific system in question (system boundaries). The following thus deals with perception spaces and resulting system boundaries for managing Sustainability Traps. As stated there are no 'right' or 'optimal' perception spaces and system boundaries, because boundary setting is subject to value judgments. As will be discussed in the following however, there are perception spaces and consequently system boundaries, which are *better suited* than others for dealing with Sustainability Traps.

a) Perception Space in time

On a very basic level, perception space in time can be differentiated in **short-term** and **long-term**. In business, long-term (strategic) is often considered to be a period of five to ten years or slightly above a decade.[172] These relatively narrow time frames in business are often driven by a focus on short-term return (maximizing shareholder value short-term) and corresponding short-term contracts (e.g. for managers or suppliers), which already has been criticized by scholars from business itself[173] (e.g. Mintzberg, Simons and Basu 2002, Burke and Cooper 2003: 9ff). The field of sustainability, which encompasses long lasting biological processes, usually associates far longer time periods with the word 'long-term', - up to future generations (see e.g. Brundtland definition of sustainability above, see also Robèrt et al. 2002)[174]. Thus, the use of the words (short-term and long-term) is relative and it is not the aim of the dissertation to define 'correct' time frames for sustainability. What is however pivotal to note with respect to Sustainability Traps is that one pitfall of Sustainability Traps lies in the fact that corporations often use *too short time-frames* (i.e. too narrow boundaries of perception space in time) and therefore do not anticipate backfiring from Sustainability Traps, which usually happen with a significant delay. Thus, it is *implicit* to the concept of Sustainability Traps that corporations get into a trap because time-frames are considered too short and thus not allow to recognize potential backfiring. [175]

*Therefore managing Sustainability Traps requires **broadening system boundaries in time**, in order to better anticipate potential backfiring.*

---

172 This is of course an average and can vary depending on the industry.
173 That is independent from a sustainbility perspective.
174 For the definition see chapter 1.2.1.
175 How these delays are produced, will be discussed in chapter 2.2.5.6.

b) Perception Space in Space

With regard to managing Sustainability Traps, the dissertation will differentiate between a **narrow, sectoral** *perception space* and a **broader, holistic** *perception space.* [176] A *sectoral* perception space is primarily focused on the **economic sector** (grey area in figure 8). Variables of the social and environmental sector - at best - are considered if they constitute obvious[177] success factors or limiting factors to economic sustainability. They are missed out, if they are only detectible as influenced and/or influencing variables with a larger perception space and with knowledge about dynamic complexity. Most importantly, - if at all - variables of the social and environmental sector are usually included in the system (model) as *exogenous* variables, so that backfiring (*endogenous*) cannot be detected. A **holistic** perception space significantly broadens boundaries beyond the economic sector and considers environmental and social factors. The transition from a sectoral to a holistic perception space is fluent and part of the learning process described above. [178] Thereby it is important to note that the term 'holistic' in this respect does not so much focus on 'the whole' as such, but rather on the *interrelations* resulting from the *embeddedness* of the economic system within the social and environmental system.

For managing Sustainability Traps the following has to be concluded with regard to sectoral and holistic perception spaces:

Because boundary setting, as stated above, constitutes a value judgment, there is no 'right' or 'optimal' perception space in reference to *space.*[179] With regard to Sustainability Traps however, it is to note that corporations often get into a trap, because of a too narrow, sectoral perspective. This is because a narrow perception space, risks taking silo-oriented sustainability measures and thus to miss out on variables from the social and ecological sector, which are impacted by corporate measures and which in turn risk to backfire on the corporation.

*Corporations caught up in a Sustainability Traps therefore often hold a too narrow, sectoral perception space and need to **broaden** system boundaries.*

It is important to point out that broadening system boundaries in space, towards a holistic perception space, does *not* imply to consider the largest relevant system possible, which would be the whole universe in order to deal with a Sustainability

---

176 Because perception spaces are based on *boundary judgments* as outlined above, there are many more possible perception spaces than the two differentiated in this dissertation. The two perception spaces however are relevant for managing Sustainbility Traps as will be outlined.
177 That is, easily detectible with orthodox, linear thinking.
178 An example from business practice will be given in the IKEA case, chapter 3.2.2.3.
179 Similar as to perception space in *time*, outlined above.

Trap. Rather, as stated, a holistic perception space stresses the point that the economic system is *embedded* in a larger social and ecological system. Broadening system boundaries hence requires a focus on variables that are responsible for *interactions* of the different sectors (economical, social and environmental), thus creating the unsustainability issue in question. Broadening system boundaries allows taking *integrated* sustainability measures, which account for interactions.

2.2.2.4.2. Changing Mental Models of Perception Space

While the above chapter has dealt with broadening boundaries of perception space, this chapter will deal with *mental models* of perception space, i.e. believes about how the space perceived (the 'relevant' world perceived) *operates*.

Mental models of perception space can equally be differentiated in *a) holistic* and *b) sectoral*. The distinction between these two mental models of perception space, that is the distinction of what perception space is considered to be the 'relevant world', can be considered to depart again comes down to deciding upon an in principle undecidable question (von Foerster 1995, chapter 2.2.1). This question here is: *'Is the economy and thus our corporation part of a larger economical-social-environmental system or is it apart from it?'*[180]

a) Holistic Mental Model of Perception Space

The underlying mental model of a holistic perception space is that the *economic sphere is part of the social sphere, which both in turn are embedded in the environmental sphere and resulting interrelations between these three fields* (see figure 10). Thus, here the 'relevant world' is not merely the economic sector, but the economic sector *embedded* in the social and environmental sector.

---

[180] This corresponds to what von Foerster formulates as one of the most decisive questions for resulting behavior of actors: The question, if someone considers himself/herself as being *apart* from the universe and merely watching the developments go by, or if someone considers himself/herself *a part* of the universe and believes to impact it whenever one acts (von Foerster 1995: 315f).

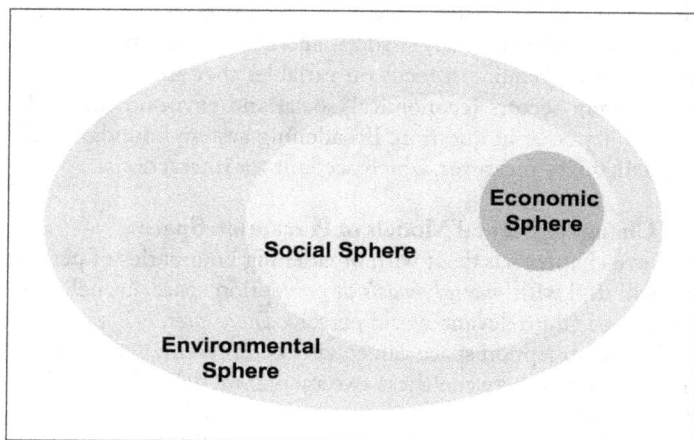

Fig. 10: Spheres Referred to in the Context of Sustainability
Source: Produced by the author

The core basis for this mental model is an asymmetrical (survival) dependency be-tween the economic, the social and the environmental sector based on the historical emergence of each field.[181] Although there exist multiple interrelations (feedbacks) between the three sectors as will be discussed later in the dissertation, this model builds on a dominant one-way "survival dependency": As Darwin (1859) has shown, human species emerged from the natural (environmental) system and there-fore depend on it for its survival and well-being. The opposite is not the case, i.e. nature can survive without humans as it did many million years before. Therefore it can be derived that the natural sector is the most fundamental one to sustain (fun-damental goal) as it constitutes the basis of all living-species. With ongoing spe-cialization human societies have constructed specialized social subsectors from which economy is one. As a social construct economy inevitably depends on the well-being of the social sector (humans) as such, which both in turn depend on the environmental sector (see figure 10).[182] "All organizations sit within larger systems – industries, communities, and larger systems. In one sense, it is illogical to think that the well-being of a company can be advanced independent of the well-being of its industry, its society, and the natural system upon which it depends" (Senge 2006: 342). Therefore, in this view, corporations when operating, in the long-run cannot *not* operate simultaneously also within the social and the environmental sector, it

---

181 See also: Sandow, Mack and Fan Tong He 2005.
182 See also Priddat (2000: 193ff) for economy as a cultural theory. And Priddat (2002) for how cultural understanding has influenced the shape of the economic system (with special focus on the German/European economy).

happens inevitably. The basic challenge is the *realization* that they do (see also Senge 2006: 342).

b) Sectoral Mental Model of Perception Space

An alternative answer to the question raised above, is to perceive economy as rather detached from the social sector and/or from the environmental sector. The 'relevant world' here, consequently is that of economy only (grey area in figure 10). Consequently the **mental model**, i.e. the belief how the 'relevant world' *operates*, is that of how the *economic system* (world) works, - including economical factors and objectives (e.g. profit maximization, focus on shareholder value, perfect price systems etc.). An example is the argumentation that the issue of depletion of minerals is regulated (driven by) mineral prices and technology improvements to harvest minerals in deeper sinks at a feasible price (or by technologies to use less of the mineral) and therefore the level of depletion of a mineral is not relevant, especially as it is hard to evaluate anyhow (see e.g. Adelman in Sterman 2002: 513 for such an argumentation).[183]

Relation between mental models of perception space and boundaries of perception space

It is important to note that there can be a *difference* between *mental models* of perception space and *boundaries* of perception space:

Social agents that hold a *holistic* mental model of perception space, usually also hold broad boundaries of perception space (*holistic* perception space). Hence, mental model of perception space and boundaries of perception space correspond in this case.

In contrast, social agents that hold a *sectoral* mental model of perception space, in many cases equally hold narrower (*sectoral*) boundaries of perception space. The pivotal point is however that these social agents oftentimes *broaden* the *boundaries* of

---

183 This sectoral mental model of perception space can prove problematic: First, from a geological point of view, any type of depletion empties the existing stock of a mineral, - technology can only slow down the process. The only exception would be a backstop technology, which "can fully substitute for all uses of the non-renewable resource at a finite price, in finite time" (Sterman 2002: 513). However, "[h]ow large the resource base is, what the costs of backstop technologies are, and whether a backstop technology can be developed before depletion constrains extraction and reduces economic welfare" are factors, which suggest that the level of depletion indeed does matter and cannot be excluded from considerations (Sterman 2002: 513). It can be added, that moreover the importance of a specific mineral for geological and biological cycles needs to be considered. Otherwise a too high depletion of a mineral, risk to put environmental systems as well as ecosystem services out of balance, which risks to impact social and – directly or indirectly - economical factors. A sectoral perspective thus risks ignoring backfiring hazards.

their perception space (e.g. after a sustainability scandal), so that they consider additional factors from the social and environmental sphere in the future. The *mental model* of perception space of these agents nevertheless remains the *sectoral* one, - *despite* broader *boundaries* of perception space[184]. That is, the belief of such a social agent of how the 'relevant world' *operates* conforms to how the agent considers the *economic* system to operate (e.g. perfect price mechanisms, maximization of profit or shareholder value as goal, etc; see also 'mineral' example above). The agent just additionally includes variables from the environmental and social sphere in his understanding of how the 'relevant world' here the economic system, works.

While the previous chapter[185] has dealt with boundaries of perception space and resulting boundaries of an individual system that is to analyze (system boundaries), this chapter will deal with mental models of perception space. More precise: Which of the two mental models of perception space (sectoral or holistic) is the one *in-use* at a corporation and resulting implications with respect to Sustainability Traps.

Deciding upon mental model of perception space in-use and resulting goals targeted

Which mental models of perception space (sectoral or holistic) a social agent holds as his mental model *in-use*[186], influences which factors he evaluates as primary **goals** and which as **conditions**. This is the case for individual corporations as well as for society as a whole. Furthermore: If something is considered a **trap**, in the sense of not reaching what is targeted through someone's measures, depends on what is considered the **goal** to be targeted, which as just stated, is determined by the **mental model of perception space**, which an agent holds. Thus there is a connection between the mental model of perception space and the goals targeted as well as - consequently - the evaluation if something is a trap.

At present, two different 'categories' of goals can be distinguished, which arose from the two different mental models of perception space described above: **Sectoral** goals and **holistic sustainability** goals.

Sectoral goals have developed *historically* within the boundaries of different societal sectors (e.g. economy, politics) without a holistic perception in mind. These goals have crystallized over time within the individual, societal sector and today implicitly, yet still fundamentally, drive agents' behavior in this sector. In the political sector for example a decisive, implicit goal, which has crystallized and which drives behavior in this sector, is 're-election' in order for the individual political party to

---

184 And consequently despite broader boundaries of the relevant system in question (broader system boundaries).
185 Chapter 2.2.2.4.1.
186 That is, which he basis his evaluations and decision on.

survive. In the business sector one *sectoral goal* that has crystallized as a decisive, implicit goal and which shall be analyzed in the dissertation is *'profit __maximization__'*[187].
Holistic, sustainability goals: In contrast to these sectoral goals, the concept of sustainability as it has been put forward by Brundtland and others, is one of the first, which poses a question that substantially reaches *across* individual sectors: What are the preconditions that the human species – or living species in general – can survive and meet their needs? Consequently the *goals of sustainability* (target-dimensions of sustainability) are disputed fiercely *throughout the different sectors*. It is not the intention of the dissertation to here present a full, accurate list of sustainability goals, because deciding upon individual goals is considered to be a social bargaining process.[188] Although further scientific and social dialogues on individual sustainability goals are needed, it can be noted however that the literature overview of the NRC (NRC 1999b: 22ff) as well as the broadly accepted Brundtland report (WCED 1987), clearly indicate that sustainability goals refer to protecting and preserve the interests from factors of (at least) two sectors, namely the *environmental* sector and the *social* sector.

What often remains unaware in debates about the 'right' goals of sustainability, - i.e. debates about which factors ought to be the *goals* and which factors are merely necessary *conditions* (means) of sustainability, - is that *underlying* the question of the 'right' goals for sustainability, is the *challenge of how to reconcile sectoral goals (e.g. profit maximization in the economic sector), which have built throughout history and new goals arising from the emerging concept of sustainability, which reach beyond sectoral boundaries.*

Furthermore the crucial implication herewith is that there is an *interdependency* between *mental models* and the evaluation what is to be considered as primary *goals* and what as conditions (means), which often remains unreflected: The validity of mental models can be evaluated according to which mental model is better suited to reach the goals desired.[189] But similarly goals vary with the mental model of perception space, which is held, as stated above.

---

187 Profit maximization thereby is only one factor often considered as primary goal in economy. Another e.g. is maximization of share holder value. It is however a key concept and one that developed over along time. Therefore, as stated in chapter 1.2.2.3, the dissertation will focus on profit maximization as the goal for economic sustainbility *exemplary*. Thereby it is pivotal to note, that the important emphasis of this concept lies in the focus of *maximizing* profit, not in the concept of profit as such.
188 For the importance and potential of *communication* for steering goals and behavior of agents see also Priddat 2005b: 200ff.
189 This interdependency has been outlined in the learning process (chapter 2.2.1.2) for mental models and goals in general. It equally applies to mental models of perception space treated here.

Because of this interdependency, there is no 'right' mental model of perception space and correspondingly no 'right' goal of sustainability. The first[190] remains a decision upon an in principle undecidable question. The different mental model of perception space held (sectoral versus holistic) and the corresponding goal followed (sectoral goals versus holistic goals of sustainability) however have different consequences. The decision, which consequences to bear, remains a normative one, in the sense of deciding upon an in principle undecidable question. Therefore the 'decision', which of the two mental model of perception space (sectoral or holistic) becomes the mental model *in-use*, i.e. the one which actions are based on, is subject to multi-stakeholder dialogues and social bargaining processes (Ulrich 1998: 7, see also Priddat 2005a).

The problem thereby lies in the pivotal point that although all agents hold and act upon one of the two alternatives, most agents never actually make a *conscious* decision about which mental model of perception space to hold (sectoral or holistic) and therefore are not aware, which mental model they base their evaluations and actions on. Von Foerster with regard to his analogous question states that he repeatedly is astonished how fundamentally different these perspectives are and that nevertheless most people never consciously reflect upon which perception they base their actions on (von Foerster 1995: 315ff).[191] Regarding sustainability it is a matter of seeing a corporation embedded in a larger system and thus inevitably influencing and being influenced by this system (holistic perception) or rather considering variables of the social and environmental sphere as exogenous, which is hardly recognized as underlying mental model of perception space *in-use*. This is the case not only in corporations but equally in society as a whole.

This leads to the important conclusion: The fact that it is hardly reflected upon which mental model of perception space is the one *in use*, is a problem, because the mental model of perception space in use (sectoral or holistic) determines what is to be considered as *goals* and consequently what constitutes a *trap* or not, as discussed above.[192]

Of particular importance thereby which is the predominant mental model of perception space in-use in a society respectively in core stakeholder groups. At present, a tendency can be observed that the *holistic* mental model of perception space is starting to gain importance in society as well as in stakeholder groups[193], i.e. considering the embeddedness of the economic sector in the social and those in turn in the environmental sector as mental model *in-use*. Consequently holistic *goals* of

---

190 That is, the 'decision' on mental model of perception space.
191 The analogous question has been noted above already, i.e. being apart or a part of the universe.
192 Depending if what has been considered the goal is reached or not.
193 For example: Consumers, NGO, media.

sustainability, i.e. meeting human needs, come into focus. If a corporation sticks to a *sectoral* mental model of perception space and remains focused on the factors (goals) that are underlying this perspective (here: profit maximization[194]), what the business 'achieves' in respect of sustainability risk to be considered as 'failed' by society (as the latter holds different goals). The 'failure' then risks *backfiring* on the corporation in form of **image damage** (e.g. failed corporate responsibility, failed ethics in business etc). It thus risks leading into a trap.

Therefore in respect of managing Sustainability Traps, it is crucial for a corporation to be aware of the mental model of perception space it holds itself as well as the mental model of perception space, which is held by particular stakeholders in a specific case. Being aware of these underlying mental model of perception space, provides leverage to analyze and better deal with a Sustainability Trap, because it uncovers inconsistencies with measures taken (behavior) based on one mental model in-use (e.g. sectoral) and *goals* of (another) mental model in-use (e.g. holistic).

For deciding upon **how to reconcile** *sectoral goals* (economic goal: profit-maximization) and *holistic goals* of social and environmental sustainability, two basic possibilities can be distinguished theoretically, departing from the two *mental model of perception space* presented:

a) Sectoral *goals* remain the primary goals. Holistic goals (social and environmental sustainability) are considered in form of *conditions* (limiting factors). The mental model of perception space *in-use* in this case remains the *sectoral* one. That is, the perception, which drives corporate behavior, is

b) how the social agent believes the *economic* system to operate.

c) Holistic *goals* (social and environmental sustainability) are considered goals. The sectoral goals are considered in form of *conditions* (limiting factors). The mental model of perception space *in-use* in this case becomes the *holistic* one. That is, the perception that the economic system is embedded in the social and the environmental system is what determines corporate behavior.

In order to avoid Sustainability Traps, it is important to be aware, which reconciliation option a corporation is following and the implications which correspond to the reconciliation option.[195]

---

194 As stated, this is used *exemplary* as a primary economic goal in the dissertation.
195 Additional annotation: It could be argued that a third reconciliation option is the one to consider sectoral goals and holistic goals as *equal* goals. This is often formulated as a win-win-win situation. It is important to realize however that there is no mental model of perception space, which corresponds to this perception. Referring to the illustration in figure 10, a mental model, which would relate to equality of sectoral and holistic goals, result in a chart,

In the following both reconciliation options will be discussed and their implications reviewed.

a) *Sectoral goals (profit maximization) remain the goal. Environmental and social sustainability are considered limiting factors (conditions) for the economic sector.*
The mental model of perception space in this reconciliation option remains the one how the *economic* system *operates*. Accordingly the goals remain the sectoral, economic goals (here: profit maximization). Social and particularly environmental sustainability are only brought into the picture as additional constraints (*limiting factors*) to how the economic system operates. Manifestations of such a refined sectoral mental model are e.g. reducing pollution and waste to zero respectively to predefined limits; or issuing a code of conduct, which states what should and what should not be done with regard to workers and communities.
The core implications of this reconciliation option are the following:

- Because in this conception social and environmental sustainability are considered constraints (limiting factors), social agents (corporations) holding this mental model of perception space focus on *reducing unsustainability* in contrast to creating sustainability.[196]
- Limits in this perception become important: Reaching an upper limit for unsustainability needs to be avoided.[197]
- The best result, which can be reached in this conception, is to minimize or reduce unsustainability to zero (e.g. zero waste, zero emission). Accord-

---

in which in which the three sectors are next to each other in a horizontal plane. But there is no theory (e.g. Darwin), which suggests this view. For a *short-time period* and/or in *specific, individual situations*, it therefore can be perfectly possible to yield goal equality in form of win-win-win *situations*. But this will always be the case for individual *situations*. On a *fundamental, normative basis* the decision, which mental model of perception space is held as mental model *in-use*, can only be decided between the *two* mental models of perception space outlined (sectoral or holistic). That is, the underlying mental model *in-use* is either the narrow perception, which focuses on the economic sector (grey colored area in figure 10) or the larger of seeing economy embedded in the larger system (surrounding areas in figure 10). The decision of which mental model is held as mental model *in-use*, i.e. the one which actions are (deliberately or unaware) based on, needs to correspond to one of the two mental models of perception space outlined, because win-win-win situations are not always possible and there needs to be a decision on a normative, general basis (deliberately or unaware), upon which goals to consider as primary goals, when taking actions. Therefore the dissertation only discusses the two options consistent with the two different mental models of perception space presented.

196 For the difference between creating sustainbility and reducing unsustainability see also chapter 2.2.4.2.

197 For limits see also chapter 2.2.4.2.

ingly there is an **ending point** for sustainability respectively for reducing unsustainability.

- The underlying mental model implicates that once sustainability problems are solved (i.e. unsustainability is reduced to zero) and limits are respected, business can go on 'as usual'.
- No substantial *changes in how the economic system operates as such* are required in this conception.

It needs to be stated that this reconciliation option (sustainability as new limiting factor/condition to business practice) is the *predominant* one existing today. Not only in business practice, but often also in scientific and public debates. This is not surprising: Looking at its origins, (environmental) sustainability can be considered to be perceived as a limiting concept in accordance to this first reconciliation concept: As has been outlined in chapter 1.2.1, Carlowitz has defined sustainability as a limit: *Only cut as much* wood *as* can re-grow again. Furthermore as has been stated, the sectoral mental model of perception space and the corresponding sectoral goal of profit-maximization have developed *historically* and cannot be expected to change in short-term.

With the exception of the systemic model, therefore all models identified in part III of the dissertation hold a *sectoral* mental model of perception space with the underlying implications identified above.

b) *Holistic goals are considered goals. Sectoral goals are considered in form of conditions (limiting factors).*

This option of reconciling holistical and sectoral goals is based on a *holistic* mental model of perception space, based on the mental model of ultimate dominate dependency outlined above: The well-being of the economic sector in an ultimate, long-term perception depends on the well-being of the social sector and the environmental sector. Consequently in this reconciliation social and environmental sustainability constitute the *goals*. And the sectoral goal of economic sustainability (profit maximization) becomes a *limiting factor* to the new goals of social and environmental sustainability. This constitutes a significant *paradigm shift*.

The concept of considering profit as a limiting factor (condition) to business and not as a primary goal is not a new idea. It has been put forward by scientific scholars as well as by business practitioners. Drucker has argued since a long-time that profit for a corporation constitutes what oxygen is for the body: It is an essential condition to survive, but not the point of life. Profit is an indicator of what is in the minds and hearts of customers (Drucker 1954 and 2003). Collins and Porras (1994) proved the viability of the approach of considering profit a condition rather than focusing on the goal of profit-maximization. The approach was one of the criteria identified in corporations that where 'built to last' and thus stood the test of time. As for business practitioners, Reinhard Springer, founder and former CEO of the highly successful advertising agency Springer & Jacoby, phrases a similar idea: Springer states that he always held the view that there is an "organic growth rate" for profit (Fischer 2006: 108). That is, a business needs a certain profit in order to maintain or grow organically, so that it will continue to be able to do, whatever it wants to do. However, what it wants to do, what it wants to achieve is something else than profit. Profit is only the condition. It is a limiting factor, in the form of 'we need at least X% profit margin, in order to go on'.[198]

If profit is the limiting factor, what is the 'something else', the goal of environmental and social sustainability that is to be targeted in this reconciliation option? As stated above, it is not the intention of the dissertation to present a full, accurate list of social and environmental sustainability goals, because this can only be reached through social bargaining processes. Rather the dissertation will refer to a broader, general understanding of the goal of sustainability: Building on the Brundtland definition cited above[199], the dissertation will refer to *meeting human needs* as social and environmental sustainability goal.

Although 'needs' are a core element of the commonly accepted Brundtland definition of sustainable development, the understanding and the implications of the concept of needs is still underdeveloped. A lot more research and social bargaining processes are required (e.g. on: Physical and social needs, present versus future needs, regional differences of needs, wants versus needs, etc.). The Brundtland commission focuses particularly on essential needs of developing countries, with needs for livelihood (employment) being the basic needs along with food, energy, water, sanitation and health care (WCED 1987: 43 and 54f). Scholars concerned with the identification of human needs however agree that the human needs go beyond physical (natural) needs. Maslow (1970) and Max-Neef (1992) for example identify entities such as love, esteem, safety or understanding, creation, affection, freedom. What is important in consideration of this dissertation, is that the goal of meeting human needs does not only imply needs for social well-being, but equally needs for environmental well-being as humans depends on functioning ecosystems.[200] Fur-

---

198 Note that this is the reversed image to the concept of considering environmental sustainability as a limiting factor; e.g. we need at least to spare X trees in order for the forest to survive.

199 See chapter 1.2.1.

200 The NRC (NRC 1999b: 23ff) suggests with respect to social sustainability e.g. cultures, groups, places and with respect to environmental sustainability e.g. earth, biodiversity, ecosystems as well as life-support systems. These specific goals mentioned might serve as specific examples. Furthermore in the view of the dissertation, humans depend on environmental well-being not only out of utilitarian reasons, but equally on 'aesthetic', emotional reasons (e.g. relaxing in nature).

thermore this understanding of needs is to clearly be differentiated from customer 'wants' in form of products and services. As the needs identified by Maslow and Max-Neef indicate it refers to fundamental human needs, which are relatively consistent over time and over different social cultures.

The conception of *meeting human needs* as an alternative, sustainability goal, (in contrast to the sectoral goal of profit maximization) is most suitable, because it is broad enough that it allows being applied to various different specific sustainability goals arising from social bargaining processes and at the same time it is concrete enough for the elaborations on the concept of a systems perspective on sustainability used in the dissertation.

The implications of this reconciliation option in significant aspects contrast the previous reconciliation option. The core implications are the following:

- The holistic mental model of perception space, stresses the aspect that economy developed out of the social sector, as a specialized, societal system. Therefore this perception stresses the view of economy as a **social construct.**
- Because economy is a construct developed by society, perceiving **economy as a vehicle (means) for meeting human needs** is a consistent (logical) conclusion.
- Perceiving economy as a vehicle for meeting human needs, allows focusing on **increasing sustainability**, rather than focusing on reducing unsustainability. As such, this process is **open-ended.**
- Perceiving economy as a vehicle for meeting human needs however requires a **paradigm shift** in the societal understanding of what business is for, i.e. the **purpose of business in society.**
- Consequently this requires substantial changes in how the economic system **operates**, including **new, alternative business models.**

As stated, this reconciliation option is not the predominant one today. However more and more concepts are developing on the basis of considering business as a vehicle for meeting human needs and consequently of considering economic goals (here: profit) as a necessary condition (limiting factor), yet not a goal. The dissertation will discuss such concepts as *Mission-Driven Enterprises* in part III, which are business models substantially based on a *holistic mental model of perception space.*

Importance for Managing Sustainability Traps

If mental models of perception space remain unclear and/or if different mental models of perception space collide, Sustainability Traps risk playing out. If for example a Mission-Driven Enterprise, which operates on a holistic mental model of perception space, is acquired by a multinational corporation, whose actions are driven primarily by a sectoral mental model of how the economic system operates, the focus of sustainability measures often becomes a different one. For example: Focus on sustainability as a market entry strategy into 'green', fair trade markets, including aggressive growth strategies to expand into this rapidly growing markets. This shift of *primary* focus, i.e. this shift of a focus on the 'laws' of a different mental model of perception space (holistic to sectoral), augment the risk to *compromise* on sustainability if economic market pressures are high. Thus turning sustainability to a condition (limiting factor), rather than sustainability being a primary goal. Various examples of Sustainability Traps, which played out in this respect in business practice, will be discussed in-depth in chapter 3.5.

Another type of Sustainability Trap risks playing out, if a corporation, which is operating on a sectoral mental model of perception space and which follows the aim of reducing unsustainability (sustainability as a limiting condition), seeks to promote its business by building an image as a sustainability leader. If the corporation claims to become a sustainability leader, its corporate operation will increasingly be observed under the lens of sustainability by stakeholders. Many of the stakeholders, which possess credibility in sustainability issues (e.g. specific NGOs, specific media and special consumer groups) however, do hold a *holistic* mental model of perception space and use this perception as the lens with which they observe activities of the corporation. As a consequence they detect many shortcomings, which in their view are incompatible with a responsible sustainability leader. In this case, the corporation in question risks being caught up in a trap: If it does not meet demands for addressing the shortcomings it risks loosing its credibility with respect to sustainability and risks being accused of Greenwashing. On the other hand overcoming the shortcomings to sustainability very often faces severe limits, because the *very business model* of the corporation has been optimized to suit the economic system. Addressing the shortcomings therefore can lead to inconsistencies with the existing business model and can lead to situations where the corporation overstrains itself. Examples from business practice of this 'Reputation Trap', will be discussed in chapter 3.4.

2.2.3 System-as-Cause Thinking
2.2.3.1 Iceberg Model

As outlined in chapter 2.1.2, what constitutes a trap is the interrelation between **mental models** and **systemic, dynamic structures**. But structures and even more so mental models often remain unrecognized by social agents due to a lack of a system's perspective. What often *is* recognized are **events** (e.g. specific sustainability scandal) or **trends** (e.g. number of non-compliances with the company's code of conduct increased by 10 percent over the last two years). Events or trends however often are **symptoms** (effects, output), which are **caused** through a specific dynamic structure of a system that is driven by the interplay of actions from social agents, which are taken based on the agents' mental models. A systems perspective thus focuses on the *system as cause* for unsustainability. It thus seeks *endogenous* explanations, - compared to orthodox thinking, which often seeks the cause for 'events' or 'trends' of failed sustainability externally, i.e. in a specific behavior of other, individual social agents (the 'causer', the 'enemy').[201]

For recognizing if a corporation is caught up in a Sustainability Trap, it therefore is helpful to differentiate between four levels of awareness: Events, Trends, Structure, Mental Models (beliefs). These levels can be represented in an Iceberg Model (figure 11) (Senge et al. 2000: 80ff, Senge et al. 1994: 96ff):

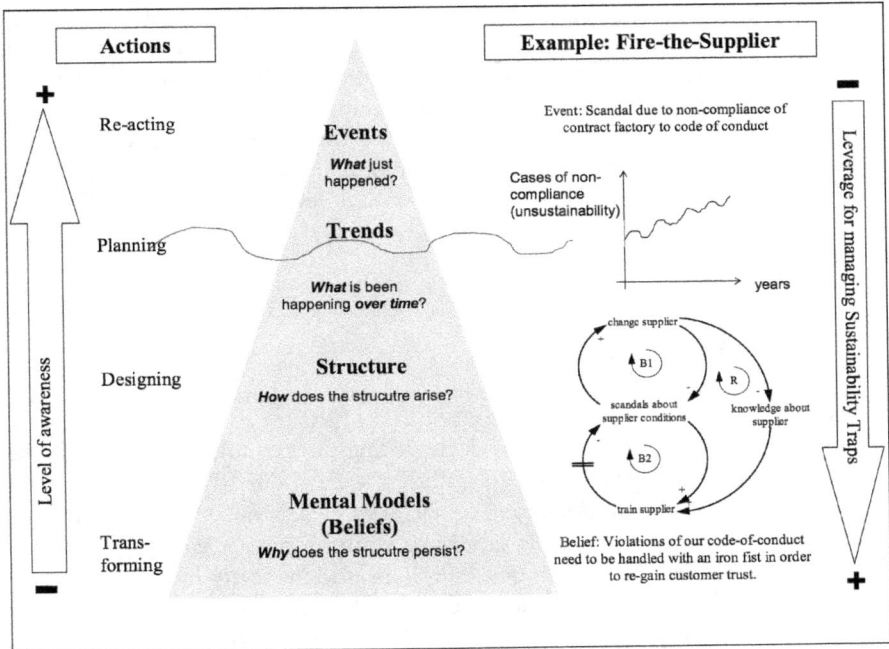

Fig. 11: Iceberg Model
Source: Produced by the author, adapted from Senge et al. 2000: 80ff, Senge et al. 1994: 96ff

The Iceberg Model outlines the interrelationship between events, trends, systemic structures and mental models (beliefs) as they play out in a Sustainability Trap. As figure 11 shows, there is a *problematic asymmetry* in regard to Sustainability Traps:

---

201 For example, the 'unethical' corporation, inefficient governmental policies, NGOs boycott/image-campaign.

While going deeper along the Iceberg *awareness* of agents for the different levels *decreases*, while *leverage* for changing the system *increases* at each level (Meadows 1999). Consequently: The levels that are easily recognized by social agents - events and trends - have almost no leverage for getting out of a Sustainability Trap. While, what has high leverage for managing Sustainability Traps – the levels of systemic, dynamics structures and mental models (beliefs) - often are hard to recognize and to identify.

In the following the *interrelationship* between the four levels - events, trends, systemic structures and mental models - and their importance for managing Sustainability Traps will be outlined, using the example of a Sustainability Trap termed Fire-the-Supplier (chapter 3.2.3). Initial point of this trap is the situation that corporations holding a Compliance Model[202] often quit suppliers (contract factories), which trigger an environmental or labor scandal by violating the code-of-conducts of the corporation. The Iceberg Model helps illustrating how and why this behavior can form a Sustainability Trap. The example of the Fire-the-Supplier Trap will therefore be used in the following to discuss the different levels of the Iceberg and to outline the contribution and implications of each level to identify and deal with Sustainability Traps. These are:

a) Events
b) Trends
c) Systemic Structures
d) Mental Models (beliefs)

a) Events

Events indicate what just has happened. Regarding the example an event would be e.g. that a corporation experienced a significant scandal due to unacceptable labor conditions in one of its overseas contract factories, which violate the corporation's code of conduct (e.g. cases of child labor in a contract factory; cases of toxic contaminations of workers at a plantation due to insufficient safety measures, concentration of toxic chemicals in the lake has doubled this month).

Events usually are what captures awareness. They tempt to look for a 'responsible' (who did what to whom?) (Sterman 2004: 10). If action is taken merely based on an event, it is no more than (unreflected) *re-action*. "The event-oriented worldview leads to an event-oriented approach to problem solving" (Sterman 2004: 10). Information about events from the 'real world' is compared with desired goals and 'appropriate' actions are taken (Sterman 2004: 10). Reacting on events thus corresponds to *single-loop learning* (chapter 2.2.1.2). A re-action regarding the above

---

202 As will be outlined in chapter 3.2, corporations holding a Compliance Model (mental model) seek to comply with the minimum customer expectations for corporate sustainability.

example is to quit the relationship to the contract factory that significantly violated the corporation's code of conduct.

b) Trends

With regard to managing Sustainability Traps it is important to analyze an event *in the context of previous events* in order to identify, if it is a single event or not. For example it makes a difference, if scandals in contract factories arose in previous times before or if this is a one time event.

If a series of similar *events over time* can be identified, a **trend** is revealed. It indicates system's *behavior over time* (Senge et al. 2000: 81f).[203] In the example used, the behavior over time graph in figure 11 indicates that cases of non-compliances in contract-factories increased in oscillating manner over time: In short-term there where amendments, which yet were offset by even more cases of non-compliance in later times. Analyzing behavior over time provides an indicator (although never a guarantee) for future behavior and facilitates planning. For example if similar scandals at contract factories happened before there is a likelihood that the corporation will face this problem again in future times.

At first sight it might seem easy to identify trends. However the classification if it is a one time event or a trend depends significantly on *boundaries judgments*. For example are violations of working hours and violations of safety measures considered similar events that form a trend? The relevance of system boundaries for defining trend and furthermore structures will be outlined in-depth in chapter 3.2.2.3 on the case study of the furniture company IKEA. However forecasting and planning on the basis of trends, still constitutes *event*-based acting (single-loop learning), only that here it are *events over time,* which are considered.

c) Systemic Structures

In a systems perspective, **systemic structures** are the crucial level to explain *how* a *trend* is produced; i.e. how the symptoms of a Sustainability Traps (or more general: system behavior, which can be observed)[204] is produced. "Behind each pattern of behavior is a systemic structure" (Senge et al. 2000: 82).[205] It thus is systemic structures that cause the system behavior which we observe.

Thereby,"[s]tructures are built out of the choices people make consciously or unconsciously, over time" (Ross, Roberts and Kleiner in Senge et al. 1994: 90). That is

---

203 A trend is also referred to as ,a pattern of behavior over time' and the graph, which illustrates it, as ,behavior over time graph (Senge et al. 2000: 82).

204 For example, oscillating behavior over time graph outlined above with respect to cases of non-compliances with a corporation's code of conduct.

205 The term 'structure' has already been defined in chapter 1.3.1 as "a set of unrelated factors that interact"

not a single agent but a set of factors (actions) and most important intrinsic *dynamics* between them contribute to structure, which produces a certain system behavior (e.g. unsustainability or sustainability). Because it are systemic structures that drive the forces, which produce the pattern of behavior observed on the higher level, *analyzing and dealing with systemic structures bears high leverage for managing Sustainability Traps*. This requires a system perspective. Orthodox thinking is focused on events and trends, so that when using principles of orthodox thinking underlying systemic structures remain unrecognized. A system perspective in contrast focuses on identifying, analyzing and dealing with systemic structures (Senge et al. 2000: 80ff). [206]

Figure 11 shows the systemic structure underlying the Fire-the-Supplier Trap, which produces the oscillating behavior over time graph (trend) with respect to cases of non-compliances with the company's code of conduct, observed above: Firing a supplier that did not comply, might ease the particular scandal, as the corporation is proactive and rigorously deals with the supplier in question. However, non-compliances often stem from diverging mental models and lack of knowledge of the supplier operating under different economic conditions and stemming from different cultural backgrounds. [207] Therefore quitting the supplier and subscribing to another in similar conditions is not suitable to solve the problem in the long-term and the problem is likely to 'pop-up' again in the future, which might lead to even fiercer accusations of media and NGOs since this happened repeatedly. [208] Furthermore, by quitting the supplier the corporation looses valuable information about the operative behavior and about short-comings of the particular contract factory, which are necessary to develop programs for overcoming non-compliances stemming form a lack of knowledge or diverging mental models. [209]

---

[206] How systemic structures can be illustrated and analyzed through causal loop diagramming as well as the particular role of dynamics in system structure, will be outlined in-depth in chapter 2.2.5. What is important to note at this point is that it are systemic structures, which produce system behavior.

[207] This is only one reason (example) for non-compliance, for further information see Nike in chapter 3.4.3.3.

[208] See oscillating behavior-over-time-graph (trend) above.

[209] The Fire-the-Supplier Trap is increasingly realized by corporations, which now start engaging in training of suppliers rather than just quitting business relationships after cases of non-compliance; see chapter 3.2.3.2.

d) Mental Models and Beliefs

The elements, which agents are most unaware of are mental models and beliefs (Senge 2006: 9)[210]. But they bear the highest leverage for change (Meadows 1999: 17ff), respectively for managing Sustainability Traps.

A mental model in the above example of contract factories that cause a scandal due to non-compliances with the code of conduct might be: "If a contract factory does not comply with our code of conduct, we need to demonstrate rigor (iron fist) and quit business relationship with them immediately in order to demonstrate to the public that we do not accept unsustainable behavior of our suppliers and punish non-compliances rigorously."[211]

Mental models as such, where defined and discussed in chapter 2.2.1. In this chapter now, what becomes important to realize is that mental models impact all other three levels of the Iceberg (structure, trends and events). "Systems often take their shape from values, attitudes, and beliefs of the people in them. That's because our mental models, our theories about how the world works, influence our actions, which in turn influence the interactions of the system" (Senge et al. 2000: 83). Redesigning a structure will therefore be ineffective if mental models (*theories-in-use*), which contribute to the 'old' problematic structure, remain unchanged as stated above (see also Sterman 2004: 10ff).[212]

Changing mental models starts with "turning the mirror inwards" (Senge 2006: 8). "Managers must learn to reflect on their current mental models - until prevailing assumptions are brought into the open, there is no reason to expect mental models to change, and there is little purpose in systems thinking" (Senge 2006: 189). As has been outlined above, changing mental models relates to *double loop learning*. A crucial condition is the realization of all agents that their world views (mental models) are *assumptions* and not facts (Senge 2006: 189, Meadows 1999: 19 and chapter 2.2.1.1). Only then mental models are open to change and can be harmonized with stakeholders: Dealing with mental models also "includes the ability to carry on 'learningful' conversations that balance inquiry and advocacy, where people expose their own thinking effectively and make that thinking open to the influence of others" (Senge 2006: 9). However, changing mental models is anything else than an easy exercise. Paradigms are hard to become aware of and even harder to change,

---

210 In the common Iceberg Model there is only the variable of mental model. As stated, the mental models dealt with in the dissertation in-line with Senge et al. constitute beliefs (see chapters 2.2.1 and 3.1.1).

211 An example of a predominant social mental model on environmental sustainability is that 'nature is a stock of resources to be converted to human purposes'. A mental model prevalent in the business community is 'growth is good' (see also Meadows 1999: 17).

212 See chapter 2.1.2: It is the interplay between mental models and systemic structures, which constitutes a Sustainability Trap.

because they are deeply rooted within the mind of agents. This becomes especially apparent if a mental model and resulting systemic structure relate to the business behavior itself. Such a case will be discussed in the case example of Nike[213], where it are not primarily a lack of knowledge or cultural differences, but the corporation's own business model of that leads into a Sustainability Traps.[214]

This chapter has outlined in detail the interrelation of events, trends, systemic structures and mental models in Sustainability Traps. It has been shown that there is an asymmetry regarding these different levels: While going deeper along the Iceberg awareness of agents for the different levels decreases, while leverage for changing the system increases at each level.

2.2.3.2   Resulting Implications for Managing Sustainability Traps

As outlined, there exist different levels of awareness for recognizing Sustainability Traps. Therefore, with regard to managing Sustainability Traps it is crucial to:

a) *Differentiate one-time events and trends*: Analyze, if an event is a one-time event or part of a trend.

b) *Analyze deeper levels of awareness*: If a specific trend is recognized (system behavior observed), what needs to be analyzed is the interplay of *systemic structures and mental models*, which produce the trend, i.e. the system behavior observed.

a) Differentiating one-time event and trends

One-time events do not necessarily need to stem from an underlying Sustainability Trap. Yet, if a pattern of behavior is visible, it is likely that there exist an underlying structure, a Sustainability Trap that is creating it. *Trends* of increasing unsustainability that backfires[215] therefore are an indicator for underlying Sustainability Traps. *The challenge lies in differentiating one-time events from trends.* If an event, which just occurred, is considered as 1) part of a series of related events (trend), i.e. the event is considered an 'old' problem that 'pops up' again caused through symptomatic solutions, or 2) if the event is considered a 'new' problem (one-time *event*), depends on *boundary judgments* of a corporation. An example was provided above (Fire-the-Supplier Trap): The trend, i.e. the system behavior observed in this case,

---

213 This business model is that of Financing Brand-Image through Low-Cost Production, see chapter 3.4.3.

214 The difficulty of changing mental models is even harder on the level of society (social paradigms). Societies "resist challenges to their paradigm harder than anything else" (Meadows 1999: 18). One of these social paradigms as it relates to consumer behavior will be discussed in chapter 3.3.2 (Efficiency Trap).

215 That is, even though it was intended to increase *sustainbility* through a specific corporate measure.

was that the number of cases of non-compliances in contract-factories, increased in an oscillating manner. If e.g. 'violations of working hours' and 'violations of safety measures' are considered similar events that form a trend, depends on system boundaries the corporation holds.[216] Hence, the challenge of recognizing *trends* and thus *Sustainability Traps*, ties in with the systems thinking skill of re-thinking boundary judgments outlined above. That is, a corporation needs to be flexible on system boundaries and particularly *broaden* its system boundaries in order to recognize a trend and hence to become aware that it is caught up in a systemic structure, which backfires (Sustainability Trap).

b) Analyzing deeper levels of awareness

If a specific trend *is* recognized (system behavior observed), what needs to be analyzed is the interplay of **systemic structures and mental models**, which produce the trend, i.e. which are responsible for creating this trend. As outlined above, events and trends are *symptoms* of Sustainability Traps (e.g. increasing number of unsustainabilities in contract factories), while it are the underlying systemic structures and mental models that are the *causes* for the trend (series of events). The *challenge* for managing Sustainability Traps here lies in the fact that events and trends usually are easy to recognize, yet re-acting upon them without being aware of underlying systemic structures and mental models has no leverage for getting out of a trap. What is needed is a system perspective, which additionally enables an analysis of underlying **systemic, dynamic structures** that usually remain unaware in orthodox thinking. The skills for an analysis of these structures will be outlined in the subsequent chapters 2.2.4 and 2.2.5.

2.2.4   Operational Thinking
2.2.4.1   Stocks and Flows

In order to understand how complex systems actually **operate**, being aware of the difference between a **stock** and a *flow* is vital. Stocks and flows form the infrastructure of a system and "provide the substrate for feedback loops to exist" (Richmond 1994: 11).[217]

"Stocks are accumulations. They characterize the state of the system and generate the information upon which decisions and actions are based" (Sterman 2004: 192). Thereby stocks are *altered* by inflows and outflows (Sterman 2004: 192).

An metaphor often used, to explain the difference of stocks and flows is a bathtub (*stock*), where the level of water is determined by the water flowing in through the tap (*inflow*) and the water flowing out through the drain (*outflow*) (Sterman 2004: 194, see also Senge 2006: 75). Following this metaphor, stocks are illustrated as

---

216 For another example, see also IKEA case in chapter 3.2.2.3.
217 See also chapters 2.2.5.6 and 2.2.5.7.

containers (boxes) and flows (inflow and outflow) are illustrated as *pipes* with a valve (see figure 12 below). The quantity of a variable (e.g. amount of water in the bathtub) is indicated by the *level* of a stock (grey area in figure 12).[218]

Increasing inflow or outflow, or more accurate the *rate* of the flow (i.e. units of flow per time interval), can be imagined as *opening the valve*, so that *more* can flow in to the stock respectively out of the stock. As a consequence, ceteris paribus the level of the stock increases respectively decreases. Correspondingly a *decrease* of a flow (rate of the flow) can be imagined as *closing the valve*, so that less can flow in to the stock respectively out of the stock.

A powerful example from the field of sustainability, which illustrates why operational thinking in stocks-and-flows is crucial, is CO_2 concentration in the atmosphere (see also Senge 2006: 344ff; Senge, Laur, Schley and Smith 2006: 15ff). CO_2 concentration in the atmosphere is a stock and can be illustrated the following way (figure 12):

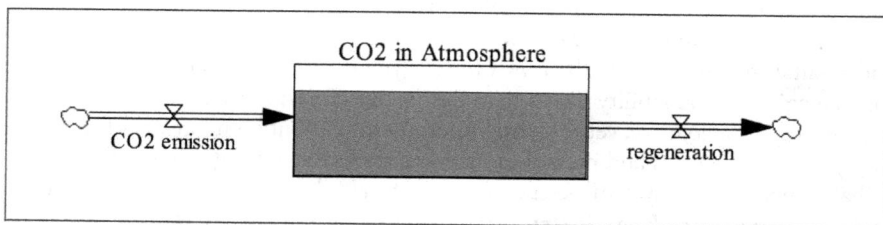

Fig. 12: CO_2 Emission as Stock-and-Flow Diagram
Source: Produced by the author[219]

While a specific level of CO_2 concentration in the atmosphere is vital to sustain life on earth, it is increasingly recognized that CO_2 emissions from human activity (combustion of fossil fuels) has pushed the CO_2 in the atmosphere to a level, which poses severe environmental problems (IPCC 2007 and 2001; Senge 2006: 346).[220]

---

218 To be precise: The level of the stock is indicated by the top-line (surface) of the grey area.

219 A strict stock-and-flow labeling would require denoting the flows as verbs ("emitting CO_2" and "regenerating"), because nouns refer to stocks. However out of reasons of simplicity and better understanding the dissertation uses the nouns. This has no impact on the conclusions.

220 Thereby it has to be stated that CO_2 is only one gas contributing to the problem of global warming (e.g. also methane). CO_2 is however a significant human-made contributor, which therefore shall further be discussed here.

When people are asked how CO_2 concentration in the atmosphere can be reduced the answer usually is 'through lowering emissions'. It is crucial to realize that this is *not* the case. When emissions are lowered, i.e. the inflow is lowered, they are still flowing into the atmosphere. The inflow is just not as high as before, i.e. emissions are flowing into the atmosphere at a lower *rate*. At the current state this implies that CO_2 concentration in the atmosphere is still *increasing* (not decreasing). And it is doing so constantly, with each emission. The reason for this is not only the fact that decreasing an inflow means that there still is something flowing into the stock. The other reason is the *outflow*, which forms the complementary part of the structure in figure 12. Therefore, in order to determine whether CO_2 concentration in the atmosphere is increasing or decreasing the **relation between inflow and outflow** has to be considered.

In the case of CO_2, the rate with which CO_2 is flowing into the atmosphere is more than double the rate it is flowing out (e.g. through absorption in the ocean or by trees) (Houghton et al. 2001, Senge 2006: 346). Therefore, even if all states sub-scribe to the Kyoto protocol (i.e. to reduce global emissions to levels of 1990) and if all states succeed, CO_2 concentration will grow forever (Senge 2006: 348). The reverse implication is even more concerning: In order just to *start* decreasing CO_2 concentration in the atmosphere the inflow would have to be reduced below the outflow, which corresponds a 50 percent or greater reduction of current emission worldwide (Senge 2006: 348). Under the current dependency of societies on the combustion of fossil fuels, this seems impossible.

The problematic is even increased when considering the feedback **dynamics** that lie within the system: Combustion of CO_2 allows for economic growth, which in turn increases CO_2 emission. This can be observed e.g. in China and India. Therefore the current outflow threatens to increase. On the other hand CO_2 emissions (along with other factors) lead to environmental damage, which in turn lowers nature's ability to reduce CO_2 concentration. Hence, the outflow (reduction of CO_2) threatens to decrease. If inflow increases and outflow decreases, CO_2 concentration in the atmosphere will rise even faster exponentially. This is one of the major challenges we are currently facing. The facts outlined might seem natural and logical, if pointed to them. But even though some of the aspects are familiar to most people, the vast majority is not trained to think in stocks and flows.

Senge tells the following anecdote from a business conference on sustainable development with around 500 attendees in Europe 2004. The attendees were knowledgeable about and engaged in many sustainability initiatives, including climate change. After having introduced the system perspective above, Senge raised the question, who knew how high the ratio between CO_2 inflow and outflow is? - The key figure for understanding the system as outlined above.

Senge comments the reaction with the following words: "I was shocked to find only about ten hands raised. At that moment I understood why we were in trouble" (Senge 2006: 346).

This anecdote once more underlies the urgency for a new thinking, which allows better understanding dynamic systems. Even the very basics of this thinking, which are reflected in the simple model above, are lacking in most parts of society including the corporate sector. Without a better systems understanding in businesses as well as at key stakeholders, the chance of reducing unsustainability in the long-term is low. As will be outlined[221], the dissertation will use causal-loop-diagramming (CLDs) for illustrating systemic structures rather than stock-and-flow diagrams. This is because it is the dissertation' intention to create a general understanding of Sustainability Traps and CLDs are far easier for actors to grasp and are understood more intuitively. The dissertation however will 'switch' to a stock-and-flow perspective, whenever it becomes necessary for a systemic understanding.

2.2.4.2 Resulting Implications for Managing Sustainability Traps

The stock-and-flow perspective enables to outline the difference between *reducing unsustainability* and *creating sustainability*. It is important to realize that currently science as well as business practice predominantly focus on **reducing unsustainability**. Unsustainability is a stock, which can be illustrated the following:

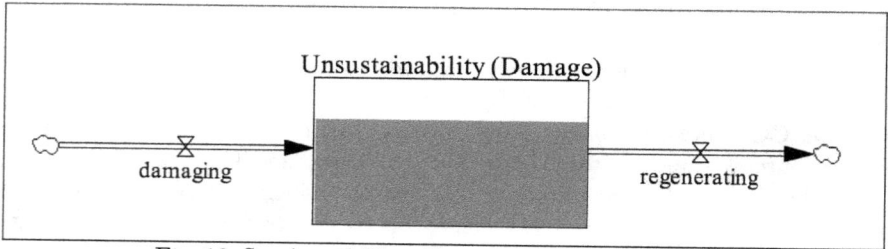

Fig. 13: Stock-and-Flow Diagram of Unsustainability
Source: Produced by the author

In this conception a sustainable development is one, where damaging (inflow) < regenerating (outflow) and thus the stock 'unsustainability' is reduced to zero.

From a stock-and-flow perspective, damaging human (corporate) activities that create environmental unsustainability can be differentiated into three categories (TNS 2000: 8 and Robèrt et. al. 2004: xxiv ff)[222]:

· *Accumulation of substances from the lithosphere in the biosphere*

---

221 See chapter 2.2.5.

222 Thereby it has to be noticed, that the earth as a sustainable system is open to flows of energy and closed to matter (based on the first and second laws of thermodynamics).

Concentrations of substances extracted from the lithosphere, i.e. the earth's crust, are continuously rising (e.g. carbon as CO_2 from fossil fuels, metals such as mercury or cadmium), because they are mined and dispersed in nature faster than they are returned (re-deposited into the Earth's crust).

- *Accumulation of substances produced by humans in the biosphere*
  Concentrations of substances produced by society, i.e. technological combination of elements into compounds (e.g. toxic chemicals, electronics, plastics) are continuously rising, because society disperses them faster than they can be broken down and built into new resources by nature (or deposited in the Earth's crust).

- *Degradation in the biosphere by physical means*
  Degradation of renewable natural resources (e.g. fish, wood) occurs by extracting more than nature can replenish, i.e. if the harvest rate is higher than the regeneration rate.[223] Furthermore degeneration can occur through other forms of ecosystem manipulation (for instance, altering the water table, soil erosion, unforeseen accidents with genetic manipulation or covering fertile land with asphalt).

It is crucial to note that most corporate sustainability measures focus on *reducing the damaging impacts* outlined above. This corresponds to the reconciliation option of *considering environmental and social sustainability as (new)* **conditions** *to existing business models.*[224]
For corporations holding this focus it is important to be aware of the following two implications:

a) The stock 'unsustainability' is only reduced, if damaging (inflow) < regenerating (outflow). If a corporation focuses only on reducing damage without being aware of the regeneration rate, unsustainability is not reduced, but only increases less fast. A focus on reducing the inflow (damage) therefore requires a focus on **limits** to unsustainability.

b) Even if corporate sustainability measures succeed and the level of the stock 'unsustainability' is reduced to zero, this does *not* equal the *creation of sustainability*.

---

223 See also von Carlowitz in chapter 1.2.1.
224 See chapter 2.2.2.4.2. This is one option of reconciling sectoral goals (e.g. profit maximization) with new sustainability goals. Another option would be to consider social and environmental sustainability the goals and economic sustainbility the condition.

These two aspects shall be outlined in the following.

a) Problems with limits

If a corporation sticks to its traditional, existing business model of aiming to maximize economic sustainability and to reduce (minimize) its environmental and social damage (sectoral mental model of perception space[225]), it needs to be aware of the fact that for actually *reducing* unsustainability the damage needs to be reduced below the regeneration rate. This often proves very difficult. As long as this does not succeed, the stock 'unsustainability' does not decrease, but *increases* - only slower. This leads to the effect that many corporations actually not focus on reducing unsustainability to zero, but aim on keeping unsustainability below a *limit* (a specific level (state)[226] of the variable 'unsustainability'). Because, as stated, if certain **limits to un-sustainability** (e.g. pollution limits) are passed, dynamics risks to be triggered that backfire.[227]

It can be differentiated between limits of environmental and limits of social unsustainability. For both spheres however, quantifying precise limits to unsustainability, which should not be passed in order to avoid backfiring is most difficult.[228] It is not the aim of the dissertation to seek to quantify limits of unsustainability. The dissertation seeks to create awareness for the point that a *focus on reducing unsustainability* as it is common to most business models, augments the risk of Sustainability Traps, because limits are hard to assess and if a corporation estimates limits wrong (to high or to low), it risks triggering dynamics in a system that backfire and create a trap.

b) Reducing unsustainability versus creating Sustainability

It is important to realize that reducing unsustainability is **not** the same as *creating sustainability*. Reducing unsustainability is illustrated in figure 13: The best, what can be achieved in this perspective is to reduce the level of unsustainability to zero. In business practice this means e.g. zero waste, zero emissions. It is crucial to realize that for *creating sustainability* other tools and business models are necessary. Creat-

---

225 See chapter 2.2.2.4.2.

226 Illustrated through the grey area in the stock ,unsustainability' in figure 13.

227 This was stated in chapters 2.1.2 and 2.1.3 b) and will also be referred to in chapter 2.2.5.

228 Although limits of environmental unsustainability are *easier* to estimate, - limits were described *relatively* above as inflow- outflow ratios, - it still remains difficult to quantify them *absolutely*. (For example: How much CO_2 should be allowed to be emitted into the air in order to avoid serious impacts from global warming?). Limits of *social* unsustainability are even harder to estimate than environmental limits as they refer to human needs and are subject to changing social values. E.g. how many hours of work or what safety measures are considered 'sustainable'/unsustainable? See also chapter 2.1.2.

ing sustainability is focused on *increasing* the level of the new stock 'sustainability' (not decreasing the level of the stock 'unsustainability'). Creating sustainability is not focused on reducing (limiting) damage, but on increasing sustainability (e.g. more trees/bigger forest versus preserving a minimum of trees required; increasing human well-being versus meeting basic/minimum needs). Creating sustainability thus corresponds to the reconciliation option of *considering environmental and social sustainability as goals and economic sustainability as a condition (i.e. based on a holistic mental model of perception space)*.[229] While corporations seeking to reduce unsustainability focus on reducing (*minimizing*) environmental and social damage within their traditional, existing business models, corporations aiming at *creating sustainability* develop new business models that enable to create additional environmental and social value through their business operations.[230]

It is important to point out that the two approaches - 'reducing unsustainability' and 'creating sustainability' - are *not* mutually exclusive, but *complementary*. What the dissertation aims to point out here is awareness for the fact that a focus of corporate measures for reducing unsustainability does *not* equal a focus of creating sustainability. The latter is open-end and faces less risk of backfiring from wrong assessment of environmental or social limits (minimum requirements) as it is focused on increasing social and environmental sustainability. If a society (through social bargaining processes) reaches the 'aim' of *increasing* social and environmental sustainability, realizing the difference is crucial. The difference between reducing unsustainability and creating sustainability will be outlined in a practice example of eco-efficiency versus eco-effectiveness in chapter 3.4.2 (McDonough and Braungart 2002a: 45ff and 67).

2.2.5 Dynamic Thinking
2.2.5.1 The Essence of Dynamic Thinking

The most crucial difference between orthodox thinking and systems thinking can be considered the difference between linear, laundry-list thinking (detailed complexity) and non-linear, dynamic thinking (dynamic complexity). This essence, which dynamic thinking constitutes for systems thinking as compared to orthodox thinking shall be outlined in the following. As will be shown, Dynamic Thinking ties together many of the aspects outlined in previous chapters, which underscores its importance for a systems perspective. This chapter provides a basic understanding of the essence of dynamic thinking (by contrasting it to orthodox thinking), while the next chapters will outline a specific language (causal loop diagramming) to illustrate and analyze *dynamic* system structures.

---

229 See chapter 2.2.2.4.2.
230 As stated, the dissertation will outline examples of this new form of enterprises (mission-driven enterprises) in chapter 3.5 (Systemic Model).

Orthodox thinking focuses on *linear cause-and-effect relations*. Since the century of enlightment (17th/18th century) we have been trained to ask for 'the cause' of an (undesired) effect we observe, in the sense 'a' has caused 'b' (figure 14). This tempts to point to 'a' as the originator for a problem and thus playing the 'blame-game'.

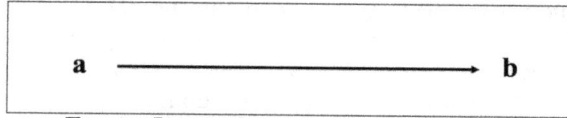

Fig. 14: Linear Cause and Effect Thinking
Source: Produced by the author

When dealing with more complicated issues, e.g. in consideration of sustainability, it has become common to focus on *additive multi-causalities*. In the sense 'a, b and c' cause 'd'. When confronted with the question "What is causing the problem of undernourishment (respectively malnutrition) in developing countries today?" most Western people are likely to come up with an additive list of causes as illustrated in figure 15 below:[231]

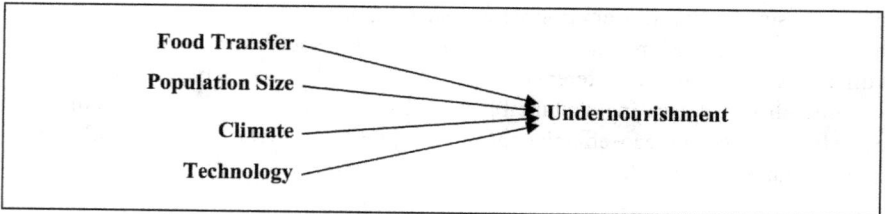

Fig. 15: Example of Additive Laundry-List Thinking
Source: Produced by the author, adapted from Richmond 1993: 117

Richmond refers to these kinds of enumerations as '*laundry lists*' (Richmond 1993: 117). Laundry lists tempt to automatically ask the question, who is 'in charge' of the different causes, - thus to identify who is the *causer*. Then, very often blame or social pressure are laid on the causer in order to change his behavior in an attempt to reduce or eliminate the causes and thus to lower the effect (e.g. undernourishment).[232]

---

231 This statement builds on Richmond, which uses the example of overpopulation (Richmond 1993: 117).

232 E.g.: *Industrial countries* do not provide enough food/money transfer; *Developing countries* need to apply more birth control technologies. *Climate* cause inferior boundary conditions for developing countries.

What yet is *not* included in this kind of thinking is how the different factors inter-relate and thus produce undernourishment.[233] At best, each factor in the list is weight, e.g. according to its importance (contribution) to the problem. Often this is represented analytically in a multiple regression equation (Richmond 1993: 117):

$$y = a_0 + a_1X_1 + a_2X_2 + \ldots + a_nX_n; \text{ where:}$$
$$y = \text{dependent variable}$$
$$X_i = \text{independent variables}$$
$$a_i = \text{coefficients (or weighting factors) for each of the independent variables.}$$

Often implications lying in this familiar way of thinking remain unreflected. Rich-mond identifies four implications (Richmond 1993: 117f):
a) One-way (linear) causality: Each factor contributes as a cause to the effect.
b) Each variable behaves and influences independently.
c) The weighting factor of each variable is fix.
d) The way, how each factor works to cause the effect is left implicit. Only the di-rection of influence (positive or negative) of a variable is indicated by the sign of its coefficient.
As a consequence of the additive laundry-list thinking, orthodox thinking focuses on developing measures for dealing with a vast number of different variables in-volved. This (i.e. a vast number of different variables involved) is the orthodox un-derstanding of *complexity*. This type of complexity can be referred to as *detailed complexity* (Senge 2006: 71). Detailed complexity often leads to an estimation of social agents that the situation is just *too* complex, meaning that there are too many different influencing variables to consider. This often triggers a series of discussions on the importance and influence of individual factors for an issue of unsustainabil-ity; or it causes a feeling of de-powerment up to frustration, because there are just 'too' many variables to consider with respect to sustainability.
Systems thinking in contrast to orthodox thinking is not focused on a weighted list of variables influencing an unsustainability issue. Rather systems thinking analyzes the ***systemic structure***, which produces the unsustainability issue observed. That is, systems thinking focuses on which variables interrelate thus that they trigger *dy-namics* in the system structure, which produce unsustainability. Figure 16 shows an example of a how a systems perspective analyzes the issue of *undernourishment*, through a focus on systemic, dynamic structures[234].

233 Often an interrelation of the factors is done *intuitively* for all or at least for part for the factors. Yet, this does not create a sufficient understanding of non-linear interrelations and resulting dynamics.
234 Figure 16 uses the language of causal loop diagramming (CLD). It is only used as an *example* to illustrate how a systems perspective looks at the issue of undernourishment: The

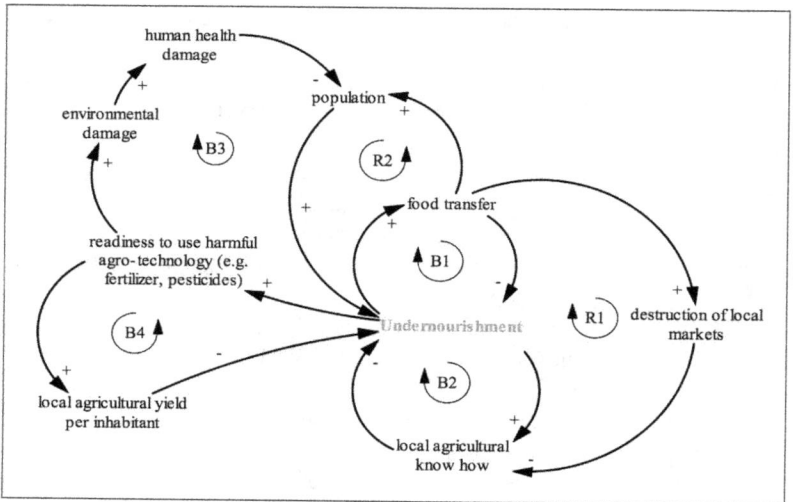

Fig. 16: Example of Dynamic Thinking
Source: Produced by the author

As can be seen in the illustration above, a structural perspective reveals how the different factors interrelate and thus create dynamics in the system, which produce undernourishment. Some examples are: *Food transfer* and *agricultural assistance (technology)* reduce undernourishment at first, but on the other hand lead to net *population* growth (due to more births, less deaths) and eventually more undernourishment (Senge 2006: 59). Furthermore food transfer leads to another additional problematic: It destroys *local markets*, which reduces local *agricultural know-how* and opposes efforts of *agricultural assistance* in the long-term (see also shifting-the-burden archetype, Senge 2006: 391). *Agricultural assistance* (technology transfer) can unfavorably impact the *environmental condition* (e.g. use of fertilizers), which in the long-run will reduce local *agricultural yields*. A bad *environmental condition* (environmental damage) in turn (e.g. water quality, less forests due to lumbering for agricultural areas) can negatively impact health and thus *population* size.[235]

---

important point here is that a systems perspective focuses on dynamic interrelations of the variables rather than on laundry list thinking. The illustration below does neither seek nor claim to fully explain the problem of undernourishment.

235 As stated, this is only used as an *example* to illustrate a systems perspective, not to discuss the issue of undernourishment: Most important: As will be outlined later, in CLD, the links (arrows) constitute **believes** (and argumentations) of a social agent of how the variables in a system interrelate, they do not constitute ‚facts'.

A systems perspective entails different assumptions to each of the four implications of laundry lists of orthodox thinking outlined above (a-d):

- Systems thinking challenges the regression analysis approach of orthodox laundry-list thinking (see implication (b) and (d) above). Systems thinking seeks for an *operational* explanation of how undernourishment is actually generated, that is *how* the different variables *interrelate* to produce unsustainability.

- Furthermore, systems thinking is focused on *circular, dynamic causality*, which contrasts the implications (a) and (b) of laundry-list thinking outlined above (linear cause-and effect and independency of influences). Richmond stresses that the shift from linear causality to circular, and thus non-linear, causality constitutes a profound change in thinking. "In effect, it is a shift from viewing the world as a set of static, stimulus-response relations to viewing it as an ongoing, interdependent, self-sustaining, dynamic process" (Richmond 1993: 118). As can be seen in figure 16, *dynamics* are produced, because variables in the systemic structure interrelate thus, that they form *closed loop interrelations*. In closed loop interrelations "each of the causes is linked in a circular process to both the effect and to each of the other causes" (Richmond 1993: 118). Therefore, it becomes possible to identify *endogenous* causes of unsustainability produced by the system, rather than seeking for an 'external' causer (enemy) (see chapters 2.2 and 2.3.2.).

- Last but not least influencing factors in orthodox thinking are assigned a static weighting (implication (c) above). In systems thinking by contrast "the strength of the closed-loop relations is assumed to wax and wane over time. Some loops will dominate at first, other loops will then take over, and so on" (Richmond 1993: 118). As a consequence, addressing a problem (Sustainability Trap) is not a one-shot deal in systems thinking. Rather, "it is considered necessary to think in terms of ongoing, interdependent relations whose strengths vary over time, partly in response to interventions that may have been implemented into the system" (Richmond 1993: 118). This aspect results to what has been outlined above: There is no one right, impeccable solution to a Sustainability Trap, rather dealing with Sustainability Trap is an ongoing learning process.[236]

*The importance of dynamics in systems thinking, leads to a focus on **dynamic complexity** rather than on detailed complexity.*

---

236 See chapter 2.2.1.2 above: Particularly double-loop learning, once a systems perspective is adopted.

Dynamic complexity is a second type of complexity, which refers to "situations where cause and effect are subtle, and where the effects over time of interventions are not obvious" (Senge 2006: 71). In cases of dynamic complexity *causes and effects are deferred in time and space*. Dörner provides the metaphor of a special chess match in order to illustrate the challenges posed by dynamic complexity (Dörner 2005: 66): An agent in a situation with dynamic complexity resembles a chess player, which has to play with a chess game encompassing multiple figures, which are connected to each other with rubber bands, so that it becomes impossible to move one figure independently. Additionally his figures as well as the figures of his adversary are moving on their own driven by rules which the player is unaware of or holds wrong assumptions of. On top of everything part of his own and his adversary's figures are standing in the dust and are only partly or not at all visible.

This metaphor reveals that in dynamic systems influencing factors are deeply interconnected. *Therefore in dynamic systems it is impossible to solve a problem by not understanding a system's structure.* This relates to more than just perceiving an *interconnection* of the different factors. *The key point is that through the interplay of factors the system produces dynamics 'on its own', which need to be understood and included in solutions.* The following chapter will outline how systemic structure can be illustrated and analyzed as well as how dynamics (dynamic complexity) are created through closed-loop interrelations in a system.

2.2.5.2 Causal Loop Diagramming as a Language for Dynamic Structures

As has been stated, circular-causality in structures is key for understanding dynamic systems that create unsustainability. A main problem, with orthodox thinking is that we are neither trained in thinking in circular causality nor do we posses an adequate *language to communicate* about it. Western language has co-evolved with the linear cause-and-effect way of thinking. The subject-verb-object construction of most Western languages makes it easy to communicate linear thinking (A causes B), but more difficult to communicate non-linear thinking of the sort "A causes B while B causes A, and both continually interrelate with C and D" (Senge et. al 1994: 88; see example undernourishment above).

Therefore a new *language* is needed for systems thinking, which allows expressing and illustrating *circular causality*. System dynamics offers two possibilities for illustrating structure: 'Causal loop diagramming' (CLD) and 'stock and-flow diagramming'[237]. The dissertation will use causal loop diagramming (Senge et al. 1994: 88ff, see also Vester 2005: 154ff, Kim 1992), because it better suites the intention of the dissertation. As outlined above, the dissertation' intention is to create awareness of the importance and implications of a systems perspective in the field of sustainabil-

---

[237] A third option can be considered mathematical equations.

ity, rather than seeking to solve a single, specific problem of unsustainability using quantitative modeling. It relates to using systems thinking as *new way of thinking* and *communicating*, i.e. systems thinking as a *language* (Senge et al. 1994: 88).

The *disadvantage* of causal loop diagrams in comparison to stock and flow diagrams is that they do not differentiate between stocks and flows, which are important for understanding how systems operate as outlined in chapter 2.3.4.[238] This disadvantage however at the same time is the great *advantage* of causal loop diagrams: Causal loop diagramming enables to illustrate and identify circular causalities and resulting dynamics *easily* and *fast*, as it consists of only three components[239]. Therefore it better meets the dissertation' requirements of an easy accessible and understandable tool for business practice. When using causal loop diagramming it is crucial however, to keep an understanding of the difference between stocks and flows in mind, even if they are not differentiated graphically. Otherwise this *leads to what Richmond calls* 'closed-loop laundry list thinking' (Richmond 1994: 11). This is the focus on '*closing the loop*' by (no matter how) linking an effect back to its cause. Yet, this is *not* how a system operates. Rather, circular causality is a consequence of how *dynamic* systems *operate*.

Therefore the dissertation will use causal loop diagramming as the main language for a systems perspective, but will 'switch' to a stock-and-flow-illustration, in cases where a stock-and-flow-perspective is inevitable for understanding crucial aspects of unsustainability, e.g. as it has been done in the CO_2 example above.

Because causal loop diagramming is a language to communicate about dynamic systems, it provides the 'vocabulary' (building blocks) to illustrate and thus to analyze many of the aspects outlined above orally, i.e. in 'conventional' language. For example, endogenous causes, dynamics and backfiring. The building blocks of causal loop diagramming allow to map dynamic structures and thus to analyze how they drive Sustainability Traps.

*The dissertation will therefore use the language of causal-loop-diagramming to illustrate and analyze dynamic, systemic structures of **Sustainability Traps in part III** of the dissertation.*

---

238 There exist several attempts to create a labelling/differentiation for stock and flows in causal-loop-diagrams, e.g. links bold, frame around stocks. Out of reason of simplicity and for a better understanding, the dissertation will stick to common causal loop diagramming, and will 'switch' to stock and flow differentiation, when relevant for aspects of unsustainability.
239 These are: Reinforcing loops, balancing loops and delays (see below).

The building blocks of causal loop diagramming, which allow to map and thus to analyze systemic, dynamic structures of Sustainability Traps and their characteristics, will be outlined in the following. These are:

- How to read *Link Polarities* (chapter 2.3.5.3)
- Positive Link Polarity and *Reinforcing Loops* (chapter 2.3.5.4)
- Negative Link Polarity and *Balancing Loops* (chapter 2.3.5.5)
- *Delays* and how they create *Dynamic Complexity* (chapter 2.3.5.6)

2.2.5.3 Link Polarities

As stated above, *circular causality* is key in a systems perspective. Circular causality occurs, if variables *interrelate* in the form of *closed loops*, as e.g. visible in figure 16 above. That is, variables are not related in a linear way of A impacts B, but in a circular (non-linear) way, so that B in turn also impacts A.[240]

In order to interpret loops and their contribution to system behavior, it is crucial to first understand how to read link polarities.

This will be outlined in the following. Link polarities indicate the impact which a variable has on another one. Link polarities can either be *positive* or *negative*. In order to outline how to read link polarities in causal loop diagrams the dissertation will use the *example of a positive link polarity* (figure 17): An example of a basic positive link polarity from the corporate sector is the causal relation between corporate profit and corporate activity (corporate operations).

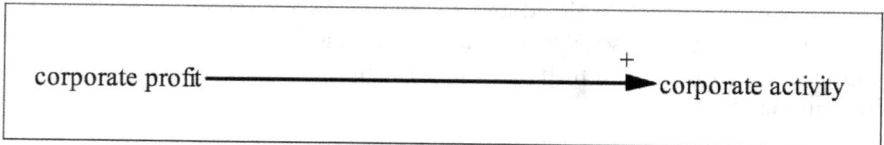

corporate profit ——————————————→ corporate activity
(with a "+" sign above the arrow near corporate activity)

Fig. 17: Positive Link Polarity
Source: Produced by the author[241]

The connecting arrow between both variables is referred to as '*link*' and indicates the direction of causality between both variables. The '+'-sign on the arrow indicates the *polarity* of the link, which in this case is positive. A link with a positive link polarity is also referred to as *positive link*.

---

240 This is the easiest form of circular relations. Usually the impact (feedback) from B to A is not direct, but occurs rather through a series of impacts on other variables (i.e. a large loop). At this moment, this simple example yet is sufficient.

241 In causal loop diagramming it is usual to use the singular form (activity). However here plural is used to stress the fact that this variable comprises several different *unsustainable* activities.

Generally, a positive link polarity is read as follows:

*A '+'-sign (**positive link polarity**) indicates that if v1 (the cause) **increases**, v2 (the effect) **increases** above what it would have been otherwise (i.e. without a change of v1). And if v1 **decreases**, v2 **decreases** below what it would have been otherwise[242] (Sterman 2004: 139).*

A simplified way of reading a positive link polarity is: That both variables are *changing in the same direction*, i.e. if v1 increases, v2 increases and if v1 decreases, v2 decreases.[243] However, there are particular cases, where this simplified mode of reading is incorrect. This has its cause in the difference between stock and flows. Appendix B outlines this point in-depth.

With regard to the specific example of figure 17, the link reads as follows:
If corporate profit (v1) increases, corporate activity increases (v2) above what it would have been otherwise, i.e. if profit would have been the same. If corporate profit decreases, corporate activity (corporate operations), decreases below what it would otherwise have been.

This simple example bears two implications crucial for reading link polarities:

a) Link polarities *represent the behavior* of a particular social agent (e.g. a corporation) depending on its *mental model in-use.*
b) Link polarities do *not* indicate any ethical evaluations.

a) Link polarities represent behavior based on mental models in-use

For link polarities in general, it is most important to notice that link polarities describe the **structure** of a system and **not the current situation** (Sterman 2004: 139). "That is, they describe what would happen **IF** there were a change. They do not describe what actually happens" (Sterman 2004: 139). Link polarities in general describe "the individual effect of a hypothesized change" in the sense of: If..., then.... (Sterman 2004: 141), Thus, the link polarity does *not* indicate that the cause variable (corporate profit, v1) is actually increasing or decreasing *at this moment*, nor if the effected variable (corporate operations, v2) is actually increasing or decreasing *at this moment*. It rather indicates what **would** happen to v2 (corporate activities), if v1 (corporate profit) is changed.

---

242 Why the addition of the formulation 'above/below what it would have been otherwise' is important as well as other aspects relating to link polarity will be outlined further below.
243 Correspondingly for a *negative* link polarity, both variables are moving in an opposite direction.

With regard to the behavior of social agents, a link polarity represents the behavior a particular social agent (e.g. the corporation) takes depending on its mental model in-use.[244]
That is, if corporate profit increases, the particular corporation analyzed behaves thus, that it increases corporate activities (corporate operations). If corporate profit reduces, corporate activities in the case of the particular corporation analyzed, will decrease below what they would otherwise have been. The link polarity thus indicates what **happens** to corporate activity, if corporate profit increases or if it decreases. The link polarity does **not** indicate the current state, that is if corporate profit currently *is* (or in the future will be) increasing or decreasing.[245] The advantage of this mode of reading is that the structure allows the 'decoupling' from events (see Iceberg Model, chapter 2.3.3) respectively the structure is accurate for different events, e.g. it is accurate in the case if profit increases and it is accurate in the case if corporate profit decreases.

b) Link polarities do not indicate any ethical evaluations
Furthermore it is important to notice that a link polarity is *independent from ethical evaluations*. That is, plus or minus signs in link polarity are not to be confounded with an *ethical* evaluation in the sense of 'good or bad' respectively 'positive or negative' (e.g. corporate profit is favorable (positive).

2.2.5.4   Positive Link Polarity and Reinforcing Loop
The above chapter has already outlined a positive link polarity, using the example of corporate profit and corporate activities (figure 17).
In addition to the positive link from corporate profit to corporate activity, there exists another positive link in so far as corporate activity influences corporate profit. If earnings per corporate activity (operation) are higher than total expenses per activity[246] it is true that the more activities a corporation can execute, the more profit it will make. Similarly, if activities are limited (less), profit will also be less than it would have been otherwise. Both positive causalities (links) belong to a reinforcing loop (figure 18). The circular causality arises on an operational level, because this is

---

244 Natural processes do not operate on mental models of course. Still here the link polarity indicates ,what hap-pens if', not the actual situation ,what is happening now'. Mental models in-use are discussed in chapter 2.2.1.
245 It is important to point this fact out thoroughly, as this often leads to confusion for beginners in causal loop modeling (Richardson 1997).
246 This is a very simplified contemplation of the causality between operations and profit (e.g. no tax considerations are included). Yet, this high level of aggregation was chosen for reason of better understanding and more details would not add to the point that is to be explained here.

how corporations seek to generate corporate growth: Profits are invested into more (or better) activities, which in turn are desired to achieve more profit, and so on.

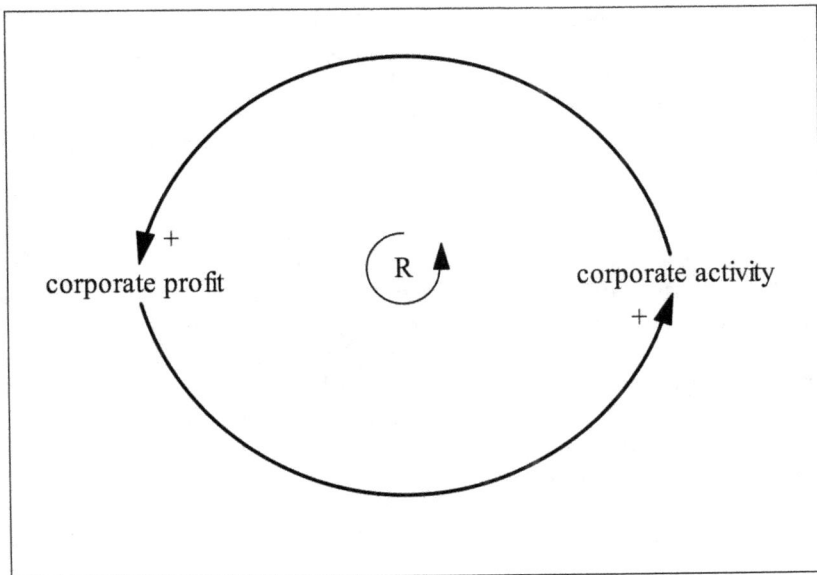

Fig. 18: Reinforcing Loop
Source: Produced by the author

The circular causality forms a closed loop (R1). It is crucial to realize that this re-ciprocal relation creates *non-linearities*[247] and *dynamic complexity*. The output of one variable flows back into it as input. Therefore one action produces a result which promotes more of the same action; e.g. corporate activity adds to corporate profit, which in turn increases corporate activity and so on. Therefore a small change, can lead to large effects – for better or worse (Senge 2006: 80). Often the analogy of a snowball running down a hill is used: A snowball starts small scale, but at the end of the hill it will be large scale.

The key here is to notice that the loop produces a ***dynamic*** behavior *'on its own'*, where a small change builds on itself, producing *'**more of the same**'* (Senge 2006: 80). Therefore such a loop is referred to as '*reinforcing*' loop (R). It has a positive *loop* polarity. A reinforcing loop does *not* necessarily need to consist of only positive links. It can also entail negative links[248]. The "quick and dirty" way of determining

---

247 Arithmetically it can be thought of as iterations.
248 A negative link is a causality, where if v1 (cause variable) increases, v2 (effect variable) decreases below what it otherwise would have been. If v1 decreases, v2 increases above would

loop polarity, i.e. determining whether a loop is reinforcing or balancing[249], is to count the number of negative links in the loop: *If the number of negative link polarities is even, the loop is positive (reinforcing)* (Sterman 2004: 144). Yet, the correct way to determine loop polarity is "to trace the effect of a small change in one of the variables as it propagates around the loop. If the feedback effect reinforces the original change, it is a positive loop [...]" (Sterman 2004: 144).

The behavior that results from a reinforcing loop is either accelerating growth (exponential growth) or accelerating decline (collapse) (Senge 2006: 82), i.e. growth or collapse continues at an ever-increasing rate. A reinforcing loop thus is not inherently good or bad, but can create virtuous cycles as well as vicious cycles depending on the values associated with them (Senge 2006: 80ff, Sterman 2004: 14). For example: If profits and corporate activities are growing exponentially, this is usually perceived as a desired, virtuous cycle. In contrast, when both are in accelerating decline, this is perceived a vicious cycle. Not all exponential growth is favorable, e.g. growth of unsustainability (waste, pollution, see also below). Reinforcing loops often accelerate so quickly that they "take people by surprise" (Senge 2006: 83). This once more is rooted in the fact that we are not used to think in dynamics. The past development of the World population is an example for exponential growth (see figure 19 below):

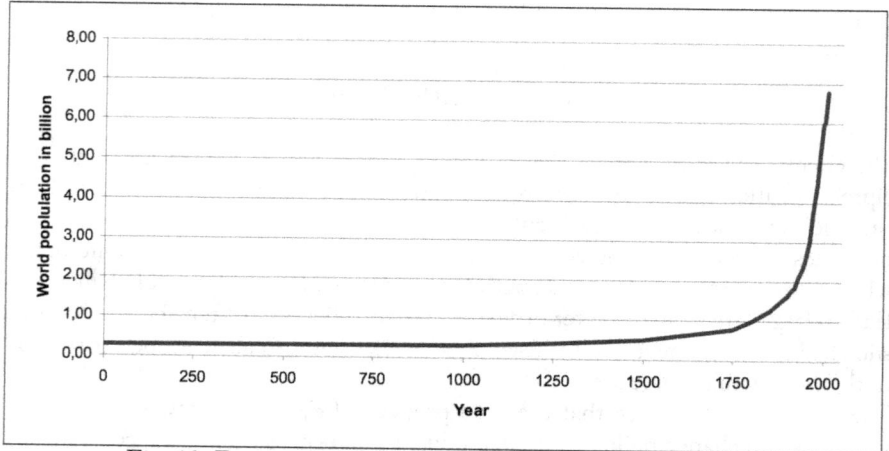

Fig. 19: Exponential Growth (Example: World Population)
Source: Produced by the author based on the data of UN (1999).

---

it would have been. Negative links will be discussed further below.
249 Balancing loops will be discussed below.

2.2.5.5 Negative Link Polarity and Balancing Loops

As has just been outlined, corporate activity can produce environmental damage. Yet, in turn environmental damage can unfavorably impact (reduce) corporate activity. Examples are lack of wood for construction or furniture industry, bad soil quality for agriculture, bad water quality for paper industry. That is

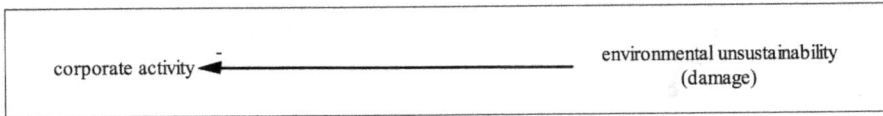

corporate activity ◄——————————————————— environmental unsustainability (damage)

Fig. 20: Negative Link Polarity
Source: Produced by the author

The '-'-sign on the arrow again indicates the *polarity* of the link, which in this case is negative. A *negative link polarity* in general means that (Sterman 2004: 139):
If v1 (cause variable) *increases*, v2 (effect variable) *decreases* below what it otherwise would have been. If v1 *decreases*, v2 *increases* above would it would have been.
Referring to the example this implies: The more environmental unsustainability (damage), the less corporate activities are possible (e.g. because there are not enough resources or because time and money has to be invested for clean-up costs before resuming the activities). Respectively: The less environmental damage, the more corporate activities are possible. Again the link polarity ('-'sign) indicates the type of causal relationship, not the current state of a variable nor an ethical statement (Richardson 1997).[250] If both of the last causal relations outlined are considered in interrelation[251] (positive and negative link with regard to corporate activity and environmental unsustainability (damage)), they form a **balancing loop** (B1), which can be illustrated the following way:

---

250 Richardson points out that with negative links this point sometime confuses readers (Richardson 1997: 249ff): When one comes to a link and says 'when C drops then D tends to rise,' some beginners have a tendency to put a positive sign on the link, signifying 'rise,' instead of a negative sign indicating 'change in the opposite direction'. This problematic can be dealt with by going to each link separately and always determining the implication of an increase in the variable at the tail of the arrow; then the direction of change in the variable at the head matches intuitively the correct polarity of the link; for example: 'If C increases, the D tends to decrease, so the link is negative'.
251 For the interrelation see also next chapter on delays, chapter 2.2.5.6.

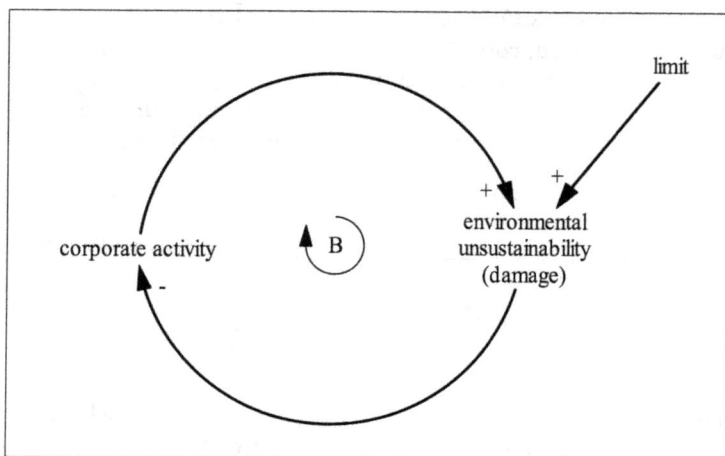

Fig. 21: Balancing Loop
Source: Produced by the author

When 'tracing' around the loop the following becomes evident: If corporate activity increases, environmental damage (unsustainability) increases (positive link polarity).[252] Yet, the more environmental damage increases, the less corporate activity becomes possible (negative link polarity). Thus, there seems to be a kind of inherent limit (goal). Obviously the limit (goal) is not one desired by the corporation (as it restricts corporate activities). It rather seems to be a goal (limit) *inherent in the system itself*.

When a corporation in the effort of "overcoming" the limit increases its efforts (activities), environmental damage increases, which in turn restricts corporate activities and drives the system back to its implicit limit (goal). Balancing loops can lead to the feeling of "no matter what we try, we can't change the system" (Senge et al. 1994: 117). They "generate the force of resistance, which eventually limits growth" (Senge et al. 1994: 117). *It is important to realize that this dynamic towards a goal is created within the system itself.* As Senge says the system seems to "have its own agenda" (Senge 2006: 84). A balancing loop 'generally has a goal-seeking behavior and results in graphs that grow or decline at a *decreasing* rate[253] (see figure 22 below). In order to determine if a loop is balancing, the "quick and dirty" way of determining loop polarity as mentioned above is to count the number of negative links in the loop: If the number is odd, the loop is negative (balancing) (Sterman

---

252 As outlined above, this is the case in this particular example (corporate activity). It does not include that all corporate activity per se, is damaging to the environment.
253 In contrast to reinforcing loops, which imply *increasing* rates (see above).

2004: 144). The correct way is to trace the effect of a change in one of the variables as it propagates around the loop: If the feedback effect opposes the original change, it is a negative loop (Sterman 2004: 144). However frustrating balancing loops that follow inherent goals can seem at first sight, because they can counter desired goals they are crucial. They are "the mechanisms, found in nature and all systems, that fix problems, maintain stability, and achieve equilibrium" (Senge et al. 1994: 117). They account for homeostasis of a system – the ability "to maintain conditions for sur- vival in a changing environment" (Senge 2006: 84). The implications of causal-loop diagrams as well as the implicit limit for the specific balancing loop outlined, will be discussed further below. At this point it is important to notice the nature of a balancing loop, which is: Counteracting disturbances and seeking for a goal (Ster- man 2004: 111). Figure 22 shows the goal seeking behavior created by a balancing loop:

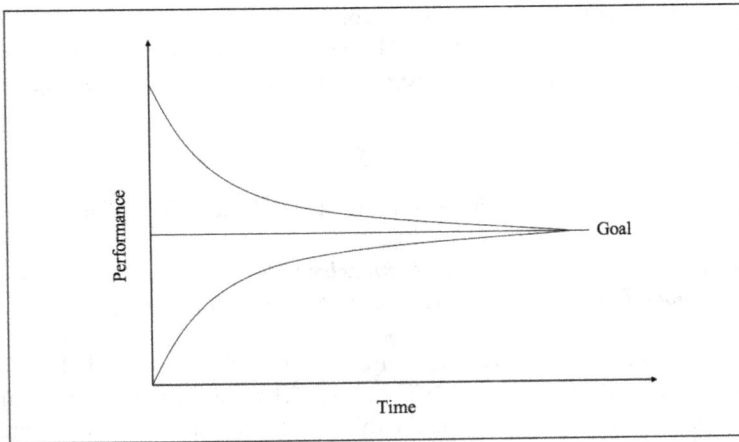

Fig. 22: Exponential Decay and Goal Seeking Growth
Source: Retrieved from Arizona State University (2001: 30, chapter 4)

The human body for example is full of balancing loops, e.g. the adjustment of body temperature to outside temperature, whereby the goal is usually 37.0 degrees Cel- sius. Another example for a balancing loop is e.g. a nuclear plant load factor (Ster- man 2004: 113).
Together the reinforcing (figure 18) and the balancing loop (figure 21) create a lim- its-to-growth structure (figure 23), where the reinforcing dynamic of corporate growth (R) is balanced through backfiring from environmental unsustainabilities (B).

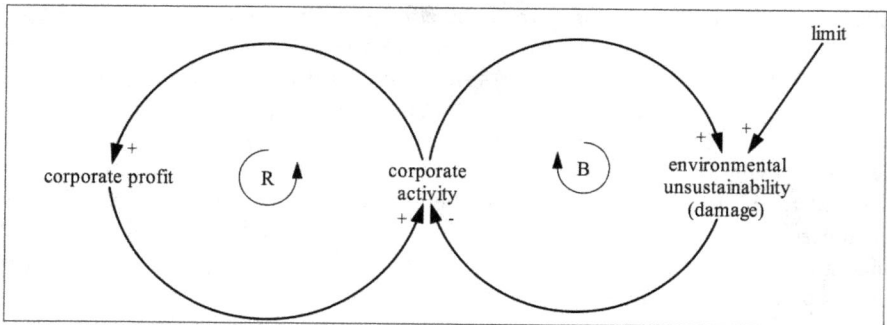

Fig. 23: Limits-to-Growth
Source: Produced by the author (for archetype see also Senge 2006: 390)

The Limits-to-Growth structure can be considered a basic Sustainability Trap.[254] For further information on Limits-to-Growth see Appendix A1. Here the structure was merely used as an example to discuss link polarities, reinforcing and balancing loops.

2.2.5.6 Delays

Delays[255] are the last – and crucial – building block of causal loop diagrams.

Delays are crucial for creating **dynamic complexity** *in Sustainability Traps, where* **cause and effect** *are not closely related, but* **distant in time and space**.

The impact of environmental damage on corporate activity outlined above usually does not happen immediately, but with a *delay*. The reason is that environmental damage (unsustainability) is a stock. At this point it is helpful to come back to a stock-and-flow diagram to illustrate the effect:

---

254 See also chapter 1.4.3 (Meadows et al. 1972, 1992 and 2004).
255 In this chapter the dissertation will focus on *balancing loops* with delay.

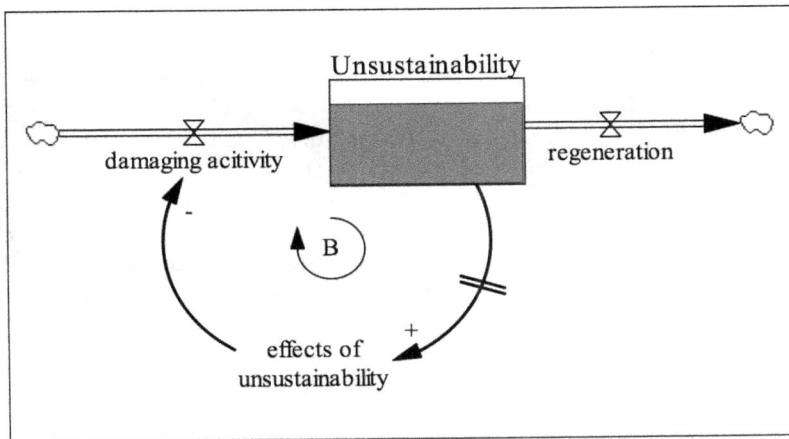

Fig. 24: A Stock Accumulates Inflows and Creates Delays
Source: Produced by the author

Stocks decouple rates of flows – into inflow and outflow (Sterman 2004: 196). In equilibrium, the total inflow to a stock equals its total outflow, so that the level of the stock remains unchanged. But as inflows and outflows usually are governed by different decision processes[256], inflow and outflow usually differ (Sterman 2004: 196). For example corporate activities that damage environment follow other 'rules' and rates, than regenerating processes, which are executed by nature (ecosystem services). As inflow and outflow differ, the stock is *accumulating*. Analytically therefore a stock in general is an integration of flows affecting it (Sterman 2004: 194):

$$Stock(t) = INTEGRAL \ (Inflow(t) - Outflow(t))$$

Thus, in the example unsustainability (environmental damage) is increasing, when the inflow (damaging) is higher than the outflow (regeneration). This currently is the case for the majority of economic activities, as stated in chapter 2.2.4.2. The grey area in the stock in figure 24 indicates the level of unsustainability accumulated. The stock thus serves as a *buffer*, which separates inflow and outflow. This creates *dis*equilibrium, which in turn constitutes *dynamic complexity*, where cause and effects are deferred in time (Sterman 2004: 192ff).
Furthermore "information about the size of the buffer will feed back in various ways to influence the inflows and outflows" (Sterman 2004: 197). This feedback of

---

256 For example: Different decision makers (human versus nature), involvement of different resources, subject to different random shocks, etc.

the buffer is crucial, because unsustainability has an **inherent limit**, which when neared increasingly releases feedback. This feedback impacts the inflow in order to reduce damaging activities that increase unsustainability. If the inflow yet still continuous and a limit is reached or even passed, backfiring will be very fierce and can risk offsetting the inflow entirely.[257] In this way, the system seeks to put itself back into balance, returning to the inherent (environmental) goal (limit). So it is a balancing process (see balancing loop above). Some of this feedback of environmental unsustainability also impacts the organization's activities (see links tracing back to corporate activities in figure 24), which as one agent contributed to the structure of unsustainability[258]. This feedback constitutes **backfiring** on the corporation.[259]

*It is important to realize that backfiring happens with a **delay**, indicated in figure 24 by the two cross-hatch lines on the link (arrow). The delay is crucial, because it diverts cause and effect in time and thus creates dynamic complexity.[260]*

Regarding environmental damage (unsustainability), this means that damaging corporate and social activities (inflow) first 'only' lead to a piling up of unsustainability in the stock, with no feedback or only low feedback. The accumulation (piling up), which causes the delay in feedback, suggests that 'nothing' is happening (Senge 2006: 90f and 389f). This delay is a paramount problem, because it tempts to the conclusion that increasing damaging corporate activity is unproblematic, since no unfavorable consequences (effects) are perceived. Yet, as damaging activity is increased the stock of unsustainability is piling up even more (faster). This will lead to an even more drastic reaction (feedback), which will occur *eventually* in order to put the system back into balance (Senge 2006: 91).

This balancing loop with delay described above (its dynamics and the effects it creates) is a basic mechanism in the field of sustainability: "That current growth rates of population and industrialization will stop is inevitable. Unless we choose favorable processes to limit growth, the social and environmental systems by their internal processes will choose for us. The natural mechanisms for terminating exponential growth appear the least desirable. Unless the world understands and begins to

---

257 This is even more the case, if the local natural system collapses and regeneration is not possible anymore as will be outlined subsequently.
258 The dissertation refers to such structures as 'unsustainable structures'.
259 See chapter 2.1.3.
260 As stated above, dynamic complexity is a type of complexity that leads to situations, where cause and effect are distant in time and space. (As compared to detailed complexity in orthodox thinking).

act soon, civilization will be overwhelmed by forces we have created but can no longer control" (Forrester 1995: 13).[261]

Additionally another dynamic is usually triggered by an accumulation of unsustainability, which also occurs with *delay*: An increase in the damage of an ecosystem reduces its capability of regeneration (Gomez-Pompa and Burley 1991: 8ff) (see additional link in figure 25). This is a ***reinforcing*** dynamic[262]: *Increased* unsustainability *reduces* a system's ability to regenerate. The more the ability to regenerate is *reduced*, the more unsustainability *increases*, which in turn *reduces* a system's ability to regenerate even more etc. This reinforcing loop adds to the problematic of the situation, because it causes unsustainability to add up even *faster* (see figure 25).

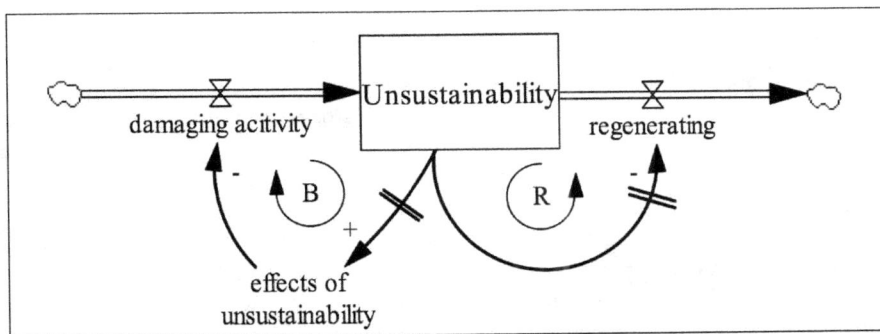

Fig. 25: Feedbacks of Unsustainability
Source: Produced by the author

If unsustainability reaches a bifurcation point, where regeneration is not possible anymore, the ecosystem collapses (e.g. collapsed lake). Because of the interconnectivity of social and economical systems to the ecosystem, social and economic system risk to be impacted as well and risk also collapsing eventually.[263]

The above chapters have shown how the language of causal loop diagramming enables to identify and analyze systemic structures by examining how exactly reinforcing loops, balancing loops and delays *interrelate*. Thereby it has been shown, which crucial role ***dynamics*** in the system structure play and why they are constitutive for Sustainability Traps as stated in chapter 2.1: Dynamics are driven by reinforcing

261 See also Limits-to-Growth structure above and in appendix A1. The limits-to-growth structure and implications will play a crucial role in the Job-Creation Trap in combination with a Trade-off Model (appendix C).
262 Reinforcing loop with two *negative* links.
263 See chapter 2.1.2. Diamond has outlined several historic examples, where collapse of ecosystems (caused by humans) has led to total collapse of societies, and thus their economic activities, depending on the ecosystem (Diamond 2005).

loops, balancing loops and delays. Reinforcing loops create a dynamic that produces more of the same (faster and faster growth or decline). Some variables are stocks, whose levels 'pile up' or decrease in the process, because inflows and outflows into a stock do not occur simultaneously and to the same amount. If the level of a stock approaches upper or lower limits, feedbacks are triggered, which backfire and seek to set the process into balance.[264] In part III, the dissertation therefore will use causal loop diagramming to identify and analyze systems, where reinforcing loops, balancing loops and delays interrelate thus, that they form a dynamic structure, which constitutes a specific Sustainability Traps. The dissertation by this means will identify and analyze dynamic structures of *eight* archetypical traps common in business practice.

2.2.5.7 Resulting Implications for Managing Sustainability Traps

As outlined above, there is a 'self-regulating' mechanism in dynamic systems, in the sense that 'while running through a loop' levels of stocks are piled up or reduced. If limits are reached, the stock variables release feedbacks (backfiring) into the system, which countervail the behavior of the system. The feedback occurs with a delay, which creates dynamic complexity in time, i.e. cause and effect are deferred *in time*. Furthermore in dynamic system cause and effect are deferred *in space* (dynamic complexity in space), e.g. when feedback impacts several variables from other sectors in the system and/or when a delay is so long that a feedback impacts other agents (e.g. future generations).

From dynamic complexity arise four crucial implications for managing Sustainability Traps:

a) Playing the Blame-Game is inefficient for managing Sustainability Traps.

b) Managing Sustainability Traps requires the 'Pogo'-attitude that the corporation is part of the problem.

c) The corporation however is only *one* part of the problem. Other social agents contribute to the systemic structure, so that managing Sustainability Traps requires cooperative approaches.

d) Managing Sustainability Traps requires orchestrating solutions (continuous learning).

In contrast to the other three a) thus discusses an aspect, which is *not* well suited for managing Sustainability Traps. Playing the blame-game however is a predominant behavior in the field of sustainability. Therefore it is most important to the dissertation to outline *that* and *why* playing the blame-game is ineffective from a

---

264 That is they countervail the reinforcing loops.

systems perspective. The points b) - d) will then outline implications resulting from dynamic complexity, which are important for managing Sustainability Traps.

a)   Playing the Blame-Game is inefficient

As stated above, feedbacks (backfiring) are produced **endogenously** by the system it-self, in such a way that if limits are reached, stocks release feedbacks (backfiring) into the system, which countervail the behavior of the system. Because backfiring of a corporate sustainability measure however occurs with a **delay**, Sustainability Trap often remain unrecognized and their backfiring seems to occur suddenly and 'out of the blue' for the corporation, as corporate measures first showed their in-tended effect. Thus, it is not surprising, if corporations lacking a systems perspective seek for a external causer ('enemy'), who caused the backfiring, which was not there before (or at such a subtle level that it remained unnoticed). The causer, i.e. the re-sponsible ('enemy'), thereby often is identified by tracing effects back to causes in a linear way (see laundry list thinking above). That is, social agents lacking a systems perspective, tend to trace an effect, which negatively impacts them, back until a 'cause' is identified as well as an agent to whom this cause is attributed (the respon-sible). Once this 'enemy' is identified, the tracing-back for causes stops, and blame and pressure is imposed on 'the enemy' in order to change its behavior (blame-game), which is negatively impacting or hindering the own actions. "[E]xperiments in causal attribution show people tend to assume each effect has a single cause and often cease their search for explanations when the first sufficient cause is found" (Sterman 2004: 28[265]). Feedback, i.e. circular causality, is not perceived in most cases (Sterman 2004: 28).

A systems perspective in contrast focuses on **circular causality**, i.e. loops. Thinking in circular causality implies, not to stop, once a cause and a causer are identified, but to identify the *systemic structure*, which creates the backfiring. This also includes to identify the different agents ('causers'), which contribute to the creation of the structure as well as *how* they contribute to it, i.e. that is through *which behavior* they contribute to the creation of the structure and *which mental models* drive their be-havior.[266] While, in dynamic systems, it is possible to identify the core structure, which produces a specific result (e.g. unsustainability), it is *not* possible to attribute single effects to single causes. This is not possible, because dynamic complexity cre-ated by the system 'itself' in the way outlined above, deferrers causes and effects. Dealing with Sustainability Traps therefore requires the realization that unsustain-ability that backfires very often is caused through dynamics in systemic structures and not through ('ill-intended') behavior of single agents. *Playing the game of blam-*

---

265 Sterman in this respect points to: Plous 1993.
266 That is through which behavior they contribute to the creation of that structure and what mental models drive their behavior.

ing 'external', individual agents ('blame-game') is a misconception of the situation posed by a Sustainability Trap and is ineffective in addressing unsustainable, systemic structures.

"However, people have a strong tendency to attribute the behavior of others [...] to character flaws rather than the system in which these people are acting" (Sterman 2004: 28). Playing the blame-game is a prevalent behavior in the field of sustainability. NGOs or activists, for example tend to blame corporations as the culprit for unsustainability, not taking into account the structure in which corporations are operating (e.g. customer behavior). Corporations on their behalf often identify (unfavorable) effects on the corporation to arise from behavior of competitors, from environmental changes or social movements; - not realizing or simply denying their own role in the contribution to these structures. A manifestation (example) for this will be given in the chapter of the trap of Financing Brand-Image through Low-Cost Production[267]: A common phenomenon is blaming social unsustainability in contract factories on the lack of knowledge and values of *suppliers* in third world countries; thereby ignoring the costs pressure which companies themselves impose on the suppliers – in order to meet customer demands for low product prices.

b) 'Pogo'-attitude

The last example points to a crucial aspect for managing Sustainability Traps: When analyzing systemic, dynamic structures as well as the different agents contributing to the structure, - it is crucial for corporations to analyze their **own** role in the contribution to the structure, which creates the backfiring that impacts the corporation. This is key, because what constitutes the core nature of a trap as outlined is: The corporation contributes to something, which eventually is backfiring on itself. Managing a Sustainability Trap therefore requires the 'Pogo-attitude': "We Have Met the Enemy and He Is Us" (Kelly 1972). Rather than blaming 'external', individual agents ('blame-game'), dealing with Sustainability Traps requires a corporation to analyze its *behavior (corporate activity/measures)*, which is contributing to the creation of the trap' structure as well as to analyze the corporation's *mental models in –use*, which are driving its behavior. Realizing and acknowledging someone's own contribution to a problem impacting someone negatively, usually however is far harder than blaming external agents as the causer. Senge summarizes the implications of a systems perspective the following way: „There is no blame. [...] Systems thinking shows us that there is no separate ‚other'; that you and the someone else are part of a single system. The cure lies in your relationship with your 'enemy'" (Senge 2006: 67). Thus, managing Sustainability Traps requires the recognition that corporations are part of the problems as well as the solutions.

---

267 See chapter 3.4.3.

c) Cooperative approaches

As just outlined for managing Sustainability Traps it is crucial that corporations recognize and analyze the vital role, which they play themselves in the creation of a trap's structure. Thus changing the corporation's behavior and corresponding mental models provides important leverage for getting out of a trap. As outlined however, a trap's structure is created through the *interplay of actions* from the corporation and its *stakeholders* (including natural, biological processes)[268]. "As our actions alter the state of the system, other people [annotation of author: and the natural, environmental system] react to restore the balance we have upset" (Sterman 2004: 10). Altering the structure thus, that it does not constitute a Sustainability Trap anymore, therefore requires cooperative approaches of all relevant agents involved. Thus, rather than blaming and imposing moral pressure for change of behavior on individual agents, it is of importance that agents – *in cooperative dialogues* – analyze how the interplay of their actions and dynamics triggered in the system, create the unsustainable structure, which produces the unsustainability issue in question.

d) Orchestrating solutions (continuous learning)

A further implication of dynamic complexity is that because of *delays,* **corporate measures can have different effects in the short-term than in the long-term** (*Senge 2006: 60*). The fatal aspect with regard to Sustainability Traps is that because backfiring of a corporate sustainability measure occurs with a delay, **behavior grows better before it grows worse**: At first the sustainability measure seems to work and to yield the intended effects (e.g. enhancement of corporate sustainability image; cost or energy reduction).[269] But at some point, backfiring (policy resistance) is perceived. If an understanding of the underlying dynamic structure of a system is lacking, this backfiring seems to occur suddenly and 'out of the blue', because previously corporate measures worked out well and showed no backfiring. System behavior thus is counter-intuitive and so are often also the leverage points for change in dynamic systems (Senge 2006: 63f, Forrester 1995).

Managing Sustainability Traps therefore does not require one-time, fix solutions, but rather dynamic solutions that 'waver' over time. Or as Meadows refers to it "dancing with systems" (Meadows 2002 and 1999).[270] A win-win-win situation in the sense of increasing economical, social and environmental sustainability *at the same time* through a specific corporate sustainability measure, – if at all possible – often only lasts *short-term*. In order to increase all three dimensions of sustainability in the *long-term* however it can be necessary to reduce one or two of the dimensions in *short-term* intervals. This is the case, because due to dynamic complexity

---

268 That is, dynamics resulting from the interplay of actions.
269 See Reputation Trap (chapter 3.4.2) and Efficiency Trap (chapter 3.3.2).
270 See also chapter 1.4.3 and 2.1.2.

behavior can *grow better before it grows worse* and similarly behavior can *grow worse before it gets better*. Therefore it is necessary to 'orchestrate' actions over time. Society in the past has focused on improving economic sustainability by compromising on environmental and social sustainability. Yet, now is the time to focus on environmental and social sustainability in order to further increase economic sustainability in the long-run.

Orchestrating 'solutions' to Sustainability Traps implies *continuous learning* as outlined in chapter 2.3.1. The third part of the dissertation will analyze various cases of Sustainability Traps, where *behavior gets better before it gets worse*, i.e. where a problem reappears over and over again often in worse form. This problem is particularly dominant in cases, where *quick fixes* are applied: These are 'solutions' that reduce *problem symptoms* in the short-term, but deteriorate the basis for fundamental solutions, thus actually *increasing* the problem in the long-term.[271] If a 'solution' to a problem caused by a Sustainability Trap is *symptomatic*, the problem will 'pop up' again, i.e. behavior will become worse in the future. If the solution is fundamental, it solves the problem 'once and for all' and thus constitutes an exit of the Sustainability Trap for the corporation.

However, due to dynamic complexity, estimating if a solution is symptomatic or fundamental is very difficult. Furthermore the problem of estimating if a solution is symptomatic or fundamental, is potentized by the fact that a differentiation between the reoccurrence of an 'old' problem 'popping up' again due to a symptomatic solution (*trend*) and the occurrence of a 'new' problem (one-time *event*) is blur, because this depends on boundary judgments of the corporation as outlined in chapter 2.3.3.

Therefore, getting out of a Sustainability Traps usually is not a 'one time shut' in the sense of a one time, fix solution, but requires continuous learning, including adaptations (changes) in systemic structures, boundary judgments and mental models. A pertinent example of such a learning process will be discussed later in the case of the furniture company IKEA, which, by running through a series of various sustainability scandals, reframed its mental models in a process of broadening its system boundaries from a formaldehyde problem in particleboards, to a formaldehyde problem in products, over to a problem of toxins in products, to environmental sustainability in general towards additionally considering social sustainability. IKEA adapted its sustainability measures accordingly and this learning process helped IKEA eventually to come out of the Sustainability Trap of 'quick-fixing' its sustainability scandals.

---

271 See chapter Quick-Fix Trap (3.2.2) and Financing Brand-image through Low-Cost Production (chapter 3.4.3). See also archetypes 'fixes that fail' (Senge 2006: 399f) and 'Shifting the burden' (Senge 2006: 391ff). A common pattern of this behavior identified in the dissertation is the Fire-the-Supplier Trap (chapter 3.2.3).

2.3 Chapter Summary (Part II)

Part II of the dissertation has elaborated the theoretical foundations of the particular systems perspective of this dissertation: The concept of Sustainability Traps.

Chapter 2.1 has *defined* Sustainability Traps and has elaborated their **concept**. Most important, Sustainability Traps are constituted by an *interdependency between mental models and systemic structures* and by *dynamics* in the system structure.

Chapter 2.2 has discussed the **characteristics** of Sustainability Traps and on this basis has identified **requirements for their management**. The four characteristics discussed are: Sustainability Traps have *endogenous* causes; Sustainability Traps *backfire* on the corporation; estimating Sustainability Traps depends on *system boundaries*; and: there is *no one right solution* to a Sustainability Trap. It has been shown that the properties of systems thinking are better suited to deal with the characteristics of Sustainability Traps than the properties of orthodox thinking.

Chapter 2.3 then has elaborated concrete **principles of a systems perspective** required **to manage Sustainability Traps**. The five principles identified, form an *integrated* set of **skills** as managing Sustainability Traps requires a continuous learning process. Each of the five chapters first discussed the concept of the specific systems thinking principle (skill) in-depth and subsequently presented the **resulting implications for managing Sustainability Traps**. The five principles discussed are:

- Thinking in Models,
- Re-thinking Boundary Judgments,
- System-as-Cause Thinking,
- Operational Thinking and
- Dynamic Thinking.

Chapter 2.3.1 Thinking in Models

The chapter provided a **definition of mental models** and distinguished *espoused mental models* and **mental models in-use**, whereby the latter is the one relevant in respect of Sustainability Traps. Subsequently it was outlined that a systems perspective has its roots in *radical constructivism*. For that reason, the basis on which 'knowledge' is build on, i.e. the understanding of 'how the world works', is a *model* and not an obvious truth. Therefore *continuous learning* and reconsideration of existing mental models is key. The learning process for dealing with Sustainability Traps elaborated in the dissertation differentiates *single loop learning*, *double loop learning* and *triple loop learning*.

Resulting implications for managing Sustainability Traps: Whereas *triple loop learning*, - in the sense of changing the way of thinking towards a systems perspective, - constitutes the underlying, inevitable basis of the learning process, *double-loop learning* constitutes the level most frequent and most relevant for managing specific, individual Sustainability Traps, because double loop learning allows *reframing mental models*. With regard to managing Sustainability Traps, double loop learning comprises two core aspects: First: Reflecting upon and changing *boundaries* of *perception space* and thus *system boundaries*. This reframes, *which variables* are considered in the analysis of a system that constitutes a Sustainability Trap. Second: Reflecting upon and reframing *how* the variables in a system are perceived to *interrelate*, thus the perceived *structure* of a system.

Reframing existing mental models (double loop learning) is key for managing Sustainability Traps, because the higher the 'fit' (matching) between the mental models (beliefs) and systemic, dynamic structures existing in the real-world, - that is, the more a corporation is aware of how unsustainability is produced in a system, - the better a corporation can avoid Sustainability Traps and increase success of its sustainability measures. If single loop learning (re-acting upon events) occurs without double loop learning the thinking of an agent (his mental model) can hold him prisoner in a trap.

Chapter 2.3.2 Re-thinking Boundary Judgments

System boundaries of a systems perspective need to be distinguished from boundaries of societal sectors, which developed historically over time: A systems perspective defines a system bottom-up, starting from an issue of unsustainability in question according to the *principle of the system boundary* and independently from existing, sectoral boundaries. A systems perspective thus allows *transcending sectoral boundaries* of the economic, social and environmental sector and permits focusing on their interrelations.

The *perception space* thereby is the space, which an agent *considers* when setting boundaries of a system, i.e. when he defines, which variables constitute the '*relevant*' system for dealing with an issue of sustainability. Both, boundaries of the perception space and consequently boundary setting with regard to a particular system in question, are subject to **value judgments**. They hence are *boundary judgments*, which require deciding upon in principle undecidable questions. Therefore there is nothing like the one right, fix system boundaries. Rather, existing boundaries need to be reconsidered and revised through the learning process described.

Resulting implications for managing Sustainability Traps: Managing Sustainability Traps requires **broadening** *perception space in **time*** (from short-term towards long-term) and *in **space*** (from sectoral towards holistic). This enables corporations to **broaden** its boundaries of a particular *system* in question and thus to better recognize potential backfiring, which in a Sustainability Trap usually occurs *deferred* in *time* and *space*.

Furthermore there are two different ***mental models*** *of perception space*. Agents holding a *sectoral* mental model of perception space, derive their goals and build their actions (including sustainability measures) upon their belief (mental model) how the *sectoral, economic* sector **operates**. Agents holding a *holistic* mental model of perception space in contrast, derive their goals and build their actions upon the *embeddedness* of the economic sector within the social and the environmental sector and upon the *interrelations* the agents believe to exist between these sectors.

The challenge many social agents are facing at present, is how to reconcile sectoral goals deriving from a sectoral mental model of perception space and holistic sustainability goals deriving from a holistic perception space. The reconciliation option predominantly *in use* at present, is to consider social and environmental sustainability as new, important *conditions (limiting factors)* to existing business, while sectoral goals (e.g. profit maximization) remain the primary goals. An alternative, but in business practice not yet frequent reconciliation option, is to consider economy (economic sustainability) as a means to increase social and environmental sustainability. This requires substantial changes in how a business operates and which sustainability measures it takes. With regard to dealing with Sustainability Traps it is important that a corporation is **aware** of which mental model of perception space it holds and of the reconciliation option it operates on, in order to avoid inconsistencies of goals and measures (conditions). Sustainability Traps as such, can play out in either of the two options.

Chapter 2.3.3 System-as-Cause Thinking

The chapter introduced the Iceberg Model to show, how different levels of awareness for Sustainability Traps relate to each other: Events, trends, system structures and mental models. The challenge for managing Sustainability Traps illustrated by the Iceberg is that lower levels hold higher leverage to deal with a Sustainability Trap, but at the same time they are harder to recognize.

Resulting implications for managing Sustainability Traps: Managing Sustainability Traps requires the analysis if an event (e.g. a negative impact on a corporation) is *a one-time event or part of a trend*. If a specific trend is recognized (system behavior observed), deeper levels need to be analyzed: The interplay of *systemic structures and mental models*, which *produce the trend*. That is: How existing *dynamic system structures*, - which so far remained unaware in the mental models the corporation holds and which the corporation itself contributes to, - cause unsustainability that backfires (system-as-cause).

Chapter 2.3.4 Operational Thinking

The chapter discussed the importance of differentiating stocks and flows.

Resulting implications for managing Sustainability Traps: A stock and flow perspective reveals the importance for the *level* of stocks and upper and lower *limits*. Furthermore a stock and flow perspective allows illustrating the *difference between reducing unsustainability and creating sustainability*. Corporations, which hold a sectoral mental model of perception space and consider sustainability as a new condition to business, need to take caution to not exceed *upper* limits of unsustainability in order to avoid triggering backfiring and getting caught up in a Sustainability Trap. The challenge here lies in the fact that it is most difficult to forecast upper limits correctly and even harder to predict the future impacts of backfiring. The *best* results these corporations, which are focused on reducing unsustainability, can accomplish, is to reach *lower* limits, i.e. to reduce unsustainability to zero, e.g. zero waste, zero use of toxic chemicals. This however is not to equal with *increasing sustainability*, which requires other, alternative business models and sustainability measures operating on the basis of a holistic mental model of perception space.

Chapter 2.3.5 Dynamic Thinking

Dynamic Thinking constitutes the essence of a systems perspective. In contrast of analyzing sustainability issues through linear 'laundry-list' thinking, it focuses *dynamic* interrelations between variables (circular, non-linear causalities). *Causal loop diagramming* has been introduced as a qualitative language to analyze dynamic system structures and thus to better communicate about Sustainability Traps. As has been set out, causal loop diagramming consists of link polarities, reinforcing loops, balancing loops and delays. These building blocks are sufficient to analyze how dynamics are created in a system and produce *dynamic complexity*. Most important, - reverting to a stock and flow perspective, - it has been shown that a dynamic system triggers dynamics that backfire 'on its own' caused through self-regulating mechanisms in dynamic systems. Dynamics and their backfiring effects are thus produced *endogenously* in the system. This insight that dynamics are produced endogenously in a system and in so doing drive system behavior, is the reason, which underlies the perception of *system* as cause for unsustainability and thus underscores the importance of *analyzing dynamic system structures* in order to deal with Sustainability Traps. The *dynamic complexity*, which in dynamic systems is produced in the endogenous way described, defers *causes* and *effects* in *time* and *space*.

Resulting implications for managing Sustainability Traps: Dynamic complexity entailed in Sustainability Traps leads to four crucial implications for their management: Playing the Blame-Game is inefficient for managing Sustainability Traps, because backfiring is caused endogenously. Instead, managing Sustainability Traps requires the 'Pogo'-attitude that the corporation is part of the problem by contributing to an unsustainable structure that backfires. The corporation however is only *one* part of the problem. Other social agents also contribute to the systemic structure, so that managing Sustainability Traps requires cooperative approaches. Furthermore Managing Sustainability Traps requires 'orchestrating' solutions. This is the case, because Sustainability Traps entail dynamic complexity, which plays out thus that *behavior gets better* (i.e. an intended sustainability measures seem to work in the short-term), *before behavior gets worse* (i.e. they backfire in the long-term). Because in a Sustainability Trap a cause (a sustainability measure) thus can have different effects in the short-run than in the long-run, there usually are no one time, fix solutions to a trap. Rather, successfully managing Sustainability Traps requires *continuous learning*, including adaptations (changes) in systemic structures, boundary judgments and mental models.

Part II of the dissertation elaborated the ***theoretical*** foundations of Sustainability Traps: Their concept, their characteristics and the systems thinking skills required for dealing with Sustainability Traps.

Part III of the dissertation will now deal with Sustainability Traps existing in ***business practice*** and will use the theoretical foundations elaborated in part II, to identify and analyze the traps from a systems perspective.

3 Part III: Archetypical Sustainability Traps in Business Practice

Part III of the dissertation will identify and discuss examples of common Sustainability Traps in business practice. That is: *Archetypical Sustainability Traps.*

The intention of part III is to show that the theoretical concept of Sustainability Traps discussed in part II, is a common phenomenon in business practice.

This entails two aspects intentioned by part III:
On the one side, to give **practice examples** of Sustainability Traps in order to underscore and endorse the theoretical concept.
On the other side, to prove the **relevance and importance** of the concept **for business practice**, i.e. for corporate sustainability measures in corporations. To this end, the dissertation will show that Sustainability Traps are no single phenomenon, but that there are very common patterns, i.e. common systemic structures of these traps, which play out in business practice again and again and countervail sustainability measures, but remain unrecognized as systemic traps. That is: **Archetypes** of Sustainability Traps.

In part II it has been elaborated that the key constitutives for a Sustainability Trap consists of the interdependency between **mental models** and **dynamic system structures**.
Consequently it is the interdependency of different specifications of these two building blocks, which needs being examined in part III, when identifying and discussing examples of Sustainability Traps through the analysis of business cases. Part III therefore will identify five mental models frequent in business practice and will identify and discuss Sustainability Traps often playing out on the basis of these mental models. The ones discussed are:
- *Trade-off Model* (historical Model): Job Creation Trap and Fighting-Enemy Trap (chapter 3.1.3)[272]
- *Compliance Model*: Quick-Fix Trap, with Special case: Fire-the-Supplier Trap (chapter 3.2)
- *Efficiency Model:* Efficiency Trap (Rebound Effects) (chapter 3.3)

---

272 The Trade-off Model differs from the other four mental models and is a special but important case, which will therefore be outlined in chapter 3.1.3.

- *Reputation Leadership Model*: Reputation Trap, with Special case: Financing Brand-image through Low-Cost Production (chapter 3.4)
- *Systemic Model*: Selling-(out) Trap (chapter 3.5)

Before outlining these different archetypical Sustainability Traps, two preliminary annotations need to be made, which will be discussed in the subsequent chapter (chapter 3.1):

- Chapter 3.1.1: Discussion of the methodology for deriving the two building blocks – mental models and archetypical dynamic structures – for business practice.
- Chapter 3.1.2: Discussion of the Trade-off Model and its underlying importance for the other models due to being the 'historical' model.

3.1 Preliminary Annotations on Methodology and Trade-Off Model

The following chapter will discuss the methodology used by the dissertation for deriving the two building blocks of Sustainability Traps for business practice and will discuss advantages and limitations of their use arising herefrom.

This results in two preliminary aspects, which provide the underlying methodology for the elaboration and discussion of the archetypical Sustainability Traps of chapter 3.2 – 3.5:

- How the *mental models* from business practice are identified (chapter 3.1.1).
- How the *archetypical dynamic structures* (Archetypes of Sustainability Traps) are identified (chapter 3.1.2).

Each of these two preliminary chapters thereby will deal with the following points:

- *Methodology* used to derive mental models respectively archetypes in the dissertation
- *Chapter structuring* resulting therefrom for chapters 3.2 – 3.5
- *Critical discussion* of the methodology and its implications for the use of the traps identified

3.1.1 Methodology for Identification of Mental Models

3.1.1.1 Methodology for Identification

The five mental models discussed in the dissertation (Trade-off Model, Compliance Model, Efficiency Model, Reputation Leadership Model and Systemic Model) are derived from a two step approach, consisting of:

Step 1: An ***initial question***, from whose different answers the mental models are derived
from in their basic form. The answers and thus the mental models are derived on a theoretical basis, yet are substantiated through existing *literature* as well as through a *Transformation Laboratory*. This results in the following points:
  a) *Elaboration of the Initial Question*
  b) *Mental Models derived*
  c) *Additional Substantiation through literature review and Transformation Laboratory*
    c1) *Literature Review*
    c2) *Transformation Laboratory at a corporation (Plug Power)*

Step 2: ***Refining*** and ***discussing*** the mental models in consideration of ***a systems perspective***. For this end, a Polarity Profile is developed on the basis of the systems thinking principles of part II.

These two steps will be outlined in the following.

Step 1: Initial Question and derived Mental Models
a) Elaboration of the Initial Question

In chapter 2.3.1 it has been explained that a mental model is an "internal conceptual representation of an external system whose structure maintains the perceived structure of that system" (Doyle and Ford (1998: 17). The external system, whose structure is relevant in this dissertation, is that of Sustainability Traps. As outlined, their structures are built through specific interrelations of variables from the three dimensions of sustainability: economic, social and environmental. A mental model in turn relates to how an agent (here: corporation) ***perceives*** the three dimensions to interrelate, i.e. a mental model corresponds to the *belief* of an agent of how the three dimensions of sustainability interrelate.

As stated, Sustainability Traps risk to play out, if corporate sustainability measures taken on the basis of the belief of the mental model about the interrelation of the three dimensions, lead to dynamic structures, where variables of the three dimensions actually interrelate thus that they create a result which *countervails* the intention of the sustainability measure taken on the basis of this mental model.

Therefore a feasible initial question, which to depart from in order to identify mental models in the context of Sustainability Traps, is:

*"How does a corporation **perceive** measures of environmental and /or social sustainability to relate to economic sustainability (here: profit maximization)?"*

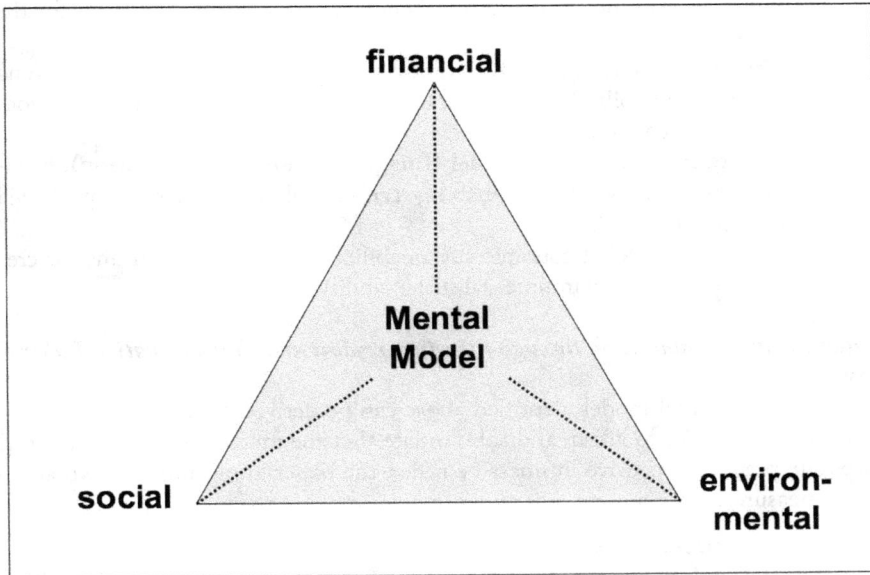

Fig. 26: Mental Model: Relation btw. Economic, Social and Environmental Sustainability
Source: Produced by the author

b) Mental Models derived

It is most important to state that the answer to this question hence constitutes (reasons) the **intention** of a *corporate measure for social and or environmental sustainability* taken, *in reference to the economic sustainability* (here: profit maximization[273]) of the corporation.

The answers to the initial question, and hence potential mental models on sustainability, are various. However it is possible to distinguish the following core groups of mental models (answers) on a theoretical basis:

- **Trade-off Model (Non-Accountability)**: Environmental sustainability and social sustainability measures reduce profit.
- **Compliance Model (Risk-Avoidance)**: Environmental sustainability and social sustainability measures do not contribute to profit, but accusation of ethical wrong doing might harm financial sustainability of our corporation. Therefore we need to comply with social and environmental sustain-

---

273 As outlined above, profit maximization was chosen *exemplary* as a goal of economic sustainbility.

ability expectations of relevant stakeholders, in order to avoid risks for the company.

- **Efficiency Model (Cost-Reduction)**: Environmental sustainability (and social sustainability) can contribute to profit, if resource efficiency goes along with cost savings.
- **Reputation Leadership Model (Image Creation and Innovation)**: Environmental and social sustainability can contribute to sales and profit via good reputation (image).
- **Systemic Model**: Economic sustainability is an inevitable means for creating social and environmental sustainability.

c) Additional Substantiation through literature review and Transformation Laboratory

As stated, the mental model identified above can be derived coherently on a theoretical basis. In order to affirm and substantiate that the models actually do exist in corporate practice and drive business behavior, the dissertation initiated two additional measures:

c1) Literature Review
c2) Conduction of a Transformation Laboratory at a corporation (Plug Power)

These two measures did not only allow substantiating the mental models identified as such, but equally provided background information for their characterization with the help of the Polarity Profile below, i.e. the development of the Polarity Profile.[274]

Both of these additional measures will be only summarized here briefly and will be discussed in-depth in the appendix M. The reason for outlining these two measures in the appendix is twofold: The commentary on the literature overview and on the Transformation Laboratory conducted is quite extensive. At the same time they form *additional* information, without which the elaboration of the mental models in the dissertation is still fully comprehensible.

Therefore in the following only a brief summary of the main points shall be given.

---

274 Thereby the literature review particularly served to substantiate the models, while the Transformation Laboratory conducted especially provided information and understanding of the characteristics of these models with respect to systems thinking. But these are only dominances. Both measures contributed to the substantiation as well as to the characterization with the help of the Polarity Profile.

ad c1) Literature Review

The work, which best backs and underlines the mental models identified is that of Griffiths, Benn and Dunphy (2003: 14ff). The authors identify a model of six developmental phases through which corporations' progress towards ecological *and* human sustainability. The phase model thus builds a historical trajectory for corporate sustainability. The authors identify the phase model through: 1) review of current empirically founded models in ecological and management literature (e.g. Austin 1999; Flannery 2001; Hoffman 1999 and 1997) and 2) additionally drawing from the authors own organizational experience and research. Through this methodology the authors identified six different phases: Rejection, non-responsiveness, compliance, efficiency, strategic proactively, the sustaining corporation.

As is already evident by the terminology, the six phases are quite similar to the five mental models of the dissertation. Thereby the phases of rejection and non-responsiveness both can be attributed to a Trade-off Model. For a more detailed overview of the correspondences and differences of these models to the one in the dissertation see appendix M.

Appendix M equally discusses further existing literature relating to the mental models identified in the dissertation.

ad c2) Transformation Laboratory

In order to gain *empirical* insight of existing mental models of sustainability and how they drive behavior in corporations the dissertation conducted a micro-world simulation.[275]

This simulation cannot be considered representative. The intention for conducting the laboratory was rather for the dissertation to gain a general understanding of how mental models of sustainability form and transform in corporations. The quality of the simulation thus is rather indicatory than descriptive. Nevertheless it was important for the dissertation to get in contact with business practice also on an empirical basis, because mental models can best be analyzed by observing corporation actions rather than through corporate statements (reports).

The Transformation Laboratory carried out is a micro-world simulation. Markets (industrial and development market) are simulated by three teams of eight participants from business practice as well as by four computer simulated corporations. Stakeholders are additionally simulated through real-life facilitators. The laboratory is especially tailored to corporate sustainability, addressing all three dimensions of environmental, social and economic satiability. The laboratory conducted was a full day session, running over a two market cycles.

---

[275] The laboratory was conducted on May 2, 2005 in Latham, USA (Plug Power headquarters).

The corporation the dissertation worked with to conduct the simulation is Plug Power, a producer of platform-based fuel-cell-systems for back-up power in telecom applications. Plug Power is based in Latham, PA, USA with branches in Washington, D.C. und the Netherlands (Plug Power 2006). Plug Power was founded in 1997 and currently has around 300 employees worldwide. Total revenues of the corporation for 2005 were US $13,5m (Plug Power 2006).[276] In cooperation with Honda Motor Co., Inc. the company is working on extending the capability of existing natural gas products to include delivering pressurized hydrogen fuel. The company is US based with international offices. Plug Power is deeply committed to the issue of sustainability and interested in systems thinking. Participants of the laboratory were employees from Plug Power as well as from their stakeholders. Thereby it was laid emphasis to include a broad basis of different personnel. A special focus however lay on employees working strategically on corporate sustainability issues, because their mental models and behavior can be considered to significantly impact mental models and behavior in the corporation. Participants included were e.g. Plug Power the Chief Executive Officer (CEO), director Product Marketing, director of Environment, Health and Safety as well as more operative employees such as Systems Engineers. Stakeholders involved people from academia, consultants as well as designers engaged with the corporation.[277]

The dissertation chose to use a micro-simulation out of the following reasons:

- Out of the reason just mentioned, conducting *interviews* is less efficient in studying mental models in-use, because the usually reveal espoused mental models. A simulation in contrast allows observing the agents in their actions.

- Studying mental models and how they drive actions in every day business practice (e.g. Action Research) usually requires long-time frames, which the dissertation could not afford. A micro-world allows to 'compress' time and space. Moreover it is feasible more feasible from a financial point of view.

The dissertation used the simulation 'Transformation: the Business Strategy Laboratory©',[278] developed by Realia Group, which has been applied and tested for ten years. It therefore is highly sophisticated and allows a large amount of flexibility. The dissertation worked closely together with Realia Group as well as with the Plug Power in order to tailor an adequate version of the laboratory. The mental models involved, the actions taken and the results, which each of the teams yielded

---

276 For further information visit: www.plugpower.com, accessed 05. March 2006.
277 For a list of participants see appendix M2.
278 Transformation: the Business Strategy Laboratory© later identified as Transformation Laboratory.

with regard to financial, ecological and social sustainability can be derived from the appendix M. The points observed by the dissertation thereby were:

- The different mental models followed by the teams, which became apparent in the team discussions as well as in their behavior in the simulation.
- The characteristics resulting therefrom, which are important for describing the different mental models.

What is more important at this point is to discuss the Polarity Profile, which the dissertation developed. Decisive for the development of the Polarity Profile are the systems thinking skills identified in part II of the dissertation. The observations on mental models, actions and decision factors made in the simulation, thereby provided further background knowledge and orientation points for the dissertation.

Step 2: Refining and discussing the mental models with respect to a systems perspective

In order to analyze the five mental models identified in reference to Sustainability Traps they need to be analyzed from a systems perspective. In order to analyze the dissertation therefore developed a Polarity Profile based on the systems thinking principles of part II in order to analyze the five mental models in the chapters 3.2 – 3.5 from a systems perspective.

A polarity profile is a well suited format to refine and characterize the mental models identified out of two reasons: First it allows characterizing each mental model within the bandwidth of two opposing poles. This is well suited, because for the dissertation there are two opposing poles relevant with respect to managing Sustainability Traps: an orthodox perspective (orthodox thinking) and a systems perspective (systems thinking). Second, the format of a polarity profile allows to quickly and easily grasping the differences between the different mental models.

The feasibility of a polarity profile for analyzing mental models is also acknowledged by other authors. Adams for example also uses a polarity profile to identify mental models in the context of sustainability (Adams 2004: 22ff). Adams thereby uses a polarity profile, which is derived from lists of adjectives, which individuals used when asked to describe the commonly held mental model with regard to sustainable consciousness in their organization. The characteristics (dimensions) of the polarity profile derived by Adams through this means are: short-term versus long-term; reactive versus creative; local versus global; separation versus systems[279]; blaming versus learning; doing/having versus being. Adams findings assorts that the foremost majority of all organizations is oriented towards the first poles of each characteristic, with a narrow zone of comfort around them (see also appendix M1).

---

[279] The term there is rather used in the colloquial sense of ‚holistic'.

The dissertation uses a polarity profile with the basic structure illustrated in figure 27, in order to characterize each of the five mental models from a systems perspective. The dissertation uses six dimensions of characteristics, which are derived from the systems thinking principles of part II.[280] Each dimension is characterized by a bandwidth of two opposing poles. These two poles contrast orthodox thinking (left side of the profile) to a systems perspective (right side of the profile) with respect to the particular characteristic. Within this bandwidth the value '3' indicates a strong disposition for a certain characteristic, the value '1' a rather latent one and 'neutral' indicates that neither of the two is applicable[281].

The six dimensions of characteristics are a *selection*[282]. But the six dimensions, - selected based on the systems thinking skills, - are sufficient to describe the main characteristics of a mental model and to discuss how these characteristics risks leading into a specific Sustainability Trap.

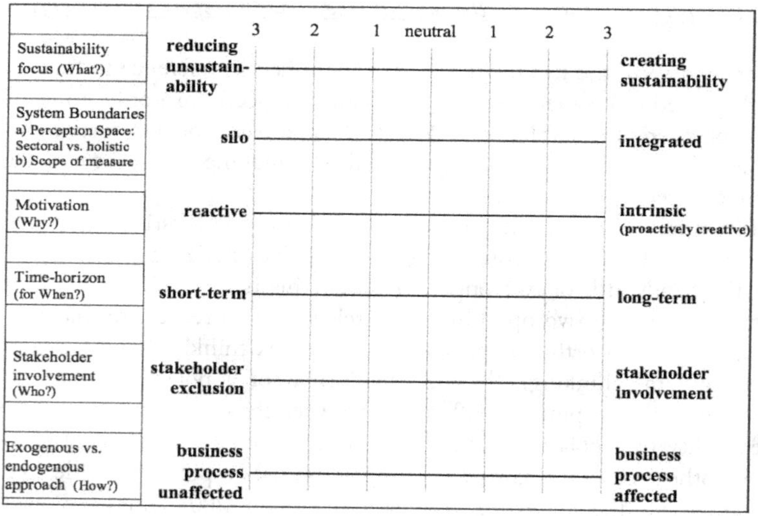

		3	2	1	neutral	1	2	3	
Sustainability focus (What?)	reducing unsustain-ability								creating sustainability
System Boundaries a) Perception Space: Sectoral vs. holistic b) Scope of measure	silo								integrated
Motivation (Why?)	reactive								intrinsic (proactively creative)
Time-horizon (for When?)	short-term								long-term
Stakeholder involvement (Who?)	stakeholder exclusion								stakeholder involvement
Exogenous vs. endogenous approach (How?)	business process unaffected								business process affected

Fig. 27: Polarity Profile: Basic Structure
Source: Produced by the author

---

280 As will be discussed, these are: Sustainbility Focus, System Boundaries, Motivation, Time-Horizon, Stakeholder involvement, exogenous versus endogenous approach.
281 For examples see respective chapters below; e.g. a value of '3' with respect to 'short-term' indicates that the time horizon considered for corporate sustainbility measures of this mental model is very short-term oriented (e.g. Trade-off Model). The value 'neutral' does not indicate being caught up between both poles, but that neither one is applicable. This is a special case that only applies for the Trade-off Model. For examples see respective chapters below.
282 That is, it is not complete and could also be extended.

Thus, the above polarity profile will be used to characterize the respective mental model relating to a Sustainability Trap in chapters 3.2 – 3.5.

The two opposing poles characterize the mental model *in-use* at a corporation, which drives corporate *sustainability measures correspondingly* and thus risk leading into a specific Sustainability Trap. The opposing poles used by the dissertation therefore will briefly be described in the following under the focus of the systems thinking skills for managing Sustainability Traps elaborated in part II.

a) Reducing Unsustainability versus Creating Sustainability?

This dimension characterizes the sustainability focus, which a corporation holding a specific mental model follows: Reducing Unsustainability versus Creating Sustainability. As has been discussed it is important to differentiate the two foci, because they result in different implications in regard to Sustainability Traps e.g. importance of limits, business model taken.[283]

b) 'Sectoral versus holistic?' and 'Silo versus integrated?'

This dimension indicates which *system boundaries* a corporation, which follows a specific mental model, is holding. The dimension is subdivided into two characteristics: a) The mental model of perception space held and b) scope of the sustainability measure.[284]

Ad a) mental model of perception space: As outlined in chapter 2.2.2.4.2, the mental model of perception space, which a corporation with a specific mental model holds, can be either sectoral or holistic. There is no bandwidth. Therefore this characteristic is not indicated by two opposing poles, but is indicates directly under the characteristic-dimension in the column all on the left.[285]

Ad b) Scope of measure: This characteristic indicates if a sustainability measure taken is rather silo-oriented or integrated. This corresponds to *system boundaries* in *space*. That is, if a particular sustainability issue is rather treated in isolation (silo-oriented) or if different sustainability measures are integrated/interwoven (e.g. environmental *and* social sustainability measures). As discussed in the systems thinking principle 'boundary judgments'[286], the *broader* system boundaries are set, the higher the possibility to take integrated approaches that reduce backfiring. Whereas in silo-oriented approaches, system boundaries in space are set narrow, thus missing out to consider backfiring risks. This second aspect is not an either or decision, but

---

283 See chapter 2.2.4.2.
284 See column all to the left, which indicates characteristic-dimension relating to the two opposing poles.
285 As stated in chapter 2.2.2.4.2 and will further be outlined, the mental model of perception space is sectoral for all models, besides of the Systemic Model, where it is holistic.
286 Chapter 2.3.2.

can vary in intensity, which is indicated by the bandwidth (silo versus integrated) with values from 1-3.

c) Reactive versus intrinsic (proactively creative)?

This dimension characterizes the *source of motivation for sustainability measures* for corporations following a specific mental model. The motivation can be either reactive, i.e. triggered by and oriented on outside pressures, for examples NGOs, customer expectations. Or the motivation can be intrinsic, i.e. driven from within the corporation. Corporations with an intrinsic motivation very often follow creative sustainability solutions pro-actively. These corporations usually are more open to *learning*, i.e. the learning process described in chapter 2.2.1.2.

d) Short-term versus long-term?

This dimension indicates which *perception space in time* a corporation[287], which follows a specific mental model, is holding and thus, which system boundaries it sets with respect to its sustainability measures: Short-term versus long-term. Broadening system boundaries in time, allows recognizing trends[288] as well as anticipating potential backfiring risks, which often occur with a delay[289].

e) Stakeholder exclusion versus stakeholder involvement?

This dimension indicates the degree to which stakeholders of corporations holding a specific mental model are excluded or included in reference to corporate sustainability measures. As has been discussed, Sustainability Traps are systemic, dynamic patterns, which are created not though the corporation alone, but through its interactions with stakeholder and dynamics arising from this interaction. Sustainability Traps therefore require cooperative approaches.[290]

f) Business process unaffected or affected?

This dimension indicates if corporations holding a specific mental model take sustainability measures, where the business process remains rather unaffected by the measures or if the measures also address core elements of the very business process of the corporation. For example conducting education and training measures at contract factories, which show unsustainabilities (e.g. sweatshops). Versus considering how the corporation's own business model contributes to create unsustainable structures.

---

287 See chapter 2.3.2.4.1.
288 See chapter 2.2.3.2 for the importance of differentiating trends and single events.
289 See chapter 2.2.5.6.
290 See chapter 2.2.5.7.

As has been outlined, dealing with Sustainability Traps requires the Pogo-attitude that the corporation is part of the problem and thus endogenous approaches.[291] The above has outlined the methodology, which the dissertation uses to identify and characterize the five mental models differentiated in regard to Sustainability Traps. It has been discussed that the dissertation departed from an initial question (Step 1) to identify the model and elaborated a Polarity Profile (Step 2), which will be used in chapter 3.2 – 3.5 to characterize the five mental models relating to a Sustainability Trap.

3.1.1.2 Resulting Chapter Structuring

Departing from the methodology described above, the dissertation in chapters 3.2 – 3.5 will discuss each of the five mental models, using a *Model Analysis* that consists of the four following parts:

- *Underlying belief about Corporate Sustainability*
  This point refers to the underlying belief about the relationship between environmental and social sustainability measures on the one side and economic sustainability (profit maximization) on the other side. These beliefs are the different answers corresponding to the initial question outlined above. In the chapters the respective belief underlying a mental model will be amended by a brief *typified line of argumentation* as it is often put forward by corporations to reason their underlying belief.

- *Underlying Model Dynamic*
  This point constitutes the mental model in the narrow sense of Doyle and Ford (1998).[292] It outlines and discusses the *dynamics* between environmental/social sustainability measures and economic sustainability (here: profit maximization), which are *assumed* by a corporation based on the underlying belief. The model dynamic represents how corporations holding a specific mental model believe 'how the world' respectively 'how sustainability measures works'. The model dynamic is thus the underlying belief that *drives corporate behavior* with respect to sustainability.

- *Model Characteristics (Polarity Profile)*
  This point constitutes the refined characterization of the mental model with the help of the Polarity Profile discussed above.

- *Relations to other Models*
  At the end of each model analysis possible relations and transitions of the respective model to the other models will be outlined.

---

291 See chapter 2.2.5.7.
292 See chapter 2.2.1.1.

3.1.1.3 Critical Discussion of Implications of the Methodology Used

Last but not least important implications of the methodology used for identifying and characterizing mental models as they arise for the dissertation will be discussed critically. The following five points are of relevance in this respect:

> *a) Three sustainability dimensions as a point of departure*
> *b) Typology of mental models is case-based*
> *c) Distinction between the mental models is a theoretical one*
> *d) Chronological Trajectory of the Mental Models*
> *e) Not focus on the one right model, but focus on Sustainability Traps*
> *f) Attribution of Sustainability Traps to one mental model is not exclusive*

These points will be discussed in the following.

a) Three sustainability dimensions as a point of departure

The three dimensional view is not without critique and discussions are raging, if this perspective is suitable for increasing sustainability (Fichter, Paech and Pfriem 2005; Norman and MacDonald 2004). Therefore it is important for the dissertation to outline why and how the three dimensional view is used in the dissertation.

As mentioned in chapter 1.2.2, the dissertation uses the three dimensions of sustainability, *not* to reinforce this perspective, but as a *starting point* to *overcome* this perspective by focusing on the interrelations between the three dimensions, i.e. perceiving the dimensions as one interactive system. The three dimensional perspective was chosen as a starting point, because it is a predominant perspective in corporate sustainability today.[293] The dissertation considers it important to depart from *commonly existing* mental models, which stemming from a historical, sectoral perspective now are seeking for some sort of relation (reconciliation) with the new concept of environmental and social sustainability.[294] Such an approach corresponds to *meeting the addressees of this dissertation (managers) on their own ground.*

This has proven to be very important in respect of learning and changing mental models as stated by many authors. "Mental models are something that cannot be imposed on somebody – every individual decides freely to accept or to reject them. Models can only be offered, and the best an author or a teacher can do is to make them as plausible as possible and to attach them to perceptions already present in the audience's mind" (Rosner 1995: 120). Adams, points out that if the change agent's starts with mental models similar to those of the receiver, then less defensiveness is generated (Adams 2004: 22). This important aspect is also underscored by Smith, who has found that in business practice, sustainability champions, who unleash their energy in direct attempts to convince others of their view, generally

---

293 See chapter 1.2.2.
294 See chapter 2.2.2.4.2.

get the opposite results. Approaches, which predict a very negative future ahead unless there is a significant change in regard to social and environmental sustainability at corporation, often lead to resistance or no actions at all from the side of the executive team. Whereas approaches, which relate aspects of social/environmental sustainability to economic sustainability of the firm, get executives to listen, because this is where their (historical) mental model sees the highest stake (Smith 2006: 31f). This corresponds exactly to the approach of the dissertation as has been outlined.[295]

b) Typology of mental models is case-based

Because the mental models are theories in-use, which drive corporate sustainability measures actually taken (corporate actions), they need *not* to be in-line with the *general* corporate sustainability strategy *espoused* by a corporation. Rather, the mental models refer to particular *cases* (*situations*), where corporate representatives adopted a certain theory-in-use with respect to a sustainability issue. Thus, when the dissertation in the following speaks of a *'corporation holding mental model 'x'*', this is an *abbreviation* and actually refers to the *corporate representatives involved in the particular case, which showed behavior that corresponds to model x*. This consequently does *not* necessarily imply that the mental model is held throughout the entire international corporation world-wide. Furthermore, the mental model executed by corporate representatives in a particular situation (case) is *not* necessarily *invariant*, but can change over time. This refers to the crucial aspect of learning and getting out of a sustainability trap as will be laid out in the cases.

Such a **case-based typology** is feasible for the dissertation, because an espoused theory might exist uniformly throughout a multi-national corporation, but theories-in-use are likely to vary, depending e.g. on cultural contexts, product type, stakeholders involved etc.[296] Identifying case-based typologies is not an uncommon method. Fichter and Arnold for example identify six types of sustainability strategies, which each refer to particular innovation projects (cases) and cannot automatically be transferred to the entire company (Fichter and Arnold 2003: 67).

c) Distinction between the mental models is a theoretical one

Furthermore the distinction between the different types of mental models is a theoretical one, based on the methodology outlined above. Making a theoretical dis-

---

295 That is, a systems perspective as intrinsic motivation to sustainbility. See chapters 2.1.3 and 2.2.3.

296 This is especially the case since the concept of sustainability is quite new to corporations and it takes a lot of time until espoused theories and theories-in-use even have the potential to be 'aligned'.

tinction is inevitable in order to conduct an analysis and to make distinctive statements.

It has to be considered however that in business practice the distinction between the five mental models is blur. The models hardly exist in pure form. Rather, in practice, a corporation – also in a specific situation - is likely to hold a blend of different mental models driving behavior. This blend (pool of mental models) is important as it bears the potential for shifting towards another mental model and slowly moving out of a Sustainability Trap as the dissertation will show. Therefore the dissertation has laid emphasis on outlining overlapping and relationships between the different mental models.[297]

However, as the business cases will show, usually one of the mental models is the *dominant, prevalent* one at a specific point in time. A corporation holding a Reputation Leadership Model for example might use eco-efficiency measures, but their theory-in-use is based on becoming the sustainability leader of its industry, which requires far more than eco-efficiency. A corporation holding an Efficiency-Model in contrast is focused on cost-reduction through sustainability measures rather than on gaining a leadership reputation on sustainability through its measures.

d) Chronological Trajectory of the Mental Models

Similar to the phases outlined by Griffiths, Benn and Dunphy (2003: 14ff, see also appendix M1) there can be considered to be a chronological trajectory of the mental models from less towards more sustainability. That is, there is a sort of chronological development from the historical, orthodox Trade-off Model over a Compliance and to Efficiency Model towards a Reputation Leadership Model, which (many) multinational corporations are running through. The Systemic Model in contrast relates to a radically different business model, based on a holistic mental model of perception space as will be outlined. Currently it can be found in small and medium size start-up companies (Mission-Driven Enterprises, see chapter 3.5).

e) Not focus on the one right model, but focus on Sustainability Traps

As will become apparent, the Systemic Model builds the end of the chronological trajectory towards sustainability, because it holds the highest promise for increasing sustainability as it is the model most in-line with a systems perspective. Because of this reason, the Systemic Model therefore is also the one, which the dissertation personally considers the most favorable for corporations to hold as mental-model in-use.

It is most important however to clearly point out that this does *not* imply that it is the dissertation' intention to praise the Systemic Model as the *impeccable* model for

---

[297] See above: *Chapter structuring* of chapters 3.2 – 3.5: Relations to other models.

sustainability. Rather the dissertation' intention is to show that every model holds the risk of creating particular Sustainability Traps. Sustainability Traps are a global phenomenon. No model is exempt from it per se. This is also the case for the Systemic Model as will be outlined (Selling-(Out) Trap).

This draws back to the dissertation' statement that 'best' intentions are not enough to avoid Sustainability Traps and to increase sustainability successfully. To stress this latter aspect is the focus of the dissertation.

f) Attribution of Sustainability Traps to one mental model is not exclusive
It is most important to state that the attribution of Sustainability Traps to a mental model in chapters 3.2 – 3.5 is not exclusive. That is: A particular Sustainability Trap can also occur in regard to other models. For example, a Quick-Fix Trap can occur not only for corporations holding a Compliance Model, but equally for corporations holding a Reputation Leadership or an Efficiency Model. The attribution made in the dissertation therefore reflects Sustainability Traps, which are especially common to a particular mental model; but the attribution is not exclusive.

The above chapter has outlined the aspects important with regard to the methodology used for identifying the *mental models* in the dissertation. The next chapter will now discuss the methodology used to analyze the complementary part of a Sustainability Trap in the business cases of chapter 3.2 – 3.5: *archetypical systemic structures*.

3.1.2   Methodology for Identification of Archetypical Structures

For each of the mental models identified, the dissertation will outline archetypical structures of Sustainability Traps, which risk occurring in combination with the specific mental model.

In the following the concept of *archetypes* will be discussed and why the dissertation uses this concept. The chapter is subdivided into the following four paragraphs:

- *Definition of Systems Archetypes*
- *Methodology used for Identification of Archetypical Structures of Sustainability Traps*
- *Resulting Chapter Design (Chapter Structuring) in chapters 3.2 – 3.5*
- *Critical Discussion of archetypes in the dissertation*

3.1.2.1   Definition of Systems Archetypes

Systems archetypes are reoccurring patterns of structure. They can be described through specific combinations of reinforcing and balancing feedbacks, which constitute a *generic* structure (Senge 2006: 92f). That is, an archetypical structure is a structure common in business practice, in the sense that it reoccurs again and again in similar manifestations. Archetypes are like "stories that get retold again and again" (Senge 2006: 93).

Senge et al. (Senge 2006: 92ff and 389ff; Senge et al. 1994: 150)[298] were the first scholars to outline system archetypes in detail using causal-loop-diagramming. The focus thereby lay on archetypes to business strategy.[299] One example is the prominent archetype of limits-to-growth, which gained popularity through the homonymous report to the Club of Rome (Meadows et al. 1972).[300] Senge et al. (Senge 2006: 92ff and 389ff; Senge et al. 1994: 150) outline twelve system archetypes, which repeatedly occur in dynamic systems in various forms. An overview and explanation of the different structures can be found in (Senge 2006: 389; Senge et al. 1994: 121ff; Kim and Lannon 1997; Braun 2002, see also appendix A[301]).

3.1.2.2 Methodology for Identification

The dissertation uses *case study analysis* to identify archetypical structures of Sustainability Traps. Sources used, thereby are existing studies, newspaper articles, corporate websites and reports. The cases analyzed thereby to the most part, use a perspective in-line with orthodox thinking to discuss the case.

In order to identify systemic traps the dissertation therefore developed and used the methodology of the following steps:

Step 1: Screening and Collecting

The dissertation screened business cases from existing empirical studies, newspaper articles, corporate websites and reports. Those cases were collected, where sustainability measures failed, showed problems or explicitly exhibited backfiring effects.

Step 2: Sorting

The dissertation took out and sorted cases into different categories, according to where 'similar stories' seem to be underlying. That is, the dissertation sorted cases into the same category, where there was an indication that a *specific archetype* of a Sustainability Trap is underlying, because in the cases of this category a similar story seems to be told again and again in slightly different manifestations.[302]

---

298 For sources of this collection of archetypes see Senge et al. 1994: 121.
299 The systems archetypes can also be applied to various other fields. (See Senge 2006: 389ff).
300 See appendix A.
301 The appendix only outlines those archetypes used in the dissertation.
302 See definition of archetypes above.

With respect to collecting and sorting of cases regarding the concept of *traps* as such, see also the elaborations in the chapter on '*derivation of the concept of Sustainability Traps*' above.[303]

Step 3: Distilling

For *each category* the dissertation then used the systems thinking principles[304], to examine and to distill out the *generics*, which are underlying the different cases. That is: The *core variables* as well as how they *interrelate* to form a dynamic structure (reinforcing loops, balancing loops and delays), which produces a specific unsustainable pattern that backfires on the corporation. This structure identified thus, constitutes the archetypical structure of a specific *Sustainability Trap*.

In order to illustrate the archetypical structure the dissertation uses causal loop diagramming.[305] Thereby some of the traps' hold a structure, which corresponds to a system archetype identified by Senge et al. and others are independent from it.

For example the Job-Creation-Trap shows behavior that corresponds to (is typical of) a Limits-to-Growth structure. It is not surprising, but even confirming, that some of the traps correspond to Senge's system archetypes, because these are behavior patterns common to various dynamic systems.[306] As will be outlined below, it is the great contribution of Senge et al. and the most valuable aspect of their system archetypes that they have been proven to exist in many different fields (e.g. business, biology, psychology). Thus it is not surprising that the dissertation also identifies them with regard to sustainability.[307]

Other traps identified in the dissertation have a structure, which does not match any of Senge's system archetype, e.g. Financing-Brand-Image though Low-Cost Production Trap, Selling-Out Trap. Nevertheless they also do form archetypes (in the sense of common patterns) for the particular field of Sustainability Traps.

Step 4: Exemplifying

: Once the specific structure of an archetype was identified, the dissertation reviewed which of the cases in the category most closely matched the generics of the archetype identified. This business case then was examined and discussed the case in-depth in the light of the archetypical trap structure identified.

---

303 See chapter 2.1.1.

304 These were elaborated in part II of the dissertation.

305 See chapter 2.2.5.

306 As will be outlined below, this is the great contribution of Senge et al. and the most valuable aspect of these system archetypes. They have been proven to exist in many different fields.

307 In the cases, where a correspondence/relation to Senge's system archetypes can be made, this is indicated in the corresponding chapter. The respective system archetype of Senge can then be found in the appendix A.

3.1.2.3   Resulting Chapter Structuring

The procedure described, has led to the following chapter design in part III (chapter 3.2 – 3.5) with respect to the archetypical trap structures:

- *Archetype of a Trap*
  - *Archetypical Trap Structure:* Identifies and discusses the archetypical structure of the specific Sustainability Trap and its implications.
  - *Dealing with the Trap:* Outlines how best to deal with the specific Sustainability Trap, reverting to the systems thinking skills outlined.
- *Business Examples:*
  - *Business Case:* Discusses the business case most pertinent in the light of the archetypical trap structure identified.
  - *Further Business Examples:* Briefly outlines other business cases, which show similar behavior with regard to the archetype identified. These further business cases can be found in the *appendix*.[308]

3.1.2.4   Critical Discussion of Implications of the Methodology Used

The following five points are important for a critical discussion in reference to the concept of *archetypes* (i.e. archetypical structures of Sustainability Traps) as it derives from the methodology used in the dissertation:

a) *Reasoning for the use of <u>archetypes</u> in the dissertation*
b) *It is the aim of archetypes to capture the generics and filter out the details*
c) *Archetypes are <u>not</u> templates that allow substituting a detailed analysis*
d) *The dissertation emphasis lies on the very <u>identification</u> of traps, not on 'solutions'*
e) *The 'family' of archetypical Sustainability Traps identified, is not complete*

a) Reasoning for the use of <u>archetypes</u> in the dissertation

The dissertation focuses on identifying different *archetypes* of Sustainability Traps rather than analyzing and quantifying one specific case in detail.

Due to financial and time restrictions the dissertation had to decide whether to analyze a single case of a Satiability Trap in all detail or whether to focus on various, archetypical structures. The first option would have the advantage that a particular case of a Sustainability Trap is analyzed in great detail. A suitable methodology would have been an extensive, complex model using a quantitative modeling technique and potentially conducting an extensive *empirical* study together with a corporation. This would correspond to the discipline of Environmental System Dynamics.

---

308 Appendices D, E, H, K, L.

As stated above already, the dissertation however followed a different intention with its work. The dissertation aimed to show that Sustainability Traps *exist as a concept, as a phenomenon*. And furthermore that it frequently remains unrecognized that it is very often *dynamic system patterns*, which drive unsustainability.

For this end it is most suitable to identify *different archetypical* structures.

b) It is the aim of archetypes to capture the generics and filter out the details

The dissertation' intention to identify archetypes inevitably requires filtering out the *generics* of each business case and to concentrate (to compress) the structure to its *core variables* and its *core structure*, which are the minimum requirement to fully explain the behavior, which can be observed in the business cases corresponding to a trap. The counter side of each archetype therefore is that in regard to a specific case there are always 'more' variables involved in a specific situation. It is indeed the dissertation' work and main contribution - by using the methodology elaborated above - to have *simplified* the archetypes as much as possible, while at the same time to ensure that they still explain the behavior observed in the business cases. This quality of being compact, but still complete, is the *essence* of the concept of an archetype and is in-line with the archetypes outlined by Senge et al. (see appendix A). As Senge states, it is precisely this quality of archetypes to distill the important generics out from the details, which makes archetypes "powerful tools for coping with the astonishing number of details that frequently overwhelm beginning systems thinkers" (Senge et al. 1994: 121). "The systems archetypes reveal incredible elegant simplicity underlying the complexity of management issues" (Senge 2006: 93).

c) Archetypes are not templates that allow substituting a detailed analysis

The core advantage of archetypes and the reason for the dissertation to use them hence is that archetypes create a basic understanding for the generics underlying a problem (a Sustainability Trap) and thus allows referring to it as an orientation point to various different situations. "As we learn how to recognize more and more of these kinds of archetypes, it becomes possible for us to see more and more places where there is leverage in facing difficult challenges, and to explain these opportunities to others" (Senge 2006: 93).

It is however important to point out that the dissertation does *not* consider the archetypes identified here to be templates, which can be imposed on any situation without further analysis of the specifics of a situation. Richmond and Richardson, criticize the Senge et al., which stress the use of archetypes as templates (1994: 121ff and 150; see also and Kim 1992; Kim and Lannon 1997). Richmond and Richardson point to the risk for agents using the templates to be tempted to 'press' a specific situation into an archetype, with the risk of missing or diverting from specific dynamics of the individual situation (Richmond 1994, Richardson 1997).

The systems structures identified by Senge et al. are built on a broad empirical basis and long-term experience, so that there validity is far more rigid than the archetypes identified in this dissertation. Therefore it is important to even more clearly state that the dissertation does *not* consider the archetypes outlined here, to be templates in the sense that once they are applied to a specific situation the analysis is *terminated* and the suggested solution[309] can be applied. Quite the contrary: When a corporation realizes that an archetype of a Sustainability Trap 'matches' its situation the analysis rather is to *start*. The intention of the Sustainability Traps archetypes in the dissertation is twofold following:

First: In their *main, scientific* intention the archetypes outline here provide ***examples*** of Sustainability Traps, which prove that their *concept* does not only exist in theory, but that there are various cases from practice

Second: With regard to the use for managers, i.e. for business practice, the archetypes serve in two ways: First, they enable managers to ***realize*** that they might be caught up in a systemic trap that backfires. Second, they point to the ***basic nature (type)*** of Sustainability Trap a corporation might be caught up in. Thus they provide a clear ***direction*** for further analysis.

For a corporation to take concrete steps to get out of a particular trap, it is therefore inevitable, to conduct an in-depth analysis, which provides for the ***specifics*** (specific variables and dynamics) of the individual situation (see Richmond 1994, Richardson 1997 above). That is, the additional variables, which an archetype does not capture, but which nevertheless might be important in reference to a specific situation. Depending on the complexity of the situation, it can be most fruitful to conduct a system dynamics computer simulation to analyze the specifics. This would be most complementary and coherent with the concept outlined in the dissertation.[310]

d) The dissertation emphasis lies on the very identification of traps, not on 'solutions'

The above explains the intention of the dissertation: As mentioned the dissertation' aim is to elaborate and discuss the concept of Sustainability Traps. That is, to prove that they exist as a phenomenon. The emphasis in part III therefore lies in the *identification* and *discussion* that there exist common patterns (archetypes) of Sustainability Traps, which risk occurring again and again, because they remain unrecognized and hold the actors prisoner.

The dissertation emphasis is *not* on providing fix, passepartout solutions to corporate sustainability. This has two reasons:

First and foremost, there simply is not a 'one right' solution to Sustainability Traps. Rather they require 'orchestrating' solutions in the sense of ***continuous learning***.

---

309 Chapter: Dealing with a trap.
310 For the compatibility and complementarity with quantitative system dynamics see chapters 1.4.2 and 2.2.5.2.

This has been reasoned in-depth in part II of the dissertation. Nevertheless this characteristic is often very hard to realize and to accept, because common business practice is dominated by 'solutions' in form of easy applicable heuristics. Understanding and internalizing the very essence of the concept of Sustainability Traps however means to realize that it is exactly *quick fix solutions*, which lead into a Sustainability Trap.

*Therefore the best 'solution' to deal with Sustainability Traps for managers is to train themselves in the **systems thinking skills** elaborated in part II, which are **specifically tailored for dealing with Sustainability Traps**.*

Second: Moreover, because the dissertation focuses on *archetypes*, providing solutions that fir a specific business case, is even less feasible. If the dissertation would discuss the case of a single Sustainability Traps in-detail and on an empirical base (see above), it would be feasible to discuss a well fitting, dynamic (i.e. learning oriented) 'solution', which fits the specifics of the individual case. As stated above however, this is *not* the intention of the dissertation.

*Therefore the chapter '**dealing with the trap**' in the dissertation can only point to general solution- **approaches**, in the sense of starting points/reference points for individual solutions, based on the systems thinking skills outlined in part II.*

Hence, these solution approaches equally are no templates: A subsequent analysis of the specific situation is inevitable as stated above and requires an individual 'solution' that fits the specifics of a particular situation.

In the focus of the dissertation therefore are not the solutions, but the identification and discussion of the traps as such and how they operate to form unsustainable patterns that backfire.

e) The 'family' of archetypical Sustainability Traps identified, is not complete

The archetypes of Sustainability Traps identified in the dissertation do not constitute a complete list of all Sustainability Traps existing. They rather are examples to illustrate the concept of Sustainability Traps in part II. It is most likely that there are far more archetypes of Sustainability Traps, which can be identified. The 'family' of archetypical Sustainability Traps discussed here, is only the tip of an iceberg (starting point) and provides potential for future research.

3.1.3 Trade-Off Model: Importance resulting as 'Historical' Model

Before outlining the different archetypical Sustainability Traps referring to the Compliance Model, Efficiency Model, Reputation Leadership and Systemic Model, - the *Trade-off Model* and corresponding traps will be outlined as a special, historical case. This is required as important underlying information.

The Trade-off Model differs from the other four following mental models of sustainability, because in this mental model, economic sustainability and environmental/social sustainability are considered Trade-Offs, i.e. a decision of either-or. The underlying belief about the relationship between economic sustainability (profit maximization) and social and environmental sustainability in a Trade-off Model is: 'Environmental sustainability and social sustainability reduce profit. Therefore businesses should not be accountable for environmental or social sustainability.' Thereby it is important to note that this view does not deny the importance of social and environmental sustainability as such. The crucial point is that this mental model does not consider improving sustainability to be a task for *corporations*, but rather that of other agents (e.g. NGOs and governments (via regulations)).

Hence, corporations holding a Trade-off Model, in contrast to the other four mental models, do not take any sustainability measures. Consequently corporations holding a Trade-off Model cannot be considered to get into a Sustainability Trap in the sense that their *sustainability measure* taken on the basis of their mental model fails and backfires on the corporation. However, the very corporate measures taken (even though – or rather *because* –) they are *not* focused on sustainability, can still cause the corporations to produce unsustainable, systemic structures, which backfire on the corporation. Common traps of this kind are the ***Job-Creation Trap*** and the ***Fighting-the-Enemy Trap***. These will be discussed thoroughly in appendix C.

Because in the Trade-off Model increasing environmental and/or social sustainability is not considered to benefit economic sustainability (profit maximization), but on the contrary to be a trade-off to it, and because consequently no sustainability measures are taken, the dissertation will outline the Trade-off Model as well as potential traps resulting from it in the appendix C.[311]

It is nevertheless important to discuss the Trade-off Model as such briefly at this point, because it is the *historical* mental model, which therefore *interferes with* respectively *underlies* other, newer mental models. Hence the term 'historical' used here with respect to the Trade-off Model is ***not*** used in the sense of overcome (sur-

---

311 Another reason for discussing the Trade-off Model in the appendix is that its model dynamic is not a mental model in the narrow sense of system dynamics, as will be outlined in appendix C.

mounted), but in the sense of being *long time established* and therefore *still exercising influence* on 'newer' models. This will be outlined in the following:

Historically, i.e. before the sustainability movement started broadly in the 1970s, the Trade-off Model was the common model in business and was accepted to be so by (Western) society. The business process of "take-make-waste" was not questioned (Doppelt 2003: 91), but considered normal. Though, from the vantage point of that time, terming it a 'trade-off' seems improper. It was less a deliberate perception of considering sustainability and profit as a trade-off. Rather there existed an ignorant indifference with regard to sustainability (see also Griffiths, Benn and Dunphy 2003[312]): Sustainability was simply not on the companies' agendas at all (at least not in today's sense of the word) and by the majority of society this was not expected to be the case either.

Today, arguing inline with a Trade-off Model has received an 'unethical touch' (see also Hart 2005: 5ff). This is, because there has been a shift in the mental models on sustainability in society and in corporations.[313] Increasing scientific knowledge about the effects of unsustainability (see e.g. Stern 2007, IPCC 2007) along with a change in social values (Svendsen 1998: 9; WVS 2005; Inglehart and Welzel 2005a and 2005b) have led to the effect that societal claims towards corporations today go beyond paying for externalities, towards actively taking on a role as a 'responsible citizen' (corporate citizenship, corporate social responsibility). These changes and corresponding stakeholder expectations were a main trigger for the new mental models on sustainability emerging in corporations, which formerly held a Trade-off Model: Many corporations are meeting some of their new responsibilities attributed to them by society in order to satisfy their stakeholders, particularly customers and investors (see Compliance Model), others start building on considerations that being more sustainable can significantly contribute to better business results (see Efficiency Model, Reputation Leadership Model).[314]

Thus, the Trade-off Model as a dominant model in pure form is loosing ground in corporations. However, because the entire economic system has developed over decades (roughly 150 years) based on a sectoral mental model of perception space with the Trade-off Model being the dominant model, the Trade-off Model cannot be expect to loose its influence over night. Society as well as many corporations is

---

312 Griffiths, Benn and Dunphy (2003: 14ff) use the term 'non-responsiveness'.

313 This refers especially to Western societies.

314 In a review of 95 academic studies of mainly U.S. companies on the relationship between corporate financial and social performance, only four of the 95 studies found a negative relationship between social and financial performance, which would support a Trade-off Model. Fifty-five studies found a positive correlation between better financial performance and better social performance (Paine 2003). For the trend of corporate orientation towards sustainbility see also Schulz, Gutterer, Geßner, Sprenger and Rave (2002).

in a phase of transition. A study (Bertelsmann Stiftung 2005) revealed e.g. that in 2005, two-third of the German companies still did not have an employee that deals exclusively with issues of corporate social responsibility. Particularly large, multinational corporations, which operated and expanded on the basis of a Trade-off Model for a long time, and which now start adopting environmental and social sustainability as new conditions to their business, therefore often still are influenced by the Trade-off Model. This is especially the case for corporations seeking to follow a Compliance Model, but also for corporations moving to an Efficiency Model or Reputation Leadership Model. As will be discussed, corporations holding a Systemic Model usually do not have a history of a Trade-off Model.

In the following chapters these four 'new' mental models of sustainability[315] will be discussed and common Sustainability Traps will be identified, which corporations following a respective mental model need to be aware of.

Thereby the chapter structuring discussed in chapters 3.1.1.2 and 3.1.2.3 will be used:

That is, first a ***Model Analysis*** of the respective mental model and subsequently a discussion of the potential ***Traps*** playing out, including a discussion of their *archetypical structure* followed by *business examples*. That is, the following structuring:

- **Model Analysis**
    - Underlying belief about Corporate Sustainability
    - Underlying Model Dynamic
    - Model Characteristics (Polarity Profile)
    - Relations to other Models
- **Traps**
    - ***Archetype of the Trap***
        - Archetypical Trap Structure
        - Dealing with the Trap
    - ***Business Case***

3.2 Traps in a Compliance Model (Risk-Avoidance)

3.2.1 Model Analysis

3.2.1.1 Underlying Belief about Corporate Sustainability

The underlying belief about the benefit of social and environmental sustainability measures for economic sustainability (profit maximization) in the Compliance Model is:

---

315 That is: Compliance Model, Efficiency Model, Reputation Leadership and Systemic Model.

"Environmental sustainability and social sustainability do not contribute to profit, but accusation of ethical wrong doing might harm our financial sustainability. Therefore we need to comply with social and environmental sustainability expectations of relevant stakeholders, in order to avoid risks for our company."

The line of argumentation, which this belief is based on, usually is similar to the following:

'Stock markets and customers do not always reward businesses, which act environmentally or socially responsible, but they *sanction* those that are accused of ethical wrong doing.[316] Thus, the wisest strategy is to do just as much as the legislator and our customers ask for, in order to avoid bad press and other risks. If risks show up, we need to deal with them quickly and efficiently, so that they do not obstruct our core business.'

3.2.1.2   Underlying Model Dynamic

As stated above, a model dynamic represents how corporations holding a specific mental model *believe* 'how sustainability works'. The model dynamic hence represents the *dynamics (the structure)* believed in, which drive corporate behavior regarding sustainability (theory-in use). It is important to note that a model dynamic as such does not constitute a Sustainability Trap. As discussed in part II, out of the specific model dynamic a corporation believes in and acts according to, can *result* specific Sustainability Traps. This is the difference between the structure held as mental model (i.e. the model dynamic) and the actual systemic structure playing out in a Sustainability Trap in the real world, due to corporate actions taken on the basis of the mental model.[317] The model dynamic, which corporations holding a *Compliance Model* believe in and act according to is, that expectations of important stakeholders are to be met, if the pressure is high enough, in order to avoid consequences, which negatively impact the business. Corporations holding a Compliance Model thus follow a strategy of satisfying. Once the issue of unsustainability is settled and stakeholder expectations are met, the corporation can 'go on with its core business'. Therefore the model dynamic of a Compliance Model corresponds to the following balancing loop (figure 28):

---

316 For corresponding research about stock markets see Litz 1996.
317 In what kind of traps corporations holding this model and acting according to it can get, will be outlined in chapter 3.2.2 and 3.2.3.

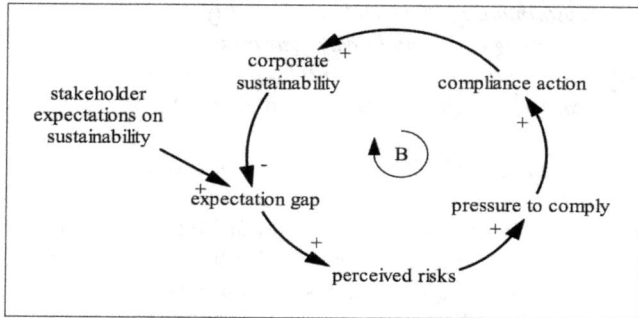

Fig. 28: Compliance Model: Model Dynamic
Source: Produced by the author

The basic dynamic, which corporations holding a Compliance Model focus on, is the following:

There is a gap between the corporation's current behavior with regard to corporate sustainability on the one side and expectations of relevant stakeholders about what the corporate sustainability of the company should consist of, on the other side. If this gap rises, so do the potential risks which the company perceives (e.g. bad press, law suits, customer boycotts). This in turn raises the pressure to comply. The company will take actions to meet the expectations and thus will be more sustainable in the sense of the stakeholders. Consequently, the expectation gap narrows and so do the perceived future risks. As the company perceives fewer risks, it feels less pressure to comply. Therefore the company will now take fewer actions towards sustainability. When the expectations are largely met and no significant risks are perceived anymore, there will be a local equilibrium and the company will not engage in any additional sustainability measures, since the external triggers have subsided.[318]

Doppelt's studies on corporate sustainability showed that this 'leveling-out' is a current phenomenon in corporations today (Doppelt 2003: 105):" All too often I find that organizations make a little progress and then begin to feel smug and content. As a result, they hit a plateau and the sustainability effort stalls."

---

[318] If the company's actions proof not to close or even to widen the gap, the company will correspondingly engage in more actions. This will happen until a local equilibrium is met.

3.2.1.3 Model Characteristics (Polarity Profile)

The model dynamics and its implications lead to the following characteristics of the Compliance Model:

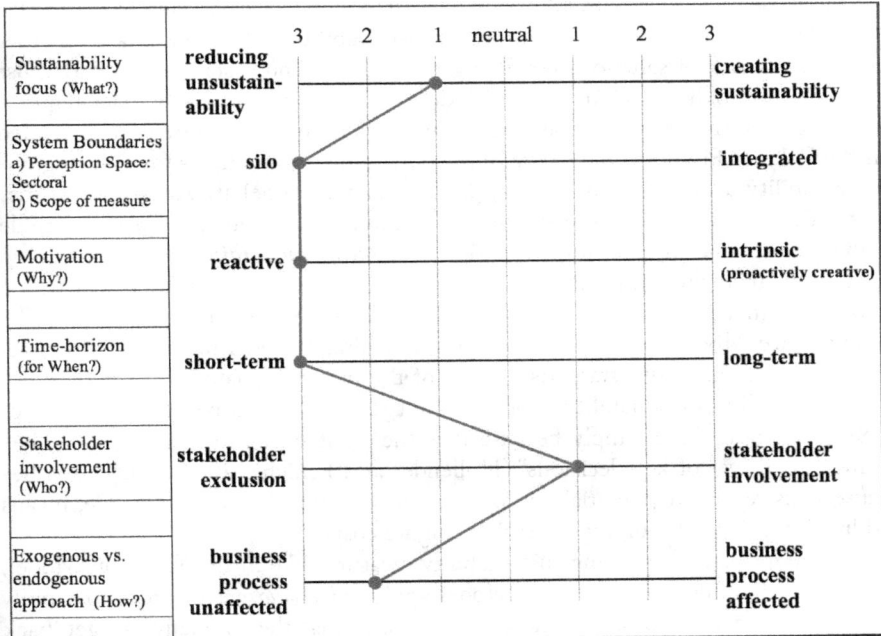

	3	2	1	neutral	1	2	3	
Sustainability focus (What?)	reducing unsustain-ability							creating sustainability
System Boundaries a) Perception Space: Sectoral b) Scope of measure	silo							integrated
Motivation (Why?)	reactive							intrinsic (proactively creative)
Time-horizon (for When?)	short-term							long-term
Stakeholder involvement (Who?)	stakeholder exclusion							stakeholder involvement
Exogenous vs. endogenous approach (How?)	business process unaffected							business process affected

Fig. 29: Compliance Model: Polarity Profile
Source: Produced by the author

The characteristics typical for a Compliance Model as they are indicated by the Polarity Profile above (figure 29) will be discussed in the following:

Corporations following a Compliance Model hold a *sectoral mental model of perception space*.[319] They consider sustainability as a condition (limiting factor) to business. In contrast to corporations holding a Trade-off Model, companies holding a Compliance Model do make *voluntary* attempts to be less unsustainable, in order to avoid risks (e.g. image loss, costs, reduction of stock value). Corporations following a Compliance Model seek to uphold what in the terminology of mining and oil industries is called a '*social license to operate*' (see Diamond 2005: 472). A representative of the oil company Chevron for example, asked what prompted the company

---

319 See left column all to the left of Polarity Profile: System Boundaries: a) Perception Space. Sectoral.

to create a large-scale conservation and development project around its fields in New Guinea, simply answered: "*Exxon Valdez*, Piper Alpha, and Bhopal"[320] (Diamond 2005: 446). That is, the main factor was the avoidance of very expensive, environmental disasters.

Griffiths, Benn and Dunphy (2003: 15), which equally identify 'compliance' as one characteristic phase in regard to corporate sustainability, state: "Compliance focuses on reducing risk of sanctions for failing to meet minimum standards."[321] Because corporations holding a Compliance Model only seek to meet stakeholder requirements, the motivation for sustainability measures is strongly *re-active* as indicated in the Polarity Profile. The important aspect thereby is that efforts for reducing unsustainability at corporations holding a Compliance Model are *minimum*, i.e. they just satisfy the minimum stakeholder expectations. Therefore the Polarity Profile indicates the value of 1, for the dimension of *reducing unsustainability*.

Risk avoidance for many multinational corporations often has been a learning process from consequences a Trade-off Model as will be discussed below. The Compliance Model can be considered a predominant model today. As Hollender and Fenichel (2004: 46) state, risk is one of the prime regulators of corporate behavior regarding sustainability. "For those not yet fully subscribed to the notion of doing the right thing simply because it is the right thing, risk management becomes the driver of key decisions" (Hollender and Fenichel 2004: 46). This is because risks represent potential costs. Attempts of being less unsustainable, means addressing risks and avoiding potentially higher costs.[322]

Therefore instead of opposing sustainability measures like in the Trade-off Model, companies holding a Compliance Model apply *quick solutions* in order to rapidly 'fix' the sustainability problem and calm critics, so that the company can get 'back to business'. Therefore, sustainability measures of corporations holding a Compliance Model usually a very *short-term* oriented as indicated in the Polarity Profile. Additionally the measures usually are very *silo-oriented* (see Polarity Profile), because they combat symptoms relating to the individual issue, where the problems happened to pop-up (reputation damage, rising costs etc.), without an overall strategy on sustainability. Once a quick-fix solution is applied and stakeholder protests subside, the corporation considers the 'sustainability issue' as settled and the corpo-

---

320 These were three main oil spills in recent history, which had not only cost the companies involved tremendous amounts of money, but also severe image damage.

321 As stated, the dissertation in contrast only refers to stakeholder expectations (particularly consumer expectations). All models, including the Trade-off Model, in the dissertation are considered to follow existing legal requirements. Respectively the dissertation does not analyze illegal corporate behavior, because it seeks to point to systemic traps that can arise even when fulfilling all legal requirements.

322 See also Stern 2007 for a macroeconomic level of this aspect.

ration to be sustainable (enough) again. Therefore a perception deeply routed at corporations holding a Compliance Model, about required sustainability in corporations is the perception, which Doppelt calls "We already do that" (Doppelt 2003: 244, see also Hollender and Fenichel 2004: 72[323]). Because the sustainability behavior of corporations holding a Compliance Model is one of fire-fighting and silo-oriented solutions, the companies each time believe that they *now* are fully sustainable once they have dealt with the problematic sustainability issue. And they consequently argue to have done a lot for sustainability by complying with sustainability expectations of relevant stakeholders.

As Doppelt found in his studies, many organizations are convinced that their existing policies and programs secure enough sustainability. In reality, Doppelt states, they do not, because underlying business models are not affected and the corporations remain in the linear take-make-waste process (Doppelt 2003: 244).

Corporations holding a Compliance Model usually seek not to affect core elements of their business process with the sustainability measures taken, because the main focus lies on meeting minimum expectations (fixing the problem/avoiding the risk) and to go on with the main business. Thus, the *business process* of sustainability measures at corporations with a Compliance Model usually remains *unaffected* to the largest extend (see Polarity Profile).[324]

Often there is a low amount of *stakeholder involvement*, especially NGO involvement. This is the case, because it most often is NGOs in cooperation with the media, which point to insufficiencies in regard to corporate sustainability at a company and thus trigger expectations of consumers, investors or even politicians for more sustainability at the respective corporation. This is often the case, if a corporation, which formerly held a Trade-off Model, moves towards a Compliance Model triggered by escalation structures with NGOs.[325]

The main stakeholder groups, which hold a sanction potential regarding unsustainabilities and corporations holding a Compliance Model seek to satisfy shall briefly be outlined in the following. This at the same time serves to outline the core aspects with regard to the main stakeholder groups, as they also apply to the other models in the dissertation (Efficiency Model, Reputation Leadership Model and Systemic Model).[326]

---

323 See there: Example provided by Dave Stangis from Intel.
324 If risks are very high and are perceived to stem directly form the business process, the particular element (issue) is sought to be fixed. However without reviewing the full business process with regard to the sustainbility issues.
325 See Fighting-the-Enemy Trap at the Trade-off Model, Appendix C.
326 Also the Trade-off Model.

Legislators

Legislators from a further stakeholder group, because corporations holding a Compliance Model seek to comply with these standards. It is important to point out however that the dissertation does *not* focus on legal requirements, because the dissertation does not seek to analyze *illegal* behavior of corporations with respect to sustainability issues, but rather on systemic traps, which also occur when legal requirements are met. Thus, the dissertation in its analyses assumes that corporations do comply with legal standards.[327]

Financial Investors

Financial investors increasingly are taking sustainability risks into account (SFI 2003). Wood (1995) points out that stock markets today not always *reward* companies, which are socially responsible, but they are likely to *penalize* ethical wrongdoing. Investors fear environmental liabilities, which are not disclosed by corporations. If something comes to light, investors might pull out of the stocks and investor trust is reduced, which makes it more difficult for a corporation to attract capital. Nevertheless the disclosure of environmental liabilities as well as the disclosure of environmental legal proceedings due to the rules of the Securities and Exchange Commission (SEC), are often *not* fulfilled: A study conducted in 2002 revealed that only 26% of the companies surveyed reported material environmental liabilities such as risks related to climate change in their SEC filings.[328] However, the group of *sustainable investors*, which pulls out and avoids stocks of unsustainable corporations, is a rapidly growing group within the investors' community (SFI 2003) and might become a relevant stakeholder group in near future.

Consumers and local communities (with media as multiplicator)

Consumers hold a sanction potential in the case of unsustainabilities since the company might face the risk of short-term losses in sales due to customer boycott and long-term risks of image damage. The media thereby serves as an important multiplicator to create consumer awareness about unsustainabilities.

When looking at production in third world countries, it is interesting to note that it often are not requests of the *local* public and of *local* communities for more sustainability in the country of manufacturing, which are in the focus of corporations holding a Compliance Model, but rather the expectations for more sustainability of *consumers in the countries of consumption* ('Western consumers'). This aspect will also play a role in the Sustainability Traps discussed in the dissertation.

---

327 This is also the case for corporations holding a Trade-off Model, see Appendix C.
328 The study examined companies from the automobile, insurance, oil, gas, petroleum and utility industry. For more information see: RFCE 2002.

Employees (including workers in contract factories)

Employees can be a further stakeholder group, driving a corporation to comply with their sustainability expectations, e.g. through strikes in order to enforce sustainability measures (e.g. health issues, family time, gender issues etc.).

One important precondition for this however is the legal right to build workers unions and the possibility of actually enforcing these rights. A crucial problem lies in the fact that in many countries these rights do not exist or cannot be enforced practically. This is especially the case in emerging and developing countries, where a lot of corporations outsource their production to (contract factories). This aspect will play an important role in regard to the Sustainability Traps outlined in the dissertation.

NGOs and International Organizations

As pointed out above already, NGOs and International Organizations (e.g. United Nations) play a crucial role in uncovering unsustainabilities and to create awareness for these unsustainabilities at other stakeholder groups (media, consumer, investor, legislator).[329] The stakeholder groups, which the dissertation will focus on, are *NGOs and International Organizations, consumers, contract factories/employees, local communities.*

3.2.1.4   Relations to Other Models

The focus on a Compliance Model usually stems from negative experiences, which companies that formerly held a **Trade-off Model** experienced personally or observed at their peers. Compliance e.g. often emerges as a result ('solution') for getting out of a Fighting-the-Enemy Trap, i.e. an escalation structure with NGOs and customer boycott.[330] Companies such as Nike, Tchibo, IKEA, or Nestlé can be observed to have made this experience. But what often happens is that in order to comply and in order to quickly get rid of 'the issue', the corporations apply symptomatic solutions, which lead into a Quick-Fix Trap (see below).[331] If this happens,

---

329 Bob Massie from the interest group CERES even states that he receives phone calls and letters form corporate employees, which inform him that they would appreciate receiving 'a little pressure' from the NGO in order to support them to foster an internal sustainability issue and thus have the argument that if the issue is not tackled, the company risks to face uproar with interest groups (Hollender and Fenichel 2004: 267). CERES is a national network of investment funds, environmental organizations and other public interest groups working to advance environmental stewardship on the part of businesses.

330 See appendix C.

331 Therefore what often can be observed is that corporations, which formerly held a Trade-off Model and got into a Fighting-the-Enemy Trap (escalation structure, see appendix C), shift into a Compliance Model and a corresponding Quick-Fix Trap (shifting-the-burden structure), as will be shown below.

i.e. corporate sustainability measures do not lead to the intended results and problem symptoms keep reappearing, this can lead to frustration and can reinforce the belief that sustainability measures are only costs. That is, the belief that environmental and social sustainability measures are a trade-off to economic sustainability risks being reinforced in this case. On the other hand, adopting a Compliance Model can be a stepping stone towards other mental models on sustainability, if compliance proves to be successful. For example a corporation, which starts applying eco-efficiency or waste reduction measures out of compliance, might realize significant potentials in cost saving and might move towards an *Efficiency Model*.

Another case, which also can be observed, is that corporations, which formerly held a Trade-off Model move only through a very short phase of compliance and leapfrog towards a *Reputation Leadership Model*. That is, a company which held a Trade-off Model and faced sustainability scandals with severe image damages, decides to make a 180 degree change in image and to become a leader towards sustainability, instead of just settling the one issue of unsustainability and 'calm' stakeholders. Such a shift can especially be observed at corporations with a strong brand image on fairness, family friendly, being 'good', high product quality etc. Being unsustainable does not match with these images.[332]

3.2.2   Quick-Fix Trap

One Sustainability Trap, which corporations holding a Compliance Model risk getting into is the Quick-Fix Trap. This will be discussed in the following.

3.2.2.1   Archetypical Trap Structure

In the model analysis above the typical dynamic targeted with a Compliance Model has been illustrated[333]: A balancing loop, where the company applies sustainability measures until risks of unsustainability are reduced.

As outlined however, these measures are often symptomatic solutions (quick fixes). Therefore, the balancing loop of the model dynamic often proofs to be the upper part (B1) of a shifting-the-burden structure[334] in which fundamental solutions are not taken[335]:

---

332 These cases will be dealt with in the chapter of the Reputation Leadership Model. One example is Nike.
333 See figure 28.
334 Shifting-the-burden is a systems archetype identified by Senge et al. (Senge 2006: 391), see appendix A2.
335 The balancing loop of the model dynamic above has been shortened to the balancing loop B1 for sake of simplicity. The assertion remains the same.

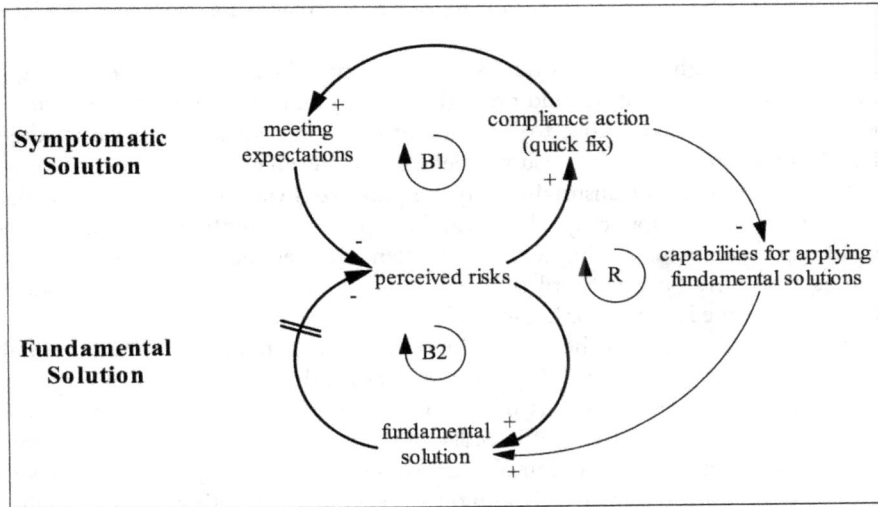

Fig. 30: Quick-Fix Trap
Source: Produced by the author

As figure 30 shows, companies holding a Compliance Model risk getting caught up into a dangerous trap: They address unsustainability only if the risks are clearly pressing. This gives them only short time to react. Therefore quick-fixes are applied. These are 'solutions', which address the *symptoms* of a (symptomatic solutions) and reduces these symptoms. As the problems symptoms subside, consumer expectations of dealing with the issue are met and the corporation goes on with 'business as usual'.

The Trap lies in the fact that, quick-fixes only reduce problems symptoms *short-term*. Because quick-fixes only tackle problem *symptoms* and not the underlying problem as such in a fundamental, holistic way, the problem symptoms reoccur in the *long-run*. Thereby the problem symptoms might appear in even worse forms: For example, if a corporation is facing a similar unsustainability issue (scandal) again, accusations of not being willing and/or capable to 'deal with the situation' are likely to increase, thus increasing the risks of consumer boycotts, loosing investor credibility and/or deteriorating corporate image. This reappearance of the sustainability problem reinforces the belief of the corporation that sustainability measures are pure 'cost factors' as their effects (successes) are only marginal. This in turn leads to the behavior that the company only adopts sustainability measures if it is forced to do so, i.e. if risks are reappearing. As a consequence, the quick-fix is applied more and more often in order to fight the problem symptom, which works out in the short-term, but in the long-turn reappears and demands for more of the quick-fix.

Corporations caught up in this trap, stay in the upper loop (B1) of repeatedly applying symptomatic solutions and fire-fighting symptoms. Furthermore it has to be pointed out that the incentive for corporations of using quick-fixes often is additionally reinforced through consumer behavior. Consumers boycott corporations, when severe scandals of unsustainability are publicized via NGOs and the media. When a corporation applies quick fixes and the problem symptoms disappear, consumer expectations for dealing with the problem are met and many consumers return as customers (at least until the next scandal), because they like the product (brand), value the low price or because of other reasons. But consumers usually also do not bother to analyze if the 'solution' applied is a symptomatic or a fundamental one. The dissertation outlines this point not to claim that every consumer ought to engage into an in-depth analysis of corporate reaction after each scandal.[336] The dissertation rather states this fact in order to outline the reinforcing nature of this trap. Corporations holding a Compliance Model tend to satisfy minimum stakeholder expectations rather than holding a strong intrinsic motivation for sustainability. Therefore, if customers return after the corporation applied a quick-fix, the corporation gets back to normal (until the next scandal).

Thus, what the dissertation seeks to point to once more is that it is not primarily 'the fault' of corporations, but that there often is a full *system*, which stabilizes unsustainabilities. There is a co-evolution between customers' behavior regarding sustainability and corporate sustainability. And what is needed is a change of perspective from corporations and stakeholders (society) alike.

Furthermore the problem of a Quick-Fix Trap can be fueled, if the application of symptomatic solutions (quick fixes) deteriorates the corporation's capability and knowledge to apply fundamental solutions (see reinforcing loop R in figure 30) as is the case in the Fire-the-Supplier Trap below.[337] In extreme cases this can even lead to an 'addiction' (strong dependence) on the symptomatic solution (see also Senge 2006: 391ff and also 399).

3.2.2.2 Dealing with the Trap

The way out of a Quick-Fix Trap apparently is to apply a 'fundamental' solution, which addresses the underlying problem, rather than the symptoms (B2). Applying a fundamental solution requires a thorough analysis of the situation. Furthermore what is needed is a holistic, integrated approach to corporate sustainability, which

---

336 The difficulty of such an analysis will be pointed out below and can best be done by an NGO if not by the corporation.
337 See chapter 3.2.3.

not only includes changing organizational processes and structures, but also mental models in-use and most importantly boundary judgments.

What makes a Quick-Fix Trap so tricky however is the *difficulty of differentiating between a symptomatic and a fundamental solution*. In order to deal with a Quick Fix Trap it is crucial to note, what causes this difficulty. The difficulty arises out of two main reasons: Dynamic complexity in time and dynamic complexity in space.[338] Dealing with these difficulties requires broadening boundary judgments. This comes down to the following two aspects important to deal with a Quick-Fix Trap:

a) *When quick-fixes are applied behavior gets better, before it gets worse. Dealing with a Quick-Fix Trap therefore requires broadening boundary judgments in time.*

b) *When quick-fixes are applied problem symptoms can reoccur in different 'forms'. Dealing with a Quick-Fix Trap therefore requires broadening boundary judgments in space.*

These two aspects will be discussed in the following:

a) First, both – symptomatic and fundamental solution – have the same effect of reducing the problem symptom.[339] The paramount pitfall of a Quick Fix Trap lies in the fact that the symptomatic solution in comparison to the fundamental solution thereby seems far more attractive in the *short-term*. This is the case, because applying fundamental solutions often requires significant investments as well as organizational changes and need time to show effect (note the delay mark in B2 in figure 30). In contrast, a quick-fix often is less cost-intensive and reduces the problem symptom in relatively short-time (no delay mark in B1 in figure 30).[340] These are the advantages (seductions) of quick-fixes.

The *problem* with quick-fixes is that *behavior gets better, before it gets worse*.[341] That is, the symptomatic solution at first 'succeeds' and reduces the problem symptom, - thus it seems to work and this even more quickly, more cost effective and with less disruptive organizational changes than the fundamental solution. Consequently

---

338 For dynamic complexity see also chapter 2.2.5.7.

339 Note that in figure 30, both variables have a negative link polarity with respect to the problem symptom.

340 In the IKEA case below for example it was far easier to shift responsibility of reducing formaldehyde in particle boards to the supplier (symptomatic solution) than to engage in costly and time-intensive research (fundamental solution) of how to eliminate formaldehyde in the entire product. The same is the case, when a corporation simply fires its overseas supplier and 'moves to the next one', if a supplier does not comply the company's code of conduct and thus produces a scandal for the company, rather than engaging in mutual learning measures of how to meet the code of conduct (see special case: Fire-the-Supplier Trap).

341 See chapter 2.2.5.7.

critics, which state that there will be 'trouble down the road' when relying (only) on this symptomatic solution have a hard stand (see also Senge 2006: 392). This is even more so the case as this 'trouble' lies in the longer-term future and current business is rather short-term oriented.

Thus, the one main challenge with regard to a Quick-Fix Trap is to resist the 'seductiveness' of only applying symptomatic solutions, because they seem cheaper and allow to quickly go on with 'business as usual' in the short-term. As e.g. the Stern review (2007) has shown, taking fundamental actions to unsustainabilities at an early stage can proof *less* costly than delaying them. It is thus here the focus of orthodox thinking of relying on short-term successes, which lies at the heart of the problem of getting into Quick-Fix Traps that backfires. Dealing with Quick-Fix Traps therefore requires the system thinking principle of *broadening system boundaries in time*.

It is important to note that the points outlined above, do not imply that quick-fixes are to avoid per se. In some cases their ability of quickly reducing problem symptoms might be harnessed, but only as a means to save time while *simultaneously* starting to apply the fundamental solution in order to remove the underlying problem.

It is when the combination with a fundamental solution is lacking, that there is a high risk of getting into a Quick-Fix Trap that backfires.

b) The second challenge, which makes it difficult to differentiate between a symptomatic and a fundamental solution, is that problem symptoms can reoccur in different 'forms'. This makes it difficult to judge, if the problems symptoms stem from the same roots and the problem is thus one, which is reoccurring again and again. This ties back to the systems thinking skill of telling apart a single event from a trend.[342] Identifying a trend, requires 'zooming out' onto a broader perception space and thus broadening system boundaries in space.[343] If a trend is identified, which indicates that a similar problem symptom is popping-up again and again, this is an indication that a systemic pattern similar to the archetypical structure of figure 30 is at play. And thus, that a corporation is caught up in a Quick Fix Trap.

Placing an unsustainability event into a larger pattern and thus realizing if a corporation is caught up in a Quick-Fix Trap thereby is easier the more a corporation possesses an overall strategy for sustainability (see IKEA case) and the more it is trained in systems thinking in order to identify systemic, dynamic structures (IKEA for example also closely engaged with The Natural Step (TNS), an NGO which intensively applies systems thinking).

---

342 See chapter 2.2.3.2.
343 See chapter 2.2.2.4.1.

A practice example for the difficulty of broadening system boundaries and recognizing a certain stream of unsustainabilities as a trend through broadening system boundaries in space, is provided in the IKEA case below. As the case will show, IKEA incrementally broadened its perception space and thus the boundary judgments on the system in question via different scandals from 1) formaldehyde in particle boards (i.e. product parts), to 2) formaldehyde in products, to 3) corporate environmental sustainability, up to 4) corporate sustainability in general (environmental *and* social sustainability).

Deliberate Greenwashing versus Systemic Traps

Last but not least it has to be stated that the differentiation between a symptomatic and fundamental solution is not always as difficult as outlined above. Rather, in some cases the borderline between a symptomatic solution (quick fix) and a mere 'smoke-and-mirror strategy', which seeks to deliberately *divert* from an underlying problem, is blur.

An example for this is Nestlé's case on breast milk substitute for developing countries, where Nestlé repeatedly violated restrictions on advertisement and promotion of the product given by the company on the basis of a code of the World Health Organization, which Nestlé signed itself (Schwartz and Gibb 1999: 42ff, IBFAN 2004: 53, UNICEF 1997). Corporations, which hold a Compliance Model and apply 'smoke-and-mirror strategies' are most likely to face Greenwashing[344] accusations and justifiably so.

Although such clear cases of Greenwashing exist without doubt, the point the dissertation seeks to make is a different one. Namely, that there also exist many cases, where similar problem symptoms of unsustainability occur again and again, because corporations are caught-up in a systemic Quick-Fix Trap. Consequently it is not necessarily always *bad will* of corporations, of not wanting to address an issue of sustainability, as NGOs frequently claim. Rather, very often it are too narrow system boundaries in time and space, which constrain corporations to address a sustainability problem in a way that the problem does not reappear again and thus to get out of a Quick-Fix Trap (see e.g. IKEA case below).

NGOs, which are not aware of the existence of systemic traps, are fast to accuse corporations of Greenwashing, because NGOs hold a larger perception space as well as a broader knowledge on sustainability and therefore have greater potential to realize the symptomatic nature of solutions. NGOs are thus more likely to recognize larger patterns and to see why a problem will pop-up again in the future, leading to a further scandal and impacting the corporation a new. Therefore NGOs are often the ones, which point to 'the trouble down the road' of symptomatic solutions. This has started being realized by investments funds as well as by corpora-

---

344 For a definition of Greenwashing see chapter 3.4.2.1.

tions themselves, which start engaging with NGOs to assess potential future risk for the corporation arising from unsustainabilities in corporate behavior (see e.g. Intel case in Hollender and Fenichel 2004: 73ff).

3.2.2.3 Business Case: IKEA

The following provides an excellent example for the difficulty of differentiating symptomatic and fundamental solutions. The case will illustrate how the company (IKEA) realized they were caught up in a Quick-Fix Trap of applying symptomatic solutions and how they successfully got out of the trap by broadening system boundaries, which enabled them to apply more fundamental solutions. The case thus will show the *learning process* the company went through, during which solutions that were considered 'fundamental' (in the sense that they eliminate a problem) needed to be reclassified as symptomatic, once the problem 'popped-up' again (although in a different format) and the company broadened its system boundaries (boundary judgments). The realization that the solutions were only symptomatic, in turn triggered the corporation to look for more fundamental solutions, until these again needed to be revised as symptomatic, etc. *This learning process can be described as one of 'going' deeper, i.e. moving from symptomatic solutions towards fundamental solutions, through incrementally broadening system boundaries.*

Key facts about first and second case of environmental unsustainability (formaldehyde)

IKEA is a global furniture retailer originated in Sweden. The company has 90,000 co-workers and operates in 44 countries in Europe, North America, Asia and Australia. Sales for the IKEA Group for the financial year 2004 totaled 14.8 billion euro.[345] In its history the company, when holding a Compliance Model, faced two shifting-the-burden structures concerning the use of formaldehyde in its products, which cost the company several million US$:

The first formaldehyde case started in 1981, when the Danish government released a new law regulating the maximum emissions allowed from formaldehyde off-gassing in particleboard (Nattrass and Altomare 2001: 50ff)[346]. Particleboard is a main component of many IKEA products. Consequently the company was affected by the law. IKEA's reaction was to simply request from their suppliers to follow the law. Hence, the company shifted the responsibility to the suppliers, without providing any further support. When Danish government tested the new law, they found that IKEA, similar to most companies in the industry, did not comply with the le-

---

345 See IKEA website: http://www.IKEA.com/ms/en_GB/about_IKEA/facts_figures/figures.html; accessed: 12. November 2005

346 If not indicated otherwise, the facts of this case are taken from Nattrass and Altomare (2001: 50ff).

gal standards. As a consequence IKEA became the focus of aggressive public campaigns. IKEA was sued by the Danish government and had to pay a fine. But what was financially far more damaging to the company, was the drop in sales: IKEA lost about 20 percent of sales in the Danish market. Additionally the company experienced severe image damage (Nattrass and Altomare 2001: 50).

As a consequence of this scandal the company decided to take more serious actions to address the problem of formaldehyde. This can be viewed as the first shift towards seeking to apply more 'fundamental' solutions. The company set up a laboratory to test its products and introduced severe requirements for their suppliers to meet. Additionally a dialogue on the topic was initiated with manufacturers (suppliers). In this dialog IKEA learned that the suppliers could not solve the problem alone, because they in turn used various subcontractors for the glue, which turned out to be the source of the formaldehyde in the particleboards. When the company subsequently addressed the glue manufacturers they still did not find a satisfactory solution. As a consequence, IKEA engaged directly with chemical companies (ICI and BASF) in order to develop a way to reduce the formaldehyde off-gassing in IKEA products. Russell Johnson, head of the quality department at IKEA, states that by finding a solution, IKEA set new standards and contributed to solutions for the whole industry in Europe (Nattrass and Altomare 2001: 51).

But in 1992 IKEA faced another formaldehyde crisis, which hit the company unexpected. This time the crisis started in Germany, IKEA's largest market, and with one of its bestseller products, the 'Billy bookshelf'. Investigative journalists from a German newspaper and television station found formaldehyde emissions, which were slightly higher than legally allowed, for the Billy bookshelf. The problem was not the particleboard itself this time, but the lacquer on the bookshelves, which was not regulated by law. But the details of legal requirements did neither matter to the press nor to the public. The case was publicized by newspapers and television stations as "the deadly poisoned bookshelves" (Nattrass and Altomare 2001: 52). The bad publicity affected IKEA around the globe and the company had to stop all production and sales of Billy bookshelves. The raw costs of tracking down the bookshelves and solving the problems were estimated between US$6 and US$7 (Doppelt 2003: 93). Additional costs arose from diverted manpower, lost sales, costs to reestablish trust at the customer side etc. (Doppelt 2003: 93). Altogether the incident cost IKEA and its suppliers tens of million of dollars (Nattrass and Altomare 2001: 52).

This crisis finally awoke senior executives at IKEA. They realized they needed to change the way the company addressed environmental issues (Doppelt 2003: 93). This realization started the move away from the pure fire-fighting mode of a Compliance Model slowly moving towards a more holistic, integrated approach. Erik Linander, former Environmental Coordinator for IKEA in Sweden, states (Nattrass and Altomare 2001: 52):" [...] from that day on, we realized that the environment is not only a technical and a legal affair but an emotional media affair. We were prepared for the technical. But when the media put in the headline 'the deadly poisoned bookshelves', I think that day we woke up. [...] If people see IKEA as a company that is polluting the environment, creating wastes or emissions, or wasting resources, then we are not living up top our mission as it is understood by people now and in the late 1980s and 1990s. That's a very strong matter."

Today IKEA is engaged with several NGO's, such as The Natural Step and the Forest Stuart Ship Council. The Natural Step framework was chosen as a foundation for the development of an environmental training program for all employees. Furthermore today there an extensive four step plan towards continually reducing environmental impacts is used.[347]

Analysis case of environmental unsustainability

The IKEA case provides a good example for the transition in mental models and structures, which a lot of companies underwent since the 1980s until today.

In the first case the corporation clearly applied a symptomatic solution. Not only did the corporation shift responsibility to the suppliers (shifting-the-burden), but it did not even care if the suppliers were willing or able to comply with the law. What the company had not realized though, was that environmental and health issues were winning great importance in society at that time. The information and risk assessment system of IKEA was not structured in a way, which reflected these risks. Therefore the company was surprised to learn that the main risks and costs did not arise out of the fine, which the company had to pay, but out of the reaction of customers and interest groups (drop in sales and image damage).

Learning from this experience, the company realized it did not only have to comply with the law, but equally with customers expectations (concerns) and reduce the formaldehyde in particleboard. But, when solving the problem, the company showed a typical behavior of companies holding a Compliance Model: IKEA firefought only the one problem in question, which was the formaldehyde concentration *in particleboard*. The company concentrated a lot of its energy and resources in order to tackle the problem quickly and once for all. This approach was clearly more fundamental than the first solution (shifting responsibility to the suppliers). By applying a more fundamental solution, the company 'dug' deeper into the issue and learned that the suppliers themselves were not the root of the problem and neither were the glue manufacturers. There simply *technically* was no glue existent yet, which complied with legal standards. As IKEA, in cooperation with its suppliers, developed a solution, the company was relieved, as it did not only reduce the formaldehyde in its particleboards, but had even function as an innovative leader

---

347 For more information see: Nattrass and Altomare (2001: 60ff).

regarding the sustainability issue in its industry. The problem, in the opinion of the company, was fixed once and for all and the company could finally go back to its 'normal business'. This stresses what was stated above: The estimation of a solution as symptomatic or fundamental is a question of defining the problem's (system's) boundaries, i.e. boundary judgments: When only looking at the problem 'formaldehyde in particleboard' the latter solution can be considered fundamental. This was the view point of the problem (system boundaries), which IKEA held. As a consequence it considered the issue as solved. The public (especially media and customers) instead held different system boundaries and were looking at a broader system. For them, the issue was about formaldehyde in products as such (no matter from which component it arose from exactly), or for some even an issue of health risks or environmental problems.

Therefore when the public at a later stage learned through the investigative journalists, that formaldehyde concentration in Billy bookshelves was higher than legal standards, the public did not at all consider IKEA to have solved the formaldehyde problem. Setting the system boundaries around 'formaldehyde values' in IKEA products in general, the action IKEA took was only symptomatic, as the company only found a solution for one component within its products (the particleboard, not e.g. for the lacquer). A fundamental solution in this respect would have been to reduce formaldehyde concentration in all components of IKEA products and in all product lines.

Analysis of second case of environmental unsustainability

Due to the severe impact the second formaldehyde case (in combination with the first one) had on the company with a loss of millions of dollars and tremendous image damage, IKEA realized that the scope of the problem (system boundaries) was not only one of formaldehyde concentration in the products, but health and environmental risks of IKEA products to the customers. That is, it set the system boundaries even broader, after the second formaldehyde case. The company furthermore understood that health and environmental risks did not comply with the image IKEA was promoting for itself in public. "As a company built on the mission to create better everyday life for the majority of the people, of course we must take environmental issues seriously" as Johnson, head of the quality department at IKEA, stated furthermore (Nattrass and Altomare 2001: 52).[348] The company realized it had to take a broader approach towards sustainability in order to match the image, which IKEA promoted from itself "to make a difference in the world" (Nattrass and Altomare 2001: 55). This broader approach proved to be a continuous process which still today is not completed yet.

---

348 See also Johnson's citations above about "waking up".

Even before the second scandal (1990), IKEA started to engage with Karl-Henrik Robèrt, founder of The Natural Step (TNS), an NGO which works to accelerate global sustainability at companies, communities and governments[349]. This happened, because Anders Moberg, President of the IKEA group realized as a private individual that "Environment is not just a new fashion, it will not just fade away, it is the new reality and we have to adapt to it" (Nattrass and Altomare 2001: 53). But, the reactions of IKEA management and employees towards the statements and suggestions of Robèrt were rather skeptical. The main problem was that although a lot of employees saw the necessity to comply with the customers' sustainability expectations (espoused theory), as a theory in-use the belief was still at play that sustainability is rather a cost factor and hinders 'going on with business'.[350] When Robèrt presented the TNS framework[351] for sustainability at an initial meeting one of IKEA's top managers responded: "Thank you very much, you have just ruined our business idea" (Nattrass and Altomare 2001: 59). He was pointing to the problem, that environmentally friendly products were known to cost more money and thus were not consistent with the IKEA idea. Therefore it was decided to create an eco-range of sustainable products called Eco-Plus line, which would be more expensive. Throughout the process the company realized however that the launch of this product range once more would have been a symptomatic solution, as there would have been about one hundred 'good' sustainable products, but people would ask "What about the 7,000 others?" (Nattrass and Altomare 2001: 60). The products of the Eco-line would have been no more than alibi products, thus also creating a danger of inadvertently creating a negative image for all the other products, which were not 'eco'. Therefore the launch of the Eco-Plus line was stopped.

Social unsustainability

In 1994 IKEA experienced yet another sustainability scandal. This time it referred to a sweatshop crisis in 1994, where pictures of children weaving carpets in Pakistan under miserable workshop conditions were broadcasted (Doppelt 2003: 93).[352] This prompted the company to set their system boundaries in reference to corporate sustainability issues even further. The company realized sustainability was

---

349 See http://www.naturalstep.org/; accessed: 08. August 2005
350 See also model analysis of Compliance Model above.
351 The TNS framework consists of system conditions which provide a scientific background of environmental problems and system conditions which indicate what need to be changed as well as concepts which provide guidance for change towards more sustainability. For further information visit the website: http://www.naturalstep.org/; accessed: 08. August 2005.
352 Although the particular pictures that started the scandal were not shot at an IKEA supplier, it turned out that many of the company's suppliers did use child labor (Doppelt 2003: 93).

not only about environmental issues, but equally about social issues. This, in combination with further sustainability issues like the use of illegal tropical wood in 1999 (Robin Wood 1999), finally led IKEA to made a shift in its mental model.

Towards broad system boundaries in environmental and social sustainability at IKEA

The company realized that everything IKEA could do to reduce its environmental impact in the rages that were potential best-sellers would make greater contribution than if the company sold 10.000 eco-sofas. This was a shift towards a fundamental solution, an 'evolutionary moment' as Nattrass and Altomare (2001: 60) call it. The company decided to take the whole range and to improve it step-by-step. The concept, which finally arose, consists of a top-down training in sustainability for all employees and co-workers through a train-the-trainer approach. Additionally the company together with TNS designed a 'stairway to sustainability', which includes four major steps or levels towards sustainability. The steps range from reducing harmful substances in products (level 1), over a sustainable product-lifecycle (level 2 and 3) to sustainable sourcing (level 4). At each level, a lot of small green steps need to be taken. Thereby IKEA targets to become known as an environmentally responsible company not by advertising itself as a green company, but by actually being one (Nattrass and Altomare 2001: 71). The company is extremely cautious not to take any actions that could be misinterpreted as Greenwashing. For example the informative brochure 'Social and Environmental Responsibility', which informs about IKEA's sustainability policies and actions, is not laid out in the stores, but is available for customers who express interest on how IKEA is dealing with sustainability issues (IKEA 2004).

That is, IKEA today can be considered heading towards a (Reputation) Leadership Model to sustainability. But they do not communicate their sustainability measures aggressively. They rather can be considered to move towards being a 'silent' leader, seeking to avoid a Reputation Trap[353]. The company is aware that it still has a long way to go to climb the full staircase and become a leader, which is fundamentally sustainbale. The company now nevertheless has gained a far clearer understanding of its inconsistencies and it has an overall concept of how to become more sustainable. As Nattrass and Altomare report from their conversations with IKEA co-workers (Nattrass and Altomare 2001: 74):" Moving toward sustainability is recognized as a very long path, consisting of thousands of small green steps. Often it is a frustrating road when the pace of change does not seem to match the urgency that is felt by many people." And also Anders Dahlvig, CEO of IKEA, concludes his message on the company's report on a humble note: "Although we are pleased with the rate of development, a lot of work still remains to be done. It is a process that

---

353 For a Reputation Trap see chapter 3.4.2.

consists of many small steps, and with each one we learn, improve and raise our ambitions" (IKEA 2005: 7).[354]

It was also crucial for the company to realize that the more fundamental a solution it seeks to apply, the more this requires a change in mental models. Dahlvig states: "We know how difficult it is to change minds and break habits, but we believe that progress can be made and goals can be reached by moving forward step by step" (IKEA 2005: 7).

3.2.3 Special Case: Fire-the-Supplier Trap

3.2.3.1 Archetypical Trap Structure

In the following a special case of a Quick-Fix Trap shall be outlined. This special form of a quick-fix can be observed so many times for companies holding a Compliance Model that the dissertation gave it a special name 'Fire-the-Supplier': As a reaction to customer expectations on social sustainability in contract factories ('sweatshops'), especially in emerging and developing countries, corporations started to launch 'code of conduct'. These codes entail directives for contract factories regarding social sustainability, such as working contracts, working hours, disciplinary methods, discrimination, health and safety, freedom of association and collective bargaining, and in some cases also environmental issues. Multinational corporations require their contract factories to meet with their code of conduct. Often an 'external' auditor is assigned to control the compliance, but the independence and effectiveness of such audits are disputed (Mamic 2004, CCC 2005b).

If non-compliance with a code of conduct at a contract factory is revealed and publicized e.g. by an NGO, and this leads to a scandal for the multinational, a common behavior of corporations holding a Compliance Model, is to quit working relations with the supplier and to move to the next one. This can be represented in the shifting-the-burden structure below:

---

354 The IKEA 2005 Report is the latest Report available as of 23. February 2007.

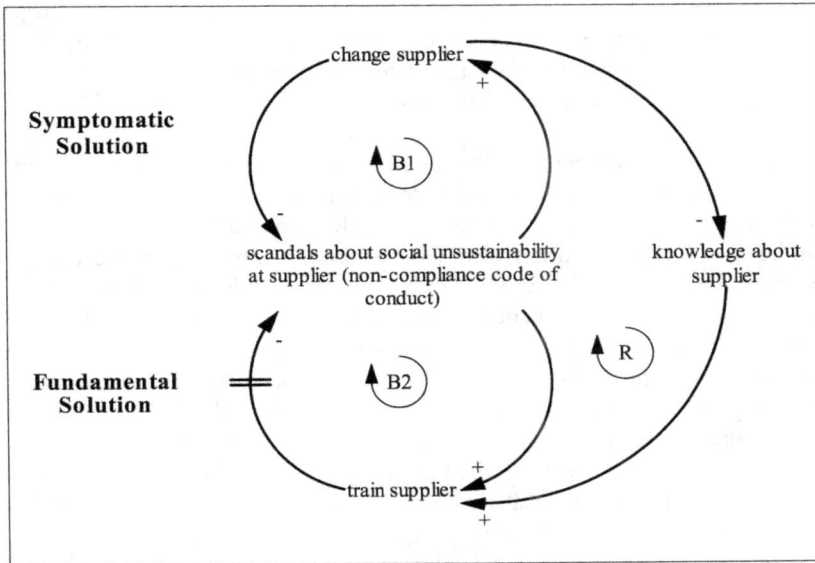

Fig. 31: Fire-the-Supplier Trap
Source: Produced by the author

If the non-compliance with a code of conduct at a contract factory (supplier) leads to a scandal for the multinational corporation sourcing from the supplier, the corporation can demonstrate to 'rule with an iron fist' by ending working relationships with the supplier. Such a behavior suggests to consumers that the corporation is true to its code of conduct and punishes non-compliance hard. – A behavior, which also quite frequently is expected and claimed for by customers, who are horrified by the pictures of child labor or physical abuses.

But quitting the supplier often proves to be a symptomatic solution (B1). This is - among others[355] - the case, because social unsustainability is not a single incident, but a broad phenomenon in developing and emerging countries, because of different legal standards, less awareness and knowledge about the issue, less financial resources as well as a different organizational culture in many contract factories. Therefore 'firing' a supplier is likely to backfire on the workers as well as on the corporation itself:

If the factory has to close down because it lost large orders from the multinational corporation, this leaves the workers unemployed. This problematic is also been re-

---

[355] See below: Very often cost-pressures resulting from the business model of the multinational itself is another main reason.

vealed by Mamic (2004: 205) in her studies for the International Labour Organization. She states that sanctions are important to enforce compliance. But, "if orders are cut to a non-compliant factory, the factory may be forced to shut down, and the now unemployed workers are likely to be worse off than before" (Mamic 2004: 205).

Furthermore for the corporation itself, a new scandal is likely to pop-up at the next supplier, because he usually works under similar conditions. Thus, changing the supplier in this case is a mere shifting-the-burden structure.

A more fundamental solution would be to engage into cooperative change and training programs with the supplier.[356] The problem of the Fire-the-Supplier Trap of not applying more fundamental training relationships with the supplier, is fueled by the fact that once the corporation quits working relationships with a supplier which faced a scandal, the corporation looses the knowledge about the supplier, which it gained in the working relationship. Additionally NGOs, which reveal non-compliances with codes of conducts often execute intensive studies and thus provide the corporation with detailed information about the specific shortcomings of the supplier. But if the relationship is quitted, this knowledge, which is most valuable to develop tailored training programs at this particular supplier, is lost. For engaging into a more fundamental solution with the next supplier this knowledge will have to be build anew. Hence possibilities of applying a fundamental solution are deteriorated even more by this behavior (see reinforcing loop R in figure 31).

3.2.3.2 Dealing with a Fire-the-Supplier Trap

In order to assess how best to deal with a Fire-the-Supplier Trap it is crucial to make a thorough analysis. As has been stated above, the 'tricky' aspect of Quick-Fix Traps, which the Fire-the-Supplier Trap is a special case of, is that an agent risks moving from one quick fix into the next quick fix, because of the difficulty to differentiate symptomatic and fundamental solutions. Thus, an assumed *fundamental* solution can turn out to be just a further *symptomatic* solution, with the problem (scandal of social unsustainability at contract factories) popping-up again. As outlined above, this moving 'deeper' into fundamental solutions is a learning process. This is also the case for the Fire-the-Supplier Trap. Here, basically four 'solutions' of how to deal with the trap can be distinguished:

a) *Applying a code of conduct*
b) *Fire the supplier*
c) *Change and train the supplier*
d) *Change sourcing practice and business model of the buyer*[357]
e) *Change consumer behavior*

---

356 See below, 'dealing with the trap'.

These different 'solutions' shall be dealt with in the following:

a) Applying a code of conduct

The very act of applying a code of conduct can be considered a quick-fix solution to comply with customer demand for social sustainability. Companies thus can point to the document and state that they are requesting their contract factories to apply to these standards. Hence, responsibility for social sustainability is shifted to the suppliers.

Additionally most corporations today also assign an external auditor to inspect compliance with the code of conduct. But the effectiveness of such audits is heavily disputed (CCC 2005b, Mamic 2004). First, because most auditing firms are contracted by the sourcing company, their independence is disputed. Second, full results of the audits usually are not publicized. Third, as will be shown in the business case below, workers are trained (or harassed) in what to answer in auditor interviews. The main reason for doubting the effectiveness of such audits in the view of the dissertation however lies in what is stated in the CCC report (CCC 2005b: 81): "But even a quality audit in and of itself can never produce change." That is, even the best, sincere and independent audit does not abolish a single case of unsustainability as long as there are no programs established of what steps to take to remedy the unsustainabilities. This is why the CCC even explicitly refers to applying a code of conduct with mere auditing as a 'quick fix' in the title of its report ("Looking for a Quick Fix", CCC 2005b).

b) Fire the supplier

Since establishing codes of conducts along with external auditors, proved not sufficient to stop scandals in contract factories, sourcing companies started to 'take action', by rigorously quitting working conditions with contract factories in the case of a scandal. The possibility of quitting the orders was used as a sanction potential to 'enforce' the code of conduct. Corporations could prove thus prove to consumers that they are willing to put the sanction (punishment) into effect by actually ending business relationships with contract factories, where cases of non-compliance are revealed.

At first sight this might seem as a more fundamental solution to eliminate scandals of social unsustainabilities, because now there is a code of how to comply and a sanction potential in the case of non-compliance. As the dissertation however seeks to show this thinking is a trap. As outlined above, firing the supplier proves to be a symptomatic solution, with backfiring in both respects, - for the workers and the corporation. Thus, how to deal with this trap? One important step is the implemen-

---

357 This will be dealt with in chapter 3.4.3.2 (Financing Brand-image through Low-Cost Production).

tation of change and training programs at the supplier as will be outlined in the following.

c) Change and train the supplier

As has been outlined above, a thorough audit needs to be coupled with measures of how to improve the situation at the supplier through change and training programs rather than quitting the supplier. These measures should be co-developed and ideally also include further stakeholders such as unions or NGOs. The CCC (2005b: 74ff) in its report proposes the following measures, which are most feasible with regard to the requirements outlined for addressing the trap:

- **Partnership with local organizations**: Unions and NGOs should not only be involved in all phases of the *implementation* of the code of conduct, but should already be consulted on how best to *organize* the entire process (planning phase).
- **Grievance and complaints mechanisms**: Complaints mechanisms provide a way to ensure direct input at any time from workers and supplement the limitations of 'snapshot auditing'. Thereby two components should be in place: A proper worker grievance handling system at the level of the supplier, and mechanisms by which workers or their representatives can take a complaint up to the level of the buyer, if it is not solved by the supplier.
- **Education and training**: In order for codes of conduct to be effective, workers need to be aware that they exist, about their rights enshrined in them and about the means available to exercise these rights. This starts by translating the codes making them available, e.g. through pasting them to the wall or through leaflets. Furthermore in-depth education and training programs need to be launched, which address and explain issues of the code of conduct, especially freedom of association (e.g. building labor unions in some countries is illegal). Thereby it proved to be crucial, how these programs are designed: First, what kind of organization gives the training and how it is delivered. Thereby workers tend to trust education delivered by their own peer group more than e.g. an international auditing or training company. Alternatives could be representatives from local unions or local NGOs. Furthermore workers are provided with the time necessary to participate in such programs, and re-assurance that they will not lose their jobs if they get involved.
- **A pro-active approach to freedom of association:** One main barrier to effective implementation of codes of conducts is the lack of comprehensive and accountable means of engaging workers into the process. A channel of representation of workers' problems through their own representatives, e.g. unions, is absent. Therefore the process of external auditing and dealing with its results

usually becomes a management issue between the suppliers and the buyers only. For an effective implementation of a code of conduct, companies therefore need to undertake concrete activities to promote freedom of association, collective bargaining and credible worker representation, such as: Improve communication channels between workers, review supplier policies and procedures (hiring, promotions, termination, disciplinary, and grievance), execute open communication of these policies to national governments, consult with external sources about the history of labor relations in the area, take into account culture specific gender issues.

- *Effective remediation (corrective action):* Remediation plans should be developed based on an analysis of root causes of workers rights violations and their impact. This process should involve workers, management and buyers. The implementation of remediation plans is a joint responsibility of suppliers and buyers. Thereby buyers need to create an environment, which enables remediation to take place (see also below).
- *Transparency:* The CCC asserts that often transparency is lacking in both, the garment industry and the auditing industry: Workers and their organizations should have access to audit reports and remediation plans. Buyers should publish whom they hire to audit which factory and how much they pay for the audit. Audit firms should put up a list of their clients, report on what methods they use and how they train their staff. As the CCC states: "Transparency is crucial to build credibility among stakeholders and the public at large, to improve the quality and effectiveness of auditing, to make complaints mechanisms work, to minimize the inefficient use of resources and in general to improve the compliance mechanisms presently under development" (CCC 2005b: 82).

The measures outlined above reveal what fundamental a change these 'training and change programs' require, in contrast to simply fire-the-supplier. For corporations holding a Compliance Model these measures constitute major steps, which actually succeed in reducing unsustainabilities at the supplier to some respect.

d) Change sourcing practice and business model of the buyer

However, as will be outlined in chapter 3.4.3, training and change programs at the suppliers' remain symptomatic solutions in respect of fully eliminate unsustainabilities, in particular social unsustainability. Therefore as will be outlined in chapter 3.4.3, brand-sensitive corporations, which seek to become a sustainly responsible leader (Reputation Leadership Model), need to go beyond changes at their *suppliers* towards analyzing how their *own business behavior (purchasing practices, business model)* contributes to unsustainabilities at their suppliers. This issue will be discussed in depth in the chapter of the Financing Brand-Image through Low-Cost Production Trap, where a corporation's very business model hinders the company to reach the sustainability reputation desired.

e) Change consumer behavior (and special role of retailers/discounters as intermediaries)

Customers themselves form part of the dilemma outlined, by demanding to decrease prices on the one side, while at the same time increasingly claiming for corporations to meet sustainability standards. This dilemma is passed onto the corporations and via them to the suppliers: Many customers today expect corporations to assure social sustainability on the one side, but on the other side have strong demand for low cost products. A survey conducted by Harris Interactive, for example, interviewed 2,594 Americans aged 18 or older and found that 79% of Americans take corporate citizenship into account when deciding whether to buy a particular company's product, with 36% considering it an important factor. The Cone Corporate Citizenship Study revealed that 86% of consumer would switch to brands associated with a good cause (behavior), but under the condition that price and quality were similar (Cone Corporate Citizenship Study 2004, see also Holliday, Schmidheiny and Watts 2002: 175; Diamond 2005: 475f).[358]

There thus also is a discrepancy on the side of consumers, who expect sustainability on the one side, but are not willing to pay more for it. The 'dilemma' of consumers, who increasingly demand sustainable, fair-trade products, but who are not ready to pay significantly more for them, is particularly high for retailers (discounters), which are focused on the low-price sector (e.g. discount-supermarkets or fashion stores).[359] Furthermore these retailers usually trade large quantities and source from multiple suppliers, which often do not have the knowledge, technology or capacity of providing sustainable products on a large scale. Therefore many retailers are 'sitting between several seats' and retailers, which do not have adopted a clear strategy regarding sustainability, risk to be overstrained with this intermediary position.

On the other hand this position offers retailers a key role regarding sustainability, because they act as an intermediary between consumers and manufacturers: On the one side they have the opportunity to influence more stainable consumer choices through the products they sell as well as how they position eco-products on their shelves and points-of-sales. Consumer demand on the other side can influence the retailers' decisions on what to list and where to source. For example as a response to

---

358 For aspects of double moral standards in consumerisms, see also Priddat 1998.
359 The dissertation therefore has picked an example of a retailer for the business case below.

increasing consumer concerns about food safety and animal treatments, a lot of supermarkets are listing organic products (Jundt 2004).[360]
Corporations ultimately will need not only to involve suppliers, but equally their
consumers in 'training and education'. But, corporations holding a Compliance
Model are unlikely to promote consumer communication about sustainability at a
broad level, because their approach is to comply with minimum expectations of
consumers regarding sustainability. The aspect of consumer behavior will further be
addressed in the chapter of the Reputation Model (chapter 3.4.3.2) and the Systemic Model (chapter 3.5.2), as consumers on their side hold the power and responsibility to develop a culture of moral consumerism, which in turn influences
corporate behavior (see also Koslowski and Priddat 2006).

3.2.3.3 Business Case: Tchibo

Originally specialized on selling coffee, the German retail chain Tchibo GmbH
(Tchibo/Eduscho) has diversified into the non-food sector and sells consumer
goods and services in its shops. These range from clothing, electronic equipment,
kitchen supply to holidays and insurances.[361] Thereby the company follows a low-
price strategy, selling the non-food products under the company's own brand,
TCM. Tchibo is the fifth largest coffee producer in the world and the second
largest producer of consumer goods in Germany after Nestlé (CCC 2006). Tchibo
is known for low-prices or 'value-for-money offers' as the company terms it on their
website.[362] One of Tchibo's highest aims is customer satisfaction, "thereby fulfilling
the trust they [note of author: customers] invest in us".[363] In order to address customer sustainability expectations with respect to its non-food products the company launched a special Non-Food Code of Conduct. Tchibo's non-food products
are produced in Germany and abroad. As the company's website states, every supplier is contractually obliged to uphold Tchibo's Non-Food Code of Conduct.
These standards are audited regularly by an independent external assessor[364]. The
following provides an excerpt of the company's Non-Food Code of Conduct as at
October 2005[365]:

---

360 See also chapter 3.5.
361 See: http://company.tchibo.de/tccom_001.jsp; accessed: 18. October 2005.
362 See: http://company.tchibo.de/company/tccom_103.jsp; accessed: 18. October 2005.
363 http://company.tchibo.de/company/tccom_103.jsp, accessed: 18. October 2005.
364 The independence of assessor is disputed, see e.g. CCC 2006.
365 See: http://company.tchibo.de/company/tccom_103.jsp; accessed: 18. October 2005. As
will be outlined below, the company launched a new more stringent code of conduct on July
2006.

"Humane Treatment
Employees must not be subjected to physical or psychological punishment, as this would impair their human dignity.

Working Hours
Working hours must not exceed legal maximum values and/or country- or job-specific values. Overtime is to be treated and recompensed separately.

Right to Peaceful Assembly and Association
The legal right of employees to form organizations of their choice, to join them or to bargain collectively must not be diminished in any way"

The Clean Clothes Campaign (CCC), an international NGO focused on improving working conditions in the global garment and sportswear industries, assigned its Bangladeshi partner organization, Alternative Movement for Resources and Freedom Society (AMRF), to conduct a study on Tchibo's contract factories in Bangladesh in 2004 (CCC 2006). The study was based on interviews with factory owners, supervisors, import/export companies as well as representatives from labor unions and NGOs. Furthermore 25 workers were inquired 'backdoor', who previously had or currently were working for contractors producing for Tchibo (CCC 2006: 17)[366]. The study revealed that at the contract factory ,Urmi Garments' 40 workers had been laid of in 2003, because they had organized in a labor union. Furthermore working hours were 80-90 hours per week, with women working overtimes up to three o'clock in the morning. Going to the bathroom required previous registration and longer waiting. Supervisors where threatening and harassing workers (CCC 2006: 19). Confronted with the accusations Tchibo admits to have sourced from Urmi Garments until 2000, where these social unsustainabilities were at place. The company however states that it had quit working relationships with Urmi Garments in 2000 due to its working conditions, so it had no stake in the issue that so many workers were laid off for joining a labor union in 2003. The study in contrast quotes workers who claim to have sewed in Tchibo's TCM Label in products at Urmi Garments up to August 2003 (CCC 2006: 10). A large range of protests were launched by the CCC, including press releases and protest campaigns in front of stores.

When exactly (in the year 2000 or 2003) Tchibo quitted the supplier due to unsustainability issues, is not the relevant point for the dissertation. Rather it is crucial to note *that* Tchibo quitted the supplier, so that unsustainabilities of this factory could no longer be attributed to Tchibo.

---

366 According to the CCC report, it was extremely hard to interview workers, as they were very scared to talk and had to work long hours, so that it was hard to get hold of them for a private conversation (backdoors).

In August 2004 Tchibo then faces a new, but similar scandal with its supplier 'Basic Apparel' in Bangladesh, which is been revealed in October 2005 through Monitor (2005)[367] and the CCC (2006: 26 and 11f). A worker from 'Basic Apparel', when interviewed backdoor about her experiences with controls of external auditors commissioned by Tchibo at her factory, states that controls may come unannounced to the supplier, but the people the controllers are allowed to talk to, are people, who previously have been instructed by the factory's supervisor accordingly (Monitor 2005). Further secret interviews reveal further non-compliances with the code of conduct: A woman reports, she was beaten when she did a mistake, because of her inability to read. A young boy states he was insulted and had to stand on a table for half an hour, because he made an error. He also indicates that sometimes the wage of the whole day is not paid, when mistakes are made. Another woman, Rina Begum, had worked for Tchibo at Basic Apparel. She was one of many workers, which in August 2004 had demonstrated in front of the factory owner's house for higher wages. Soon the police drove up and started to arrest the demonstrators, thereby several were hurt. Rina Begum was put to jail for nine days. When released, she returned to the factory in order to continue her work. But she was not allowed to. Furthermore the factory management had made a poster with photos of the protesters and had posted them at other factories, indicating that these were protesters. She did not find work at another factory at the time of the Monitor report (Monitor 2005, see also CCC 2006). Altogether around 230 workers were laid of by Basic Apparel in August 2004, because they organized in a labor union and protested against their working conditions (CCC 2006: 26).

When Monitor (2005) confronts Tchibo with their findings in the documentation, the company is not ready for a full interview, but launches the statement that the company will review the accusations and will stop sourcing from Basic Apparel during this process.[368]

This statement suggests that Tchibo intends to deal with the issue once more with the behavior of firing-the-supplier, if Tchibo's own investigations would support the accusations. While the Tchibo management is still elaborating how to deal with the Basic Apparel issue, yet another case of unsustainability is reported by the CCC. This time Tchibo's Bangladeshi supplier Factory A-One laid off 219 workers in September 2005, because they established a Worker Representation and Welfare Committee in their factory to lobby for better working conditions (CCC 2006: 26 and 11f).

In December 2005 Tchibo meets with the CCC for the third time and in the light of the accumulation of issues of social unsustainability, declares a paradigm shift

---

367 The facts of this particular case are based on a documentation from the news magazine Monitor, if not indicated otherwise. (MONITOR 2005).

368 This statement was reported in the TV-documentary of Monitor (not on the webpage).

(CCC 2006: 11f): The representative of the newly established department for 'Corporate Social Affairs' declares that Tchibo would now actively seek to support its contract factories in meeting the code of conduct. First steps will be to reemploy the workers laid of at Basic Apparels and Factory A-One. Then steps will have to be developed with the owner of the factories, of how to promote working conditions. Furthermore social responsibility should be anchored in Tchibo's organizational culture itself (CCC 2006: 12). In March 2006 the CCC and Tchibo meet for the fourth time, where Tchibo presents its plans for establishing social responsibility within the organization's culture as well as in its communication. As for contract factories, Tchibo declares to pay a bonus to suppliers, which meet the code of conduct and to incrementally reduce its numbers of suppliers in order to concentrate on a few factories with which to engage into longer-term working and training relationships (CCC 2006: 12). In July 2006, Tchibo has launched its new, more stringent and precise code of conduct on its webpage.

Thus, although Tchibo still has a very long way to go, the acknowledgement that severe violations of Tchibo's code of conduct in their contract factories, is a reoccurring pattern (trend) - and not single events, which consequently cannot be solved by quitting working relationships with a particular supplier - is a step toward for moving out of the trap and thus out of reoccurring sustainability scandals. Taking over responsibility in so far as to stick to the suppliers, where scandals occurred, and to engage in longer-term training relationships with them in order to meet the code of conduct is an important measure for addressing this Sustainability Traps as outlined above. But, as also stated above, mere training of the suppliers will stay a symptomatic solution as long as the business model of Tchibo is focused on 'low-cost' pressure. According to the CCC, Tchibo negotiates prices with their supplier every six month anew. Thereby Tchibo assigns more and more of its orders via Internet-auctions, where the cheapest bidder (supplier) gets the order (CCC 2005c: 7). The relevance of the company's *own* behavior for their unsustainability problems as well as for resulting image-damaging scandals (Pogo-attitude), seems far of being recognized and addressed at Tchibo.

Appendix D provides an overview of further business examples of Quick-Fix Traps (including Fire-the-Supplier) in order to underline the broad diffusion of these traps in business.

3.3 Traps in an Efficiency Model (Cost-Reduction)
3.3.1 Model Analysis
3.3.1.1 Underlying Belief about Corporate Sustainability
The underlying belief about the benefit of social and environmental sustainability measures for economic sustainability (profit maximization) in the Efficiency Model is:

"Environmental sustainability (and social sustainability) can contribute to profit, if resource efficiency goes along with cost savings."

The line of argumentation, which this belief is based on, usually is similar to the following:
'Investing in eco-efficiency in the sense of a reduction of material input and by-products (e.g. waste, pollution), actually reduces costs while contributing to (environmental) sustainability. It is on these win-win opportunities that businesses need to focus on. That is, making (saving) money by doing 'the right thing'. Technological and process *innovation* thereby are key factors for harnessing this potential.'

3.3.1.2 Underlying Model Dynamic
The model dynamic, which corporations holding an Efficiency Model (resource efficiency) *believe* in and *act* according to (theory in-use) is that of the following reinforcing loop (R1):

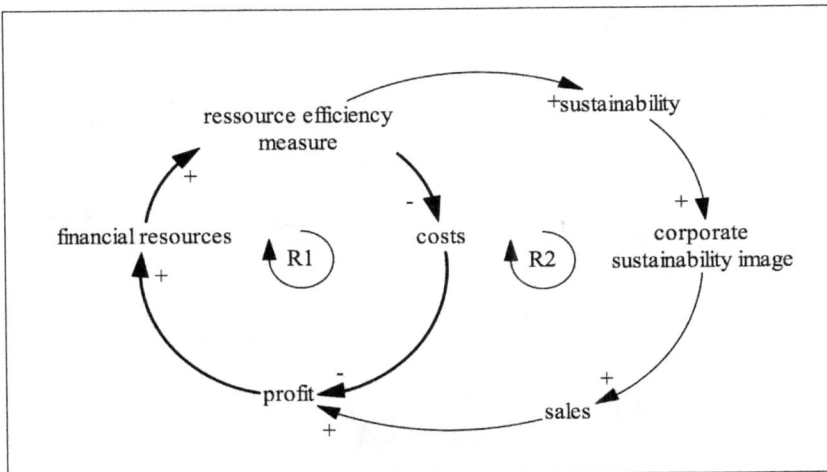

Fig. 32: Efficiency Model: Model Dynamic
Source: Produced by the author

The main loop is R1, which assumes that investing into resource efficiency, i.e. reduction of material input required, reduces costs and augments profits (ceteris paribus). This leads to additional financial resources, which can be invested into additional innovation and/or technology for reducing resource efficiency.

R2 illustrates an additional loop, which is often strived for as a beneficial 'side-effect' in combination with resource-efficiency: Resource efficiency in the sense of a reduction in material inputs of renewable and non-renewable natural resources, leads to more (environmental) sustainability, which augments the sustainability image of the corporation, which (after a delay) might lead to increased sales, thus contributing to profit additionally. Hence, R2 relates to (combines with) a Reputation Leadership Mental Model.[369]

3.3.1.3 Model Characteristics (Polarity Profile)

The Efficiency Model can be considered to hold the following typical characteristics:

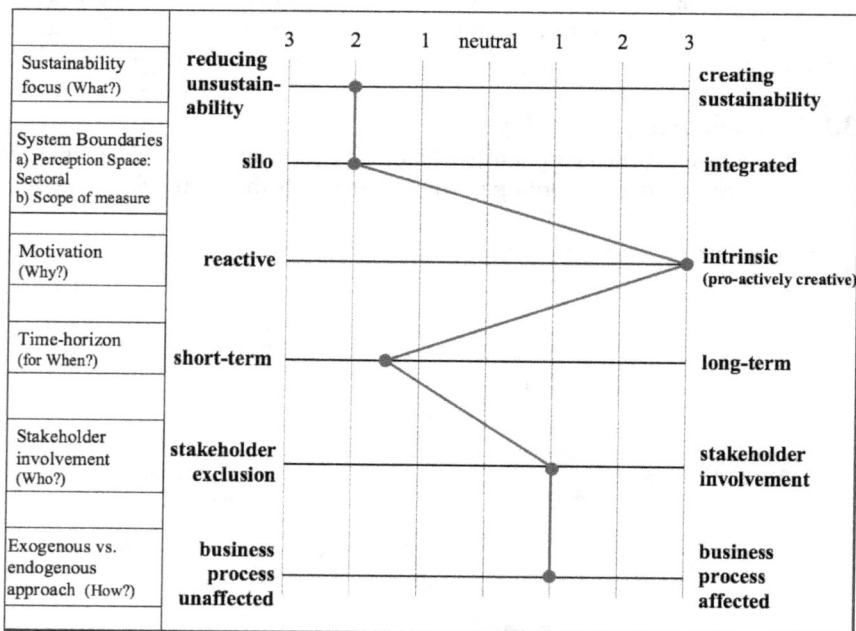

Fig. 33: Efficiency Model: Polarity Profile
Source: Produced by the author

---

369 See also chapter 3.4 and below 3.3.1.4 for the difference between the two models.

The conception of the Efficiency Model as well as its characteristics as they are illustrated in the Polarity Profile above, will be outlined in the following:

Conception of the Efficiency Model

The focus of the Efficiency Model usually lies on the environmental dimension (eco-efficiency). Social sustainability if at all is considered as a favorable 'side-effect' (see below). The World Business Council for Sustainable Development defines eco-efficiency as follows: "[E]co-efficiency is achieved by the delivery of competitively priced goods and services that satisfy human needs and bring quality of life, while progressively reducing ecological impacts and resource intensity throughout the life-cycle to a level at least in line with the Earth's estimated carrying capacity" (WBCSD 2006a: 3, see also DeSimone and Popoff 2000: 47 and WBCSD 2000). Furthermore the WBCSD stresses that eco-efficiency focuses on environmental improvements, which yield parallel economic benefits. Hence, eco-efficiency is concerned with "creating more value with less impact" (WBCSD 2006a: 3).[370]

Eco-efficiency is concerned with saving material and energy input as well as reducing by-products (side-output) like waste and pollution (DeSimone and Popoff 2000: 47ff; Schmidheiny and Timberlake 1992: 9f). A popular tool for quantifying environmental impacts over full product-life-cycles is Life-Cycle Assessment (SETAC 1991 and 1993; ISO 14040).

At a macro-economic focus, the emphasis of eco-efficiency is to decouple 'the use of nature' from human welfare. The European Environment Agency defines eco-efficiency as "a concept and *strategy* enabling sufficient de-linking of the '*use of nature*' from economic activity needed to meet human needs (*welfare*) to allow it to remain within carrying capacities; and permit equitable access and use of the environment by current and future generation" [emphasis by original] (EEA 1999: 4). Factor Four, which has been mentioned above[371], was one prominent approach to reach this goal. (Weizsäcker, Lovins and Lovins 1997, for special reference to eco-efficiency see also Bleischwitz and Hennicke 2004).

The dissertation' emphasis lies on the micro-economic view. Schaltegger and Sturm argue for calculating eco-efficiency as the economic value added by a firm in relation to its aggregated ecological impact (Schaltegger and Sturm 1998). The main focus of eco-efficiency for businesses traditionally lay within concepts of remanufacturing and demanufacturing[372]. Today, it comprises the full product life cycle, e.g.

---

370 It is striking to note, that this new brochure of the WBCSD (2006) at no point discusses the problematic of rebound-effects (Efficiency Trap).

371 See chapter 1.4.6.

372 Demanufacturing describes a disassembly process. While remanufacturing is the broader approach, disassembly is only the first step followed by steps as cleaning and examining components, replacing or remanufacturing those components and finally reassembling the

including sourcing, design, marketing, distribution, disposal (Schmidheiny and Timberlake 1992: 10 and 97ff, WBCSD 2006a: 73ff).

The concept of efficiency as such historically always has been a prevalent one within economy. Therefore it seems not surprising that the Efficiency Model (eco-efficiency) is one of the most broadly accepted and applied models for corporate sustainability today (Dyllick and Hockerts 2002: 20, WBCSD 2006a).[373] But as will be shown below, it is precisely the historical understanding, which is problematic and risks leading into a Sustainability Trap.

Characteristics of the Efficiency Model as in Polarity Profile

Because of its focus on reducing material input and/or waste, the Efficiency Model clearly is focused on *reducing unsustainability*. In the polarity profile (figure 33), the value of two (2) is indicated, instead of three (3), because the corporation's main focus lies on efficiency measures, i.e. measures that *simultaneously* reduce costs, rather than on reducing unsustainability as such. This focus on win-win situations is crucial with respect to the Sustainability Trap, as will be discussed below.

The *mental model of perception space* of an Efficiency Model is sectoral, as economic sustainability remains the primary goal and measures of sustainability are only taken, if they promise to yield (short-term) win-win situations. The sustainability measures as such can be considered *silo-oriented* rather than integrated, because the primary focus lies on economic and environmental sustainability only (see definition above, see also DeSimone and Popoff 2000: 47, Dyllick and Hockerts 2002: 5, WBCSD 2006a: 87). *Social* sustainability at best results as a favorable side-effect. For example if the use of toxic chemicals is reduced as a measure of efficiency, which reduces health impact on the workers. A practice example for this is Chiquita, which reduced toxic chemical in its banana plants.[374]

For corporations holding an Efficiency model the motivation for taking eco-efficiency measures is an *intrinsic* one, because it promises to reduce costs respectively increase profitability. As a matter of fact, the very concept of eco-efficiency was developed by business for business and has been promoted through the World Business Council for Sustainable Development, WBCSD (DeSimone and Popoff

---

product to operate like a new one.

373 The chemical company Dupont for example reduced energy use by one-third at one of their facilities saving over $17 million per year on power, while reducing greenhouse gas pollution per pound of product by half. In 2000, the company saved almost $400 million due to resource and productivity improvement. SC Johnson in five years increased production by 50% while waste emissions were cut by half, resulting in annual cost savings of more than $125 million and United Technologies Corporation's sites eliminated almost 40,000 gallons per year of waste water and saved over US$50,000 per year due to a fundamental change in managing test cells, underground storage tanks and waste streams (WBCSD 2006a: 3).

374 See chapter 3.4.2.3.

2000: 2; Weizsäcker, Seiler-Hausmann and Liedtke 2004: 9f). Because eco-efficiency measures very often relate to the production process as such as well as to the
product life-cycle, the **business process is affected** (WBCSD 2006a: 4). But since
eco-efficiency does not comprise issues of *social* sustainability the dissertation has
indicated only a low value (value 1) for the variable 'business process *affected*' in the
polarity-profile above.
Eco-efficiency can be implemented without stakeholder involvement, e.g. changes
in the manufacturing process. Quite often however, **stakeholders are involved**; especially stakeholders, which can contribute to the development and implementation
of technologies and innovations. These can be stakeholders from the market place,
such as suppliers, investors or competitors, in order to engage in joint developments. Or it can be stakeholders from research, such as universities and scientific
communities, in order to cooperate with in regard to research and development (innovations) (DeSimone and Popoff 2000: 136f). In the polarity-profile the dissertation therefore has indicated a low value of stakeholder *involvement* (value 1), because stakeholder involvement is usually restricted to close business partners (stakeholders of the market sphere) or stakeholders in the field of research. [375]
Eco-efficiency measures are **short-term** oriented. This lies within the nature of the
concept: Once the measure is implemented, material or energy input is saved
and/or waste and pollution are reduced, which leads to direct cost savings. This
characteristic of showing short-term results is the main advantage of eco-efficiency
and constitutes its popularity in business practice.

3.3.1.4   Relations to Other Models

Because of its ability to save costs, the Efficiency Model provides a feasibly entry
model into corporate (environmental) sustainability. The financial savings pose a
counter argument for a trade-off argumentation and might convince corporations
holding a **Trade-off Model** to move towards sustainability. In turn, cost reductions
for corporations following an Efficiency Model provide a competitive advantage
over corporations following a Trade-off Model.
Corporations holding a **Compliance Model** might apply measures of eco-efficiency
in order to meet stakeholder expectations regarding environmental sustainability,
e.g. reducing pollution and waste. In contrast to the Compliance Model however,
corporations following an Efficiency Model hold an *intrinsic* motivation for eco-ef-

---

[375] Furthermore businesses can engage and promote the development of policy frameworks
on national or international level or they can work with NGOs or communities to "add to
the quality of life and to make social investments in the human and physical development of
their neighbors" (DeSimone and Popoff 2000: 137). However especially the last concept is
one that goes beyond the common understanding of eco-efficiency (see above).

ficiency, as outlined above. That is, they actively inquire and innovate for realizing more efficiency potential and do not shy away from significant investments.

Although – or better *because* – corporations holding an Eco-Efficiency Model are realizing significant resource savings, they might not see a pressing need to further engage into sustainability.[376] On the other hand, benefits realized through eco-efficiency, might *stimulate* and *sensitize* corporations following an Efficiency Model to for further engage into sustainability and e.g. move towards a Reputation Leadership Model.

Corporations already holding a **Reputation Leadership Model** are likely to apply eco-efficiency as *one measure* among others. In contrast to corporations with a Reputation Leadership Model, a corporation holding an Efficiency Model focuses on cost reduction through efficiency, rather than on the aim of becoming a sustainability leader in its industry sector, which would require also engaging in other fields of sustainability (social sustainability).

3.3.2 Efficiency Trap (Rebound Effects)
3.3.2.1 Archetypical Trap Structure

The Sustainability Trap of a rebound-effect within the context of eco-efficiency is well documented and builds on many studies, especially in the field of energy economics (Hertwich 2005a: 85; Binswanger 2001: 121; Khazzoom 1980, Greening and Greene 1997). The dissertation builds on this work in order to look at rebound-effects from a systems perspective.

As has been stated in the model analysis above, a main reason for the appreciation of eco-efficiency in corporations is the fact that the very concept of 'efficiency' has been known and valued within the business sector since long time.

*It is most crucial to realize however that the new concept of efficiency in (environmental) sustainability (**eco-efficiency**) is **different** from the concept of efficiency known historically from **economy**. It is the lack of realizing this difference, which is key in Efficiency Traps.*

Sanne (2001: 121) points to the difference: "But two meanings of resources are at play here. Mainstream economic theory accepts budgets as temporary limits but not natural resources limits as ceilings." The important difference of the two efficiency conceptions in economics and in sustainbility lies in the following:

Efficiency in economics: That is, the underlying, historical mental model about efficiency in economics is that efficiency is 'good', because it releases (financial) resources, which then can be *invested into producing 'more'*, i.e. more of the same or

---

376 That is, the denial mechanism for sustainability "We already do that" (Doppelt 2003: 244; see also above).

other products/services. The economic mental model of efficiency hence is basically a *reinforcing loop of economic growth and value creation*: Savings due to efficiency are invested into new endeavors and these, after a time, will release further potential for efficiency etc.

Efficiency in sustainbility: The concept of efficiency in (environmental) sustainability is an entirely different one: The focus does not lie on financial resources, but on *natural resources*[377]. Efficiency here is considered 'good', because it *diminishes depletion of natural resources*, which possess limits.

The problematic situation arises due to what has already been outlined on a more general basis for chapter 2.3.2.4.2[378]: A historically emerged, sectoral understanding of a concept in *business (economics)* encounters a new understanding of this concept within the context of *sustainability*. The specific concept in question here is 'efficiency'. The problem, which is similar to the one outlined in chapter 2.2.2.4.2, is that it is not questioned, which mental models are underlying the sectoral concept of efficiency and which mental models are underlying the sustainability concept of efficiency, in contrast. As has just been showed, these two mental models differ significantly.

But what happens in the far most cases is that the concept of 'efficiency' as it is known from economics nevertheless is transferred – undistinguished - to the concept of 'efficiency' in sustainbility. Consequently, short-term win-win situations are proclaimed and strived for with the reasoning that environmental efficiency (e.g. energy reduction) simultaneously leads to economic efficiency.

This alleged win-win situation however can turn into a loose-loose situation in the *long-term*, because the inconsistency between the different underlying mental models risks leading into a Sustainability Trap as will be outlined in the following. In order to understand the trap, two aspects are crucial:

a) *Eco-efficiency (in contrast to eco-effectiveness) is a <u>symptomatic</u> solution, whose only main advantage with respect to resource depletion (environmental unsustainability) is to save time.*

b) *Rebound effects moreover risk diminishing or (in extreme cases) even tipping this only advantage of eco-efficiency.*

These aspects will be discussed in the following:

---

377 That is, in the economic mental model, savings in natural resources are translated into finical resources (cost savings). This does not happen within the mental model of (environmental) sustainability.
378 Sectoral and holistic mental model of perception space.

a) Eco-efficiency is a symptomatic solution

In order to outline the Sustainability Trap it is necessary come back to what has been discussed in chapter 2.2.4 on operational stock-and-flow thinking and chapter 2.2.5.6 on dynamic thinking:

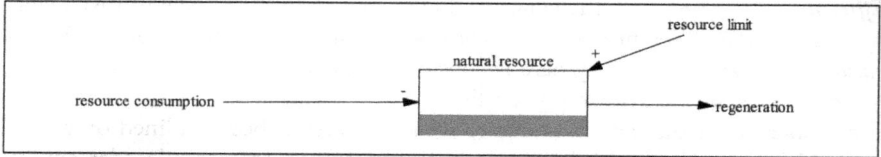

Fig. 34: Reduction of Resource Consumption
Source: Produced by the author

A reduction in resource consumption, e.g. through eco-efficiency, only has the effect that the *depletion rate* is lowered. The stock of *non-renewable natural resources* continuous to diminish inevitably until limits[379] are reached.[380] For *renewable resources* the outer limit for harvesting as outlined is the regeneration rate, i.e. consuming the income, not the capital (Hawken, Lovins and Lovins 1999).[381] Many reservoirs of renewable resources in specific places today however are depleted to such a large extend that the capital (i.e. the stock) as such needs to be increased (e.g. fish, wood, clean water). Therefore in many cases sustainable harvesting needs to even lie significantly *below* the regeneration rate.[382]

To illustrate this point, an example of Dyllick and Hockerts can be used. If for example the Thai fishing industry reduces the number of sea turtles caught accidentally per kilogram of shrimp, this would increase its *eco-efficiency*. In a world with abundant sea turtles this might be irrelevant from an ecological point of view. But if the sea turtle population is very close to the level of extinction the only *eco-effective*[383] action would be to ban fishing until the population has recovered (Dyllick and Hockerts 2002: 24).

Thus, the crucial factor for evaluating eco-efficiency is the *level of the stock in reference to its limits*: If the stock is near a limit even a small amount of depletion (or in the case of waste or pollution a small addition), might cause the system to pass a threshold and potentially even to collapse. "It makes [...] a difference whether an emission is released into a system that is still largely unpolluted, or whether the re-

---

379 That is until all known resource reserves are emptied or until the resource cannot be harvested at a competitive price.
380 It only happens *slower*.
381 See chapter 2.2.4.2.
382 Hence, the rates – similar to other sustainability 'limits' – are subject to social bargaining processes.
383 That is, from a *sustainbility* point of view (not from an economic point).

ceiving systems is already so close to its carrying capacity that the extra emission will cause the whole system to break down" (Dyllick and Hockerts 2002: 21f).

In the light of the facts that 1) non-renewable resources inevitably deplete through consumption and 2) the situation that many renewable resources have been harvested over their regeneration rate and their stocks are low, the first shortcoming of an Efficiency Model becomes evident: In the foremost most cases, *eco-efficiency only transfers the unsustainability problem into the future* through reducing the depletion rate, *but does not tackle the problem as such*. "Eco-efficiency is an outwardly admirable, even noble, concept, but it is not a strategy for success over the long term, because it does not reach deep enough. It works within the same system that caused the problem in the first place, merely slowing it down [...]. It presents little more than an illusion of change" (McDonough and Braungart 2002a: 62). Eco-efficiency therefore is a *symptomatic solution*, whose only advantage in regard to environmental sustainability is to safe time.

The dissertation states this point not to off-set eco-efficiency efforts entirely. Eco-efficiency can be used as a quick-fix[384] in order to *save time* in respect of resource depletion and its effects, which is important. But what is crucial to realize, is that eco-efficiency does not constitute a *fundamental* solution to sustainability.

*The crucial point for addressing unsustainability lies in how resources gained through eco-efficiency (e.g. time, finances) are **used (reinvested)** and not in eco-efficiency itself. This pivotal point often remains unreflected in the enthusiasm for eco-efficiency.*

It is most important to note that investing the time gained through eco-efficiency into new technologies for even more eco-efficiency constitutes an investment into a *symptomatic solution* with diminishing marginal utility in regard to the goal of increasing corporate sustainability, and *not* an investment into more sustainability. For businesses practicing extensive eco-efficiency (Eco-Efficiency Model) and therefore claiming to contribute to sustainability, this difference is important to realize.

McDonough and Braungart (2002a) introduce the concept of *eco-effectiveness* to stress this difference. As the authors state, "eco-efficiency only works to make the old, destructive system a bit less so" (McDonough and Braungart 2002a: 62). Eco-effectiveness in contrast, means working on the right things, i.e. on products, services and systems that create sustainbility, in stead of making wrong things less bad (McDonough and Braungart 2002: 76). Once the right things are done, "then doing them 'right', with the help of efficiency among other tools, makes perfect sense" (McDonough and Braungart 2002a: 76). Hence, the difference between eco-effi-

---

384 See also chapter 3.2.2 for quick fixes.

ciency and eco-effectiveness relates to the crucial difference between reducing un-sustainability and creating sustainability outlined in chapter 2.2.4.2.

The importance of the difference between efficiency and effectiveness is valued in business since long-time, for example Peter Drucker, whom McDonough and Braungart also refer to, pointed out that management is concerned in 'doing things right', while it is the job of leadership (executives) to make sure that the 'right things are done' (Drucker 2001 and 2002). But with respect to corporate sustain-ability this difference and its implications have not yet broadly diffused in manage-ment practice and management science (Dyllick and Hockerts 2002: 29).

b) Rebound Effects

Being unaware about the symptomatic nature of eco-efficiency and its difference to eco-effectiveness is the first aspect, which risks leading corporations holding an Ef-ficiency Model into a Sustainability Trap (Efficiency Trap).

*The crucial 'fatal' aspect of an Efficiency Trap lies in the problematic that due to rebound-effects even the ability of eco-efficiency as a symptomatic solution, i.e. to diminish the problem symptoms[385] and thus to save time in regard to resource depletion, is **diminished** and in extreme cases might even tip the system and **fuel** resource depletion.*

This problem of an Efficiency Trap can be illustrated by drawing on a parallel from traditional business (Dyllick and Hockerts 2002: 22f): Increasing the efficiency of the distribution system of a corporation, i.e. increasing the number of products a sales agent can sell within a given period of time, in most cases makes economic sense. But if the corporation has a negative contribution margin, i.e. production costs per product are higher than the market price, such a strategy proves fatal, be-cause the more products the corporation sells, the higher its losses will be. Corpo-rations subscribing to eco-efficiency "run a similar risk of fuelling rather than re-ducing ecological degradation" (Dyllick and Hockerts 2002: 22f, the authors in this respect also point to Senge 1999: 178).

Figure 35 shows the basic structure of an Efficiency Trap, which will be analyzed in the following. The example below focuses on *depletion* of natural resources. A simi-lar structure can be considered to apply for the *accumulation* of waste or pollution.

---

385 That is resource depleting.

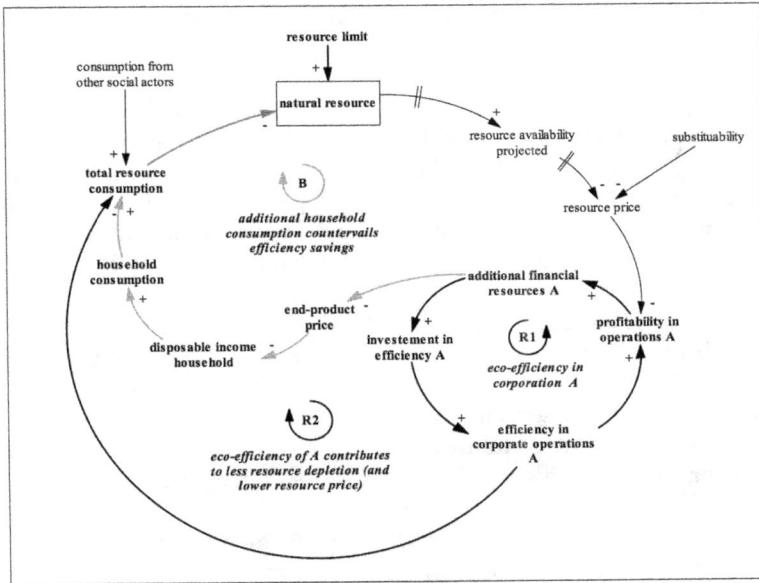

Fig. 35: Efficiency Trap
Source: Produced by the author

The reinforcing loop R1 corresponds to the dynamic of the mental model of an Efficiency Model outlined above: *Efficiency measures in operations* (activities) of the corporation, lead to better *profitability* due to cost savings and thus *additional financial resources* become available, which can be invested; e.g. into *further efficiency measures* to fuel the process (R1). R1 represents the economic win (economic sustainability) of an individual corporation associated with efficiency measures.[386]

R2 indicates the dynamics associated with eco-efficiency in the wider system: Efficiency measures have the (intended) effect that *total resource consumption* is reduced. This is the 'contribution to sustainability' commonly attributed to eco-efficiency.

---

386 The *additional* dynamic of benefits due to better image for the corporation, which are indicated in the mental model of the Efficiency Model above, are left out in figure 35 for reasons of simplicity.

As has been stated above however, even a reduced consumption in the foremost cases[387] still *reduces* the stock of *natural resources* (note the link in red color in figure 35).[388]

The dynamic, which often remains unrecognized, is the 'rebound effect':

Gains due to eco-efficiency are invested into greater consumption, which countervails resource savings (Sanne 2001: 121, Radermacher 1997, Brand 2003). Therefore reduction in resource consumption is *less* than proportionally to changes in physical resource efficiency. The rebound effect therefore is typically quantified as the extent of the deviation from proportionality (Small and van Dender 2006: 1). As stated above, in extreme cases the rebound effect can even lead to a counter-effect, which fuels resource depletion, i.e. which empties the stock of a resource faster.

As will be further outlined below, the rebound effect can play out in many different facets (types). One of these types is illustrated in the balancing loop 'B' in figure 35 above, which refers to subsequent household consumption. This example has been chosen to stress the point that unsustainability is not only caused through corporate behavior, but through *structures* to which also other social agents contribute too.[389]

The crucial part of the balancing loop (B) is highlighted in orange color in figure 35: All or a part of the corporation's savings due to efficiency measures is passed on to consumers in form of lower prices for the end-product. These lower prices augment the disposable income of the consumer (household), which he/she invests in more of the *same* product (direct rebound-effect, e.g. second cell-phone, second car, twentieth pullover) or in *other* products for example an additional holiday or short-trip (secondary rebound-effect).

A problem arises, if this additional product or service consumed in turn, requires the input of the natural resource in question in order to be produced. Then the additional consumption countervails the very resource savings accomplished due to the eco-efficiency measure in the first place: Note that the two links contributing to the variable 'total resource consumption' have opposing link polarities (reducing (-) and increasing (+)). It obviously depends on the *relation of these two parameters*[390] to

---

387 As outlined above, this is always the case for non-renewable resources and very often the case for renewable resources as their stocks currently are substantially reduced (consumption rate > regeneration rate).

388 As for the dashed links in figure 35: see below. They signify potential backfiring on the corporation, but refer to a macroeconomic perspective. At this point first the rebound-effect as such will be outlined.

389 Another outplay of the rebound effect occurs e.g. if a corporation uses the money saved through eco-efficiency to invest in the development and manufacturing of other products, which require the same or another scarce natural resource.

390 That is: Reduction of resource consumption due to corporate efficiency and increase of resource consumption due to increased household consumption.

evaluate, if the rebound-effect only *reduces* resource savings[391] or (in extreme cases) actually *annihilates* the resource savings and thus even accelerates resource depletion. In both cases the rebound-effect countervails efficiency measures. Therefore depletion of the *natural resource* due to the rebound effect *inevitably* happens faster than if the full savings of eco-efficiency could play out.

That the rebound effect actually exists, today is accepted as fact. What yet remains disputed is its magnitude (Binswanger 2001: 120, Sanne 2001: 122f). The magnitude cannot be stated generally, but depends on factors such as the type of resource, the consumption patterns etc. The magnitude of the rebound effect will further be discussed below. At this point it is crucial to realize that the effect exists and that corporations, which seek to contribute to sustainability, need to individually analyze the effect in order not to fall pray to an Efficiency Trap.

In order to analyze potential backfiring of rebound effects on the individual corporation, it is necessary to look at a macro-economic scale or at least at an industry scale.[392] This is the case, because underlying this structure is a tragedy-of-the-commons situation (see Senge 2006: 397f and Senge et al. 1994). In a tragedy-of-the-commons situation, individual gains rise *short-term*, but the depletion of the commons (i.e. the natural resource) due to all agents involved, risks to backfire on all agents relying on the commons in the *long-term*.

This industry level (macro level) is outlined in the dashed links in figure 35[393]: If resource efficiency is applied by many corporations in the industry (as in many industries currently is the case) and if significant rebound effects occur, scarcity of the resource will be projected earlier than previously expected. Respectively the 'resource availability projected' will diminish. As the delay mark in figure 35 indicates, correction of prognoses will only happen with a delay, because they will only be corrected if the effect shows to play out for a significant period of time (trend). Depending on other factors, such as substitutability of the natural resource, the reduc-

---

391 That is, reduction in resource consumption is *less* than proportionally to changes in resource efficiency.

392 There might be cases, where backfiring of a rebound effect directly plays out on a corporation (e.g. in the case of a very specific resource and a large buyer). But in most cases, if backfiring occurs it is likely to do so via a macro level.

393 That is, other corporations and social actors (consumers) in the industry showing the same behavior as the one outlined here, are represented in the variable 'consumption from other social actors'. This has been done for reasons of simplicity. That is, the situation (corporation) exhibited here is a cut out of the industry. Appendix F outlines a structure, which includes an additional corporation, which invests its financial resources in the production of a new product, which needs the same natural resource. Also these two corporations are representations (a cut-out) of the industry that illustrates the main dynamics. That is, similar too the tragedy of the commons archetype outlined by Senge et al. (Senge 2006: 397) only two corporations are outlined as representatives to illustrate the structure.

tion in resource availability forecasted, this can lead to the effect that the resource price rises, thus reducing the profitability for corporations depending on the resource.[394] This, in turn, raises the incentive for these corporations to even further increase resource-efficiency. - A vicious circle, as long as rebound effects are not addressed on a macro-level. The problematic and fatality of tragedy-of-the-commons structures, that is the depletion of common resources, is know since a long time, e.g. in the fishery industry (see e.g. Gordon 1954, for the concept as such see Hardin 1968).

More important than the potential backfiring on corporations, however is the fact that resource-efficiency is only a symptomatic solution to sustainbility and can – in extreme cases – even fuel depletion (orange colored part of the loop in figure 35).

As has been outlined above, rebound-effects are the trap most studied already with respect to sustainability so far. Thereby it needs to be stated that in contrast to the Efficiency Trap outlined by the dissertation above, analyses of rebound-effects usually do not point to the divergence in the underlying mental model of efficiency[395] and to the symptomatic nature of eco-efficiency measures. Rather they concentrate only on the rebound effect as such, i.e. gains due to eco-efficiency are invested into greater consumption, which countervails resource savings. Therefore the Efficiency Trap as it is outlined in the dissertation is a larger conception of what commonly is referred to as rebound-effect (e.g. in energy economics, such as Greening and Greene 1997, Greening, Greene and Difiglio 2000).

Further discussion of rebound effects

Now that basic structure of an Efficiency Trap has been outlined from a systems perspective on sustainbility, further important aspects relating to rebound-effects in particular shall be discussed, as they have been examined in fields of sustainbility, particularly in energy economics. These aspects equally apply to the concept of an Efficiency Trap elaborated above.

Greening et al. differentiate three categories of rebound effects (Greening and Greene 1997, Greening, Greene and Difiglio 2000[396]):

---

394 If resource scarcity and consequently higher prices will play out on the specific corporation in question depends on the length of the delay. In some cases it does, in many cases it can be expected to backfire on future generations. But, if rebound-effects are significant as they seem to be in some cases (e.g. energy consumption) backfiring on economy as such will happen eventually.

395 That is, the different understanding of the conception of efficiency in economics and in sustainbility.

396 The later paper 'splits' the 'direct rebound effect' in differentiating between the substitution and income effect. But for the purposes in this dissertation the concept of 'direct rebound effect' is sufficient.

- *Direct Rebound Effect*: The goods or services affected by the price drop enabled through eco-efficiency are consumed more.
- *Secondary Rebound Effect*: Savings are used to consume other products.
- *Economy Wide Effect*: Changes in the price of one good due to efficiency (e.g. energy-efficiency), leads to changes in prices of other goods, which then are consumed more.
- *Transformational Effects:* Changes in technology alter consumers' preferences, social institutions and the organization of production.

The concept of rebound effects in reference to efficiency originated in energy economics and thus this constitutes the field, where rebound effects are most studied in (Hertwich 2005a: 85; Binswanger 2001: 121; Khazzoom 1980). Therefore the dissertation builds on findings within this field. As stated above, the existence of the rebound-effect – especially in regard to energy-efficiency - is widely acknowledged by now, yet its magnitude and thus its magnitude remain heavily disputed (Binswanger 2001: 120, Sanne 2001: 122f). With respect to the magnitude (significance) basically three cases can be differentiated (Hertwich 2005a: 86):

- *Weak rebound effect*: Efficiency measures are not as effective as expected.
- *Strong rebound effect*: Most of the expected savings do not materialize.
- *Backfire effect*: The efficiency measure leads to increased energy demand.[397]

The findings of empirical studies on the magnitude (weak, strong, backfiring) of the different types of rebound effects (direct, secondary, economy-wise and transformational) will be outlined in the following. As stated, the findings are conflicting in part and the magnitude of rebound effects remains disputed. This is particularly the case for the magnitude of the last three types (secondary, economy-wise and transformational).

a) Magnitude of direct rebound effects

Most studies on the magnitude of rebound-effects within the field of *energy*-efficiency focus on *direct* rebound effects, because especially the macro-economic types (Economy Wide Effect and Transformational) are hard to track (Hertwich 2005a: 87). The survey of studies in the United States of Greening et al. (2000) point to a rebound effect of *energy*-efficiency of around 0% for white goods, 50% for space cooling and on average less than 30% for space heating, lighting, automotive transport. A study on road transport in Germany and Italy indicates rebound effects between 30% and 50% (Walker and Wirl 1993). It can be stated that in general, em-

---

397 Note, that this conception of „backfiring" in contrast to the dissertation' discussion above, does not explicitly imply that energy prices increase accordingly. But his is likely to bet he case in a free market situation.

pirical studies suggest that the rebound effect is indeed of empirical relevance, but its size varies significantly depending on the data and the method used in the studies (Binswanger 2001: 123f). Binswanger in his survey of different studies draws the conclusion that "[g]enerally, the rebound effect seems to be somewhere between 5 and 50% implying that energy saving technologies will still lead to a reduction in energy consumption, but that part of the saving potential is lost because of the induced increase in service demand" Binswanger (2001: 123f).

Thus, in respect of *direct* rebound effects, empirical studies indicate that the effect exists as a rebound, but not as a backfiring in the sense that it leads to faster resource depletion. That is, eco-efficiency indeed does lead to a *net*-reduction of the rate of resource depletion and therefore is a valuable too to save time. But due to the rebound effect, the reduction of the rate of resource depletion does not occur to its full extend, but only to a certain percentage. Thereby the offsetting due to rebound effects varies depending on different product types. This is also the conclusion drawn in the recent survey of Hertwich (2005a: 90).

b) Magnitude of secondary rebound effects

Whereby empirical studies support the usefulness of eco-efficiency in decelerating resource depletion, findings about the usefulness or harmfulness (backfiring) of the *indirect (secondary) rebound effect* and the two *macro-effects* are not conclusive as Hertwich states in his analysis of existing studies (Hertwich 2005a: 90).

Sanne states that if the primary rebound effect is limited, the secondary effect is correspondingly large, with a 20% direct rebound effect entailing an 80% budget replenishment for the household, which correspondingly is available for alternative consumption (Sanne 2001: 122). This is reasoned on the basis of satiation effects of households for one good, so that the household rather invests in other goods (Sanne 2001: 121ff).

c) Magnitude of macro-effects (economy-wide and transformational rebound effects)

Findings of different studies are even more heterogeneous, when it comes to macro-effects.

One of the first two scholars to come up with a model for assessing *rebound effects on a macro-level* was Saunders (1992, see also 2000), by applying a neo-classical one-sector growth model with three factors of production (labor, energy and capital) using Cobb-Douglas production functions. His findings pointed to an increase of resource consumption due to efficiency improvements, i.e. to an existence of a rebound effect.

Schipper and Grubb (2000) however, review decomposition analysis for energy demand in seven industrialized economies. That is, the contribution of changes in underlying variables, such as population size, economic structure, and efficiency, to changes in energy use or any other aggregate variables (Hertwich 2005a: 88ff). This analysis does not support the existence of macro-rebound effects (Hertwich 2005a: 89).

Grepperud and Rasmussen (2004) analyzed the effect of autonomous energy effi- ciency improvements in the Norwegian economy. The analysis identifies "strong re- bound effects in the paper and chemical industries, weak or no rebound effects in finance, fisheries, and transportation, and a backfire effect in the metals industry" (Hertwich 2005a: 89).

Washida et al. use a general equilibrium model for the appraisal of rebound effects due to environmental policies in the Japanese economy (particularly on CO_2 emis- sions). The study disaggregates the economy into 33 industrial sectors inclusive of energy sectors (coal products, oil products, electricity and gas supply). The model indicates the economy-wide rebound effect to be significant ranging 35% to 70% in Japan economy (Washida 2004).

A most recent study stems from Barker and Foxon et al. (2006: 51ff), who exam- ined the macroeconomic rebound effect for the UK economy arising from UK en- ergy efficiency policies and programs for 2000-2010 using an energy-economy-en- vironment models. Their findings indicate that the reduction in energy demand in 2010 is around 11% less than expected due to rebound effects. Thereby higher macroeconomic rebounds in the energy-intensive industries sector (25%) are offset by lower macroeconomic rebounds in road transport, commerce and household sec- tors.

These findings again point to significant differences of rebound effects depending on the industry sectors. Senge also points to a likelihood of rebound-effect on a macro-scale: "It is possible for resource productivity to improve and for natural sys- tems to decline. Indeed, some industry studies have indicated that just this is hap- pening. [...] Rapid growth at less resource intensity is not even necessarily a step forward: if the growth rate swamps the productivity improvement rate (especially on a global scale), total resource extraction may actually increase" (Senge 1999: 178).

Outlook: Need for further research
Concluding, it needs to be stated that the assessment of rebound-effects especially indirect and foremost macro-effects are very hard to measure and still extensive studies need to be undertaken in this new and important field (see also Washida 2004: 300). Difficulties of assessing macro-effects do not only lie in scope (e.g. sub- stitutability, behavior patterns), but equally in time. Economy-wide and transfor- mational effects are likely to play out with a significant delay, because there needs to be a period of adjustment (Sanne 2001: 122).

Other authors such as Binswanger (2001) have argued to also account for a time-rebound effect, where the additional time saved through efficiency measures (e.g. faster transportation) is used for more consumption (see also Jalas 2002, 2005 and Perrels 2002). Hertwich has pointed out that future analysis need to focus on more than just one environmental problem, such as energy consumption. "It is not generally true that all effects are reduced simultaneously. Instead, the general case is that a technical measure reduces some environmental pressures while increasing or keeping constant other environmental pressures" (Hertwich 2005a: 90). He therefore argues to broaden the focus of rebound effects and to extend it to cover negative side effects, spillover effects and also co-benefits (Hertwich 2005a).

Conclusions for the dissertation

As stated the dissertation' motivation is not to discredit eco-efficiency. Rather it seeks to outline the limitations and possible risks, which corporations holding an Efficiency Model need to be aware of. It has been outlined that limitations and risk vary for different industries and there still need to be further investigation in this crucial issue. This is especially the case, because, as pointed out, eco-efficiency is one of the most prevalent measures in corporate sustainability. It needs to be taken care of that corporations, which seek to contribute to sustainability through eco-efficiency as well as society as a whole, which is in support of eco-efficiency, are not "chasing their tail in the pursuit of sustainability" as Sanne calls it (Sanne 2001: 120). It has been the aim of the above chapter to create awareness for the following three aspects, which if unaware can lead a corporation – as well as society - into a Sustainability Trap:

- Recognition of the different underlying mental models (sectoral versus holistic) of efficiency: 1) Efficiency as a measure for economic growth through more consumption versus 2) efficiency as a measure for decelerating resource depletion or accumulation of waste/pollution.
- Realization of the difference between eco-efficiency and eco-effectiveness. Eco-efficiency itself is not a fundamental solution to sustainability.
- Awareness for the existence of rebound-effects, which countervail resource savings/pollution reduction or in the case of backfiring can even lead to faster depletion/increased accumulation.
- Also important is the recognition that the conflicting mental models of efficiency (sectoral versus holistic), which drive behavior, are not only a problem of business, but all the same for customers and other social agents involved.

3.3.2.2 Dealing with the Trap

With regard to possible ways out of the efficiency trap, two basic approaches can be distinguished, which are complementary:

a) Changing mental models (value and behavioral-driven) and
b) changing processes and technologies (technological-and-design-driven).

Both lines of approaches contribute to the aim expressed above, to further decouple human welfare from unsustainable consumption (dematerialization), thereby avoiding rebound-effects or at least significantly reducing them.

The foremost approaches refer to unsustainable consumption of *natural* resources, while unsustainable consumption of *social* resources still hold a shadowy existence in literature on rebound-effects (for a discussion of the latter issue with regard to working hours see: Sanne 2001: 124ff).

a) Changing mental models from material growth two qualitative growth

As outlined, for escaping a Sustainability Trap long-term, there usually are no quick-fix solutions, but it is inevitable to reflect and change underlying mental models – a task, which usually is very difficult and requires continuous work and consideration on one's own behavior. The problematic mental model, which drives the Efficiency-Trap is that of using efficiency gains (e.g. financial, timewise or others) for further *material* consumption, as has been shown.

Many scholars therefore argue for a concept of 'sufficiency' (Sanne 2001, Bartelmus 1999, Princen 2005, Lamberton 2005 Sachs 1995, Dyllick and Hockerts 2002, Daly 1996, Schumacher 1989, see also Ecological Economics chapter 1.4.7[398]). Because the idea of sufficiency in the sense of 'enough' as opposed to 'too much' is a very general one, the concept of sufficiency consequently is argued for with respect to various issues, such as economic growth, consumption, pollution, population size, level of affluence etc. (for an in-depth discussion of the concept see Princen 2005). What is of particular relevance here are approaches to the concept of sufficiency in regard to material consumption (of private households and of corporations), which is coupled with sufficiency in quantitative economic growth as such.

This ties back to the understanding of efficiency in economics outlined above, that the benefit of efficiency lies in the fact that it allows for economic growth. Sanne (2001: 121) therefore states: "The economist's observation that a lower price leads to higher consumption (and the adherent valuation that this is good) cannot be passively accepted; it challenges politics to match it with a conscious policy of moderation. An ecologically responsible economy is needed, an economy that can manage thriftiness by combining efficiency with a policy of sufficiency" Bartelmus

---

398 It has to be noted that many authors, arguing for the concept 'sufficiency' do not particularly relate the eco-efficiency and potential rebounds effects, but rather to the fact that natural resources as such are limited.

(1999: 11) draws a similar conclusion: "It is generally held, however, that technology alone cannot be the savior: it needs to be reinforced by more or less voluntary restriction in consumption levels. 'Ecoefficiency' in production needs to be combined with 'sufficiency' in final consumption".

Approaches of sufficiency in material, quantitative growth are often accompanied by approaches towards *qualitative development* (growth) (Costanza et al. 1997, Daly 1996 and 2005). The dissertation considers concepts for alternative qualitative growth most crucial, because the dissertation' normative assumption is that it lies within the nature of human beings to strive for growth and progress, not for sufficiency. Therefore concepts which proclaim *anti*-consumerism and *anti*-growth *as* behavioral *targets* (i.e. limitation/sufficiency as the *goal*) risk scaring off agents from sustainability (see also Zavestovski 2001, who compares values basis of anti-consumerism and environmentalism). A *re-direction* of growth towards *qualitative targets* in the sense of increasing human well-being (quality-of-life) instead of material wealth offers *alternative* goals and therefore in the view of the dissertation holds a higher potential for aspiration.

Although qualitative growth is widely argued for, understandings of qualitative growth differ significantly throughout literature and a reconciliation in form of an alternative vision to quantitative growth is still to be reached. Two concepts can be distinguished, which are complementary:

> *a1) Qualitative growth as an increase of human well-being (quality-of-life) instead*
> > *of material wealth and*
> *a2) qualitative growth as increasing immaterial services (dematerialization).*

These two will be discussed in the following.

a1) Qualitative growth as an increase of human well-being (meeting human needs)

Some authors, as does the dissertation, refer qualitative growth rather to the increase of human well-being (quality-of-life) instead of material wealth. These approaches lay emphasis on *social sustainability*, in the sense of promoting non-physical fundamental human *needs*, instead of focusing on meeting economic *wants*, which require excessive resource input (*environmental unsustainability*). Michaelis (2000), who deals with ethics of consumption, for example argues for developing ideals of 'good life', which can be met without excessive material consumption. This relates to concepts of sustainable life-styles (see e.g. Thogersen 2005, Devuyst, Hens and Lannoy 2001). Peet and Peet argue to move away from evaluating development processes via measures of quantitative growth (e.g. GDP), towards an indicator of qualitative growth of people. According to this conception, "the best development process will be the one which allows the greatest improvement in people's

240

quality of life" (Peet and Peet 2000: 1[399], see also Max- Neef 1997). The concept of non-physical human needs, such as love, esteem, safety or understanding, creation, affection or freedom, has already been mentioned above.[400] As outlined, Maslow (1970) and particularly Max-Neef (1992) worked on identifying fundamental human needs. However, far more extensive research on needs especially in reference to sustainability is still required. Furthermore emphasis on specific needs is likely to differ locally e.g. industrialized versus developing countries.

a2) Qualitative growth as increasing immaterial services (dematerialization)

Many scholars define qualitative development (as opposed to quantitative growth) rather in an economic-technical sense (e.g. increasing immaterial services, dematerialization). Daly argues that a sustainable economy must stop growing at a point, because if economy's expansion encroaches too much on its surrounding ecosystem, society will begin to sacrifice natural capital (such as fish, minerals and fossil fuels), which is worth more than the man-made capital (such as roads, factories and appliances) added by the growth (Daly 2005: 100). If this happens, it will come to what Daly calls *uneconomic* growth, i.e. "producing 'bads' faster than goods - making us poorer, not richer" (Daly 2005: 100).

Although quantitative growth is limited in a sustainable economy, it can grow by developing qualitative improvements in design of products, which can increase GDP without increasing the amount of resources used (Daly 2005: 100). Hennicke argues in the same line. He claims for a radical structural change in the patterns of growth, towards qualitative growth, e.g. dematerialization; service orientation; closed loop economies; up cycling; zero emissions. Otherwise, "mankind seems to be captured in a deadlock" (Hennicke 2003: 1). This is the case, because if the growing population in the South tries to copy the per capita resource consumption of the North, then further deterioration of nature seems inevitable. On the other, growth in goods and services, as well as in profits and personal incomes, is most important in order to increase living standards, to overcome poverty and to reduce unemployment, - especially in the South (Hennicke 2003: 1).

Concludingly it can be stated that understandings and aspects of 'qualitative growth' still vary significantly. In order to become theories in-use for consumers and corporations (sustainable consumption and production) they need to crystallize *through social bargaining processes*, which lead to a change of mental models and of underlying values. In this respect there still seems to be a very long way to go in a sense of developing common and accepted concepts of qualitative growth. Heiskanen and Pantzar (1997) point to the difficulties of changing moral values and corresponding behavior on a broad level, i.e. throughout society: First, because experi-

---

399 The authors explicitly refer to Max-Neef.
400 See also chapter 2.2.2.4.2.

ence has shown that a change in beliefs, attitudes or values does not necessarily lead to lifestyle change. Second, the authors argue that value change is needed, but new values need significant time to disseminate to a significant degree – at least a hundred years. Therefore the authors argue that although sustainable consumption is needed there is no time to wait until the concept crystallizes and disseminates, therefore emphasis should be laid on technical possibilities of a shift to less resource intensive types of consumption.

b) Changing processes and technologies (technological-and-design-driven)
The last point of the above paragraph, leads over to the second type of approaches, which are rather technological and design-driven. As stated above, these can be used complementary to a change in mental models. From a technology and design driven point of view, the combination of the following two aspects is feasible for dealing with Efficiency Traps:

b1) Eco-effectiveness, that is *what* is produced (or consumed[401]) and
b2) Cradle-to-cradle (closed-loop-cycles), which refer to processes (*how*) over a product life-cycle.[402]

b1) Eco-effectiveness
The concept and importance of eco-effectives as opposed to eco-efficiency has been outlined extensively above (see also McDonough and Braungart 2002a, Dyllick and Hockerts 2002, Stahlmann and Clausen 2000). McDonough and Braungart identify the following aspects as a crucial decision-basis for eco-effectiveness, i.e. how to decide on 'what' to design and to produce (2002a: 81): "Eco-effective designers expand their vision from primary purpose of a product or system and consider the whole. What are its goals and potential effects, both immediate and wide-ranging, with respect to both time and place? What is the entire system – cultural, commercial, ecological – of which this made thing, and way of making things, will be part of?" Thus, from a systems perspective, the authors refer to apply the systems thinking skills of broadening system boundaries and of reflecting on the dynamics (dynamic complexity) in time and space.

---

401 Eco-effectiveness is usually referred to within a corporate context (McDonough and Braungart 2002a, Dyllick and Hockerts 2002, Stahlmann and Clausen 2000). But there is no reason, why a similar concept could not equally apply to consumption. However, in line with existing literature the dissertation focuses on the corporate side.
402 McDonough and Braungart 2002a consider these two approaches identical. The dissertation however considers them as two separate, but complementary aspects relating to *what* is produced and *how* is it produced.

b2) Cradle-to-cradle

The concept of cradle-to-cradle (McDonough and Braungart 2002a and 1998) entails two main approaches, which will be discussed in the following:

b2.1) *Closed-loop-cycles and*
b2.1) *Product of service*

b.2.1) Closed-loop-cycles (keeping biological and technical metabolism separated)

The concept of closed-loop-cycles is most prominent within the field of *industrial ecology*, where e.g. waste of one industry becomes the input for another as outlined in chapter 1.4.6. The closed-loop cycles, which shall be introduced in the following, constitute a particular one, referred to as *cradle-to-cradle* and developed by McDonough and Braungart (2002a and 1998). The authors argue that basically there are two discrete metabolisms on earth: The biological metabolism, which is the cycle of nature (biosphere) and the technical metabolism (technosphere), the cycle of industry, including the harvesting of technical materials from natural places (McDonough and Braungart 2002a: 104ff). What economy currently is doing, is to mix up the flows of both metabolisms by designing products as hybrids, with the effects that: 1) Technical (toxic) elements are released into the biosphere via waste and pollution, and 2) due to this 'loss' more and more resources need to be harvested and processed.

The authors propose to radically change this process, by 1) keeping the two metabolisms separate and 2) to introduce close-loop-cycles for the technosphere ('cradle-to-cradle' instead of 'cradle-to-grave' life-cycle-processes) thus mimicking the biosphere, which aboriginally possesses closed-loop-cycles[403].

The authors use an example of a television in order to illustrate such a transition: An average television is made of 4,360 chemicals. Some of them are toxic, but others are valuable nutrients for industry, which are wasted when the television ends up in a landfill. If these chemicals would be isolated from biological nutrients, this allows to upcycle the chemicals, rather than to recycle them. Upcycling thereby means to "retain their high quality in a closed-loop industrial cycle" (McDonough and Braungart 2002a: 110). This would mean that a plastic computer case will continually circulate as a computer case; or as some other high-quality product (e.g. a car part or a medical device), instead of being downcycled, e.g. into soundproof barriers and flowerpots" (McDonough and Braungart 2002a: 110).

b2.1) Product of service

A further crucial concept of cradle-to-cradle is *product of service*. This implies that instead that a consumer possess a product, in the sense that he/she buys, owns and

---

403 This overlaps with the concept of biomimicry, i.e. imitation of natural processes. For more on biomimicry see Benyus 1997.

disposes it, consumers become *users*, who purchase the *service* of a product for a defined user period. In the example of the television, this would mean that customers purchase e.g. ten thousand hours of television viewing, instead of the television itself. This has the advantage that customers do not need to pay for complex materials, which they will not be able to use after the product's current life anyway. When customers finish with the product or want to up-grade to a newer version, the manufacturer replaces it. He takes the old model back, breaks it down can use its complex materials as food for new products (McDonough and Braungart 2002a: 111). A corporation applying 'product of service' is Interface, which today is the largest carpet manufacturer worldwide and is perceived as a sustainability pioneer in its industry.

It can be concluded that in order to deal with an Efficiency Trap and thus to actually reach a broader decoupling of human welfare and resource consumption, both is needed: A change in *mental models* and a change in *technologies/processes* – at private households as well as at corporations. This means: Sustainable production *and* consumption[404]. Looking at systemic structures enables agents to look at mental models as well as at processes and technologies. Furthermore it allows analyzing patterns, which emerge from the interactions of corporations and private households as has been shown.

3.3.2.3   Business Case: Energy Sector

A case of rebound-effects studied quite intensively, which shall be used as a reference here, is that of *fuel-efficiency* (fuel economy).[405] Even though fuel efficiency so far had its peek in the 1980s, the topic remains a major area of public and policy interest in the future (Heavenrich 2006: ii and vi). Building more fuel-efficient cars for example via hybrid-technology is increasingly considered a long-term growth market by many automobile companies, e.g. Toyota (Toyota Prius), Honda (Honda Insight).

Rebound effects with regard to fuel-efficiency play an important role in determining the effectiveness of policy measure aiming at reducing car use – and thus reducing congestion and CO_2 emission. For example rebound effects play an important

---

404 See also the Marrakech process, a 10-year framework of programs for sustainable consumption and production worldwide hosted by the UN (M'hamed Elmurabit, H., Bohn, V. 2003). See also the UNEP/Wuppertal Institute Collaborating Centre on Sustainable Consumption and Production (CSCP), which seeks to implement projects on sustainable consumption and production; homepage: http://www.scp-centre.org, accessed: 14. December 2005.

405 In all studies reviewed, the rebound effect lies primarily on the environmental impact (due to increased use of fuel) (see rebound definition below), not particularly accounting for effects on individual car manufacturers (e.g. increased use of fuel rises demand for fuel-efficient cars, increased oil-prices raise resource input).

role in US Corporate Average Fuel Economy (CAFE) regulations (Portney, Parry, Gruenspecht and Harrington 2003). These regulations aim at regulating and improving average fuel economy of cars and light trucks (expressed in miles per gallon) by imposing penalties on manufacturers that do not meet fuel efficiency standards. Besides its importance for economy and politics, the example of rebound effects in fuel economy shall be used, because there are studies, which deal with dynamic complexity of the rebound effect, in the sense of a differentiation between long and short term effects.

Small and van Dender define the rebound effect with respect to fuel economy the following (2006: 1): "For motor vehicles, the process under consideration is use of fuel in producing vehicle-miles traveled (VMT). When vehicles are made more fuel-efficient, it costs less to drive a mile, so VMT increases if demand for it is downward-sloping. That in turn causes more fuel to be used than would be the case if VMT were constant; the difference is the rebound effect." Thus, the rebound effect can be considered the negative of the cost-per-mile elasticity of driving. One of the first scholars to examine the rebound effect based on aggregate data from 1957-1989 in the US was Greene (1992), whose studies estimate the rebound effect to be around 12,7%, with no differentiation between short- and long-term estimations (see also Greening, Greene and Difiglio 2000). Jones (1993) re-examined the data of Greene taking into account inertia (lagged variables) and showed that long-run estimates of the rebound effect (around 31%) exceeded short run estimates (around 11%). The main significance of the rebound effect in theses studies turned out to arise from the costs of 'externalities' due to the increased amount of driving, namely congestion and traffic accidents.

Small and van Dender (2006) introduce an interesting enhancement of these studies. The authors studied the rebound effect for the US in 1966-2001. Their findings support the former data, indicating a discrepancy between estimates of the short-run rebound effect (4.5%) and the long-run (22.2%). What is interesting though, is that the authors' findings suggest that the rebound effect as such *decreased* over the period, due to rising real income and potentially due to falling fuel prices (Small and van Dender 2006: 2 and 22ff, 31): With variables at 1997-2001 levels, the estimates for the rebound effect are only 2.2% and 10.7% (Small and van Dender 2006: 2).

In contrast to prior studies, the model of Small and van Dender allows for endogenous changes in fuel efficiency. Fuel efficiency thereby is determined jointly by consumers and manufacturers accounting for the price of fuel, the regulatory environment, and their expected amount of driving. This process can include manufacturers' adjustments to the relative prices of various models, consumers' adjustments via purchases of various models, consumers' decisions about vehicle scrappage, and driving habits (Small and van Dender 2006: 7). The rebound effect is allowed to vary with income, urbanization, and the fuel cost of driving (Small and van Dender 2006: 23). Behavioral inertia is allowed for by including one-year lagged values of the dependent variables (vehicle miles traveled, vehicle stock divided by adult population and fuel intensity).[406] Strong inertia is found e.g. in expanding or contracting the vehicle stock (Small and van Dender 2006: 19).

Regarding the rebound effect, findings indicate that a 10.5 percent increase in real income reduces the magnitude of the short-run rebound effect by about 0.58 percentage points. The authors conclude from this that "higher incomes make people less sensitive to fuel costs" (Small and van Dender 2006: 23). Urbanization has a smaller effect (a 10 percentage-point increase in urbanization reduces the rebound effect by about 25%). Fuel cost raises the rebound effect as expected, but only modestly and according to the authors without statistical significance (Small and van Dender 2006: 23). Most interestingly the findings indicate that the magnitude of the rebound effect has *declined* between the time periods 1966-1989 and 1990-2001. The authors see the reason for this stemming most likely from increases in real income over these time periods; falling fuel prices might have contributed to a smaller extend (Small and van Dender 2006: 21ff). Thus, the rebound effect diminishes with income, and possibly increases with fuel cost of driving. Furthermore results indicate that the response to fuel prices has become increasingly dominated by changes in fuel efficiency rather than changes in travel. Whether this remains the case after 2001 depends on how incomes and fuel costs of driving evolve (Small and van Dender 2006: 24). The authors conclude that the rebound effect is likely to diminish still further as rising incomes reduce the significance of fuel costs in decisions about travel. But this may be offset to some extent by increases in fuel prices (Small and van Dender 2006: 31).

Critically to this study it has to be pointed out that fuel prices can be expected to increase in the long-run (see stock argumentation above), so that the magnitude of the rebound effect might as well diminish less again or might rise above 10,7%. Furthermore the model holds the theoretical restriction that people react to changes in cost per mile in the same way whether those changes arise from variations in fuel prices or in fuel efficiency (Small and van Dender 2006: 30), which can equally be questioned. Last but not least, it needs to be considered that energy efficiency gains are not only reinvested for increased driving, but also on comfort and safety devices, accompanied by increased weight and increased direct energy use of cars on the market (for an overview see: Throne-Holst 2003). A survey on fuel-efficiency in the US from 1975 to 2006 by the Environment Protection Agency found that gains in fuel, where offset by increase of vehicle growth and performance, so

---

406 See Small and van Dender 2006: 8ff for an in-depth discussion of the model dynamics; also for a list of independent variables.

that fuel economy has remained constant (Heavenrich 2006). Schipper and Meyer (1992: 124f) indicate similar effects for Europe and Japan.

The findings outlined, once more point to the difficulty of assessing rebound-effects, because the effects (especially macro-economic effects) are very broad due to the increasing complexity of consumption patterns. So far evidence of existing studies underscores that rebound effects also in regard to fuel-efficiency are higher in the long-term than in the short-term[407], which is what constitutes the additional 'tricky' part of Efficiency Traps.

3.4 Traps in a Reputation Leadership Model (Image and Innovation)

3.4.1 Model Analysis

3.4.1.1 Underlying Belief about Corporate Sustainability

The underlying belief about the benefit of social and environmental sustainability measures for economic sustainability (profit maximization) in the Reputation Leadership Model is:

Environmental and social sustainability can contribute to sales and profit 'indirectly' via good reputation (brand image).

The line of argumentation, which this belief is based on, usually is similar to the following:

Because consumers today increasingly demand environmental and social sustainability, a good reputation regarding sustainability will strengthen our brands and the company's image. This will contribute to the loyalty of our customers and might attract new ones. Therefore we should seek to gain a sustainable reputation fast, in order to get a first-mover-advantage of being more sustainable than our competitors.

3.4.1.2 Underlying Model Dynamics

The model dynamic, which corporations holding a Reputation Leadership Model *believe* in and *act* according to (theory in-use) is that of the following reinforcing loop (R1):

---

407 This is so far also the evidence of Small and van Dender, although here it is less than in previous studies (i.e. the long-term impact reduces).

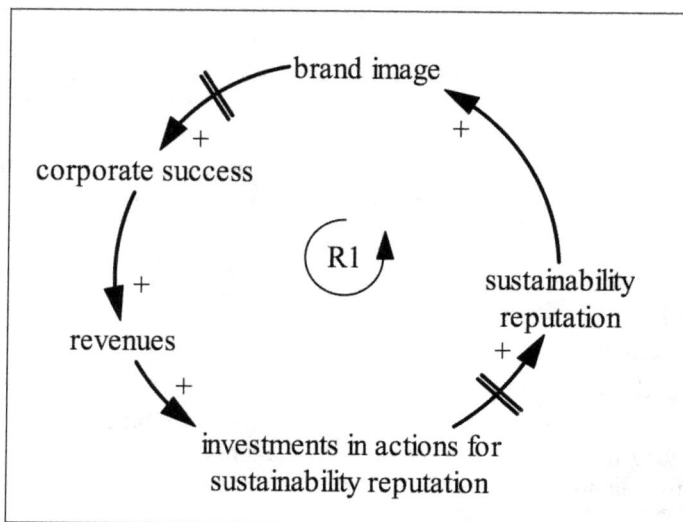

Fig. 36: Reputation Leadership Model: Model Dynamics
Source: Produced by the author

The corporation makes investments in actions, which aim to demonstrate that the company is sustainably responsible. When following a Reputation Leadership Model, such actions are often ones that promote public awareness, e.g. engaging with prominent NGOs in order to reduce unsustainability, labeling products, aiming at sustainability awards, sponsoring of media-effective sustainability initiatives. After some time (note the delay mark in figure 36) the reputation of being sustainably responsible rises. This positively impacts the brand image, which (after some time) will lead to higher corporate success. The corporate success leads to higher revenues, from which a part can be reinvested in building a sustainability reputation.

Regarding the activities invested in, to build a reputation of being sustainably responsible, it is most important to point out that the Reputation Leadership Model is *not* to equate with Greenwashing, i.e. with deliberate or negligent disinformation.[408] Rather companies following a Reputation Leadership Model seriously engage in sustainability in order to gain a *competitive advantage* through the reputation of being sustainably responsible. This subtle, but important distinction between a Reputation Leadership Model and Greenwashing will be outlined in-depth further below, because it is crucial with respect to a Reputation Trap.

---

408 See chapter 3.4.2.1 below for an in-depth explanation of Greenwashing.

3.4.1.3 Model Characteristics (Polarity Profile)

The model dynamics and its implications lead to the following characteristics of the Reputation Leadership Model:

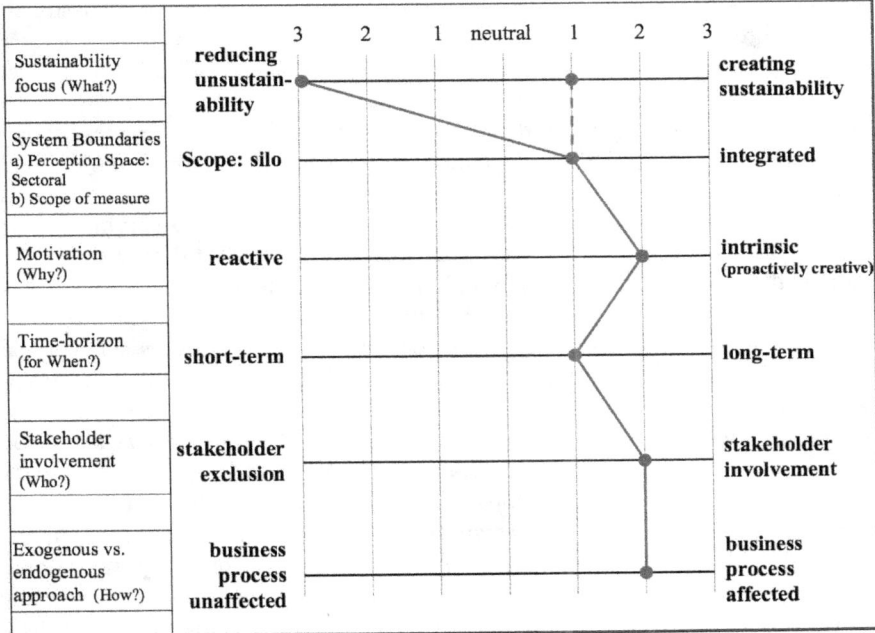

		3	2	1	neutral	1	2	3	
Sustainability focus (What?)	reducing unsustain-ability								creating sustainability
System Boundaries a) Perception Space: Sectoral b) Scope of measure	Scope: silo								integrated
Motivation (Why?)	reactive								intrinsic (proactively creative)
Time-horizon (for When?)	short-term								long-term
Stakeholder involvement (Who?)	stakeholder exclusion								stakeholder involvement
Exogenous vs. endogenous approach (How?)	business process unaffected								business process affected

Fig. 37: Reputation Leadership Model: Polarity Profile
Source: Produced by the author

The conception of the Reputation Leadership Model as well as its characteristics as they are illustrated in the Polarity Profile above, will be outlined in the following:

a) Conception of the Reputation Leadership Model

The aspect of reputation, particularly brand image, plays an ever increasing role for securing competitive advantage and economic success. Thereby *sustainability* is becoming a weightily factor in reputation (brand image). According to the Hill and Knowlton survey (2001) "Corporate Reputation Watch" 94% of the business leaders interviewed, considered reputation to be very important for achieving their strategic business objectives. [409] Corporate reputation is an asset, because it is linked to brand equity (Schwartz and Gibb 1999: 10), an intangible entity that measures consumer value of a particular product and is now widely regarded as "any organi-

---

409 The survey interviewed a total of 611 business leaders.

zation's most valuable and vulnerable asset" (Hollender and Fenichel 2004: 44). Raimondo Boggia, expert in brand management, suggests that nowadays the corporate name (connected directly to company reputation) and brand equity (connected to consumer value of a particular product) are *merging*, because consumers have begun to look to *a brand as a way to judge and express their own views of right and wrong*, rather than seeing brand-image as an individual indicator of product quality (Schwartz and Gibb 1999: 11). This role of brand-image as an expression of values is particularly crucial in the field of sustainbility, because it reaches beyond product qualities towards judging corporate behavior as such in regard to social and environmental issues.

As stated in the chapter on the Compliance Model, there still is an asymmetry of *punishing* unsustainability rather than *honoring* sustainability. But there are clear indications that the latter point is gaining importance and hence that sustainbility is becoming a *competitive advantage* rather than an inevitable minimum requirement. This is the case not only on the *consumer* side, but also on the *investor* side (capital market). Therefore it is especially corporations, which are focused on a strong brand-image that is associated with attributes like sportive, fair, family-friendly, progressive, innovative, which start perceiving sustainbility as a crucial factor for gaining credibility and a competitive advantage for their brand.

According to a survey on CSR trends, the company British Telecom for example has calculated that its social and environmental performance accounts for more than 25 percent of its overall business and reputation. It consequently is the second biggest factor, which drives change in customer satisfaction for the corporation (Hollender and Fenichel 2004: 47). Researchers from the company Philips Electronics, found that linking the attributes of energy reduction, materials and toxic reduction (lower-cost), immaterial (convenience) and emotional (quality-of-life, feel-good) raised consumer purchase interest by 60% (Ottman 2000).

Similarly in the capital market, following a Reputation Leadership Model, can prove to be a competitive advantage: The SAM Indexes, which together with STOXX Limited launches the Dow Jones Sustainability Indexes, claims that a growing number of investors sees sustainability is a catalyst for enlightened and disciplined management and hence as a crucial success factor.[410] Frank Dixon, managing director for research at the socially conscious investment firm Innovest Strategic Value Advisors, has observed that a corporation's environmental and social performance has become the perfect proxy for management quality in general. Because handling complex environmental and social issues requires sophisticated communication skills, a corporation successful in this field can also be assumed to

---

[410] See: http://www.sustainability-indexes.com/htmle/other/aboutus.html; accessed: 11. October 2005.

handle other complex issues well, which gives them a better risk-to-return profile (Hollender and Fenichel 2004: 48f).

b) Characteristics of a Reputation Leadership Model as illustrated in the Polarity Profile

From the above it becomes clear, that the **motivation** for sustainability measures of corporations holding a Reputation Leadership Model is an **intrinsic** one (see polarity profile).

Corporations holding a Reputation Leadership Model are ready to also engage into innovative sustainability measures, even if they require substantial investments, as long as they promise to promote brand-image. When further looking at sustainability measures, what seems striking in the polarity profile above, is the two dots regarding the reduction of unsustainability and the creation of sustainability. The dissertation chose to represent it in this way, because the Reputation Leadership Model often encompasses both. As will be outlined in the following, the emphasis however clearly lies on **reducing unsustainability** (see value three (3) in polarity profile).

In regard to sustainability reputation, consumers often differentiate between two corporate responsibilities (GlobeScan 2005):

a) Citizenship responsibilities, *where corporations holding a Reputation Leadership Model engage in* **creating sustainbility**

b) Operational responsibilities, *where corporations holding a Reputation Leadership Model focus on* **reducing unsustainability**

These two responsibilities, which are important to distinguish with respect to a Reputation Leadership Model, will be discussed in the following.

a) Citizenship Responsibilities

Citizenship responsibilities relate to issues, which are considered rather deferred from the actual business process (operations) of a corporation, such as solving social problems, reducing the divide between rich and poor or tackling human rights abuses (GlobeScan 2005). Fewer than half of the consumers hold corporations fully responsible for these issues. Companies, which take on citizenship responsibilities however can differentiate themselves and boost their reputation.

Corporations following a Reputation Leadership Model very often engage in citizenship activities, which are focused on *creating sustainability*, e.g. financing schools/education, reforestation in developing countries. Therefore the polarity profile indicates a dashed mark on creating sustainability with the value '1' (see figure 37)

b) Operational Responsibilities

Operational responsibilities are issues considered closely related to the operational business process itself, e.g. product safety, environmental protection, fair treatment of employees and ensuring an ethical supply chain (GlobeScan 2005). Failure to fulfill operational responsibilities can seriously damage a company's reputation. More than 70 per cent of consumers in the 21 countries surveyed by GlobeScan hold companies completely responsible for these. Operational responsibilities are thus the main ones in regard to achieving a sustainbility reputation.

Consumers are more likely to punish corporations seen as performing poorly on the operational side than reward companies, which exceed their expectations on the citizenship side. Therefore, a lack of responsibility at the operational level cannot be compensated for by more socially oriented citizenship activities (GlobeScan 2005).

Corporations holding a Reputation Leadership Model do apply sustainability measures, which address issues on their operational level. That is, measures, which *affect their business process* (see polarity profile).

It is important to note however that these measures are not yet focused on creating sustainability in the sense of 'doing the right things' (eco-effectiveness[411]). But they are focused on *reducing unsustainabilities* within their *existing business model*. The focus of corporations holding a Reputation Leadership Model therefore is to not only meet minimum requirements for sustainbility, but to *maximize their reduction of unsustainabilities* (see polarity profile value thee (3)). That is e.g. being the first corporation in its industry to reduce pollution by 70% or even to zero, zero land-fill, zero waste programs.

The crucial point, which is to be noted thereby, is that the focus of maximizing the reduction of unsustainability for corporations holding a Reputation Leadership Model refers to their *existing business model*. The *business model as such* is *not* changed. That is, the *mental model of perception space* remains a *sectoral* one. Because the sustainbility measures taken affect (change) only businesses processes within the existing business model and not the underlying business model as such, the polarity profile indicates only the value two (2) and not the value three (3) for the variable 'business process affected'.

The fact that in corporations holding a Reputation Leadership Model, the underlying business model as such remains unreflected and unchanged with respect to sustainbility, is most important to note. A problem (dilemma) is created, if the business model of the corporation is contributing to the very unsustainabilities, which the corporation seeks to minimize. This can lead into a malicious Sustainability Trap as will be outlined below.[412]

---

411 For eco-effectiveness see chapter 3.3.2.2.
412 See: Financing Brand-Image through Low-Cost Production Trap.

It is the *disparity* in the way of addressing *operational* responsibilities on the one side and *citizenship* responsibilities on the other side, which is a striking characteristic for corporations holding a Reputation Leadership Model. That is, the disparity between 1) focusing on reducing unsustainabilities within the existing, unchanged business model when it comes to operational responsibilities and 2) the new focus on creating sustainbility when it comes to citizenship responsibilities, which are perceived as something *apart* from the operational business process.[413]

The following will discuss the remaining characteristics of the Reputation Leadership Model:

The scope of measures applied to reduce unsustainabilities for corporations holding a Reputation Leadership Model can be considered narrow in so far, as sustainability measures are selected according to their impact on the company's image, - according to the motto 'do good and talk about it'. Because the factors, which shape a company's image, are numerous however, companies following a Reputation Leadership Model often realize that they have to apply sustainability measure on a broad band in order to receive a credible reputation for being sustainably responsible. Therefore the Reputation Leadership Model can be considered rather *integrated* than silo-oriented (see polarity profile).[414]

Furthermore corporations holding a Reputation Leadership Model, very often proactively engage in *stakeholder involvement*, particularly with NGOs (see polarity profile). Engaging with NGOs can strengthen the corporations' credibility regarding sustainability, particularly when the corporation is dealing with legacy problems of former unsustainability. Furthermore NGOs possess high knowledge on how to promote corporate sustainability, which is most valuable for corporations holding a Reputation Leadership Model.

The time-horizon considered in regard to sustainability measures, are rather *long-term* oriented than short-term for corporations holding a Reputation Leadership Model, because building an image takes time. But many corporations, which formerly held a Trade-Off or Compliance Model and which now seeks to change its image from being unsustainable into becoming a sustainably responsible leader (e.g. Chiquita, Nike), strive to build up this sustainbility reputation as fast as possible.

---

413 This is exactly what constitutes the main difference of the Reputation Leadership Model to a Systemic Model. For corporations holding a Systemic Model, the disparity between operational activities and citizenship activities closes more and more, because they are build as mission-driven enterprises. That is, the very business model of these corporations is conceptualized thus, that it focuses on the citizenship-mission of creating social and/or environmental sustainability. Operational and citizenship activities therefore are aligned in the sense that operational activities serve as a means to enhance citizenship responsibilities (i.e. holistic mental model of perception space). Thus, the two responsibilities are not conflicting as it is often the case for corporations following a Reputation Leadership Model.

414 But not as much as the Systemic Model.

Therefore the time-horizon of the Reputation Leadership Model can be classified as rather *long-term* oriented than short-term oriented, but still far from the foresight of companies holding a Systemic Model. The polarity profile above (figure 37), correspondingly indicates the value one (1) for the time-horizon considered.

The time discrepancy between 1) the corporations' intention to change their image with regard to sustainability[415] *fast* and thus to *early* communicate their sustainability measures initiated and 2) the rather *long* time it takes for fundamental measures implemented to actually 'show effect' due to limitations, will be crucial for the Reputation Trap discussed below.[416]

3.4.1.4   Relations to Other Models

As has been outlined in chapter 3.1.1.3, there exists a 'historical trajectory' of improving sustainability measures in respect of the models outlined so far (see also what Griffiths, Benn and Dunphy 2003: 14). That is, there is a sort of chronological development from a historical, orthodox Trade-off Model to a Reputation Leadership Model, i.e. a development from 'Saulus to Paulus of sustainability', which many multinational corporations are running through at present. [417]

Thereby a corporation does not need to progress through all phases, but can also leapfrog phases (see also Griffiths, Benn and Dunphy 2003: 14). This is especially the case for brand-sensitive corporations, which often seek to quickly move from a formerly held Trade-off Model to a Reputation Leadership Model in order to gain competitive advantage in the emerging field of sustainable products. Thereby the phase of adopting a Compliance Model in this 'trespassing' is rather short and measures of eco-efficiency in contrast to the Efficiency Model are adopted as one measure among others within a sustainability strategy.

While discussing the relation of the Reputation Leadership Model to other models in this chapter, therefore also the 'historical trajectory' shall be outlined using the sportswear company 'Nike' as an example, in particular Nike's 'labor issue' in sourcing from contract factories in developing countries.[418] Figure 38, shows the corresponding historical trajectory:

---

415 That is from 'unsustainable' to 'sustainable'.

416 See chapter 3.4.2.

417 As stated, the Systemic Model in contrast relates to a radically different business model with a holistic perception space and currently can be rather found in small and medium size start-up companies (mission-driven enterprises) and not yet in multinational corporations.

418 Details of this historical development can be found in Appendix I.

Nike's "labor issue" in contract factories		
Trade-off Model	**Compliance Model**	**Reputation Model**
• Aiming at cheap production costs without consideration of labor conditions	• Acknowledgement of corporate responsibility for labor issues (launch of Responsibility Report)	• Perception of sustainability as an open-end process
• Corporation as job creator in poor countries (= social sustainability)	• Engagement with NGOs and advocates to rebut image	• Broadening scope of responsibility
• Corporations not the accountable institutions for sustainability (instead legislation, NGOs etc.)	• First steps towards transparency	• Shift from monitoring as a main instrument towards learning/training and involvement
• NGOs as molesters	• Code of conduct and commitments combined with monitoring program as bulwark against accusations of unsustainability	• Analysis of root causes
		• NGOs and researchers as learning partners
	• Focusing reasoning for non-compliance on external causes (legislation, fraud, incapability of factory personnel)	**Eco-Efficiency Measures** • Waste elimination/recycling
		• Reduction of material input (particularly harmful substances)

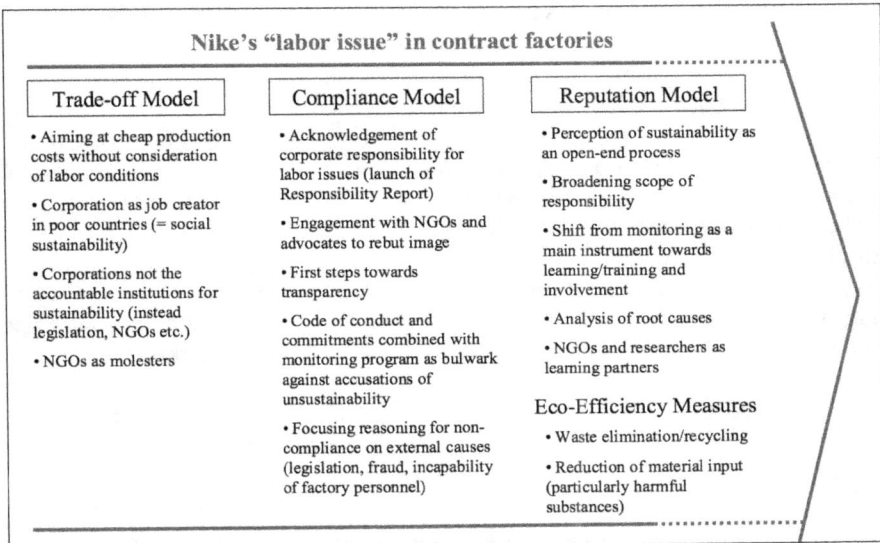

Fig. 38: Historical Trajectory of Changes in Mental Models
Source: Produced by the author; Example: Corresponding behavior regarding
Nike's 'labor issue'

Trade-off Model: As stated, the Trade-off Model was the historical, orthodox mental model of business with respect to sustainability, as neither the corporation nor the majority of society held business accountable for unsustainabilities.

Also Nike started with a clear Trade-off Model, especially regarding social sustainability. The company deliberately sought for cheapest labor in order to maximize profits and reinvest in brand building and design. Accusations of unsustainability were countered with statements like the one that the workers should be lucky that Nike provides jobs to the regions and that unsustainability is not the companies' business, but rather one for the United Nations[419] - a clear rejection of corporate accountability for unsustainabilities. NGOs raising labor issues were not considered stakeholders, but rather molester for the ongoing business.

Compliance Model: As outlined in chapter 3.2, due to NGO pressure and a change in values of society as a whole, corporations today start moving away from a Trade-off Model towards a Compliance Model. Thereby corporations very often apply symptomatic solutions, which get them into Quick-Fix Traps, where scandals that harm corporate image keep on reappearing despite the measures applied.

---

419 For statements see Nike case below (chapter 3.4.3.3 and appendix I).

This was also the case for Nike. With former CEO Phil Knight's "mea culpa" speech in 1998 and Nike's first Corporate Responsibility Report in 2001, the company induced a shift towards a Compliance Model, after years of severe NGO's protests, several law suits, customer boycotts and increasing damage on the Nike brand. Nike started to engage with NGOs, even with one of its fiercest critics "Global Exchange". But it was apparent that Nike made sure to have some control over the NGOs or advocates with which the company interacted more deeply, such as the Fair Labor Association (see below) or in the case of the UN Ambassador Andrew Young[420]. In addition Nike launched a list of commitments along with a Code of Conduct for contract factories and initiated a rigorous monitoring program to ensure compliance with the Code. But as is characteristic for companies holding a Compliance Model, Nike used the Code of Conduct and the monitoring as a quick fix, in the sense of shifting-the-responsibility (burden) away from Nike towards the suppliers: When accused of unsustainability, Nike now reacted by pointing out that it did have a code of conduct and it even imposed a rigorous monitoring program.

Efficiency Model: Both, Efficiency Model as well as Reputation Leadership Model apply sustainability measures as a tool to gain competitive advantage. Whereas the Efficiency Model strives to reduce costs of unsustainability, the Reputation Leadership Model aims at increasing image and sales through sustainability measures. As stated above, corporations holding a Reputation Leadership Model thereby often adopt measures of eco-efficiency as one sustainability measure among others.

Nike for example seeks to adopt cradle-to-cradle approaches, and currently is applying eco-efficiency measures such as energy reduction, waste elimination and more efficient use of input-materials.

Reputation Leadership Model: While corporations holding a Compliance Model follow a minimizing (satisfying) strategy regarding sustainable reputation, corporations holding a Reputation Leadership Model follow a maximizing strategy regarding a sustainable reputation, as stated.

Regarding the chronological trajectory, corporations, which 'stick' to a Compliance Model are often ones that deal with unbranded ('white products'), low-price products (see Tchibo case[421]). As stated above, brand-sensitive corporations in contrast often leapfrog from a Trade-off Model towards a Reputation Leadership Model, with only a short period of Compliance Model.

Also Nike can be considered one of these latter corporations: Nike's Corporate Responsibility Report 2004 indicates that the company has started to move towards a

---

420 The civil rights activist Young was hired by Nike to toured its Asian factories, but received a lot of critics, because the translators as well as the guides he used for the tour were supplied by Nike (Hollender and Fenichel 2004: 190).
421 Chapter 3.2.3.3.

Reputation Leadership Model, where the company is willing to adopt significant changes in order to not only comply with sustainability expectations, but where the company also seeks to gain a competitive image-advantage over its industry peers, by proactively addressing sustainability issues and setting sustainability standards for its industry. The company now views sustainability as an open ended process, where benchmarks of what is considered to be sustainable, are likely to rise continuously. The company took another huge step regarding transparency by being the first of its industry to publicly disclose the lists of its contract factories. Nike started, even though not yet systematically, to consider itself responsible for payback of workers' wages in specific cases. Furthermore Nike diffidently starts analyzing root causes of unsustainability. All these are clear indications that Nike started moving towards a Reputation Leadership Model. But the company still has some distance to cover in order to overcome accusations of 'sweatwashing' and being successful with a Reputation Leadership Model.

As will be discussed in the Nike business case below, Nike can be considered to have moved away from a trap of Quick-fixes and Fire-the-Supplier of a Compliance Model.[422] But is now starting to realize that it is caught up in the trap of Financing Brand-Image through Low-Cost Production and faces the challenge to address its very business model as a root cause to its sustainbility problems.

Systemic Model: Companies holding a Systemic Model also usually promote an image of being sustainable. But these cases are not to equate with a Reputation Leadership Model. As has been stated in the model analysis above[423] and as will be discussed in-depth in chapter 3.5, the Systemic Model can be considered a significant breach (leap) in the model trajectory: The Systemic Model relates to a radically different business model, which is based on a holistic mental model of perception space and currently can be rather found in small and medium size start-up companies (mission-driven enterprises) and not yet in multinational corporations. Also Nike is still far from reaching a Systemic Model.

3.4.2 Reputation Trap
3.4.2.1 Archetypical Trap Structure

One of the most significant risks for companies following a Reputation Leadership Model is what the dissertation calls 'Reputation Trap': Being caught up in a spiral of increasing sustainability expectations form NGOs and customers. This risk especially refers to corporations, which have shifted from a former attitude of unsustainability towards a Reputation Leadership Model. – What the dissertation above has referred to as the historical trajectory of seeking to move from 'Saulus to Paulus of sustainability'. The critical point is that these corporations hold significant legacy

---

422 See chapter 3.4.3.3 and appendix I.
423 See footnote in chapter 3.4.1.3

problems regarding their credibility of sustainability. Therefore, if these companies engage into sustainability, their sustainability measures are screened all the more thoroughly by NGOs and interested consumers. If shortcomings to sustainbility are detected, these companies face a particularly high risk of *being accused of Greenwashing*, which would *countervail* the intended image improvement.

The Oxford English Dictionary defines Greenwash as "disinformation disseminated by an organization so as to present an environmentally responsible public image" (Concise Oxford English Dictionary 2001). Disinformation can thereby refer to deliberately wrong information or deliberately withholding important information on failures in sustainbility.[424]

These cases need to be distinguished from cases, where only partial information, in form of sustainbility *successes* are communicated, because the corporation does not perceive *shortcomings*, due to **too narrow system boundaries in time and space**. This can often be observed for corporations coming from a Trade-off Model or Compliance Model and now seeking to follow a Reputation Leadership Model. They engage into substantial projects and measures for reducing unsustainability, which for the corporations constitute a large step. Because the corporations follow a Reputation Leadership Model, they then are eager to communicate their progresses with respect to sustainbility *early*, in order to *quickly* change their reputation and gain a more sustainable image.

Because these companies often still hold quite narrow system boundaries on sustainability, they very often communicate their success (sustainbility project/measures), *without pointing to shortcomings and inconsistencies* that still exist. Especially often the case can be observed that corporations seeking to follow a Reputation Leadership Model engage into **pilot projects**, which go far beyond mere compliance and are substantially innovative with respect to sustainbility. But as the concept of a pilot project implies, it does not yet apply to the core business processes. In order to foster the reputation as a leader corporations tend to communicate successful pilot projects, without addressing the shortcomings of their core business process and product.

A problem arises, because many stakeholders, especially NGOs and pertinent media, which are critical regarding the credibility of a sustainbility reputation of the corporations, hold **broader** system boundaries than the corporations.

These stakeholders measure corporate sustainability behavior according to their own (absolute) standards on sustainability, which are based on these broader system boundaries. Therefore they perceive shortcomings and inconsistencies in corporate

---

424 A survey of 80 pro-environmental claims (e.g. on labels) such as 'for every tree felled, at least two are planted' found that 77 of the claims could not be substantiated at all, 3 only partially, and almost all were withdrawn when challenged (Diamond 2005: 472f). These are examples of deliberate misinformation.

behavior with respect to sustainability, which – particularly in change processes – often occur.[425]

The discrepancy in system boundaries can lead to the danger that stakeholders attribute higher expectations on sustainability on a company claiming to be sustainably responsible, than currently intended in the corporate conception of sustainability. Thus, NGOs seem to ask for "more and more", while the company at this point seeks to feed its reputation on the present achievements. This can lead corporations holding a Reputation Leadership Model and communicating their sustainability measures/improvements at an early state, into the following Reputation Trap (figure 39):

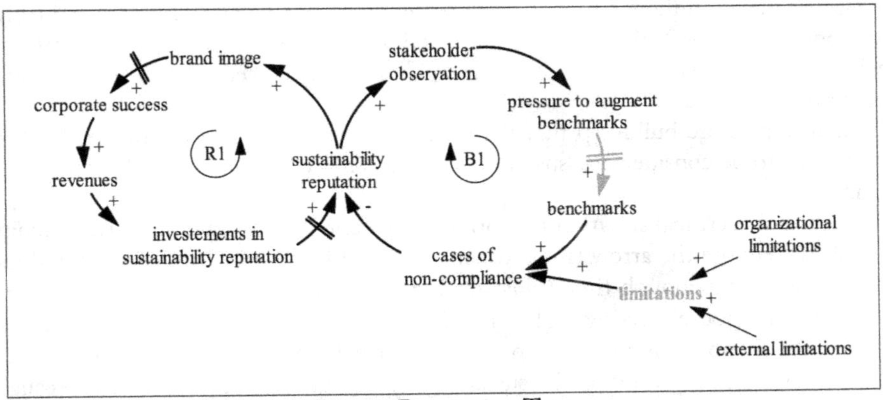

Fig. 39: Reputation Trap
Source: Produced by the author

The growth dynamic, which can enhance sustainability reputation (R1) corresponds to the model dynamic of the Reputation Leadership Model outlined above (chapter 3.4.1.2): The company, especially when it historically comes from a Trade-off Model and holds legacy problems, engages into serious measures for becoming a sustainability leader. Thereby the measures are no obvious quick-fixes, but substantial, rather fundamental investments (e.g. engaging in a training and learning relationship with a supplier), because the company seriously seeks to gain credibility as a sustainable company. But these more fundamental measures need a rather *long* time to show effect (note the delay mark in figure 39).

---

425 For example having an eco-line/fair-trade line of product X, while the majority of the products are still produced far more unsustainably. For example IKEA, which planned an eco-product line, but would still manufacture most of its products in the orthodox way. Another example is Unilever, which experiences with an organic, fair-caught fish-line.

On the other hand, the corporation seeks to early communicate the initiatives and measures it has launched in order to *rapidly* change its 'Saulus'-image of sustainability, because it hopes to thus increase sales. A part of these additional revenues can than be reinvested into further measures for creating a sustainable image, etc.

But this reinforcing dynamic is often moderated by the following balancing dynamic (B1): As the reputation of the company to be sustainably responsible rises, stakeholders (NGOs, media and consumers)[426] increasingly start observing the company's activities through the lens of sustainability. Due to this closer observation, shortcomings regarding sustainability show up (e.g. through studies by NGOs or by investigative journalists). This is often the case because 1) the stakeholders (NGOs) have a different (broader) understanding of company that is 'sustainably responsible' and/or 2) the rather fundamental measures initiated by the corporation, which formerly held a Trade-Off or Compliance Model, need time to show the effect 'promised'.

Therefore pressure builds up that the corporation has to raise its benchmarks if it still seeks to be considered a 'sustainably responsible' company by NGOs and consumers.[427]

This often is a critical situation for corporations following a Reputation Leadership Model (therefore the arrow is marked in orange in figure 39). If the company does not allow a long enough time (illustrated by the delay mark) to *account for limitations*, which oppose meeting higher sustainability benchmarks, the number of cases where the company is not able to meet the benchmarks (non-compliance) rises. This then negatively impacts the sustainability reputation of the company, because it did not meet its benchmarks communicated e.g. in its code of conduct[428] and thus did not 'hold its promises'.

In extreme cases, a sudden harsh or repeated damage on brand-image due to sustainability reputation might (after a time-delay) even tip the reinforcing dynamic (R1), which the company primarily used as a means to *growth*, into a reinforcing dynamic, which *decreases* brand-image and thus corporate success.[429]

Kramer describes the essence of the balancing dynamic (B1) of the Reputation Trap to the point. He outlines that Weyerhaeuser, Starbucks, and Nike all made

---

426 These can also comprise further stakeholders, e.g. investors. But the focus here lies on the consumer side.

427 E.g. statements like:" As long as the company does eliminate y or does not do x, it cannot really be considered to be sustainably responsible."

428 As pointed out above, the interpretation of the code of conduct might be influenced by (absolute) indicators of NGOs that usually are stricter than those of corporations.

429 That is: Brand image decreases, hence corporate success decreases (e.g. less sales, deceived employees, drop out of investors), thus less revenues and thus less money to invest in actions to rebuild sustainability reputation (even though in this situation more money is needed to rebuilt the reputation).

similar experiences. Once they starting engaging into sustainbility, the more they were observed and pressured to augment their efforts. Therefore Kramer stresses the point that corporations leading the ethical-business charge remain prime targets of advocacy groups, who point to shortcomings of their measures, so that applause is seldom far from a Greenwashing charge (Kramer 2000). Vogel in his analysis has also identified this risk and states that the more a corporation trumpets its social or environmental engagement, the more vulnerable it is to challenges by activists when its behavior fails to meet their expectations (Vogel 2005a and 2005b).[430]

It is important to point out that it is *not* the intention of the dissertation to come to the defense of corporations, which, although having achieved substantial progress, still hold serious unsustainabilities. Just as little it is the intention of the dissertation to call on NGOs or on critical consumers to satisfy themselves with the progress these companies have made in their industry and for NGOs to stop pointing to further unsustainabilities. The identification of these unsustainabilities is important and most crucial for a shift into a less unsustainable society.

The intention of the dissertation rather *is* to address managers of corporations seeking to follow a Reputation Leadership Model. The dissertation seeks to outline to these managers a common trap (Reputation Trap) their companies risk to face, when seeking to turn 'from Saulus to Paulus' and become a sustainably responsible leader in order to gain a competitive advantage in its industry. In the following the dissertation therefore will outline, how corporations can best address respectively avoid a Reputation Trap, when seeking to follow a Reputation Leadership Model.

3.4.2.2 Dealing with the Trap

As figure 39 indicates the crucial aspect in this limits-to-growth structure are the *limitations*, which hinder to increase the sustainability benchmarks *in-use*, i.e. those actually used.[431] For dealing with this trap, two measures are existent, which need to be applied in combination in order to avoid a Reputation Trap:

> *a) Transparent communication*: If the elimination of limitations takes time (which it usually does), but the corporation at a point still wants to go ahead and start communicating its campaign for becoming a sustainably responsible leader, the corporation can seek to avoid a Reputation Trap through thorough transparency (transparent communication). *As long as the time gained is used to address the limitations fundamentally.*

---

430 Vogel however, draws the conclusion that corporations should therefore abstain from a Reputation Leadership Model on sustainbility altogether. This view is not shared by the dissertation. Rather as will be outlined, transparent communication along with addressing root causes builds a way for avoiding getting into this trap.

431 For a limits-to-growth structure see Senge 2006: 390 and appendix A1.

b) Address and eliminate the limitations (external and organizational: This
is the core measures, which, when not taken simultaneously with transparent communication, will lead the corporation into a Reputation Trap.
While transparent communication is a *symptomatic* solution, which gains
time; addressing limitations is the *fundamental* measure.

In the following both measures will be discussed.

a) Transparent communication
In order to execute transparent communication, many measures are possible. The
dissertation will discuss two, which have gained popularity:

> ***a1) Labelling***: That is, certification through NGOs. [432]

> ***a2) Sustainbility reports***: That is, the corporation practices transparent
> communication itself, through corporate sustainbility reports.

a1) Labelling (NGO certification)
Quite often corporations engage with NGOs in order to certify their products or
business processes to be sustainably responsible. This provides a more neutral, official recognition of being sustainably responsible.
Using accredited eco-labels from reliable and well-known NGOs can help overcome a potential "credibility gap" between business and consumer (Holliday,
Schmidheiny, Watts (2002): 178). The German Blue Angel was the first eco-label.
It started in 1978 and now covers 4,885 products (Holliday, Schmidheiny, Watts
(2002): 178). One of the best-known labels is the Fair-trade label and the one
from the Forest Stewardship Council (FSC), which today is used e.g. by Ikea and
others. The restaurant chain *fish!* was the first restaurant to use labels from the Marine Stewardship Council (MSC) in 2001. In the dissertation the case of Chiquita
will be discussed below, which successfully qualified for a certification of the Rainforest Alliance.
As Holliday, Schmidheiny, Watts (2002: 180) argue, eco-labels can increase sales.
Far East and Northern Europe suggest that eco-labeling does work, especially with
promotion at point-of-sales (Holliday, Schmidheiny, Watts (2002): 180). The risk
of being accused of Greenwashing is lower than with merely sponsoring or promotion activities, because NGOs are involved as independent partners. However, form
a systemic point of view, it must be pointed out that eco-labeling and certification
can only work out efficiently to increase sustainability, if customers on the other
side posses knowledge about the implications of different labels. Customers need to
be able to differentiate between reliable, independent labels from NGOs and non-
substantiated labels.

---

432 Other, similar measures are e.g. prices for sustainability or direct consumer interaction.

Furthermore it has to be pointed out that labels usually concentrate on a specific aspect of sustainability. Therefore a label, even a reliable one, does not automatically mean that a corporation is sustainably responsible in an omnibus way. Thus, renowned labels can increase a corporation's credibility regarding one sustainability aspect, but if unsustainabilities in other areas occur, the company might still get into a Reputation Trap.

a2) Sustainbility Reports

A second measure for increasing transparency, is transparent communication of the corporations themselves, e.g. in sustainability reports. As mentioned, above transparent communication requires communicating sustainability successes *in the context of* corporate *deficiencies to sustainability*.

In order to identify deficiencies, corporations following a Reputation Leadership Model need to *broaden system boundaries on sustainability in time and space*. Transparent communication needs to clearly indicate where the company actually stands with respect to sustainability and how far it still needs to go. Showing a balanced picture (successes and shortcomings) and placing this picture into a comprehensive context is one of the most effective ways for creating transparency and along with this, credibility. Corporations following a Reputation Leadership Model need to move beyond compliance and need to regard corporate sustainability as an *open-ended process*, in which the company still has quite a learning journey to go.

As the business examples will show, most multinational corporations just start to make first experiences with such types of transparent communication, including a disclosure of existing unsustainabilities – and so do their customers. For example it will be most interesting to see how customers will assess a company like Philip Morris, which proactively communicates the unsustainability of their own products. Customers - all the same like corporations - need to learn how to deal with a marketing (or communication), which does not only present the 'sunny and nice side' of the customers' beloved high-image products, but also openly reveals problems of unsustainability. Chiquita for example in its Corporate Responsibility Report for 2002 (Chiquita 2003), addresses cases of forced labor[433], discrimination and even work-related fatalities. Following this path means building a new kind of relationship of transparency and trust, but also of new responsibilities with customers. As

---

433 In 2000 assessors found that ship captains held crewmembers' passports and identification papers, which is a common industry practice, to make processing easier for the captain at foreign ports when immigration officials inspect identification documents for each seafarer as Chiquita states. Yet it can be misused for forced labor. Therefore Chiquita's Code of Conduct prohibits any requirement that employees must deposit identity papers with the company at the start of employment (Chiquita 2003: 45). But as the company does not prevent the collection of documents on a voluntary basis, a risk of misuse remains.

Boggia states "Building brand equity is no longer as it was in the 1950s and 1960s, a matter of 'make up'. The game of advertising is over. It is now about communicating what you really are in an intelligent way" (Raimondo Boggia, expert for brand-image, cited in an interview by Schwartz and Gibb 1999: 11).[434]

b) Addressing limitations

Above, transparency has been discussed as a measure for addressing a Reputation Trap. While transparent communication about shortcomings still existent in the corporation is important to avoid a Reputation Trap, it alone is not sufficient. As long as the limitations, which hinder the corporation to overcome the shortcomings to sustainability, are not addressed *simultaneously* by corporations following a Reputation Leadership Model, transparency remains a *symptomatic solution* and the corporations still face a high risk of getting into a Reputation Trap.

Therefore the issue of addressing limitations will be discussed in the following. As indicated in figure 39 limitations basically can be:[435]

> **b1) internal** as well as
> **b2) external.**

b1) Internal limitations

Internal limitations can further be distinguished between *cultural* limitations and *organizational* limitations: If sustainability is a rather new concept to the corporation and a system perspective is lacking, chances are high that the corporation's approach is not holistically enough and crucial dynamics with respect to sustainability are not identified yet. As a consequence incomplete or even inconsistent approaches are taken, which then seem as Greenwashing to other agents (e.g. NGO), which hold a more holistic mental model. Second and most crucial the organization even if holding a consistent approach regarding a sustainability issue, faces organizational limitations such as sourcing practices, organizational structures, sustainability know how, which hinder a *quick* change.

b2) External limitations

External limitations with regard to contract factories refer e.g. to local legislations, local cultures, beliefs and behavior of managers of contract factories, capabilities and knowledge of workers in contract factories, etc.

---

434 The issue will be discussed deeper in the Chiquita case below (see chapter 3.4.2.2).
435 This distinction, as any distinction, is a theoretical one used for explanatory purposes and depends on boundary judgments.

External versus internal limitations
As the dissertation will show in the business cases below, organizational limitations and external limitations are often interdependent. External limitations can pose severe obstacles and are not to underestimate. But the key role for corporations lies in *organizational limitations*, because they are easier for companies to influence and control and they can furthermore effect external limitations.

Nonetheless if companies do consider limitations to more sustainability at all, the focus often lies on *external* limitations rather than internal limitations/barriers. This is because external limitations are often easier to detect (for example prohibition of labor unions (e.g. China) or allowance of low ages for factory workers). Furthermore they provide a convenient opportunity for corporations to play the blame game and shifting the responsibility to other agents involved.

Above it has been discussed that addressing external limitations at contract factories through engaging in learning and training at the suppliers' is a more fundamental solution than merely codes of conduct and firing-the-supplier.[436]

The subchapters below will show that addressing external limitations remains a symptomatic solution, as long as *internal limitations* of the very corporation (buyer) are not addressed. This problematic can be observed so often that it will be addressed in a separate chapter as a special case. In this case, the very business model of Financing Brand-Image through Low-Cost Production constitutes the trap.[437]

3.4.2.3 Business Case: Chiquita

Some readers might be surprised to read about Chiquita Brands International, Inc. in the chapter of the Reputation Leadership Model. Chiquita and particularly its predecessor United Fruit Company hold a record of fiercest Trade-Off (Heuer 2006, Klawitter 2006).[438] After a period of compliance, today Chiquita has started to shift to a Reputation Leadership Model and – within its industry - is becoming one of the sustainably responsible leaders. The specific *details* of the history of Chiquita's transition from Trade-Off to Reputation Leadership can be traced in-depth in appendix G. For the following case of the Reputation Trap, which Chiquita risks facing currently, only individual, relevant outcomes of this transition will

---

436 See chapter 3.2.3.2.

437 This chapter thus ties in with chapter 3.2.3.2, where the problematic of sourcing from contract factories with serious unsustainabilities has been discussed as a special case in the light of a Quick-Fix Trap for corporations holding a Compliance Model.

438 Most prominent was e.g. the case that United Fruit Company has been accused of supporting political forces in the U.S. in overthrowing the democratically elected government of Jacobo Arbenz of Guatemala in 1954 (Schlesinger and Kinzer 2005, Taylor-Robinson and Redd 2003). Here however Chiquita shall be analyzed, not its predecessor United Fruit Company.

be referred to. The dissertation chose to discuss the Chiquita case as an example for the Reputation Leadership Model, especially *because* of the history of unsustainability it possesses. This is not to deny that Chiquita still does have a lot of unsustainabilities it needs to address. Chiquita here rather is an interesting case of a company with serious legacy problems of unsustainability, which seeks to become a sustainably responsible leader in its industry and currently is just on the verge of moving away from a Compliance Model towards a Reputation Leadership Model. This is what makes the Chiquita case, particularly interesting in reference to a Reputation Trap. As the dissertation will outline, the sustainably responsible leadership thereby is to see in comparison to Chiquita's industry peers, i.e. the ‚orthodox' fruit industry, in particular banana industry, not the bio/organic and fair trade industry.

Chiquita's achievements with regard to sustainbility reputation

Chiquita is undertaking significant investments and managed to reach substantial improvements in respect of reducing unsustainabilities. The company spends US$3 Mio. per year for Infrastructure and improved working processes as well as US$3 – US$4 Mio. per year as bonus to their suppliers to foster ecological and social behavior (Heuer 2006: 24; see also Taylor and Scharlin 2004). In the last quarter 2005, Chiquita started to launch an image campaign for Chiquita as the 'better' banana. That is, Chiquita as a brand, which is environmentally as well as socially one of the most aware in its industry (Reputation leadership in its industry). Thereby the company strongly relies and advertises its long-term partnership with the Rainforest Alliance, a NGO aimed at protecting rainforest and other ecosystems, which significantly contributed to Chiquita's turnaround.

Chiquita's achievements particularly in the field of environmental sustainbility have opened up a path for Chiquita to gain reputation as a sustainably responsible leader in its industry as is targeted by the company: Chiquita's banana farms in Costa Rica were the first major agricultural operation in Central America to earn SA8000 certification in 2002. In 2002, the company earned recertification of all company-owned farms to Rainforest Alliance standards (Chiquita 2003: 4). In 2003 Chiquita received the Corporate Conscience Award for Innovative Partnership of Social Accountability International. The award recognizes outstanding corporate social and environmental initiatives.[439]

And even more corporate-critical organizations acknowledge that Chiquita took some progressive measures for sustainability in comparison to its industry peers: "Chiquita has excelled past its competitors by using Rainforest Alliance environmental standards in banana production" (The Responsible Shopper[440]). Melo and Wolf (2005) in their empirical assessment of eco-certified farms in Ecuador found

---

439 http://www.rainforest-alliance.org/news/rainforest-matters/november2003.html, accessed: 16. January 2006.

that certified farms, including Chiquita farms, significantly outperform non-certified farms on all environmental assessment criteria. Werre (2003) in his case analysis of Chiquita assigns the company to have successfully implemented its corporate responsibility structure, by identifying a consistent understanding of corporate responsibility based on four core values (integrity, respect, opportunity and responsibility) and by aligning the corporation's action to the values. Alsever from Business 2.0 Magazine states that Chiquita is becoming a study in corporate responsibility, rather than a counterexample (Alsever 2006).

Chiquita facing a Reputation Trap
As the dissertation will show in the following, Chiquita is getting into a Reputation Trap, where Chiquita's campaign along with its achievements risks to be discredited as mere Greenwashing (see also Heuer 2006: 25; Vogel 2005b). Leaving the company in a spiral of the need for ever increasing its sustainability measures; but as these are running behind the expectations released through the campaign, they are likely to be discredited as Greenwashing as well.

As the dissertation elaborated above, it is key for corporations, which hold credibility problems from their past to 1) conduct *transparent communication* of shortcomings still existent, while 2) simultaneously *addressing the limitations,* which hinder the corporation to overcome the shortcomings.

What the dissertation will therefore show in the following is that engaging with an NGO and achieving certification for its farms (suppliers) as well as reporting on shortcomings still existent (transparent communication), as Chiquita does, still remains a symptomatic solution and will not avoid getting into a Reputation Trap as long as *root causes (limitations)* are not started to be addressed *simultaneously.*

By these the dissertation refers to *organizational, internal limitations,* which lie within the very business process of Chiquita itself, e.g. how suppliers are chosen, purchasing prices etc. Furthermore the dissertation will also point to problems or barriers of addressing these internal limitations for Chiquita, which arise from *external limitations* and reveal the complexity of the issue.[441]

---

440 http://www.coopamerica.org/programs/rs/profile.cfm?id=202, accessed: 24. November 2006.

441 It needs to be mentioned, that the Chiquita case equally is a case of the special-case of Financing Brand-image through Low Cost Production (see chapter 3.4.3). The emphasis in this chapter however, lies in pointing out that *transparent communication* (i.e. achieving certification from NGO and sustainbility reporting) proves to be *symptomatic* solutions, as long as root causes (limitations) are not addressed. Chapter 3.4.3 (including Nike case), will then lay emphasis on analyzing the case that the very business model is an organizational limitation to sustainbility and how this trap can be addressed.

Unsustainabilities (shortcomings) are countered through transparent communication
Chiquita gained a lot of achievements regarding environmental sustainbility. However, particularly with regard to *social* sustainability (workers rights at farms), the company still faces serious shortcomings. Chiquita is using the measure of transparent communication in order to address these shortcomings and by doing so seeks to maintain credibility of its measures for sustainbility – and thus to avoid the Reputation Trap of Greenwashing accusations popping-up repeatedly.

What is interesting to note however, is that the efforts for transparent communication have subsided in recent time, so that the risk for Chiquita to staying caught-up in a Reputation Trap is even higher.[442]

In the field of social sustainbility, Chiquita still faces serious shortcomings, which various critics point to and which thus risk undermining the credibility of the sincere achievements, which Chiquita gained so far and which it seeks to build its leadership reputation on:

Stephen Coats, executive director of U.S. LEAP, which advocates for Latin American worker rights states that there have been clear and important improvements, regarding workers rights, but the situation is still far from perfect (Alsever 2006). In 2002 Human Rights Watch published reported cases of child labor at farms contracted by Chiquita, Del Monte and Dole, whereby the children were also exposed to toxic chemicals (Klawitter 2006). In 2006 workers at a farm in Panama contracted to Chiquita, laid down their work, because they were not paid their wages (Klawitter 2006). Moreover Chiquita needed to spend two days renegotiating workers' contracts after disputes with Honduran labor unions (Alsever 2006).

Chiquita started to address its non-compliances with the certification standards of the Rainforest alliance in a respectively transparent manner beginning 2000 in Corporate Responsibility Reports. Chiquita's Corporate Responsibility Report 2002 provides transparent overviews of the Rainforest Alliance's audits (Chiquita 2003: 16) as well as assessments against the SA8000 standard (Chiquita 2003: 24). Cases of non-compliance are addressed, such as forced labor, discrimination (Chiquita 2003: 47) and even work-related fatalities (Chiquita 2003: 26). The report also even mentions the fact that three farms in Honduras were temporarily decertified from the Rain Forest Alliance, after a surprise audit uncovered two major non-conformances (Chiquita 2003: 11). Furthermore the report shows that all banana divisions audited had at least one non-compliance with SA8000 standard regarding health and safety of the workers and in all divisions, administrative personnel routinely exceeded the maximum allowable overtime hours (Chiquita 2003: 24). Michelle Lapinski, director of food and agriculture advisory services at the nonprofit Business for Social Responsibility with respect to Chiquita starting to publish its Corporate Responsibility Report in 2000 states:" They were really transpar-

---

442 Aside from the problematic that Chiquita does not address (organizational) limitations.

ent. [...]. When someone admits they weren't perfect, you trust them a little more" (Alsevere 2006).

It is most interesting to note however that Chiquita's efforts for transparent communication, are subsiding.

Chiquita announced the next Corporate Responsibility Report for the year 2005 (see Chiquita 2005a: 18). But up to date, i.e. February 2007, the company has not launched such a report yet and the Annual Report 2005 does not even mention a separate Corporate Responsibility Report anymore (Chiquita 2006: 22). Instead, Chiquita since 2003 is publishing issues of corporate responsibility, within a very brief section of its annual report (Chiquita 2004: 14f), where basically only achievements are communicated. Chiquita seems to have made a shift of fully relying on successes of certification with NGOs, without outlining existing shortcomings and corporate measures of how to address these anymore. But this single sided communication, which only emphasizes successes of the corporation, risks undermining its credibility and to get Chiquita into another 'round' of the Reputation Trap as will be outlined.[443]

The latest Annual Report (Chiquita 2006: 21) stresses that this is the "sixth straight year with 100 percent of our owned banana farms in Latin America certified to the Rainforest Alliance environmental [...]. In addition, 93 percent of the bananas we source from independent grower farms in Latin America were also Rainforest-Alliance certified, up from 83 percent in 2004. Moreover, 100 percent of our owned farms in Latin America were certified to the Social Accountability 8000 labor and human rights standard and to the EurepGAP food safety standard." A large part of the corporate responsibility section furthermore deals with the success of the Nogal Nature and Community Project in Costa Rica, an environmental reforestation and education project in cooperation with the Rainforest Alliance and the Deutsche Gesellschaft für Technische Zusammenarbeit (GTZ), a German organization for sustainbale development.[444]

This one-sided communication backfires on the Chiquita. Suchanek (2005)[445] in Bio100, discredits the Nogal Nature and Community Project as mere Greenwashing as long as unsustainabilities persist at Chiquita's farms and mourns that these

443 That is, Greenwashing accusations popping up again.
444 For details see Appendix G.
445 As the platform (Bio100) where the article is published indicates, this article is rather biased as Chiquita is no organic company at all. The dissertation chose to nevertheless cite this article, because it represents the argumentation of many NGOs, blogger and internet sites, which accuse Chiquita of Greenwashing activities. In the light of the scientific articles cited above, it becomes clear that the facts on which this article draws its conclusions on are substantiated. It is the conclusion of mere 'Greenwashing' from the sights of NGOs and/or 'ethical' consumers, which often forms the understanding of corporate sustainability of orthodox consumers, which is critical here.

unsustainabilities are not addressed in the context of the Nogal Nature and Community Project. The article even discredits the NGO 'Rainforest Alliance'. Klawitter even accused Chiquita with its Greenwashing activities to go as far as to influence independent magazines and to deliberately conceal unsustainabilities still existing at the "new role model company" (Klawitter 2006).

Engaging with NGOs and reaching certification thus is not enough for reaching and sustaining a reputation as sustainably progressive. On the contrary, if unsustainabilities keep showing up and are not communicated proactively and thoroughly, this risks even to discredit the NGO the corporation is working with.

Chiquita in the view of the dissertation is facing a tipping point: The company has yielded substantial achievements in reducing *environmental* sustainability, which not only has led to company savings (eco-efficiency), but has also boosted the corporate image as shown above. But only harvesting the achievements the company made so far (focus on the re-inforcing loop R1, figure 39) without addressing limitations to further improvement of a sustainable brand-image, which is the crucial factor Chiquita relies on when holding a Reputation Leadership Model, risks to erode the ground for a sustainable reputation in the future.

The next threshold (limitation point) the company is now facing relates to *social* sustainbility. But instead of taking the corresponding measures for avoiding a 'next' round of a Reputation Trap[446], the company is withdrawing from communicating these shortcomings openly and – most important – seems not ready to address limitations to social unsustainability (see also Alsever 2006).

Addressing limitations (internal and external)

Similar as Chiquita needed to address *limitations* with regard to environmental sustainability by engaging with NGOs and their farmers and by taking the measures outlined[447], which took the company over 10 years, Chiquita now faces the next *limitations*. That is, Chiquita is getting anew into the balancing loop B of figure 39. These limitations hinder the company to further increase their reputation in respect of sustainability. Similar as Chiquita first shied away from taking substantial measures for addressing the limitations provided to reducing environmental sustainability, it now seems to shy away to take this 'next step' of addressing further limitations to sustainability.

As the dissertation will show, this 'next step' would be to address limitations, which arise form the corporation's own business process, not primarily conditions at the suppliers alone. Addressing these internal, organizational limitations encompasses most importantly *sourcing practices* of Chiquita.

---

446 That is, Greenwashing accusations popping up again.
447 See also Appendix G.

Because these in turn are embedded into a larger system. Thus, it is understandable that these measures will require further, large change processes and that these will take a significant time span to show effect.

The dissertation in the following will first discuss the internal, organizational limitations and subsequently the larger context of external limitations these are embedded in.

Addressing internal limitations (sourcing practices)

The main *limitation* for Chiquita in gaining its desired reputation in the view of the dissertation lies in Chiquita's very business practices. But the company does not seem to be ready yet to address this as the dissertation will outline in the following. As quoted above, Chiquita has reached a substantial amount of certifications for sustainbility (Chiquita 2006). However these certifications refer farms, *owned* by Chiquita. Due to a restructuring process the company however *outsourced* a significant number of farms. As stated above, 93 percent of the bananas, which are sourced from these independent grower farms in Latin America are also Rainforest-Alliance certified. But only 14% of the contract farms hold the SA8000 certification for acceptable working conditions (Heuer 2006), i.e. for *social* sustainability.

These shortcomings regarding social unsustainability, risk discrediting the achievements the corporation reached so far with regard to environmental sustainability and to the social sustainbility standards in the company-owned farms.

The limitations (threshold) for these social unsustainabilities in the view of Chiquita are to be found in process efficiency. Chiquita in its last Corporate Responsibility Report states that it operates in an environment focused on strict cost reduction and therefore plans to tackle the issue of social unsustainability at its supplier farms by process efficiency, which will safe time and thus allows reducing overtime (Chiquita 2003: 26).

While process inefficiency might contribute to the problem, the root causes of the problems however are likely to result from cost pressure, - that is related to Chiquita's very business model. But the company does not yet seem ready to address root causes thoroughly. The statement above clearly indicates the corporation's main focus on cost reduction and consequently the pressure on low cost production, which is laid on suppliers. The suppliers in turn seek to fulfill these requirements through longer working hours and low wages.[448] Furthermore the company states that it has not yet integrated social and environmental performance criteria into their selection and evaluation processes for strategic materials suppliers (Chiquita 2003: 9). This underscores that Chiquita faces serious shortcomings in its sourcing practices. This is also supported through the next statement: George Jaksch[449], states that in-

---

[448] See cases of social unsustainabilities at Chiquita suppliers above and in appendix G.

creasing compliance with the SA8000 standard at external suppliers has high priority at Chiquita, but there is no specific timeline.

Tying in organizational limitations and external limitations in regard to a Trap

So what are the reasons why the corporation shies away from addressing its sourcing practices? When looking at answers to this question they reveal that the problematic is more systemic than 'bad will/unethical behavior' of a corporation or mere
profit-seeking, as it often colloquially is put forward. This is not to deny that profit-
maximization is one aspect. But as will be outlined in the following, there are many
more reasons, which interact:

Capital markets

Outsourcing its farmers and broadening its product range[450], has been part of a re-
capitalization concept for the company. Since 1996 the company was making losses
and in 2001 it had to betake itself to a program for protection of creditors. Even
during these critical times, the path towards reducing unsustainability was considered crucial and was pushed forward even when this meant making critical decisions, as interims- CEO Cyrus Freidhams pointed out in 2003. But the resort via
outsourcing poses a limitation to the company's sustainability, as Heuer points out.
Therefore Chiquita's corporate dilemma regarding sustainability can be summed up
the following way: The more external partners Chiquita has, the better for their financial situation, because the stock market values outsourcing, but on the other
hand it gets harder to convert and to certify 'external' farmers (Heuer 2006: 28).

Consumer behavior

Another factor apart from the stock market is consumer behavior: Chiquita started
its sustainability campaign with the Rainforest Alliance in nine European countries
(Austria, Belgium, Denmark, Finland, Germany, the Netherlands, Norway, Sweden
and Switzerland) (Chiquita 2005b[451]), because customers in the American market,
Loeb, president of Chiquita Fresh Group Europe, states, are not ready yet for sustainable products (Heuer 2006: 28). In order to create and foster a market for sustainability, large enough to ensure the company's growth, Chiquita engages in customer education for sustainability. Loeb states that they invite consumers to exam-

---

449 Jaksch is responsible for Corporate Responsibility at Chiquita's European headquarter
(see Appendix G).
450 The company now also sells pineapples, melons, kiwis, grapes etc. through acquisition of
the brand "Fresh Express".
451 Press release from: Chiquita Brands International, Inc. "Chiquita Brands International
Launches The First 'Rainforest Alliance-Certified' Fruit In Europe" 10/18/2005, available
at: http://www.csrwire.com/article.cgi/4569.html; accessed: 12. December 2005.

ine, why a cheap banana is so cheap. He states that consumers need to learn, that today there is more to premium quality than appearance and taste – namely the conditions under which a fruit is produced (Heuer 2006: 28). The company thereby applies various measures, such as product information (flyers next to the supermarket shelves), website information, and also the Nogal Nature and Community Project[452].

Supplier shortages
Furthermore Chiquita faces not only shortcomings from the demand side, but also from the supply side. The company sources from multiple suppliers and has difficulties of identifying and/or developing suppliers, which meet the standards for certification of the Rainforest Alliance and other programs. Chiquita faces the challenge to reorganize its sourcing as well as the conditions at its suppliers thus, that the company is able to deliver the new sustainably-responsible products to its entire former market (Heuer 2006: 28). This requires a tremendous shift, as the market Chiquita serves, is by far larger than that of mission-driven enterprises, which start-up right from the beginning as bio and fair-trade businesses.

The company stresses the fact that it is no Bio and Fair-Trade company (Heuer 2006: 28). Chiquita follows an 'intermediary' strategy of offering a 'better' banana, i.e. more sustainable than the orthodox banana, but the banana still is no organic and fair-trade banana.[453] The company would not find a sufficient capacity of organic suppliers to meet the large quantities Chiquita needs to serve its full market. At present the situation is particularly fierce as there are serious bottlenecks of organic suppliers due to an increasing demand on organic products.[454]

Conclusion

The dissertation in this chapter sought to outline the difficulties a company with strong legacy problems, but a strong brand, faces when seeking to move towards a Reputation Leadership Model.

As has been discussed Chiquita can be considered to have moved far beyond smoke-and-mirror strategies of mere Greenwashing. But in order to get out of the Reputation Trap of repeatedly being accused of Greenwashing accusations the corporation needs to engage into transparency measures and most importantly needs

---

452 For the project, see above.
453 The company aimed however at certifying a 200 hectares plant in Honduras by the Fair-Trade-Organization, in order to offer them at the US bio-supermarket chain "Wild Oats" on a trial basis (Heuer 2006: 28). But plans were called off when a hurricane wiped out the plantation and workers were laid off. See also 'responsible shopper' at: http://www.coopamerica.org/programs/rs/profile.cfm?id=202, accessed: 30. November 2006.
454 See also chapter 3.5.

to address limitations to further increase its sustainability reputation. Thus, the above ties up identifying 'solutions' as *symptomatic solutions* and incrementally eliminating more and more *limitations* through *fundamental solutions* in order to further increase sustainability reputation and to reach their target of becoming/staying a sustainably responsible leader, is a learning process for corporations.

Because corporations holding a Reputation Leadership Model, seek to become a sustainability leader in their industry, they need to go beyond solutions, which can be considered 'fundamental' for corporations holding a Compliance Model[455]: They need to address root causes and need to be ready to restructure and innovate their own business practices in order to gain credibility as a sustainability leader.

The chapter above has outlined different root causes, which are limitations and hinder sustainability within the business process.

Further examples of corporations dealing with cases of a Reputation Trap are outlined in appendix H.

3.4.3 Special Case: Financing Brand-Image through Low-Cost Production

3.4.3.1 Archetypical Trap Structure

The following will outline a special case of a Reputation Trap, where the root cause (internal, organizational limitation to sustainbility) lies in the very business model of the corporation: A lot of companies focused on brand-image (particularly from the apparel industry) tend to 'finance' their investments in brand-building through sourcing from unsustainable, but cheap suppliers. But this business model risks backfiring on the very brand-image the corporation is focusing on (figure 40):

---

455 These would be training suppliers.

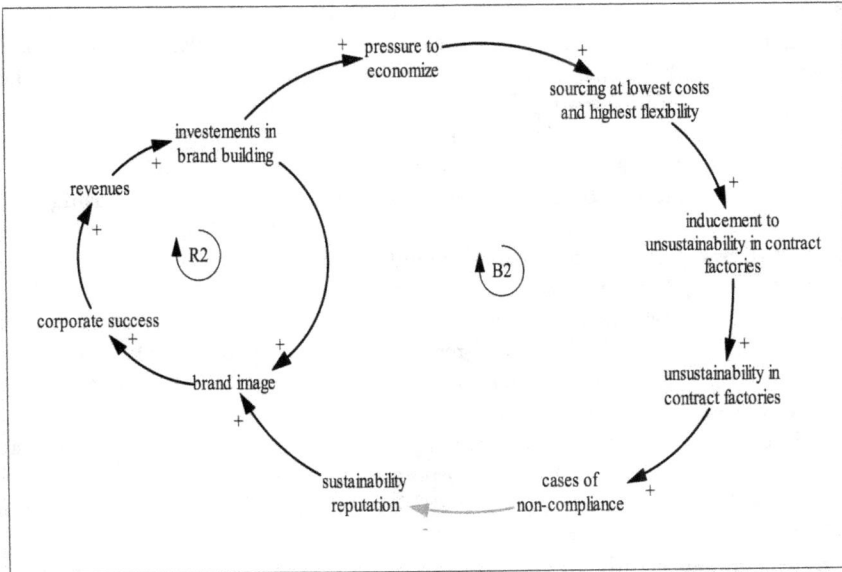

Fig. 40: Financing Brand-Image through Low-Cost Production Trap
Source: Source: Produced by the author

The company invests a significant part of its financial resources in design and marketing, which (after some time) raises brand image. This in turn again leads to corporate success, which results in higher revenues that allow investing even more into brand building (R2).

But as large sums are invested into design and brand building, this raises the pressure for the company to economize in other operating areas. Often this is done through outsourcing production, and sourcing from overseas suppliers at lowest costs. This cost pressure is passed onto the management of the contract factories, in form of a pressure to lower unit prices. Often the pressure to lower prices is accompanied by pressures to shorten delivery lead-times, which reduces inventory costs and enables to provide consumers with the latest fad (Connor and Dent 2006: 57, CCC 2005b).

The pressures applied through the company's purchasing practices, in turn augments the inducement of suppliers (contract factories) to meet the demand for low-cost and flexible sourcing through unsustainable working conditions, such as excessive working hours, short-term working contracts or no contracts at all, poverty wages, insufficient health protection from toxic materials or noise, physical and verbal harassment of workers, impediment of trade unions etc.). These unsustainabilities are then sought to be hidden with regard to compliance with the code of conduct e.g. through subcontracting to other suppliers, through false time records, influencing workers being interviewed etc. Figure 41 provides an overview of the factory manager's dilemma arising from the code of conduct on the one side and the corporation's purchasing practices on the other side.

But unsustainabilities at contract factories usually cannot be hidden fully and/or long-term. Thus, auditors or independent media/NGO's, detect an increasing number of cases of non-compliance with the code of conduct. That is, as the structure in figure 40 shows, pressures for unsustainabilities are built way up the supply chain through the company's own corporate investment decisions and thus persist *despite* a code of conduct, which the company launched in order to prevent unsustainability at contract factories.[456] The MSN report in their analysis of CSR reports state that some corporations start to acknowledge that "different departments of their companies often make conflicting demands on suppliers, insisting on code compliance while at the same time also pressuring suppliers to make their products faster and cheaper" (MSN 2005: 8). These corporations are e.g. Nike, adidas, Puma and Gap (MSN 2005: 8, Connor and Dent 2006: 57, Oxfam, CCC and Global Unions 2004: 60, see also Nike case below).

The non-compliance with the code of conduct poses a serious problem to corporations holding a Reputation Leadership Model, as they have communicated the 'promise' to be a sustainably responsible leader. As figure 40 shows, non-compliance with the code of conduct risks to negatively impact the company's reputation regarding sustainability, which in turn damages the brand image. This problem is likely to increase as customers start caring *how* the product they wear, was produced and if its production had negative impacts on other human beings or on the environment. If in turn, even more financial resources are directed into restoring brand image without tackling the organizational root-causes of unsustainabilities, a vicious circle is created. Thus, the *limitations* that drive the balancing loop of the Reputation Trap[457] here are created through the very business model of the corporation of Financing Brand-Image through Low-Cost Production. That is, a business model of financing brand image through low-cost production risks to *back-fire on the brand itself*. This is a problem, which companies increasingly face today, as will be outlined in the business cases below.

---

456 As will be outlined in the Nike business case below, codes of conduct can even put the suppliers into a worse dilemma, if root causes for unsustainability inherent in the business model of the company are not changed accordingly.
457 See also figure 39.

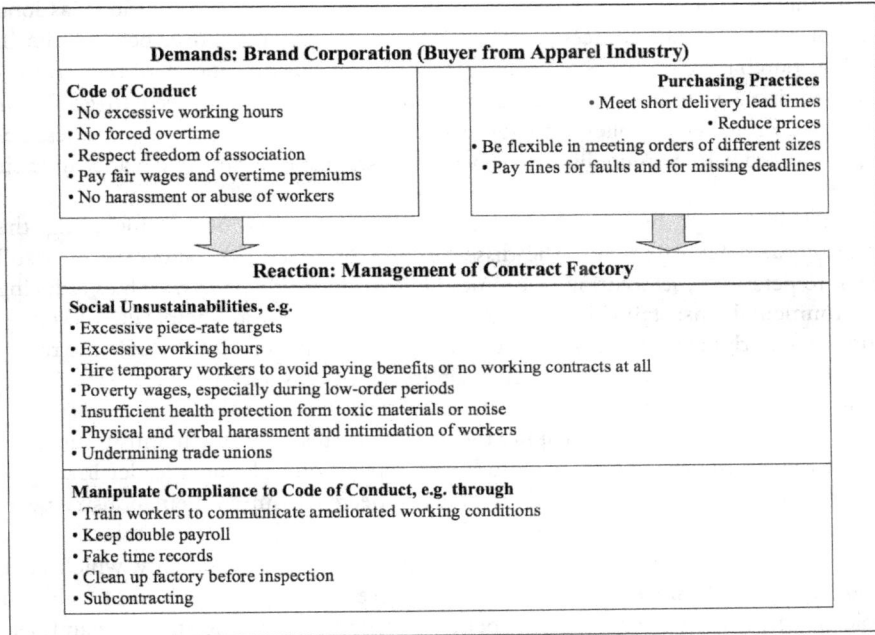

Demands: Brand Corporation (Buyer from Apparel Industry)	
Code of Conduct • No excessive working hours • No forced overtime • Respect freedom of association • Pay fair wages and overtime premiums • No harassment or abuse of workers	**Purchasing Practices** • Meet short delivery lead times • Reduce prices • Be flexible in meeting orders of different sizes • Pay fines for faults and for missing deadlines

Reaction: Management of Contract Factory

Social Unsustainabilities, e.g.
• Excessive piece-rate targets
• Excessive working hours
• Hire temporary workers to avoid paying benefits or no working contracts at all
• Poverty wages, especially during low-order periods
• Insufficient health protection form toxic materials or noise
• Physical and verbal harassment and intimidation of workers
• Undermining trade unions

Manipulate Compliance to Code of Conduct, e.g. through
• Train workers to communicate ameliorated working conditions
• Keep double payroll
• Fake time records
• Clean up factory before inspection
• Subcontracting

Fig. 41: Factory Manager's Dilemma
Source: adapted from Oxfam, CCC and Global Unions 2004: 61

3.4.3.2 Dealing with the Trap

While chapter 3.4.2 above (including the Chiquita case), stressed the aspect that transparent communication is a *symptomatic* solution for addressing a Reputation Trap, this chapter will focus on the aspect that internal, organizational limitations for applying *fundamental* solutions to a Reputation Trap arise from a corporation's own business model.

As stated above, this special case of a Reputation Trap, ties up to the special case of a Quick-Fix Trap 'Fire-the-Supplier-Trap' referring to unsustainabilities in contract factories.[458] As has been outlined in this former chapter, there exists a learning process of moving away from applying symptomatic solutions, where scandals of unsustainabilities keep 'popping'-up, towards more fundamental solutions.

As has been discussed for corporations holding a Compliance Model, engaging into trainings with suppliers can be considered a more fundamental solution than firing-the-supplier with respect to social unsustainabilities in contract factories.[459]

---

458 See chapter 3.2.3.
459 See chapter 3.2.3.2.

Nevertheless trainings at the suppliers still remain symptomatic solutions, as long as root causes are not addressed, which stem from corporate buyer behavior itself, such as purchasing practices or even further the very business model of the buyer.

Corporations with a Reputation Leadership Model therefore need to go *beyond* trainings with their suppliers and address root causes within their *own* business behavior in order to gain credibility of being a sustainable responsible leader in their industry.

Nevertheless most brand-sensitive multinational corporations, - including the *sports apparel industry*, which the dissertation will focus (Nike and others), - still seem to persist at the 'solution' to promote *changes at their suppliers*, such as reducing environmental unsustainabilities (e.g. reducing use of toxic chemicals, recycling) and workers rights (e.g. applying safety measures, abolishing child labor). The readiness for addressing root-causes, which lie in the buyer's very business behavior, in contrast, is hardly developed.

Currently corporations, which apply rigorous measures for reducing unsustainabilities at their contract factories, still do hold a reputation of being a leader in corporate responsibility compared to their industry peers.[460] But as their industry peers are catching up on these measures (MSN 2005: 8), leaders need to take the next step of addressing *internal, organizational limitations* to sustainability, which arise from their own business model. Otherwise these corporations will not be able to hold up the targeted reputation of being a 'leader' of reducing unsustainabilities. Their communication of being a leader, then risks to get them in a Reputation Trap, where they are not able to meet increasing benchmarks for sustainability, i.e. transparently communicate shortcomings that still exist – particularly in social sustainability – and present a plan of how the company seeks to address the shortcomings.

A first step for addressing root causes thereby is to address the corporation's purchasing practices. But also the business model itself needs to be taken under examination, which determines the purchasing practices, here: Financing Brand-Image through Low-Cost Production.

In the following measures regarding the **purchasing practices** with regard to this business model shall be outlined, which enable corporations to address respectively to avoid the trap. As will be shown in the business cases of the sportswear industry below (Nike and others), corporations are now just starting to recognize and analyze the trap. Currently corporations however remain in the status of analysis. Specific measures to address the trap, - as the ones outlined here, - are not yet implemented in a comprehensive approach by any of the companies analyzed.

---

460 As stated above, this does not imply that they are considered 'sustainable' enterprises as such; i.e. as corporations holding a Systemic Model.

An extensive study by the international NGO 'Oxfam'[461] on twelve sportswear corporations found that purchasing behavior within the (sports) apparel industry is characterized by (Connor and Dent 2006: 57, CCC 2005b):

- *Shorten delivery lead-times,*
- *lowering unit prices* paid for the products, and
- striving for *high flexibility* through placing smaller orders more frequently.

Consequently, the following seven measures can be taken to ease the pressure arising from purchasing practices and thus contribute to further reduce (social) unsustainability at contract factories:

a) Establishing long-term relationships with suppliers

Developing long-term relationships with their suppliers enables managers of contract factories to invest into safety as well as training measures for its personnel, as they receive more planning reliability (Connor and Dent 2006: 61f, see also CCC 2005b: 81). The Oxfam report thereby stresses the point that commitments to maintain ongoing orders have to be in *writing*, so that legal security is guaranteed (Connor and Dent 2006: 57).

A problem is that most contracts are bargained short-term in order to assure flexibility. The CCC report on Tchibo (2005a: 78f), e.g. found that the retailer negotiates prices anew every six month, which hardly gives a supplier time to make any substantial investments without fearing to lose the client. Suppliers in turn pass on this insecurity to their workers by employing them as daily workers, on short-term contracts or with no contract at all (Connor and Dent 2006: 61). About 80% of the workers in the garment industry are women (Connor and Dent 2006: 100), who often do not have any other working alternatives (Connor and Dent 2006: 61) and whose incomes are most vulnerable under these work arrangements. Additionally short-term contract "discourage workers organizing into trade unions, because workers fear their contracts will not be renewed if they are a trade union member" (Connor and Dent 2006: 61). Oxfam therefore argues that buyers should

---

461 The report analyzes corporate behavior of twelve sports brands with regard to social unsustainability at their Asian contract factories. Research was conducted between July 2005 and April 2006 and executed in five main phases: a) Selecting workplaces to be featured as case-studies. The report contains nine case studies of workplace issues in three Asian countries. B) Seeking input from sportswear companies highlighted in the report. The sports brands examined are: adidas, ASICS, FILA, Kappa, Lotto, Mizuno, New Balance, Nike, Puma, Reebok, Speedo and Umbro. C) Researching and writing case studies of particular workplaces. D) Assessment of sportswear companies' trade union rights programs in Asia. E) Extensive consultation with stakeholders, such as workers, other NGOs, unions etc. For more information on the research methodology see Connor and Dent 2006: 17ff.

ban or severely limit the use of short-term contracts by their suppliers (Connor and Dent 2006: 62).

In the sportswear industry Reebok has taken the lead in this respect. In contrast to its industry peers the company, - although it does not ban the use of short-term contracts, - has a policy limiting the use of such contracts in order to cover peak periods of production (Connor and Dent 2006: 62).

b) Giving more lead time in orders

Neil Kearney, General Secretary of the International Textile, Garment and Leather Workers' Federation, states that delivery times often are so short, that they can only be met, when the machines run 24 hours at seven days a week (Monitor 2005). The pressure on overtime worked in contract factories, therefore can be reduced if more lead times in orders would be given (CCC 2005b: 79). Additionally short delivery times further induce managers of contract factories to impede freedom of association of their workers (e.g. labor unions). Factory owners are very wary of having to deal with a workforce, which has the power to collectively withhold its labor when an urgent order needs to be filled, because they fear to miss deadlines (Connor and Dent 2006: 57).

Therefore sports brand companies, which are serious about respecting workers right of freedom of association, can support these buy providing more lead time in orders and to abstain from unreasonably tight deadlines currently demanded in the industry. (Connor and Dent 2006: 57).

c) Providing for living wages

There is substantial evidence that apparel brand companies lay pressure on lowering unit prices paid for the products, so that the prices, which they currently pay to their suppliers are insufficient to provide for wages that meet workers' basic needs (living wages) (CCC 2005b: 40, Connor and Dent 2006: 57, MSN 2005: 8). Oxfam therefore argues for sports brand owners to provide workers' representatives with information regarding the unit price they are paying for goods (Connor and Dent 2006: 57). This would enable workers to negotiate a collective bargaining agreement, including a wage increase.

Furthermore buyers could require factory management to provide full financial information to workers as part of a commitment to negotiating in good faith. But the study by Oxfam found that no one of the twelve sports brand companies reviewed, is currently willing to provide workers' representatives with purchasing price information or to require suppliers to disclose company financial records to worker representatives (Connor and Dent 2006: 58). Only Puma and adidas claimed at least to take into account the costs of observing labor standards when they negotiate prices with their suppliers (Connor and Dent 2006: 57).

d) Incorporating social sustainability as a criterion in sourcing decisions

Another important step constitutes corporations including the information on compliance with their code of conduct (e.g. from the audits), as a further criterion for their sourcing decisions (see also MSN 2005: 8). This would have the effect that corporations shift sourcing towards more sustainable suppliers.

Nike for example announced to apply a balanced scorecard approach, where the suppliers' compliance scores are introduced as a further criterion in their sourcing decisions, in addition to traditional measures such as cost, delivery time and quality.[462] But what will be crucial to observe are cases, where compliance will form a trade-off to cost, delivery time and quality. That is, where due to compliance unit prices rise or strikes of workers lead to delays.[463]

e) Purchasing from countries with trade union rights

The importance of freedom of association and trade union rights as such has been become apparent above. There are however substantial problems with the *regulation* and *enforcement* of trade union rights in almost every country in Asia, where the majority of the apparel industry is sourcing from (Connor and Dent 2006: 58ff). Even in those countries where trade unions are legal, there are multiple problems with enforcement, e.g. due to a lack of financial resources of workers in taking a case through the legal system and/or due to corruption in labor courts (Connor and Dent 2006: 58).

Buying companies serious about respecting these rights, therefore at a minimum should adopt a policy of maintaining existing sourcing relationships and establishing new production only in countries, which give legal effect to these rights. Additionally buyers should make this policy clear to all national governments involved, which prohibit trade unions (CCC 2005b: 79ff, Connor and Dent 2006: 58).

But the opposite appears to be the case: Companies are sourcing much of their production from countries and free trade zones, where it is legally forbidden or extremely difficult for workers to organize themselves into trade unions (CCC 2005b: 79f, Connor and Dent 2006: 59): adidas sources just over half of its sportswear production in such countries. Puma sources more than half of its sports shoe production and New Balance almost all of its Asian production in these countries. Nike has significantly reduced the proportion of its sports shoes made in countries where these rights have legal effect, although the company made a public commitment to ensuring respect for trade union rights in 1998 (Connor and Dent 2006: 101).

---

462 See Nike business case below for further information.
463 See also paragraph 'building trusted relationships' below.

f) Building trusted relationships with suppliers

Establishing change processes at suppliers inline with changes in purchasing processes requires a close and trusted relationship between the buyer and the supplier (CCC 2005b: 79). Building this relationship cannot be done through third parties, like external auditors or NGOs alone, but requires active part from the corporations. Building relationship with suppliers, which will help improve compliance, requires the integration of employees at the multinationals, who are familiar with the buying process and also the procurement (ILO 2005 cited in: CCC 2005b: 79).

An additional problem of coordinating mutual, in-depth relationships is posed through the fact that very often

1) corporations source from a variety of suppliers,
2) one supplier works for several brands and
3) orders are passed on through several levels of subcontractors (CCC 2005b: 25, Oxfam 2004: 60f, Connor and Dent 2006).

This can be countered by prohibiting subcontracting and focusing an a few suppliers, engaging with them into longer-term relationships. Nike for example does prohibit subcontracting to home-based workers (Connor and Dent 2006: 81). As for the issue that one supplier is serving multiple brands, the brand corporations can coordinate their efforts of reducing unsustainability at the supplier. This has been done for example at an apparel project in Bulgaria, including adidas, Nike, Levi's and H&M cooperating with the European Trade Union Federation of Textiles, Clothing and Leather, the Bulgarian Ministry of Labor and the consultant firm Just Solutions (Connor and Dent 2006: 82, Nike 2005, adidas 2005: 36). The project involved around 140 stakeholders of 10 different factories, which received focused training on corporate responsibility issues, social dialogue, corporate codes, local and international laws and possible local implications. Through 'improvement circles' the workers directly involved shared what they had learned with more than 500 other workers in their factories.

Most important for building a trusted relationship is that suppliers, which invest into measures of reducing unsustainabilities, receive an assurance that the corporation will keep its purchasing orders for a longer-term. However, here also the opposite seems to occur at least in a significant number of cases. Connor and Dent refer to this behavior as "[d]oing the right thing and then walking away" (Connor and Dent 2006: 82). In their report for Oxfam the authors have documented examples, where sportswear workers sought to form trade unions and campaigned for better wages and conditions, but then experienced that their factory loses orders from major sports brand owners or else that factory management closes the factory and relocates the production to a zone where there is no union (Connor and Dent 2006: 61). In the case of the Bulgarian project described above for example, Nike significantly reduced its sourcing in Bulgaria and reduced or cut orders to the factories which took part in the project.[464] Another example is Puma, which helped stop discrimination against union members in a factory in Thailand and then stopped ordering from the factory on the grounds that its products were too expensive (Connor and Dent 2006: 72ff).

g) Consumer education

As has been stated above[465], organizational limitations very often are embedded into larger external limitations. This is also the case for the purchasing practices in cases of production outsourcing as is dealt with in this chapter. One crucial factor in this respect is *consumer behavior*.[466]

The report by the Clean Clothes Campaign on the apparel industry hints to the dilemma corporations face (CCC 2005b: 78[467]): "Companies need to address the conflicting logic of simultaneously pursuing lower prices and shorter delivery times whilst at the same time pursuing compliance with labour standards."

Problematic consumer behavior thereby is the rising demand for low prices, which especially affects brands 'for the masses'[468]. Further consumer behavior that ties in with this problematic are: Behavior of fast turnover, where 'old fashion' is thrown away and there is a desire to quickly wear the latest fad just presented on the catwalks. Moreover there still is a broad indifference on the side of consumers of how products are produced and a lack of willingness to align buying practices with ethical standards espoused to care for[469].

Therefore corporations holding a Reputation Leadership Model will also need to engage into customer education and training, in order to harness their competitive advantage of more sustainable production conditions. This is done by several corporations already, e.g. Gap (MSN 2005: 4).

The dissertation considers consumer 'education' as an additional crucial measure for dealing with the trap.[470] The focus of this chapter however lies on the corporation's very business model (especially purchasing practices), which needs to be reconsid-

---

464 For details, see Nike case below.

465 See chapter 3.4.2.2.

466 Another factor is e.g. shareholder value, i.e. capital markets. Because of the focus on reputation for the Reputation Leadership Model the dissertation however concentrates on consumer behavior.

467 The report also points to CCC 2005a and Mark 2005.

468 That is, no luxury brands, but brands as e.g. outlined in the sports industry (like Nike and others) or the apparel industry (Gap, Zara, etc.).

469 See e.g. study by Harris Interactive 2001 outlined above.

470 This does not imply that lower prices or high flexibility are incompatible with reducing unsustainabilities per se. What is crucial with regard to consumer behavior is consumer awareness for the impact of their purchasing practices on the corporation, on the supplier and ultimately on the workers.

ered by corporations, which follow a Reputation Leadership Model in order to avoid the trap described. Consumer behavior will play a more crucial role in the next main chapter of the Systemic Model.

Conclusion

While a number of sports brand owners, including Nike, adidas and Puma, start to openly admit, that their buying practices are contributing to unsustainabilities, such as excessive working hours or low wages (Connor and Dent 2006: 57, MSN 2005: 8f, Oxfam, CCC and Global Unions 2004: 60), the corporations' measures taken to address these root causes are still underdeveloped and often not free of inconsisten-cies[471]. The risk of getting into a trap, where the own business model builds the lim-itations for further reducing unsustainabilities and increasing sustainbility reputa-tion, thus is still a crucial unsolved issues in many corporations holding a Reputa-tion Leadership Model.

3.4.3.3   Business Case: Nike

The following business case illustrates how financing brand-building through low-cost and unsustainable production can backfire and thus can actually impact brand-image negatively. The example is based on the case of 'labor issues' at the sports wear company 'Nike'.

Nike thereby is another typical example of a brand-oriented company, which made the transition from a Trade-off Model (including escalation structures with NGOs and customer boycotts) to a Compliance Model and that is now moving towards a Reputation Leadership Model. The main steps of this transition have been ad-dressed in chapter 3.4.1.4 (figure 38).[472] *Details* of this transition can be traced in-depth in appendix I.

As stated above, transparent communication alone is not enough for dealing with a Reputation Trap. A company, which does not similarly analyzes root causes for un-sustainability and accounts for limiting factors, will not be able to raise its perfor-mance regarding sustainability and thus risks to damage its sustainability reputa-tion or even being accused of Greenwashing. While Nike starts realizing and also communicating that its own business behavior is contributing to the unsustainabili-ties disclosed in the Corporate Responsibility Report (see above, Connor and Dent 2006: 57, MSN 2005: 8f, Oxfam, CCC and Global Unions 2004: 60), the corpora-tion has not yet applied fundamental solutions to account for these limitations.

---

471 See above: For example: Communicating freedom of association and simultaneously moving production to countries that prohibit trade unions; or engaging into trainings with suppliers and then moving away, if prices get to high.
472 Chapter on ,Relations to other models', chapter 3.4.1.4.

Nike's sustainbility measures therefore contain inconsistencies, which risk getting the corporation into another 'round' of a Reputation Trap.[473]

When looking at Nike's latest Corporate Responsibility Report (Nike 2005), the two very frequent areas of non-compliance with the code of conduct are non-compliance with **working hours** and non-compliance with **minimum wage standards**. Nike itself speaks of a 'disturbing trend' regarding the non-compliance with minimum wage standards (Nike 2005: 45). The dissertation argues that the reason for this trend lies in the corporation's own business model.

Nike therefore is an excellent example to illustrate the trap of Financing Brand-Image through Low-Cost Production (see figure 40[474]):

Nike concentrates the money it earns from its profits on design and brand building: Nike spends more money on advertising and promoting reputation than most other companies in the world. Celebrities like e.g. Michael Jordan, Andre Agassi, Tiger Woods, Carl Lewis are paid huge sums of money for advertising Nike products. In 1998, for example, Nike paid Michael Jordan US$ 45 million, Andrew Agassi US$ 10 million and Tiger Woods US$ 28 million in endorsements (Jensen 2000: 41A see also de Haan and Schipper 1999).

To counter the high costs in design and brand building, Nike has outsourced its production and strives to keep manufacturing costs (respectively sourcing costs) as low as possible. This business model is also pointed out by Beder: "This cheap labor enables Nike to spend a great deal on design and marketing, pay large executive salaries, maintain large profits, and still keep the cost of the shoes affordable to the middle classes in affluent countries" (Beder 2002). This in turn produces a pressure on the contracted factories to pay less than the minimum wages or/and let the employees work overtime. Nike so far considered back pay of outstanding wages to the workers due to non-compliance to be an issue of the supplier: "When we find payment below what is due to them, we direct the factory to pay back wages. Although we have not tracked this issue systematically across our supply chain, in FY04 a pilot initiative in our North Asia region led to more than $720,000 returned to workers as back pay following the discovery of non-compliant compensation practices by our M-Audit team" (Nike 2005: 46).

Thus many suppliers found themselves in the dilemma of complying with the code of conduct, but at the same time to meet Nike's low cost approach. [475] But without

---

473 For pervious ‚rounds' in the loop of a Reputation Trap see Nike's historical trajectory in appendix I.

474 Archetypical structure of the Trap 'Financing Brand-Image through Low-Cost Production'.

475 This dilemma has clear parallels with the dilemma of complying with the working hours and meeting the short delivery times, described in the chapter of the Compliance Model (Tchibo case, chapter 3.2.3.3).

Nike's cooperation factory management is not able to address conflicts, which arise further up the supply chain through conflicting demands of Nike (purchasing practices versus code of conduct) (see also figure 41).

Therefore as long as long as Nike does not address root causes arising from its own business model, unsustainabilities will keep arising and will keep countervailing image campaigns which Nike is financing. That is the corporation will keep caught up in the trap of Financing Brand-Image through Low-Cost Production (figure 40[476]).

The problematic that many unsustainabilities, which impact the brand-image negatively, arise due to the corporation's own business decisions is started to being realized and acknowledged by Nike: "The limitation of most monitoring tools is that they identify problems, but are often inadequate in identifying root causes. For example, to understand overtime, one must examine the buyer-seller relationship, including manufacturing timelines, pricing, quality demands and their associated downstream impacts on the worker. We need to understand better how our business decisions may contribute to negative impacts on workers" (Nike 2005: 24).

As the report states, Nike for this purpose plans to engage with a research team from the Sloan School of Management at the Massachusetts Institute of Technology, which is to examine a range of questions around the business drivers and outcomes (Nike 2005: 24). In this way the company hopes gaining insights about the whole of the business process, which will help Nike and contract factories better manage production flows and factories manage hours of work (Nike 2005: 24). It remains to be seen how Nike will react, if the analysis should reveal that main root causes lie in its very business model, which would require substantial changes[477].

Up to date findings of the research have not yet been disclosed. Neither has a new Corporate Responsibility Report been published so far (as of February 2007). But statements of Nike representatives and the corporation's behavior so far indicate that there still is not a comprehensive approach on addressing root causes and corporate behavior still implies inconsistencies regarding sustainability. In an interview with MSN for example, Dusty Kidd, Nike's vice president of compliance, argues that "workers should be paid what they deserve, but the current business model makes it difficult for a single company on its own to ensure that workers receive

---

476 Appendix J shows a structure, which entails the similar information as figure 40, but which explicitly illustrates the structure of the Reputation Trap (figure 39) and that of the structure of Financing-Brand Image through Low-Cost production (figure 40). The figure entails no additional information, only a more detailed illustration of this specific case.

477 As in the IKEA case discussed in the chapter of the Compliance Model, managers often react with resistance, when their business model seems to be questioned from a sustainability point of view; e.g. the reaction of the manager in the IKEA case discussed: Thank you very much, you have just ruined our business idea.

wages that meet their basic needs" (MSN 2005: 9). While Nike starts engaging into multi-stakeholder projects for reducing unsustainabilities, Kidd claims that increasing productivity and moving to lean manufacturing is a more viable solution for improving wages in the short term (MSN 2005: 9). Hannah Jones, Vice President Corporate Responsibility at Nike, argues into a similar direction of increasing efficiency: "There's no point in Nike having 96 monitors on a factory floor day in and day out monitoring overtime, if overtime is being caused way up the supply chain" (statement at the conference "Making Globalization Work for All", MIT-World 2005). Jones concludes that Nike had to provide incentives to suppliers to become part of business decision-making and convince suppliers that creating efficiencies does not mean "squeezing labor costs" but "squeezing time to market" (MITWorld 2005[478]).[479]

As has been outlined above, these measures are rather unlikely to tackle the root causes underlying the trap. Rather, 'squeezing time to market' is part of the very problem. This indicates that Nike has not yet realized the root causes, which drive the trap in which the company is caught up in or – at best – that the company is not yet ready to apply fundamental changes for addressing root causes. The corporation's behavior concerning sustainability therefore remains full of *inconsistencies*: By joining the Fair Labor Association in 1998 for example, Nike committed itself to making sure that workers' rights to freedom of association and collective bargaining are respected in the company's supply chain. But as the Oxfam report indicates on basis of Nike's data, the proportion of Nike production of sport shoes in countries which give legal protection to those rights has fallen from 52% to 38% between 1998 and 2005. As Connor and Dent (2006: 59) state, Nike by far is not the only corporation in the industry showing this trend and "Nike deserves credit for making this information public". But, as stated above, while transparency is crucially important, it does not provide a fundamental solution to inconsistencies.

Another inconsistency with regard to Nike's corporate sustainability are cases, where the company cuts orders at factories, which increased workers rights often with the investment and contribution of Nike itself (e.g. in the case of the Bulgarian apparel project outlined above[480]). Another exemplifying case seems to have occurred at the Indonesian factory PT Doson (Connor and Dent 2006: 38ff, CCC 2003): Since 1993 Doson was exclusively producing for Nike and in 2001 the factory, at Nike's suggestion, invested in an extra plant and equipment to increase production capacity (Connor and Dent 2006: 38). In February 2002 Nike then

---

478 The video is available at: http://mitworld.mit.edu/video/312, accessed: 12. June 2006.
479 It is interesting to note that Chiquita's suggestion for addressing root causes pointed into a similar direction: In its report the company argues for increasing process efficiency, which will safe time and thus allow reducing overtime for workers (see chapter 3.4.2.3).
480 See chapter 3.4.3.2 f).

abruptly announced to cease all orders to Doson within a period of nine month, which resulted in the factory's closure and the 7,840 workers unemployed (Connor and Dent 2006: 38).

Yeheskiel Prabowo a representative of the trade union of the worker's at Doson argues that Nike's decision to cut all orders to the factory was linked to the worker's campaign and strike for better wages and conditions held in October 2001. The union then threatened to slow-down action in February 2002, the same month Nike announced plans to cut orders (Prabowo 2003). Nike in contrast argues that ceasing order was a pure business decision based on delivery and quality performance issues, rather than price, which might have resulted from higher wages. Nike furthermore argues that over the last years were several work stoppages and strikes within a number of Nike's suppliers, most of which are still producing for Nike (Connor and Dent 2006: 38). While the dissertation does not consider the data sufficient in order to finally assess what has been the terminal factor for Nike's decision of terminating business relationships with Doson, it nevertheless needs to be noted that not only wages but equally delivery times can interrelate with strikes. A problem seems to lie in Nike's balanced scorecard, which does not account for the interrelations of workers rights enforcement (thus increasing compliance with code of conduct) and union prices and delivery times.[481] This can lead to inconsistencies of corporate behavior, similar to the case of the factories included in the project in Bulgaria pointed out above, where e.g. adidas in contrast to Nike even augmented orders in 2005 by 15 percent on the previous year (Connor and Dent 2006: 82).

The Nike case above has illustrated the trap, which many brand-sensitive corporations, coming from a Trade-off Model and following a Reputation Leadership Model face. Although the company starts realizing that root causes lying in its own business behavior are countervailing their desired image of becoming a sustainably responsible leader, the corporation seems not yet to have analyzed the trap in which it is caught up to its full extend and consequently has not yet developed a comprehensive approach of addressing root causes, particular purchasing practices. Therefore inconsistencies within the corporation's sustainbility measures exist, which bear the risk for Greenwashing accusations and thus undermine the sustainbility image, which the corporation seeks to pursue.

Further Business examples of the Trap of Financing Brand-Image through Low-Cost Production can be found in Appendix K.

---

481 As stated above, Nike applies a balanced scorecard approach, where the suppliers' compliance scores are introduced as a further criterion in their sourcing decisions, in addition to traditional measures such as cost, delivery time and quality. See chapter 3.4.3.2 d) and appendix I.

3.5 Traps in a Systemic Model and Mission-Driven Enterprises

3.5.1 Model Analysis

3.5.1.1 Underlying Belief about Corporate Sustainability

The underlying belief about the benefit of social and environmental sustainability measures for economic sustainability (profit maximization) in the Systemic Model is:

Economic sustainability is a powerful means for creating social and environmental sustainability.

This belief is usually based on the following line of argumentation:
Economy is a social construct designed to meet and satisfy human needs. As such, economy is a vehicle to social sustainability. Because human and thus society's wellbeing relies on the wellbeing of the natural system and because humanity share this planet with other species, social sustainability depends on environmental sustainability. Both are interdependent and symbiotic.

3.5.1.2 Underlying Model Dynamics

The model dynamic, which corporations holding a Systemic Model *believe* in and *act* according to (theory in-use) is that of reinforcing loops between economic, social and environmental sustainability while thereby accounting for balancing processes (limits to 'material-intensive' growth):

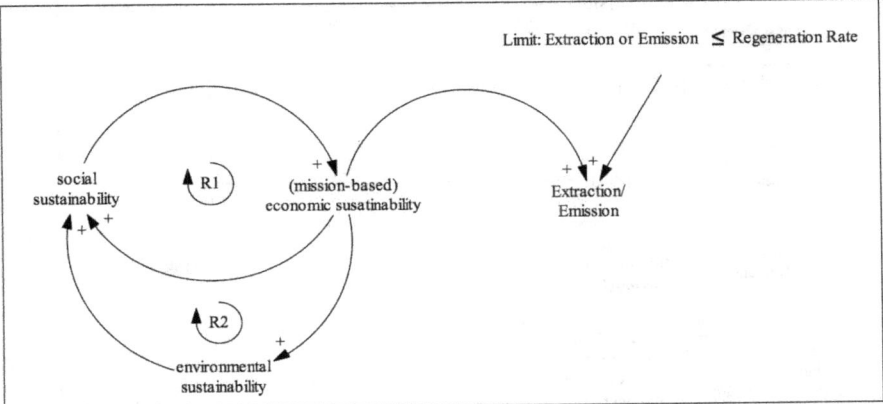

Fig. 42: Systemic Model: Model Dynamic
Source: Produced by the author

According to the Systemic Model, economic activity aims at increasing social (R1) and environmental sustainability (R2) for human wellbeing, which in turn allows to engage in even more mission-based economic activities. While the aim is to increase social and environmental sustainability, this does not exclude that there is some sort of environmental 'unsustainability' in form of harvesting of natural resources or even some sort of emission. The crucial factor is that limits are screened regularly and extraction respectively emission stays below or at most equals the regeneration rate, so that backfiring in form of a balancing loop does not kick-in. (In figure 42, backfiring would imply a negative link from the variable 'extraction respectively emission to 'environmental sustainability', impacting both reinforcing loops unfavorably.)

Thus, the Systemic Model seeks to foster sustainability while thereby accounting for balancing processes. As becomes apparent in the causal-relationships illustrated, the Systemic Model has a different understanding of the purpose of economy (corporations) than the other models before as will be outlined more in-depth in the polarity profile below.

3.5.1.3 Model Characteristics (Polarity Profile)

The Systemic Model holds the following characteristics:

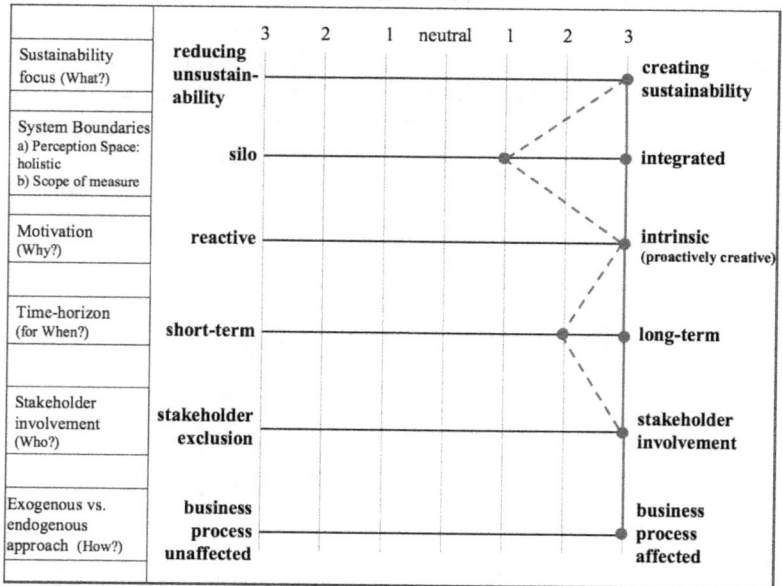

Fig. 43: Systemic Model: Polarity Profile
Source: Produced by the author

The polarity profile, which indicates all factors (characteristics) on the right in their maximum value (3) simultaneously, surely is an idealized representation of the Systemic Model. This arises from the problematic that a Systemic Model bases its behavior on *dynamic* thinking, which cannot be properly illustrated in form of a polarity profile, which is a linear format.

As stated, a systems perspective requires *'orchestrating'*.[482] That is, concentrating on and fostering one factor more intensively (e.g. environmental sustainability) at the expense of another (e.g. social or economic sustainability) *for a given period of time* (short-term), in order to take advantage of dynamics at play in order to increase social and environmental sustainability in the ***long-term*** (see also model dynamics above). Therefore approaches can also be less ***integrated***[483] for a given short-term period, which is indicated by the dashed profile above.

The most crucial difference to the previous models described is that the Systemic Model is based on a ***holistic mental model of perception space***.[484] That is, the mental model of perception space underlying the Systemic Model is that of economy being part of and depending on society, which ultimately is part of and depending on the natural environment (biosphere). Thereby the understanding is *not* that of three sectors, but that of one interdependent system.

As stated, a holistic mental model of perception space, furthermore makes it possible – even suggests – to reevaluate the relationship between economic, social and environmental sustainability in terms of goals and means[485]: The holistic mental model of perception space suggests that social sustainability - and along with it inevitably environmental sustainability - are considered *goals* (mission) of corporations. Consequently the motivation for sustainability is highly ***intrinsic***. The social and/or environmental mission, the company pursues 'comes first', i.e. it is considered central (Bamburg 2006). These kinds of corporations therefore can be referred to as **Mission-Driven Enterprises** (Bamburg 2006).

In mission-driven enterprises consequently the entire ***business process*** is geared to (affected on) ***creating sustainbility***. Mission-driven enterprises usually practice ***intensive stakeholder involvement***, particularly of those, who the corporation's mission is targeted on.[486]

---

482 See chapter 2.2.5.7.

483 That is: More silo-oriented in the sense of emphasizing one aspect, while thereby nevertheless keeping the optimization of the whole system in mind.

484 Note the indication 'holistic' on the left in the polarity profile (figure 43) under system boundaries a).

485 See chapter 2.2.2.4.2.

486 For example: Community, particular groups in society (e.g. disabled, poor), environmental NGOs etc.

3.5.1.4 Relations to Other Models

The most crucial difference of the Systemic Model to all previous models discussed so far, as stated, is the holistic mental model of perception space.

Previous models (Compliance Model, Reputation Leadership Model, Efficiency Model) referred to *reducing unsustainability* within their existing, orthodox business model based on a sectoral perception space. Social and environmental sustainability here became a new condition (limiting factor). Mission-driven enterprises in turn are start-ups build *from scratch* with a Systemic Model of sustainability in mind (i.e. on a holistic perception space). Environmental and/or social sustainability lie at the very heart of the business model.

The difference between orthodox business models of multinational corporations holding a Reputation Leadership Model and mission-driven enterprises holding a Systemic Model is the following: Orthodox businesses did not start out as sustainable businesses, but turned to sustainbility as a means for reaching competitive advantage, once managers discovered the cost, innovation and marketing benefits of steering their corporation towards sustainbility, as has been discussed in-depth. In contrast, mission-driven enterprises are designed to be sustainbale in process and products from scratch, as a start-up, and, furthermore intended to socially transform the industrial sector in which they are operating towards sustainable development. This difference between orthodox business models and mission-driven enterprises is consistent with the difference of ‚green business' and ‚green-green business', which Isaak outlines (2005: 14).[487]

It is important to note, that founders, usually build their mission-driven enterprises enterprise explicitly as *alternatives* to orthodox business models, particularly multinational corporations. This new, alternative approach to business is stressed through the term '*enterprise*' (mission-driven enterprise) used here. The term 'entrepreneur' originated in France in the 17th and 18th centuries. The French economist Jean Baptiste Say in the 19th century provided a characterization of an entrepreneur, which shapes this understanding until present: An entrepreneur being someone, who shifts economic resources out of an area of lower into an area of higher productivity and greater yield, thus creating additional value (Say 1803). Such entrepreneurs are leaders of innovation, who in the sense of Schumpeter trigger creative-destructive processes in the economic system and shape new models (forms) of business (Schumpeter 1934).

Although there does not yet exist an example of a mission-driven enterprise, which meets all the characteristics outlined above, 'The Body Shop' (cosmetics) and Ben & Jerry's' (ice cream) can serve as examples, which come close to this concept (see also Isaak 2005: 14).

---

487 In contrast to the dissertation Isaak however only refers to environmental sustainbility.

While the dissertation personally considers the Systemic Model and the corresponding concept of mission-driven enterprises the most desirable of the five models outlined with regard to sustainability it is *not* the intention of the dissertation to present the Systemic Model as the impeccable 'solution' to sustainability, as stated above.[488]

Rather the dissertation seeks to show that also corporations holding a Systemic Model hold a risk of getting into Sustainability Traps. That is, best intentions regarding environmental and social sustainability and a corresponding Systemic Mental Model are not a guarantee and alone are not sufficient for sustainability. In order to produce results, which actually create sustainability, corporations holding a Systemic Model – similar as the other models - need to *continuously* screen and reflect on systemic structures in cooperation with their stakeholders in order not to get into Sustainability Traps.

The following sustainability trap outlined here, is most likely not the only one with regard to a Systemic Model. While there currently might already exist others, it is likely that even more will become apparent in the future, since the concept of mission-driven enterprises is still very young and most literature focuses on their superiority over orthodox business regarding sustainability, rather than on outlining that also they can fall prey to Sustainability Traps.

3.5.2 Selling-(out) Trap
3.5.2.1 Archetypical Trap Structure
Trend: Mission-driven enterprises are sold to multinational corporations

In recent years a phenomenon can be observed, which meanwhile occurred so many times that it can be considered a trend: Mission-driven enterprises with a strong brand image on sustainability are sold to respectively brought by precisely these 'orthodox', multinational corporations, which the start-ups in their beginnings considered a counter-model to their business approach. This trend is also described by Hollender and Fenichel (2004: 230ff), Jundt (2004), Goodman (2003) as well as Harrison (2006).

However none of the authors provides an explicit dynamic explanation for the phenomenon. Jundt (2004) stresses the relevance of the 'green middle class' for mainstreaming ethical consuming (see below). Hollender and Fenichel (2004: 230ff) concentrate on outlining problems, which occur when mission-driven enterprises go public and issue stocks – either independently or due to an acquisition of a listed multinational corporation. The dissertation in contrast will focus on a shift in mental models and resulting dynamics triggered, when a mission-driven enterprise is acquired by a multinational corporation, which can lead to the result that the indi-

---

488 See chapter 3.1.1.3.

vidual corporate sustainability in-use is reduced (*trap*), while still contributing to mainstream ethical consuming. The dissertation in this way seeks to further contribute to analyze the phenomenon by providing a *dynamic* explanation.

Most prominent case examples of the phenomenon outlined are The Body Shop, which has been sold to L'Oréal and Ben & Jerry's Homemade (ice cream) now owned by the multinational corporation Unilever. But there exist many more examples.[489]

This has earned founders of mission-driven enterprises like Anita Roddick (The Body Shop) or Ben Cohen and Jerry Greenfield (Ben & Jerry's) the accusation of surrendering or 'selling-out' their principles to the counter-business-model (the 'enemy').[490]

Considering however that the concept of sustainability has been - as Anita Roddick phrases it – in the DNA of the founders (The Body Shop 2006, Anita Roddick) and their enterprises since decades and considering the number of cases in which the phenomenon occurred, the explanation of founders suddenly giving up on their principles and selling out simply out of personal financial interest[491] seems hollow and superficial and – at best – incomplete. So the question remains what other underlying reason for this trend exists and what does it means for corporate sustainability?

The dissertation in the following will show, why it is justified to speak of selling in the sense of an economical transaction (deal), rather than of selling-*out* in the sense of betraying. The dissertation therefore has placed the suffix 'out' into brackets and uses the term: ***Selling-(out) Trap.***

Is it however just to speak of a *trap*? The dissertation argues that it risks being a trap for the *individual* mission-driven enterprise, which is being sold, because it compromises on its sustainability in-use, and on the promotion of an alternative business model. On the other hand, the development might be beneficial on a larger, macro-economic scale in terms of further democratizing (diffusing) the sustainability movement into the so called new 'green middle class'[492].

---

489 See below and especially appendix L for further business examples.
490 See e.g. statements in business cases below.
491 Ben Cohen is reported to have received nearly $40 million (Hollender and Fenichel 2004: 213), Anita Roddick and her husband £120m (€173m) (Pitman 2006), while Roddick explicitly stated that she wanted to channel most part of this sum into a human rights foundation, rather than having it 'caught-up' into shares of The Body Shop (Steinbichler 2006: 3).
492 The term is derived from Jundt 2004. The dissertation yet subsumes under this term not only customers concerned about environmental, but also about social sustainability issues. The green middle class consumes organic and fare trade food, yet does not possess extensive background knowledge on sustainability and is far more passive than the consumer group of ,active, ethical consumers' (see below for further explanation).

Diverging intentions associated with growth by the acquisition
In regard to a Selling-(out) Trap, it is important to note that one main reason for the acquisition on side of the mission-driven enterprises as well as on the side of the multinational corporation is **growth**. That is, growing the mission-driven enterprises in scale. The pivotal point however is to differentiate the **intention** *associated with this growth*, which is different for the mission-driven enterprises and the multinational corporation. These different intentions arise from the difference in the mental model of perception space and are constitutive for the Selling(-out) Trap. This will be discussed in the following:

a) **Mission-Driven Enterprise:** The mission-driven enterprise seeks to grow through the acquisition by the multinational corporation, in order to *spread its alternative business model on large scale*. That is, its business model, which is based on a *holistic mental model of perception space*.

b) **Multinational Corporation:** The multinational corporation seeks to grow the mission-driven enterprise after the acquisition in order to gain *market share in the rapidly growing market of organic and ethical products*. It is crucial to note that the *mental model on perception space* thereby is still the *sectoral* (orthodox economic) one, which the mission-driven enterprise opposes.

These two different intentions of growth based on the different mental model of perception space will be discussed in-depth in the following.

a) Mission-Driven Enterprise: Growth through selling (acquisition) as a way to leapfrog an alternative, sustainbale business model on large scale
In order to explain the trap, it is crucial to start with the different motivations and intentions of a mission-driven enterprise on the one side and those of a multinational corporation on the other side.

While the reasons of founders of mission-driven enterprises for selling to a multinational corporation surely are manifold, one reason seems to play a key role in the cases analyzed: **growth**. The engagement with a multinational corporation is considered as an opportunity to raise capital to finance growth and thus to take the mission-driven enterprise that began as a start-up several years ago to 'a next level' for the future.

Peter Saunders CEO of The Body Shop for example clearly states that this acquisition is about growth opportunities (The Body Shop 2006, Saunders[493]). Asked for the opportunities he sees in the L'Oréal acquisition he states (The Body Shop 2006, Saunders): "I think that there are a number of things that they do that we don't do,

---

493 This is a transcript of an interview with Peter Saunders by the Body Shop International PLC, 17 March 2006, available at http://w3.cantos.com/06/rose-603-6k9y5/bodyshop/pjx-d138-transcript.php?language=en, accessed: 03. November 2006; in the bibliography under: The Body Shop 2006, Saunders.

shop-in-shop for example. They operate in many department stores, whereas we operate in very few, and I think we can learn a lot from that. They're in countries that we're not in. We're not in Latin America or South America. They clearly have strong positions there. And so I'm sure our entry into those parts of the world would be greatly enhanced. [...T]hey are a little bigger than we are. So I think that we have to understand that the scale they have, the dimension they have, gives us a competitive advantage that we wouldn't normally have."

Stonyfield Farm, a manufacturer of natural and organic yogurts and ice cream was brought by Danone in 2001. Their statement can serve as another example: "Stony-field Farm sought, in a strategic partner, a company that could lend cost-saving synergies, but who also had the foresight to allow Stonyfield Farm to continue growing its brand through mission driven initiatives" (the company's website[494]).

It is most crucial to note that the intention and motivation for 'growth' on the side of mission-driven enterprises goes *beyond* increasing profits through market share: The founders of mission-driven enterprises possess a deep conviction that they have developed sustainable products and an alternative, innovative business model, which should spread in the economy in order to transform the way business is done and to offer more sustainable consumer choices. The selling to a multinational corporation therefore, is not considered a surrender, but rather a way to propel the spreading of sustainable products and alternative business behavior.

The engagement with a multinational corporation is considered a *continuation* of the creative, disruptive process in economy intended from the beginning, but now with the possibility to diffuse and change the system 'on large scale'.

As outlined, many things have changed since the first mission-driven enterprises were founded as alternatives to multinational corporations in the 1970's and 80's. Progressive multinational corporations today are starting to engage into the issue of sustainability and show some impressive changes in their products and processes. This new attention and interest of multinational corporations in the topic, is considered by many mission-driven enterprises as a tremendous leverage for diffusing sustainability.

Anita Roddick, founder of The Body Shop, for example when asked why she sold The Body Shop to L'Oreal argues the following:" I want to look for a house for it [annotation of the author: The Body Shop], to shape it in the next 30 years. And we all grow. [...W]ith L'Oréal now, the biggest cosmetic company in the world, for them to partner with us on our projects in 35 countries in the world, I think it's amazing, amazing. They could work with our Nicaraguan farmers who sell us 70 tons of sesame oil. How many tons could they use? A thousand? I mean it's mind

---

494 See company's website at: http://www.stonyfield.com/AboutUS/StonyfieldDanone.cfm, accessed: 06. November 2006.

blowing in the terms of poverty eradication. Small-scale support of family farms is wonderful" (The Body Shop 2006, Roddick[495]).

Ben Cohen and Jerry Greenfield, co-founders of Ben & Jerry's Ice-cream, with respect to their acquisition by Unilever stated: "Neither of us could have anticipated, twenty years ago, that a major multinational would some day sign on, enthusiastically, to pursue and expand the social mission that continues to be an essential part of Ben & Jerry's" (Hollender and Fenichel 2004: 226[496]). On the company's webpage Ben & Jerry's argues: "The people who work here are passionate about the company and its unique vision. Having the resources of a much larger company to draw upon is an opportunity to expand the reach of that vision to the local, national, and global community."[497] "We continue our PartnerShop program, support for farmers [...], sponsorship of events which contribute to community wellbeing, and protection of the environment in all of our activities. We are optimistic that the Unilever connection will help us project this social awareness on to a much larger canvas."[498]

Samuel Kaymen, founder of Stonyfield Farm had built the enterprise to feed his six kids and in order to escape the dominant culture (Brady 2006). Gary Hirshberg, CEO and 'co-founder' of Stonyfield Farm, is quoted by Hollender and Fenichel to have set up the deal with Danone to "keep the company independent in spirit, if not in fact" (Hollender and Fenichel 2004: 234). Hirshberg has made it his mission to infect Danone with his own life's work and message, that is selling the value of organic agriculture, for human health as well as for the environment (Hollender and Fenichel 2004: 233f).

---

495 This is a transcript of an interview with Anita Roddick by the Body Shop International PLC, 17 March 2006, available at http://w3.cantos.com/06/rose-603-6k9y5/bodyshop/pjx-d136-transcript.php?language=en, accessed: 03. November 2006; in the bibliography under: The Body Shop 2006, Roddick.

496 See also the company's official press statement: http://www.benjerry.com/our_company/press_center/press/join-forces.html, accessed: November 2006

497 Cited from company's webpage at: http://benjerry.custhelp.com/cgi-bin/benjerry.cfg/php/enduser/std_adp.phpp_sid=aJjNZYli&p_lva=&p_faqid=136&p_created=955568704&p_sp=cF9zcmNoPSZwX2dyaWRzb3J0PSZwX3Jvd19jbn-Q9MjMwJnBfcGFnZT0x&p_li=, accessed: November 2006

498 Cited from company's webpage at: http://benjerry.custhelp.com/cgi-bin/benjerry.cfg/php/enduser/std_adp.php?p_sid=lUTyi-Zli&p_lva=136&p_faqid=174&p_created=986217851&p_sp=cF9zcmNoPTEmcF9ncm-lkc29ydD0mcF9yb3dfY250PTI0JnBfc2VhcmNoX3RleHQ9R-WZmZWN0IG9mIFVuaWxldmVyIGFjXVpc2l0aW9uIG9uIGNvbXBhbnkgdmFsd-WVzJnBfc2VhcmNoX3R5cGU9MyZwX2NhdF9sdmwxPX5hbnl_JnBfc2VhcF9i-eT1kZmx0JnBfcGFnZT0x&p_li= accessed: November 2006

297

From the quotes above a most important aspect becomes evident: One core argument for founders of mission-driven enterprises to sell to a multinational corporation is seen in the *potential of promoting and diffusing alternative, sustainable business processes on large scale* (see also O'Rourke 2006), by growing the mission-driven enterprise as such and potentially also influencing the multinational corporation towards sustainbility from bottom-up.

b) Multinational Corporation: Growth through acquisition as a way to enter and to gain market share in the new rapidly growing market of organic and ethical products

The motivation of *multinational corporations* for acquiring mission-driven enterprises in turn might seem only slightly different from the motivation of mission-driven enterprises at first sight, but the difference refers to underlying *mental models* and is crucial, because it can release *dynamics* that form a trap from the vantage point of the mission-driven enterprise, as the dissertation will show.

The motivation of multinational corporations for acquisitions of mission-driven enterprises with respect to 'growth' in the cases analyzed were the entry into the rapidly expanding ,green' or ,ethical' market, which they identified as a new trend. The organic market according to a report of the Organic Trade Association (OTA 2005) based on a survey of industry research organizations and long-time member companies currently posses a 20 percent average annual sales growth, which is five times as fast than the orthodox food market (Hollender and Fenichel 2004: 231). According to the survey, the organic market is expected to grow further over the next 20 years, although at a slower pace (OTA 2005). The average consumer household in 2025 will buy organic products on a regular basis, which will include food items as well as organic clothing, household cleaning products, and personal care items. Survey participants indicated a clear trend of organic food being sold through mass market grocery outlets such as Wal-Mart[499] as well as in regular restaurants up to fast-food chains like McDonalds, hospitals or day care centers (OTA 2005: 17, see also Jundt 2004 below).

This is a growth potential, which receives strong interest of the multinational corporations. But because of their legacy it is extremely hard for multinational corporations to build a brand within this new market, which posses the credibility of being 'truly' sustainable and does not fall pray to Greenwashing accusations.[500] Therefore what is most interesting for a multinational corporation acquiring a mission-driven enterprise is the strong *brand name*, which possesses credibility and influence within the new green, ethical market.

---

499 Wal-Mart this year (2006) announced to become a center of affordable 'organics for everyone' and has started by doubling its organic products at 374 stores nationwide (Brady 2006).

500 See also Reputation Trap above.

North Castle Partners, which acquired Avalon Natural Products (personal care products) in 2002, for example states: "With the dramatic rise of consumer interest in healthy living and social responsibility, 'natural and organic' personal care is the fastest growing segment of the personal care industry. Growing to $5 billion in 2004, the natural personal care market recorded 3 straight years of double-digit growth and a 50 percent increase since 2000. The organic segment has been growing even faster. [...] The North Castle team is working closely with Avalon management [...] to identify key opportunities in their market, build brand equity through strong positioning and overall brand strategy including the introduction of new products and entry into new channels of distribution, as well as to continue to strengthen Avalon's leadership position in its core health food channel."[501]

Another example is provided by Richard Goldstein, President of Unilever Foods North America, who at the time of the Ben & Jerry's acquisition said: „Unilever believes the super premium segment of the ice cream market will continue to grow and that the Ben & Jerry's brand will lead that growth. [...] Furthermore, we feel that Ben & Jerry's has a significant opportunity outside of the United States. Unilever is in an ideal position to bring the Ben & Jerry's brand, values and socially responsible message to consumers worldwide. These opportunities strongly support Unilever's stated strategy for expanding the ice cream category globally."[502]

Danone expresses a similar reasoning for their acquisition of Stonyfield Farm: "Similarly, the partnership enables Danone to participate in the rapidly growing organic and natural dairy segment, which has enjoyed strong double-digit growth in an otherwise low growth overall yogurt category."[503]

Jean-Paul Agon, CEO of L'Oreal, has outlined plans to more than double the number of Body Shop stores around the world from 2,000 stores to 5,000 in a few years, with special interest on China, India, Brazil, Argentina and Chile (Jones 2006). Forbes news with respect to the L'Oréal's acquisition of The Body Shop reports the strategy outlined above: "Yet it looks as though the iconic Body Shop will become L'Oreal's much-trumpeted 'ethical' brand, allowing the French company to penetrate the lucrative liberal-middle-class guilt market" (Noon 2006).

Mueller summarizes the strategy of multinational corporations the following: Through the acquisition, the multinationals are buying a foot in the door in the new market segment. An acquisition holds the advantage that they can take something, which has shown some market success and continue to leverage that equity

---

501 See the company's webpage at: http://www.northcastlepartners.com/portfolio/avalon.php, accessed: 06. November 2006.
502 Press Release from 12 April 2000, available at the company's webpage: http://www.ben-jerry.com/our_company/press_center/press/join-forces.html, accessed: 06. November 2006.
503 http://www.stonyfield.com/AboutUs/MoosReleases_Display.cfm?pr_id=36, accessed: 06. November 2006.

in a larger way. Multinational corporations therefore provide financial and marketing resources, in order "to leverage the smaller brands onto the mainstream stage in the longer term" (Mueller 2000).

When looking at this motivation of *acquiring strong brands for getting a foot into growing new ethical markets*, it seems coherent that multinational corporations will **lay high emphasis on preserving the brand image**, which the mission-driven enterprise has build.

This logic is clearly expressed by Peter Saunders, CEO of the Body Shop with respect to the L'Oreal acquisition: „I think that it's been very clear in terms of everything that's been discussed with the Board, that what they're buying is a wonderful brand, The Body Shop. And the last thing that anyone is going to do is to tamper with what they've invested in. We are what we are. We are different from other retailers. We're different from other cosmetics brands. And to change that would basically, probably not get anywhere near the full momentum of the brand that they think they can get" (The Body Shop 2006, Saunders).

The main step taken for preserving brand image after the acquisition thereby is to ensure *operational independence* of the mission-driven enterprise. Adrian Bellamy, Executive Chairman of The Body Shop, for example states: „ L'Oréal have agreed for us to continue operating as an independent entity within their total corporation. Our Chief Executive, Peter Saunders, will remain Chief Executive. Our whole executive team will stay in place. I will stay in place as the Chairman of the company. And all the policies, values and general growth plans that we have will continue unchanged from where they are today. So we have the great benefit of the association and partnership with L'Oréal without having to disturb, in any significant way, our management or our strategic directions" (The Body Shop 2006, Bellamy[504]).

Also the press release of Unilever's acquisition of Ben & Jerry's stresses this point[505] as well as the one of Danone and Stonyfield Farm.[506].

c) Implication of diverging motivations for growth: Shift to brand-orientated consumer expectations

The implication, which arises from these two different motivations for growth discussed and which is pivotal with regard to the Selling-(Out) Trap is the following: The multinational corporation, when following a Reputation Leadership Model, is

---

504 This is a transcript of an interview with Adrian Bellamy by the Body Shop International PLC, 17 March 2006, available at http://w3.cantos.com/06/rose-603-6k9y5/bodyshop/pjx-d137-transcript.php?language=en , accessed: 03. November 2006; in the bibliography under: The Body Shop 2006, Bellamy.
505 Press Release from 12 April 2000, available at the company's webpage: http://www.ben-jerry.com/our_company/press_center/press/join-forces.html, accessed: 06. November 2006.
506 See business case below for further information.

clearly oriented towards *customer* expectations, while the mission-driven enterprise, holding a Symbiotic Model, is rather oriented towards an *absolute, intrinsical* motivation driven by a vision for an *alternative way of doing business*.

Therefore, after an acquisition very often a shift of emphasis occurs: While the historical mission-driven enterprise (i.e. before the acquisition) has laid strong emphasis on its absolute, intrinsic vision and principles of sustainability, usually driven by its founders intention of changing the way business is done, the acquisition of a multinational corporation requires a stronger emphasis on *customer-oriented brand management* in order to foster the desired growth.

Tom McMakin, former CEO of Great Harvest Bread Company and currently principal in Thrive Capital partners, a mission-focused private equity firm, supports this observation. He states that there is a tremendous distinction between commitment to the customer and commitment to sustainbility (community). Therefore, when multinational, strategic buyers acquire mission-driven enterprises, they will lay emphasis on the commitment to the customer, while the commitment to sustainability (to the community, to workers, to the environment, to a particular group) risks getting out of focus and becomes hard for them to keep. (Bamburg 2006: 68).

Jerry Gorde, founder of Vatex, a socially responsible promotional apparel firm, in reference to other founders, which he observed selling to multinational corporations, states that the founders of these firms lost big, not in a financial sense but the objective of a company as a force for change in the world, this mission is lost (Kelly 2003).

d) Selling-Out Trap as a consequence of diverging motivations for growth (different mental models)

The crucial question therefore is, if through an acquisition of a multinational corporation, the independency of management and operation of the mission-driven enterprise can be kept up in order to hold or even foster it's sustainability in-use, while growing to large scale.

In regard to this question the dissertation argues that there is a risk of the mission-driven enterprise *compromising* on its high *sustainability in-use*, while on the other hand the acquisition allows growth and a further diffusion of sustainable products and processes. Put it pointedly: *Rapid growth and diffusion of more sustainable products and/or processes (democratizing the ethical economy) are achieved on the expense of compromising on the sustainability behavior (theory-in-use) of the individual corporation, whereby its sustainability behavior still remains significantly above industry average.* This is the problematic, which lies at the heart of the **Selling-(Out) Trap**, as the dissertation will argue.

The dissertation reasons this not through an ‚unethical nature' of multinational corporations per se, that will hollow-out the principles of a mission-driven enterprise deliberately. Rather, the dissertation argues this through the difference in the mental models outlined above and the dynamics, which are released through this difference after an acquisition.

In the following these dynamics of a Selling-(out) Trap will be discussed (figure 44):

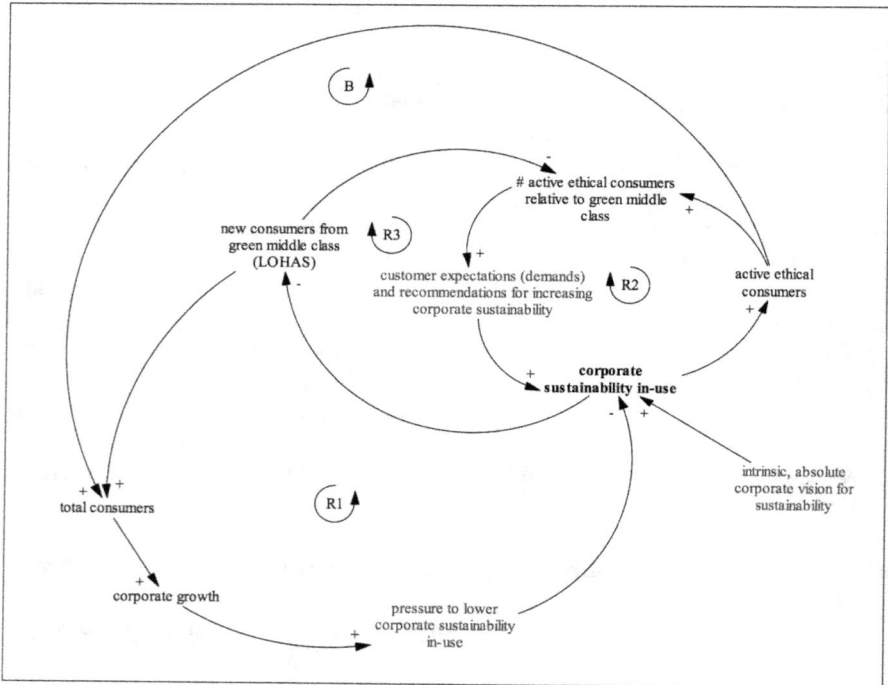

Fig. 44: Selling-(Out) Trap
Source: Produced by the author

The core variable this structure is centered around is the 'corporate sustainability in-use' at the mission-driven enterprise, i.e. corporate behavior regarding sustainability as theory-*in-use* (not as espoused theory).

While still staying at a level above average, the 'corporate sustainability in-use' after a sale to/an acquisition by a multinational corporation often is *reduced* in significant points inherent to the business model (concept) of the mission-driven enterprise.

In a lot of cases, this reduction in sustainbility in-use at their enterprise, is considered a *trap* by the founders (as well as by previous customers or employees) of the mission-driven enterprise.

With the above structure (figure 44), the dissertation seeks to show, that this reduction in corporate sustainability in-use is **not** something deliberately intended by the multinational corporation nor by the sustainable enterprise, but very often results from the following dynamics[507]:

Figure 44 identifies three influencing factors driving 'corporate sustainability in-use', marked in *blue*:

a) *'pressures to lower corporate sustainability in-use'*
b) *'customer expectations and recommendations for increasing corporate sustainability behavior'*
c) the corporation's *'intrinsic, absolute vision for sustainability'*

The last two influencing factors have already been mentioned above.

The first influencing factor opposes the previous two and constitutes in 'pressures to lower corporate sustainability in-use'. As the dissertation will argue in the following, very often the latter factor ('pressures to lower corporate sustainability in-use') is augmented, whereby the previous two factors diminish, resulting in an overall reduction of 'corporate sustainability in-use'.

In the following the underlying dynamics driving these factors will be elaborated for each of the three variables:

a) *'Pressures to lower corporate sustainability in-use'*

For the variable 'pressures to lower corporate sustainability in-use' the dissertation refers to such pressures, which arise from the corporation's intention for rapidly growing large scale. This dynamic is represented in the growth loop R1: As has become apparent in the quotations from business practice above, one core intention of the acquisition is to speed up large scale growth of the mission-driven enterprise. But rapid, large growth can lead to various *pressures for lowering sustainability in-use* in order to reach the growth targets, for example:

- A main pressure at present is that there are not enough organic farmers (suppliers) to meet mass demand on large scale, which raises the pressure to lower standards or source from farmers with less organic standards.
- A further pressure, which can result is a pressure for reducing 'fair' payments to farmers in order to quickly amortize the purchase price for the mission-driven enterprise in order for the stock price to stay high (avoid take-over, see also Hollender and Fenichel 2004: 230ff).

---

507 Similar as in all previous structures, this does not imply that this structure is the only explanation for this phenomenon or that it will play out evidentially, as soon as a mission-driven enterprise is acquired by a multinational corporation. It rather is an archetypical structure, which caused the phenomenon in a number of cases.

- Listing products in supermarkets or discounters with questionable reputation in regard to social responsibility to their employees, but which promise a larger turn-over of the products (e.g. Wal-Mart).[508]
- Introducing more hierarchies with salary-discrepancy as the corporation grows (see also Hollender and Fenichel 216).
- Compromising on cost-intensive, but more sustainable ingredients to keep prices moderate.

As mentioned above, such pressures for lowering sustainability in-use in order to grow more rapidly are countervailed by two main factors: *customer expectations and recommendations* for increasing corporate sustainability behavior and the *corporations' intrinsic motivation* for continuously improving its sustainability behavior.

The pivotal point of this Sustainbility Traps is that *while pressures to* **lower** *sustainability in-use risk to* **rise** *due to the reasons mentioned, both of these* **countervailing** *factors, which could still hold up the sustainability in-use despite of the pressures, risk to* **decrease** *after an acquisition.* This will be elaborated in the following.

b) 'Customer expectation and recommendation'

'Customer expectation and recommendation' for increasing corporate sustainability behavior risks *decreasing* after an acquisition due to the following dynamics:

The mission-driven enterprise in its history usually has acquired a large basis of '*active, ethical consumers*'. Active, ethical consumers only buy products of companies, whose corporate behavior is inline with their morals (see also moral consumption in Priddat 2005a: 175ff, Koslowski and Priddat 2006). Ethical consumers share a Symbiotic Model (holistic mental model of perception space) and through their consumption seek to particularly support mission-driven enterprises in their endeavor of introducing alternative products and business models. They posses high background knowledge on sustainability issues, read relevant literature and visit pertinent websites. They refer to "advocates of deep sustainability" and want to know, who owns the business; how they make decisions; and what this means about wealth and power (Goodman 2003).

Most importantly, these consumers actively interact with 'their' mission-driven enterprise (e.g. via e-mail, feedback-letters, blogs, campaigns, etc.) in order to approve actions, point to shortcomings or to bring in new ideas and suggestions for further improving sustainability (see reinforcing loop R2).

After a sale to a multinational corporation however, many of these 'active, ethical consumers' turn away from the mission-driven enterprise, because they fear that

---

508 Wal-Mart this year (2006) announced to become a center of affordable 'organics for everyone' and has started by doubling its organic products at 374 stores nationwide (Brady 2006).

with the multinational corporation 'behind their back' the mission-driven enterprise will not be able to keep up its high sustainability in-use. Therefore these consumers turn to other independent mission-driven enterprises (see customer quotations in business cases below).

On the other hand new *consumers from the 'green middle class'* are won as new customers in the attempt of growing and spreading the mission-driven enterprise after the acquisition (see R1 above), e.g. through listing products in supermarket/discounters, introduce cheaper products, or simply through 'mainstreaming' the brand via intensive marketing.

The term 'green middle class' is derived from Jundt (2004). It corresponds to what has become also known as LOHAS (Lifestyles of Health and Sustainability) consumers, who are focused on health and fitness, the environment, personal development, sustainable living, and social justice (see also The LOHAS Journal). Thus the dissertation does not only subsume environmentally, but also socially responsible consumers under this term.

The term 'green *middle class*' is adopted in the dissertation in order to stress the aspect of *mainstreaming* within the green/ethical market (see Jundt 2004) in differentiation to the other customer group of 'active, ethical consumers'. Consumers from the green middle class buy organic, bio or fair-trade goods also at grocery outlets (e.g. Wal-Mart, Safeway, Plus or REWE) in order to contribute to their own and their family's health as well as to strengthen their cultural identity as conscious consumers with environmental and/or social concern.

The green middle class however possesses a far more passive attitude than the active, ethical consumers. Their background knowledge on sustainability issues is far lower, they tend to buy food with a ,bio'-label at a supermarket or discounter, without questioning what lies behind the label, most important they hardly feedback to their producer in terms of where and how to further increase sustainability – out of lack of priority for the subject or simply out of missing knowledge.

The crucial point is that after an acquisition, the number of active, ethical consumers relative to consumers from the green middle class tends to drop significantly, with the consequence that customer expectations as well as knowledgeable, innovative suggestions of how to further increase sustainability is reduced (see R2 and R3 in figure 44).

Balancing Loop B could work as a limit-to-growth, if sustainability in-use is reduced and if the drop-out of active ethical consumers actually reduces the total number of consumers, then growth slows down, which reduces pressures to lower sustainability in-use (e.g. because the number of organic farmers is now sufficient to meet the reduced demand). However, this balancing dynamic only plays out, if the number of ,active ethical consumers' dropping-out cannot be countered by an increasing number of consumers from ,green middle class'. (Note that in figure 44, both variables - 'active, ethical consumers' and 'new consumers from green middle class' - run into the variables of 'total consumers').[509]

But as the dissertation argues, in most cases a large number of new consumers from green middle class can be gained, so that they easily offset the drop-out from active, ethical consumers. Consequently the number of total consumers raises and the intended growth succeeds.

The crucial point now is that this shift in the consumer-structure (see variable: 'number of active, ethical consumers relative to green middle class') leads to the effect that 'customer expectations (pressure) and recommendations for increasing corporate sustainability in-use' is *decreasing*, because the green middle-class is satisfied with a lower level of sustainability than the active, ethical consumers and have less knowledge and/or interest to actively engage into interaction with the corporation in how to further improve their sustainability in-use.

c) Intrinsic, absolute vision for sustainability of the corporation

The third variable influencing corporate sustainability in-use is the corporation's *intrinsic, absolute vision for sustainability*. This factor usually is grounded in the founders' personal values and vision to develop an alternative, unorthodox business model focused on sustainability, and thus revolutionizing the way business is done. It usually provides the intrinsic motivation for continuously improving the corporation's behavior with respect to sustainability.[510] After an acquisition, the founders usually stay connected to the enterprise and serve as an advisor. Due to changes in management however, their influence on driving the enterprise often is diminished

---

509 The reader might wonder why both variables enter with the same link polarity (+), but still yield countervailing effects. This is because the countervailing effect plays out earlier in the loops: The *decrease* of the variable 'corporate sustainability in-use' has *opposing* effects on the two consumer groups:

1) When the variable 'corporate sustainability in-use' decreases, the number of 'active, ethical consumers' *decreases* (positive link polarity (+)), which in turn *reduces* the variable 'total consumers'.

2) When the variable 'corporate sustainability in-use' decreases, the number of 'consumers from green middle class' however *increases*. (This can be reasoned by the following exemplary measures: More of the corporation's financial resources are directed to marketing and augmenting brand-awareness (rather than in sustainability initiatives), products are listed in discounters with questionable social sustainability standards (e.g. Wal-Mart), supply sources are compromised on so that larger amounts are available etc.) The increase in the number of 'consumers from green middle class' *increases* the number of 'total consumers'.

The two countervailing-effects described, constitute of course the dominant (stereotyped or theoretical) effects; in reality there are far more effects. As the statements and analysis in the business cases below will show however, these two countervailing effects show in many cases and are crucial for the dynamics discussed.

510 Note that this is an external, absolute variable (see figure 44).

(see below e.g. Unilever's decision to appoint a CEO specialized in sales instead of another candidate with strong commitment to social values proposed by Ben and Jerry's advisory board, see business case below).

Due to the difference in mental models on sustainability of the original mission-driven enterprise and the multinational corporation described above, the influencing variable 'independent, absolute vision' (i.e. vision for a new sustainable business model), looses on influence in expense of an orientation towards customer expectations (brand management) in order to grow (R1).[511]

The crucial point thereby is that 'customer expectations and recommendations for increasing sustainability in-use' is an *internal, dependent* variable (in contrast to the rather independent, absolute vision or principles introduced by the founder). What therefore happens is that customer expectations and recommendations for increasing sustainability in-use *lower*, because of the dynamics described (shift in customer structure).

Summary of dynamics driving the Selling-(out) Trap

The above dynamics (figure 44) can be summed up the following:

The declared goal of the acquisition to grow 'large scale' in a rather short time augments specific pressures for compromising on sustainability in-use. Countervailing these pressures are

1) the intrinsic, absolute dedication (vision) for holding up sustainability in-use even to the expense of growth or other factors (e.g. profit) and

2) customer expectations that need to be regarded for.

After an acquisition there is a significant risk that there is a shift of emphasis [512] on acquiring new customers through brand building and to grow, rather than focusing on the vision of an alternative business practice. That is, a shift from dominant influence of 1) towards a dominant influence of 2).

The pivotal point is that this second variable (customer expectation and recommendation), which now dominantly influences corporate sustainability in-use, *decreases*. This is the case, because there is a *shift in consumer structure* in the way that more and more 'active, ethical consumers' are leaving and on the other hand more and more consumers of the 'green middle class' can be won as new customers in a grow-

---

511 This is no case of 'either – or'. As figure 44 shows, both variables ('customer expectations and recommendations for increasing sustainability in-use' and 'intrinsic, absolute corporate vision of sustainability') still remain influencing factors for the variable 'corporate sustainability in-use'. But what happens is a *shift* in the *dominance* of the two variables.

512 This is *not* to say, that one is given up for the other. As stated, this is a shift of *emphasis* (dominance) and became apparent in the business cases analyzed. Furthermore this shift evidentially refers to a theory-in-use and is unlikely to be espoused as a shift explicitly.

ing market. The green middle class however is less interested and less knowledge-able with respect to sustainbility expectations and recommendations.

This dynamics can lead to the effect that 'corporate sustainability in-use' is lowered over-time in regard to significant points.[513] That is, 'corporate sustainability in-use' is lower in certain respects (e.g. sourcing practices, farmers' compensations etc.) as well as less radical/innovative in its business approach, compared to the mission-driven enterprise before the acquisition by the multinational corporation.

It is insofar that it can be spoken of a *Sustainability Trap*: That is, 'falling back' from a Systemic Model with a holistic perception space as a driver, towards a Reputation Leadership Model, where credible brand-image dominates.

On the other hand however, as pointed out, many of the acquisitions have led to higher brand recognition and have won new customers, thus mainstreaming 'sustainable consumerisms' and growing the 'green middle class'. This is an important achievement, which needs to be recognized and valued. Building a 'green middle class' is key for moving towards a transformation to sustainable consumption and production. As Jundt states, although the trend of multinationals acquiring mission-driven enterprises and thus compromising on the business model that was an important part of the original ideal might seem concerning, it needs to be acknowledged that the trend as served to greatly expand the market for organic foods (Jundt 2004: 11).

3.5.2.2   Dealing with the Trap

It is important to point out once more that it is not the intention of the dissertation to discredit selling to a multinational corporation per se. The point the dissertation makes, is that it is crucial for founders (managers) of mission-driven enterprises to realize that leapfrogging growth through selling to a multinational corporation, bears the risks described. As stated, this is the case, not because of deliberate 'bad' intentions of multinational corporations, but because multinationals work on a different mental model than mission-driven enterprises, which triggers the dynamics described above and leads to the results of: Growth in mainstream market, but compromising on corporate sustainability in-use.

It remains a question of individual judgment if these results are considered to be a trap or not:[514]

---

513 Although reduced, the sustainbility in-use however usually still remains at a level above average.

514 That is: On the one side the individual mission-driven enterprise after an acquisition often turns out to compromise on its sustainbility standards. On the other side, the trend of acquisitions of mission-driven enterprises and consequently their growth on large scale, contributes to a mainstreaming of the sustainbility movement.

For founders or managers of mission-driven enterprises, who consider rapid growth into mainstream markets important for promoting sustainability and which, in turn, are ready to risk compromising on their sustainability in-use and on a radically, alternative business model, for such founders selling to a multinational corporation makes perfect sense.

Hirshberg (Stonyfield Farm) for example argues that founders should not 'sit on their high horses' and refuse activities just because they are not ecologically perfect, rather it would be crucial to rapidly grow in order to become a powerful force in the industry, even if this meant compromising to some respect (Brady 2006). This seems a reasonable and legitimate argumentation, since corporate sustainability in-use usually still stays above average and a rapid diffusion of the products and the 'sustainable messages' contribute to an awareness for the issue.

As will become apparent in the business cases below however, there are many *founders* of mission-driven enterprises, who welcome the growth of the green/sustainable market, but who do consider their *individual* enterprise to have gotten into a trap after having sold to a multinational corporation. Not only because individual aspects of sustainbility in-use of the enterprise were compromised on, but primarily because the enterprise did not contribute to the disruptive process of changing the way business operates as such, anymore.[515] The enterprise now rather operates under the similar rules as the multinational mother company, i.e. on a sectoral mental model of perception space.

The dissertation in the following will therefore discuss two measures, which can serve as alternatives to selling to multinational corporations and thus to keep up the high level of sustainbility in-use and most important to preserve the vision of an alternative business model, which serves as a disruptive force in orthodox economy.

The two measures thereby are rather mutually exclusive. Thereby, none of the measures is 'right' or 'wrong', both are suitable to avoid getting into the trap described. Rather, the alternative measures depend on the question whether a mission-driven enterprise values large scale growth as a measure to sustainbility in the first place or if it does not:

    a)   ***Alternative ways to grow large scale:*** If a mission-driven enterprise values large scale growth as a way to push the sustainability movement forward, it needs to evaluate alternative ways to grow, than selling to a multinational corporation. This paragraph will discuss financing alternatives, which allow growing and still preserving the high level of sustainbility in-use.

---

515 That is, change towards what the dissertation has termed a holistic mental model of perception space.

b) *Questioning large scale growth* as a feasible means towards sustainbility: From organization-centered to society-centered mission-driven enterprises.

These two measures will be discussed in the following.

a) Alternative ways for growth (organic growth)

There is a growing number of founders/managers of still independent mission-driven enterprises, who express their dissatisfaction with the results described above and with what has become of other mission-driven enterprises acquired by multinational corporations (Hollender and Fenichel 2004: 230ff and 236ff, Bamburg 2006).

These founders therefore start looking for other ways of how to grow and thereby still guard their *alternative* business model, in order to penetrate the market with mission-driven business models (based on a Systemic Model) and thus to promote a 'real', revolution of how we conduct business.[516] This process referred to as 'institutionalizing social mission' (Harrison 2006, Kelly 2003), currently is a hot topic discussed within the community of mission-driven enterprises.

One crucial question thereby is how to *finance* growth alternatively?

Going public bears the problem that investors do not share the values and pressure for short-term profit. And even investors who do share the values, at one point will want to exit and cash their profits. At this time there is a risk that they sell to other investors, who do not share the values (see e.g. Ben & Jerry's case[517]).

Bamburg (2006) examined several success factors for growing mission-driven enterprises. Her analysis has shown, that the best way to grow and still hold up the initial vision of a highly sustainable, alternative business model is to grow *organically*, i.e. slowly and without outside investor capital (Bamburg 2006: 10). "Mission-driven businesses tend to grow more slowly, and *need* to grow more slowly" (Bamburg 2006: 10).

For mission-driven enterprises bootstrapping, i.e. financing business growth largely out of revenues, is the best option of financing investments, because it preserves independence (Bamburg 2006: 10 and 57ff).

The advantages of organic growth identified by Bamburg are (Bamburg 2006: 54ff):

- It reduces the reliance of mission-driven enterprises on outside investors and thereby enables them to maintain their commitment to mission.
- Furthermore it allows founders and employees to grow into their job and continuously reflect upon and further develop their mission over time.

---

516 See e.g. statement by Gorde in Kelly 2003 cited above.
517 See appendix L.

- Corporate culture can better be established and maintained over time.
- Last but not least an organic pace better allows employees to maintain their health and well-being.

As Bamburg states organic growth however is *not*, slow. "It is simply slow*er*" (Bamburg 2006: 55).

Nevertheless there are situations, where organic growth is very difficult, for example when a market is growing rapidly and attracts significant competition (see e.g. organic food market below). Mission-driven enterprises in this situation need to decide whether to meet the challenge or settle into a niche (or a series of niches) (Bamburg 2006: 54ff). If large investments into marketing or manufacturing are necessary, this usually requires outside investors. If outside investments are required or desired, it is crucial to choose the investors carefully. Thereby the enterprise should seek to build mission into its value proposition, i.e. to seek building the company's values into the ownership structure (Bamburg 2006: 68). Ideal investors thereby are of course those, who share the values.

Currently more and more 'socially responsible investors' are emerging. Bamburg e.g. introduces Investor's Circle, a network of angel investors with a commitment to provide slow money or patient capital to businesses in energy and the environment, food and organics, community and international development, education and media, and health and wellness (Bamburg 2006: 64).

Hollender and Fenichel (2004: 230ff) point to investment funds like the planned Upstream 21. Such funds aim to put investors' capital to work in local communities by purchasing small, successful progressive companies thereby especially designed to making sure that those companies are not required to maximize wealth for shareholders at the expense of employee, the community, and the environment.

Another possibility suggested by Bamberg are employee stock ownership programs (ESOPs), because the employees usually share the mission and thus will also have a strong say in the business they helped to build. Furthermore Bamberg argues to be creative and invent new instruments for financing, e.g. innovative debt-equity combinations (Bamburg 2006: 69). One example could be the way Ben and Jerry's raised their capital initially, by selling shares to citizens of Vermont. Ben and Jerry's however did not provide for a feasible exit strategy for their investors, which caused serious problems.[518]

It can be summarized that organic growth is a more feasible way for promoting mission-driven enterprises and their mission.

It has been known since quite a time that going public can proof problematic for mission-driven enterprises, because shares can be sold to investors, which do not share the values and press for short-term profit. Compared to this, selling to (being

---

518 See Ben and Jerry case in appendix L.

acquired by) a multinational corporation with interest for the 'ethical market', seemed to be a feasible new alternative, because the multinational corporation is in the same business and espouses a similar emphasis on sustainability.

The dissertation however sought to show why this also can turn out to be problematic (a trap). The above provided alternative ways to fund growth, which are currently emerging on a broad basis.

b) From organization-centered to society-centered mission-driven enterprises

Another line of argumentation about how to avoid the trap outlined, can be centered around the question, if large scale growth as such – even organic growth – is a main leverage for promoting sustainability.

When growing organically, pressures for reducing sustainability in-use can be withheld to some extent. But at some point even organic growth is likely to be confronted with serious pressures, e.g. when local sourcing cannot meet the demand anymore and global sourcing becomes necessary, which implies serious environmental stresses due to transportation (Woodward 2001). Therefore in the view of the dissertation, questions to whether the emphasis on growth as such is feasible for promoting sustainability are legitimate (see e.g. Schumacher 1989; Meadows et al. 2004). An alternative to growing some mission-driven enterprises large scale could be the promotion of many local, smaller-scale enterprises.

The dissertation sees a main reason why mission-driven enterprises focus on growing large scale in order to spread sustainability, therein that their business-model still is what the dissertation refers to as 'organization-centered'. Being 'organization-centered' augments the risk of getting into the trap described, which departs from the intention of growing large scale in order to promote sustainability. The term 'organization-centered' is used by the dissertation to refer to business models, whose core purpose is still centered around a – sustainable - vision for the organization itself (e.g. to become the world's first organization with fully organic ice cream, to be the largest provider of sustainable energy supply, to be the enterprise with the highest support for renaturating rain forests). Organization-centered business models can be distinguished from society-centered business models, which consider an enterprise as a *social construct (vehicle) developed to meet **human needs***.

Society-centered business models are built to address problems of social unsustainability respectively of social wellbeing. Organization-centered business models in contrast are primarily centered around selling a specific product or service and by doing so to meet an *organizational* goal or vision of sustainability (e.g. to be the first enterprise to built product X from fully remanufacturable components). Therefore even if the full business model and product life-cycle of a mission-driven enterprise are sustainable in every respect imaginable, there remains a difference between organization-centered and social-centered enterprises, which lies deeper and refers to the 'purpose' and self-awareness of an enterprise.

The difference lies in the point if the *core* purpose of the enterprise is to preserve and grow *itself*, or if the enterprise is considered a social construct to serve human needs (based on the mission) and to grow *social sustainability* as such. Critics are likely to argue that this is not a matter of either-or, but that both aspects are inter-dependent when speaking about sustainability. And the dissertation fully acknowledges the interdependence, but the question lies in the conscious decision, which aspect is considered fundamental (constitutive) for the enterprise. For example, Ben & Jerry's are widely considered to be a mission-driven enterprise[519]. However it can be questioned, if ice cream as such is a sustainable product. A society-centered enterprise in contrast would not have been centered around ice cream.

Therefore the dissertation argues that very often no distinction between organization-centered and society-centered enterprises is made in literature and different business models holding a Systemic Model are 'lumped' together (see e.g. also in Bamburg 2006).

With respect to the trap described above however, this distinction becomes relevant. The business model of organization-centered mission-driven enterprises still relies on the aspect of orthodox economics that rapid, large scale growth is important. However, organization-centered mission-driven enterprises, which focus on changing the economic system via growing their own, alternative business model large scale rapidly, have a higher risk of getting into the Sustainbility Trap described, because they will nevertheless meet the pressures of large scale growth described above at some point.

Society-centered enterprises in contrast are less focused on growing the enterprise as such large scale, but rather on growing the mission, e.g. via many small-scale, local initiatives, which thus avoid pressures of rapid, large scale growth. Moreover society-centered mission-driven enterprises lay substantial care on the fact that their product or service as such is one, which promotes sustainbility, - i.e. their sustainability mission -, by meeting human needs.

Because the society-centered form of mission-driven enterprises is radically new and different from orthodox-business models, there are no examples of pure forms of these types of mission-driven enterprises. However, in contrast to Ben & Jerry's ice cream for example, the following mission-driven enterprises can be considered rather society-centered:

Honey Care Africa, is a Kenyan enterprise focused on sustainable community-based beekeeping for production of natural honey.[520] The company trains small

---

519 At least before the acquisition by Unilever.
520 For information see the company's website at: http://www.honeycareafrica.com/index.php, accessed 02. November 2006.

scale farmers in commercial beekeeping and buys their honey at a guaranteed price, with the explicit mission to increase income and education of rural farmers (social sustainbility). The enterprise thereby trains farmers on modern beekeeping methods using the Langstroth hives, which although more expensive, give cleaner honey and wax, produce less disturbance of the queen bee and the brood and is comparatively less destructive to trees than the traditional hives[521] (environmental sustainbility). Problematic, is that Honey Care Africa distributes the honey not only locally, but also internationally, which bears sustainbility issues with respect to transportation.

Another most prominent examples of a society-centered mission-driven enterprise is the Grameen Family of Enterprises founded in Bangladesh, whose original enterprise, the Grameen Bank, and its founder Muhammad Yunus were assigned the Nobel Peace Prize for 2006.[522] While Grameen Bank provides micro-credits to rural poor, Grameen Shakti (GS) is an energy company, which supplies renewable energy to unelectrified villages, with the mission not only to provide renewable energy services, but also to create employment and income-generation opportunities in rural areas.

The distinction of organization-centered and society-centered mission-driven enterprises, draws back on a meeting of representatives from small and midsize corporations dedicated to sustainability, NGOs, scientists and representatives from developing countries (local communities) in Boston, USA, March 2006[523]. There, a concept of so called mission-based enterprises (MBE) was discussed as a radically new form of enterprise, which is focused on meeting human needs and fostering environmental well-being by working on a small-scale level, which allows staying in contact with local needs and vulnerabilities as well as to work in small, flexible units.

The concept of Mission-Based Enterprises is still on a working level, so that a full business model cannot be laid out at this time. To the dissertation it was important to point out that there seems to be a difference between organization-centered and society-centered business models, with the former holding a higher risk of getting into the trap described as it is still focused on rapidly growing the organization large scale.

---

521 This is because an average of one tree is cut down for each traditional hive constructed unlike for Langstroth where only already sawn timber is used.
522 For further information see the website at http://www.grameen-info.org/grameen/gknit/index.html, accessed: 02. November 2006.
523 Participants among others were: Peter Senge (Massachusetts Institute of Technology), Stuart Hart (Cornell University), Wolfgang Stark (University Duisburg-Essen), Macharia Waruingi (Director Kenya Development Network Consortium), Sara Schley and Joe Laur (SoL and Seed System), Michael Dupee (Green Mountain Coffee Roasters), Don Seville (Sustainability Institute), Dean Cycon (Dean's Beans), Simone Ambre (SEED at Schlumberger), the author of this dissertation.

3.5.2.3   Business Case: Stonyfield Farm

The business case, which will be outlined more in-depth in the following, is that of Stonyfield Farm.

The beginnings and background of the founders

The enterprise was founded by Samuel Kayman, a Brooklyn-born head of an organic-farming school in Wilton, New Hampshire, in order to feed his six kids and to escape the dominant culture business is operating in (Brady 2006). Kayman produced his yogurt as a showcase for the virtues and practicality of organic agriculture (Goodman 2003).

But the farm was not running well financially. This is why in 1982 Kayman asked the 29-year-old Gary Hirshberg to run the farm in a more businesslike manner, turning it into an enterprise Stonyfield Farm (Hollender and Fenichel 2004: 234[524]). Hirshberg, who describes himself as "a former windmill-building hippie" (Goodman 2003), was an environmental activist, windmill-maker, author and entrepreneur (the company's website[525]). When starting out, Hirshberg and Kayman milked 19 cows every day, getting up at five in the morning often in subfreezing weather and produced milk according to strict organic principles, i.e. chemically-free and all-natural (Hollender and Fenichel 2004: 234, Goodman 2003). They nearly went bankrupt before the organic market started sky rocking, growing around 20 percent a year throughout the 1990s (Goodman 2003, see also above).

Sustainbility at Stonyfield Farm

Stonyfield farm always laid strong emphasis on improving sustainability through their business. They seek to serve as "a model that environmentally and socially responsible businesses can also be profitable."[526] Stonyfield lays special emphasis on supporting local, organic farmers and supporting family farms throughout New England, USA, in turning their farms into organic farms. Stonyfield became the first dairy processor in the United States to pay farmers for not using a synthetic hormone (rBST) and sued the State of Illinois for preventing them from labeling their products rBST-free (the company's website[527]). In contrast to the vast major-

---

524 See also company's webpage: http://www.stonyfield.com/AboutUs/MemoryLane/index.cfm, accessed: 09. November 2006.

525 See company's webpage at: http://www.stonyfieldfarm.com/AboutUs/OurStory.cfm, accessed: 09. November 2006.

526 See company's mission statement at http://www.stonyfield.com/AboutUs/OurStory.cfm, accessed: 09. November 2006.

527 See company's webpage at:
http://www.stonyfieldfarm.com/AboutUs/setting_the_record_straight.cfm, accessed: 09. November 2006.

ity of other food producers, Stonyfield significantly invests in the farms, which supply them, improving their soil, water and sanitary conditions, thus fueling their mission of a shift towards organic farming (Arena 2004: 52).

By 2004 Stonyfield had encouraged 120 farms in New England to convert to organic (Hollender and Fenichel 2004: 234f), which means far less pesticides going into the ground, less cows being fed with genetically modified food and ultimately less health risks for the farmers themselves. As Hirshberg claims, the farmers now can "hug their children at the end of a work day because they're not covered in toxic white dust, and they can swim in clean ponds and enjoy a life free of sprays and mounting health problems" (Arena 2004: 52).

Stonyfield moreover quantifies the impact created by all its environmental and social activities in form of an ecological footprint. The company monitors total water and energy consumption company-wide as well as the amount of CO_2, solid waste and airborne emissions caused of the manufacturing process on a quarterly basis (Arena 2004: 53). The monitoring has not only led to significant reduction of resource use, but also to product and packaging innovations, such as replacing the lids on top of its products by thin foil seal, making the plastic containers as light as possible and recyclable (Arena 2004: 53, Hollender and Fenichel 2004: 235).

The company's plant near Manchester, New Hampshire, posses recycled wood floors, uses ultra-efficient lighting and bathrooms with recycled plastic stalls (Hollender and Fenichel 2004, Goodman 2003).

Furthermore Stonyfield lays strong emphasis on interacting and also educating consumers about the value of protecting the environment.[528] For this purpose Hirshberg introduced the concept of using the plastic yogurt containers as 'mini-billboards' in order to inform about issues such as fighting oil drilling in Alaska or long-term implications of global climate change (Hollender and Fenichel 2004: 235, Goodman 2003). The company donates 10 percent of its profits to organizations and projects, which work to protect and restore the earth. In 2005, for example, nearly US$ 713,420 were given to non-profit and educational organizations in the US to support their innovative environmental and organic programs, e.g. supporting bicycling as a means of transportation and a four-year university dedicated to saving the ecosystems of the tropics.[529]

---

528 See also the company's mission statement at:
http://www.stonyfieldfarm.com/AboutUs/OurStory.cfm, accessed: 09. November 2006.
529 http://www.stonyfield.com/EarthActions/GivingProfitstothePlanet.cfm, company's webpage, accessed: 09. November 2006.

Acquisition by Groupe Danone

Hirshberg had financed the growth of the enterprise through a few hundred investors (297), primarily family, friends and venture capitalist, who shared the vision of promoting environmental and social sustainability. As stated above, the company developed very successfully with the organic market booming through the 1990s. But this very success became a problem, because some of the investors – the largest one being a socially responsible venture capitalist – wanted to cash in at a share price, which was more than Hirshberg and the company could afford to pay (Hollender and Fenichel 2004: 234, Goodman 2003).

Hirshberg started pondering his options and at the end got positively excited about the deal arranged with Groupe Danone, the French parent company of The Dannon Company, Inc. Negotiations were tough and took two exhausting years, because Hirshberg repeatedly threatened to call off the deal, if his preconditions were not met. Hirshberg backed off the deal several times, because he feared conditions, which held the risk of losing control of the company's social mission (Rose 2001).

Finally the two parties agreed on gradually phasing in the acquisition: In 2001 Danone acquired a 40 percent stake in Stonyfield, by then being the largest organic yogurt brand in the United States, for an estimated US\$ 125 million (Goodman 2003, Hollender and Fenichel 2004: 233). With Hirshberg's approval Danone then in phase two of the acquisition, purchased all non-employee owned shares of Stonyfield stock, enabling it to achieve majority ownership (85%) of the company in December 2003 (the company's website[530], Brady 2006). His friend Ben Cohen had previously expressed his dissatisfaction of having sold Ben & Jerry's to a multinational corporation, but Hirshberg strongly believed in the potential of engaging with a multinational corporation if only the conditions were set right. Hirshberg considered Ben Cohen's deal to have been a too cautionary one and deliberately set out a deal with Danone, which in Hirshberg's view was 'something different' (Hollender and Fenichel 2004: 236).

The awareness for the problematic of forming a deal, which allows the mission-driven enterprise to keep up its sustainbility in-use after an acquisition by a multinational, is also reflected on Stonyfield's webpage, which concerning the Danone acquisition claims that the Stonyfield Farm/Danone deal is a special one within the current climate of food industry consolidation. Stonyfield points to the trend, that numerous smaller, natural and organic products companies have been acquired by multinationals, which through these brands seek to fuel growth in fast-growing market niches. As Stonyfield further points out, thereby many of those examples have resulted in changes of control and management of the acquired firm, for example Kraft/ Boca Burger, Nestle/Power Bar, Kellogg's/Kashi, Unilever/Ben

---

530 http://www.stonyfield.com/Aboutus/StonyfieldDanone.cfm, accessed 09. November 2006.

& Jerry's. Stonyfield states to have recognized this problem and therefore the deal with Danone is staged as a partnership, which enables both firms to "walk before they run" and "has been engineered not only to ensure Stonyfield's continued management autonomy, but also to ensure that its ambitious organic, environmental and social missions will be unimpeded as well."[531]

Hirshberg consequently has been positively excited about the deal made with Danone, stating to his friend Jeffrey Hollender, CEO of Seventh Generation:" The deal with Danone is turning out to be an unbelievable deal. It's the solution to money-raising problem you and I have been working on for decades. I've got total influence, total control, and total freedom from having to worry about money!" (Hollender and Fenichel 2004: 236).

This freedom however was all dependent on Hirshberg's ability to generate results as a business. In order to remain CEO and guarantee Stonyfield's independence, Hirshberg has to meet double-digit growth targets (Goodman 2003).[532] Further key elements of the partnership included (Goodman 2003, the company's website[533]):

- Establishing two Danone appointees, including Danone's worldwide head of Dairy on Stonyfield's five-member board.
- Stonyfield's sales, brand and marketing strategies remain independent from Danone and there will be no changes to Stonyfield Farm employees, facility and operations.
- Stonyfield's corporate-giving program 'Profits for the Planet', in which 10% of prior year's profits are donated to environmental causes (see above) is continued and will be supported for at least a decade beyond Hirshberg's tenure.

---

531 See company's webpage: http://www.stonyfield.com/AboutUS/StonyfieldDanone.cfm, accessed: 06. November 2006.

532 More precisely, repercussions on Stonyfield's independence would officially only came to play if in two consecutive years Hirshberg would come in below budgeted revenues by more than 20 percent, whereby if he stumbled in the first year, the adjusted second-year goals would be a reduction from the first year results (Hollender and Fenichel 2004: 236). With the boom in the organic market it was no question to Hirshberg that he would meet these requirements:" So in order to fail that badly, I would have to go on heroin and become a complete junkie and do something really irrational, and I would have to do it for more than a year" (Hollender and Fenichel 2004: 236).

533 A full list of the key elements of the partnership can be found on the company's webpage at: http://www.stonyfield.com/Aboutus/StonyfieldDanone.cfm, accessed: 09. November 2006.

Diverging motivations for growth through the acquisition (different mental models)
As stated in the analysis of the archetypical structure of a Selling-(Out) Trap above, the motivations for fueling large scale growth after an acquisition are different at the mission-driven enterprise and the multinational. While the mission-driven enterprise seeks to fuel the growth in order to infiltrate and change the orthodox way of how business is done at large scale; the multinational seeks to penetrate a new market segment with a brand, which has already owned customer credibility in this segment. This divergence is also visible in the Stonyfield/Danone case.

What made Hirshberg passionate about the deal with Danone was the prospect of leveraging "economies of scale to spread the gospel of organic farming and organic food to a broader, global market" (Hollender and Fenichel 2004: 236). Hirshberg sought to accomplish this by expanding Stonyfield internationally[534] and saw tremendous potential in instilling the concept of organic food into the much larger parent company, by considering himself like a "Trojan horse within their company [...] and introduce organics through their many product lines" (Goodman 2003). Furthermore Hirshberg was convinced that his personal values are 'genetically encoded' in the product so that their future is safeguarded no matter who controls Stonyfield (Goodman 2003, Hollender and Fenichel 2004: 236).

Franck Riboud, chairman and CEO of Groupe DANONE comments the acquisition with a clear emphasis on market growth: "Through this unique partnership, Danone will build upon and expand Stonyfield's leadership in the U.S. natural and organic yoghurt segment as we provide pivotal assistance in terms of manufacturing, purchasing, logistics and other efficiencies. We believe it is important for Stonyfield to continue to grow its market share while maintaining its commitment to social responsibility."' ('Danone buys US functional yoghurt' 2001).

Ethical stakeholders, who pushed sustainbility in-use, leave (change in stakeholder structure)
Samuel Kaymen, original founder of Stonyfield, presuming the changes associated with the Danone deal, felt less enthusiastic about the acquisition than Hirshberg, and retired shortly before Danone bought the shares. "I never felt comfortable with the scale or dealing with people so far away" he states, he nevertheless acknowledges that Hirshberg so far has managed to uphold the company's original principles (Brady 2006).

Furthermore many active, ethical consumers stopped purchasing products from Stonyfield, especially since Danone is listed on the ban-list of the 'Responsible Shopper' of Co-Op America, an NGO for global research and action to stop corporate abuse, which is most renowned and widespread in the sustainability commu-

---

534 For example Stonyfield's entrance into the European market, see Awbi 2006.

nity.[535] It has to be stated clearly however, that the 'Responsible Shopper' specifically does *not* refer to Stonyfield, but to another market segment of Danone (bottled water). Some active, ethical consumers however deliberately stop purchasing Stonyfield products in order not to support crosswise a company (Danone), which is considered to be unsustainable in another market segment or simply because they fear Danone will 'negatively' influence Stonyfield.[536]

Rapid large scale growth and pressures to compromise on sustainbility

Hirshberg so far has managed to reach his required minimum growth rate. Stonyfield has enjoyed a compounded growth rate of over 26% for each of the last 14 years and today is the third largest brand in the US with expected annual revenues in 2006 of $250 million[537].

The company currently is working on a major expansion by entering the European market. For this purpose, a European subsidiary (Stonyfield Europe) has been created in which Danone owns 80 per cent, while Stonyfield Farm owns the remaining 20 per cent (Heller 2006 and the company's website[538]). As a first step, Stonyfield Europe brought over a third of the family-owned Irish company Glensik, which it considers a pacesetter for organic dairy in Europe (Heller 2006 and the company's website[539]). Danone is reported to have invested US$ 66 Mio. into the Stonyfield plant in New Hampshire, US, in order to increase production capacity to cope with the new export market and to capitalize on growing demand for organic dairy products (Heller 2006). But the tremendous growth of the market of about 20 percent per year starts producing severe shortages of organic supplies. This in turn raises pressures on sustainability start-ups like Stonyfield to compromise on their original sustainability in-use in order to meet the soaring demand and fulfill the growth targets agreed on with the parent company. In the US for example, dairy producers estimate that demand for organic milk is at least twice the current available supply (Brady 2006, see also Heller 2006). Brady describes the challenge ahead: In order to meet demand, the number of organic cows in the U.S. would have to more than double to 280,000 over the next five years. This poses a tremen-

---

535 See http://www.coopamerica.org/programs/rs/profile.cfm?id=235, accessed: 08. November 2006.

536 For an example see
http://slowlysheturned.blogspot.com/2005_11_01_slowlysheturned_archive.html, accessed: 08. November 2006

537 See company's webpage at: http://www.stonyfield.com/AboutUs/MoosReleases_Display.cfm?pr_id=122, accessed o9. November 2006.

538 See: http://www.stonyfield.com/AboutUs/MoosReleases_Display.cfm?pr_id=122, accessed 09. November 2006.

539 http://www.stonyfield.com/AboutUs/MoosReleases_Display.cfm?pr_id=122, accessed 09. November 2006.

dous challenge, since the number of dairy farms has shrunk to 60,000, from 334,000 in 1980 according to the National Milk Producers Federation. Furthermore, almost half the milk produced in the U.S. comes from farms with more than 500 cows, - a size, which many organic advocates rarely support (Brady 2006). In the United Kingdom to name another example, organic milk sales grew 91 per cent in the last 12 months (since November 2005) and had grown 30 per cent per year for the decade before that, with sales now topping £100m - producing severe shortages on the market (OMSC 2006: 4ff). Amarjit Sahota from the British consultancy firm Organic Monitor states that the lack of organic milk has caused many retailers to have empty shelves throughout the year (Heller 2006). For the reason mentioned, the problematic sourcing situation of raw materials might even seriously endanger Stonyfield's targeted success in the European market (Heller 2006). As a result to these pressures, Stonyfield drastically cut the percentage of organic products in its line (Brady 2006). Hirshberg also has scaled back annual sales growth from almost 40 percent to 20 percent (Brady 2006). Stonyfield acknowledges the underlying problematic: „As our loyal customers know, due to the enormous demand for organic dairy products, over the past two years, we could not source enough organic milk to make our products. In fact, we had to convert two of our product lines to non-organic as a result" (Hirshberg 2006). Hirshberg states that Stonyfield is working closely with its supplier Organic Valley to dramatically increase the organic milk supply in the US and Stonyfield in 2007 aims to purchase 50 percent more US farmer organic milk than in 2006 (Hirshberg 2006). Nevertheless even this capacity lurks to be insufficient, increasing the pressure to source globally to meet demand and keep up growth. The problem with organic farming in regard to meeting accelerating mass demand is twofold: Converting orthodox farms to organic farms takes time and supply can be volatile. Organic farming requires more land per animal as well as know-how on alternative substances and processes. Furthermore no hormones, chemical fertilizers or antibiotics can be used in order to speed up the process if demand soars (see also Brady 2006). This increases pressures to source globally in order to meet demand and enable growth. As Hirshberg states: „However, because of the severe shortage of organic milk in the US, we have engaged in conversation with a New Zealand dairy cooperative about the possibility of importing organic milk powder. We have not purchased any organic milk powder from New Zealand – or anywhere outside the US – and it could be we never will. But in light of the severe milk shortages over the past two years, it is our responsibility to our consumers, customers and employees to examine all options to allow us to keep making yogurt" (Hirshberg 2006). Stonyfield already imports strawberries from China, apple puree from Turkey, blueberries from Canada, and bananas from Ecuador (Brady 2006). Sourcing from *local* family farmers in the US however has been a trademark of Stonyfield (Hirshberg 2006, see also above).

If in order to meet growth pressures within the next year Stonyfield would expand their sourcing at global scale, this can therefore be considered a significant change in operations. The crucial problem with global sourcing lies in the following: Substantial global sourcing would dramatically increase Stonyfield's ecological footprint in regard to energy-intensity and CO_2 emissions due to transportation. A study by the UK Department for Environment, Transport and the Regions (DETR) for example has indicated that a shopping basket of 26 imported organic products can have traveled 241,000 kilometers and released as much CO_2 into the atmosphere as an average four bedroom household does through cooking meals over eight months (DETR 2001). Lawrence Woodward, director of the Elm Farm Research Centre, whose research has pointed to similar problems for the organic industry when increasing global sourcing, therefore argues to introduce the proximity principle into organic certification schemes, e.g. by providing incentives to produce locally via reduced costs for certification or via added premiums for locally produced products (Woodward 2001: 8).[540] Hirshberg with respect to the argumentation on the problematic of global sourcing, makes the point that there are some ingredients like organic cocoa, banana, and vanilla, which cannot be grown in the U.S. and consequently need to be imported. Furthermore Hirshberg states that Stonyfield's imports of organic ingredients, which could also be grown in the U.S. at present, make up less than 2% of their organic ingredient purchases (Hirshberg 2006). While this is the case today, looking at the growth rates forecasted for the organic market as well as the statements outlined above, pressures for global sourcing are likely to further increase for Stonyfield. Therefore the company's commitment of making a 'different deal', with Danone, which enables Stonyfield to "walk before it runs" (see above) and thereby easing pressures arising from growth, is at stake, when considering the growth rates targeted for the European expansion on the one side and the supply shortages on the other side.

Conclusion
The conversion of two product lines to non-organic, which has been undertaken already, as well as the likelihood to further expand global sourcing, which is a clear contradiction to the company's commitment to local farming, underscores the as-

---

540 With special respect to social sustainbility in sourcing, the following can be pointed out: Hirshberg's sister, Nancy, who is vice-president of natural resources, ordered a social audit to check worker conditions before sourcing from the farm in northeastern China (Brady 2006). While it is surely valuable to promote local family farming also in far-off developing and emerging countries as Hirshberg argues, it however remains a common challenge to make sure standards are met in overseas farms as well as to assure the credibility to the customers (see chapters 3.2.3 and 3.4.3; see also Brady 2006). See also the argumentation for New Zealand http://www.stonyfield.com/AboutUs/setting_the_record_straight.cfm, accessed 09. November 2006.

sumption that Stonyfield is caught up in the trap described above, where Stonyfield's expansion (growth) is fueled through compromising on its original sustainability in-use. Appendix L, discusses further business cases, where the Sustainbility Trap outlined did play out (Ben & Jerry's/Unilever; Odwalla/Coca-Cola; Body Shop/L'Oréal). The number of cases of mission-driven enterprises being acquired by multinational corporations, which seek to get into and expand the market for sustainable products, is vast. Figure 45, indicates ownership structures for the organic industry, which reveals the significance of this trend (see also Hollender and Fenichel 2004: 299ff, Sligh and Christman 2003: 26). The dissertation does not have the resources to examine, where in all these cases of figure 45, the Sustainbility Trap described did play out. The figure however reveals the significance of the trend and thus the relevance of being aware of the Trap outlined, which proved to have played out at least in the cases analyzed (see also Appendix L).

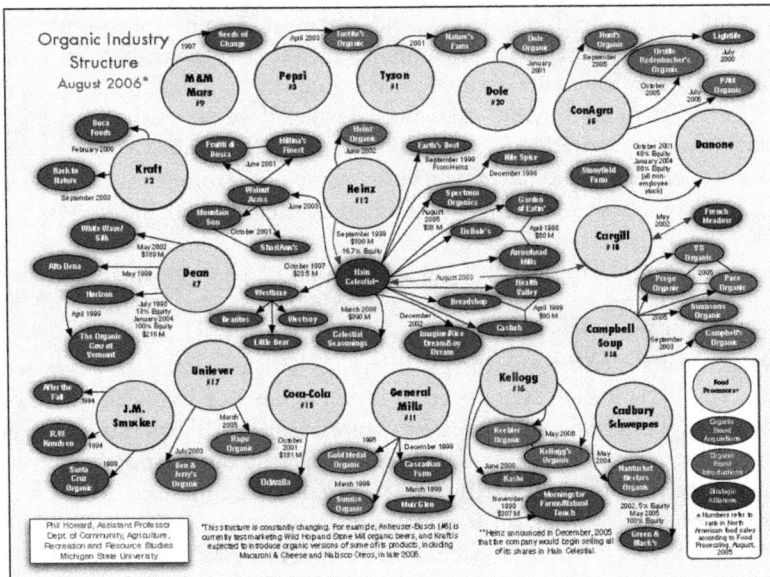

Fig. 45: Organic Enterprises Acquired by Multinational Corporations
Source: Howard, P. (2006) Department of Community, Agriculture, Recreation and Resource Studies, Michigan State University (August)[541]

541 Retrieved online at: http://www.msu.edu/%7Ehowardp/OrganicChartAug06.pdf , accessed: 13. Nov. 2006.

3.6 Chapter Summary (Part III)

The aim of part III was to show that the concept of Sustainbility Traps as it has been elaborated in part II on a theoretical level, does exist in business practice. The dissertation sought to demonstrate that the concept actually is a common phenomenon, which often remains unrecognized in business practice due to a lack of a systems perspective. The aim of part III therefore laid in the identification of different types of Sustainbility Traps as they commonly exist in business practice (archetypes of Sustainbility Traps).

Part III started out with preliminary annotations on the methodology used to identify the mental models as well as the archetypical structure of sustainbility traps (chapters 3.1.1 and 3.1.2). Subsequently the Trade-off Model was discussed, because of its importance as 'the historical model' (chapter 3.1.3).[542]

In addition to the Trade-off Model, the dissertation identified four mental models of sustainbility common in business practice, depending on how a corporation considers environmental and social sustainbility measures to contribute to economic sustainbility. These five mental models on sustainbility build a chronological trajectory with respect to sustainbility measures: Trade-off Model, Compliance Model, Efficiency Model, Reputation Leadership Model and Systemic Model.

The dissertation identified archetypical Sustainbility Traps, which corporations holding a specific mental model prove to often be caught up in, in business practice (chapter 3.2 – 3.5).

Because Sustainbility Traps result from an interplay of a specific mental model held and systemic structures playing out on the basis of this model, the dissertation analyzed in each chapter first the characteristics of each mental model and second, the archetypical trap structures, which risk emerging with regard to corporate sustainbility. Subsequently a case example from business practice has been discussed indepth in the light of the archetypical structure identified. Further business examples are outlined in the appendix. In the following, the different archetypical Sustainbility Traps identified by the dissertation will be summarized. These different archetypical Sustainbility Traps, frequently play out in business practice, but very often remain unrecognized as a systemic pattern.

a) Quick-Fix Trap
b) Special case: Fire-the-Supplier Trap
c) Efficiency Trap
d) Reputation Trap
e) Special Case: Financing Brand-Image through Low-Cost Production
f) Selling-(Out) Trap

---

542 Appendix C, additionally discussed Sustainbility Traps, which risk playing out for corporations following a Trade-off Model: Job-Creation Trap and Fighting-the-Enemy Trap.

a) Quick-Fix Trap

The *Quick-Fix Trap* particularly risks occurring for corporations holding a *Compliance Model*. These corporations have no overall concept or interest for sustainability, but apply quick fixes to issues of unsustainability in order to reduce risks and/or to complying with customer expectations.

But, because boundary judgments regarding these issues are set too narrow in time and space, the solutions applied prove to only address the symptoms (symptomatic solutions), so that the unsustainability problem pops up again and the risks for the corporation prevail. The challenge of this trap lies in the fact that, due to dynamic complexity, the problem reoccurs *deferred* in time (i.e. first the symptoms subside) and in space (i.e. the problem can occur in different forms). Dealing with this trap therefore requires broaden system boundaries as has been shown in the business case of IKEA.

b) Special case: Fire-the-Supplier Trap

A special case of a Quick-Fix Trap is the *Fire-the-Supplier Trap*. In the Fire-the-Supplier Trap, a corporation seeks to demonstrate its 'iron fist' and is quick in quitting contracts with overseas supplier in the case of an unsustainability scandal, in order to comply and avoid bad press. But this leaves workers of the contract factory unemployed and often without any compensation for their outstanding wages.

Also for the corporation itself quitting the supplier usually constitutes a symptomatic solution, because further scandals are likely to occur with new suppliers, since many of the shortcomings similarly exist in various overseas contract factories. Corporations caught up in this trap therefore risk getting into a series of scandals.

As a consequence these companies, instead of gaining an image as starting to address existing unsustainabilities in their production with an 'iron fist' and thus complying with consumer expectations, on the contrary risk gaining an image of not being capable or willing to address unsustainabilities at their contract factories effectively with the problem symptom turning up repeatedly.

The business case discussed in-depth with respect to this trap, is the one of the German retailer Tchibo.

Addressing this trap requires engaging into cooperation and training with the supplier instead of quitting working relationships. Measures include: Grievance and complaints mechanisms, education, freedom of association, transparent communication to worker representatives, partnerships with local organizations (NGOs) and effective remediation.

c) Efficiency Trap

Corporations following an *Efficiency Model*, risk to release so called rebound effects (*Efficiency Trap*). This is the case when resource savings lead to higher consumption and thus to more use of a resource. As a consequence the reduction of unsustainability is lowered or in extreme cases rebound effects can even lead to an increase of unsustainability, i.e. to faster resource depletion.

Because of the pivotal role of consumer behavior in this structure, dealing with Efficiency Traps requires not only changes in corporate behavior, but notably also in consumer behavior (sustainbale consumption). As an example the dissertation discussed the case of fuel-efficiency.

For addressing this trap it is crucial to realize that eco-efficiency is a symptomatic solution, whose only benefit is to safe time in regard to resource depletion. Therefore the key for dealing with this trap does not lie in increasing eco-efficiency evermore, but in how the resources saved through eco-efficiency (time, finances) are used to create sustainbility. This is the concept of eco-effectiveness, which focuses on 'doing the right things' to create sustainbility. As one instrument to eco-efficiency, the dissertation introduced the cradle-to-cradle approach.

d) Reputation Trap

Corporations formerly holding a Trade-off Model or Compliance Model and now moving towards a *Reputation Leadership Model*, risk getting caught up in a *Reputation Trap*:

In order to demonstrate its progressive approach to sustainability, the company propagandizes its sustainability successes. But the more the company positions itself as progressive regarding sustainability, the more activists, NGOs, media and consumers observe the company's behavior in this respect to sustainability and are likely to point to ('reveal') shortcomings. If a company is not able to address these shortcomings quickly and successfully, there is a significant risk of being accused of Greenwashing.

For dealing with this trap, transparent communication is important, i.e. communicating the successes in sustainbility within the context of the shortcomings still existent.[543] In turn, transparent communication remains a symptomatic solution, if root causes for the limitations to sustainability are not addressed. Limitations thereby can be external as well as internal. In respect of credibility of a sustainable image, addressing internal limitation to sustainbility, i.e. limitations arising from business operations, is key. The business example discussed in this respect is that of Chiquita's case of 'the better banana'.

e) Special Case: Financing Brand-Image through Low-Cost Production

A particular Reputation Trap results when *Brand-Image is financed through Low Cost Production*. This can particularly be observed in brand-focused corporations in

---

543 This enables to communicate successes at an early stage, thereby saving time until sustainbility measures taken also meet the shortcomings still existent.

the apparel and fashion industry. High expenses for brand-image (e.g. marketing and design) are compensated by outsourcing production overseas and pressing on low production cost and short delivery times. Contract factories react by compromising on sustainability in order to meet these requirements. But this augments the number of non-compliances with the company's code of conduct and negatively impacts brand-image, so that even more money is needed to 'restore' brand image.

The key for dealing with this trap, lies in analyzing how the own business model contributes to the unsustainabilities. Dealing with this trap therefore requires to change the own business behavior, particularly purchasing practices, not only training and education at the suppliers. The business case used as an example to discuss the trap is that of the sportswear company Nike.

f) Selling-(Out) Trap

It was crucial to the dissertation to point out that also corporations holding a *Systemic Model* can get into Sustainability Traps. The *Selling-(Out) Trap* analyzed here refers to mission-driven enterprises, which are sold by their founders to a multinational corporation, with the aim of 'infiltrating' the existing industry and spreading an alternative model based on high sustainability in-use through rapid growth of the enterprise.

But rapid growth often *augments* specific pressures for compromising on sustainability in-use. Similarly two factors, which could countervail these pressures for compromising on sustainability in-use risk *diminishing*: 1) the company's absolute, intrinsic dedication to sustainability originated from the vision of its founders, because the founders lose influence and 2) the expectations and recommendations for increasing sustainability from the peer group of active, ethical customers of the enterprise, because they stop buying form the company.

As a result of this structure, rapid large-scale growth is achieved after the acquisition at the expanse of compromising on sustainbility in-use at the enterprise.

The business case used as an example to illustrate the trap, is that of the organic yoghurt farm Stonyfield Farm, which has been acquired by Groupe Danone.

Measures to avoid getting into this trap are alternative measures to finance growth, particularly organic growth via bootstrapping. As mission-driven enterprises, which follow this strategy still seek to use large scale growth as a measure disrupt the prevailing, orthodox economy with sustainable business models, the pressures of the trap arising from growth prevail. So called society-centered mission-driven enterprises (mission-based enterprises) in contrast hold a far lower risk of getting into the trap described, because they are focused on meeting human needs and fostering environmental well-being by working on a small-scale level, with many local, flexible initiatives.

As has been stated, the different archetypes identified above are most likely only the tip of an Iceberg of traps of unsustainability, which frequently play out in business practice, but very often remain unrecognized as a systemic pattern.

This is the case for corporations (business practice) as well as for science, which does not have analyzed them as a particular phenomenon before. Therefore the concept of Sustainbility Traps provides interesting potential for future research as well as important benefit for business practice, which will be outlined in the following part IV of the dissertation.

4 Part IV: Conclusion and Directions for Future Research

It was the goal of the dissertation to discuss the importance of *a systems perspective* and its potentials for improving corporate sustainability.

The systems perspective on sustainability discussed in the dissertation is that of systemic, dynamic *Sustainability Traps*. The dissertation developed the concept and characteristics of Sustainability Traps and elaborated systems thinking principles for identifying and managing Sustainability Traps. Concluding the dissertation used the systems thinking skills to identify archetypical Sustainability Traps existing in business practice and discussed how to deal with them from a systems perspective.

The individual findings of the dissertation shall *not* be repeated at this point, as these are already available in the individual chapter summaries.[544] Rather, this chapter will discuss the ***contributions of the dissertation' findings*** for

- the scientific community (chapter 4.1),
- for business practice (chapter 4.2) as well as
- for NGOs, international organizations and interested individuals (chapter 4.3).

4.1 Scientific Contribution and Directions for Future Research

The dissertation in the following first will discuss *contributions*, which the dissertation' work provides for science and subsequently will discuss potentials for *future research* arising from the dissertation' findings.

Scientific contribution of the dissertation

As the dissertation is interdisciplinary its findings provide contributions to different scientific fields. Besides the dissertation' *cross*-disciplinary contribution of bringing together the fields of sustainability and systems science, the dissertation makes contributions to three particular scientific fields: Organizational Learning/Systems Thinking, Sustainability Science and existing value-based, 'normative' approaches to corporate sustainability like CR, CSR and Business Ethics. These contributions will be outlined in the following.

The dissertation elaborated an ***overview*** of existing scientific approaches, which use principles from system science to analyze issues of sustainability. This is the first ex-

---

544 That is, chapter summary part I – III.

tensive overview in this respect and shows the broadness of the scientific context of a systems perspective on sustainability already existing today.[545]

As has been stated, the dissertation heavily builds on the field of Organizational Learning of Senge et al. While the five learning disciplines outlined by Senge et al., primarily relate to the area of strategic management in general, a rising number of scholars in the field are starting to expand these concepts to the field of sustainability (see Senge, Laur, Schley and Smith 2006; Senge 2006: 341ff). The dissertation sought to make a contribution to this new area of *Organizational Learning for Sustainability*, which is developing particularly at the Massachusetts Institute of Technology and within the Society for Organizational Learning.

While the existing works mentioned (Senge, Laur, Schley and Smith 2006; Senge 2006: 341ff), discuss individual cases and issues of sustainability from a systems perspective, the contribution of the dissertation lies in outlining a *general concept*, which specifically discusses the phenomena of systemic patterns of unsustainability, i.e. Sustainability *Traps*. The dissertation thereby outlined *archetypical* patterns of Sustainability Traps in order to show that there is a whole 'family' of Sustainability Traps, which emerged in several business cases and risk to reoccur in future cases as long as they remain unrecognized. Furthermore the dissertation elaborated specific systems thinking skills, which differ from the learning skills of Senge et al. (Senge 2006 and Senge et al. 1994), and which are specifically tailored for dealing with *traps* of corporate sustainability.[546]

As stated, the dissertation positions itself within the field of *Sustainability Science*. As the dissertation discussed, Sustainability Science has taken most interesting approaches for addressing sustainability issues from a systems perspective. The focus of Sustainability Science however currently lies on global issues. As argued by the dissertation, the concept of *Organizational Learning for Sustainability*, which provides a focus on *organizations* (particularly corporations) and on *learning*, can be considered a crucial enlargement for the field of Sustainability Science. The dissertation through its elaborations hence has provided arguments for synergies between these two specific scientific areas.[547]

At present, research in management science (business) with respect to sustainability is dominated by approaches with a strong value-based, normative emphasis, such as *Corporate Responsibility, Corporate Social Responsibility and Business Ethics* (Cannon 1992, Carroll 1999, Ferrell, Fraedrich and Ferrell 2002, Hawkins 2006, Moir 2001, Priddat 2005a, Trevino and Nelson 2004, Velasquez 2006). As stated, these approaches are most important because they provide value-based orientation points for corporate sustainability. However these approaches do not address the impor-

---

545 For the overview see chapter 1.4. For the potentials of future research see also below.
546 For a detailed overview of the differences between the learning skills see chapter 1.4.3.
547 For details see chapter 1.4.1. See also directions of future research below.

tance of systemic, dynamic structures for the success of corporate sustainability. It is the contribution of the dissertation to have examined the crucial interrelation between value judgments and the development of systemic, dynamic structures with respect to corporate sustainability. Furthermore the dissertation has elaborated the implications of this interrelationship for managing Sustainability Traps.[548]

Directions for future research
From the dissertation' findings arose various aspects, which could not further be addressed by this dissertation. They constitute interesting potential for further research. Three main areas for future scientific inquiry and studies can be considered to arise from the dissertation' findings:

a) Refine the overview of scientific fields that use systems thinking (system science) for sustainability and identify synergies of findings as well as collaboration potential.

b) Examination and elaboration of the importance of boundary judgments for the emergence of unsustainable, dynamic structures.

c) The concept of systemic Sustainability Traps: 'Expanding the family'.

a) Refine the overview of scientific fields using systems thinking for analyzing sustainability
The overview of scientific disciplines applying systems thinking to sustainability provided by the dissertation, as stated, is the first of this kind. The overview is however tailored to and discussed in reference to positioning this particular *dissertation* in its scientific context.

It would be most valuable and fruitful, to discuss differences as well as synergy potentials between the different fields identified in the overview independently from this dissertation. For example there is a promising potential of including *global dynamics* identified by Earth System Science into the analysis of *local* dynamics (structures) examined e.g. in the fields of systems ecology, environmental dynamics and organizational learning for sustainability.

Furthermore the overview outlined can and should be *amplified*. For example many approaches of Biomimicry rely on principles from system science, because Biomimicry builds on how natural systems operate (Benyus 1997). These Biomimicry approaches could be discussed in-depth as an additional field in the dissertation.[549]

---

548 See skill: Re-thinking Boundary Judgments; see 2.2.2 and corresponding examples of business cases in part III, particularly IKEA case in chapter 3.2.2.3.
549 The dissertation only mentions Biomimicry in the context of Systems Efficiency and Industrial Ecology, see chapter 1.4.6.

Bringing together resources and findings from the different scientific fields more-over bears the promise of stressing the crucial importance of systems science for sustainability and of increasing the influence of systems science within 'mainstream' sustainability literature (e.g. on CSR, business ethics etc.). Not as an alternative to the latter, but as a crucial *complement*.

b) Examination and elaboration of the importance of boundary judgments

As discussed in the dissertation, the issue of boundary judgments is often neglected in systems thinking, although boundary judgments crucially influence how (mental) models are defined. As has been argued and shown by the dissertation, boundary judgments cannot only be used as boundary critique in the field of sustainability as argued by Ulrich (1993, 1994, 1998, 2005), but do play a far more *extensive* role in the field of sustainability: Boundary judgments are of particular importance for corporate sustainability, because they address the challenge for corporations for changing (broadening) their perception spaces and system boundaries, i.e. to reconsider their value-based boundary *judgments* in the new light of sustainability. This is necessary because boundary judgments determine corporate sustainability measures and thus their contribution to the emergence of unsustainable structures that backfire. The dissertation has laid the theoretical basis to explain these interrelations and has outlined individual examples from business practice based on case study research.

The dissertation however considers this only to be a drop in a bucket. The importance of boundary judgments for the development of dynamic system structure, which produce unsustainability, is barely investigated. Far more research is needed with respect to this pivotal issue. Particularly *empirical studies* of how boundary judgments with regard to sustainability are determined in corporations. Furthermore, which *factors* trigger *revisions* of these boundary judgments and how these tie in with *backfiring effects* of unsustainable dynamic structures, which are caused by the corporation itself, due to its actions driven by the underlying boundaries judgments existing in the corporation. These studies will need to use research methods, which allow studying ill-structured, subliminal processes in organizations, such as action research (Reason and Bradbury 2001) or grounded theory (Glaser and Strauss 1967). Findings of these studies should 1) provide indicators of how to determine boundary judgments (in time and space), which minimize the risk of unsustainable structures that backfire[550] and 2) should provide leverage points for a

---

550 The dissertation showed that it usually is important to *broaden* system boundaries in regard to Sustainbility Traps. Empirical studies however could reveal more precise indicators for system boundaries with respect to time and space. This would then need to be examined for different archetypical Sustainbility Traps individually, e.g. the backfiring effect Y of Sustainbility Trap X usually plaid out after 5 years. Therefore, system boundaries considered by

corporation of how to actually change (broaden) boundary judgments in its organization.

c) Expanding the concept of Sustainability Traps

The third, and to the dissertation the most dearest, area that provides future research potential is the concept of Sustainability Traps itself. The traps outlined in this dissertation are likely to only present the tip of an iceberg. Three fields for further research result from the concept of Sustainability Traps elaborated in the dissertation: *Refining* the Sustainability Traps outlined, *expanding* the family of *corporate* Sustainability Traps, *transfer* the concept of Sustainability to other non-corporate areas.

Refining the concept: It would be most valuable to refine the archetypes outlined through *empirical studies*, which would need to be on a broad basis and long-term, because backfiring of unsustainable occurs deferred in time and space. Suitable research methods here would equally be action research or grounded theory. As stated, the dissertation had neither the time nor the financial resources to conduct such research for a significant number of cases. The archetypes in the dissertation are based on case study research. The main contribution of the dissertation was to reveal and elaborate the concept of Sustainability Traps as such.

Expanding the family: Second, the 'family' of Sustainability Traps identified needs to be enlarged through future studies. It is most likely that there are far more archetypes of Sustainability Traps than outlined here in the dissertation. Such frequent patterns of unsustainability need to be identified in order to promote corporate sustainability and avoid frustration or resistance to sustainability in corporations, because of backfiring. Ideally this identification of further traps should also occur on the basis of empirical studies. If this is not possible however due to temporal or financial restrictions, case study research as conducted in the dissertation, is also suitable for a first identification of another archetype existing.

Transfer the concept to other areas: Furthermore Sustainability Traps do not only exist in the corporate sphere. It would therefore be most interesting to conduct research about Sustainability Traps in regard to politics or in regard to the non-profit sector. The dissertation has mentioned the example of combating undernourishment with free food supply, which can turn to a Sustainability Trap.[551] This example can also be associated with the developmental field.

---

the corporation in this respect should not be below 5 years. As stated, there are no fix, impeccable system boundaries and a continuous learning process is inevitable. However, empirical studies could provide more precise indications for suitable system boundaries, which lower the risk of creating unsustainable structures that backfire.
551 See chapter 2.2.5.1.

At present, a group of experts from systems thinking/organizational learning and sustainability – including Peter Senge, Stuart Hart, Macharia Waruingi, Don Seville and others including the author of this dissertation - is forming, in order to 'add to the family' of Sustainability Traps. The focus thereby lies on how to build so called Mission Based Enterprises[552] that avoid getting into systemic traps by being trained in sustainability and systems thinking. The emphasis thereby lies in using Mission Based Enterprises as a powerful means to leverage human development and environmental sustainability in developing countries. The traps focused on therefore are referred to as Development Traps. The emphasis of this project planned thereby does not only lie in the identification of potential development traps, but on how to create organizational and social learning spaces for a systems perspective on sustainability (Learning Labs). The project is planned as an action research project.

The above outlined the contribution of this dissertation to different scientific fields, particularly organizational learning/systems thinking, sustainability science and existing value-based, 'normative' approaches to corporate sustainability (e.g. CR, CSR and Business Ethics). Furthermore potentials for future research were discussed, which arise out of the findings of the dissertation. These are: Amending the overview of scientific approaches using system science to analyze sustainability; further research on the importance of boundary judgments for the emergence of unsustainable structures; refining and expanding the very concept of Sustainability Traps.

4.2 Contribution to Business Practice

As stated, corporate sustainability is crystallizing as one of the core future topics for meeting the challenges of global change. Corporations that fall short in successfully and credibly addressing issues of unsustainability, increasingly encounter a risk of loosing their social license to operate, facing higher risk-premiums from investors or being confronted with regulations from policies in the future. The concept of how to identify and how to address systemic, dynamic patterns of unsustainability, which the corporations operate in, - thus the concept of Sustainability Traps as such - in the view of the dissertation will play a key role in successfully managing corporate sustainability. As long as managers do not analyze the systemic structures of unsustainability, which they are operating in, corporate sustainability measures risk to fall short or even to backfire on the corporation.

The dissertation' contribution to business practice will be referred to in the following four points:

    a)   Creating awareness for the importance of dynamic system structures for the success of corporate sustainability measures

---

552 These equal Mission Driven Enterprises, yet hold a particular focus on developing countries.

b) A reference book of common Sustainability Traps, which a corporation risks getting into
c) Backfiring as an intrinsic motivator for corporate sustainability
d) Elaborations on the limitations of the concept of Sustainability Traps in business practice

a) Creating awareness for the importance of dynamic system structures

The dissertation thereby laid great emphasis on stressing the point that Sustainability Traps are not primarily a matter of multiple-agents or multiple-causes, which contribute to unsustainability, but that the crucial examination of Sustainability Traps needs to lie on a) *how* behavior of the corporation and their stakeholders interacts (*system structure, pattern*) and b) which self-organizing *dynamics*, i.e. which reinforcing and balancing loops, are created in the structure that drive behavior (dynamic system structure). Only looking at multiple-causes and at the different social agents 'responsible' for the causes, leads to laundry-list thinking and to playing the 'blame-game' in sustainability. It is the awareness for and the analysis of the *dynamics* in a system that constitutes the main contribution and extension of a systems perspective for corporations in order to successfully address the challenges of sustainability and to avoid Sustainability Traps. Thus, the first contribution of the dissertation to business practice is to create awareness for the fact that dynamic Sustainability Traps, which backfire on corporations, do exist and to outline systems thinking skills for identifying, illustrating and analyzing these traps.

b) Archetypes

Furthermore the dissertation identified different archetypical Sustainability Traps that are common to business practice. These archetypes can be used by managers as orientation points for potential traps, which their organization risks to get caught up in, depending on which mental model of sustainability an organization pursues in a specific situation. Thereby dissertation sought to acknowledge the fact that the believe about and the motivation for sustainability measures are not homogeneous, but can vary, depending on the corporate culture as well as on a specific situation (issue) in question. Therefore the dissertation sorted the traps according to different common mental models of sustainability. The dissertation hence can be used as a sort of *reference book* for Sustainability Traps that risk playing out depending on specific mental models of sustainability followed and as a guide book of how specific traps can be addressed.

As will be outlined in the following, the archetypes can be used first, as a means to realize that a corporation is caught up in a trap and second, to avoid getting caught up in a Sustainability Trap in the first place.

Realizing being caught up: First, the archetypes can help a corporation to *realize* that it currently *already is* caught up in a Sustainability Trap and how to *deal* with it. As has been outlined (Iceberg Model)[553], what is often recognized and acted upon by corporations, are the *symptoms* of a trap (event, trends). The archetypes do not only outline the symptoms (backfiring, effects), but also explain dynamics underlying these symptoms and thus provide support for a *systemic* analysis of underlying *patterns*. These are necessary to get out of a trap.

Avoiding getting caught up: Second, the archetypes can serve as early warning-systems for corporations to *avoid* getting caught up in frequent Sustainability Traps in the first place. Thus avoiding the backfiring-risks of the traps on the corporation and successfully achieving the reduction of unsustainability respectively the creation of sustainability targeted by the corporation. Early warning-systems of potential sustainability traps can be particularly interesting for corporations moving along the 'trajectory' of the different mental models and being in the transformation stage towards a different mental model of sustainability (e.g. moving from Compliance to Reputation Leadership).[554] Here the archetypes can provide reference points for potential, systemic traps, which a corporation needs to be aware off, when moving towards another model, e.g. a Reputation Trap.

c) Backfiring as an intrinsic motivator for corporate sustainability

The contributions outlined above, refer to a general corporate praxis on how to better address the challenges of sustainability emerging for corporations. When looking at the specific situation of managers or employees dealing with issues of sustainability in corporations today (e.g. managers from CR, CSR, Sustainability, Marketing), they are very often still considered dealing with 'soft, moral' issues that do not form part of the core business process. A systems perspective and in particular the Sustainability Traps outlined, provide an argumentation basis for these managers to put corporate sustainability also on the *strategic agenda* in corporations. This is because the concept of systemic Sustainability Traps, particularly its focus on *backfiring* on the corporation, points to the systemic, strategic nature of many sustainability topics. Therefore the archetypes and the corresponding business examples given can be used by these managers to better illustrate systemic structures and their impact on corporations (e.g. Financing Brand-Image through Low-Cost Production Trap with respect to unsustainabilities and sourcing practices from contract factories).

---

553 See chapter 2.3.3.
554 See chapter 3.4.1.4.

d) Limitations to the use in business practice

As mentioned, there are several limitations to the approach outlined in the dissertation: First, the number of mental models as well as the number of Sustainability Traps outlined, is not terminal. The Sustainability Traps outlined constitute Sustainability Traps most common in business practice, but there exist many more.

Second, the attribution of the traps to specific mental models in the dissertation is not fix. As has been outlined in chapters 2.2.1 and 2.2.3, mental models constitute the deepest level in Sustainability Traps and being aware of the dominant mental model in-use, which a corporation is acting upon in a specific situation, is key for addressing a trap. The dissertation therefore departed from mental models of sustainability common in business practice and outlined traps that often play out on the basis of these models. As has been stated however, the occurrence of the traps is not restricted to the individual mental models a trap is attributed to in chapter 3: A corporation following an Efficiency Model for example can equally get caught up in a Quick-Fix Trap.

This ties in with the last limitation that is to mention: As has been outlined, the archetypical Sustainability Traps do not constitute *templates*. They were used by the dissertation to illustrate the principles of the concept of Sustainability Traps. The archetypes as such can provide orientation points (hints) for potential Sustainability Traps, but they cannot substitute an individual analysis. Ideally such an individual analysis of the systemic structures, which a corporation is dealing with in regard to its sustainability measures, should be mapped out and analyzed in cooperation with the stakeholders involved. For managers that seek to further engage into systems thinking skills and approaches and to adopt them to Sustainability Traps and beyond[555], chapter 1.4 of the dissertation provides an extensive overview of further approaches.

4.3 Contribution to NGOs, International Organizations and Interested Individuals

Although the main addressees of the dissertation are managers from business practice, a systemic approach inevitably also comprises corporate stakeholders. Stakeholders emphasized on in the dissertation are NGOs, international organizations in general and consumers (individuals).

The contribution the dissertation makes for these groups is twofold:

a) Critical review of moral argumentations
b) Importance and contribution of these groups for supporting corporations in avoiding Sustainability Traps

---

555 That is to other aspects of sustainability.

a) Critical review of moral argumentations

As stated moral argumentations based on specific values as they are often put forward by representatives of NGOs, international organizations or ethical consumers are pivotal to sustainability (see e.g. Moore 2000). As been shown, these moral argumentations however need to be reviewed in the context of their interdependence with dynamic system structures. The dissertation in this respect has particularly shown the following to points:

First stressing the point that 'good' (moral) intentions of social agents (e.g. corporations) are *important*, but not *sufficient* to leverage corporate sustainability. It is pivotal to realize that Sustainability Traps can occur regardless of 'good' or 'bad' intentions regarding sustainability (e.g. Trade-Off and Systemic Model). Thus, well-intended measures alone are no guarantee for actually improving sustainability.

Second, corporate sustainability measures often do not fail or fall short primarily due to 'bad intentions' of a corporation, but far more often due to unsustainable, systemic patterns existing. Therefore playing 'the blame-game' as it is still done by some NGOs and individuals[556], alone is not efficient to leverage corporate sustainability.

b) Importance and contribution for supporting corporations in avoiding Sustainability Traps

NGOs, international organizations and ethical consumers can significantly support corporations in avoiding Sustainability Traps and thus increasing success of corporate sustainability measures.

Many NGOs, international organizations and individual consumers already adopted aspects of systems thinking skills intuitively or even deliberately. The dissertation thereby provides a *structured* overview of systems thinking skills relevant for sustainability and thus can further complement a systems perspective on sustainability for these groups. Most important here is again the emphasis on *dynamic structures*, which often still remain unnoticed or unrecognized. The language of Causal Loop Diagramming and the archetypical Sustainability Traps outlined, provide tools and an argumentation basis for groups, which engage in communication and/or consulting of corporations in respect of sustainability.

NGOs, international organizations and consumers hold great potentials in supporting corporations in identifying Sustainability Traps. This is because, as has been outlined, these groups often do hold *broader perception spaces* (holistic mental model of perception space) than corporations with regard to sustainability and therefore hold high competence in identifying the *symptomatic nature* of sustainability 'solutions' that can lead into a trap. A systems perspective and the systems thinking learning skills outlined in the dissertation, therefore are of specific value for inter-

---

556 See e.g. appendix C, chapter 2.2.5.7, Moore (2000).

national organizations and NGOs that follow approaches, which seek to leverage sustainability through for-profit entrepreneurship, such as the approach of 'Human Development through the Market' (HDtM) of the United Nations Environmental Program (see CSCP 2006, Pratt 2007) or the approach of Mission-Based Enterprises of the NGO 'Kenya Development Network Consortium' (Pratt 2006, KDNC 2006). Knowledge about systemic, dynamic structures is crucial to success-fully develop *alternative* business models that avoid triggering Sustainability Traps. Concluding this dissertation it remains to state the many different disciplines and approaches outlined in the overview have proven through their work the potential and importance, which systems thinking (systems science) holds to leverage sustainability. Their findings and concepts show that systems science holds the potential for looking at sustainability with *"new eyes"* as voted for by Marcel Proust, whose quote was cited prefatory. The concept of Sustainability Traps developed throughout this dissertation, thus is one more spot in the landscape of sustainability, which can be seen through these new glasses (eyes) of systems thinking.

It consequently seems apt to end the dissertation with a quote. The following quote already referred to before, is most fitting to conclude this dissertation, because it underscores that seeing with new eyes requires changing the way we *think* about the problems we are facing. It has been the aim of the dissertation to show that in respect of the challenges of sustainability we are facing today, a new way of thinking, a new perspective, which holds large potential in improving sustainability is: A *Systems* Perspective on Sustainability.

"The significant problems we face cannot be solved at the same level of thinking we were at when we created them."
(Albert Einstein)

Bibliography

Achbar, M., Abbott, J. and Bakan, J. (2003) *The Corporation*. Video. Ontario, Canada: Big Picture Media Corporation.

Adams, J. (2004) Mental Models @ Work: Implications for Teaching Sustainability. In C. Galea (Ed.), *Teaching Business Sustainability: From Theory to Practice* (pp. 20-33). Sheffield, UK: Greenleaf Publishing.

Adams, W.M. (1990) *Green Development: Environment and Sustainability in the Third World*. London: Routledge.

Adelman, M.A. (1993) *The Economics of Petroleum Supply*. Cambridge, MA: MIT Press.

Adidas (2005) *Social and Environmental Report 2004, Taking on the Challenges, Wherever we Operate*. Herzogenaurach: adidas Salomon AG.

Aghion P. and Howitt, P. (1998) *Endogenous Growth Theory*. Cambridge MA: MIT Press.

Alsever, J. (2006, October 2) Chiquita Cleans Up Its Act. *Business 2.0 Magazine*, 7(7) Retrieved online December 15, 2006 from Business 2.0 Magazine electronic database: http://cnn.com/business2.

Anderson, W. and Ross, R. (2005, Winter) The Methodology of Profit Maximization: An Austrian Alternative. *The Quarterly Journal of Austrian Economics*, 8(4), 31-44.

Andres, M.S. (2003, January) Ben, Jerry und der große Fisch. *brand eins 1*, 22-27.

Arena, C (2004) *Cause For Success: 10 Companies That Put Profits Second and Come In First - How Solving the World's Problems Improves Corporate Health, Growth, and Competitive Edge*. Novato, CA: New World Library.

Argyris, C. (1999) *On Organizational Learning* (2nd ed.). Malden, MA: Blackwell.

Argyris, C. and Schön, D. (1996) *Organizational Learning II*. Reading, MA: Addison-Wesley.

Arizona State University (2001) *System Dynamics Methods: A Quick Introduction*. Retrieved online 12. August 2006 from http://www.public.asu.edu/~kirkwood/sysdyn/SDIntro/ch-4.pdf.

Ashby, W. R. (1956) *Introduction to Cybernetics*. London: Methuen.

Austin, J. (1999) *Strategic Collaboration Between Non-Profits and Business*, Working Paper. Harvard: Harvard University.

Avise, J. (2004) *The Hope, Hype, & Reality of Genetic Engineering*. New York: Oxford University Press.

Awbi, A. (2006, May 11) Danone Brings US Organic Yoghurt to Europe. *Food Navigator Europe*. Retrieved online October 16, 2006 from Food Navigator electronic database http://www.foodnavigator.com.

Ayres, R.U. and Ayres L.W. (1996) *Industrial Ecology: Towards Closing the Materials Cycle*. Cheltenham, UK: Edward Elgar.

Ayres, R.U. and Ayres L.W. (Eds.) (2002) *A Handbook of Industrial Ecology*. Cheltenham, UK: Edward Elgar.

Bailey, K. (2005) Fifty Years of Systems Science: Further Reflections. *Systems Research and Behavioral Science*, 22(5), 355-361.

Bamburg, J. (2006) *Getting to Scale: Growing Your Business Without Selling Out*. San Francisco: Berrett-Koehler Publishers.

Banathy, B.H. (1996) *Designing Social Systems in a Changing World.* New York: Plenum Press.

Barker, T. and Foxon, T. J. (2006, April) *The Macro-economic Rebound Effect and the UK Economy, Report for Defra.* Cambridge: Cambridge Centre for Climate Change Mitigation Research (4CMR), with Cambridge Econometrics, Policy Studies Institute (PSI) and Dr Horace Herring.

Bartelmus, P. (1999, November) Economic Growth and Patterns of Sustainability. *Wuppertal Papers Series, 98.* Wuppertal: Wuppertal Institute.

Bar-Yam, Y. (1997) *Dynamics of Complex Systems.* Reading, MA: Addison-Wesley.

Bateson, G. (2000) [original 1964 and extended 1971] The Logical Categories of Learning and Communication. In: G. Bateson (2000) [original 1972] *Steps to an Ecology of Mind* (pp. 279-308). Chicago: The University of Chicago Press.

Baum, H.-G., Coenenberg, A. G., Günther, T. (2006) *Strategisches Controlling* (4th ed.). Stuttgart: Schäffer-Poeschel.

Becker, G. (1964) *Human Capital* (1st ed.). New York: Columbia University.

Beder, S. (2002, March, 22) Nike Greenwash Over Sweatshop Labour. *The Ecologist.* Retrieved online November 13, 2006, from The Ecologist electronic database: http://www.theecologist.org.

Behrens W. (1973) The Dynamics of Natural Resource Utilization. In D. L. Meadows and D. H. Meadows (Eds.), *Toward a Global Equilibrium*, Collected Papers (pp. 141 - 162). Cambridge, MA: Productivity Press.

„Ben and Jerry's: Interview with Ben Cohen". (2000, 30. September). Retrieved online 28. October 2006 from http://usatoday.com/news/ndsthu09.htm.

"Ben and Jerry's to Roll Out in Europe" (2002, March 14) *In Eurofood.*

"Ben and Jerry's Goes Organic" (2003, June 20). In *Ice Cream Reporter*, E-journal. Retrieved online August 28, 2006 from http://goliath.ecnext.com/coms2/summary_0199-3074455_ITM .

Ben and Jerry's (2005) *Social and Environmental Assessment Report 2004.* South Burlington, Vermont: Ben and Jerry's Homemade Inc.

Ben and Jerry's (2006) *Social and Environmental Assessment Report 2005.* South Burlington, Vermont: Ben and Jerry's Homemade Inc.

Benyus, J. (1997) *Biomimicry: Innovation Inspired By Nature.* New York: William Morrow

Berkes, F (1985) Fishermen and The Tragedy of the Commons. *Environmental Conservation, 12*(3), 199-206.

Bertalanffy, L. v. (1968) *General Systems Theory: Foundations, Development, Applications* (rev. ed.). New York: George Braziller.

Bertelsmann Stiftung (2005) *Die gesellschaftliche Verantwortung von Unternehmen - Dokumentation der Ergebnisse einer Unternehmensbefragung der Bertelsmann Stiftung.* Oelde: Festge.

Binswanger, M. (2001) Technological Progress and Sustainable Development: What About the Rebound Effect?. *Ecological Economics, 36*,119-132.

Black, S.E. and Lynch, L.M. (1996) Human Capital Investments and Productivity. *American Economic Review, 86*(2), 263-267.

Blank, J.E. and Clausen, H. (2001) "Sustainable Development". In W.F. Schulz, C. Burschel, M. Weigert, C. Liedtke, S. Bohnet-Joschko, M. Kreeb et al. (Eds.) *Lexikon Nachhaltiges*

Wirtschaften (Lehr- und Handbücher zur ökologischen Unternehmensführung und Umweltökonomie) (pp. 374-385). Munich: Oldenbourg.

Bleischwitz, R. and Hennicke, P. (Eds.) (2004) *Eco-Efficiency, Regulation, and Sustainable Business: Towards a Governance Structure for Sustainable Development*. Cheltenham, UK: Edward Elgar.

Boulding, K. (1956, April) General Systems Theory - The Skeleton of Science. *Management Science, 2*(3), 197-208.

Bourg, D. and Erkman, S. (Eds.) (2003) *Perspectives on Industrial Ecology*. Sheffield: Greenleaf Publishing.

Brady, D. (2006, October 16) The Organic Myth: Pastoral ideals are getting trampled as organic food goes mass market. *BusinessWeek Online*. Retrieved online November 05, 2006, from BusinessWeek Online electronic database: http://www.businessweek.com/magazine.

Brand, R. (2003) *Co-evolution Toward Sustainable Development - Neither Smart Technologies nor Heroic Choices*. Doctoral Dissertation at the University of Texas at Austin, USA. Ann Arbor, MI: UMI.

Braun, W. (2002) *The Systems Archetypes*. Retrieved online September 15, 2006 from http://wwwu.uni-klu.ac.at/gossimit/pap/sd/wb_sysarch.pdf.

Brinckerhoff, P. (2000). *Social Entrepreneurship: The Art of Mission-Based Venture Development*. New York: John Wiley.

Brown, J. (2006, May 11) Roddick Targets Nestlé After Corporate 'Sell-out'. *The Independent/UK*. Retrieved online November 12, 2006, from The Independent/UK electronic database: http://www.independent.co.uk.

Brown, M. (2004) A Picture is Worth a Thousand Words: Energy Systems Language and Simulation. *Ecological Modelling, 178*, 83-100.

Bruno, K. and Karliner, J. (2002) *Earthsummit.biz*: The Corporate Takeover of Sustainable Development. Canada: Institute for Food and Development Policy and CorpWatch.

Buncombe, A. (2006, August 30) Big Problems for Oil Giant BP. *The New Zealand Herald*. Retrieved online September 06, 2006, from The New Zealand Herald electronic database: http://www.nzherald.co.nz.

Burke, R. J. and Cooper, C. L. (Eds.) (2003) *Leading in Turbulent Times*: Managing in the New World of Work. Oxford: Blackwell.

Callenbach, E., Capra, F., Goldman, L., Lutz, R. and Marburg, S. (1994) [original 1992]. *Innovations - Ökologie. Strategien für umweltbewußtes Management*. Frankfurt: Ullstein; Englisch Edition (1993) *EcoManagement: The Elmwood Guide to Ecological Auditing and Sustainable Business*. San Francisco: Berrett-Koehler.

Cannon, T. (1992) *Corporate Responsibility*. London: Pitman.

Capra, F. (1982) *The Turning Point*. New York: Bantam Books

Capra, F. (1996) *The Web of Life: A New Synthesis of Mind and Matter*. London: HarperCollins

Capra, F. (2000) [original 1975] *The Tao of Physics: An Exploration of the Parallels Between Modern Physics and Eastern Mysticism*. Boston, MA: Shambhala Publications.

Capra, F. (2002) *The Hidden Connections: Integrating The Biological, Cognitive, and Social Dimensions of Life Into a Science of Sustainability*. New York: Doubleday.

Capra, F. (2003) *The Hidden Connections: A Science for Sustainable Living*. London: Flamingo.

Capra, F. and Pauli, G. (Eds.) (1995) *Steering Business Toward Sustainability*. Tokyo: United Nations University Press.

Capra, F., Matus, T., Steindl-Rast, D. (1992) *Belonging to the Universe: New Thinking About God and Nature*. Harmondsworth, UK: Penguin Books.

Carlowitz, H.C. v. (1713) *Sylvicultura Oeconomica oder Haußwirthliche Nachricht und Natur-mäßige Anweisung zur wilden Baum-Zucht*. Reprint Freiberg: TU Bergakademie (2000).

Carroll, A.B. (1999) Corporate Social Responsibility: Evolution of a Definitional Construct. *Business & Society, 38*(3), 268-295.

CCC (Clean Cloth Campaign) (2003) *Nike in Indonesia: Doson Workers Down to Eating Rice with Salt, but still Nike Refuses to Pay*. Retrieved online December 04, 2005 from http://www.cleanclothes.org/companies/nike03-02-03.htm.

CCC (2005a) *Freedom of Association and the Right to Collective Bargaining - A Clean Clothes Campaign Primer Focusing on the Global Apparel Industry*. S. l..: Clean Clothes Campaign.

CCC (2005b) *Looking For a Quick Fix. How Weak Social Auditing is Keeping Workers in Sweatshops*. Amsterdam: CCC.

CCC (2005c) *Tchibo - Jede Woche eine neue Welt?* [Brochure]. Wuppertal: CCC.

CCC (2006) *Tchibo - jede Woche eine neue Welt?*. Tübingen und Berlin: Terre de Femmes and Ver.di.

CCSP (Climate Change Science Program and The Subcommittee on Global Change Research) (2006) *Our Changing Planet: The U.S. Climate Change Science Program for Fiscal Year 2006*. Washington, D.C.: National Science and Technology Council.

Chambers Concise Dictionary (1999). Edinburgh: Chambers Harrap.

Checkland, P.B. (1981) *Systems Thinking, Systems Practice*. Chichester: John Wiley.

Checkland, P.B. and Scholes, J. (1990) *Soft Systems Methodology in Action*. Chichester: John Wiley.

Chiquita (2003) *Corporate Responsibility Report 2002: Sustaining Progress*. Chiquita Brands International, Inc.

Chiquita (2004) *Annual Report 2003*. Chiquita Brands International, Inc.

Chiquita (2005a) *Annual Report 2004*. Chiquita Brands International, Inc.

Chiquita (2005b, October 18) *Chiquita Brands International Launches the First Rainforest Alliance-Certified Fruit in Europe* [Press Release]. Chiquita Brands International, Inc.

Chiquita (2006) *Annual Report 2005*. Chiquita Brands International, Inc.

Churchman, C.W. (1968) *Challenge to Reason*. New York: McGraw-Hill.

Churchman, C.W. (1982) *Thought and Wisdom*. Seaside, CA: Intersystems Publications.

Clark, W.C. (2003) *Sustainability Science: Challenges for the New Millennium*. An address on 4 September at the official opening of the Zuckerman Institute for Connective Environmental Research and the Third Sustainability Days, 4-10 September 2003, Norwich, United Kingdom: University of East Anglia.

Clark, W.C., Crutzen, P. and Schellnhuber H. (2003) Science for Global Sustainability. In H. Schellnhuber et al. (Eds.), *Earth System Analysis for Sustainability: Toward a New Paradigm* (pp. 1-28). Cambridge, MA: MIT Press.

Claussen, M. (2001) Earth System Models. In E. Ehlers and T. Kraft (Eds.), *Understanding the Earth System: Compartments, Processes and Interactions* (pp. 147-162). New York: Springer

343

Cogan, D. 2006 *Corporate Governance and Climate Change: Making the Connection.* Boston: Coalition for Environmentally Responsible Economies (CERES).

Cohen, B. and Greenfield, J. (1998) *Ben Jerrys Double Dip: How to Run a Values Led Business and Make Money Too.* New York: Fireside.

Coke Buys Odwalla (2001, October 30) *CNNmoney.* Retrieved online November 14, 2001 from available online: http://money.cnn.com/2001/10/30/deals/coke_odwalla/.

Collins, J.C. and Porras, J.I. (1994) *Built to Last: Successful Habits of Visionary Companies.* New York: Harper Business.

Concise Oxford English Dictionary (10th ed.) (2001). Oxford: Oxford University Press.

Cone (2004) *Cone Corporate Citizenship Study.* Boston: Cone.

Connor, T. (2001) *Still Waiting For Nike To Do It.* San Francisco: Global Exchange.

Connor, T. and Dent, K. (2006) *Offside! Labour rights and sportswear production in Asia.* Oxford, UK: Oxfam International.

Contreras, M. (2004) *Corporate Social Responsibility in the Promotion of Social Development: Experiences from Asia and Latin America.* Washington: Free Hand Press.

Cook, D. (2004) *The Natural Step Towards a Sustainable Society.* Darlington, UK: Green Books.

Costanza, R. (Ed.) (1991) *Ecological Economics. The Science and Management of Sustainability.* New York: Columbia University Press.

Costanza, R., Cumberland, J. C., Daly, H. E., Goodland, R. and Norgaard, R. (1997) *An Introduction to Ecological Economics.* Boca Raton, FL: St. Lucie Press.

CSCP (UNEP Wuppertal Institute Collaborating Center on Sustainable Consumption and Production) (2005a) *Making the Marrakech Process Work.* Discussion Paper 2nd International Expert Meeting on The 10-Year Framework of Programmes on Sustainable Consumption and Production San José, Costa Rica, 5-8 September 2005.

CSCP (2005b) *Sustainable Energy Consumption.* Background Paper European Conference under the Marrakech Process on Sustainable Consumption and Production (SCP) Berlin, 13-14 December 2005.

CSCP (2006) Background Paper of the UNEP 9th High-level Seminar on Sustainable Consumption and Production (SCP9) *Creating Solutions for Industry, Environment and Development,* Arusha, Tanzania, 10-12 December 2006.

Currying Favor With the Green Lobby (2002, October 12) Editorial, *Washington Times.* Retrieved online November 10, 2006 from Washington Times electronic database: http://www.washtimes.com.

Cushing, J.M., Dennis, B., Desharnais, R.A., and Costantino, R.F. (1996) An Interdisciplinary Approach to Understanding Nonlinear Ecological Dynamics. *Ecological Modelling,* 92, 111-119.

Daily, G. (Ed.) 1997 *Nature's Services: Societal Dependence on Natural Ecosystems.* Washington, D.C.: Island Press.

Daily, G.C, Alexander, S., Ehrlich, P.R., Goulder, L., Lubchenco, J., Matson, P.A., Mooney, H.A., Postel, S., Schneider, S.H., Tilman, D., Woodwell, G. M. (1997, Spring) Ecosystem Services: Benefits Supplied to Human Societies by Natural Ecosystems. *Issues in Ecology,* 2, 1-16.

Daly, H. (1991) [original 1977] *Steady-State Economics* (2nd. ed.) Washington DC: Island Press.

Daly, H. (1996) *Beyond Growth: The Economics of Sustainable Development*. Beacon Press: Boston.

Daly, H. (1999) *Ecological Economics and the Ecology of Economics: Essays in Criticism*. Cheltenham, UK: Edward Elgar.

Daly, H. (2005, September) Economics in a Full World. *Scientific American, Special Issue: Crossroads for Planet Earth, 293*(3), 100-107.

Daly, H. and Cobb, J. (1986) For *the Common Good: Redirecting the Economy toward Community, the Environment and a Sustainable Future*. Boston: Beacon Press.

Daly, H. and Farley, J. (2003) *Ecological Economics: Principles and Applications*. Washington D.C.: Island Press.

"Danone Buys US Functional Yoghurt" (2001, October 05). In *Nutraingredients.com Europe*. Retrieved online November 09., 2006 from http://www.nutraingredients.com/news/ng.asp?id=33713-danone-buys-us.

Darwin, C. (1859) *On the Origin of Species by Means of Natural Selection*. London: Murray.

Davidz, H., Nightingale, D. and Rhodes, D. (2004) Enablers, *Barriers, and Precursors to Systems Thinking Development: The Urgent Need for More Information*. International Conference on Systems Engineering 2004, Las Vegas. Boston: MIT.

De Haan, E. and Schipper, V. (1999) *Nike: Company Profile of Clean Clothes Campaign*. Retrieved online September 12, 2006, from www.cleanclothes.org/companies/nikecase99-11-2.htm

Deaton, M.L. and Winebrake, J.J. (2000) *Dynamic Modelling of Environmental Systems*. New York: Springer-Verlag.

Defourny, J. (2001) From Third Sector to Social Enterprise. In C. Borzaga and J. Defourny (Eds.) *The Emergence of Social Enterprise* (pp. 1-28). London: Routledge

DeSimone, L. and Popoff, F. (2000) [original 1997] E*co-Efficiency: The Business Link to Sustainable Development*. Cambridge: MIT Press.

DETR, UK Department for Environment, *Transport and the Regions* (2001) The Draft UK Climate Change Program. London: HMSO.

Devuyst, D., Hens, L., De Lannoy, W. (Eds.) (2001) *How Green Is the City? Sustainability Assessment at the Local Level*. New York: Columbia University Press

Diamond, J. (2005) *Collapse: How Societies Choose to Fail or Succeed*. New York: Viking Penguin.

Diamond, J. 1999 [original 1997] *Guns, Germs and Steel: The Fates of Human Societies*. New York: Norton Paperback

Dobson, A. (1998) *Justice and the Environment: Conceptions of Environmental Sustainability and Dimensions of Social Justice*. Oxford, Oxford University Press.

Doppelt, B. (2003) *Leading Change Toward Sustainbility: A Change-Management Guide for Business, Government and Civil Society*. Sheffield, UK: Greenleaf.

Doppelt, B., and Nelson, H. (2001) *Extended Producer Responsibility and Product Take-Back: Applications for the Pacific Northwest*. Portland: The Center for Watershed and Community Health, Mark O. Hatfield School of Government, Portland State University.

Doppelt, B., and Watson, L. (2000) Jus*t Plain Good Business - The Economic and Environmental Benefits of Sustainability as Exemplified by One Hundred Sixty Case Examples*. Paper from the Center for Watershed and Community Health. Portland, Oregon: Portland State University.

Dörner, D. (1980) On the Difficulties People have in Dealing with Complexity. *Simulation and Games 11*(1), 87-106.

Dörner, D. (2005) [original 2003] *Die Logik des Misslingens* (4th ed.). Reinbeck: Rowohlt. English version: *The Logic of failure* (1996). New York: Metropolitan Books/Henry Holt.

Doyle, J. and Ford, D. (1998) Mental Model Concepts for System Dynamics Research. *System Dynamics Review, 14*(1), 3-29.

Drucker, P.F. (1993) [original 1954] The Practice of Management; New York: Harper-Collins.

Drucker, P.F. (2001) The Effective Decision. Harvard Business Review On Decision Making. *Harvard Business Review Paperback Series* (pp. 1-19). Harvard: Harvard Business Press.

Drucker, P.F. (2002) [original 1967] *The Effective Executive*. New York: Harper Collins.

Drucker, P.F. (2003). *The Essential Drucker: The Best of Sixty Years of Peter Drucker's Essential Writings on Management*. New York: Harper Business.

Dunphy, D. and Benveniste, J. (Eds.) (2000) *Sustainability: The Corporate Challenge of the 21st Century*. St. Leonards, N.S.W: Allen & Unwin Academic.

Dunphy, D., Griffiths, A., and Benn, S. (2003) *Organizational Change for Corporate Sustainability: A Guide for Leaders and Change Agents of the Future*. London: Routledge.

Dyllick, T. and Hockerts, K. (2002) Beyond the Business Case for Corporate Sustainability. *Business Strategy and The Environment, 11*(2), 130 - 141. Retrieved online from: http://www.iwoe.unisg.ch/org/iwo/web.nsf/SysWebRessources/UMS_Corporate_Sustainability_Beyond_the_business_case/$FILE/DyHo_CorporateSustainability.pdf.

EEA (European Environment Agency) (1999) *Making Sustainability Accountable: Eco-efficiency, Resource Productivity and Innovation.* Topic Report No 11, Proceedings of a Workshop on the Occasion of the Fifth Anniversary of the European Environment Agency (EEA) 28 - 30 October 1998 in Copenhagen.

Ehlers, E. and Krafft, T. (2001) Understanding the Earth System: From Global Change Research to Earth System Science. In E. Ehlers and T. Krafft (Eds.) *Understanding the Earth System: Compartments, Processes and Interactions* (pp. 3-16). New York: Springer.

Ehrenfeld, J. and Gertler, N. (1997) Industrial Ecology in Practice: The Evolution of Interdependence at Kalundborg. *Journal of Industrial Ecology, 1*(1), 67-79.

Ehrlich, P.R. and Ehrlich, A.G. (1992) The Value of Biodiversity. *Ambio 21*, 219-226.

Elkington, J. (1997) *Cannibals with Forks*. Oxford: Capstone Publishing.

Enquete-Kommission 'Schutz des Menschen und der Umwelt' (1998) *Konzept Nachhaltigkeit. Vom Leitbild zur Umsetzung.* Abschlußbericht der Enquete-Kommission 'Schutz des Menschen und der Umwelt - Ziele und Rahmenbedingungen einer nachhaltig zukunftsverträglichen Entwicklung' des 13. Deutschen Bundestages. Bonn: Deutscher Bundestag.

Epstein, J. M. (2008) *Making Sustainability Work*, Sheffield, UK: Greenleaf

Esbenshade, J.L. (2004) *Monitoring Sweatshops: Workers, Consumers, and the Global Apparel Industry*. Philadelphia: Temple University Press.

Eskildsen, J., Dahlgaard, J., and Norgaard, A. (1999) The Impact of Creativity and Learning on Business Excellence. In *Total Quality Management, 10*(4-5), 523-530.

346

Esty, K., Griffin, R. and Schorr-Hirsch, M. (1995) *Workplace Diversity: A Managers Guide to Solving Problems and Turning Diversity into a Competitive Advantage.* Massachusetts: Adams Publishing.

Evan, T. (1999) Odwalla. *Public Relations Quarterly, 44*(2), 15-17.

Fava, J.A. et al. (Eds.) (1991) *SETAC Workshop Report: A Technical Framework for Life Cycle Assessments,* August 18-23 1990, Smugglers Notch, Vermont, USA.

Ferrara, J. (1999) Revolving Doors: Monsanto and the Regulators. *The Ecologist, 28*(5), 280-286

Ferrell, O.C., Fraedrich, J. and Ferrell, L. (2002) *Business Ethics: Ethical Decision Making and Cases* (5th ed.). Boston, MA: Houghton Mifflin.

Fichter, K. and Arnold, M. (2003) *Nachhaltigkeitsinnovationen: Nachhaltigkeit als Strategischer Faktor - eine explorative Untersuchung von Unternehmensbeispielen zur Berücksichtigung von Nachhaltigkeit im strategischen Management.* Bericht aus der Basisstudie 'Nachhaltigkeit im strategischen Management' im Rahmen des vom BMBF geförderten Vorhabens Sustainable Markets eMERge (SUMMER), Berlin/Oldenburg.

Fichter, K., Paech, N. and Pfriem, R. (2005) *Nachhaltige Zukunftsmärkte. Orientierungen für unternehmerische Innovationsprozesse im 21. Jahrhundert.* Marburg: Metropolis-Verlag.

Fischer, G. (2006) Wir wollen vom Büfett immer nur die Sahnetorte. Interview mit Reinhard Springer. *brand eins, 5,* 102-108.

Flannery, T. (2001) *The Eternal Frontier: An Ecological History of North America and its People.* Melbourne: Text Publishing Company.

Flood, R.L. and Jackson, M.C. (1991) *Creative Problem Solving: Total System Intervention.* Chichester: John Wiley.

Flood, R.L. and Romm, N.R.A. (1996) *Diversity Management: Triple Loop Learning.* Chichester: John Wiley.

Flood, R.L. and Romm, N.R.A. (1997). From Metatheory to Multimethodology. In J. Mingers and A. Gill (Eds.), *Multimethodology: The Theory and Practice of Combining Management Science Methodologies* (pp. 291-322). Chichester: John Wiley.

Foerster, H. v. (1979) Cybernetics of Cybernetics. In K. Krippendorff (Ed.), *Communication and Control in Society.* New York: Gordon and Breach.

Foerster, H. v. (1995) *Ethics and Second-order Cybernetics.* Opening address for the International Conference, Systems and Family Therapy: Ethics, Epistemology, New Methods, held in Paris, France, October 4th, 1990. Reprinted from the original unpublished English version in *Stanford Humanities Review, 4*(2), 308 – 319.

Ford, A. (1999) *Modeling the Environment - An Introduction to System dynamics Modeling of Environmental Systems.* Washington, DC: Island Press.

Ford, A. and Cavana, R.Y. (Eds.) (2004) *Special Issue on Environmental and Resource Systems, System Dynamics Review, 20*(2).

Forrester, J.W. (1961) *Industrial Dynamics.* Cambridge, MA: MIT Press.

Forrester, J.W. (1969) *Urban Dynamics,* Cambridge: MIT Press.

Forrester, J.W. (1971) *World Dynamics.* Cambridge: Wright-Allan Press.

Forrester, J.W. (1989) *The Beginning of System Dynamics.* Banquet Talk at the International Meeting of the System Dynamics Society, Stuttgart, Germany, July 13, 1989.

Forrester, J.W. (1991). System Dynamics and the Lessons of 35 Years. In K. B. De Greene (Ed.), *The Systemic Basis of Policy Making in the 1990s.* Cambridge, MA: MIT Press.

Forrester, J.W. (1992) *System Dynamics and Learner-Centered-Learning in Kindergarten through 12th Grade Education.* Paper D-4337, Cambridge, MA: MIT.

Forrester, J.W. (1994). *Learning through System Dynamics as Preparation to the 21st Century.* Keynote Address for System Thinking and Dynamic Modeling Conference for K-12 Education. Concord, MA: Concord Academy.

Forrester, J.W. (1995) *Counterintuitive Behavior of Social Systems.* MIT System Dynamics Group Working Paper D-4468, updated version. Original paper in Technology Review 73(3), 52-68, January 1971.

Forrester, J.W. (1999) System Dynamics: The Foundation Under Systems Thinking. *Working Paper Sloan School of Management.* Cambridge, MA: MIT.

Frey, D. (2002, December 8) How green is BP?. *New York Times Magazine.* Retrieved online April 18, 2006 from New York Times Magazine electronic database: http://www.nytimes.com/pages/magazine.

Funding Universe (2006) *Odwalla Inc.: Company History.* Retrieved online October, 14, 2006 from Funding Universe corporate information: http://www.fundinguniverse.com/company-histories/Odwalla-Inc-Company-History.html.

Fung, A., O'Rourke, D. and Sabel, C.F. (2001) *Can We Put an End to Sweatshops?: A New Democracy Form on Raising Global Labor Standards.* Boston: Beacon Press.

Gabler Wirtschaftslexikon (1994) (13th rev. ed.). Wiesbaden: Gabler.

Gallagher, M. and McWhirter, C. (1998, May 3) Chiquita Secrets Revealed. *The Enquirer.* Retrieved online May 25, 2006 from The Enquirer electronic database: http://news.enquirer.com.

Garrett, A. (1998, August 23) From Agent Orange to Tampered Genes: Monsanto's Life Cycle. *The Observer.* Retrieved online October 12, 2005 from Observer electronic database: http://observer.guardian.co.uk.

Gaston, K. and Spicer, J. (2004) *Biodiversity: An Introduction* (2nd. ed.). Oxford: Blackwell Science.

Gatewood, B. (2005, October 1) To Drink or Not To Drink?. *The Green Dartmouth Magazine,* 4(1), Retrieved online January 12, 2006 from http://www.dartmouth.edu/~tgm/2005/10/01/to-drink-or-not-to-drink/.

Georgescu-Roegen, N. (1971) *The Entropy Law and the Economic Process.* Cambridge, MA.: Harvard University Press.

Georgescu-Roegen, N. (1976) *Energy and Economic Myths.* New York: Pergamon.

Georgescu-Roegen, N. (1977) The Steady State and Ecological Salvation. *Bio Science, 27*(4), 266-270.

Georgescu-Roegen, N. (1992) Georgescu-Roegen About Himself. In M. Szenberg (Ed.), *Eminent Economists: Their Life Philosophies* (pp. 128-159). Cambridge: Cambridge University Press.

Gerlagh, R. and Keyzer, M. (2001) Limits-to-Growth Theory. In G.H. Kuper, E. Sterken and E. Wester (Eds.), *Coordination and Growth, Essays in Honour of Simon Kuipers* (pp. 219-232). Dordrecht: Kluwer Academic Press.

Gilbert, J.A., Stead, B.A. and Ivancevich, J.M. (1999) Diversity Management: A New Organizational Paradigm. *Journal of Business Ethics, 21*(1), 61-76.

Gill, R.A. (1998a) *Exploring Transdiciplinary Themes.* Working Paper, Centre for Ecological Economics and Water Policy Research at the University of New England, Australia.

Gill, R.A. (1998b) *Research Agenda for Ecological Economics in Australia*. Working Paper, Centre for Ecological Economics and Water Policy Research at the University of New England, Australia.

Gladwin, T., Kennelly, J., Krause T.S. (1995) Shifting Paradigms for Sustainable Development: Implications for Management Theory and Research. *Academy of Management Review, 20*(4), 874-907.

Glaser, B.G. and Strauss, A.L. (1967) The Discovery Of Grounded Theory: Strategies For Qualitative Research. Chicago: Aldine.

Glasersfeld, E. v. (1995) *Radical Constructivism: A Way of Knowing and Learning*. London: Falmer.

Glasersfeld, E. v. (2003) Konstruktion der Wirklichkeit und des Begriffs der Objektivität. In H. Gumin and H. Meier (Eds.), *Einführung in den Konstruktivismus* (7th ed.) (pp. 9-39). München: Piper.

GlobeScan (2005) *Corporate Social Responsibility Monitor*. Toronto, Canada and London, UK: GlobeScan Inc.

Goethe, J.W. (1797) *Der Zauberlehrling* [Poem]. Reprint (1999) München: Middelhauve.

Gomez-Pompa, A. and Burley, F.W. (1991) The Management of Natural Tropical Forests. In A. Gomez-Pompa, T.C. Whitmore and M. Hadly (Eds.) *Rain Forest Regeneration and Management (Man and the Biosphere Series Vol. 6, UNESCO)* (pp. 3-20). Park Ridge, NJ: Parthenon.

Goodland, R. (2002) Sustainability: Human, Social, Economic and Environmental. In *Encyclopedia of Global Environmental Change*. New York: John Wiley.

Goodland, R. and Daly, H. (1996, November) Environmental Sustainability: Universal and Non-Negotiable. *Ecological Applications, 6*(4), 1002-1017.

Goodman, D. (2003, January/February) Culture Change. *Mother Jones Magazine*. Retrieved online September 19, 2005 from Mother Jones Magazine electronic database: http://www.motherjones.com.

Goodstein, E., Doppelt, B., and Sable, K. (2000) *Salmon Economics Report: Saving Salmon, Saving Money: Innovative Business Leadership in the Pacific Northwest*. Paper from the Center for Watershed and Community Health. Portland State University. Portland, Oregon.

Gordon, H.S. (1954) The Economic Theory Of A Common Property Resource: The Fishery. *Journal of Political Economy, 62*, 124-142.

Goyder, M. (2006 May, 25) The Body Shop and L'Oreal: Why Can't Big be Beautiful?. *Ethical Corporation Magazine, 2006*. Retrieved online June 12, 2006 from Ethical Corporation Magazine electronic database: http://www.ethicalcorp.com.

Graham, M. (2002) *Democracy by Disclosure*: The Rise of Technopopulism. Washington, DC: Brookings Institution.

Gray, S. (1999, May 13) Companies Popular With Teens Deny Sweatshop Contracts. *Wiscasset Newspaper*. Retrieved online October 18, 2006 from Wiscasset Newspaper electronic database: http://www.wiscassetnewspaper.maine.com.

Greene D.L. (1992) Vehicle Use and Fuel Economy: How Big is the Rebound Effect?. *Energy Journal, 13*(1), 117-143.

Greening L.A., Greene, D.L. and Difiglio, C. (2000) Energy Efficiency and Consumption - The Rebound Effect - A Survey. *Energy Policy, 28*, 389-401.

349

Greening, L.A. and Greene, D.L. (1997) *Energy Use, Technical Efficiency, and the Rebound Effect: A Review of the Literature.* Report to the Office of Policy Analysis and International Affairs, US Department of Energy, Washington, DC.

Greenpeace (2000, August 10) *BP runs to Court to Avoid Publicity About Fueling Global Warming.* Greenpeace Statement, Anchorage, Alaska.

Grepperud, S. and Rasmussen, I. (2004) A General Equilibrium Assessment of Rebound Effects. *Energy Economics 26*(2), 261-282.

Griffiths, A., Benn, S. and Dunphy, D. (2003) *Organisational Change for Corporate Sustainability: A Guide for Leaders and Change Agents of the Future.* London: Routledge

Gurney, W.S.C and Nisbet, R. (1998) *Ecological Dynamics,* Oxford: Oxford University Press.

Hagan, J.O. and Harvey, D. (2000) Why Do Companies Sponsor Arts Events? Some Evidence and a Proposed Classification. *Journal of Cultural Economics, 24*(3), 205-224.

Hardin, G. (1968) The Tragedy of the Commons. *Science, 162,* 1243-1248.

Hargens, J., and Schlippe, A. v. (Eds.) (1998). Das *Spiel der Ideen. Reflektierendes Team und systemische Praxis.* Dortmund: Borgmann.

Harris Interactive (2001) *Corporate Citizen Watch Survey.* Rochester, NY: Harris Interactive.

Harrison, R. (2006, July 18) When Ethical Companies are Taken Over. *Philosophy for Business e-journal,* 31, November 11, 2006 from http://www.isfp.co.uk/businesspathways/issue31.html.

Hart, S. (1997, Jan-Feb.) Beyond Greening: Strategies for Sustainable World. *Harvard Business Review, 75*(1), 66-76.

Hart, S. (2005). *Capitalism at the Crossroads: The Unlimited Business Opportunities in Solving the World's Most Difficult Problems.* Upper Saddle River, NJ: Wharton.

Hart, S. and Milstein, M. (2003) Creating Sustainable Value. *Academy of Management Executive, 17*(2), 56-69.

Harvard Business Review on Corporate Responsibility (2003) *The Harvard Business Review Paperback Series.* Boston: Harvard Business School Press.

Hawken, P. (1993) *The Ecology of Commerce: A Declaration of Sustainability.* New York: HarperCollins

Hawken, P., Lovins, A.B. and Lovins, L.H. (1999) *Natural Capitalism: Creating the Next Industrial Revolution.* New York: Little Brown and Co.

Hawkins, D. (2006) *Corporate Social Responsibility: Balancing Tomorrow's Sustainability And Today's Profitability.* New York: Palgrave Macmillan.

Heap, B. and Kent, J. (Eds). 2000 *Towards Sustainable Consumption: A European Perspective.* London: The Royal Society.

Heavenrich, R.M. (2006) *Light-Duty Automotive Technology and Fuel Economy Trends: 1975 Through 2006.* U.S. Environmental Protection Agency, Office of Transportation and Air Quality, Advanced Technology Division, EPA420-R-06-011.

Hein, K. (2006, February 22) A Journey in Every Bottle. *Brandweek Magazine.* Retrieved online August 27, 2006 from Brandweek Magazine electronic database: http://www.brandweek.com.

Heiskanen, E. and Pantzar, M. (1997) Towards Sustainable Consumption: Two New Perspectives. *Journal of Consumer Policy, 20,* 409-42.

Heller, L. (2006, June) Danone and Stonyfield Create European Organic Dairy Firm. *Food Navigator Europe, 20.* Retrieved online November 09, 2006 from Food Navigator electronic database: http://www.foodnavigator.com.

Hennicke, P. 2003 *Decoupling Well-being from GDP - Towards a New Kind of Technological Progress.* Paper of the 5th International Conference on Ethics and Environmental Policies Business Styles and Sustainable Development, Kyiv, April 2-6, 2003.

Herbert, B. (1998, May 21) Nike Blinks. *New York Times.* Retrieved online July 23, 2006 from New York Times electronic database: http://www.nytimes.com/.

Herring, H. and Roy, R. (2002) Sustainable Services, Electronic Education and the Rebound Effect. *Environmental Impact Assessment Review, 22,* 525-542.

Hertwich, E. (2005a) Consumption and the Rebound Effect, An Industrial Ecology Perspective. *Journal of Industrial Ecology, 9*(1-2), 85-98.

Hertwich, E. (2005b) Lifecycle Approaches to Sustainable Consumption: A Critical Review. *Environmental Science and Technology, 39*(13), 4673 - 4684.

Hertwich, E. and Katzmayr, M. (2003) *Examples of Sustainable Consumption: Review, Classification and Analysis.* Final Report to the Society for Non-Traditional Technology, Japan/IIASA Laxenburg.

Heuer, S. (2006, January) Ein bisschen Bio und gar nicht böse. *Brand Eins,* 18-28.

Heylighen, F. and Cliff, J. (1995) "Systems Theory". In R. Audi (Ed.) *Cambridge Dictionary of Philosophy* (pp. 784-785), Cambridge MA: Cambridge U. Press.

Hill and Knowlton (2001) *Third Annual Corporate Reputation Watch*, CEOs on Corporate Reputation, New York: Hill and Knowlton.

Hilty, L. (2005) Electronic Waste - An Emerging Risk?. *Environmental Impact Assessment Review, 25*(5), 431-435.

Hilty, L. and Gilgen, P. (Eds.) (2001) *Sustainability in the Information Society.* Marburg: Metropolis-Verlag.

Hilty, L. and Ruddy, T.F. (2000) Towards a sustainable information society. *Informatik/Informatique, 4,* 2-7.

Hilty, L. and Ruddy, T.F. (2002) Resource Productivity in the Information Age. *Futura, 2,* 77-85.

Hilty, L., Köhler, A., Schéele, F. v., Zah, R. and Ruddy, T. (2006, March) Rebound Effects of Progress in Information Technology. Poiesis and Praxis: *International Journal of Technology Assessment and Ethics of Science, 4*(1), 19-38.

Hirshberg, G. (2006) Setting the Record Straight. Retrieved online November 09., 2006 from http://www.stonyfield.com/AboutUs/setting_the_record_straight.cfm.

Hirshleifer, J. (1980) *Price Theory and Applications.* Englewood Cliffs, N.J.: Prentice-Hall.

Hoffman, A.J. (1997) *From Heresey to Dogma: An Institutional History of Corporate Environmentalism.* San Francisco: New Lexington Press.

Hoffman, A.J. (1999) Institutional Evolution and Change: Environmentalism and the US Chemical Industry. *Academy of Management Journal, 22*(4), 351-357.

Hoffman, S. (2003, November/December) Does Odwalla Go Better with Coke? An Interview with Odwalla President Shawn Sugarman. *GreenMoney Journal.* Retrieved online November, 14, 2006 from GreenMoney Journal electronic database: http://www.greenmoneyjournal.com/.

Holiday, C.O., Schmidheiny, S., Watts, P. (2002) *Walking the Talk: The Business Case for Sustainable Development*. Sheffield, UK: Greenleaf.

Hollender, J. and Fenichel, S. (2004) *What Matters Most: How a Small Group of Pioneers is Teaching Social Responsibility to Big Business, and Why Big Business is Listening*. New York: Basic Books.

Homer-Dixon, T.F. (1999) *Environment, Scarcity, and Violence*. Princeton, NJ: Princeton University Press.

Houghton, J.; Ding, Y.; Griggs, D.; Noguer, M.; van der Linden, P. and Xiaosu, D. (Eds.) *2001 Climate Change 2001: The Scientific Basis, Contribution of Working Group I to the Third Assessment Report of the Intergovernmental Panel on Climate Change (IPCC)*, Cambridge, UK: Cambridge University Press.

Howard, T. (2005, October 16) Ben & Jerry's Returns to Social Issues. *USA Today*. Retrieved online October, 22, 2006 from USA Today electronic database: http://www.usatoday.com/.

Hunkeler, D. and Rebitzer, G. (2005) The Future of Life Cycle Assessment. *The International Journal of Life Cycle Assessment, 10*(5), 305-308.

IHDP (International Human Dimension Programme on Global Environmental Change) (2005) *Annual Report 2004/2005*. Bonn: Köllen Druck.

IKEA (2002) *The IKEA Way of Preventing Child Labour*. Retrieved online September 14, 2005 from http://www.ikea.com/ms/en_GB/about_ikea/social_environmental/preventing_child_labour.pdf

IKEA (2004, January) *Social and Environmental Responsibility*. Brochure. IKEA Group.

IKEA (2005, August) *Social and Environmental Sustainability Report 2005*. IKEA Group.

ILO (International Labour Organization) (2005, June) *Social Auditing in Bulgaria, Romania and Turkey - Results from Survey and Case Study Research*. Ankara: International Labour Office.

Inglehart, R. and Welzel, C. (2005a) Liberalism, Postmaterialism, and the Growth of Freedom: The Human Development Perspective. *International Review of Sociology, 15*(1), 81-108.

Inglehart, R. and Welzel, C. (2005b) *Modernization, Cultural Change and Democracy: The Human Development Sequence*. Cambridge: Cambridge University Press

IPCC (Intergovernmental Panel on Climate Change) (2001) *Third Assessment Report: Climate Change 2001: Synthesis Report*. Geneva, Switzerland: IPCC.

IPCC (2007) *Fourth Assessment Report: Climate Change 2007*. Geneva, Switzerland: IPCC.

Isaak, R. (2005) The Making of the Ecoprenuer. In Schaper, M. (Ed.), *Making Ecopreneurs: Developing Sustainable Entrepreneurship*. Hampshire, England: Ashgate.

IUCN/UNEP/WWF (1980) *World Conservation Strategy: Living Resource Conservation for Sustainable Development*. Gland, Switzerland: IUCN.

It's Official: Odwalla, Fresh Samantha to Merge. (2000, February, 7) *Brandweek Magazine*, Retrieved online April 14, 2006 from Brandweek Magazine electronic database: http://www.brandweek.com.

Jackson, M. (1992). *Systems Methodology for the Management Sciences*. New York: Plenum.

Jackson, M. (2000) *Systems Approaches to Management*. New York: Kluwer Academic/Plenum Publishers

Jalas, M. (2002) A Time Use Perspective on the Materials Intensity of Consumption. *Ecological Economics*, *41*, 109-123.

Jalas, M. (2005) The Everyday Life-Context of Increasing Energy Demands: Time Use Survey Data in a Decomposition Analysis. *Journal of Industrial Ecology*, *9*(1-2), 129-146.

Jensen, H. (2000, July 2) Low Pay, High Desire: A Tale Of 2 Swooshes in Indonesia. *Denver Rocky Mountain News*, 41.

Johansen, D., Brown, A. and Kalambi, S. (1998, November/December) Shopping Around. In *Tomorrow Magazine*, 26-27.

Johnson-Laird, P. (1983) *Mental Models: Towards a Cognitive Science of Language, Inference and Consciousness*. Cambridge, MA: Harvard University Press.

Jones, A. (2006, October 03) L'Oréal Sold on Expanding Body Shop. *Financial Times*. Retrieved online October 07, 2006 from Financial Times electronic database: http://www.ft.com.

Jørgensen, S. and Bendoricchio, G. (2001) *Fundamentals of Ecological Modelling* (3. ed.). Amsterdam: Elsevier.

Jucker, R. (2002) *Our Common Illiteracy - Education as if the Earth and People Mattered*. New York: Peter Lang.

Jundt, T. (2004, Spring) A Shopping Trip: How Consumer Culture has Sustained the Environmental Movement. *Watershed Magazine*, 7-13.

Kates, R.W., Clark, C.W., Corell, R., Hall, J. M. Jaeger, C. C., Lowe, I., et al. (2000) *Sustainability Science*. Research and Assessment Systems for Sustainability Program Discussion Paper 2000-33. Cambridge, MA: Environment and Natural Resources Program, Belfer Center for Science and International Affairs, Kennedy School of Government, Harvard University.

Kates, R.W., Clark, C.W., Corell, R., Hall, J. M. Jaeger, C. C., Lowe, I., et al. (2001) Sustainability Science. *Science*, *292*, 641-642.

Kates, R.W., Parris, T.M., and Leiserowitz, A. A. (2005, April) What is Sustainable Development? - Goals, Indicators, Values, and Practice. *Environment: Science and Policy for Sustainable Development*, *47*(3), 8-21.

Kelly, M. (2003, Summer) The Legacy Problem: Why Social Mission Gets Squeezed Out of Firms When They're Sold. *Business Ethics*, *17*(2). Retrieved online July 07, 2006 from Business Ethics electronic database: http://www.business-ethics.com.

Kelly, W. (1972) *Pogo: We Have Met the Enemy and He Is Us*. New York: Simon and Schuster.

Khazzoom, J.D. (1980). Economic Implications of Mandated Efficiency in Standards for Household Appliances. *Energy Journal*, *1*(4), 21-40.

Kiger, P. (2005, April) Corporate Crunch. *Workforce Management*, 32-38.

Kim, D.H. (1992) *Systems Archetypes I: Diagnosing Systemic Issues and Designing High-Leverage Interventions*. Waltham, MA: Pegasus Communications.

Kim, D.H. and Lannon, C. (1997) *Applying Systems Archetypes*, Waltham, MA: Pegasus Communications.

Klassen, G.K. and Opschoor, J.B. (1990). Economics of Sustainability or the Sustainability of Economics: Different Paradigms. *Ecological Economics*, *4*, 93-116.

Klawitter, N. (2006, June 31) Public Relations: Meister der Verdrehung. *Der Spiegel*, 72-76.

Klir, G. (2001) *Facets of Systems Science* (2nd ed.). IFSR. International Series on Systems Science and Engineering,. Vol. 15. New York: Plenum Press.

Kluge (2002) *Etymologisches Wörterbuch der deutschen Sprache* (24th ed.), rev. ed. edited by E. Seebold. Berlin: de Gruyter.

Kondratyev, K., Savinykh, V., Varotsos, C. and Krapivin, V. (2004) *Global Ecodynamics: A Multidimensional Analysis.* Chichester: Springer/Praxis.

Kopfmüller, J., Coenen, R., Jörissen, J., Langniß, O., and Nitsch, J. (2000) *Konkretisierung und Operationalisierung des Leitbildes einer nachhaltigen Entwicklung für den Energiebereich.* Wissenschaftliche Berichte, FZKA 6578. Karlsruhe: Forschungszentrum Karlsruhe Technik und Umwelt.

Koslowski, P. and Priddat, B.P. (Eds.) (2006) *Ethik des Konsums.* Munich: Fink.

Kotler, P. and Lee, N. (2005) *Corporate Social Responsibility: Doing the Most for Your. Company and Your Cause.* Hoboken, NJ: Wiley & Sons.

Kramer, A. (2000) Greenwashing Charges Make Businesses Blue, *Sustainable Industries Journal.* Retrieved online July 05, 2006 from Sustainable Industries Journal electronic database: http://www.sijournal.com.

Kristof, N.D. and WuDunn, S. (2000, September 24) Two Cheers for Sweatshops. New *York Times.* Retrieved online July 14, 2006 from New York Times electronic database: http:// www.nytimes.com.

Kuhndt, M., Geibler, J. v., Türk, V. and Ritthoff. M. (2003) Wie ressourceneffizient ist die Informationsgesellschaft? In Angrick, M. (Ed.*) Auf dem Weg zur nachhaltigen Informationsgesellschaft* (pp. 87-103). Marburg: Metropolis.

Kuhndt, M., Tuncer, B. and Lietdke, C. (2003) *Life-Cycle Approaches to Sustainable Consumption Matching Consumer Acceptance and Business Preparedness.* Final Report. Triple Innova and Wuppertal Institute.

Kuhns, B. (2004) Developing Communities, People and Business: In Search of a Model of Community Based Enterprises. In H. P. Welsch (Ed.) *Entrepreneurship: The Way Ahead.* New York: Routledge.

Kyoto Protocol (1997) *Kyoto Protocol to the United Nations Framework Convention on Climate Change,* U.N. Doc. FCCC/CP/1997/7/Add.1, adopted Dec. 1997, Kyoto - Japan, United Nations, 1998.

Lamberton, G. (2005) Sustainable Sufficiency - An Internally Consistent Version of Sustainability. *Sustainable Development, 13*(1), 53 - 78.

Lash, J. (2005, December 14) *Environmental Stories to Watch in 2006.* Washington: World Resource Institute.

Lash, J. (2006, December 19) *Environmental Stories to Watch in 2007.* Washington: World Resource Institute.

Laszlo, E. (1996) *The Systems View of the World: A Holistic Vision for Our Time* (2nd rev. ed.). Cresskill, NJ: Hampton Press.

Laszlo, E. (2001) *Macroshift: Navigating the Transformation to a Sustainable World.* San Francisco, CA: Berrett - Koehler.

Laszlo, E. (2003) *You Can Change the World. The Global Citizen's Handbook for Living on Planet Earth: A Report of the Club of Budapest.* New York: Select Books.

Laszlo, E. (2006) *The Chaos Point: The World at the Crossroads.* Charlottesville, VA: Hampton Roads.

Laszlo, E. and Seidel, P. (Eds.) (2006) Global Survival: The Challenge and Its Implications for Thinking and Acting. New York: Select Books.

Laszlo, E., and Laszlo, A. (1997) The Contribution of the Systems Sciences to the Humanities. *Systems Research and Behavioral Science, 14*(1), 5-19.

Leadbeater, C. (1997) *The Rise of the Social Entrepreneur.* London: Demos.

Levidow, L. and Carr, S. (2000) UK: Precautionary Commercialization?. *Journal of Risk Research, 3*(3), 261 - 270.

Light, J. (1998, December 11) *Sweatwash: The Apparel Industry's Efforts to Co-opt Labor Rights.* Special to CorpWatch. Retrieved online November 04, 2005 from http://www.corpwatch.org/article.php?id=239.

Liptak, A. (2003, September 13) Free Speech: Nike Move Ends Case Over Firms' Free Speech. *New York Times,* Retrieved online December 19, 2005 from New York Times electronic database: http:// www.nytimes.com.

Litvin, D. (2003) *Empires of Profit: Commerce, Conquest and Corporate Responsibility.* New York: Texere.

Litz, R. (1996) A Resource Based View of the Socially Responsible Firm: Stakeholder Interdependence, Ethical Awareness and Issue Responsiveness as Strategic Assets. *Journal of Business Ethics, 15,* 1355-1363.

Loomis, R. and Salter, S. (2006, September) Can BP Come Clean? *World Energy Monthly Review.* Retrieved online December 19, 2005 from World Energy Monthly Review electronic database: http://www.worldenergysource.com.

Lotter, D., Braun, J. (2011) *Der CSR-Manager,* München: ALTOP Verlag

Lovelock, J. (2000) [original 1979] *Gaia: A New Look at Life on Earth.* New York: Oxford University Press.

Lovelock, J. (2006) *The Revenge of Gaia: Why the Earth Is Fighting Back - and How We Can Still Save Humanity.* Santa Barbara, CA: Allen Lane.

Lovins, A.B., Lovins, L.H. and Hawken, P. (1999) A Road Map For Natural Capitalism. *Harvard Business Review, 77*(3), 145-158.

Luhmann, N. (1986) *Oekologische Kommunikation. Kann die moderne Gesellschaft sich auf ökologische Gefährdungen einstellen?.* Opladen: Westdeutscher Verlag.

M'hamed Elmurabit, H. and Bohn, V. (2003) Summary Report of *International Expert Meeting On The 10-Year Framework Of Programmes For Sustainable Consumption And Production,* Marrakech, Morocco, 16-19 June 2003.

Mamic, I. (2004) *Implementing Codes of Conduct: How Business Manages Social Performance in Global Supply Chains.* Sheffield, U.K./Geneva, Switzerland: Greenleaf and International Labour Organization.

Maplecroft (2005) *Company Report Review by Maplecroft: Nike, Corporate Responsibility Report 2004.* Bradford on Avon, UK: Maplecroft.

Margulis, L. (1998) *Symbiotic Planet: A New Look at Evolution.* London: Weidenfeld & Nicolson.

Markl, H. (1986) *Natur als Kulturaufgabe - Über die Beziehung des Menschen zur lebendigen Natur.* Stuttgart: DVA.

Markl, H. (2001) *Man's Place in Nature - Past and Future.* In E. Ehlers and T. Krafft (Eds.) Understanding the Earth System: Compartments, Processes and Interactions (pp. 81-96). New York: Springer.

Marsden, C. (2000) The New Corporate Citizenship of Big Business: Part of the Solution to Sustainability?. *Business and Society Review*, *105*(1), 9-25.

Marshall, R.S. and Brown, D. (2003) Corporate Environmental Reporting: What's in a Metric?. *Business Strategy and the Environment*, *12*, 87-103.

Martin, S. (2002) Sustainability, Systems Thinking and Professional Practice. *Planet*, *4*, 20-21.

Martin, S. (2005) Sustainability, Systems Thinking and Professional Practice. *Systemic Practice and Action Research*, *18*(2), 163-171.

Martin, S. and Hall, A. (2002) Sustainable Development and the Professions. *Planet*, *3*, 17-18.

Martin, S., Cohen, J. and Martin, M. (2004) *Opportunities For Sustainable Development in the Learning and Skills Sector: A Policy Analysis*. London, UK: The Learning and Skills Development Agency.

Martinelli, K. and Briggs, W. (1998) Integrating Public Relations and Legal Responses During a Crisis: The Case of Odwalla, Inc. *Public Relations Review*, *24*(4), 443-460.

Martorella, R. (1996) *Art and Business: An International Perspective on Sponsorship*. Westport, CT: Praeger.

Maslow, A. (1970) *Motivation and Personality* (2nd ed.). New York: Harper.

Mathews S, and Hendrickson C. (2001) Economic and Environmental Implications of On-line Retailing in the United States. In L. Hilty and P. Gilgen (Eds.), *Sustainability in the Information Society* (pp. 65-72). Marburg: Metropolis.

Matten, D., Crane, A. and Chapple, W. (2003) Behind the Mask: Revealing the True Face of Corporate Citizenship. *Journal of Business Ethics*, *45*(1-2), 109-120.

Maturana, H. and Varela, F. (1980) *Autopoiesis and Cognition: The Realization of the Living*. Boston: D. Reidel.

Maturana, H. and Varela, F. (1987) *The Tree of Knowledge: The Biological Roots of Human Understanding*. Boston: Shambhala.

Max-Neef, M. (1992) Development and Human Needs. In P. Ekins and M. Max-Neef (Eds.), *Real Life Economics: Understanding Wealth Creation* (pp. 197-213). London: Routledge.

McDonough, W. and Braungart, M. (1998) The Next Industrial Revolution. *The Atlantic Monthly*, *282*(4), 82-92.

McDonough, W. and Braungart, M. (2002a) *Cradle to Cradle: Remaking the Way We Make Things*. New York: North Point Press.

McDonough, W. and Braungart, M. (2002b, July-August) From Inspiration to Innovation: Nike's Giant Steps Towards Sustainbility. *Green@work Magazine*. Retrieved online December 19, 2005 from Green@work Magazine electronic database: http://www.greenatworkmag.com.

Meadows D.H. and Robinson J. (1985) T*he Electronic Oracle: Computer Models and Social Decisions*. Chichester: John Wiley.

Meadows D.H. and Robinson J. (2002) The Electronic Oracle: Computer Models and Social Decisions. *System Dynamics Review*, *18*(2), 271-308.

Meadows, D. L., Behrens III. W. W., Meadows, D. H., Naill, R. F., Randers, J. and Zahn, E. K. O. (1974) *The Dynamics of Growth in a Finite World*. Cambridge MA: Productivity Press.

Meadows, D.H. (1980) The Unavoidable a Priori. In J. Randers (Ed.), *Elements of the System Dynamics Method* (pp. 23-57). Waltham, MA: Pegasus Communications.

Meadows, D.H. (1991) *The Global Citizen*. Washington DC: Island Press.

Meadows, D.H. (1999) *Leverage Points: Places to Intervene in a System*. Vermont: The Sustainability Institute.

Meadows, D.H. (2002) Dancing With Systems. *The Systems Thinker, 13*(2).

Meadows, D.H., Meadows, D.L., Randers, J. (1992) *Beyond the Limits: Confronting Global Collapse*, Envisioning a Sustainable Future. Vermont: Chelsea Green Publishing.

Meadows, D.H., Meadows, D.L., Randers, J. and Behrens, W.W.III. (1972) *The Limits to Growth*. New York: Universe Books.

Meadows, D.H., Randers, J., Meadows, D.L. (2004) *Limits to Growth: The 30-Year Update*. Vermont: Chelsea Green Publishing.

Meadows, D.H., Richardson, J. and Bruckmann, G. (1982) *Groping in the Dark: The First Decade of Global Modelling*. Chichester: John Wiley.

Meadows, D.L. and Meadows, D.H. (1973) *Toward Global Equilibrium*. Cambridge, MA: Wright-Allen Press.

Melo, C. and Wolf, S. (2005) Empirical Assessment of Eco-Certification. *Organization and Environment, 18*(3), 287-317.

Merk, J. (2005) *Fair Purchasing Practices: Some Issues for Discussion*. Amsterdam: Clean Clothes Campaign.

Michaelis L. (2000) *Ethics of Consumption*. Oxford: Centre for Environment, Ethics and Society.

Michaelis L. (2003) The Role of Business in Sustainable Consumption. *Journal of Cleaner Production, 11*(8), 915-921.

Midgley, G. (Ed.) (2003) *Systems Thinking* (Volumes I-IV). London: Sage Publications.

Milmo, C. (2006, April 10) Body Shop's Popularity Plunges After L'Oreal Sale. *The Independent/UK*. Retrieved online September 07, 2006, from The Independent/UK electronic database: http://www.independent.co.uk.

Mintzberg, H, Simons, R. and Basu, K. (2002) Beyond Selfishness. *Sloan Management Review, 44*(1), 67-74.

Mitchell, R.B. and Lankao, P.R. (2004) Institutions, Science and Technology in the Transition to Sustainbility. In H. Schellnhuber, P.J. Crutzen, W.C. Clark, M. Claussen and H. Held (Eds.), *Earth System Analysis for Sustainbility* (pp. 387-408) Cambridge, MA and London, UK: MIT Press/Dahlem University Press.

MITWorld (2005) *Making Globalization Work for All*. Conference Video at Sloan School of Management at the Massachusetts Institute of Technology on October 7, 2005. Cambridge MA: MITWorld.

Moir, L. (2001) What Do We Mean by Corporate Social Responsibility?. *Corporate Governance, 1*(2), 16 - 22.

Mokhiber, R. and Weissman, R. (2003, September 23) Nike Gets a Pass. *ZNet*. Retrieved online August 09, 2005 from http://www.zmag.org/content/print_article.cfm?itemID=4235&sectionID=1.

Monitor (2005) Schöne, billige Kleidung - und das Elend dahinter. *Monitor, 539* [TV-Documentation] broadcasted October 13, 2005; a written documentation is available online,

retrieved October 18, 2005 from http://www.wdr.de/tv/monitor/beitrag.phtml?
bid=742&sid=136.

Monsanto (2006) *Third Quarter 2006 Financial Results*. Monsanto

Mooney, H. A. and Ehrlich, P. R. (1997) Ecosystem Services: A Fragmentary History. In
G.E. Daily (Ed.), *Nature's Services: Societal Dependence on Natural Ecosystems* (pp. 11-19).
Washington: Island Press.

Moore, P. (2000): Environmentalism for the Twenty-first Century. *IPA Review, 52*(3), 3-8.

Morhardt, J.E., Baird, S. and Freeman, K. (2002) Scoring corporate environmental and sustainability reports using GRI 2000, ISO 14031 and other criteria. *Corporate Social Responsibility and Environmental Management, 9*, 215 - 233.

Mort, G.S., Weerawardena, J. and Carnegie, K. (2003) Social Entrepreneurship: Towards
Conceptualization. *International Journal of Nonprofit and Voluntary Sector Marketing, 8*(1),
76-88.

MSN (2005) CSR Reports: Ratcheting Up Transparency Standards?. *Codes.Memo, 19*, 1-10.
Toronto: Maquila Solidarity Network (MSN).

Mueller, P. (2000) Guess Who's is Coming to Dinner?, *Mirus e-newsletter*. Retrieved online
September 15, 2005 from
www.merger.com/pdfs/newsletter_800.pdf+Mueller+Guess+who%27s+coming+to+din-
ner.

Müller-Christ, G. (Ed.) (2006) *Unternehmen und Nachhaltigkeit. Zwischen Selbst- und
Fremdsteuerung*. Karlsruhe: Vereinigung für Ökologische Ökonomie.

Munro, D. (1995) Sustainability: Rhetoric or Reality. In T. Trzyna (Ed.), *A Sustainable
World: Defining and Measuring Sustainable Development*. Sacramento and London: California Institute of Public Affairs and Earthscan for IUCN.

NASA (1986) *Earth System Science*. Report of the Earth System Science Committee (Francis Bretherton, Chair), NASA Advisory Council.

Nattrass, B. and Altomare, M. (2001) *Natural Step for Business: Wealth, Ecology and the Evolutionary Corporation* (2nd ed.). British Columbia, Canada: New Society Publishers.

Nike (2005) *Corporate Responsibility Report Fy04*. Portland: Nike Inc.

Nocera, J. (2005, September 10) On Oil Supply, Opinions Aren't Scarce. *New York Times*,
Retrieved online December 12, 2005 from New York Times electronic database: http://
www.nytimes.com.

Noon, C. (2006, March 10) Organic Growth for Body Shop. *Forbes*, Retrieved online April
28, 2006 from Forbes electronic database: http://www.forbes.com.

Norman, D.A. (1983) Some Observations On Mental Models. In D.R. Gentner and A.L.
Stevens (Eds.), *Mental Models* (pp. 7-14). Hillsdale, NJ: Erlbaum.

Norman, W. and MacDonald, C. (2004) Getting to the bottom of triple bottom line. *Business Ethics Quarterly, 14*(2), 243-262.

NRC (National Research Council) (1999a) *Global Environmental Change: Research Path-
ways for the Next Decade. Report of the Committee on Global Change Research, Board on
Sustainable Development, Policy Division, National Research Council*. Washington D.C.:
National Academy Press.

NRC (1999b) *Our Common Journey: A Transition Toward Sustainability*. Washington DC:
National Academy Press.

NRC (2001) *The Science of Regional and Global Change: Putting Knowledge to Work. Report of the Committee on Global Change Research.* Washington, D.C.: National Academy Press.

O'Rourke, D. (2006, April 5) Selling Out or Buying In?. *The Boston Globe*, Retrieved online April 22, 2006 from The Boston Globe electronic database: http://www.boston.com/news/globe/.

Odum, E.P. and Barrett, G.W. (2005) *Fundamentals of Ecology* (5th ed.). Belmont, California: Thomson Brooks/Cole.

Odum, H.T. (1983) *Systems Ecology: An Introduction.* New York: John Wiley.

Odum, H.T. (1994). *Ecological and General Systems: An Introduction to Systems Ecology* (2nd rev. ed.). Niwot, Colorado: University Press of Colorado.

Odwalla (1998) *Annual Report 1998.* Dinuba, CA: Odwalla Inc.

OMSC (2006) *The Organic Milk Market Report 2005.* Somerset, UK: Organic Milk Suppliers' Co-operative (OMSC).

Ossimitz, G. (1995) *Denken und Modellbilden.* Working Paper of the Institute for Mathematics, Statistics and Didactic of Mathematics. Klagenfurt: University Klagenfurt.

Ossimitz, G. (1997) *The Development of Systems Thinking Skills Using System Dynamics Modeling Tools.* Working Paper of the Institute for Mathematics, Statistics and Didactic of Mathematics. Klagenfurt: University Klagenfurt.

Ossimitz, G. (2003) *Systems Thinking and System Dynamics Modeling: a new perspective for math classes?* In Proceedings of the International Conference on Technology in Mathematics Teaching. Klagenfurt: University Klagenfurt.

OTA (2005) *The Past, Present and Future of the Organic Industry: A Retrospective of the First 20 Years, a Look at the Current State of Organic and forecasting the next 20 Years.* Greenfield MA: Organic Trade Association (OTA).

Ottman, J. (2000, September/October): It's not just the Environment, Stupid. *Business Magazine*, 31.

Oxfam International (2004) *Trading Away Our Rights: Women Working in Global Supply Chains.* Australia: Oxfam.

Oxfam, CCC and ICFTU/Global Unions (2004) *Play Fair At The Olympics.* Oxford: Oxfam GB.

Paine, L. S. (2003) *Value Shift: Why Companies Must Merge Social and Financial Imperatives to Achieve Superior Performance.* New York: McGraw-Hill.

Parker, S.C. (2006) *The Economics of Entrepreneurship.* Cheltenham: Edward Elgar.

Parris, T.M. and Kates, R.W. (2003) Characterizing and Measuring Sustainable Development. *Annual Review of Environment and Resources, 28,* 559-586.

Parson, E. and Clark, W.C. (1995) Sustainable Development As Social Learning. In L.H. Gunderson, C.S. Holling, S.S. Light (Eds.), *Barriers and Bridges to the Renewal of Ecosystems and Institutions* (pp. 428-460). New York: Columbia University Press.

Pearce, D., Markandya, A. and Barbier, E.B (1989) *Blueprint for a Green Economy.* London: Earthscan Publications.

Pearce, D.W. and Atkinson, G. (1992) *Are National Economies Sustainable? - Measuring Sustainable Development.* Centre for Social and Economic Research on the Global Environment (CSERGE) GEC Working Paper 92-11. London: University College.

Pearce, D.W. and Turner, R.K. (1990) *Economics of Natural Resources and the Environment.* London: Harvester Wheatsheaf.

Peet, K. and Peet, J. (2000) *Poverties and Satisfiers: A Systems Look at Human Needs - Creating a New Democracy.* Conference Paper, Devnet Conference - Poverty, Prosperity, Progress. Wellington, 17-19th November 2000.

Perrels, A. (2002) *Understanding Consumption Patterns - Including Time Use, Skills, and Market Failures.* In Workshop Proceedings Life-Cycle Approaches To Sustainable Consumption. Laxenburg, Austria: International Institute for Applied Systems Analysis.

Peters, G. (2003) *A Society Addicted to Paper: The Effect of Computer Use on Paper Consumption*, School of Computing Science. Working Paper. Vancouver, Canada: Simon Fraser University.

Pirages, D.C. (1977) A Social Design For Sustainable Growth. In D.C. Pirages (Ed.), *The Sustainable Society - Implications for Limited Growth.* New York: Praeger.

Pitman, S. (2006, March 22) L'Oreal's Body Shop Acquisition Meets With Mixed Reaction. *Cosmetics Design Europe.* Retrieved online November 20, 2006 from http://www.cosmeticsdesign-europe.com/news/printNewsBis.asp?id=66584.

Plous, S. (1993) *The Psychology of Judgment and Decision Making.* New York: McGraw Hill.

Plug Power (2006) *Annual Report 2005.* Latham: Plug Power.

Pohl, M., Tolhurst, N. (Eds) (2010) *Responsible Business – How to Manage a CSR Strategy Successfully*, West Sussex: John Wiley & Sons

Portney, P., Parry, I., Gruenspecht, H. and Harrington, W. (2003) *The Economics of Fuel Economy Standards.* Discussion Paper RFF DP 03-44, Washington: Resources for the Future (RFF).

Prabowo, Y. (2003) *Presentation to the Globalization and Labour Rights Panel.* Public Eye on Davos Conference, 27 January 2003, Davos/Switzerland.

Prahalad, C.K. (2004) *The Fortune at the Bottom of the Pyramid: Eradicating Poverty Through Profit*, Philadelphia, PA: Wharton School Publishing.

Prahalad, C.K. and Hammond, A. (2002) Serving the World's Poor, Profitably. *Harvard Business Review, 80*(9), 48-57.

Prahalad, C.K. and Hart, S.L. (2002) The Fortune at the Bottom of the Pyramid. *Strategy+Business, 26*, 54-67.

Pratt, N. (2006) *Learning Laboratories for Mission-Based Enterprises.* Presentation at the 2nd KDNC WorldBank Workshop, April 07-08, 2006. Washington D.C.: WorldBank.

Pratt, N. (2007) [forthcoming] *Sustainable Agriculture.* Workshop Report UNEP 9th Seminar on Sustainable Consumption and Production, 10-12 December 2006, Arusha, Tanzania: United Nations Environmental Program.

PRB (2006) *World Population Data Sheet.* Washington: Population Reference Bureau (PRB).

Priddat, B.P. (1998) *Moralischer Konsum. 13 Lektionen über die Käuflichkeit.* Stuttgart: Hirzel.

Priddat, B.P. (2002) *Theoriegeschichte der Wirtschaft*, Neue Ökonomische Bibliothek, Vol. 2. Munich: Fink (UTB).

Priddat, B.P. (2005a) *Moral und Ökonomie*, Sozialphilosophische Studien, Vol. 8. Berlin: Parerga.

Priddat, B.P. (2005b) *Unvollständige Akteure. Komplexer werdende Ökonomie.* Wiesbaden: VS-Verlag.

Priddat, B.P. (Ed.) (2000) Beyond Equilibrium. Kultur als Hintergrund/Vordergrund der Ökonomie. In B.P. Priddat (Ed.), *Kapitalismus, Krisen, Kultur* (pp. 189-218). Marburg: Metropolis.

Princen, T. (2005) *The Logic of Sufficiency*. Cambridge, MA: MIT Press.

Pringle, P. (2003) *Food, Inc.: Mendel to Monsanto - The Promises and Perils of The Biotech Harvest*. New York: Simon and Schuster.

Radermacher F. J. (2004a) *Balance or Destruction: Ecosocial Market Economy as the Key to Global Sustainable Development*. Vienna: Ecosocial Forum Europe.

Radermacher, F.J. (1997) Building The Information Society. In R. Sturm, G. Weinmann, O. Will (Eds.), *Information Society and the Regions in Europe*, Tagungsband No. 14. Tübingen: University of Tübingen.

Radermacher, F.J. (2004b) Ökosoziale Grundlagen für Nachhaltigkeitspfade - Warum der Marktfundamentalismus die Welt arm macht. *Gaia - Ecological Perspectives for Science and Society, 13*(3), 170-175.

Reason, P. and Bradbury, H. (2001). Handbook of Action Research: Participative Inquiry and Practice. Thousand Oaks, California: Sage.

Reddy, A. (2003, September 13): Nike Settles Commercial Speech Case Over False Advertising. *The Washington Post*. Retrieved online October 23, 2005 from The Washington Post electronic database: http:// www.washingtonpost.com.

RFCE (2002) *The Environmental Fiduciary: The Case for Incorporating Environmental Factors into Investment Management Policies*. Oakland, CA: Rose Foundation for Communities and Environment (RFCE).

Richardson, G. (1986) Problems with Causal Loop Diagrams. *System Dynamics Review, 2*(2), 158-170.

Richardson, G. (1991) *Feedback Thought in Social Science and Systems Theory*. Philadelphia, PA: University of Pennsylvania Press.

Richardson, G. (1997) Problems in Causal Loop Diagrams Revisited. *System Dynamics Review, 13*(3), 247-252.

Richmond, B. (1993) Systems Thinking: Critical Thinking Skills for the 1990s and Beyond. *System Dynamics Review, 9*(2), 113-133.

Richmond, B. (1994) *System Dynamics/Systems Thinking: Let's Just Get On With It*. Paper delivered at the International Systems Dynamics Conference in Sterling, Scotland.

Robèrt, K.H., Basile, G., Broman, G., Byggeth, S., Cook, D., Haraldsson, H. et. al. (2004) *Strategic Leadership Towards Sustainbility* (2nd ed.). Karlskrona, Sweden: Blekinge Institute of Technology.

Robèrt, K.-H., Schmidt-Bleek, B., Aloisi de Larderel, J., Basile, G., Jansen, J.L., Kuehr, R., Price-Thomas, P., Suzuki, M., Hawken P. and Wackernagel, M. (2002) Strategic Sustainable Development - Selection, Design and Synergies of Applied Tools. *Journal of Cleaner Production, 10*(3), 197- 214.

Robin Wood (1999, June 24) *What is the Elk Doing in the Tropical Forest?*. Press Release. Hamburg: Robin Wood.

Romme, A.G.L. and Witteloostuijn, A. v. (1999) Circular Organizing and Triple Loop Learning. *Journal of Organizational Change, 12*(5), 439-453.

Rose, J. (2001, December 03) Selling His Soul to Dannon? *Fortune Small Business*. Retrieved online August 12, 2006 from Fortune Small Business electronic database: http://magazine-directory.com/Fortune-Small-Business.htm.

Rosner W.J. (1995) Mental Models for Sustainability. *Journal of Cleaner Production, 3*(1), 107-121.

Sachs, J.D. (2005) *The End of Poverty: Economic Possibilities for Our Time*. New York: The Penguin Press.

Sachs, W. (1995) From Efficiency To Sufficiency. *Resurgence*, 171, 6-8.

Sandow, D., Mack, M. and Fan Tong He (2005) *The Secret Economics of Wellbeing: First Steps toward a Natural Economic System*, Unpublished Manuscript, Oregon.

Sanne, C. (2001) Are We Chasing Our Tail in the Pursuit of Sustainability. *International Journal of Sustainable Development*, 4(1), 120-133.

Sanne, C. (2002). Willing Consumers - Or Locked-In? Policies for a Sustainable Consumption. *Ecological Economics*, 42(1-2), 273-287.

Saunders, H.D. (1992) The Khazzoom-Brookes Postulate And Neoclassical Growth. *Energy Journal*, 13(4), 131-148.

Saunders, H.D. (2000) A View From the Macro Side: Rebound, Backfire, and Khazzoom-Brookes. *Energy Policy*, 28(6-7), 439-449.

Say, J.B. (1803) *Traité d'économie Politique, ou Simple Exposition de la Maniére dont se forment, se Distribuent, et se Consomment les Richesses*. Paris: Calmann-Lévy.

Schaltegger, S. and Sturm, A. (1998) *Eco-Efficiency by Eco-Controlling*. Theory and Cases. Zürich: vdf.

Schaltegger, S., Burritt, R. and Petersen, H. (2003) *An Introduction to Corporate Environmental Management: Striving for Sustainability*. Sheffield UK: Greenleaf.

Schauer, T. (2003) *The Sustainable Information Society*. Vision and Risks. Ulm: Universitätsverlag.

Schellnhuber H. and Wenzel V. (Eds.) (1998) *Earth System Analysis. Integrating Science for Sustainability*. Berlin: Springer.

Schellnhuber H., Crutzen, P.J., Clark W.C., Claussen, M. and Held, H. (Eds.) *Earth System Analysis for Sustainbility* (2004) Cambridge, MA and London, UK: MIT Press/Dahlem University Press.

Schellnhuber, H. (2001) Earth System Analysis and Management. In E. Ehlers and T. Krafft (Eds.) *Understanding the Earth System: Compartments, Processes and Interactions*. (pp. 17-56). New York: Springer.

Schipper, L. and Grubb, M. (2000) On the Rebound? Feedback Between Energy Intensities and Energy Uses in IEA Countries. *Energy Policy*, 28(6-7), 367-388.

Schipper, L. and Meyer, S. (1992) En*ergy Efficiency and Human Activity: Past Trends, Future Prospects*. Cambridge: Cambridge University Press.

Schlesinger, S. and Kinzer, S. (2005) B*itter Fruit: The Story of the American Coup in Guatemala* (rev. and exp. ed.). Cambridge: Harvard University Press.

Schley, S. and Laur, J. (1998) *Creating Sustainable Organizations: Meeting the Economic, Ecological, and Social Challenges of the 21st Century*. Waltham, MA: Pegasus Communication.

Schlippe, A. v. and Schweitzer, J. (2003) *Lehrbuch der systemischen Therapie und Beratung* (9th ed.). Göttingen: Vandenhoeck and Ruprecht.

Schlippe, A. v., El Hachimi, M., Jürgens, G. (2004) *Multikulturelle systemische Praxis. Ein Reiseführer für Beratung, Therapie und Supervision* (2nd ed.). Heidelberg: Carl Auer Systeme.

Schmidheiny, S. and Timberlake, L. (1992) *Changing Course: A Global Business Perspective on Development and the Environment*. Cambridge: MIT Press.

Schulz, W.F., Burschel, C., Weigert, M., Liedtke, C., Bohnet-Joschko, S., Kreeb, M., Losen, D., Geßner, C., Diffenhard, V., Maniura, A. (Eds.) (2001) *Lexikon Nachhaltiges Wirtschaften* (Lehr- und Handbücher zur ökologischen Unternehmensführung und Umweltökonomie). Munich: Oldenbourg.

Schulz, W.F., Geßner, C., Kölle, A. (2006) Nachhaltiges Wirtschaften in Unternehmen: Ein Überblick. E. Tiemeyer and K. Wilbers (Eds.), *Berufliche Bildung für nachhaltiges Wirtschaften : Konzepte, Curricula, Methoden, Beispiele Bildung für nachhaltiges Wirtschaften - Konzepte und Praxisbeispiele* (pp. 57-70). Bielefeld: Bertelsmann.

Schulz, W.F., Gutterer, B., Geßner, C., Sprenger, R.U. and Rave, T. (2002, August) *Nachhaltiges Wirtschaften in Deutschland. Erfahrungen, Trends und Potenziale, Oekoradar.* Holzkirchen: Denkmayr druck&design.

Schumacher, E.F. (1977) *A Guide for the Perplexed.* New York: Harper and Row.

Schumacher, E.F. (1989) [original 1973] *Small is Beautiful - Economics as if People Mattered.* New York: Harper and Row.

Schumacher, E.F., Candre, H., Echeverri, J.A. (1998) *This I Believe, and Other Essays.* Dartington Totnes, UK: Green Books.

Schumpeter, J. A. (1934) *The Theory of Economic Development.* Cambridge, MA: Harvard University Press.

Schwartz, N. (2006, October 31) Can BP Bounce Back?. *CNN Money*.Com, Retrieved online November 21, 2006 from http://money.cnn.com/magazines/fortune/fortune_archive/2006/10/16/8388595/index.htm.

Schwartz, P. and Gibb, B. (1999) *When Good Companies do Bad Things: Responsibility and Risk in an Age of Globalization.* New York: John Wiley.

Schweitzer, J. and Schlippe, A. v. (2006) *Lehrbuch der systemischen Therapie und Beratung II - Das störungsspezifische Wissen.* Göttingen: Vandenhoeck and Ruprecht.

Seiler-Hausmann, J.D., Liedtke, C. and Weizsäcker, E. v. (Eds.) (2004) *Eco-efficiency and Beyond - Towards the Sustainable Enterprise.* Sheffield: Greenleaf Publishing.

Senge, P. (1999) Letter to the Editor. *Harvard Business Review,* 77(4), 178-179.

Senge, P. (2006) [original 1990] T*he Fifth Discipline: The Art and Practice of the Learning Organization* (rev. ed.). New York: Doubleday.

Senge, P., Cambron-McCabe, N., Luca, T., Smith, B., Dutton, J. and Kleiner, A. (2000) *Schools that Learn: A Fifth Discipline Fieldbook for Educators, Parents, and Everyone Who Cares About Education.* New York: Doubleday.

Senge, P., Kleiner, A., Roberts, C., Richard, R. Bryan, S. (1994) *The Fifth Discipline Fieldbook: Strategies and Tools for Building a Learning Organization.* New York: Doubleday.

Senge, P., Kleiner, A., Roberts, C., Richard, R. Roth, G., Bryan, S. (1999) *The Dance of Change: The Challenge of Sustaining Momentum in Learning Organizations.* New York: Doubleday.

Senge, P., Laur, J., Schley, S. and Smith, B. (2006) *Learning for Sustainability.* Cambridge, MA: Society for Organizational Learning (SoL).

Senge, P.; Scharmer, O.; Jaworski, J.; Flowers, B.S. (2004) *Presence: Human Purpose and the field of the Future.* Cambridge, MA: The Society for Organizational Learning.

SETAC (1993) *Guidelines for Life-Cycle Assessment: A Code of Practice.* Workshop Paper Sesimbra, Portugal, March 31 - April 3. Brussels and Pensacola, Florida: Society of Environmental Toxicology and Chemistry (SETAC).

SFI (2003) *Report on Socially Responsible Investing Trends in the United States 2003.* Washington, D.C.: Social Investment Forum.

Sharma, S. and Aragon-Correa, A. (Eds.) (2005) *Corporate Environmental Strategy and Competitive Advantage.* Northampton, MA: Edward Elgar Academic Publishing.

Shell (1998, May) *The Shell Report, Profits and Principles - does there have to be a choice?.* London: Royal Dutch/Shell International.

Sligh, M., and Christman, C. (2003) Who Owns Organic? *The Global Status, Prospects, and Challenges of a Changing Organic Market.* Pittsboro, NC: Rural Advancement Foundation International.

Small, K. and Van Dender, K. (2006, March 21) *Fuel Efficiency and Motor Vehicle Travel: The Declining Rebound Effect.* Economic Working Paper, Department of Economics. Irvine, CA: University of California.

Smith, B. (2006) Engaging the Future. In P. Senge, J. Laur, S. Schley and B. Smith (Eds.) *Learning for Sustainability* (pp. 26-43). Cambridge, MA: The Society for Organizational Learning (SoL).

Smith, J. (2000) *Redesigning Education Programs for Business Sustainability.* Presentation at the International System Dynamics Society Conference, 6-10 August 2000, Bergen Norway.

Socolow, R, Andrews, C, Berkhout, F. and Thomas, V. (Eds.) (1994) *Industrial Ecology and Global Change.* Cambridge: Cambridge University Press.

Solow, R.M. (1973) Is the End of the World at Hand? *Challenge, 16*(1), 39-50.

Spangenberg, J. and Bonniot, O. (1998) *Sustainable Indicators: A Compass on the Road Towards Sustainability.* Wuppertal Paper No. 81. Wuppertal: Wuppertal Institute for Climate, Environment, Energy.

Stahlmann, V. and Clausen, J. (2000) *Umweltleistung von Unternehmen. Von der Öko-Effizienz zur Öko-Effektivität.* Wiesbaden: Gabler.

Steffen, W., Sanderson, A., Tyson, P.D., Jäger, J., Matson, P.A., Moore III, B. et al. (Eds.) (2004) *Global Change and the Earth System: A Planet Under Pressure,* Global Change - The IGBP Series. New York: Springer.

Steinbichler, K. (2006, October 21) Wirtschaft heute - das ist Finanzfaschismus, Interview mit Anita Roddick. *Süddeutsche Zeitung.* Retrieved online November 10, 2006 from Süddeutsche Zeitung electronic database: http://www.sueddeutsche.de.

Steltenpohl, G. (2005, March-May) Will Big Business Save the World? *What Is Enlightenment? 28.* Retrieved online April 12, 2006 from What Is Enlightenment? electronic database: http://www.wie.org/magazine/.

Sterman, J.D. (1991). A Skeptic's Guide to Computer Models. In G. O. Barney (Ed.), *Managing the Nation: The Microcomputer Software Catalog* (pp. 201-229). Boulder, Colorado: Westview Press.

Sterman, J.D. (1994) Learning In And About Complex Systems. *System Dynamics Review 10*(2/3), 291-330.

Sterman, J.D. (2002) All Models Are Wrong: Reflections On Becoming A Systems Scientist. *System Dynamics Review, 18*(4), 501-531.

Sterman, J.D. (2004) Business Dynamics: *Systems Thinking and Modeling for a Complex World* (international ed.). Singapore: McGraw Hill.

Stern, N. (2007) *The Economics of Climate Change - The Stern Review*. Cambridge, UK: Cambridge University Press.

Stivers, R. (1976) *The Sustainable Society: Ethics and Economic Growth*. Philadelphia: Westminster Press.

Stroh, D. (2000) Leveraging Change: The Power of Systems Thinking in Action. *Reflections*, 2(2), 51-66.

Suchanek, N. (2005) Chiquita, BMZ und GTZ: Greenwashing mit Entwicklungshilfegeldern. *Bio100*. Retrieved online November 12, 2006 from http://www.kommunikationssystem.de/news/Mittelamerika/Fw:-%5Bbio100%5D-Chiquita,-BMZ-und-GTZ:-Greenwashing-mit-Entwicklungshilfegeldern-19569.pdf.

Sussdorff, M. (2000, February 13) Ethics Frozen Out in the Ben & Jerry Ice Cream War. CSR Europe. Retrieved online October 14, 2006: http://intranet.csreurope.org/news/csr/one-entry?entry_id=114425.

Svendsen, A. (1998) *The Stakeholder Strategy*. San Francisco, CA: Berrett-Koehler.

Svoboda, S. and Whalen, J. (2005) Using Experiential Simulation to Teach Sustainability. *Greenbiz*, Retrieved online January 12, 2006 from http://www.greenbiz.com/toolbox/howto_third.cfm?LinkAdvID=53072.

Swank, W.T. and Tilley, D.R. (2000) Watershed Management Contributions to Land Stewardship: Case Studies In *The Southeast*. In *Proceedings of the Land Stewardship in the 21st Century: The Contributions Of Watershed Management*. 2000. March 13-16; Tuscon, AZ. P-13: U.S. Department of Agriculture, Forest Service, Rocky Mountain Station: 93-108.

Swieringa, J. and Wierdsma, A. (1992) *Becoming a Learning Organization - Beyond the Learning Curve*. Wokingham, England: Addison-Wesley.

SWOP (1995) *Intel Inside* New Mexico: A Case Study of Environmental and Economic Justice. Albuquerque, NM: South West Organizing Project (SWOP).

Taylor, G. and Scharlin, P. (2004) *Smart Alliance: How a Global Corporation and Environmental Activists Transformed a Tarnished Brand*. New Haven: Yale University Press.

Taylor-Robinson, M. and Redd, S. (2003) Framing the Poliheuristic Theory of Decision: The United Fruit Company and the 1954 U.S.-Led Coup in Guatemala. In A. Mintz (Ed.) *Integrating Cognitive and Rational Theories of Foreign Policy Decision Making*. New York: Palgrave Macmillan.

The Body Shop (2006, March 17) *Interview with Adrian Bellamy*, Executive Chairman. Body Shop International PLC. Retrieved online November 03, 2006 from http://w3.cantos.com/06/rose-603-6k9y5/bodyshop/pjx-d137-transcript.php?language=en.

The Body Shop (2006, March 17) *Interview with Anita Roddick*, Non-Executive Director. Body Shop International PLC. Retrieved online November 03, 2006 from at http://w3.cantos.com/06/rose-603-6k9y5/bodyshop/pjx-d136-transcript.php?language=en.

The Body Shop (2006, March 17) *Interview with Peter Saunders*, Chief Executive Officer. Body Shop International PLC. Retrieved online November 03, 2006 from at http://w3.cantos.com/06/rose-603-6k9y5/bodyshop/pjx-d138-transcript.php?language=en.

The Climate Greenwash Vanguard: Shell and BP Amoco (2000) *Greenhouse Market Mania, Corporate Europe Observatory.* Retrieved online July 25, 2006 from http://www.corpora-teeurope.org/greenhouse/greenwash.html

The Social Learning Group (2001) *Learning To Manage Global Environmental Risks* (Volumes I-II). Cambridge: MIT Press.

Thiel, R. E. (2003) Editorial: What Developmental Impact? *Magazine for Development and Cooperation, 4.*

Thogersen, J. (2005) How May Consumer Policy Empower Consumers for Sustainable Lifestyles?. *Journal of Consumer Policy, 28*(2), 143-177.

Thogersen, J. and Olander, F. (2002) Human Values and The Emergence of a Sustainable Consumption Pattern: A Panel Study. *Journal of Economics Psychology, 23,* 605-630.

Thompson, A. (2002) Unilever's Acquisitions of Slimfast, Ben & Jerry's, & Bestfoods. In A. Thompson and A. Strickland (Eds.) *Strategic Management: Concepts and Cases* (13th ed.) (pp. C470-501). Boston: McGraw-Hill/Irwin.

Thomsen, S. and Rawson, B. (1998) Purifying a Tainted Corporate Image: Odwalla's Response to an E.Coli Poisoning. *Public Relations Quarterly, 43*(3), 35-46.

Throne-Holst, H. (2003) *The Fallacies of Energy Efficiency: The Rebound Effect?* Paper presented at the Strategies For Sustainable Energy Technology Workshop in Trondheim, November 20-21, 2003. Trondheim, Norway: The SAMSTEMT Programme Of The Norwegian Research Council.

TNS (2000) *The Natural Step Framework Guidebook.* Sweden: The Natural Step (TNS).

Tokar, B. (1998) Monsanto: A Checkered History. *The Ecologist, 28*(5), 254-261.

Trevino, L. and Nelson, K. (2004) *Managing Business Ethics: Straight Talk About How To Do It Right.* New York: John Wiley.

Tuncer, B. and Kuhndt, M. (2006) *Elements of System Innovations for Sustainable Consumption & Production.* In M. M. Andersen and A. Tukker (Eds.) Proceedings of Workshop of the Sustainable Consumption Research Exchange (SCORE!) Network, Perspectives on Radical Changes to Sustainable Consumption and Production, April 20-21, 2006, Copenhagen, Denmark.

Turner II, B.L., Clark, W.C., Kates, R.W., Richards, J.F., Mathews, J T. and Meyer, W.B. (Eds.) (1990) *The Earth as Transformed by Human Action: Global and Regional Changes in the Biosphere over the Past 300 Years.* Cambridge: Cambridge University Press.

Turner, R. K. (1992) *Speculations on Weak and Strong Sustainability.* Working Paper GEC 92-2. Norwich UK: Centre for Social and Economic Research on the Global Environment (CSERGE).

Ulrich, H. and Probst, G. (1991) *Anleitung zum ganzheitlichen Denken und Handeln: Ein Brevier für Führungskräfte* (3rd ed.). Bern: Paul Haupt.

Ulrich, W. (1983) *Critical Heuristics of Social Planning: A New Approach to Practical Philosophy.* Bern: Haupt.

Ulrich, W. (1987) Critical Heuristics of Social Systems Design. *European Journal of Operational Research, 31*(3), 276-283.

Ulrich, W. (1993) Some Difficulties Of Ecological Thinking, Considered From A Critical Systems Perspective: A Plea For Critical Holism. *Systems Practice, 6*(6), 583-611.

Ulrich, W. (1994) Can We Secure Future-Responsive Management Through Systems Thinking And Design?. *Interfaces, An International Journal of The Institute of Management*

Sciences and the Operations Research Society of America, Special Section: In Celebration of C. West Churchman's 80 Years, 24(4), 26-37. Retrieved from: Prepublication version 1993 and 2002 by W. Ulrich, The Institute of Management Sciences.

Ulrich, W. (1998) Systems Thinking as if People Mattered: Critical Systems Thinking for Citizens and Managers. Working Paper No. 23. Lincolnshire: Lincoln School of Management, University of Lincolnshire & Humberside.

Ulrich, W. (2000) Reflective Practice In The Civil Society: The Contribution Of Critically Systemic Thinking. Reflective Practice, 1(2), 247-268.

Ulrich, W. (2002) Boundary Critique. In H.G. Daellenbach and R.L. Flood (Eds.), The Informed Student Guide to Management Science (pp. 41-42). London: Thomson.

Ulrich, W. (2003) A Brief Introduction to Critical Systems Thinking for Professionals & Citizens. Online Paper. Retrieved online September 12, 2005 from http://www.geocities.-com/csh_home/downloads/ulrich_2003b.pdf.

Ulrich, W. (2005). Can Nature Teach Us Good Research Practice? A Critical Look At Frederic Vester's Bio-Cybernetic Systems Approach (book review). Journal of Research Practice, 1(1), article R2.

UN (1972) Report of the United Nations Conference on the Human Environment, 5-16 June 1972. Stockholm, Sweden: United Nations.

UN (1983) General Assembly Resolution A/RES/38/161. Process of Preparation of the Environmental Perspective to the Year 2000 and Beyond. December 19, 1983, New York: United Nations.

UN (1992) UN Conference on Environment and Development (Earth Summit), Agenda 21, 3-14 June 1992, Rio de Janeiro.

UN (1995) Report of the World Summit for Social Development, A/CONF.166/9, March, 6-12, Copenhagen, Denmark: United Nations.

UN (1999) The World at Six Billion. Population Division, Department of Economic and Social Affairs, ESA/P/WP.154, 12 October 1999, New York: United Nations Secretariat.

UN (2000) Millennium Declaration. Adopted by the UN General Assembly, 8th Plenary Meeting, Document A/RES/55/2, September 8. United Nations.

UNCED (1992) The Convention on Biological Diversity, United Nations Conference on Environment and Development. United Nations.

UNDP (2006) Human Development Report 2006, Beyond Scarcity: Power, Poverty and the Global Water Crises. Hampshire: Palgrave.

UNEP (2006) GEO Year Book 2006: An Overview of Our Changing Environment. Hertfordshire, UK: Earthprint.

UNEP and UNDESA (2003) International Expert Meeting On the 10-Year Framework of Programmes For Sustainable Consumption and Production, Summary by the Co-Chairs of the Meeting, June, 16-19, Marrakech, Morocco.

UNEP and UNDESA (2005) Second International Expert Meeting On the 10-Year Framework of Programmes For Sustainable Consumption and Production, Summary by the Co-Chairs of the Meeting, September, 5-8, San José, Costa Rica.

Van Den Bergh, J. and Janssen, M. (2005) Economics of Industrial Ecology: Materials, Structural Change, and Spatial Scales. Cambridge: The MIT Press.

Velasquez, M. (2006) Business Ethics: Concepts and Cases (6th ed.). Upper Saddle River, NJ: Prentice Hall.

Vester, F. (1988) The Bio-Cybernetic Approach as a Basis For Planning Our Environment. *Systems Practice, Special Issue: C. West Churchman 75 Years*, W. Ulrich (Ed.), *1*(4), 399-413.

Vester, F. (1999) [original 1978] *Unsere Welt - ein vernetztes System* (10th ed.), Munich: dtv.

Vester, F. (2001) [original 1973] *Denken, Lernen, Vergessen* (28th ed.). Munich: dtv.

Vester, F. (2002) [original 1980] *Neuland des Denkens: Vom technokratischen zum kybernetischen Zeitalter* (12th ed.). Munich: dtv.

Vester, F. (2005) [original 1999] *Die Kunst vernetzt zu denken. Ideen und Werkzeuge für einen neuen Umgang mit Komplexität* (5th ed.). Munich: dtv.

Vickers, G. (1970) *Freedom in a Rocking Boat*. London: Penguin Books.

Vogel, D. J. (2005a) The Low Value of Virtue. *Harvard Business Review, 83*(6), 26-36.

Vogel, D. J. (2005b) *The Market for Virtue: The Potential and Limits of Corporate Social Responsibility*. Washington, D.C.: Brookings Institute.

Vries, B. J. M. (2013) *Sustainability Science*, Cambridge: Cambridge University Press

Walker, I.O. and Wirl, F. (1993) Irreversible Price-Induced Efficiency Improvements: Theory And Empirical Application To Road Transportation. *The Energy Journal 14*(4), 183-205.

Wallich, H. C. (1972, March 13) More on Growth. *Newsweek*, 86.

Warwick, H. (1998) Agent Orange: The Poisoning of Vietnam. *The Ecologist, 28*(5), 264-265.

Washida, T. (2004) *Economy-wide Model of Rebound Effect for Environmental Efficiency*, Proceedings of International Workshop on Sustainable Consumption (pp. 292-301), March 5-6, 2004, Leeds, UK: University of Leeds.

WBCSD (2000) *Measuring Eco-Efficiency: A Guide to Reporting Company Performance*. Geneva, Switzerland: World Business Council for Sustainable Development (WBCSD).

WBCSD (2004) *Doing Business With The Poor - A Field Guide*. Geneva, Switzerland: World Business Council for Sustainable Development (WBCSD).

WBCSD (2006a) *Eco-Efficiency - Learning Module*. Hertfordshire, UK: Earthprint.

WBCSD (2006b) *From Challenge to Opportunity: The Role Of Business In Tomorrow's Society*, Switzerland: Earthprint.

WBGU (1994) *Annual Report 1993: World in Transition: Basic Structure of Global People-Environment Interactions*. German Advisory Council on Global Change. Bonn: Economica Verlag.

WBGU (1995) *Annual Report 1994: World in Transition: The Threat to Soils*. Bonn: Economica Verlag.

WBGU (1997) *Annual Report 1996: World in Transition: The Research Challenge*. Berlin: Springer Verlag.

WBGU (1999) *Annual Report 1997: World in Transition: Ways Towards Sustainable Management of Freshwater Resources*. Berlin: Springer Verlag.

WBGU (2000) *Annual Report 1998: World in Transition: Strategies for Managing Global Environmental Risks*. Berlin: Springer Verlag.

WBGU (2001) *Annual Report 1999: World in Transition: Conservation and Sustainable Use of the Biosphere*. London: Earthscan.

WCED (1987) *Our Common Future*. New York: Oxford University Press.

Merriam Webster's Collegiate Dictionary (2004) (11th ed.). Springfield, MA: Merriam Webster.

Weizsäcker, E.U., Lovins, A.B., and Lovins, L.H. (1997) *Factor Four: Doubling Wealth, Halving Resource Use*. London: Earthscan.

Werre, M. (2003) Implementing Corporate Responsibility: The Chiquita Case. *Journal of Business Ethics, 44*(2-3), 247-260.

Wheatley, M.A. and Kellner-Rogers, M. (1996) *A Simpler Way*. San Francisco, CA: Berrett-Koehler.

Wheeler, D. and Elkington, J. (2001) The End of the Corporate Environmental Report? Or The Advent of Cybernetic Sustainability Reporting and Communication. Business *Strategy and the Environment, 10*(1), 1-14.

Wiedmann, T., Minx, J., Barrett, J. and Wackernagel, M. (2006) Allocating Ecological Footprints To Final Consumption Categories With Input- Output Analysis. *Ecological Economics, 56*(1), 28-48.

Wiener, N. (1948) *Cybernetics, or Control and Communication in the Animal and the Machine*. New York: John Wiley.

Wilson, E. and Peter, F. (Eds.) (1988) *Biodiversity*. Washington: National Academy Press.

Wolstenholme, E.F. (1990) *System Enquiry: A Systems Dynamics Approach*. Chichester, UK: John Wiley.

Wood, D. (1995) Stakeholder Mismatching: A Theoretical Problem in Empirical Research on Corporate Social Performance. *The International Journal of Organization Analysis, 3*(3), 229-267.

Woodward, L. (Ed.) (2001) *Eating Oil*, Summary Report. Berkshire: Elm Farm Research Centre.

WRI, (1999) Are Business and Industry Taking Sustainability Seriously? , Online Paper of t h e *World Resources Institute* (WRI). Retrieved online January 12, 2005 from http://earthtrends.wri.org/features/view_feature.php?theme=5&fid=2.

WTO (2005, August 1) *European Communities - The ACP-EC Partnership Agreement - Recourse to Arbitration Pursuant To The Decision of 14 November 2001*, WT/L616, Geneva, Switzerland: World Trade Organization.

WVS (2005) *World Values Survey 2005*. Ann Arbor, Michigan: World Values Survey Association.

Zavestovski, S. (2001) Environmental Concern and Anti-Consumerism in the Self-Concept: Do They Share The Same Basis?. In M.J. Cohen and J. Murphy (Eds.), *Exploring Sustainable Consumption* (pp. 173-190). Amsterdam: Pergamon.

Internet Sites of Corporations and Organizations Used

The following provides a summary of the main corporate internet sites visited in respect to the business cases. The following indicates the *main* sites. The particular (sub)page, from which information has been retrieved from, is given in the respective text passage as a footnote. These footnotes also entail the date at which the respective internet site was addressed.

Clean Clothes Campaign	http://www.cleanclothes.org
Club of Rome	http://www.clubofrome.org
CSCP	http://www.scp-centre.org
Dow Jones Sustainbility Indices	http://www.sustainability-indexes.com
Ethiscore	http://www.ethiscore.org
Global Exchange	http://www.globalexchange.org
Grameen Family of Enterprises	http://www.grameen-info.org
Greenpeace	http://www.greenpeace.org
Honey Care Africa	http://www.honeycareafrica.com
IKEA	http://www.IKEA.com
Intel Corporation	http://www.intel.com
Jessie Smith Noyes Foundation	http://www.noyes.org
KarstadtQuelle	http://www.karstadtquelle.com
Nike	http://www.nike.com
North Castle Partners	http://www.northcastlepartners.com
Odwalla	http://www.odwalla.com
Organic Consumers Association	http://www.organicconsumers.org
Plug Power	http://www.plugpower.com
Rainforest Alliance	http://www.rainforest-alliance.org
Realia Group	http://www.realiagroup.com
Royal Dutch Shell	http://www.shell.com
Stonyfield Farm	http://www.stoneyfield.com

Sustainability Institute	http://www.sustainabilityinstitute.org
SWOP, South West Organizing Project	http://www.swop.net
System Dynamics Society	http://www.systemdynamics.org
Tchibo	http://company.tchibo.de
The Body Shop	http://www.nike.com/index.jhtml
The Kalundborg Centre for Industrial Symbiosis	http://www.symbiosis.dk
The Natural Step	http://www.naturalstep.org
The Responsible Shopper	http://www.coopamerica.org/programs/rs
Threshold 21	http://www.threshold21.com
Unilever	http://www.unileverusa.com
Wal-Mart	http://walmartstores.com

Appendices

Appendix A: Archetypes

As stated, the dissertation in the chapters 3.2.2, 3.4.2 and appendix C refers to systems archetypes identified by Senge et al. All information on the archetypes below is taken from Senge 2006 and Braun 2002.

Appendix A1: Limits-to-Growth

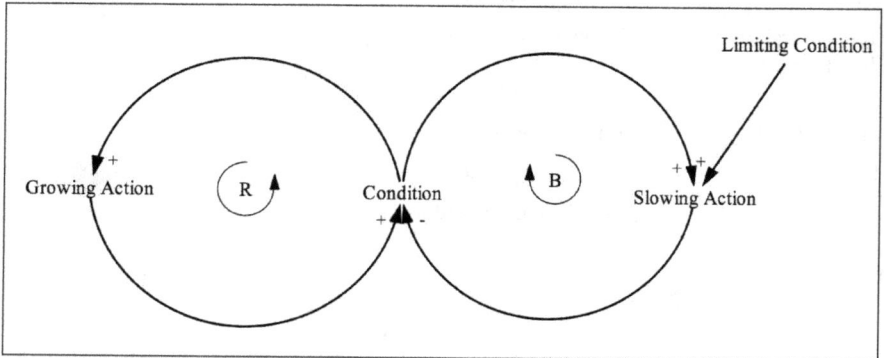

Fig. 46: Archetype: Limits-to-Growth
Source: Adapted from Senge 2006: 390

The following annotations to the Limits-to-Growth archetypes are taken from Senge 2006 (390f):

"Description: A process feeds on itself to produce a period of accelerating growth or expansion. Then the growth begins to slow [...] and eventually comes to a halt, and may even reverse itself and begin an accelerating collapse. [...]

Early Warning Symptom: 'Why should we worry about problems we don't have? We're growing tremendously.' (A little later, 'Sure there are some problems, but all we have to do is go back to what was working before.' Still later, 'The harder we run, the more we seem to stay in the same place.')

Management Principle: Don't push on the reinforcing (growth) process, remove (or weaken) the source of limitation."

Appendix A2: Shifting-the-Burden

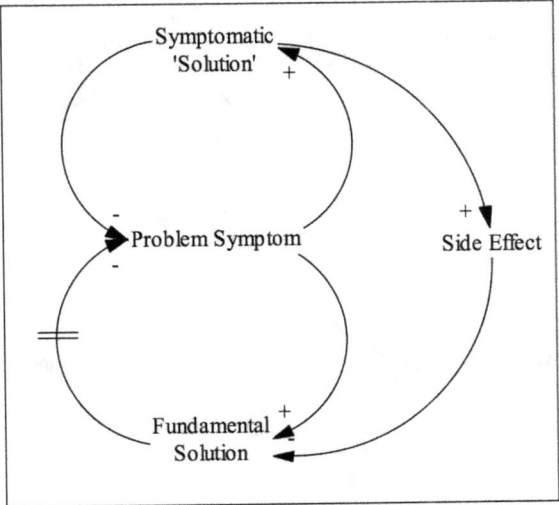

Fig. 47: Archetype: Shifting-the-Burden
Source: Adapted from Braun 2002: 4, see also Senge 2006: 392

The following annotations to the Limits-to-Growth archetypes are taken from Senge 2006 (391f):

"Description: A short-term 'solution' is used to correct a problem, with seemingly positive immediate results. As this correction is used more and more, more fundamental long-term corrective measures are used less and less. Over time, the capabilities for the fundamental solution may atrophy or become disabled, leading to even greater reliance on the symptomatic solution.

Early Warning Symptom: 'Look here, this solution has worked so far! What do you mean, there's trouble down the road?'

Management Principle: Focus on the fundamental solution. If symptomatic solution is imperative (because of delays in fundamental solution), use it to gain time while working on the fundamental solution."

Appendix A3: Escalation

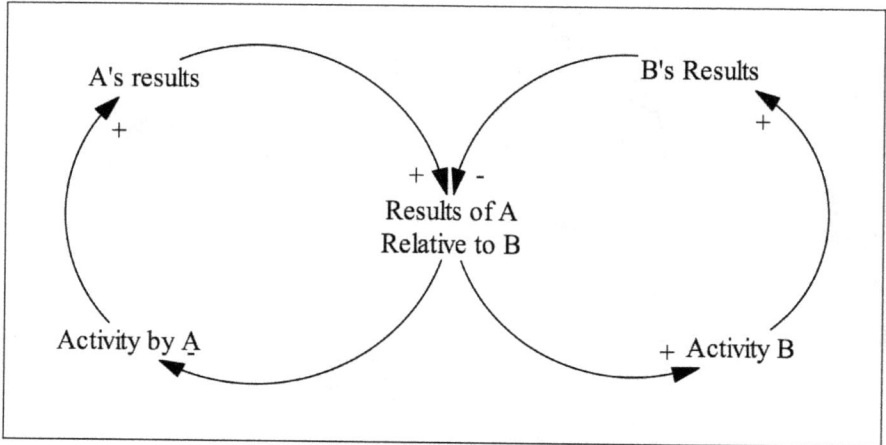

Fig. 48: Archetype: Escalation
Source: Adapted from Senge 2006: 395

The following annotations to the Limits-to-Growth archetypes are taken from Senge 2006 (395f):

"Description: Two people or organizations each see their welfare as depending on a relative advantage over the other. Whenever one side gets ahead, the other is more threatened, lead-ing it to act more aggressively to reestablish its advantage, which threatens the first, increas-ing its aggressiveness, and so on. Often each side sees its own aggressive behavior as a defen-sive response to the other's aggression; but each side action "in defense" results in a buildup that goes far beyond either side's desires.

Early Warning Symptom: "If our opponent would only slow down, then we could stop fighting this battle and get some other things done."

Management Principle: Look for a way for both sides to "win", or to achieve their objec-tives. In many instances, one side can unilaterally reverse the vicious spiral by taking overtly aggressive "peaceful" actions that cause the other to fell less threatened."

Appendix A4: Tragedy-of-the-Commons

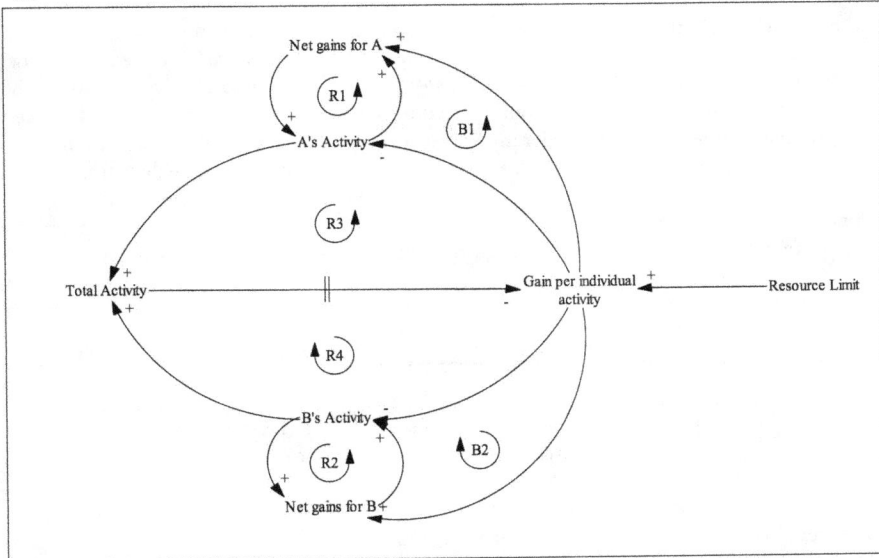

Fig. 49: Archetype: Tragedy of the Commons
Source: Adapted from Braun 2002: 12f, see also Senge 2006: 397

The following annotations to the Limits-to-Growth archetypes are taken from Senge 2006 (398):

"Description: Individuals use a commonly available but limited resource solely on the basis of individual need. At first they are rewarded for using it; eventually, they get diminishing returns, which causes them to intensify their efforts. Eventually, the resource is significantly depleted, eroded, or entirely used up.

Early Warning Symptom: 'There used to be plenty for everyone. Now things are getting tough. If I'm going to get any profit out of it this year, I'll have to work harder.'

Management Principle: Manage the 'commons' either through educating everyone and creating forms of self-regulation and peer pressure, or through an official regulating mechanism, ideally designed by participants."

The concept of Tragedy of the Commons was originally outlined by Hardin (1968).

Appendix B: Annotation on Reading Link Polarities

In the following the importance of the appendix used in the explanation of link polarity (i.e. that a change in v1 increases/decreases v2 *above/below what v2 would have been otherwise*) shall be discussed more in depth Sterman (2004: 138ff). In order to clarify this aspect, the dissertation will use a positive link often referred to in the field of sustainability. As has been outlined, many current corporate operations (especially in the industrial sector) produce environmental damage (unsustainability), e.g. in form of waste, pollution or exhausting natural resources. In this case, it can be stated: If corporate operations increase (get more), environmental damage increases above what it otherwise would have been. If corporate operations decrease (get less), environmental damage decreases below what it otherwise would have been.

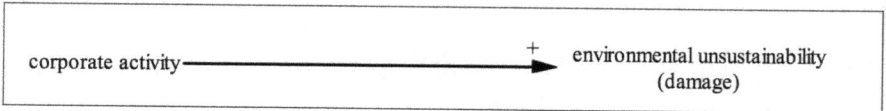

Fig. 50: Differentiating Stocks and Flows (Example)
Source: Produced by the author

In order to understand the importance of the appendix[557], it is necessary to switch into a stock-and-flow perspective: Environmental unsustainability (damage) is a stock, while corporate activity is a flow, which *always adds* to the stock (i.e. to environmental unsustainability).

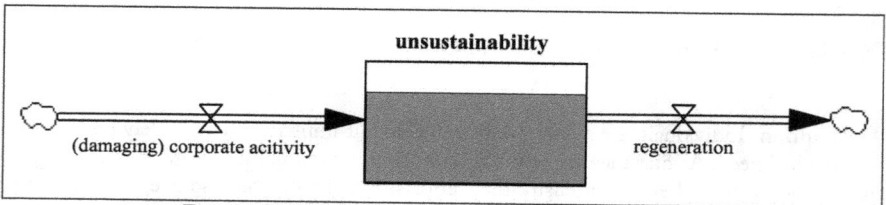

Fig. 51: Stock-and-Flow Diagram of Unsustainability
Source: Produced by the author

Even if corporate activity is reduced (less), it still *adds* to unsustainability. That is, the stock environmental unsustainability increases (not decreases). However, environmental unsustainability increases *less high (less fast)*, i.e. corporate activity *adds less* to environmental unsustainability.

In other words: If corporate activity (v1) *would not* be reduced, but would flow in the stock at the same rate, the level of environmental unsustainability (damage) would be higher than with the change (the reduction).

If environmental unsustainability however *is* reduced (i.e. flows into the stock at a lower rate), the *level* of environmental damage *decreases below what it otherwise would have been*, - but the stock environmental unsustainability as such still increases (only *less fast*) (Sterman

---

557 That is, the expression 'above/below what it otherwise would have been'.

2004: 139). Why this differentiation is crucial for the field of sustainability, was revealed in the CO_2 example (chapter 2.2.4.1 on operating thinking).

The equivalent is the case, when a flow *substracts* from a stock in a ***negative link***: The flow always substracts. If v1 (the cause variables) is reduced, it *substracts less* than otherwise, but it results in a reduction of v2 and not in an increase (Sterman 2004: 139).[558]

The simplification of 'same' and 'opposite' direction

It was important to the dissertation to outline, that there is a differentiation between stocks and flows. This difference is important, because causal-loop-diagrams, which the dissertation uses, do not reveal if a variable is a stock or a flow. Therefore it is important to use the signs "+"and "-" and explain, what they imply (i.e. annotations of appendix above).

Quite frequently instead of '+' and '-', the signs 'S' and 'O' are used in causal-loop-diagramming (e.g. in Senge et. al 1994 and Kim 1992). This means the following: In the case of a positive link, polarity v2 ***moves in the same ('S') direction*** as v2, and in the case of a negative link polarity v2 ***move in the opposite ('O') direction***.

The advantage of this wording is that it is easier to understand and in the foremost cases is correct. It thus provides a mnemonic. – But as has been outlined above, it is not correct in all cases. Richardson has pointed to the problematic of using S and O and the corresponding wording of 'moving in the same direction' respectively 'moving in the opposite direction' (Richardson 1986 and 1997).[559]

Therefore inline with Richardson and Sterman, the dissertation uses the signs +/- and has explained their implications, i.e. the appendix (above/below what v2 otherwise would have been) thoroughly. Out of reasons of simplicity, the dissertation does not always mention this appendix, when outlining causalities in systems (especially in part III of the dissertation). However, the appendix is always to be added in the mind of the reader, when tracing causal-loop-diagrams.

---

558 In the CO2 example, e.g. unsustainability always reduces (unfavorably impacts) regeneration. If unsustainability (environmental damage) is reduced, there is still damage, which reduces the rate of regeneration. But the reduction of the rate of regeneration will be less strong (high). Therefore the regeneration rate will increase above what it otherwise would have been.

559 Richardson (1997) suggests using the following wording: A positive link (arrow) from v1 to v2 indicates that v1 adds to v2 (additive influence), or, that a change in v1 causes a change in v2 in the same direction, i.e. a positive correlation, (proportional influence). A negative link from v1 to v2 indicates that v1 subtracts from v2, or, a change in v1 causes a change in v2 in the opposite direction. The wording used in the dissertation with the appendix (above/below what v2 otherwise would have been) is equally correct, as outlined by Sterman (2004: 138ff).

Appendix C: Traps in a Trade-off Model (Non Accountability)

C1) Model Analysis

Underlying belief about Corporate Sustainability

The underlying belief about the relationship between economic sustainability (profit maximization) and social and environmental sustainability is:

> *Environmental sustainability and social sustainability reduce profit. Therefore, businesses should not be accountable for environmental or social sustainability.*

The argumentation of this belief of a Trade-off Model is similar to the following: "Caring for people and the environment is important, but it is not the tasks of businesses. Environmental and social sustainability reduce profit. Businesses cannot be held accountable for environmental or social sustainability. It is not without reason that our society is based on the division of labor. There are other institutions, such as legislators or interest groups/NGOs, which are responsible for environmental protection and social care. Beyond this, each of our employees is free to commit his/her spare time to environmental protection or social aid.
It would be irresponsible of us to spent money on planet and people, thus reducing profit and endangering the jobs we provide. There is a fierce competition out there on the market and if we do not concentrate on our profits we will be out of the game pretty soon."

Underlying Model Dynamic

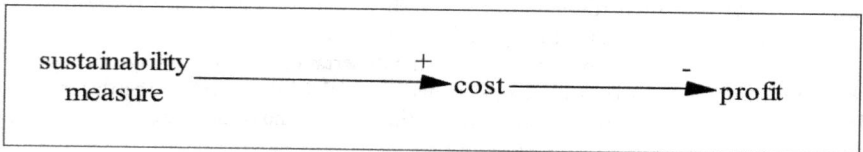

Fig. 52: Trade-Off Model: Model Dynamics
Source: Produced by the author

The 'Model Dynamic' corporations holding a Trade-off Model believe in and act according to, is no dynamic in the narrow sense, as there is no feedback. Consequently a Trade-off Model does not meet Doyle and Ford' minimum requirement for a mental model that it is a closed' system, i.e. two variables and two causal relationships (Doyle and Ford 1998: 18). The Trade-Off Model rather is based on a *linear* belief that sustainability measures lead to higher costs (not investments), which reduce profit without any return for the corporation (see figure 53). The model dynamic of the Trade-off Model is often coupled with the argumentation, that reducing unsustainability/creating sustainability is not the task of corporations (non-accountability argumentation), but rather that of NGOs, governments or other social agents.

Model Characteristics (Polarity Profile)

The following polarity-profile provides an overview of the characteristics of the Trade-off Model. The individual characteristics will be discussed in the following below.

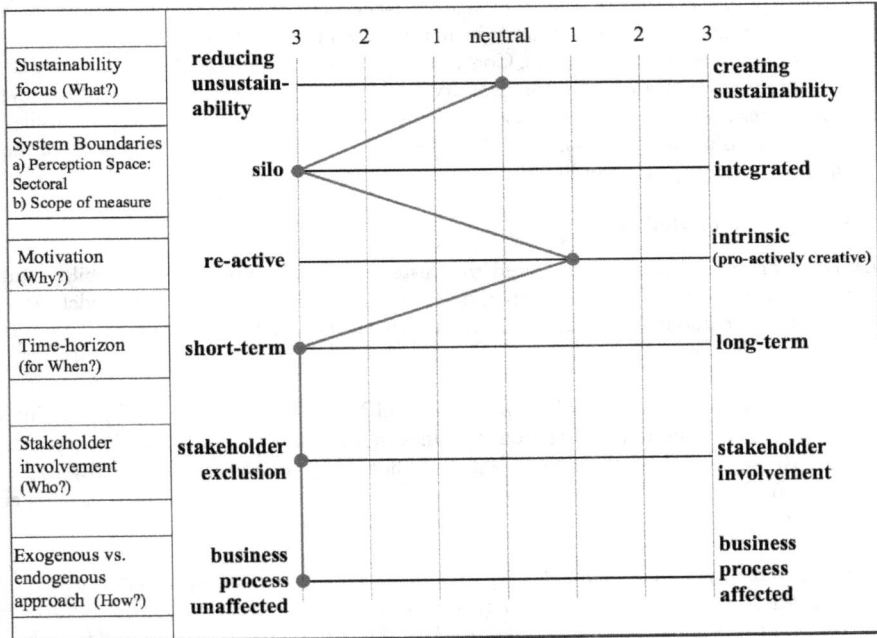

Fig. 53: Trade-Off Model: Polarity Profile
Source: Produced by the author

A trade-off encompasses an either-or-decision: Either spend money on sustainability or increase profit. Achieving both simultaneously is not possible according to this model. The Trade-off Model clearly is based on a *sectoral mental model of perception space* (see polarity profile). Furthermore, the Trade-off Model is a strongly *silo-oriented* concept as all focus lies on increasing economic sustainability. Companies holding a Trade-off Model do not engage in any voluntarily sustainability measure[560]. The focus of corporate measures (actions) lies *neither in reducing unsustainability nor in promoting sustainability*. This is indicated in the polarity profile through the value zero (neutral) for this point. To the contrary, the companies oppose sustainability initiatives. Consequently, companies that hold a Trade-off Model, lobby against sustainability regulations, because the companies fear that sustainability regulations will augment their costs. As the companies lobby actively against regulations on sustainability, the Trade-off Model can be considered slightly *pro-active* (polarity-profile).

---

560 The dissertation presumes that corporations holding a Trade-off Model (and all other models) do comply with legal requirements regarding sustainability. Thus the dissertation does not treat deliberate illegal behavior of corporations.

The *business process* thereby remains fully *unaffected*. If regulations are enforced nevertheless, the focus of the company is to implement the regulations at the lowest costs possible. A Trade-off Model does not consider ecological and social sustainbility inevitable in order to stay profitable in the long run. The focus is *short-term* profit oriented (see polarity-profile). Companies holding a Trade-off Model do not engage in sustainability measures (besides those that cannot be bypassed legally). Consequently, there is no *stakeholder involvement* regarding sustainbility measures. To the contrary, there is rather the tendency of withholding information regarding unsustainability, as the companies fear bad press (see polarity-profile). If the company is accused of unsustainability, it considers the case to be a private issue of the company and deals with it accordingly.

Relations to Other Models

The Trade-off Model can be considered the 'historical' mental model of sustainbility and therefore still has influence, when corporations formerly holding a Trade-off Model move towards other mental model of sustainbility. This has been outlined in-depth above in chapter 3.1.3.

As also stated above, corporations holding a Trade-off Model have a high risk of getting into Sustainbility Traps. The traps differ from the ones in other models insofar as the traps are triggered through corporate operations, which do not target to increase sustainbility in the first place. In the following two traps common to corporations, holding a Trade-off Model will be outlined.

*In line with the dissertation' aim of showing that it is often systemic structures, which create Sustainability Traps rather than individual agents, the dissertation will outline traps, which are caused through **systemic structures** created through the interactions of a **corporation and its stakeholders**. In these cases, playing the blame-game of accusing the corporation as the sole usurpator consequently would be a misconception of the situation.*

In the following two Sustainbility Traps will be discussed, which are very common for corporations following a Trade-off Model. These are:

- *Job-Creation Trap (chapter c2)*
- *Fighting-the-Enemy Trap (chapter c3)*

C2) Job-Creation Trap

Archetypical Trap Structure

The Job-Creation Trap can result from a corporation's interaction with local communities and governments. The trap risks to arise, when creating jobs (social sustainability) through business (economic sustainability), yet thereby putting up with environmental sustainability as a trade-off.

The slogan 'social is, whatever creates jobs' was one largely used by various political parties in the German federal elections of 2005[561] and underscores the actuality of this attitude, not only in emerging and developing countries, but also in Western societies. Underlying is the belief that measures of environmental sustainability (or other measures of social sustainability) are a trade-off to economic sustainability and thus to job creation.

Creating jobs and economic growth at the expense of environmental sustainability is a trap that risks backfiring on the community as well as on the company and eventually can even lead to a future *reduction* of jobs as will be outlined below. The structure of the trap is that of a limits-to-growth. This trap can be considered a particular manifestation (type) of the basic limits-to-growth structure.[562] The trap has occurred multiple times in history and is therefore well known, although hardly analyzed in its archetypical structure.

The Job-Creation Trap provides a good structure to start with in outlining Sustainability Traps, because compared to further traps it is quite simple. The following causal-loop-diagramming using systemic structures illustrate the trap:

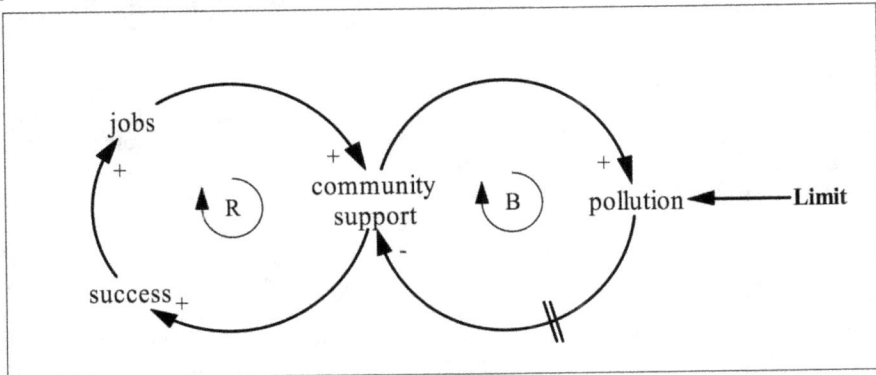

Fig. 54: Job-Creation Trap
Source: Produced by the author

---

561 The slogan stems from the Initiative New Social Market Economy (Initiative Neue Soziale Marktwirtschaft), which is known to support the corporate lobby (German wording of the slogan: Sozial ist, was Arbeit schafft).
562 See appendix A1.

The above dynamic (structure) of the job creation trap can be described as follows: When a major business announces that it plans to open a production facility in a certain country/ region, the different local communities, especially the local governments, of that region often try to outstrip each other with tax-benefits, investments in infrastructure and innovative ideas. The community, where the business finally settles, considers itself a 'winner', local government is considered successful and the business is welcomed enthusiastically.

All because of the one reason: The business provides jobs for the region. A contribution to positive image or other factors can also contribute to the enthusiasm, but most of the time job creation stands first place. Thus, the community supports the business: People from the community start to work motivated, local government provides additional infrastructure and tax benefits, local businesses (e.g. catering services, cleaning services) offer their services, etc. This community support contributes to the business' success and growth. As the corporation grows, it employs more people, which in turn increase the community's enthusiasm and support for the business, which in turn fosters the business' success. The loop on the left thus reinforces the company's growth through the support of the community (reinforcing loop R). The company grows and grows and become an additional or even the solely "light house" of the region - a success example.

However, as the business grows so does the pollution and waste the business creates. , because in this structure both - corporation and community - ignore environmental sustainability and/or consider it a trade-off. In a growth situation not only the intended output (products, services) grows, but also the 'negative' outputs such as noise, waste, destruction of forests or grasslands[563]. When the amount of pollution exceeds a certain tolerated limit, the community's support for the business starts to decrease. There will be resistance from the side of the community, which in turn threatens to lower the success of the business (Balancing Loop B). This will not occur suddenly, but gradually (note the delay mark). The limit here is the social license to operate depending on the perceived environmental damage and its effects. If the community's apprehensions though are not addressed by the business fast enough or not in the scope considered necessary, the community support might *inverse* into community resistance, such as threat of rigid regulations, strikes of the workers, public protests or even activists attacks or others. In this case the former growth-structure can reverse into a downward spiral. Instead of exponential growth, the reinforcing loop (the former 'growth loop R' on the left) will lead to exponential decline: Because of the community's resistance, the success of the company is reduced, which at some point will lead to dismissals. This reduction in jobs in turn will increase the community's protests against the company, which will lead to less success for the business etc.

At the end, the community often does not notice that it is fighting something, which it contributed to itself, as it was the community, which provided the conditions for corporate growth that is now causing problems, because of to much pollution. *Therefore, responsibility can not only be laid on the corporation alone, but equally lies in the behavior of the community that contributes to the above structure.* The situation the community finds itself in reminds of the 'Zauberlehrling' in the homonymous poetry of Johann Wolfgang von Goethe: "The ghosts I called I can't get rid of now" (Goethe 1797).

---

563 For example due to construction.

As mentioned, the process described is an idealized one. Often a minority of the community, which is sustainably responsible, will point to possible pollution risks of an industrial plant right at the beginning. But usually these groups are not taken seriously. Often they are considered troublemakers, which might endanger the settlement of the company and thus the outlook of job creation. Correspondingly, when the support within the community tips, because more and more people are concerned about health risks due to the pollution of the plant, there often remains a minority within the community that still supports the company. These might be politicians which consider the settlement of the company their personal success and want to keep the success story going, by accepting pollution as an inevitable side-effect. Other politicians might sense the change in public opinion and press the company to take measures of pollution reduction. Employees are often caught up in between. On the one side the company is providing their jobs and stricter regulations on pollution will lead to higher costs for the company and the success of the company might be endangered as the global competition is fierce.[564] On the other hand, the workers are concerned about their health and those of their families living in the community.

Dealing with the Trap

The structure of the trap described above is not inevitable when companies grow, of course. However, it is very likely to occur, if the business and the community do not deal with the *limits of pollution*. In principle, there are two points when to intervene in the structure of the system:

One possibility of dealing with the structure is to intervene when the limit has already kicked in and the community starts to complain about the pollution. This is a very common point of intervention in the system, because it is based on the reaction to *symptoms* of the structure (the complaints of the community). Knowledge about the underlying structure is not necessary. Although this point of intervention might still be early enough to avoid the inversion of the reinforcing loop into a downwards-cycle, it is still a late stage at which to intervene in the system. It bears the following disadvantages: The pollution has already piled up over the limit (the variable 'pollution' in the structure is a stock[565]). Therefore, business and community will have to deal with legacy problems: They will not only have to reduce the pollution, which occurs in the current production process, but will also have to dismantle the 'old' pollution, which has piled up over the time. Once the old pollution has reached a tipping point in the eco-system, e.g. waters have turned over, soil is salinated, animal population is extinct etc., the restoration can proof very expensive. Besides these direct costs, the business has to deal with its tattered community relationships and possible bad press. As long as the pollution is somewhere near the limit (or threatens to rise up again), the community is likely to be resistant. Even when unsustainability is reduced significantly, it is likely to take a considerable amount of time until the trust between both parties is restored. It is also likely, that it takes much longer re-established the original enthusiastic atmosphere. Until then, the

---

564 This is what is also often stated by the company inline with its mental model of a Trade-Off.

565 See also chapter 2.2.4.

business has to deal with the lack of support of the community and negative image, which risks to affect the business unfavorably.

A more effective and most of the time cheaper solution would be to account for limits right at the beginning. This presumes that both sides are aware of the limits-to-growth structure and its implications: It is important to understand that nothing can grow exponentially forever. If there is a reinforcing loop that promotes growth, there inevitably will be a limit to growth (Senge 2006: 96).

Environmental pollution is surly not the only limit, but it is an important one. So how can the social parties deal with this pollution-limit? A twofold approach is necessary, which consists of first defining the limits and second take actions to prevent their surpassing:

First, both parties (business and community) need to come together and identify possible limiting factors in cooperation. These need not only to be limits in the field of environmental sustainability, but also in the field of social sustainability. It might be helpful to consult with experts (such as universities, NGOs, etc.). Subsequently both parties should agree on quantitative or qualitative limits in the areas identified, which the company agrees to keep or not exceed. These limits can and most likely will differ from the limits in legal regulations and even from the limits that the company might have set for itself[566].

Second, the parties will have to talk about how not to exceed the limits. These can be additional investments in technologies, change of procedures etc. Last but not least, a control mechanism needs to be installed that monitors the process and indicates, if limits have to be adjusted.

If the corporation manages to keep below the limits, the likelihood of steady growth is higher.[567] Corporate growth might be slower than when not providing for the limits (as this takes time and investments), but in turn there will be no sudden crash, which leads to decline or at best levels the growth.[568] This procedure though, implies a shift away from the Trade-off Model. The planning period is long-term rather than short-term, as the business will need to consider the future limitations of unsustainability by broadening system boundaries in time. In addition, the business will need to shift its perception from sustainability measures as costs, towards a view of seeing them as an *investment* for contributing to future growth. Furthermore, the business will need to learn to include stakeholders, the community and probably some experts (NGO, researcher) in its planning process.

It might be objected, that setting limits to unsustainability is not enough. And yes, it has to be admitted that 'more' is possible than suggested above. Instead of setting *limits to unsustainability*, it can proof to be more effective to focus on *targets for sustainability*. This would mean neither a goal like "we plan not to exceed limit x", nor a goal like "we plan to reduce y

---

566 Even though a company holding a Trade-off Model is unlikely to have defined such limits in their company policy.

567 Even though it is almost impossible to think of all the possible limits, reducing the unsustainability-limit is an important step. Furthermore, growth itself might not be the only factor for success of the business.

568 Note, that this is a case of 'orchestrating' solutions in the sense that with the same measure, the (financial) situation gets worse, before it gets better. The essential idea of investments, which is a measure in-line with dynamic complexity. For dynamic complexity see chapter 2.2.5.7.

by 20%". Nevertheless, it would imply creating conditions for a dynamic, which leads to more sustainability. The reason why the dissertation did not put forward such a solution is that it is likely to overstrain a company holding a Trade-off Model and thus might lead to failure. The suggested solution already asks for tremendous changes from the corporation as pointed out above. As mentioned, moving towards sustainability is an incremental process. If reducing unsustainability and involving stakeholders proofs to be successful for the company, it might take further steps. Some companies in emerging markets even identify an integrated set of possible contributions they can offer to communities beforehand and use this as an argument to gaining admission and support in these areas (Diamond 2005: 441ff).

Business Examples of Job Creation Trap
Business Case: Intel

In 1980, Intel announced plans to build a new chip fabrication plant just outside Rio Rancho near Albuquerque in New Mexico, USA. By 2002, Rio Rancho had become Intel's largest manufacturing plant. The site is primarily a manufacturing site, currently developing flash memory chips, as well as Intel® Celeron® and Intel® Pentium® processors.[569] Today, Intel employs approximately 5,200 employees at the Rio Rancho plant[570] and is the largest private-sector industrial employer in Albuquerque[571]. Intel has become the 'light-house' of the area.[572] The following case deals with one of the biggest expansion processes at the Rio Rancho side in Intel's history and how Intel experienced limits-to-growth due to toxic soil and air pollution. The dissertation will discuss the effects of the structure on workers and on the community's support/resistance and eventually on Intel itself.

Back in 1992, Intel and the state of New Mexico announced an enormous expansion of the Rio Rancho plant, funded by the launch of a bond issue, which was the largest one ever floated in the state. By 1995, it amounted US$ 10 billion. The expansion was fully implemented. The Southwest Organizing Project (SWOP), based in Albuquerque, held a critical view on Intel's expansion and its support by the state. SWOP is a statewide multi-racial, multi-issue, community based membership organization, founded in 1980. SWOP's mission is "working to empower our communities to realize racial and gender equality and social and economic justice."[573] SWOP had found that Intel had been a major pollutant at former production plants. Intel's first factory in the United States in Mountain View, had become the second largest area with underground toxic pollution in Santa Clara County and threatened the San Francisco Bay. The Environmental Protection Agency (EPA) estimated it could take up to sixty years to do a full cleanup of the toxic solvent trichloroethylene (TCE) underground plume spreading from it (Hollender and Fenichel 2004: 63). On the Rio Rancho plant toxic elements were also registered which can lead to organ damages, blood poisoning,

---

569 http://www.intel.com/jobs/usa/sites/RioRancho/; accessed: 10.Sept.2005.

570 http://www.intel.com/jobs/usa/sites/riorancho/facts.htm; accessed: 10.Sept.2005.

571 http://www.intel.com/jobs/usa/sites/RioRancho/; accessed: 10.Sept. 2005.

572 The facts about the following case are taken from the Intel website (www.intel.com, accessed 12. September 2005) as well as from Hollender and Fenichel 2004, if not indicated otherwise specifically.

573 http://www.swop.net/aboutswop.htm; accessed: 10.Sept.2005.

miscarriages and others. These pose not only health concerns for the community, but consequently also threaten to reduce the productivity of the workers.[574]

SWOP executive director Jeanne Guana perceived the situation as an exploitation of the community, mainly consisting of Spanish-Americans as well as a cultural clash, which she was not willing to accept. She stated that "working class people of color have paid the historical price of disproportionate and adverse affects of toxic chemicals in and around the communities where we live, work and play" (Hollender and Fenichel 2004: 64-65). The Governor, Bruce King, in contrast held a different view regarding the expansion of the Rio Rancho plant. He considered the toxic pollution as price of a trade-off, which had to be paid in order to provide jobs for the people in the community (Hollender and Fenichel 2004: 64): "If we let the land be ruined, it's usually ruined forever. Nevertheless, we cannot afford to forget the people who need a chance to make a living. You've got to decide how high the return has to be in terms of payroll to make it worthwhile to accept damage to the land." This argumentation is clearly inline with the Trade-off Model. The trade-off view is especially evident here, since the Governor was not unaware of the pollution (e.g. due to lack of knowledge). He even considered the long-term implications of the pollution (the land will usually be ruined forever) and deliberately accepted them as an inevitable trade-off for new jobs. In his statement, the governor strictly avoids a systemic argumentation, not mentioning that damage to the land most likely means damage to the people, but choose to put forward the silo-oriented view of a trade-off.

SWOP reacted by publishing a booklet entitled "Intel Inside New Mexico" in 1995 (SWOP 1995), that documented Intel's environmental track record. In the report, SWOP proposed the view that tax breaks and other financial benefits, which were made in the context of the issuing of the bond were so enormous that they outgrew the financial benefits of job creation and hence where a burden for the taxpayers of the county. Furthermore, the report raised serious questions about the amount of water used in the manufacturing process (especially since New Mexico is a desert) as well as about the quality and character of emissions into the air. Last but not least, it expressed doubt about whether the new jobs, which were to be created, would truly be given to New Mexicans as has been promised.
SWOP's request to meet with Intel representatives to discuss the issues where turned down by the company, until local press started to report about the issue and public concerns grew. Intel finally agreed to meet with Jeanne Guana alone, which she rejected, as she did not feel that a many-to-one meeting was a fruitful atmosphere to address the problems. Guana turned to her friend and supporter Stephen Viederman, president of the Jessie Smith Noyes Foundation in New York, to seek advice on what step to take next. The Jessie Smith Noyes Foundation had shifted its focus to family planning and environmentalism by the mid-1980s and held Intel stocks in their portfolio. The foundation promotes a sustainable and just social and natural system by supporting grassroots organizations and movements committed to this goal.[575] From Viederman's perspective, SWOP was the ideal Jessie Smith Noyes grantee,

---

574 A full list of toxics still emitted by the plant today and possible health risks can be found at: http://www.swop.net/chemlist.htm; accessed: 10.Sept. 2005.
575 http://www.noyes.org/; accessed: 10. September 2005.

as it was a relatively new grassroots-organization concerned with environmental and social aspects, which was well organized and managed. He was impressed by the environmental reporting in the "Intel Inside New Mexico" report (Hollender and Fenichel 2004: 66). Viederman held the view that "the more pressure we put on big corporations to become better social agents the better, [...] because I don't believe that they will do anything that they don't have to do" (Hollender and Fenichel 2004: 67). Therefore, Viederman considered the highest leverage for a partnership with SWOP was to use the foundation's Intel stocks as a vehicle for action.

In May 1994, Viederman and Guana showed up at Intel's annual shareholders meeting and demanded to know why Intel was not responding to SWOP's "Intel inside New Mexico" report. Andrew S. Grove, back then the chief operating officer, and later the chief executive officer at Intel, commented: "We at Intel do not deal with vocal minorities" (Hollender and Fenichel 2004: 64). In the fall of 1994, Noyes filed a shareholder resolution to be voted on at Intel's 1995 annual shareholders meeting. The resolution instructed Intel to revise its Environmental, Health and Safety (EHS) policy to commit the company to sharing information with community-based organizations. This was an attempt to shift Intel's perception form a shareholder to a broader stakeholder model. For until then, Intel's EHS policy committed it to share knowledge with employees, customers, the scientific community and the government only, but not with the community. Furthermore, the foundation granted SWOP money to purchase Intel stock, in order to make SWOP not only a stakeholder, but also a shareholder. Filing the resolution got SWOP on Intel's agenda. In December 1994, an Intel corporate vice president and the manager of the New Mexico site traveled to New York in order to meet with Viederman. As Viederman describes it, the gentlemen "pulled thick notebooks from their briefcases, filled with data on water usage, air emissions, and the like, as the basis for a discussion of the issues raised by SWOP" (Hollender and Fenichel 2004. 69). Viederman refused to get into a discussion with them. He explained that the foundation's concern was Intel's accountability and transparency to its community and that the community should be the one talking to. Viederman also noted that he felt that there was a culture at Intel that needed to change and that SWOP could be an aid in this regard.

As a result of this conversation Intel initiated facilitated discussions with SWOP in January 1995, which continued for most of the year. Both parties learned more about each other's cultures. Viederman later explained: "A continuing issue was Intel's culture of secrecy concerning such things as their suppliers and subcontractors" (Hollender and Fenichel 2004: 70). Noyes Foundation filed a second shareholder resolution in order to include information sharing with communities into Intel's EHS policy. The resolution received support from 5 percent of the shareholders voting, with 8 percent abstaining. By the early fall 1995 Viederman simply refiled his resolution from the prior year for the annual meeting in 1996. In December 1995, Viederman finally received a draft of a revised EHS policy that included information sharing with the community as requested. Thus, the resolution for 1996 was withdrawn.

Intel started to move away from their Trade-off Model at least in the sense that they started to accept the community (respectively SWOP) to be a legitimate stakeholder of the company. Viederman points out: "Intel became much more open with us on a number of issues of accountability and transparency. They have been more receptive to SWOP and other communities' approaches to them, and have often provided information before SWOP had to request it. Intel, however, still has a distance to travel. Sharing information is not yet intuitive for them" (Hollender and Fenichel 2004: 71). Thus Intel started to shift away from the rigid Trade-off Model towards a Compliance Model, where it was considered more feasible to cooperate with the community, start to listen and try to comply with their demands, - than having to deal with new resolutions and bad press at the annual shareholder meetings. This step of opening up, created an atmosphere at Intel, which made it possible for a young EHS officer in the company, Dave Stangis, to establish - against quite some resistance – the function of a 'Manager Corporate Responsibility' at Intel. His goal was to create a single point of contact for corporate accountability and social responsibility issues at Intel. In the position of a Corporate Responsibility Manager, Stangis planned to initiate stakeholder engagement in CSR issues; manage (together with Investor Relations Department) relationships with socially responsible stock indices and holdings; monitor for impact to Intel's reputation and communicate new CSR strategies proactively. The main barrier Stangis encountered when struggling to create the position as he states, was the belief of his superiors that "we were doing this stuff already" (Hollender and Fenichel 2004: 72). This is a common denial mechanism identified by Doppelt (Doppelt 2003: 244). Stangis was finally granted the position on condition that he would not create a whole bureaucracy to manage this new function.

At first Stangis was disappointed with this decision until he realized its potential. Stangis had to implement his plans in accordance with the low-hierarchy and low-bureaucracy culture at Intel. He was forced to design his function in line-with the existing intra-organizational structure. Stangis realized this would have to be in form of a virtual network. In practice, he had to pull people from all over the company who might be right, whenever he needed to mount a new program or initiative. This kind of internal structure had the great advantage that people from different parts of Intel got involved in sustainability initiatives temporarily and could later act as sustainability incubators in their area. It was a grass-root approach, which worked effectively in the Intel culture. This internal structure efficiently facilitated the shift away from a Trade-off Model towards other less conflicting or even supportive mental models regarding sustainability by actually engaging people within the organization. Stangis explains: "I can say with some confidence that everyone I've met inside Intel sincerely *wants* to do the right thing. They just don't necessary know what that is. I see my job as helping them to figure that out. We found that a lot of people in the company cared deeply about this stuff, but had nowhere to go until we gave them an outlet" (Hollender and Fenichel 2004: 73).

Stangis did not only design the internal structure fittingly to a new mental model on sustainability, but he also changed the structure in stakeholder interaction so that it too would support a different mental model. He visited communities and NGOs throughout the country to find out what were Intel's sustainability issues according to these groups. He knew that some organizations, as SWOP, had studied Intel for years and had valuable data, which could help him in his work. Stangis actually sought potential confrontations as he learned that this knowledge could pay enormous dividends not only in the field of risk reduction, but also on Intel's reputation.[576] Stangis has proven to be the best insurance policy against CSR risk to the company (Hollender and Fenichel 2004: 74). Knowing that NGO engagement is "a process with no end" (Hollender and Fenichel 2004: 74), Stangis repeats his travels and interactions with the NGOs several times a year. Instead of touring every one of Intel's fifteen major production centers in seven countries, he engaged local communities and especially the socially responsible investing community, to do some of the research for him. Hollender and Fenichel judge Stangis' achievements the following way (Hollender and Fenichel 2004: 74):" It's not just that Intel now dodges shareholder resolutions before they arise, or that they're just being clever about keeping NGOs off their backs. The real moral of the story is that by opening up this channel of communication, [...] Intel is now not only 'talking to vocal minorities' [...] but actively listening to them, and learning from them as well."

Today Intel's focus of engagement within communities is education, for which the company runs multiple projects all over the world.[577] Intel however has still some way to go: SWOP lists over 80 toxic chemical compounds, with possible health risks, which the company is still emitting today.[578] Also Intel's Corporate Business Principles do not refer to communities or the environment directly, when stating who is to benefit from Intel's actions: "In our complicated work environment, we often face challenging and ambiguous issues. It is our responsibility to work through those issues in a disciplined fashion and reach the right result for Intel, its shareholders and employees."[579] The Intel case provides an insightful example how mental models on sustainability, if supported by corresponding structures, can change the results of a company. At the beginning, pollution was a limiting factor to Intel's success as it faced severe stakeholder and shareholder resistance. Today, having shifted away from the Trade-off Model and engaging with the 'sources of resistance', the community and interest groups, pollution reduction has become a vehicle for Intel to learn about sustainability, stakeholder communication, risk reduction, driving innovation and other fields.

Further Business Examples of Job Creation Trap

If a company does not at all react to limits of sustainability put forward by the local community, this can lead to a complete stop of the operations. This happened to the **Bougainville copper mine** 1989 (Papua New Guinea), was shut down by angry landowners because of environmental damage. Despite the efforts of the country's police force and army, the mine could never reopen. Instead, the police and army intervention provoked a civil war (Diamond (2005): 448).

Sustainability limits need not only concern the environment or health risks. They also concern e.g. aspects of aesthetical living in the community, of atmosphere and feel good, as the following example shows: **Costco**, a wholesale corporation, faced strong opposition from merchants and community leaders in the city of Cuernavaca, Mexico. The company was ac-

---

576 See also Compliance and Reputation Leadership Model.
577 see: http://www.intel.com/community/; accessed: 10. Sept. 2005.
578 see: http://www.swop.net/chemlist.htm; accessed: 10. Sept. 2005.
579 http://www.intel.com/intel/finance/docs/CBP%20-%20Intro.pdf; accessed: 10. Sept. 2005.

cused of destroying historical sides of the central city by locating one of its big-box stores right in downtown Cuernavaca (Hollender and Fenichel 2004: 39).

Thus, in this example Costco faced the limits at the community of Cuernavaca right from the start. It is an interesting example of a community that does not hold a Trade-off Model and confronts the business holding a Trade-off Model with sustainability issues right from the start. However, looking at a larger system, this example can also be considered a limits-to-growth within a longer-term process, because Cuernavaca realized how Costco behaved in other regions where stores were already settled. If Costco had approached communities differently right from the start, they might have not faced the limits they did in Cuernavaca.

Hollender and Fenichel in their book suggest a more sustainable solution (Hollender and Fenichel 2004: 40): "What if Costco offered to restore a whole city block and weave its 'big box' into the fabric of the neighborhood and its architecture, persuading critics that its presence downtown would be an asset, not a blight?" The authors state that this solution might cost more money in the short-term, but is more likely to be beneficial (for both sides) in the long-run. This becomes especially apparent, when considering the costs for waging such a "fight" with the community and the media for the company. This aspect will be discussed in-depth in the chapter of the interaction with NGOs, the public and the media.

C3) Fighting-the-Enemy Trap

Another Sustainbility Trap, besides the Job-Creation Trap, which corporations following a Trade-off Model, often get into is the Fighting-the-Enemy Trap. This trap will be discussed in the following.

As mentioned above, the shift away from the Trade-off Model started when NGOs like Greenpeace, Robin Wood, Human Rights Watch and others were successful in calling customers for boycott. The media was an important distribution organ in that matter. As mentioned in the introductory chapter, the Trade-off Model was historically the predominant model in corporations. Thus when NGOs started to call for corporate accountability, businesses dismissed such claims initially and argued publicly that this were neither the tasks of businesses nor had they the possibilities to influence these cases (e.g. because they were sourcing their materials form other corporations). As already mentioned, society was no longer willing to pay for externalities of businesses nor did customers like to use products, which were produced in an unsustainable way (e.g. child labor). These differing mental models of corporations and of their customers (respectively the NGOs and the public) regarding sustainability[580], often let to *escalation structures* of 'Fighting-the-Enemy' between corporations and NGOs. When customers joined into the dynamic and boycotted products identified by NGOs, the companies hit a limit. They realized that the NGOs holding the support of the customers and the media had the longer perseverance in the escalation structure.

A lot of multinational corporations recognized that continuing to argue alongside a Trade-off Model bears a minor risk of having negative impact in the short-term (losing sales temporarily through customer boycott), but particularly in the long-term (damaging image) (see Schwartz and Gibb 1999: 43). Due to this recognition of social change corporations are looking for alternatives to the Trade-off Model and many corporations are moving towards a Compliance Model (see chapter 3.2). Other businesses have shifted towards mental models that even go beyond compliance. As a consequence a lot of companies today are much more open to critics and claims of NGOs and have gained knowledge in the field of sustainability themselves. Today even a significant number of companies and NGOs work on projects together (see e.g. Chiquita and the Rainforest Alliance[581]). Therefore *historically* the escalation structure can be considered an effective structure in the sense that it 'forced' companies to put sustainability issues on their agenda, which in the past were not considered the responsibility of a business. As the dissertation will outline, *today* a broad spectrum of alternative modes of interactions on sustainability emerged, so that an escalation structure (as one of the first interaction structures between corporations and NGOs) is not the most efficient structure anymore and its disadvantages often predominate. Because of the new, alternative modes of interaction arisen getting into an escalation structure of 'Fighting-the-Enemy' can be considered a trap today. Avoiding escalation does not imply that NGOs shall not criticize corporations any longer. Quite the contrary, the difference is that it has become more effective doing so in a trusted relationship rather than through escalation, because corpora-

---

580 E.g. Trade-off Models on the corporate side and other models e.g. Moral Obligation Model on the customer (respectively public side).
581 Chapter 3.4.2.3.

tions started to listen and NGOs started to realize the challenges corporations face towards sustainability.

This chapter seeks to show the problems of an escalation structure and thus its inferiority in many situations compared to other structures that exists today out of which some will be discussed in the dissertation.

Archetype of a Fighting-the-Enemy Trap

'Fighting-the-Enemy' possesses two inferiorities (disadvantages), which make this structure a trap: First, enforcing a corporate behavior towards sustainability through an escalation structure often risks being a short-term success, because it does not effectively change the *activating* mental models (theories-in-use) of a corporation in the long run. Instead, the escalation structure is turned into a shifting-the-burden structure. This structure consists of vicious circles, where the company is fire-fighting unsustainability in one part of the company, but it reoccurs in other parts of the company. This dynamic will be analyzed in-depth in the chapter of the Compliance Model. Furthermore, an escalation structure might at the end lead to some kind of reduction of *unsustainability* at the company, but it is not suited for the creation of *sustainability*, which requires a pro-active organizational mental model for sustainability (see Systemic model). The second disadvantage (inefficiency) of an escalation structure lies in its resource-intensiveness for both parties. The belief underlying an escalation is that the party which has the longer perseverance will finally succeed. Yet this often results in a total expenditure on both sides and often the outcome proofs unsatisfying for both sides (Senge, P. (1990): 384f). An example is the case of the oilrig Brent Spar that will be discussed as a business example below.

A significant problem presently arises out of the fact that mental models on sustainability that drive corporate behavior today are very diversified and subtle. Also not all NGOs are activists that strive for confrontation, but today a significant number are large organizations themselves and deeply interested in working together with companies. An enormous problem though seems to be that there is a lack of awareness for these developments as well as a lack of a language to talk about the diverse models and structures existing today. Although from today's standpoint, an escalation structure often proofs less effective compared to other structures possible, escalation can often be observed. Triggers for creating a Fighting-the-Enemy Trap thereby do not only lie within corporations that oppose sustainability, but the problem equally can lie on the side of NGOs that deliberately strive for escalation as the most appropriate matter. The dissertation in the following will therefore also lay an emphasis on outlining the NGOs role in the creation of a Fighting-the-Enemy Trap. The structure 'Fighting-the-Enemy' still seems to promise the myth of the "small group of activists that strives for good" in solidarity with the customers and achieves a hilarious victory against the "huge, fatal monstrosity" of a multinational corporation. This is an inappropriate myth, because reality has changed and is far more diverse. Still today, some NGOs deliberately strive for the inefficient structure of escalation and thereby are supported by parts of the public[582].

---

582 There are also companies that still strive for an escalation structure, but they are getting less and less, because of risk of bad press as outlined above. Therefore, the dissertation wants to focus on the NGOs' side, which is less being observed and sanctioned for striving for an

This is because they do not notice the recent development (unaware or deliberately) and are still grounded in the historical belief system that corporations per se do hold a Trade-off Model and therefore escalation is the most effective structure to reach results. As Patrick Moore, co-founder and 15 year long leading member of Greenpeace states about some of his former colleagues:" They rejected consensus politics and sustainable development in favor of continued confrontation and ever-increasing extremism" (Moore 2000: 4).

The Fighting-the-Enemy Trap can play out in many different facets. The structure that ana-lyzed in the following is a common one, namely about winning public approval on a sustain-ability matter between a business holding a Trade-off Model and an environmental or social interest group holding corporations accountable for sustainability. Often this "war" is carried out via the media, but also through campaigns and demonstrations. The following causal loop diagram (CLD) illustrates an escalation structure of media campaigns between an in-terest group and a company (see figure 55 and the archetypical structure of escalation in ap-pendix A.3).

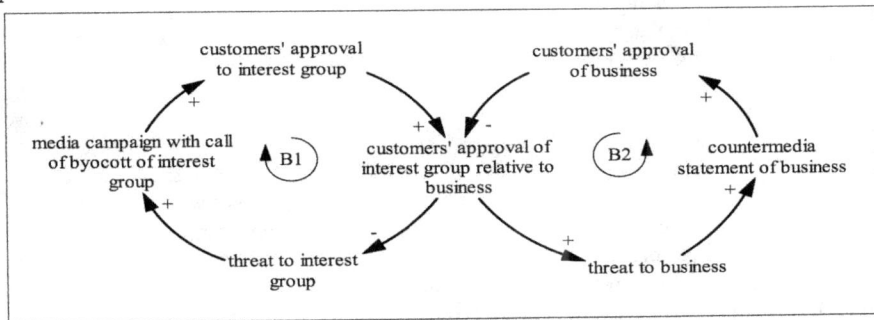

Fig. 55: Fighting-the-Enemy Trap
Source: Produced by the author

The above structure of the Fighting-the-Enemy Trap can be described as follows: The inter-est group realizes that customers are not aware of the (in their view) unsustainable behavior of a business. Thus, they launch a media campaign in order to inform customers and to call for boycott of the products. Some of the customers that read the materials[583] of the interest group approve of the group's complains and adopt a critical attitude towards the company (Balancing Loop B1). As the customers' approval of the interest group rises, the business feels threatened. It reacts by launching a counter-media statement, pointing out for example why the business can not be held accountable for the situations founded fault by the NGO or stating that the argumentation of the interest group is misleading and based on incom-plete data. Some of the customers consider the arguments of the business convincing and stay loyal or return (Balancing Loop B2). As the customers' approval of the interest group relative to the business decreases, the interest group in turn sees its positions threatened. It

---

escalation structure by the media or the public.
583 Of course it does not necessarily has to be a print campaign. Often NGOs e.g. Green-peace use spectacular actions (e.g. occupations of ships or buildings) to get media attention.

393

launches another media statement where it e.g. presents why its initial statement is accurate or provides additional data that supports its position. Thus, the dynamic continues anew. Through the increasing media presence, more and more existing and potential customers gain attention of the situation.

Dealing with the Fighting-the-Enemy Trap

The big winner of the structure described above is the media, as both sides are steadily increasing their media statements. What both sides achieve through their actions in the first place, is to increase media statements, which eventually turn out to be very expensive. The leverage per dollar for sustainability in the escalation structure is quite low compared to a bilateral voluntary agreement, because a lot of money has to be put into - potentially - reaching a small amount of action from reluctant businesses. The leverage per dollar (resource) is far more likely to be higher in a cooperative structure (see e.g. Efficiency model or Systemic model), as here the money of both sides is spent in creating more sustainable behavior of the business, instead of investing it into fighting each other.

An additional problem regarding an escalation structure is that animosities on both sides increase, thus decreasing trust and the ground for direct communication and collaboration. Instead, the blame game is at play. Businesses are stating something like:" Instead of investing all their money in a campaign to harm us, the NGO should invest the money to improve matters on sustainability. If they would just stop these inaccurate and false accusations against us, we might find a way to work things out. They just do not understand the situation our business is in." The interest group on the contrary may argue:" We would work together with the company and help them to become more sustainable. However, they will not let us. The company refuses to provide the information we asked for. Furthermore, the company has to acknowledge that their unsustainable behavior is wrong and where it is leading too. Instead they are undermining the credibility of our arguments." It is the nature of an escalation that often both parties get so involved in argumentation and counter-argumentation that the base for real listening to the other party and improving the situation for both, is eroding (Senge 2006: 395f). Sharing relevant and truthful information is necessary on both sides in order to engage in sustainability initiatives together. Continuous sharing of relevant information is unlikely to happen in an escalation structure though, as a basis for trust cannot be established.

The point the dissertation seeks to make is not to deny successes that have also been reached through escalation structures triggered by NGOs and consumers in the past as will be discussed in the example of the Shell business case below. The point the dissertation seeks to make is that *today* engaging in an escalation structure constitutes a trap, because it is less efficient than other modes of interaction currently existing. Several more efficient cooperative measures of interaction have emerged, which allow cooperations as well as NGOs a bigger leverage than an escalation. Examples for such cooperative interactions will be given in the chapter on the Reputation Leadership Model (chapter 3.4). As stated by Moore (2000, see below), today an escalation structure is rather followed by NGO's than by multinational corporations. Because of the increase of public awareness for sustainability, many multinational corporations engaged in escalations in the past, today seek to avoid escalation and start engaging in structures that are more cooperative. This is also the case for Shell, as will be outlined in the case. Another example is Chiquita and the Forest Stewardship Council (chapter 3.4.2.3).

Business Examples for Fighting-the-Enemy Trap

Business Case: Shell

The case that will be outlined in the following is a very prominent one about the oilrig Brant Spar. What the case became popular for is a David-against-Goliath myth of sustainability: The 'small, good' NGO (Greenpeace) that with large support of the public brings the 'bad, big' multinational corporation to its knees and forces it to a more sustainable behavior. While the case surely marked a landline for corporate sustainability, this account of the case however, represents a classical blame-game point of view.[584] Looking at the situation from a *structural* analysis point of view reveals another quality of the case and points to the problems of an escalation structure. The dissertation therefore decided to use exactly this prominent example not in order to recount the linear, orthodox view of 'David's success over Goliath', but in contrast to reveal an aspect of the case that becomes apparent when looking at it from a systems perspective on structures. The focus is placed on analyzing how *both* parties – in particular also the NGO Greenpeace – found themselves in an escalation *structure* which triggered both parties to move into directions (actions) that were counterproductive and eventually also backfired on them.

If not indicated otherwise the facts for the case are taken from the Greenpeace website[585], as well as from the Shell website[586], which provides various links to newspaper articles and independent sources: In 1995 Greenpeace learned that the UK government announced approval for deep sea disposal of the Shell oil rig "Brent Spar" into the North Atlantic Ocean. Greenpeace stated that there were hundreds of tones of petroleum wastes on board of the Brent Spar, some of these radioactive. Greenpeace occupied Brent Spar and organized a consumer boycott of Shell. Shell denied the Greenpeace accusations, stating that investigations showed that the Greenpeace evaluation of the waste situation and its environmental impact was not correct. Consequently, Shell began to tow Brent Spar to the deep Atlantic disposal site. However, the public and political opinion in continental northern Europe strongly opposed. The German Chancellor, Helmut Kohl, denounced the British government's decision to allow the dumping. Customers started to boycott Shell internationally. Protesters in Germany threaten to damage 200 Shell service stations. 50 were subsequently damaged, two firebombed and one raked with bullets. Meanwhile the scientific debate on the most sustainable solution intensified, with growing support for the Shell approach of deep-sea disposal. Nevertheless, despite the scientific evidence and support from the UK government, Greenpeace as well as a large part of the public further on disagreed with the suggested option.

---

584 For Blame-Game see chapter 2.2.5.7.
585 http://www.greenpeace.org/international/about/history/the-brent-spar; accessed: 12 February 2005.
586 http://www.shell.com/home/Framework?siteId=uk-en&FC2=/uk-en/html/iwgen/about_shell/brentspardossier/zzz_lhn.html&FC3=/uk-en/html/iwgen/about_shell/brentspardossier/dir_brent_spar.html; accessed: 12 February 2005.

Shell recognized that it needed to change its approach as the Brent Spar case was continuously damaging their reputation[587]: "We recognized that while good science and regulatory approval are essential, they are not sufficient to win public acceptance of our actions. We needed to engage with society, understanding and responding to people's concerns and expectations." Shell Expro set up the initiative `Way Forward' to find a solution for Spar disposal or re-use.

Finally, the decision was made for a "one-off" re-use as a Norwegian Ro/Ro ferry quay. The project was effectively completed when cut and cleaned ring sections of Spar's hull were placed on the seabed at Mekjarvik to form the base of a new quay. The study of the independent Norwegian foundation Det Norske Veritas (DNV) commissioned by Shell UK, revealed that the Greenpeace allegations, which stated that Spar contained 5,550 tones of oil, were wrong. Greenpeace admitted that it had used inaccurate data, which had created a strong argument for the rejection of the deep-sea disposal. Greenpeace apologized to Shell about this.

The DNV study further reached a similar conclusion as the study of the Best Practicable Environmental Option (BPEO). According to this study, the deep-sea solution was *preferable* to the onshore dismantling from a sustainability point of view. The reasons for this were based on the attributes, engineering complexity, and safety to the workforce, environmental impact, acceptability and cost. According to the BPEO, sinking the Brent Spar was more straightforward and less hazardous to the workforce than on-shore dismantling. Sinking the Brent Spar would "only" have a localized impact in a remote deep-sea region, and this was the cheapest option.[588]

In the following, the benefits as well as the problems of the escalation structure shall be analyzed. The benefits regarding sustainability were on the one hand the start of awareness for sustainability at Shell. Today there are still various sustainability aspects that the company needs to resolve, yet Shell has tackled a significant number of sustainability projects since the Brent Spar case, e.g. in the area of community work, energy efficiency, water management, biodiversity and others.[589] Greenpeace on the other side has gained enormous popularity through this case. As Greenpeace states, the Brent Spar case is remembered as one of the most significant Greenpeace successes of the 1990s.[590] Another important result according to Greenpeace was that the Brent spar case "led to a ban on the ocean disposal of such rigs

---

587 From:" Information on the decommissioning of Brent Spar" on the Shell website. Available online: http://www.shell.com/home/Framework?siteId=uk-en&FC2=&FC3=/uk-en/html/iwgen/about_shell/brentspardossier/brent_spar_280405.html; accessed 12 February 2005.

588 Greenpeace itself had purposely sunk its own ship off the coast of New Zealand in 1986 (Moore 2000: 5).

589 For an overview of the different projects visit: http://www.shell.com/home/Framework?siteId=royal-en&FC2=/royal-en/html/iwgen/leftnavs/zzz_lhn7_0_0.html&FC3=/royal-en/html/iwgen/environment_and_society/dir_environment_and_society.html; accessed: 12. February 2005.

590 See: http://www.greenpeace.org/international/about/history/the-brent-spar; accessed: 12. February 2005.

by the international body which regulates ocean dumping."[591] The ban has been Greenpeace's long-term goal, beyond the single Brent Spar case, as Brent Spar was the first of nearly 400 North Sea oil platforms scheduled for decommission in the upcoming years (Hollender and Fenichel 2004: 53). Thus, the case was a precedent.

Despite of the considerable achievements just mentioned, there were also significant problems that arose from the escalation structure. The problems lay in the costs for both sides as well as in the inferior result of the structure. As mentioned above the media war cost both sides tremendous resources. Additionally *both* sides were so involved in the argumentation in favor of their side (their loop in the CLD) that they got enravished to a behavior that damaged their image: Shell because the company did not react to the NGO and customer apprehensions at first and continued to prepare for a deep-sea disposal. Greenpeace because they manipulated data in order to foster their argumentation. The actual result that arose out of the escalation structure proofed also problematic in important aspects. The result (solution) was suboptimal with respect to the goals of both sides. Greenpeace strived to achieve the best environmental solution. Shell aimed for the most economical, legal solution and after customer boycotts also for a more sustainable solution. As the studies mentioned above indicate, the solution that resulted out of the escalation structure was more expensive *and* potentially less sustainable than other solutions.[592] Often these problems remain forgotten in the afterthought and subsequently the Brent Spar case is solely considered as a hilarious victory in the sustainability movement. *This perception bears the risk of considering an escalation structure as one of the most effective structures for sustainability today.* As reasoned in the previous chapter, this is not the case anymore. Today the disadvantages of an escalation often outrun its positive results, which can often be reached more efficiently and more long-term with other structures.

Yet as outlined there are still some NGOs that did (unaware or deliberately) neither notice the changes in the mental models on sustainability within corporations nor the structural changes between some corporations and the sustainability movement. Thus, they still consider confrontation and an escalation structure to be the most effective approach, but often achieve less successful results regarding sustainability or pay a far higher price for success compared to other structures. Patrick Moore, an environmentalist himself,[593] even considers

---

591 See: http://www.greenpeace.org/international/about/history/the-brent-spar; accessed: 12. February 2005

592 It is an interesting curiosity that the company held a Trade-off Model (which only later shifted to a compliance model). Nevertheless, the situation itself did not contain a trade-off: The more sustainable solution (according to the study) was also the cheaper solution. Thus, the Trade-off Model of Shell did not apply; the company did not need to reveal to pick the cheaper solution in trade-off of the more sustainable solution. However, the public was conditioned in a way that it held an inverse Trade-off Model: The more sustainable solution is the more expensive one; it cannot be the cheaper one. This special type of Trade-off Model as well as the belief that Greenpeace was more reliable regarding sustainability (see also reputation model) led to the fact that the public contributed to a less favorable solution.

593 As mentioned above Moore is a Greenpeace co-founder and held leading positions within the organization for 15 years.

the mainstream of the environmental movement to be caught up in this trap (Moore (2000): 8):" It's easy to see that the mainstream of the environmental movement has fallen prey to misguided priorities, misinformation, dogmatism and self-interest." Moore identifies two aspects that in his opinion many environmental movements still lacks today: First, the realization that sustainability is only achievable through the co-operation and involvement with various parts of society, i.e. government, industry and academia (Moore 2000: 4). Second, he criticizes that initiatives are not sustainable that focus exclusively on environmental issues and do not consider social aspects (Moore 2000: 4). Moore is harsh in its critics. He states that there is a tendency in the movement "to abandon science and logic and to get the priorities completely mixed up through sensationalism, misinformation and downright lies". Moore provides an important reason why some people strive for an escalation structure. As he experienced in his own life, he states, it is something different and far more difficult to strive *for* something and create new conditions, than to simply oppose something and fight *against* it (Moore (2000): 4 and 8). Striving for confrontation often is less complex than engaging with the other side and finding solutions that enhance the whole system – ecological, social and financial. This problematic applies all the same to the corporate side, if companies consider it the easier way to denial accusations than to look into the subject raised together with the interest group.

It is important to point out that the dissertation does not seek to declare that a fierce confrontation per se is never effective. The Dissertation wants to emphasize that corporations and NGOs should to analyze the systemic, dynamic structures and reflect on the danger of being trapped up in a resource intensive escalation structure that risks being less *efficient*. As mentioned above, Shell presently engages into multiple cooperative measures of corporate sustainability.

Further Business Examples for Fighting-the-Enemy Trap

A further example of an escalation of 'fighting-the-enemy' once again Shell shall be used as an example. This is done out of two reasons: First, it stresses the point that one corporation can get into a similar trap a couple of times (learning process). Second, it reveals the difficulty that similar traps can 'pop-up' in many different facets. The following is an escalation structure that relates to environmental and social sustainability and highlights how closely both are interlinked.

Shell faced an additional escalation structure in 1995, which also became quite prominent. In this year, the well-known book- and TV author Ken Saro-Wiwa was hanged in Nigeria. Saro-Wiwa was not only an opponent of the Nigerian military regime, but also criticized Shell for alleged environmental exploitation of the River State region and for the way the oil revenues were distributed by the government (Schwartz, Gibbs (1999): 27). Saro-Wiwa and his associates asked that more of the government's share of oil generated by Shell in Ogoniland should return to the locals in order to develop their community. The Abacha regime in power convicted Saro-Wiwa and nine activists of murder and hanged them in November 1995 (Schwartz, Gibbs (1999): 27). The trial was considered a political staging. Shell at this time pursued a no-intervention strategy regarding internal conflicts governmental issues of the countries in which they operated, which was a common procedure in the industry. Human rights organizations in turn did not accept such a position and accused Shell of having failed to use its influence to overturn the death sentences as well as to support the practices of the Nigerian regime. Protests broke out around the world, including customer boycotts as well as attacks on Shell stations. Even children of company employees were harassed at school. As Schwartz and Gibbs state (Schwartz, Gibbs (1999): 28):"There was wide-spread comment from the press and public to the effect that Shell's behavior exemplified the stereo-type of the irresponsible, indeed evil, multinational." As mentioned in the earlier chapter, Shell has started to change its attitudes tremendously since then. Today Shell spends US$ 60m for community projects in Nigeria - almost three times more than 1995. Shell changed its non-intervention strategy, so that due to the pressure of the company the Nigerian government is returning 13% to the oil producing regions in the Nigerdelta. In 1995, it had only been 3% (Thiel 2004, Litvin 2003).

A corporation that still today gets into escalation structures of fighting-the-enemy is **Monsanto** Co., a leader in the bioengineering industry. Most prominent was the escalation with Vietnam veterans about the toxic herbicide Agent Orange, which not only caused large de-forestation in Vietnam, but also led to serious health effects (including birth defects) of the local population and US veterans. Monsanto reached a $180 million settlement with veterans, but image remains damaged until today (Garrett 1998, Warwick 1998). Currently the corporation can be considered to be in an ongoing escalation structure with NGOs and the public with regard to disclosure of genetic engineering of ingredients offered in supermarkets (Levidow and Carr 2000, Pringle 2003, see also Ferrara 1999 regarding political ties). The resistance to transparency augments suspicions at NGOs and the public, thus fueling concerns as well as fears and long-term hammering the possibility to point to potential benefits of genetic engineering in a credible and trustworthy way (Levidow and Carr 2000, for potential benefits see: Avise 2004). Furthermore, since 1998 many retail chains have excluded genetically engineered ingredients from their own-brand lines due to consumer protests (Levidow and Carr 2000). Although Monsanto regarding some issues can be considered to have shifted towards a Compliance Model (e.g. air toxins, which were communicated actively and cut drastically, Graham 2002), the number of escalations Monsanto has been and is still trapped in is long (see e.g. Garrett, A. 1998, Tokar 1998). Financially the co-operation has not been affected so far.[594] However, as stated above, behavior often gets better before it gets worse[595] and indicators for Monsanto being caught in an escalation trap are increasing significantly. Monsanto currently is considered one of the weakest corporations with regard to sustainability. There exist a 'Millions Against Monsanto' campaign[596] and the company is continuously underperforming on indicators measuring sustainability risks (see e.g. Cogan 2006 or ethiscore[597]). Furthermore, trends in the food industry, which is central for Monsanto, clearly point to increasing consumer awareness and the fastest growing sector, the organic sector, excludes genetically engineered products. It remains to be seen how long

---

594 Monsanto's gross profit over nine month in 2006 totaled US$ 3,068M an increase of 22% compared to 2005; source: Monsanto 2006: 4.
595 Chapter 2.2.5.7.
596 See http://www.organicconsumers.org/monlink.cfm, accessed: 21. November 2006.
597 See www.ethiscore.org, 21. November 2006.

Monsanto will stick to corporate behavior that fosters escalation due to a lack of transparency and more cooperative modes of interaction.

The list of multinational corporations having turned away from escalations with NGO, the public and other stakeholders, and seeking more cooperative modes of interaction is long. One of the newest, 'candidates' is **Wal-Mart**, which equally had serious image problems resulting from unsustainabilities. Wal-Mart now seeks to engage into aspects of sustainability such as energy and waste-saving technologies as well as listing organic food.[598] Nevertheless, many competitors that reacted earlier to the increasing sustainability awareness now are leaders in their industry. Many multinationals formerly holding a Trade-off Model and engaged into escalations structures, now have turned towards a Compliance Model. Nonetheless, sustainability scandals continue to emerge because the corporations lack knowledge regarding sustainability and apply quick fixes and the Trade-off Model as a theory in-use[599] has not been overcome.

Other multinationals, which in the past also were in an escalation structure of fighting-the-enemy, today even seek to move to a Reputation Leadership Model in cooperation with the NGO. Examples for this are **Nike** and **Chiquita**, which will be outlined in the following.[600] As will be shown in this chapter, these corporations yet face crucial legacy problems from the escalation trap (fighting-the-enemy). First, because trust between the former 'enemies', i.e. the corporation and the NGO, has to be established. Second, because the corporation has bad sustainability records in the past and their image concerning sustainability is damaged, they face a high risk of getting into a Reputation Trap and being accused of Greenwashing. As a most recent consequence, multinationals start to acquire mission-driven enterprises (start-ups), like Stonyfield Farm or The Body Shop, which possess brands with high sustainability awareness. However, as will be shown in chapter 3.5, this equally is not without problems.

---

598 See chapter 3.5.
599 See chapter 2.2.1.1 for theory-in-use.
600 Chapter 3.4.

Appendix D: Further Business Examples of Quick-Fix Traps

In the following, further business examples of Quick-Fix Traps as well as their special case of Fire-the-Supplier Traps will be outlined, in order to underline the broad pervasiveness of these kinds of Sustainbility Traps in business practice.

The list of companies which installed a code of conduct, which yet repeatedly faced scandals due to non-compliances with their code of conduct 'popping-up' again and again is long. As outlined above, the vast majority of companies holding a code of conduct meanwhile have applied social audits to check compliance, yet with little to no effect. So that they remain a quick fix (CCC 2005b).

As outlined above, cases where codes of conduct along with social audits remain quick-fixes, because they are not embedded into more fundamental solutions of training and education, and the reaction to non-compliance scandals often still is to fire-the-supplier, remains particularly fierce with **unbranded retailers**. Besides the Tchibo case outlined above, the same problematic has been observed at **KarstadtQuelle**[601] or **Wal-Mart** (CCC 2005b: 13). As the CCC report (2005b: 13) with respect to the latter two states: "The impact of these programs on working conditions is at best superficial. Their approach seems for the most part to be minimalist—they tend to invest as little time and money as possible, and more worryingly, they seem to be promoting a 'lowering of the bar', in order to make it easier to tell consumers that they are meeting goals for treating workers responsibly." This 'lowering of the bar' behavior refers to the less thorough screening methods of auditors working for those retailers in comparison to auditors from companies with high brand image (see examples at CCC 2005b: 13ff). KarstadtQuelle communicates the following commitment to sustainability on its website (espoused theory): "We seek to shape the future in a responsible manner. The term sustainability stands for an economically successful, socially just society and an undamaged environment. These values depend on the way we conduct ourselves day-by day – what we buy, consume, how we work together and do business."[602] Jörg Howe from KarstadtQuelle's communication department reveals the following understanding of the group's responsibility regarding sustainable sourcing, when being confronted with intolerable labor conditions at one of the group's suppliers (Monitor 2005[603]): "It is not possible, to fully monitor the producers. We can not do this, nor can the companies that do the auditing for us. So. They of course rely on their experience and can put the finger in the wound. But I tell

---

601 KarstadtQuelle (German) is one of Europe's biggest department-store and mail-order companies.
602 Company's website: http://www.karstadtquelle.com/englisch/nachhaltigkeit/4878.asp, accessed: 14. June 2005
603 http://www.wdr.de/tv/monitor/beitrag.phtml?bid=742&sid=136, accessed 20. October 2005; translated from German to English by the author, original German text: "Es ist nicht möglich, Produzenten vollständig zu überwachen. Das können auch wir nicht, das können auch die Firmen nicht, die das Auditing für uns machen. So. Die sind natürlich auf ihre Erfahrungen angewiesen und können hier und dort den Finger in die Wunde legen. Aber wir sind nicht in der Lage, sag ich ganz ehrlich, 24 Stunden am Tag dafür zu sorgen, dass alle Vorschriften eingehalten werden, das ist ja selbst in der Bundesrepublik nicht möglich."

you honestly, we are not capable 24 hours a day to see to that all regulations are met, this is even not possible in Germany." Responsibility is thus shifted to external auditors and to the suppliers. In regard to Wal-Mart things seems to get into motion with respect to sustainability, as the company currently is launching its highly-publicized initiative on sustainable supply chains (Wal-Mart Sustainability: Starting the Journey[604]) and has set the goal of becoming a distributor for organic products.[605] Results and effectiveness of these measures remain to be seen. It is striking to note that Wal-Mart's large initiative of sustainable supply chains focuses on environmental sustainability, while issues of social sustainability remain underrepresented[606]. This once more points out the challenge of broadening boundary judgments and applying a holistic concept of sustainability.

Companies with a strong brand-image, have already made the experience that argumentations like the one cited above from the KarstadtQuelle representative, Howe, is not accepted by NGOs and consumers as sufficient, as scandals of social unsustainability reappear in their contract factories. The sportswear producer adidas-Salomon after having faced various scandals of social unsustainability, similar to many of its peers, has made another calculation: If the company engages into more fundamental solutions of issuing programs of training and workers rights, compliance can be enhanced without controlling suppliers '24 hours a day'. As Holliday, Schmidheiny and Watts (2002: 119) state, **adidas-Salomon** strategy is "based on a long-term vision of self-governance for suppliers, as adidas does not wish to be forever in the position of looking over the shoulders of its suppliers. Therefore, training forms an important part of the process, more so than monitoring [...]." More than reducing controlling efforts, suppliers can become a valuable provider of ideas or necessities of how to further reduce unsustainability. If in a longer-term relationship, the suppliers learn that the company will not automatically quit the contracts, if the supplier perceives a conflict between the purchasing practices of the company and the code of conduct, which often poses a dilemma for suppliers[607], trust is built. The supplier together with the corporation (buyer) can identify conflicting areas, which in turn will help the company to optimize its process of sustainable sourcing and to solve problems, which are likely to come up with other suppliers similarly. The issue of a corporation's own business model contributing to unsustainabilities at the supplier will be discussed in-depth in chapter 3.4.3.

Also **IKEA** was trapped into a Fire-the-Supplier Trap with regard to social unsustainability (child labor). Yet, inline with its incremental, yet broad sustainability approach outlined above, the company has realized the complexity of the issue and the risk of shifting-the-burden. In its declaration of the 'IKEA way of preventing child labor', the company states that

---

604 See the company's website at: http://walmartstores.com/microsite/walmart_sustainability.html and http://www.walmartstores.com/GlobalWMStoresWeb/navigate.do?catg=347, accessed: 27. November 2006.
605 See chapter 3.5.
606 See the company's website at: http://walmartstores.com/microsite/walmart_sustainability.html, accessed: 27. November 2006.
607 See the statement of Neil Kearney, General Secretary of the International Textile, Garment and Leather Workers' Federation above.

if "[c]hild Labour is found in any place of production, IKEA will require the supplier to implement a corrective action plan" (IKEA 2002: 2). Only if the plan is not implemented in
the agreed time-frame or if repeated violations occur, IKEA will terminate business with the
supplier (IKEA 2002: 2). IKEA specifically states the risk of merely shifting-the-burden
through quick fixes: "Care shall be taken not merely to move Child Labour from one supplier's workplace to another, but to enable more viable and sustainable alternatives for the
children" (IKEA 2002: 2).

The statement of spokesperson Irma Melwani from the apparel company **Guess,** points to
another popular strategy of shifting the responsibility for unsustainability not to the supplier,
but to the local government of the country sweatshops are located in. She states that foreign
subcontractors are held to the laws of their own countries (Gray 1999[608],[609]). But often these
laws are not sufficient to ensure sustainability in working conditions (particularly freedom of
association) and environmental issues, because governments of developing countries often
deliberately use low sustainability regulations as a competitive advantage to create jobs in the
area (CCC 2005b, Connor and Dent 2006, see also appendix C). The inefficient local regulations in turn provide an opportunity for corporations to shift the responsibility to local governments. Melwani states: "It is up to each individual country whether their labor laws are
adequate. Guess can't lobby other counties about their minimum wage" (Gray 1999). Melwani states the example of India. The minimum employment age in India is 13 as Melwani
states. "'No manufacturer is going to go in there and say you can't hire 13-year-old children
or young adults,' she said. 'They are supporting their families.'" (Gray 1999). Regarding these
arguments it has to be said, that insufficient local regulations are no argument of not requir-
ing suppliers to meet corporate standards which go beyond local regulations. Arguing the
way Melwani and others do, means to stabilize unsustainability through a structure of government and corporation. The governments apply insufficient standards to attract investors,
in order to create job and thus ensure their power. Companies can thus produce at very low
costs and still argue that they meet legal requirements. Yet this view ignores an important aspect, which destabilizes the structure. More and more companies start to realize this aspect:
The critical requirement to ensure customer support is *not* to meet the *legal* requirements on
sustainability of the *developing countries*, but the sustainability *expectations* of the *customers* in
first-world countries. This is especially true for companies following an image strategy. Nevertheless, awareness for these interdependencies and readiness to address the issues are only
starting to emerge. A recent study of Oxfam on major sports-wear companies, found that
only Reebok goes beyond local laws regarding workers rights issues (Connor and Dent 2006:
3). Thus, there still remains a long way to go.

---

608 The following facts are taken from this newspaper article: http://wiscassetnewspaper.-
maine.com/1999-05-13/sweatshops.html, accessed: 18. October 2005.
609 For the Guess case see also website of UNITE, the Union of Needletrades, Industrial &
Textile Employees at: http://www.unitehere.org/about/apparel.asp?offset=0; accessed: 18.
October 2005

Appendix E: Further Business Examples of Efficiency Traps

Another area of rebound effects due to efficiency is the Information Communication Technology (ICT). The most prominent examples within this area is that the introduction of computer on average increased paper consumption rather than decreasing it (Peters 2003, for further potential and problems with regard to resource efficiency in the ICT see Kuhndt, Geibler von, Türk, and Ritthoff 2003). The Factor 10 Visions project at the UK Open University further is examining the environmental impacts of three higher education systems offered at the University (Herring and Roy 2002): Orthodox campus, print-based distance learning course and electronically based distance-learning course. Results point to a rebound effect such that energy savings from the e-learning course due to reduced travel and facility heating, are partly offset by greater energy and emissions from student purchase and use of computers (including additional time spent on-line), rebound effects from printing from Internet sites and more additional home heating. Particularly the e-learning course indicates to be less energy efficient than the print-based distance learning course, where printed material is already provided to the students (Herring and Roy 2002: 537ff). Hilty et al. (Hilty et al. 2006, Hilty 2005, Hilty and Ruddy 2002, Hilty and Gilgen 2001, Hilty and Ruddy 2000) find that ICT can reduce energy use via substitution and optimization effects. Yet, these effects are offset by the induction-effect arising from the globalization of markets enabled through ICT (telecommunication networks). One reason is that ICT supports global division of labor, thus increasing energy use through transport. A rebound effect in ICT due to transport is supported by a study of Mathews and Hendrickson (2001), who examined internet book retailing in the United States and found that about two thirds of energy use and emissions were caused by book delivery through trucks and planes. Therefore selling books over the Internet does not lead to energy savings, compared to buying books at traditional bookshops, especially when books are transported with airfreight.

Another reason for the induction-effect stated by Hilty et al. is that the short innovation cycles within ICT increase waste disposal. Schauer (2003: 9ff) also points to the increasing waste problem of electrical and electronic equipment, which according to a directive of the European Commission is increasing three times higher than the growth of the average municipal waste. Schauer argues that the waste problem is additionally increased through miniaturization of electronic devices in the sense, that smaller devices tempt consumer to dispose them in garbage cans, thus significantly increasing hazardous content in municipal waste (e.g. chrome, nickel, tin, cadmium and halogenated organic compounds). Schauer also identifies further potential environmental rebound effects due to the miniaturization of electric and electrical devices (2003: 9ff): The fact that devices are getting smaller allows for more people to store devices at home or carry them around, which increased consumption. Furthermore – similar to the effects outlined for fuel-efficiency above - savings in material-input due to smaller size of devices are countervailed by an increase in features and performance of devices, which demand for higher energy consumption. For example Intel processors from the Pentium III series with 1 GHz consumed between 26.1 and 29.0 Watt max, while this amount increased for Pentium IV processors increased to 54.7 - 57.9 Watt (1.5 GHz) or even 71.8 - 75.3 Watt (2 GHz). Energy consumption of an intelligent refrigerator from Electrolux, which scans refrigerator content and orders supply via the internet possesses a 12.5 Watt higher energy consumption than orthodox refrigerators.

The different cases outlined, illustrate the importance of studying rebound effects triggered through corporate efficiency measures, - not only in the energy sector. Thereby it remains crucial to realize that efficiency is only a symptomatic solution and that alternative technologies and processes are needed that ensure eco-effectiveness (e.g. cradle-to-cradle).

Most importantly the cases of rebound effects outlined above, once more make obvious that for corporate sustainability to show effect[610] a systemic perspective is needed that also includes behavior of other social agents, particularly consumer behavior. Rebound effects thus stress the importance of the respectively new scientific focus on 'sustainable consumption' (see Wiedmann, Minx, Barrett and Wackernagel 2006, Hertwich and Katzmayr 2003, Thogersen and Olander 2002, Heap and Kent 2000; Kuhndt, Tuncer and Lietdke 2003; Tuncer and Kuhndt 2006, Hertwich 2005b, Sanne 2002). The cases above made it clear that *integrated* processes are needed in order to deal with the trap, i.e. sustainable production *and* consumption (see also the 'Marrakech Process' UNEP and UNDESA 2003 and 2005; CSCP 2005b). As has been outlined, a systems perspective can be most valuable in this respect, as it addresses mental models of corporations and consumers. As has been shown furthermore a system perspective allows illustrating and analyzing systemic patterns arising from the interactions of producers and consumers based on specific mental models.

---

610 That is, for corporate sustainability measures to actually contribute to reducing unsustainability/increasing sustainability.

Appendix F: Efficiency Trap (extended)

Figure 56 shows a structure that includes an additional corporation, which invests its financial resources in the production of a new product, which needs the same natural resource. In addition, these two corporations are representations (a cutout) of the industry that illustrates the main dynamics. That is, similar too the tragedy of the commons archetype outlined by Senge et al. (Senge 2006: 397) only two corporations are outlined as representatives to illustrate the structure.

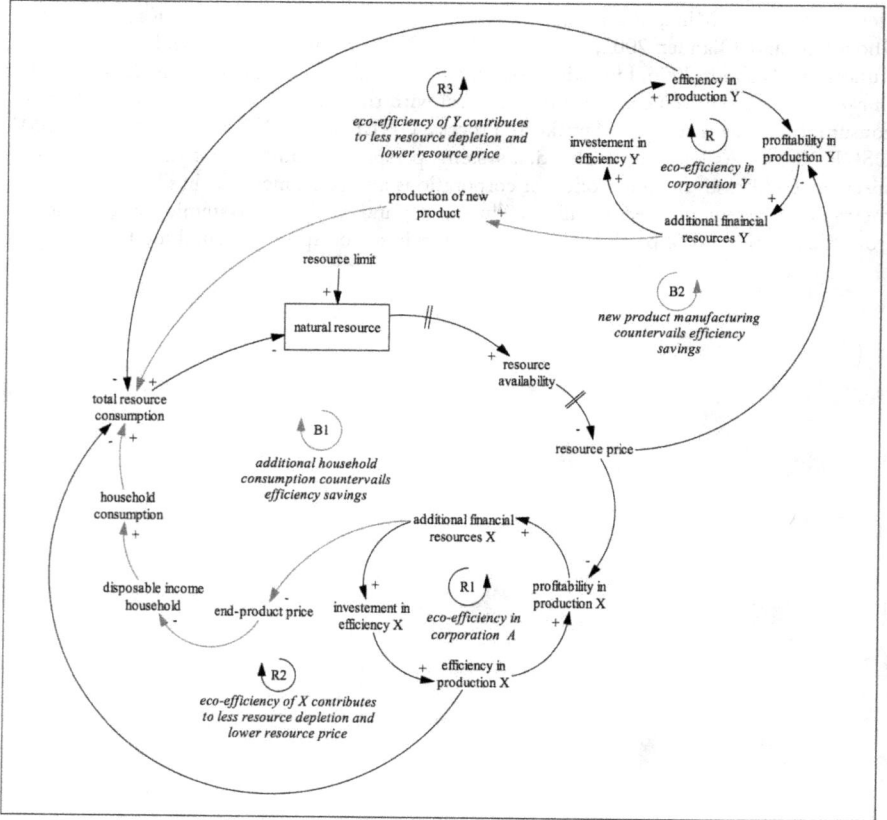

Fig. 56: Efficiency Trap (Extended)
Source: Produced by the author

Appendix G: Transition at Chiquita

The following traces in-depth Chiquita's transition from a Trade-off Model, over a Compliance Model towards a Reputation Leadership Model.

Transition from a Trade-off Model to a Compliance Model

Up to the 1990s Chiquita's focus regarding its plantations was simple: To produce as much bananas as possible. Health or safety matters of farm workers were just as little an issue as was environmental protection. A worker describes the former conditions at a Chiquita plant in Costa Rica: "Tons of blue plastic bags soaked with insecticides were spread all over the plantations; if chemicals were sprayed, workers just held their hands before their mouth and nose; the rain rinsed fertilizers, plastic waste and chemicals into the Rio Sucio and ultimately into the ocean (Heuer 2006: 20-21). In 1992, after protests of NGOs and the public, the company slowly started its turn around away from a Trade-off Model, which took up more then ten years and cost the company around $50 Mio. (Heuer 2006: 21, see also Alsever 2006). The company engaged with the former 'enemy', which in Chiquita's case was the Rainforest Alliance, an NGO aimed at protecting rainforest and other ecosystems[611]. This new partnership was substantially pushed by Dave McLaughlin, recently appointed Chiquita's senior director of environmental and social performance at Chiquita, which back then had to push very hard against intra-organizational barriers within its company (Alsever 2006): In 1992 the Rainforest Alliance sent banana companies including Chiquita, a list of environmental and worker-rights standards required to gain its certification. But Chiquita's officials dismissed the proposal as too expensive. So that at the beginning McLaughlin even had to meet with the environmentalist in secret, i.e. without knowledge of his superiors to get the partnership growing (Alsever 2006).

The first aim of this new partnership was forest protection, which seriously was endangered through plantations (Taylor and Scharlin 2004). Together standards for sustainable plantations were developed and in 1994, the first two Chiquita farms qualified for a certification of the Rainforest Alliance. This proofed successful for both sides: Environmental damage was reduced and Chiquita was impressed to learn that the efficiency at these plants had actually increased (Taylor and Scharlin 2004). According to Chiquita, productivity in the Latin-American farms rose by 25%, while costs were reduced by 10% (Heuer 2006: 25).

The company's turn around regarding *social* sustainability was triggered by a further scandal in 1998. The Cincinnati Enquirer, a newspaper of the city of Chiquita's headquarter, revealed that Chiquita bribed foreign officials, evaded foreign nations' laws on land ownership, as well as made extensively use of toxic chemicals, which allegedly even caused death among the workers, prevented workers from unionizing as well as exerted influence on political issues (Gallagher and McWhirter 1998). Although the newspaper had to withdraw the article because the reporters obtained their information through illegally hacking into the company's voice-mail system, the findings let to an uproar, which seriously affected the company's image.

In the late nineties Chiquita started to undergo a turn-around in social issues under its CEO Steve Warshaw. In 1998 Warshaw started his first meeting with Social Accountability

611 Website: www.rainforest-alliance.org; accessed: 24. October 2005

International (Heuer 2006: 23), a NGO committed to promoting human rights for workers. Today Chiquita is aiming at certifying its own farms as well as associated plantations with the SA8000 (Chiquita 2003: 4), a certification issued by Social Accountability International, based on international workplace norms in the International Labour Organization conventions and the United Nation's Universal Declaration of Human Rights and the Convention on Rights of the Child. These measures as well have brought significant advantages with regard to the economic sustainbility for Chiquita: A key success factor is the increased working moral within the company, according to George Jaksch, responsible for Corporate Responsibility at Chiquita's European headquarter in Antwerpen. Young people that formerly could not have imagined working for Chiquita are applying (Heuer 2006: 21). Working days lost due to strikes have decreased by a quarter from 2001 to 2002 (Chiquita 2003: 54) and the following year even by 70% (Heuer 2006: 26)[612].

These achievements in reducing unsustainability required substantial investments for Chiquita: The company spends $3 Mio. per year for Infrastructure and improved working processes as well as $3 – $4 Mio. per year as bonus to their suppliers to foster ecological and social behavior (Heuer 2006: 24; see also Taylor and Scharlin 2004).

Furthermore, Chiquita opened the Nogal Nature and Community Project in Costa Rica in 2004 with the help of Swiss retailer Migros and the Rainforest Alliance. In 2005 the Deutsche Gesellschaft für Technische Zusammenarbeit (GTZ), a German organization for sustainbale development, helped to expand the project. The project encompasses 100 hectares (250 acres) of forest, a visitor center, a botanical garden and educational trails through the forest (Chiquita 2006: 21f) . The project further provides environmental education to nearby elementary schools, research opportunities for university students from Latin America and Europe as well as small business assistance for local women's groups. It is further planned to link Nogal with the Mesoamerican Biological Corridor and to expand the education program (Chiquita 2006: 22).

Moving to Reputation Leadership Model

In the last quarter 2005, Chiquita started to launch an image campaign for Chiquita as a brand, which is environmentally as well as socially aware. Thereby it strongly advertises its long-term partnership with the Rainforest Alliance.

Chiquita spent tens of million on the campaign only in the starting quarter 2005 and has doubled its marketing budget until at least 2006 (Heuer 2006: 28). Also the statements of Cyrus Freidheim, former Chairman and CEO of Chiquita, in the Corporate Responsibility Report 2002, emphasize that Chiquita is following a Reputation Leadership Model (Chiquita 2003: 4): "We're committed to corporate responsibility because it's the right thing to do, and because we believe it's good for business, employees and the communities where we op-

---

612 This case also relates to the unsustainability-as-limits-to-growth structure through community resistance discussed in the chapter of the Trade-off Model. Formerly Chiquita experienced severe strikes due to unsustainable working conditions, which also included violence from both sides and which were a burden for the company. With the enforcement of new labor standards Chiquita now accounted for these limitations to its growth.

erate. [...] We also achieve intangible – yet equally real – benefits to our brand and corporate reputation. And while few customers today select Chiquita solely on the strength of our corporate responsibility standards and performance, many are increasingly sensitive to issues, which we know will increase in importance over time."[613]

The last sentence clearly points out the longer-term approach, typical for a Reputation Leadership Model as outlined in the model characteristic above. Inline with studies cited in the dissertation, Chiquita experiences that corporate responsibility is currently not yet a crucial factor in most consumer decision, but that the impact of this factor is increasing. Therefore, the company considers a sustainability orientation to be a crucial factor for the future and targets to increase its market share through sustainability reputation. As is typical for a Reputation Leadership Model the company seeks to be a sustainability leader (a role model) within its industry and to ensure first mover advantage. "Of course we hope other producers will follow our example regarding sustainability. It would be nice, if we could lay back in 20 years and say: Now everyone is making it.' [...] 'But no one shall catch up with us so fast" says George Jaksch, responsible for Corporate Responsibility at Chiquita's European headquarter (Heuer 2006: 28).

Need for action for Chiquita arises especially through the fact that the European Union transfers its quota-system on banana imports to a toll-per-ton system (WTO 2005), which will open the European market further for cheap 'dollar –bananas' imported from Latin-America and thus increase competition. Thus, Chiquita seeks for a *competitive advantage*, which it has found in sustainability. Michael Loeb, president of Chiquita Fresh Group Europe, outlines the company's strategy: Chiquita does not sell its premium bananas to discounters, and others have already taken the pure bio and fair trade niche. The area which remains for Chiquita to increase market share in the future is a differentiation as 'the better' (the good) banana in the high-price segment (Heuer 2006: 28).

Before launching the campaign for the 'better' banana together with the Rainforest Alliance in Europe, Chiquita according to its own statement, wanted to make sure all structures were adapted and the company could meet what it was promising. "We wanted to create facts first, to state with a clear conscience: For sure, each banana deserves the certificate" (Heuer 2006: 28[614]). Thus, the company was well aware of the risk of being accused of Greenwashing. As the dissertation will outline however, Chiquita is getting into a Reputation Trap.

---

613 As has been outlined, Chiquita also applies many efficiency measures.
614 Translation from German into English by the author. Original German text: „Wir wollten zuerst Fakten schaffen, um Guten Gewissens sagen zu können: Garantiert jede Banane verdient das Gütesiegel."

Appendix H: Further Business Examples of Reputation Traps

British Petroleum (BP) can be considered to be caught up in a Reputation Trap. The corporation seeks to achieve a leadership reputation of being sustainably responsible in its industry through its 'Beyond Petroleum'- campaign (Buncombe 2006). However, the company is facing serious Greenwashing accusations. BP argues that for the company 'Beyond Petroleum' means "the development of new ways in which to produce and supply oil and gas – through clean fuels, through greater efficiency and through substitution – particularly of gas for coal in the power sector." [615] Special emphasis thereby lies on natural gas as a 'cleaner' fossil fuel. Bruno and Karliner (2002: 82f) argue that the slogan (Beyond Petroleum) is a deliberate misuse of how the term is used by environmentalists. In this context, the term is used in the sense of moving away from fossil fuels in general (including gas) into renewable energy solutions. This once more reveals the discrepancies in system boundaries of corporations on the one side and NGOs on the other side – whether deliberately instrumentalized or applied unaware. BP however also started moving into the field of renewable energy particular solar energy. Through its acquisition of Lucas Energy Systems in 1980 and Solarex (part of BP's acquisition of Amoco) in 2000[616], BP Solar according to its account has become the second largest solar producer worldwide (Buncombe 2006). Additionally BP adopted other measures such as installing solar panels on selected gas stations, a pilot project in wind energy[617], investments into bio-fuel and hydrogen, and customer education through its CO2 footprint calculator and the possibility for customers to off-set their CO2 emissions via the NGO 'target neutral'.[618]

Bruno and Karliner (2002: 85) argue that, "BP is still an oil company dedicated to growing its oil and gas business. That makes its fancy rhetoric mainly Greenwash". While BP indeed still heavily relies on fossil fuels – as this historically has been its core business – the dissertation argues that BP invested substantially into issues of sustainability in reference to its industry, so that their actions go beyond the definition of Greenwashing outlined above. As BP spokesman Ronnie Chappell states: "While that is a small amount compared to our base, compared to anyone, and I mean anyone, we are a big player in the world of alternative energy" (Buncombe 2006). BP's credibility of building renewable energies as a new important branch and thus being a leader in its industry is undermined by its lack of transparency in addressing shortcomings as well as the unsustainable nature of its core business model. The major oil spill in Prudhoe Bay, Alaska in March 2006 is just the end of a list of sustainability scandals popping-up at BP. The spill of estimated 267,000 gallons of crude oil leaked out slowly over time from an almond-sized hole caused by corrosion constitutes the largest spill to date on the North Slope (Loomis and Salter 2006). After the detection of a further leak, BP needed to shut down its Prudhoe Bay oil field operations indefinitely, which according to

---

615 See the corporation's website online: http://www.bp.com/sectiongenericarticle.do?categoryId=9010219&contentId=7019491, accessed: 14. November 2006.
616 See company website for further information http://www.bp.com/sectiongenericarticle.do?categoryId=9012889&contentId=7025482, accessed: 14. November 2006.
617 Wind energy supply for 20.000 homes in Rotterdam, Netherlands in 2004.
618 See the company's website: http://www.bp.com/sectiongenericarticle.do?categoryId=9008205&contentId=7015200, accessed: 12. November 2006.

World Energy Monthly Review "could cut the North Slope production by half for the next three to four months" (Loomis and Salter 2006). BP had to disclose extensive corrosion in the Prudhoe Bay transit lines presumably due to maintenance insufficiencies (Buncombe 2006, Loomis and Salter 2006), which yet are rejected by the company (Buncombe 2006). Several acres of the North Slope of Alaska were contaminated. Damaged was confined through the fact that the spill did not significantly contaminate flowing surface waters, through which the oil could have been diffused even a much longer distance. Nevertheless, environmental damage is understood to be extensive and costly to remediate. Besides the clean-up costs, the scandal significantly impacted BP's image and the "single blow, undid the green reputation CEO John Browne had meticulously crafted for BP over the past decade" (Schwartz 2006). John Kenney, worked for the Ogilvy & Mather advertising agency that helped BP rebranding to 'Beyond Petroleum', claims that BP's environmental concerns were genuine. Yet that the statement of 'beyond petroleum' were unrealistic. "I think 'Beyond Petroleum' is simply absurd because they are an oil company and that is not beyond petroleum ... I think those words go too far" (Buncombe 2006). In the evaluation of Kenney, BP overstrained itself with claiming to target 'beyond petroleum' its campaign and thus lost credibility of their efforts. It was a 'promise', which the company due to its current business model and processes according to Kenney will not be able to meet for a long time to come (Buncombe 2006).

Shell equally started investing into renewable energy[619]. The company equally has been accused of Greenwashing as Shell spends only around 0.6 percent of its annual investments into this energy branch (Bruno and Karliner 2002: 109). What is interesting to mention in this respect though is that Shell itself states that a sustainable oil company is a contradiction in itself (Shell 1998). This illustrates that some oil producers start to openly admit that their core business mode is unsustainable as such.[620] Even though this is espoused theory, the very fact that the company openly addresses this issue in an official document is to be valued. Most oil producers are still far from exposing such a statement (see also above). The statement reveals the diremption for not getting into a Reputation Trap and maintaining a social license to operate in the future.

Concluding a particular issue within a Reputation Trap shall briefly be outlined. This is the case when a corporation's credibility is undermined by the fact that the company spends more on *advertisement* of a specific sustainability measure (e.g. pilot project) than on the measure (project) itself. **BP** for example faced such Greenwashing charges with regard to its 'Beyond Petroleum' Campaign, where the campaign itself was expected to cost the company US$100 million a year, which would have been three times what its' actually spending annually on solar power (New York Times Magazine 2000, "Currying Favor With the Green Lobby" 2002)[621]. In addition, **Chiquita** faced similar charges with respect to its campaign

---

619 See company website at: http://www.shell.com/home/Framework?siteId=rw-br, accessed: 12. November 2006.
620 See also chapter 3.4.3.2 on addressing root causes
621 The company has announced plans to invest US$8bn in electricity from solar, wind, hydrogen and natural gas the next 10 years (Buncombe 2006). The dissertation could however

with the Rainforest Alliance.. A further example is **Chevron** with respect to a nature conservation project (Bruno and Karliner 2002: 87). Concerning this problematic (special issue),
it has to be stated that – as has been outlined above – corporations following a Reputation
Leadership Model gain their motivation for sustainability through profiling their brand (image) as a sustainably responsible leader in its industry. As has been stated, these corporations
cannot be referred to as 'sustainable companies' as they still hold a sectoral perception space
and their very business model is not sustainable yet. Yet, as has been equally outlined thoroughly above, it is crucial to distinguish multinationals with a former 'Saulus' behavior that
today start engaging in sincere pilot projects or measures of sustainable development, from
corporations that are merely Greenwashing in the definition used above or even disclaim
crucial aspects of sustainability.[622] **Exxon Mobil** for example belongs to the group that argues
that oil supply will not have any problems to outstrip increasing demand, in the near to
midterm future. Thus leaving oil prices moderate and oil a secure energy source for the future
(Nocera 2005). While oil availability is indeed very hard to forecast, geologists consider the
oil industry working at its peak today, with refineries operating at 96 percent and no new refinery being built for some 30 years (Nocera 2005). In order to get out (avoid) a Reputation
Trap and to either undermine their own credibility and/or to overstrain themselves with regard to sustainability, corporations need to gain sustainability knowledge (including broader
system boundaries) and the courage for transparency. As the business examples shows this is
something corporations just start to realize. In regard to investing more money into sustainability campaigns than the actual pilot projects entail, transparency requires to a) outline pilot projects as such and to b) stress the point why core business products or processes are still
problematic (limiting) in regard to sustainability and to c) outline how the corporation seeks
to address these limitations in the future. Change processes for corporations with a former
Trade-off Model/Compliance Model towards a sustainably responsible leaders require time-
and financial resources as well as learning processes. – Similar to other *corporate change processes*. The corporations rely on their 'cash cows' (core business), which often are based on historical, unsustainable products and processes. Sustainable products and processes for many
corporations in reference to the BCG-Matrix[623] can be considered to still constitute 'question marks' from a business point of view, with the potential of becoming 'stars' in the future.[624] Thus, it is understandable from a business point of view that multinationals are not
redirecting all their resources into sustainable products and processes immediately. Thus it is

---

not find newer data that relates BP's yearly expenses on the Beyond Petroleum campaign
with regard to its investments in renewable energies. The important fact here however is that
BP did face these Greenwashing charges based on the argumentation above, when announc-
ing its campaign.

622 Thereby it can not be precluded per se that also corporations holding a Reputation
Leadership Model diffuse deliberate misinformation (Greenwashing definition) in individual cases. As has been equally outlined however, corporations holding a Reputation Leadership Model usually seek to avoid these situations as it negatively impacts their image. Rather,
these corporations communicate single-sided, by outlining only progresses and successes. –
Which can happen particularly in the case of narrow system boundaries.

623 The BCG-Matrix is a tool for strategic controlling. For further information see e.g.
Baum, Coenenberg and Günther 2006.

not surprising that sustainable products still constitute a small fraction of the corporations' product range. Transparency of these problematics therefore is key, by setting pilot projects (e.g. renewable energies, an organic product line etc.) into the context of the corporation's core business.

In this respect **IKEA** can be presented as a further alternative, which rejected plans for launching an eco-furniture line, because of the "danger of inadvertently drawing negative attention to the rest of its products range" (Nattrass and Altomare 2001: 59f). Thus, the company anticipated the dynamics of a Reputation Trap. Instead IKEA chose to reduce environmental impacts by 5-15 percent throughout its whole product range, i.e. its core business. "They [annotation of the author: IKEA] reasoned that everything that IKEA could do to reduce their environmental impact in those products would make a greater contribution than if they sold 10,000 eco-sofas." Combining pilot-projects of 'fully' sustainable products and reducing unsustainability in the core product range could equally be an option. Nike can be considered an example of another corporation that targets to reduce unsustainability in its core business, by introducing at least of 5% of organic cotton in their regular garments by 2010.[625] The aspect of addressing limitations that arise from root causes, i.e. which lie in the core products and/or core business models of corporations itself, will be dealt with in-depth in the following chapter. Necessities as well as challenges for addressing root causes will be outlined. The dissertation thereby will concentrate on the special case of the common business model of Financing Brand-Image through Low-Cost Production.[626]

---

624 This happened e.g. in the industry of organic food products (see chapter 3.5.2), which shows high market growth and where many multinational corporations seek to get into the market.
625 See appendix I and chapter 3.4.3.3.
626 See chapter 3.4.3.

Appendix I: Transition at Nike

The following discusses Nike's transition from a Trade-off Model over a Compliance Model towards a Reputation Leadership Model in the case of Nike's 'labor issue'.

Trade-off Model

After sensing the public's increasing concern on environmental sustainability, Nike rather proactively engaged in this field by launching the Nike Environmental Action Team (NEAT) in 1993, focused on recycling and environmental education (Hollender and Fenichel 2004: 187). Since then the company has worked with recognized experts in this filed, e.g. Paul Hawken, Bill McDonough and the Natural Step (Hollender and Fenichel 2004: 188). One of Nike's most spectacular projects is Reuse-A-Shoe[627]: Customers can return their worn-out shoes, which are then demounted and reused: The rubber from the outer-soles is turned into playing surface for soccer, football and baseball fields, granulated foam from the mid-soles is turned into synthetic basketball and tennis courts and granulated fabric from the uppers becomes part of basketball floors. The almost three million kilograms of contract manufacturing footwear scrap has been used by licensees. Nike uses the royalty monies from the licensees to help donate NikeGO sports surfaces to communities in need (Nike 2005: 73).

Despite its efforts on environmental issues, Nike disregarded *social* sustainability for over a decade. The issue of intolerable working conditions in sweatshops of Nike suppliers, internally called 'the labor issue' at Nike (Hollender and Fenichel 2004: 190), first surfaced in 1988 for the corporation. An Indonesian Trade Union published a detailed investigative report on poor working conditions at a south Korean manufacturer producing running shoes for Nike (Hollender and Fenichel 2004: 190). Soon more and more cases of workers exploitations were revealed and Western media (such as the New York Times, International Herald Tribune, Economist, CBS-TV and others (Hollender and Fenichel 2004: 190)) spread the information on intolerable working conditions in Asia to Nike's Western customers. The exploitations consisted not only of insufficient wages, but on health damage by toxic chemicals, harassment and intimidation (see Global Exchange 2001). When confronted with the investigations Nike initially responded with positions clearly related to a Trade-off Model/Accountability Model (Schwartz, Gibbs (1999): 52):

" a. the workers are lucky…it's better than having no job.

b. it is not the companies' business … you should be asking that question of the United Nations.

c. they [note of author: Nike] are indeed dealing with the problem, giving concrete instances of action taken."

Compliance Model

For over a decade, Nike addressed the 'labor issue' with a fire-fighting mentality, typical for a Compliance Model: A Code of Conduct and a Memorandum of Understanding for contractors was launched. External auditors like Ernst and Young were hired to conduct social audits, but negative incidents continued to show up, so that Nike was accused of sweatwash-

---

627 See company's website: http://www.nikereuseashoe.com; accessed: 04. November 2005

ing (Hollender and Fenichel 2004: 190)[628]. This led to a situation in which the brand reputation was seriously damaged and the brand 'Nike' had become a "synonymous with slave wages, forced overtime and arbitrary abuse" as Phil Knight, former CEO of Nike, later admits (Hollender and Fenichel 2004: 195, see also Herbert 1998). Nike was by far not the only company subcontracting its production overseas at manufacturers with questionable working conditions. But Nike became one of the companies most criticized in the industry. This basically had two reasons: One reason - outlined by the interest group 'Global Exchange' which is one of Nike's fiercest critics - is that Nike is the leading corporation in its industry, making substantial profits, so that according to Global Exchange it can afford being more sustainable and simultaneously can be a role model for the industry.[629] The second, probably more substantial reason, is the brand-image that Nike gives itself: Being sportive, fair and innovative. The perception of such a leader producing its shoes under intolerable human conditions contradicts the image targeted. When - a decade after the first accusations - Phil Knight realized the negative impact these social issues had on Nike's image, he launched a dramatic speech to the National Press Club in 1998. Knight acknowledged not having understood the depth of public concern on the issue of worker exploitation (Schwartz, Gibbs (1999): 54) and announced several commitments on improving the conditions (Hollender and Fenichel 2004: 194), which inter alia comprised meeting standards of the U.S. Occupational Safety and Health Administration (OSHA) for indoor air quality, rising minimum wages, including independent NGOs for monitoring and an education program for Nike's workers.

Moving away from Compliance

Five month before his speech, Knight hired Maria Eitel, a former employee of Microsoft's Corporate Affairs department, for the position of Vice President for Corporate Responsibility. Eitel started engaging with NGOs, some of them, like Global Exchange, being Nike's severe critics. She focused on the creation of a set of guidelines and business practices for the contractors in combination with a rigorous monitoring system (Hollender and Fenichel 2004: 197). Eitel clearly states that she wanted Nike to move away from the fire-fighting attitude of a Compliance Model: "What we didn't want was a superficial or short-lived response to a specific initiative. Our goal was substantive transformation and anything less than that would not be considered a success" (Hollender and Fenichel 2004: 197). Also the recent Corporate Responsibility Report clearly identifies and proclaims the shift away from the fire-fighting attitude of a Compliance Model towards fundamental changes within a coordinated plan: "Over the past decade we have primarily focused on compliance-related issues, and often in a state of continuous crisis. In regards to the environment and community, innovations have continued to emerge from across the company, but often without the benefit of a comprehensive and coordinated plan. Therefore setting focused, strategic goals is new to our team as well as a key challenge for us going forward" (Nike 2005: 10).

---

628 An analogy to the term of Greenwashing, which refers to sweatshop abuses (see: Light 1998).
629 http://www.globalexchange.org/campaigns/sweatshops/nike/faq.html, accessed: 12. September 2006.

Despite these changes of attitude and despite new guidelines and rigorous monitoring efforts in the new millennium, sustainability problems kept to show up and Nike was continuously blamed of Greenwashing respectively sweatwashing. The most prominent case was the 'Marc Kasky' case. Marc Kasky, a labor activist, and Alan Caplan, a San Francisco attorney, filed a suit against Nike in April of 1998 (Liptak 2003 and Reddy 2003).[630] The suit claimed that Nike's assertions about good labor conditions in its Asia factories, including the one that workers in Nike's overseas supply factories made double the local minimum wage and were protected from physical and sexual abuse, amounted to false advertising.[631] Nike in contrast argued that its statements were not commercial speech, but free speech in a public debate on globalization and thus were protected by the First Amendment. Commercial speech in contrast would be subject to truth-in-advertising laws, and could be regulated by the government and companies could be sued over false statements. The case was finally settled by both parties out of court in September 2003. As part of the settlement, Nike agreed to make a contribution of US$ 1.5 million to the Fair Labor Association (FLA) for a program to strengthen workplace monitoring and factory worker education. Critics moaned that Nike was part of the FLA and that thus, the group was not independent enough (Mokhiber and Weissman 2003).

The Kasky case was not the only critics Nike had to face in recent times: In his book "Still Waiting For Nike To Do It" Tim Connor (2001) examines Nike's labor performance three years after Phil Knight's commitments in his speech to the National Press Club and reveals achievements as well as insufficiencies. The Workers Rights Consortium published a report on deficiencies in a Nike factory in Thailand in 2004. Also in 2004 Oxfam, Global Unions and the Clean Clothes Campaign published a report on the labor rights conditions in the sportswear industry, which also (among others) outlined successes and failures of Nike (Oxfam, CCC and ICFTU. 2004).

Due to these and many other critical reports, accusations of Greenwashing respectively sweatwashing against Nike persist and argumentations similar to the ones in the article from Sharon Beder in The Ecologist (Beder 2002) can be found: Beder considers Nike a textbook study in greenwash. Beder argues that Nike's response to all the criticisms directed at it has been largely superficial. The company failed to address the underlying issues and rather employed mere reputation management (Beder 2002).
The dissertation considers the view of pure Greenwashing to be to short-sighted. Rather the dissertation considers Nike to be caught up in a trap, where Nike's own business model hinders the corporation of reaching the sustainability reputation it desires (see below). In the following the dissertation will therefore outline that Nike indeed has taken some innovative

---

630 If not indicated otherwise, the information on the case Kasky versus Nike are derived from these two articles.
631 Nike had published a report by Goodworks International, commissioned by Nike, which basically supported Nike's statements of good conditions for its workers. Simultaneously the company tried to oppress far more critical findings of the Ernst & Young audit of a Nike factory in Vietnam in 1996 mentioned above.

approaches, which go beyond mere compliance to sustainability and which are also valued by NGOs as 'taking a lead'.

Reputation Leadership Model

Despite all the critics, Nike has also repeatedly been acknowledged a leader of its industry in certain sustainability aspects. Nike for example was the first company to eliminate 100% of the polyvinyl chloride (PVC) in their shoes (Nike 2005: 66). Furthermore Nike is working together with organic cotton growers to fund an organic cotton association with the goal of greatly expanding the world's supply of organic cotton and has launched a collection of all-organic cotton clothing (Hollender and Fenichel 2004: 192, McDonough and Braungart 2002b). Nike started to use organic cotton in all its products and aims at containing at least 5% in their regular garments by 2010 (Hollender and Fenichel 2004: 192). This can be considered a fundamental approach in which the goal is to change products on a large scale.

But Nike does not communicate this trail on a broad basis, as the company fears critics of only using such a small percentage of organic cotton (Hollender and Fenichel 2004: 192). The main problem thereby lies in sourcing opportunities. At the scale on which Nike is operating, there is not sufficient organic cotton being grown worldwide at present (Hollender and Fenichel 2004: 192). This problematic of supply shortages for large-scale changes has also been addressed in the Chiquita case[632] and plays a crucial role in chapter 3.5.

However, the interesting point to notice here, is that Nike based on its experiences of former Reputation Traps before, has chosen not to communicate its project on large scale in order to avoid getting into a Reputation Trap another time.

Nike furthermore has engaged with McDonough and Braungart's design firm MBDC in order to move towards cradle-to-cradle manufacturing and product life cycle system (McDonough and Braungart 2002b). In 2000 a two-phase collaborative effort was launched for setting new design guidelines and auditing all of the company's major material suppliers. Since 2001, research has focused on the chemicals used in the manufacturing process in order to identify a 'positive list' of materials to use and Nike has began to align the life-cycles of all its products as closely as possible with natural cycles. Once a palette of chemicals and materials to use is identified, the aim is to then flow products in discrete biological and technical cycles, thus nourishing the soil or circulating as high quality technical nutrients from producer to consumer and back again (McDonough and Braungart 2002b, see also cradle-to-cradle approach in chapter 3.3.2.2). By 2020 Nike among other things aims to eliminate the concept of waste, to abolish all substances known or suspected to be harmful to human health or the health of natural systems and to develop financial structures, which promote greater product stewardship in design, engineering and manufacturing (McDonough and Braungart 2002b).

Nike also took a lead in more transparent communication regarding sustainability. Nike, after a year long struggle, now has come to consider sustainability as an open-ended process. Maria Eitel, former Vice President for Corporate Responsibility, states: "On one subject' [...] 'I am a total maniac: the idea that in this area, there truly is no finish line. There is no perfect factory, just as there is no perfect community" (Hollender and Fenichel 2004: 201).

---

632 See chapter 3.4.3.2.

The aspect, which earned Nike credit in regard to transparent communication in its industry is that Nike was the first global apparel company to publicly disclose the names and locations of their suppliers of Nike-branded goods (Nike 2005: 12; Maplecroft 2005: 4). Although the corporation has not yet disclosed the suppliers of other brands owned by Nike and its subsidiaries, also NGOs assign Nike a lead in this respect (MSN 2005: 1, Connor and Dent 2006: 55 and 101). Puma and Reebok followed Nike's lead and released the addresses of all suppliers of their branded products later in 2005 (Connor and Dent 2006: 55). Furthermore Nike in its latest Corporate Responsibility Report 2004 (Nike 2005) introduces its 'balanced scorecard' approach, in which compliance with the code of conduct is integrated in the scorecard as a forth criterion to evaluate purchasing decisions at suppliers alongside with Nike's three traditional measures of product price, delivery time and quality (Nike 2005: 26ff). What however is not guaranteed in this approach is that ameliorations in the code of conduct are not offset through lower scores in the other dimensions (e.g. when strikes lead to later delivery times or higher wages lead to an increase in unit price). In these cases the scorecard could lead to actually *reduce* orders from factories which ameliorate social sustainability, compared to other factories, which score better on product price and delivery time due to unsustainabilities.

As a further progress in transparency, Nike's Corporate Responsibility Report 2004 (Nike 2005) reveals findings of non-compliance at internally audited factories, as well as those identified by independent audits, which indicate severe unsustainabilities. Although one might argue that the verbal explanations to the numerical data presented, are phrased too favorably or too positively, the openness of the report has to be acknowledged. As stated above, corporations, which choose following a Reputation Leadership Model and openly discuss their unsustainability have to fulfill a tightrope-walk between communicating the unsustainabilities too positively and being accused of Greenwashing and – on the other side -communicating them too negatively and scaring of customers or risking to be charged legally[633]. Customers might be repelled to learn, about the cases of non-compliance at contracted suppliers of their 'beloved' Nike brand, ignoring that it is a problem found in the whole industry. Nike nevertheless openly discusses issues of unsustainability in its Corporate Responsibility Report 2004, for example that Nike intensively operates in many countries, where freedom of association is prohibited by law, including China and Vietnam (one or more instances in up to 25% of audited factories), that Nike auditors have found cases of excessive overtime (over 60 hours per week), non-compliance with minimum wage standards and that contractors faced cases of physical, verbal as well as sexual harassment (Nike 2005: 15-48).

---

633 Nike for example deliberately did not disclose any sustainability reports during the time the Kasky case was still running; see also Nike Responsibility Report 2004: 2.

Appendix J: Financing Brand-Image through Low-Cost Production (extended)

Figure 57 shows a structure, which entails the similar information, but which explicitly illustrates the structure of the Reputation Trap (figure 39) and that of the structure of Financing-Brand Image through Low-Cost Production (figure 40). The figure entails no additional information, but only a more detailed illustration of this specific case.

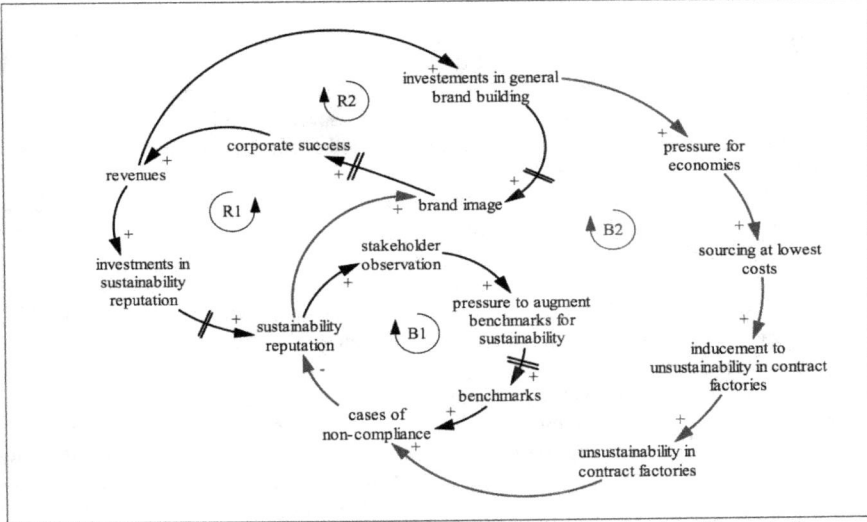

Fig. 57: Financing-Brand Image through Low-Cost Production (Extended)
Source: Produced by the author

Companies following a Reputation Leadership Model as Nike invest in actions to rise their reputation on sustainability (R1), the more they do so, the higher the benchmarks for still being called sustainably responsible rise (B1), so that the company needs to address limitations that hinder meeting higher sustainability benchmarks (cases of non-compliance), if it still wants to be considered sustainably responsible.

One core limitation of meeting higher sustainability benchmarks, as in the Nike case, often lies in the company's own corporate decisions: The company invests a huge part of its profits in general[634] brand building (marketing and design), this fosters its brand image, which increases corporate success and leads to higher revenues, which in turn can be reinvested in brand building activities (R2). But as these investments are 'financed' through low-cost, unsustainable sourcing, this *limits* the cases of compliance with sustainability codes (i.e. cases of non-compliance rise), which damages the sustainability reputation of the company and in turn damages the company's brand image (B2).

---

[634] The term 'general' was added in order to distinguish these brand building measures from 'investments in sustainability reputation', which are only one aspect of building brand image (other aspects regarding Nike are e.g. sportive, leadership etc.).

Appendix K: Further Business Examples for Brand-image/Low-Cost Prod. Traps

The trap of *Financing Brand-Image through Low-Cost Production* is particularly common in the brand-intensive apparel industry, where unsustainabilities at contract factories triggered through unsustainable buyer behavior, which backfires on the company's brand and impacts their image.

The sportswear company '**adidas-Salomon**' equally can be considered to be caught up in the trap of Financing Brand-Image through Low-Cost Production. Adidas' expenditures on advertisement amounted to US$ 775 million in 2004 (Oxfam, Clean Clothes Campaign and ICFTU/Global Unions. 2004: 32). The company faced several scandals with respect to unsustainabilities at contract factories that backfired on its brand (Connor and Dent, K. 2006: 76ff, Oxfam, Clean Clothes Campaign and ICFTU/Global Unions 2004). Although adidas, similar to Nike, can be considered rather progressive in reference to its industry in addressing limitations of sustainability, the company equally is far from rigorously tackling root causes that enable the trap to retain: The supply chain of adidas used to be very large and complex, making it hard to work with and monitor suppliers as well as to engage into long-term relationships. In 2002 the company had about 570 suppliers worldwide (Holliday, Schmidheiny, Watts 2002: 119). The company has realized this problematic and since the past four years is working on consolidating its supply chain, i.e. placing larger orders with fewer factories and engage into long term partnerships (Connor and Dent 2006: 78). While the company thus lays emphasis on the stability of the business relationship in order to reduce unsustainabilities, according to Oxfam the company still rejected claims that other buying practices of the company (e.g. prices and lead times) significantly impact worker's social sustainability, particularly union rights (Connor and Dent 2006: 78, see also 57ff). As for adidas sourcing practices regarding freedom of association and thus collective bargaining opportunities, the company states to source 32.4% of its global production from Asia-Pacific countries with corresponding laws, while approximately 52% of adidas production takes place in Asia-Pacific countries, which do not give legal force to these rights (Connor and Dent 2006: 77). Adidas "expects suppliers to develop a 'strategic compliance plan' which includes the provision of training to workers in Freedom of association and collective bargaining standards" (Connor and Dent, K. 2006: 76[635]). The problem here is that the focus lies on self-governance of the suppliers (see also Holliday, Schmidheiny, Watts 2002: 119), which yet not guarantees that suppliers have the knowledge and the willingness to train their workers on their rights to freedom of association. Yet, there are many indicators that adidas is now seeking to closer engage NGOs with regard to providing training as well as to monitor the implementation of factory compliance plans. For example in 2004 adidas cooperated with Reebok in order to arrange for an NGO to provide training to workers involved in welfare committees, which included providing information regarding the process of union formation under the law of Thailand (Connor and Dent 2006: 68). With regard to other social sustainability issues, particularly fair wages, adidas states that "labour costs — including basic wages, anticipated overtime payments, costs associated with maintaining health and safety requirements and other legal requirements — are included as a separate line item when ne-

---

635 According to the authors the information is based on adidas-Salomon Response to Oxfam Letter, 12 and 20 August 2005.

gotiating manufacturing prices with factories" (Connor and Dent 2006: 78[636]). Additionally the company in times has paid an additional amount on top of negotiated prices to help cover the costs associated with comprehensive implementation of social security of the workers under the law (Connor and Dent 2006: 78). The company yet did not reveal the methodology of how living costs are calculated and how exactly they are integrated in negotiation processes. Thus, while the very fact that measures to ensure social sustainability are disclosed and considered specifically, the process as such remains intransparent.

Puma has spent approximately US$ 107 million in 2004 for its advertisements (Oxfam, Clean Clothes Campaign and ICFTU/Global Unions. 2004: 32). The company has been buying from 83% of the 116 factories in Asia for more than two years (Connor and Dent 2006: 74), which in the industry can be considered rather long-term. Yet Puma reports that there exist no written commitment that would guarantee suppliers sourcing security for this time period, as flexibility for both the brand and the factory is crucial for the business (Connor and Dent 2006: 74). This yet exactly points to the problematic of the trap outlined above that emphasis on flexibility - and thus often sourcing-insecurity and short lead-times – can lead to unsustainabilities (see e.g. example of excessive overtime due to short-lead times in Indonesian Factory D producing for Puma in Oxfam, Clean Clothes Campaign and ICFTU/Global Unions. 2004: 38). Puma along with its industry peers need to investigate in the dynamics triggered through their own business behavior regarding sustainability scandals that impact their brands. Although root causes thus are hardly tackled, it can be stated in regard to transparency that Puma has followed Nike and displays a full list of suppliers producing Puma-branded products (although not yet for other brands the company produces), which positively underscores its reputation as a sustainably responsible leader. "Puma's release of its full supplier list marks the company as one of the leaders among sports brand owners in terms of transparency" (Connor and Dent 2006: 75). Inline with what has been outlined in respect of a Reputation Trap, the NGO Oxfam argues for Puma to go further in taking a lead and to also disclose "the proportion of production placed per year with each supplier [...], as it would be possible to trace whether workers who form unions and negotiate better wages and conditions are being punished by having orders to their factory reduced" (Connor and Dent 2006: 75). This once more illustrates that dynamic forces that drive the Reputation Trap and the problematics of addressing limitations that drive the balancing loop outlined (here: root cause, business model).

The corporations outlined above can be considered rather progressive in addressing limitations and moving out of the trap. Other corporations in the apparel industry are far more intransparent, hardly releasing any of the above information outlined with regard to social unsustainabilities (e.g. purchasing practices, names of supplier, amount of products sourced from countries that do not give legal force to these rights). For example with regard to the extensive study conducted by Oxfam et al. (Connor and Dent 2006), many corporations e.g. **Umbro**, **New Balance**, **Mizuno** and Pentland provided no or only very limited information (notably the brands less popular in Western countries). Very often the argumentation was

---

636 Based on adidas response to relevant sections of Oxfam's draft report (received by Oxfam via email on 8 February 2006).

put forward that the company does not possess this information, which points to the fact that mechanisms for inquiry and transparency regarding social sustainability issues through the supply chain still are hardly existent or at best insufficient. These corporations often still focus on laying blame for unsustainabilities elsewhere. **Pentland** (brand: Lacoste, Speedo and others) for example stated that it holds the view that "it is the lack of capacity of local institutions and organizations in sourcing countries which is the main impediment to making progress" (Connor and Dent 2006: 91).

Last but not least it needs to be stated that although the trap is common to the apparel industry, which the dissertation concentrated on, because of its strong focus on brand-image, getting caught up in the trap is not restricted to this industry as has been pointed to e.g. in the Chiquita case.[637]

---

637 Chapter 3.4.2.3.

Appendix L: Further Business Examples of Selling-(Out) Traps

Ben & Jerry's (Unilever)

Ben & Jerry's Homemade was founded by Ben Cohen and Jerry Greenfield in 1978. After four years in business and the enterprise 'taking off' they started to seriously engage into aspects of sustainability with the aim of being "value-led rather than profit-driven" (Hollender and Fenichel 2004: 220, Cohen and Greenfield 1998: 29ff).

They started to give away 10 percent of their annual profit to social courses, taking political stands on social issues and sought to implement value-driven behavior in their daily business behavior (Cohen and Greenfield 1998, Hollender and Fenichel 2004: 220ff). With social mission and business running well, the founders soon had the desire to grow in order to disrupt the system and leverage their alternative business model on large scale. "We believed that the best way to make Ben & Jerry's a force for progressive social change [...] was to grow bigger so we could make more profits and give more money away" (Hollender and Fenichel 2004: 221). After pondering different options of raising money for financing the growth, they decided on the innovative idea of an unusual public stock offering restricted to the citizens of Vermont. The reason behind it was that they wanted to investors who shared their vision and valued their community work. Although professional experts highly recommended against it, Cohen and Greenfield went ahead and sold their stock not through orthodox brokers, but through adds in local newspapers near the grocery coupons, so that ordinary people could see them and advertised for being into their mission. The unorthodox idea took off and Ben & Jerry's first public stock offering sold out in a few days, priced at US$ 126 for twelve shares at US$ 10,50 (Hollender and Fenichel 2004: 222).

What happened over time was that people who had bought into the initial idea, overtime sold their stocks to investors more interested in the profit than the values. By 1998 Cohen and Greenfield realized they had lost control over the company, as the stock price was quite low and larger buyers got interested in a takeover (Hollender and Fenichel 2004: 222). They ended up looking for a 'white knight', i.e. a friendly investor that would support the company's mission and allow it to remain independent and Unilever was identified as the best option (Hollender and Fenichel 2004: 223). When Ben & Jerry's was acquired by Unilever many active, ethical consumers turned away from the brand. Protests and boycotts of the products already started when plans became public to sell to a multinational corporation. Protest rallies at the company's facilities in Vermont were organized and a number of Ben & Jerry's franchise owners organized a protest campaign named 'Save Ben & Jerry's Coalition' with a website on which consumers could express their displeasure and to help mount a public relations campaign to block a sale (Hollender and Fenichel 2004: 224, Thompson 2002: C-489). Hundreds of messages were posted at the site, most of which expressed concern that the company would lose its social values and the alternative way the company conducted business (Thompson 2002: C-489). One message for example asserted: "My friend and I will not buy Ben & Jerry's again if you sell out. It would not taste the same" (Thompson 2002: C-489) and even Vermont's governor sympathized with the campaign stating (Thompson 2002: C-489). Furthermore the socially responsible private equity firm Meadowbrook Lane Capital filed an alternative, yet lower price offer for the shares. Cohen supported the Meadowbrook bid, yet after stating so, three shareholder groups sued Ben & Jerry's under the provision of federal law that it is director's responsibility to maximize shareholder return in the short term (Hollender and Fenichel 2004: 224, see also Sussdorff 2000). The Meadowbrook deal collapsed and finally in August 2000 Ben & Jerry's was sold to Unilever for US$ 326 million (Hollender and Fenichel 2004: 224). Key points of the agreement asked Unilever to: "Maintain the company as an independent entity, with a board of directors independent from Unilever. [...] Make a substantial donation to Ben & Jerry's Foundation in support of the company's social agenda, and to maintain an annual gift of at least $1 million a year. Buy rBGH (recombinant bovine growth hormone)-free milk from local farmers. Increase the number of suppliers who use Fair Trade. Explore the opportunity for an organic line of ice cream" (Hollender and Fenichel 2004: 225f[638]). Cohen and Greenfield remained as company employees and members of a separate advisory board, which should focus on providing leadership for Ben & Jerry's social mission and brand integrity. In the press release Cohen and Greenfield comment the deal as follows: "In commenting on the transaction, Ben Cohen and Jerry Greenfield, the co-founders of Ben & Jerry's, said: "Neither of us could have anticipated, twenty years ago, that a major multinational would some day sign on, enthusiastically, to pursue and expand the social mission that continues to be an essential part of Ben & Jerry's and a driving force behind our many successes. But today, Unilever has done just that. While we and others certainly would have preferred to pursue our mission as an independent enterprise, we hope that, as part of Unilever, Ben & Jerry's will continue to expand its role in society."[639] Richard Goldstein, President of Unilever Foods North America, in his statement stresses the intention for growth: "Unilever believes the super premium segment of the ice cream market will continue to grow and that the Ben & Jerry's brand will lead that growth [...]. Furthermore, we feel that Ben & Jerry's has a significant opportunity outside of the United States. Unilever is in an ideal position to bring the Ben & Jerry's brand, values and socially responsible message to consumers worldwide. These opportunities strongly support Unilever's stated strategy for expanding the ice cream category globally."[640] Cohen today states his dissatisfaction of having sold to Unilever. USA Today cites Cohen: „Ben & Jerry's will become just another brand like any other soulless, heartless, spiritless brand out there – that's my concern" ('Ben & Jerry's: Interview with Ben Cohen' 2000). Hollender and Fenichel quote: "Ben Cohen's less-than-satisfying experience with Unilever has prompted him to offer some timely advice for socially responsible corporations: ‚Don't do it!' he told *Mother Jones*. ‚Stay independent. I certainly tried to keep Ben & Jerry's independent. I lost that battle. Butt hat doesn't mean that other people can't win it.'" (Hollender and Fenichel 2004: 231, see also 214). First disputes between the former owners and Unilever started, when Unilever refused appointing a CEO favored by the advisory board, including Cohen and Greenfield, for his commitment to the social mission, and instead nominated Yves Cou-

---

638 See ibid for further information and the company's homepage at: http://benjerry.custhelp.com/cgi-bin/benjerry.cfg/php/enduser/std_adp.php?
p_sid=aJjNZYli&p_lva=&p_faqid=136&p_created=955568704&p_sp=cF9zcmNoP-
SZwX2dyaWRzb3J0PSZwX3Jvd19jbnQ9MjMwJnBfcGFnZT0x&p_li, accessed: 10. November 2006.
639 Official press release Wednesday, April 12, 2000, available online at: http://www.benjerry.com/our_company/press_center/press/join-forces.html, accessed: 10. November 2006.
640 Official press release Wednesday, April 12, 2000, available online at: http://www.benjerry.com/our_company/press_center/press/join-forces.html, accessed: 10. November 2006.

ette, a twenty-four-year Unilever veteran specialized in sales (Kiger 2005, Hollender and Fenichel 2004).[641] The acquisition agreement included that there would be no layoffs for two years. After this timeline, in May 2002 two facilities, a factory and a sales-center, in Vermont were closed and 124 people laid off, in October the same year 52 jobs in the headquarter were cut (Andres 2003, Goodman 2003). Cohen openly expressed his concern that „the ostensibly ironclad commitments made by Unilever to maintain the company's social policies were not as legally binding as he had been led to believe" (Hollender and Fenichel 2004: 227).

However, it has to be stated that 55 jobs out of the 124 were compensated by offers in another factory. Furthermore, a former employee stated that plans for closing the factory already existed before the Unilever acquisition (Andres 2003). Furthermore, it could be augmented – as CEO Yves Couette did - that keeping extensive, inefficient overhead costs is (economically) unsustainable (Andres 2003). Yet, the fact that the 20% cut-off staff included the entire sales force (Hollender and Fenichel 2004: 216), which is a crucial part of communicating company values, can be seen as an indicator for the different marketing emphasis followed by Unilever. Furthermore payments to Vermont dairy farmers since the Unilever acquisition are less generous than before (Hollender and Fenichel 2004: 216[642]), the support of family farming having been an emphasis of Cohen and Greenfield. Last but not least Cohen expressed his discontent that the completion of the ‚social audit' agreed on took longer then envisaged to be implemented ('Ben & Jerry's: Interview with Ben Cohen' 2000). The independent financial expert, James E. Heard, who prepared the company's social audit (before and after the acquisition), in the social audit for 2001 asserts that there are no indications of Ben & Jerry's giving up on their social mission, but he constitutes that management is behaving less unorthodox than before (Andres 2003). In the social audit 2004 Heard gets even more explicit. While he constitutes that Ben & Jerry's overall managed to keep up their social mission as well as promoting it through the introduction of Fair Trade Certified coffee extract and continued support for the organic flavors, Heard unmistakably expresses serious concern about the development of Ben & Jerry's social mission (Ben and Jerry's 2005: 3): Heard asserts that retail operations of Ben & Jerry expanded in North America and abroad, which provided new opportunities for expression of the Social Mission, but otherwise there were few new initiatives. Heard states that "[o]verall, however, the absence of new Social Mission initiatives is disappointing, given the economic successes the company is now enjoying "(Ben and Jerry's 2005: 3). In 2004 Ben & Jerry's was completely reorganized in respect to its business structure, including sales, operations, and the announcement of changes to come in finance and information systems. Heard expresses his concern about these structuring for the Social Mission, because key decisions will now involve the North American Ice Cream Group in Green Bay, Wisconsin, which has no demonstrated commitment, and no track record, in supporting the Social Mission. In Heard's view this leads to enormous repu-

---

641 Couette resigned in 2004 and became Senior Vice President for Unilever's Beverages Category. He was succeeded by Walt Freese, formerly Chief Marketing Officer for Ben & Jerry's for the past 3 ½ years, i.e. after the Unilever acquisition. See: http://www.unileverusa.com/ourcompany/newsandmedia/pressreleases/2004/bjnewCEO.asp, accessed: 11. November 2006.
642 Hollender and Fenichel refer to Oligarchy Watch, 15. April 2003.

tation risks if Ben & Jerry's fails to live up to its mission in the future. Last but not least, Heard states that the future will show, if "Ben & Jerry's is a company operating in alignment with its Statement of Mission, or simply a Unilever marketing operation using the brand's reputation for social responsibility to promote sales" (Ben and Jerry's 2005: 3). The newest social and environmental assessment report for 2005 (Ben and Jerry's 2006) appeared only in late 2006, i.e. almost a year later as former reports. It is now available online, structured in various different specific sections. But it does not include a statement of the social auditor (formerly Heard) anymore, but instead a statement by the CEO, Walt Freese, which is roundabout positive in respect to Ben and Jerry's social mission. The only critical points, mentioned in one sentence are that the restructuring process had frayed our employee community and that the rapid growth in the network of shops impacted the company's ability to deliver the ice cream and the support to the company's franchisees (Ben and Jerry's 2006). [643] These statements indicate the clear market perspective of the social mission is turning towards and furthermore stresses the shortcomings due to rapid growth.

The different points outlined above, provide some clear indications that sustainability in-use has been compromised on significantly in comparison to the mission-driven enterprise before the acquisition, - moving further away from the founders intrinsic, absolute sustainability vision, towards a tempered, ,tamed' customer oriented brand-management. However, as stated in the archetypical dynamic this does *not* mean that Ben & Jerry's has turned to mere Greenwashing. Sustainability in-use still after the acquisition can be considered significantly above industry average. It is the ,shift' from compromising individual, original sustainability in-use in favor of diffusing sustainability rapidly to larger scale that the dissertation points to.

The acquisition by Unilever has made it possible for Ben & Jerry's to grow significantly and to diffuse the brand, thus also transporting the message and values to far more people (see also social audit, Ben and Jerry's 2005, above). In March 2004 the company announced to significantly expand its presence in the European market ("Ben and Jerry's to Roll Out in Europe": 2002), while retail operations were also expanded in North America as well as globally since the acquisition (Ben and Jerry's 2005, and also previous social audits 2001-2003). Furthermore the company since the acquisition has managed to develop and introduce notable progresses in the field of R&D and eco-efficiency. The most prominent undertaking was – as stated in the acquisition agreement - the introduction of a fully organic product line in 2003 ("Ben & Jerry's Goes Organic" 2003). Further projects include [644]: Conversion of pints in unbleached paperboard Eco-Pint containers as well as usage of unbleached bags, napkins, cone-wraps, sundae bowls & cake boxes in the scoop shops (started 2000, has been already planned before the acquisition). Reduction of plastic packaging in 2003. Furthermore the company established a greenhouse gas reduction goal of 10% by 2007, to be achieved via a three part energy strategy aimed at reducing total energy con-

---

643 http://www.benjerry.com/our_company/about_us/social_mission/social_audits/2005_se ar/sear05_1.0.cfm, accessed 12. February 2007.

644 See the company's environmental history timeline, available at: http://www.benjerry.-com/our_company/about_us/environment/enviro_timeline/index.cfm, accessed: 13. November 2006. At date the environmental timeline didn't include announcements for the years 2004 and 2005. Yet, further information is provided in press releases.

sumption and CO_2 emissions companywide. Or a rather strange, promotion-oriented innovation announced in 2003: The company is working on the development of a working thermoacoustic refrigeration prototype - an environmentally friendly, alternative refrigeration technology that chills out to sound waves ("Wouldn't it be cool if the music of the Grateful Dead could keep Cherry Garcia ice cream cold?"[645]). On this year's Fair Trade month (October 2006) Ben & Jerry's announced that it is expanding its Fair Trade certified ice cream flavors.[646] Thus, an innovative spirit for sustainability as in a Reputation Leadership Model (including eco-efficiency) is still clearly visible, while the approaches can be considered rather orthodox and mainstream compared to pre-acquisition (see also social audits Ben & Jerry's 2001-2004 and Andres 2003). The problematic of Ben & Jerry's moving away from the founder's mission towards mediocrity and mainstream, while active, ethical consumers are turning away, has been identified last year by the company's new CEO Walt Freese. "CEO Walt Freese admits that Ben & Jerry's has been soft in recent years on continuing its founders' tradition of social consciousness" (Howard 2005). USA Today quotes the new CEO: "Ben & Jerry's has tremendous heritage in leading with its values. Over the last few years, we've honored our values, but we haven't stepped out there boldly the way that (founders) Ben Cohen and Jerry Greenfield taught us to lead" (Howard 2005). Freese has started out to rebux the social mission by launching a $5 million dollar campaign to save small family farms last year. Yet, if a return to pre-acquisition, high-profile sustainability in-use will be possible as part of a multinational corporation with a different mental model and the dynamics released still at play – pressure from unchanged growth target and not only active, ethical consumers, but even the founders, who incorporated the initial social vision, turning away from the company - seems a more than daunting task. It will have to be observed within the next years.

Odwalla (Coca-Cola Company)

Another case example is Odwalla, a producer of natural, premium juices, brought by Coca-Cola Company for $181 million in October 2001 ("Coke buys Odwalla" 2001). Odwalla was founded by three friends, Greg Steltenpohl, Gerry Percy, and Bonnie Bassett, in 1980, who used $200 hand-juicer to squeeze fresh juice in a shed behind their house and delivered it to local restaurants.[647] Steltenpohl, who held a degree in environmental science from Stanford University laid emphasis on contributing to healthy living, Odwalla being all natural using non-pasteurized, fresh juice. The organization's culture was democratic and entrepreneurial, employees were essentially trained to manage themselves and could also design their own jobs to an extent (Funding Universe 2006). The company's vision is expressed in form of a

---

645 http://www.benjerry.com/our_company/about_us/environment/enviro_timeline/index.cfm, accessed: 13. November 2006.

646 See http://home.businesswire.com/portal/site/benjerry/index.jsp?epicontent=GENERIC&newsId=20061011005271&ndmHsc=v2*A1104584400000*B116344 1121000*C4102491599000*DgroupByDate*J2*N1002521&newsLang=en&beanID=37038 6346&viewID=news_view, accessed: 13. November 2006.

647 See company's homepage: http://www.odwalla.com/whoweare.asp?p=whoweare&id=3, accessed: 14. November 2006.

poem.[648] Since its beginning the founders focused on community support and environmental sustainability. In later years (1997) e.g. Odwalla converted most of its delivery trucks to run on compressed natural gas, for which it won the Clean Air Award from the American Lung Association (Funding Universe 2006 and Odwalla[649]). Yet, as for sustainability it has to be stated that the company experienced a serious scandal while it was not yet acquired by Coca-Cola (Martinelli and Briggs 1998; Hoffman 2003; Thomsen and Rawson 1998; Evan 1999): In October 1996 some of Odwalla's apple juice products were found to be contaminated with E. coli due to neglected safety procedures with non-pasteurized juice, resulting in some 70 infections and one death of a 16-month-old toddler. The company received the highest food injury penalty ever so far and sales plummeted by more than 90 percent. The company launched a recall of its products, covered medical costs of those made ill and introduced the technology of flash pasteurization into its manufacturing processes, which eliminates harmful bacteria without the associated taste and nutritional loss accompanying traditional pasteurization. Due to this good crisis management and the launch of various new products (shakes, energy bar and nutritionals) Odwalla was able to regain consumer trust and after around two years returned to profitability. Thus, Odwalla can be considered to have compromised on sustainability even before it went public and was acquired by Coca Cola. However the dissertation argues that this case is of different quality than the archetypical dynamic outlined above. The E.coli case was a one time scandal, whereas what the dissertation treats to below is a slower, yet continues reduction of sustainability in-use as perceived by active, ethical consumers and the founder.

In 1993 Steltenpohl arranged for the company's initial public offering in order to raise capital for growth (Funding Universe 2006). It was after going public that the company started to significantly feel the pressures for compromising on their business model (sustainability in-use) as Steltenpohl states (Kelly 2003; see also Steltenpohl 2005). In 2000 Odwalla merged with Fresh Samantha, another mission-driven enterprise producing high-end natural juice with similar values on sustainability and community, which seemed like a good fit ("It's Official": 2000).

In 2001, Coca Cola bought the combined company for around $181 million. Odwalla was made a part of the Minute Maid division, both brands were expanded nation wide. In 2003 the Fresh Samantha was phased out in order to focus on building the Odwalla brand and increasing distribution on a national level. For this reason also the distribution of Odwalla products through Coca-Cola's distribution networks has been started to test-market (Hoffman 2003). Shawn Sugarman, formerly working for business development for Minute Maid (Coca-Cola) and the key figure for promoting the acquisition became president of Odwalla. This year Coca Cola announced to heavily invest promotion in order to mainstream the brand, using the tagline 'for every body' (Hein 2006). Chief operating officer Steve Mc-Cormick states: "Consumers are becoming more and more aware and educated around health and wellness needs for themselves. [...] We play right in that strike zone. Consumers are reading labels more. They're more educated about how they live" (Hein 2006).

---

648 To read the poem, go to the company's website at:
http://www.odwalla.com/whoweare.asp?p=whoweare&id=0, accessed: 14. November 2006.
649 See company's homepage at: http://www.odwalla.com, accessed: 14. November 2006.

As in the previous cases the results can be interpreted twofold: On the one side it can be val-
uated positively that the organic brand along with a 'sustainability message' is diffusing
through the help of Coca-Cola. Sugarman states (Hoffman 2003): "Odwalla has certainly
benefited from a capability standpoint. Odwalla was a small business that was capital con-
strained. We're now able to attract better talent. We're getting more people from Coke but
also more people joining our company with an eye toward a career. Also, Coca-Cola can help
us expand distribution of Odwalla products. At a minimum we are looking for help in terms
of penetrating new account opportunities. In some cases where we would have looked for a
third-party distributor to start a new market, now we're going to work with Coke, which has
tremendous penetration and breadth. Coke has already helped us in penetrating colleges and
universities. In Atlanta, where Odwalla didn't have any infrastructure, we are now running
through Coca-Cola enterprises, and they're making the investment in trucks, coolers and
people. [...] The idea is to be more efficient and that efficiency will create resources for further expansion. One thing I think Coke has done very well is to consider the culture of
Odwalla as integral to the brand. It has done a nice job of allowing us to maintain that culture through our vision and values. [...] Now, you can see all the big companies channeling
money into the natural foods industry because it's good business and consumers are increasingly voting with their dollars. As the mainstream consumer begins to gravitate toward more
natural, sustainable products, the capital will follow. [...] When I see a natural foods company succeeding, I view that as a good thing overall. And I don't think it's a bad thing when
a company improves its product to become more sustainable. That's happening in all the big
companies now. If Pepsi or Nestle or Kraft really invested in the natural foods business, that
changes everything - and they are investing. It's a transformational time" (Hoffman 2003).
Similar as in the previous cases active, ethical voices of consumers and pertinent websites after the acquisition by Coca Cola turned away from Odwalla and/or argued not to buy
Odwalla anymore. What thereby is particularly criticized is the fact that the Odwalla website (in contrast to the other two cases above) does not openly address and discuss the acquisition by Coca Cola (Gatewood 2005, see also Responsible Shopper[650]).[651] The original
founder, Steltenpohl, also judges less enthusiastic about the development. Steltenpohl resigned from his position as CEO in November 1998, but it was agreed on that he continued
as chairman and would provide consulting services to Odwalla for the next two years
(Odwalla Inc. Annual Report 1998). Steltenpohl with respect to Odwalla concludes that it is
the function of large corporations to concentrate power and wealth (Steltenpohl 2005). He
furthermore states (Steltenpohl 2005): "There was an incompatibility between the founders'
values and the values of the new investors that came in when we went public. [...] Eighteen
months after I left as chairman, Odwalla was sold to Coca-Cola. And if you look at other
examples, like Ben and Jerry's or The Body Shop or Stonyfield Farms, you'll find that all of
them are now either directly owned and controlled by a big corporation or well on their way."

---

650 Coca Cola profile including Odwalla association at: http://www.coopamerica.org/pro-
grams/rs/profile.cfm?id=204, accessed: 14. November 2006.
651 As an example of consumer reaction after the acquisition see e.g. the blog: http://word-
press.com/tag/pharmacy/feed/, accessed: 14. November 2006; comment: "If you are trying to
drink something healthier, stay away from Odwalla".

Thus, as in the previous cases, the founder can be considered to remain with the feeling of having got into a trap and with a feeling of – unintendedly - having 'sold-out', at least partly, on their initial mission. What is yet crucial to the dissertation to point to, is that this 'trap' is *not* one intentionally laid, but one that develops due to the dynamics involved. That is, are *neither* the founders that deliberately surrender and 'betray' their vision when agreeing of selling to/being brought by a multinational corporation, *nor* is it the multinational corporation's intention to 'hollow' out the enterprise to mere Greenwashing, as can often be read in 'activist' articles or consumer website. Rather it is crucial for all parties involved to be aware of and understand the dynamics that risk playing from a systems perspective.

The number of cases of mission-driven enterprises being acquired by multinational corporations, which seek to get into and expand the market for sustainable products is vast, other examples besides the ones mentioned are: Seeds of Change (pasta) by M&M-Mars UK/ Europe in 1998, Cascadian Farm (organic) by General Mills in 1999, Natural Boca Burger (veggie burger) by Kraft (Altria Group/Philip Morris) in February 2000, Odwalla (premium juice) by Coca Cola in October 2001, PJ Smoothies (drinks) by Pepsi in February 2005, Green & Blacks (Chocolate) by Cadbury Schweppes in May 2005, Tom's of Maine (natural toothpaste) by Colgate Palmolive in March 2006. See also figure 45 of acquisitions in the organic industry.[652]

The Body Shop (L'Oréal)

One of the most recent, prominent examples is the acquisition of The Body Shop, by L'Oréal in 2006. While it is yet to early for judging on the sustainability in-use and despite the founder's conviction that the values will not dilute, because they are encoded in the DNA of the enterprise, there exist clear indications for an enrollment of the archetypical pattern (Selling-(out) Trap) outlined above: As outlined above, the main goal of the acquisition is rapid growth, with first growth-projects already on the agenda.[653] On the other hand active, ethical consumers are turning away from the brand, fueled by the notion that L'Oréal is owned to 26% by Nestlé (Milmo 2006), which in the sustainability community possesses an unsustainable image in many respects[654]. The daily BrandIndex found that since the announcement of the deal Body Shop's "satisfaction" rating has dropped by 11 points to 14, another index that tracks public perception of more than 1,000 consumer brands found that "satisfaction" with Body Shop had slumped by almost half since the acquisition and ethiscore (Ethical Consumer) has downgrade its own rating from 11 out of 20, to 2.5 (Milmo 2006). Boycotts against Body Shop products are running (Milmo 2006). While it can be questioned if these ranking actually reflect an experienced reduction of sustainability in use or rather are an expression of discontent and concern about future development, they yet clearly show how sensible and quick moving the peer-group of active, ethical consumers is. One consumer for example notes: "I have purchased Body Shop products for many years, for its stance against animal testing, its fair trade principles, its attitude towards women's self-esteem, its attitude towards the ridiculous beauty industry. But now, on learning of this

---

652 See chapter 3.5.2.3.
653 See chapter 3.5.2.1.
654 See company profile at 'Responsible Shopper' at:
http://www.coopamerica.org/programs/rs/profile.cfm?id=269, accessed: 13. November 2006.

takeover by L'Oreal, a company part-owned by Nestle, and one that I have never looked favourably upon for any reason, I will no longer be purchasing anything from The Body Shop. [...] From now on, I will be purchasing products from small, local companies with strong ethical principles, organically produced ingredients as far as possible, and no desire to be associated with huge corporations that swallow and swamp everyone in their wake. 'Growth' is not always a positive thing."[655] Concerns over the ethical record of Nestlé meanwhile were equally expressed by Anita Roddick after the acquisition and notable customer boycotts (Brown 2006). While as stated it is yet too early to judge on the results, there exists a justifiable risk that the archetypical structure outlined above will also play out in the case of The Body Shop. Thereby on the one hand mainstreaming the brand and diffusing its sustainability messages, while on the other hand compromising on the company's original sustainability in-use – potentially leaving the founder, Anita Roddick, with the feeling of having gotten into a 'trap' with regard to her original vision of an alternative business model that changes the way business is done (Systemic Model).

---

655 Retrieved from Anita Roddick's homepage, posted May 9, 2006, available online at: http://www.anitaroddick.com/readmore.php?sid=545, accessed: 13. November 2006.

M1) Literature Overview of Mental Models on Sustainability

In the following a short literature overview shall be given. There exist a variety of literature on corporate strategies and approaches on corporate sustainability, but these constitute espoused theories. Literature on mental models as theories-in-use about corporate sustainability is far more limited. This corresponds to business practice, where the issue of mental models as underlying beliefs that drive behavior are hardly addressed.

Doppelt, who researched corporate sustainability behavior regarding leadership of various multinational organizations (see below) notes (2003: 16): "During my research I found that discussions about *what* to do – for example, which new technologies and policy instruments to apply – dominate public dialogue on sustainability. Practitioners place comparatively little emphasis on *how* organizations can change their internal thought processes, assumptions and ingrained behavior to embrace the new tools and techniques. This void accounts for many of the problems organizations face when seeking to operationalise sustainable development."

In the following literature findings on mental models of corporate sustainability shall be outlined with relevance to the dissertation. Adams (2004: 21f) discusses the importance of mental models as theories-in-use that drive sustainability behavior in corporations: [...H]ow we think is a strong influence on how we act, and our actions, in turn, are strong influences on the results we get. Trying to get different results (e.g. more sustainable management practices) while continuing to think in the "same old ways" is not likely to lead to much change. Our mental models, in other words, tend to be both self-reinforcing and self-fulfilling. [...W]e are generally unaware of the mental models we use. So, an early priority in any sustainability education program must be to raise awareness of the mental models being used and then to encourage responsible and conscious choice about adopting more appropriate mental models. If our attempts to teach sustainability in academic and corporate classrooms are to lead to significant action, we must help learners to understand and address their own default mental models [...]." Adams uses a collection of lists of adjectives indicated by individuals, that describe the commonly held mental models in the organization of these individuals to identify a polarity profile of six characteristics (dimensions) of a sustainable consciousness, which are: short-term versus long-term; reactive versus creative; local versus global; separation versus systems; blaming versus learning; doing/having versus being (Adams 2004: 22ff). Adams findings assorts that the foremost majority of all organizations is oriented towards the first poles of each characteristic, with a narrow zone of comfort around them. Adams argues that we need to develop learning and a new way of thinking to move towards the other side of the pole. The dissertation similar to Adams will use a polarity profile to characterize different mental models of sustainability. However, as the dissertation considers systems thinking to be the new way of thinking needed for sustainability, the characteristics (poles) of the polarity profile in the dissertation will refer to elements arising from the different systems thinking skills described.

Schley and Laur (1998) outline existing mental models of corporate sustainability based on their consulting work with corporations and contrast them to sustainable mental models:

‚The Economic System Is the Entire System' versus ‚The Earth Is the Source of All Profits'; ‚Industrial Processes Are Linear' versus ‚Product Development Is a Cyclical Process'; ‚There Are Infinite Resources for the Production of Goods, So We Can Throw Wastes Away' versus ‚We Do Not Have an Unlimited Supply of Raw Materials'. Smith (2000) identifies five exemplary mental models on corporate sustainability: Sustainability is a hassle, a cost for business; It's too hard, too complicated, too many issues; I'll go bankrupt if I do it before my competitors; I can just move my business overseas; Laws aren't being enforced.

Doppelt reviewed major US-based corporations (e.g. Chiquita, Xerox, Starbuck, Nike), European and Canadian corporations (e.g. Henkel, Swisscom, IKEA) as well as governmental sustainability initiatives from various countries and has identified six denial mechanisms for corporate sustainability, which are: ‚We don't have to do that'; ‚We already do that'; ‚The success are mostly anecdotal so we'll wait for more hard data'; ‚It's too costly (or time-consuming, complicated etc.)'; ‚Ist [name]'s fault, not our' (Doppelt 2003: 241ff). Doppelt's denial mechanisms and the other mental models outlined will in part tie into the mental model characteristics identified in the dissertation.

The mental models outlined by Rosner (1995) can be considered a valuable complementation to the dissertation. While the dissertation departs from the relationship between economic, social and environmental sustainability for identifying mental models of sustainability and analyses corresponding Sustainability Traps using systems thinking, Rosner refers to mental models in the sense of existing dogma of economy (market ‚laws') and challenges them in the context of environmental sustainability using systems thinking. Dogma discussed by Rosner (1995: 114ff) are for example: ‚The market will solve it'; ‚treatment of free goods[656]'; ‚competition prohibits cooperation'; ‚technology will solve it'. Rosner also discusses different feedbacks that can drive corporate behavior with respect to sustainability, such as liabilities, market forces, compliances with legislation and ethics (1995: 118f). The dissertation however, has laid an emphasis on not only outlining *recognized* feedbacks that drive corporate behavior, but the dissertation particularly laid emphasis on systemic structures, where certain dynamic feedbacks often remain *un*recognized and therefore can form Sustainability Traps.

Griffiths, Benn and Dunphy (2003: 14ff) outline a phase model for environmental *and* social sustainability in order to characterize different phases of corporate sustainability. The authors distinguish six phases, which are very similar to the ones outlined in the dissertation.

- *Rejection:* "There is a strong belief that the firm simply exists to maximize profits and any other claims by the community are dismissed as illegitimate" (2003: 15). The corporation actively opposes any attempts of governments or activists to place constraints on corporate behavior. This phase is comparable to the *Trade-off Model* used in the dissertation. It has to be kept in mind that the dissertation refers to mental model in-use (i.e. theory in-use).

---

656 Underlying belief: Goods that are not yet scarce are not valued by the market and are thereby free; as a good is expected to become scarce, it either becomes occupied and traded or a public good.

- *Non-responsiveness:* This phase "results from lack of awareness or ignorance rather than active opposition" (2003: 15). Sustainability is ignored and business is pursued 'as usual'. There exists no corresponding mental model in the dissertation. The reason is that the dissertation assumes that today every corporation (at least the large multinationals referred to here) has been confronted with the issue of sustainability. If sustainability is thus ignored, the dissertation considers this as a 'deliberate' decision[657], which then is subsumed under the *Trade-off Model*.
- *Compliance:* Compliance focuses on reducing risk of sanctions for failing to meet minimum standards derived from legal requirements or community expectations. This phase corresponds to the *Compliance Model* used in the dissertation, whereby the dissertation only refers to stakeholder (particularly consumer) expectations. All models, including the Trade-off Model, in the dissertation are considered to follow existing legal requirements. Respectively the dissertation does not analyze illegal corporate behavior, because it seeks to point to systemic traps that can arise even when fulfilling all legal requirements.
- *Efficiency:* The corporation realizes advantages of corporate sustainability, in particular reduction of costs and increase of efficiency. This corresponds to the *Efficiency Model* used in the dissertation.
- *Strategic proactively:* Sustainability is an important part of the corporation's business model. The corporation seeks to position itself as a leader in sustainability business practice. The motivation for sustainability yet still lies on maximizing longer-term corporate profitability. This phase corresponds to the *Reputation Leadership Model* used in the dissertation.
- *The sustaining corporation:* The ideology of working for a sustainable world is internalized. It is still a 'for-profit'-company, but it "voluntarily goes beyond this by actively promoting ecological sustainability values and practices in the industry and society generally. Its fundamental commitment is to facilitate the emergence of a society that supports the ecological viability of the planet and its species and contributes to just, equitable social practices and human fulfillment" (2003: 16). This corresponds to the *Systemic Model* in the dissertation. The dissertation thereby stresses the point that the Systemic Model is based on a holistic perception space and is build on a radically different business model (mission-driven enterprises).

The different phases in the model of Griffiths, Benn and Dunphy also constitute a sort of 'historical trajectory' of improving sustainability measures. Thereby a corporation does not need to progress through all phases, but can also leapfrog phases (Griffiths, Benn and Dunphy 2003: 14). As will be outlined below, also the mental models identified in the dissertation can be considered a 'historical trajectory' in this sense.

Last but not least a portfolio of four main strategies of corporate sustainability shall be outlined as identified by Hart (Hart 2005 and 1997; Hart and Milstein 2003). These are strategies and thus constitute espoused theories (although as mentioned above, some might also exist as theories-in-use). The strategies will be outlined more in-depth here, since *the portfo-*

---

657 Even though not necessarily explicit, yet deliberate at least to some significant extend.

lio builds the basis for the computer-simulated corporations used in Transformation Laboratory by the dissertation (see Appendix M2 below).

Hart used a Shareholder Value Model with two axis to stretch out a portfolio with four quadrants (see figure 58): The *vertical* axis reflects the corporation's challenge to manage to-day's business while simultaneously building markets and technology for the future. This captures the tension between the need to realize short-term results on the one hand and ful-filling expectations for the future on the other hand (Hart 2005: 60). The *horizontal* axis il-lustrates the challenge to promote and protect organizational skills and technologies, while simultaneously engaging with outside stakeholders to create sustainability. This dimension il-lustrates the tension created by the need to ran and harvest existing technologies without distraction, while similarly remaining open to new, disruptive models and technologies (Hart 2005: 60).

Within this framework of these two axis, the authors (Hart 2005; Hart and Milstein 2003) sorted buzzwords of corporate sustainability such as eco-efficiency, waste reduction, ISO 14001, biomimicry, closed loops, corporate social responsibility, full cost accounting, take back, sustainable development, base of the pyramid, civic entrepreneurship.

These clusters led to the following four subordinated Strategies: *Pollution Prevention, Clean Technology, Product Stewardship, Sustainability Vision* (Hart 2005: 65ff, see figure 58).

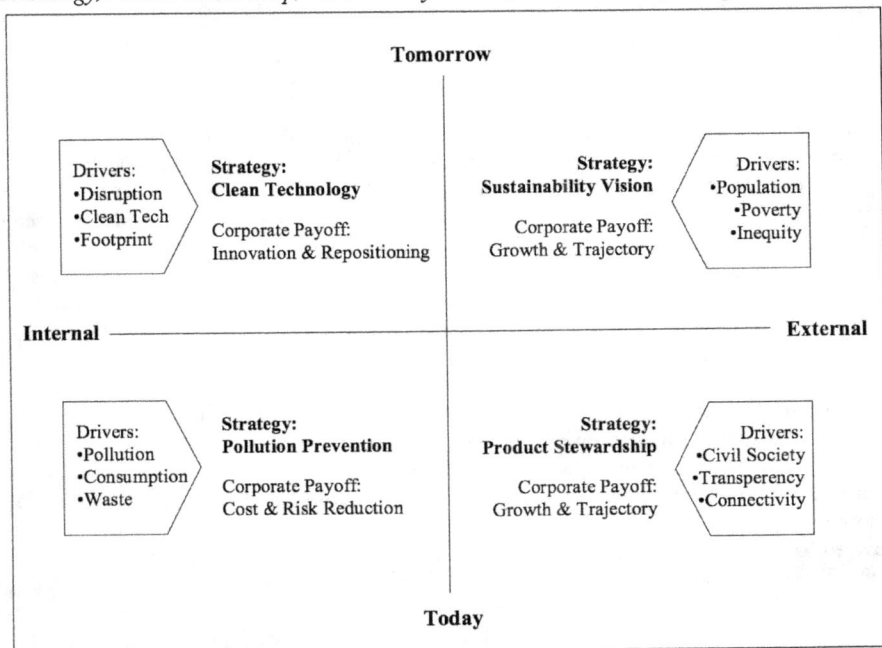

Tomorrow

| Drivers:
•Disruption
•Clean Tech
•Footprint | **Strategy:**
Clean Technology

Corporate Payoff:
Innovation & Repositioning | **Strategy:**
Sustainability Vision

Corporate Payoff:
Growth & Trajectory | Drivers:
•Population
•Poverty
•Inequity |

Internal ———————————————————— **External**

| Drivers:
•Pollution
•Consumption
•Waste | **Strategy:**
Pollution Prevention

Corporate Payoff:
Cost & Risk Reduction | **Strategy:**
Product Stewardship

Corporate Payoff:
Growth & Trajectory | Drivers:
•Civil Society
•Transperency
•Connectivity |

Today

Fig. 58: Sustainable Value Framework
Source: Adapted from Hart 2005: 65 (see also Hart and Milstein 2003)

The strategy of *pollution prevention* is focused on growing profits and minimizing risks through reducing waste and emissions of current operations, e.g. through eco-efficiency measures (Hart 2005: 66). „Less waste means better utilization of inputs, resulting in lower costs for raw materials and waste disposal. Effective pollution prevention also requires extensive employee involvement, continuous improvement, and quality management capability" (Hart 2005: 66). In the simulation developed by Hart and Svoboda and used in the dissertation to identifying and verifying mental models of sustainability, the pollution prevention strategy is adopted by the computer-simulated corporation Excelsior (see Appendix M2). In the dissertation Pollution Prevention is related to ‚Efficiency Model' identified in the dissertation.

Product stewardship is focused on enhancing reputation and legitimacy through corporate sustainability measures. While pollution prevention focuses more on inner processes, product steward ship aims at listening and integrating the voices of stakeholders such as suppliers, customers, regulators, communities, NGOs and the media. Thus lowering environmental impacts across the value chain and enhancing the corporations reputation and legitimacy towards the stakeholders (Hart 2005: 67). In the simulation product stewardship will be applied by the simulation corporation Vanguard (Appendix M2). Product stewardship is related to the Reputation Leadership Model identified in the dissertation, but the latter is more far reaching focusing on a leadership role of sustainability in its industry and also focusing on social sustainability (not only environmental sustainability).

While pollution prevention deals with incremental improvement, *Clean Technology* refers to innovations that leapfrog routines and knowledge (e.g. biomimicry, nanotechnology, renewable energy) and may even allow repositioning (Hart 2005: 69ff). In the simulation (Transformation Laboratory) clean technology will be followed by the simulated corporation TechnoSphere (see Appendix M2). Regarding the mental models of the dissertation, clean technology is related the Reputation Leadership Model, which is ready to apply innovations in order to gain sustainability leadership reputation in its industry. In particular cases it can also refer to the Efficiency Model. It is key that new technologies are not only driven by internal tech- and design ‚freaks', but if integrated into products meet customer needs.

Sustainability Vision therefore focuses on sustainable innovations that meet stakeholder needs, whereby they can open up new market and mark a corporation's growth path according to Hart (2005: 71). Such new markets can arise from customer groups conventionally overlooked by corporations, e.g. environmentalists, shantytown dwellers or rural poor in developing countries. That is groups, which form the base of the pyramid and only now are discovered as new customers (Hart 2005: 71ff, see also Hart 1997, Prahalad and Hammond 2002, Prahalad and Stuart 2002). In the simulation (Transformation Lab) this strategy is represented by the computer-simulated corporation 'Provisio'. With respect to the dissertation this approach is related to the Systemic Model. However, sustainability vision is still focused on multinational corporations, while the dissertation focuses on Mission-Driven-Enterprises.

The following chapter (Appendix M2) will outline the simulation, which uses the Hart framework outlined.

M2) Simulation: Transformation Laboratory

As stated above, the simulation was used as an additional exemplifying method in order to *refine the mental models* and *important characteristics of mental models* (polarity profile), which the dissertation derived through the methodology outlined in chapter 3.1.1.

The Transformation Laboratory (simulation) conducted on May 2, 2005[658] offered the possibility to actually observe business behavior (theories-in-use) with regard to sustainbility and thus to refine the characteristics associated with the different mental models used in the dissertation (see polarity profile). The dissertation used a preliminary version of the polarity profile presented below, to observe the simulated corporations in a structured way. In the following the lab design shall briefly be summarized and its findings outlined.

The laboratory can not be considered significant due to a low data volume, so that it can only provide additional information. However, as will become apparent, a wide band-with of different mental models was at play in the simulation, which founded a solid basis to observe and outline their different characteristics. That is, which mental model crystallized for a specific corporation (team) throughout the simulation? And how did this mental model manifested itself though a specific behavior (characteristic) of the corporations throughout the simulation?

Background of the Transformation Laboratory (Simulation)

The simulation used is a business simulation designed for the field of corporate sustainability, which has been developed by Susan Svoboda working with Stuart Hart (Cornell University), and Richard Duke (University of Michigan) in 1997.

It has since been used for academia as well as for consulting in business practice (see also Svoboda and Whalen 2005).[659] The facilitator the dissertation worked with to execute the laboratory session, Susan Svoboda, has carried out the laboratory with hundreds of groups in business schools, corporations, government organizations, and nonprofit organizations over the past seven years and thus possesses a deep knowledge about the process. In the following the simulation in general and the specific one used in the dissertation shall be outlined.[660]

The intention of Transformation Laboratory is experiential learning for corporate sustainability, aimed to train corporate representatives on adaptability and openness rather than only eco-efficiency. Creating sustainable business solutions requires seeing a business as part of a much larger system involving a wide variety of stakeholders. Transformation Laboratory therefore is designed as a micro world which requires a perspective from participants that incorporates social and environmental dimensions as well as economics, and requires a flexible, adaptable, and inclusive approach. Simulated corporations need to face the challenge and struggle of reconciling dynamic natural systems and complex social processes with control-oriented management systems, they are used to.

---

658 The session ran full day.
659 For further information see www.realiagroup.com (accessed: 12. October 2006).
660 The description given is based in part on the information provided by Realia Group (see also website above).

The participants form teams of 5-8 people, which represent corporations seeking a sustainable-enterprise business strategy that will enable their company to enhance its corporate citizenship profile while it conducts a profitable business. Individual team members take on executive management roles within their companies (Strategic Planning Director, Manufacturing Director, Marketing & Sales Director, Product Design Director, Communications, Finance Director, Sustainable Development Director, Consultant).[661]

Each team makes a product and runs their corporation in the context of life-like conditions such as time pressures, budgetary constraints, unpredictable stakeholder interventions, changing market conditions and limited information. At the end of the decision cycle, participants sell their product in dynamic markets - industrialized countries (market 1) and/or developing countries (market 2). It allows companies to take market share from one another, and to record their decisions that result in Profit and Loss Statement, Balance Sheet and Environmental reports.

Participant teams are scored on their performance and benchmarked against four computer-simulated corporations that face the same challenges as the lab participants. These four computer-simulated corporations were designed to each follow one of the four sustainability strategies identified by Hart in the Sustainable Value Framework (see figure 58 above), i.e. Pollution Prevention, Product Stewardship, Clean Technology and Sustainability Vision.

The products on the market are vehicles built by the participants out of K'nex construction components. Thereby the corporations need to balance the economic, environmental and social impact of the components. The final product is evaluated on how it meets several performance criteria and the company is evaluated on leadership and management issues such as being proactive, transparent and innovative. Reflecting the real world, the management teams often find they are working with incomplete, changing or conflicting information.

The facilitators role-play different stakeholders, influencing the proceedings proactively and in response to company actions. These stakeholder-interventions require the participants to react to changing circumstances and allow the simulation to be highly flexible. A more detailed description of the laboratory process can be found below.

Corporation: Plug Power

The particular laboratory used in the dissertation was carried out with high-level employees from the company 'Plug Power' and their stakeholders in May, 2 2005 in Latham, PA, USA.

Plug Power was founded in 1997, currently employs around 300 people and is based in Latham, PA, USA with branches in Washington, D.C. und the Netherlands (Plug Power 2006).[662] Plug Power produces platform-based fuel-cell-systems for back-up power in telecom applications. In cooperation with Honda Motor Co., Inc. the company is working on extending the capability of existing natural gas products to include delivering pressurized hy-

---

661 For further information, see below.
662 For further information visit: www.plugpower.com, accessed 05. March 2006.

drogen fuel. This solution will provide electricity and heat for the home and hydrogen for fuel cell vehicles. Plug Power is not only aiming at producing a sustainable product, but targets to promote sustainability in the full product-life-cycle including zero-land-fill. The corporation is engaged in several initiatives to anchor this commitment to sustainability not only within the internal organizational culture, but similarly within stakeholders' organizations. The company states on its website „[...] Plug Power is striving to meet longer-term objectives of delivering economic, social, and environmental benefits in terms of reliable, clean, cost-effective power and, ultimately, sustainability – preserving and protecting the earth's natural resources" (Plug Power 2006[663]). Hence, the issue of sustainability is anchored within the corporation, with special emphasis on environmental sustainability.

Methodological annotations to the laboratory carried out

The laboratory used in the dissertation has been designed by Realiagroup, Plug Power and this dissertation in close collaboration. It ran over two business cycles (with a cycle being equivalent to one financial year) and was conducted by Susan Svoboda from Realia Group as a facilitator. In the following the key methodological aspects in regard to the simulation shall be outlined.

First it needs to be stated why the dissertation decided on using a simulation, instead of interviews or action theory/grounded research.

   a) *Interviews*: Interviews are likely to reveal espoused theories. A simulation in contrast, offers the possibility to actually *observe* behavior and thus to reveal theories in-use (mental models) and their characteristics.
   b) *Action theory/grounded research*: While these approaches would have been very well suited to study mental models and their characteristics, they require substantial resources with respect to time and finance, which were not available for this dissertation. A simulation offers the best proxy to such approaches, because a simulation allows to condensate processes (business behavior) in time and is more affordable financially.

Second, it needs to be argued, why the dissertation decided to use this specific simulation of 'Transformation: the Business Strategy Laboratory©' from Realia Group. The reason for this is threefold:

   a) First it is one of the view simulations existing, which particularly are designed with respect to corporate sustainability.
   b) Second, as the term laboratory suggests, it has been designed with the most degrees of freedom possible so that participants are free to act and play out their mental models (theories-in-use), rather than being restricted or guided by too many rules.
   c) Last but not least the facilitator, Susan Svoboda, is very experienced running the lab for years now and thus could provide valuable input of the corporation's behav-

---

663 Quoted from the corporations' website at http://www.Plug Power.com/company/profile.cfm, accessed: 17. January 2005; see also the corporations' environmental policy at http://www.Plug Power.com/will/policy.cfm, accessed: 12. July 2006

ior with respect to the polarity profile and could also benchmark it with behavior of teams in previous labs.

The reason for the dissertation to conduct the simulation with a single corporation (Plug Power) and its stakeholders were twofold:

a) On the one side time and financial constraints, as organizing such a full day meeting with participants from various corporations would have been very challenging and far more costly.

b) As from the content side working together with one corporation had the advantage that most participants knew each other, shared a similar culture and could act as teammates closely to 'real-life' behavior, which increased plausibility for the simulation as an authentic micro-world. It therefore was agreed on with the facilitator and Plug Power to build two 'Plug Power teams' (BioSphere and SphereThis) build of corporate members and an external stakeholder in the role of a consultant as well as a competitor team made out of 'externals' (Spheres of Influence).

As stated, it was the aim of the dissertation to identify and observe, different mental models operating within the simulation and their characteristics playing out. The basis for this, thereby was formed by the five mental models identified by the dissertation in chapter 3.1.1.1.

The dissertation analyzed the theories-in-use of the different corporations and their characteristics through observing participants actions as well as their argumentations throughout the simulation.

All interactions were tape-recorded so that they could further be analyzed in-depth again. Furthermore the dissertation engaged in follow-up interviews with participants and in particular with the lab facilitator in order to clarify and refine the findings.

The simulation carried out included high-ranking, strategically focused personnel from Plug Power including the Chief Executive Officer (CEO), director Product Marketing, director of Environment, Health and Safety as well as more operative employees such as Systems Engineers. Stakeholders involved people from academia, consultants as well as designers engaged with the corporation.

These Participants formed the following three teams (simulated corporations) of 8 people each in the simulation: BioSphere, SphereThis and Spheres of Influence. A full list of all participants, their ‚real-life' relationship to Plug Power as well as their roles in the simulation is presented in the following.

Overview of Participants Transformation Laboratory

As can be seen in the table below, the participants were senior as well as diverse, stemming from the Plug Power itself as well as from the company's stakeholder organizations. The assignment to the positions in the teams has been carried out in cooperation with Plug Power in order to best match the position in the laboratory with the real position:

Position Transformation Lab.	Team A (Green) SphereThis! Position at Plugpower	Team B (Yellow) Biosphere Position at Plugpower
Strategic Planning Director	Manager of Product Assurance, GenCore Programs	Chief Executive Officer
Manufacturing Director	Director of Manufacturing and Facilities	Manager of Production
Marketing & Sales Director	Director of Government Relations	Director of Product Marketing
Product Design Director	Manager of Honda Program	Systems Engineer
Communications Director	Mechanical Engineer	Director of Human Resources
Finance Director	Program Manager	Manager of Technology Delivery
Sustainable Development Director	Manager of High Temperature Program	Manager of Environment, Health, and Safety
Consultant	President of Brownlie Design[664] (Stakeholder)	President of The Initiatives Group, LLC (Stakeholder)[665]

Table 1: Teams Transformation Laboratory I
Source: Produced by the author

---

664 Brownlie Design, is a design company, which designs the fuel cell systems for Plug Power. Both companies are engaged in close working and training relationships with regard to sustainability.
665 The Initiatives Group, LLC is a consulting company, associated with military, which advises Plug Power with respect to strategic business management.

Position Transformation Lab.	Team C (Pink) Spheres of Influence	Expertise and Relationship to Plug Power
Strategic Planning Director	Dr. Peter Senge Senior Lecturer at the Massachusetts Institute of Technology	Research and consulting in the field of organizational learning and systems thinking
Manufacturing Director	Dan Robeson, PhD Student	Research associate from Lally School of Management and Technology
Marketing & Sales Director	Prof. George Richardson Professor at University at Albany, SUNY; President of the System Dynamics Society	University at Albany, SUNY, from which several employees of Plug Power have been hired from.
Product Design Director	Dr. Roger Varden Managing Director of Strata-gems	Strategic consultant to Plug Power
Communications Director	Prof. Richard Leifer Professor at University at Albany, SUNY and director of the MBA Program	Director of the MBA Program from which several employees of Plug Power have been hired from.
Finance Director	Prof. Pradeep Haldar Professor at University at Albany, SUNY and Director of Energy and Environment within the Nanotechnology Center	Scientific cooperation with Plug Power for fuel cells in nano-applications.
Sustainable Development Director	Joe Laur Senior Partner SEED Systems	Sustainability Consultant to Plug Power
Consultant	Katrina Fritz Intwala	Government Programs Manager at Plug Power

Table 2: Teams Transformation Laboratory II
Source: Produced by the author

Summary of the Results of the Simulation

In the following, the findings of the simulation shall be summarized[666]. That is, the mental models followed by the different corporations (teams) and their characteristics observed.
The following shows an overview of the main outcomes for each of the seven teams within cycle 1 and 2 and within the two possible markets (market 1: industrialized country, market 2: developing country).

Team	Cycle 1 Unit Sales	Cycle 2 Unit Sales	Cycle 1 Market Share	Cycle 2 Market Share	%Δ Mkt Share	Cycle 1 Profit (millions)	Cycle 2 Profit (millions)	%Δ Profit	Cycle 1 Mfg. Pollution	Cycle 2 Mfg. Pollution	%Δ Mfg. Poll.
Market 1											
Excelsior	30,039	30,298	30,00%	20,00%	-33,00%	14.2	19.6	38,00%	163	142	-13,00%
Vanguard	21,798	29,324	22,00%	20,00%	-10,00%	-7.4	14.3	293,00%	250	144	-42,00%
Sphere This!	19,169	--	10,00%	--	--	16.0	--	--	278	--	--
BioSphere	16,418	57,282	16,00%	38,00%	133,00%	-15.9	61.3	486,00%	189	126	-33,00%
Spheres of Influen	12,576	33,096	13,00%	22,00%	75,00%	-18.3	19.5	207,00%	392	354	-10,00%
Market 2											
TechnoSphere	123,077	87,155	31,00%	15,00%	-53,00%	54.6	39.1	-28,00%	2034	1492	-27,00%
Provisio	276,923	314,781	69,00%	52,00%	-24,00%	-19.8	-14.3	-28,00%	1621	307	-81,00%
Sphere This!	--	188,065	--	31,00%	--	--	50.6	216,00%	--	709	155,00%

Table 3: Matrix of Results Transformation Laboratory
Source: Realia Group[667]

In the following a summary of the key findings for each corporation will be given, in respect of the mental model followed and the characteristics that correspondingly played out for this corporation throughout the simulation. Additional written material form the observation of the simulation as well as audio-material is available upon request. The dissertation decided to only outline the main findings for the corporations in the simulation here. This is, because the laboratory findings only build additional information.

What is important with regard to the dissertation is the characteristic of each of the five mental models in chapters 3.2 – 3.5[668]. This will be done in-depth in the respective chapter, using the polarity profile elaborated. The following findings of the laboratory thereby only provide additional information with respect to the characteristics important to describe the different mental models.

---

666 The following findings presented are the outcome of close collaboration of the author with Susan Svoboda.
667 Note: Blue-shaded boxes are the best in that market – either highest (as in profit) or lowest (as in pollution). Since SphereThis! changed markets between cycles, the percent change column for their market share is blank as this is an apple-to-oranges comparison, unless you are looking at world market share.
668 See also appendix C for characteristics of Trade-off Model.

Mental Models and Characteristic behavior as it played out for the different Corporations

a) Excelsior

The first simulated company in the laboratory, Excelsior, is a company focusing primarily on Pollution Prevention strategies.[669] This company, selling in M1, focused on activities to reduce manufacturing pollution. But they had little concern for total lifecycle costs, little interest in external stakeholders, innovations or new markets. The approach was clearly silo-oriented, focused on reducing environmental unsustainability in the existing business process. Furthermore Excelsior was short-term oriented.

The company can be considered to have followed a Compliance Model, with emphasis on eco-efficiency strategies. The corporation yielded strong sales and profits in Cycle 1, which were surpassed by other companies that were moving beyond pollution prevention strategies.

b) Vanguard

The second simulated company, Vanguard, focused on Product Stewardship. This company, selling in M1, focused on lifecycle pollution and stakeholders, but not on new markets or products. Their approach was still silo-oriented, but showed a clear commitment to stakeholder involvement. Vanguard can be considered to be moving from a Compliance Model towards a Reputation Leadership Model. This company's profitability improved in Cycle 2 due to stakeholder and lifecycle activity, while the company managed to still reduce its pollution. This is especially the case for the production from manufacturing, which is particularly observed and valued for corporations, which follow a Reputation Leadership. The company however did not manage to take a leadership in that position (reducing manufacturing pollution), but is significantly surpassed by the company Proviso.

c) TechnoSphere

TechnoSphere focused primarily on Clean Technology strategies. The corporation can be considered following an Eco-efficiency Model. Their approach remains silo-oriented, because of missing stakeholder involvement. This company, selling in M2, was not concerned with stakeholder and lifecycle issues.

However due to substantive innovations their approach was longer-term than the previous two. This company, with operations in M2 (which made 5 times more pollution than factory standards in M1) had strong profits in Cycle 1 but was almost matched by BioSphere in Cycle 2.

d) Provisio

Provisio focused on Sustainable Vision strategies. This company, selling in M2, is working to develop a new business model that would foster innovation of new products for new markets with infrastructure support to suit the needs of the community. Their approach is very

---

669 To be precise, Excelsior is the product of that company build here. Out of reasons of simplicity, the dissertation will use the name of the company and the name of product as synonyms.

much long-term oriented and integrated, dealing not only with environmental but equally with social sustainability.

Provisio can be considered to have followed a Systemic Model. The company reduced its manufacturing pollution by 81% and total pollution by 67%. Profits however were still nega - tive, which can be explained with the long-term strategy of the company.[670] The situation however is ameliorating from cycle 1 to cycle 2, which suggests a positive development.

e) BioSphere

BioSphere was focused very proactively on measures of eco-efficiency and reducing unsus - tainabilities. The company can be considered to have followed an Eco-Efficiency Model. The team came prepared to take advantage of a strategic opportunity to gain preferred access to a resource – the recycled components. BioSphere designed a product made entirely from re - manufactured and recycled parts – thereby reducing labor, energy and manufacturing waste. Furthermore the corporation worked with the Community Redevelopment Association (NGO) to avoid disposal of several of their components, thereby improving profitability.

Their engagement with stakeholders was very intensive at the beginning, with particular em - phasis on stakeholder expectations, but faded with time. Furthermore the corporation fo - cused much more on environmental sustainability than social sustainability, which however can be explained by the fact that it operated entirely in the industrialized market (market 1), where labor and community issues are low. The corporation over time got more and more in - novative, while thereby still focusing on clean technology and pollution prevention: The cor - poration innovated when conducting research and development to make additional compo - nents remanufacturable, which according to the facilitator is rather unusual (only 1 in 15 teams). Furthermore they developed a program to take-back old SphereMovers and offered them for resale in Market 2, thereby developing an additional revenue stream of $1.6 mil - lion.

---

670 The laboratory ran only over two cycles.

f) SphereThis!

SphereThis can be considered to have followed a Reputation Leadership Model. The corporation invested early in Biomimicry and even though so far their project broke-even, they did get some new spin off technologies from the investment.

One of the spin-off technologies, was a patented, never before seen white wheel that integrated the company's technology and the current fad while saving the company money. The corporation continuously engaged in conversations with their customers throughout both cycles in addition to the Market Research initiatives. The corporation stayed on the innovation edge, by developing concept cars and promoting and testing the concepts with customers. It looked for sources of creativity by inviting employees in to review design plans and offer comments and suggestions. Stakeholder involvement, specifically from customer side, was very extensive, seeking to move from reducing unsustainability to actually create sustainability. SphereThis moved their factories also into developing countries (market 2), but only in cycle 2, when they were also selling their product there.

SphereThis hired a third-party firm to monitor working conditions in their market 2 factories. However, it can be stated that the corporation focused its innovative emphasis on building a customer-focused, environmentally friendly product rather than on improving social sustainability issues. However, there were several hints that the corporation might have engaged more into social issues in a potential third cycle, as the corporation started to become aware of social unsustainabilities through their monitoring process and also through their conversations with market 2 customers.

g) Spheres of Influence

As the name indicates, Spheres of Influence showed a clear dedication towards creating sustainability (towards a Systemic Model). The actions of Spheres of Influence's were clearly long-term focused. The corporation made large investments into sustainability measures that would rather play out in the long-term, but Spheres of Influence missed out on some of the 'quick wins' through redesign and pollution prevention.

The corporation demonstrated their interest in becoming a learning organization, by making investments in market 2 factories and villages to learn about the market in order to enter it in future cycles. Furthermore the corporation initiated a take-back program that would be facilitated through an exclusive agreement with a national retail chain, certifying personnel at each center for quality and to improve customer relations. It trained their supply chain on best practices in safety and quality. Furthermore the corporation invested in fuel cells which, while not successful, generated spin-off technology that could have been used in Cycle 3. Throughout all these activities the corporation quite intensively engaged with stakeholders.

Due to its investments, the corporation made significant losses in cycle 1 (-18.3 Mio.), but recovered in cycle 2. The corporation was the only one to get assigned the 'Green Label'- an industry award for environmental sustainability. The corporation can be considered to have followed a rather holistic approach investing into greener technologies and particularly into social sustainability (worker training, safety measures, community work). However, similar to the corporation 'Provisio', their investments would play out in the long-run, leaving the corporation with weak financial performance during early product cycles.

Last but not least it can be stated, that the teams were rather progressive with respect to corporate sustainability and a clear Trade-off Model could not be identified. This can be explained by the focus, particularly on environmental sustainability of Plug Power outlined above, which revealed to also drive the participant's theories-in-use in the simulation.

The different strategies, the teams followed and the characteristic behavior observed thereby, served the dissertation for the elaboration and refinement of the polarity profile for the different mental models outlined above. A detailed explanation of the polarity profile and the description (characterization) of the different models is given above in part III of the dissertation.

Additional information material on Transformation Laboratory (Realia Group)

The following provides additional information on the Transformation Laboratory carried out at Plug Power. It constitutes the material, which was handed out to the participants of the Laboratory. All material in the following has been produced by 'Transformation: the Business Strategy Laboratory©' from Realia Group. For further information visit also the website at: www.realiagroup.com[671].

Laboratories are routine in chemistry, architecture, engineering and art education. Perhaps because labs aren't standard in business coursework, they generally aren't part of sustainability training. Within a Transformation: The Business Strategy Laboratory session, teams are formed which represent companies seeking a sustainable enterprise business strategy that will enable their firm to enhance its corporate citizenship profile while it conducts a profitable business. Individual team members take on executive management roles within their companies. Each team defines its own strategy to run their company in the context of lifelike conditions such as time pressures, budgetary constraints, unpredictable stakeholder interventions, changing market conditions and limited information.

At the end of the decision cycle, participants sell their product in a dynamic market that allows companies to take market share from one another, and to record their decisions that result in P&L, Balance Sheet and Environmental reports. Participant teams are scored on their performance and benchmarked against computer-simulated firms that face the same challenges as the lab participants and respond with discrete Pollution Prevention, Product Stewardship, Clean Technology and Base of the Pyramid strategies.

[Annotation of the author: The following provides the manual, which has been distributed to the participants before the Laboratory. It provides additional information on the specifics of the laboratory. Because the manual has been produced by Realia Group and not by the author, the pagination is a different one.]

---

671 Accessed: 17. October 2006.